SOCIAL SERVICE
ORGANIZATIONS

The Greenwood Encyclopedia of American Institutions

Each work in the *Encyclopedia* is designed to provide concise histories of major voluntary groups and nonprofit organizations that have played significant roles in American civic, cultural, political, and economic life from the colonial era to the present. Previously published:

1. *Labor Unions*
Gary M Fink, Editor-in-Chief

The Greenwood Encyclopedia of American Institutions

Social Service Organizations

editor-in-chief PETER ROMANOFSKY

advisory editor CLARKE A. CHAMBERS

Volume 2

GREENWOOD PRESS
Westport, Connecticut • London, England

Library of Congress Cataloging in Publication Data
Main entry under title:

Social service organizations.

(The Greenwood encyclopedia of American institutions; no. 2)
Bibliography: p.
Includes index.
1. Charitable societies—History. 2. Charities,
Medical—United States—History. 3. Social service—
Societies, etc.—History. 4. Charitable societies—
Directories. 5. Charities, Medical—United States—
Directories. 6. Social service—Societies, etc.—Direc-
tories. I. Romanofsky, Peter. II. Chambers, Clarke A.
III. Series.
HV88.S59   361.7'0973   77-84754
ISBN 0-8371-9829-1 (set)

Library of Congress Catalog Card Number: 77-84754
ISBN: 0-8371-9829-1 (set)
        0-8371-9902-6 (vol. 1)
        0-8371-9903-4 (vol. 2)

First published in 1978

Greenwood Press, Inc.
51 Riverside Avenue, Westport, Connecticut 06880

Printed in the United States of America

10 9 8 7 6 5 4 3 2

FOR MY PARENTS, FRED AND HELEN ROMANOFSKY

Contents

B _____

D _____

E _____

F _____

G _____

H _____

I _____

J

L

SOCIAL SERVICE ORGANIZATIONS

N

NATIONAL ASSEMBLY OF NATIONAL VOLUNTARY HEALTH AND SOCIAL WELFARE ORGANIZATIONS, INC., THE (NANVHSWO). In the second decade of the twentieth century, after many national social service agencies had been organized, there developed a concern for better coordination among these social welfare agencies. There was also a concern for the general improvement of social services by the leading national agencies. In 1919, the American Association for Organizing Family Social Work* (AAOFSW) appointed a committee to work with the American National Red Cross* (ANRC) to work to avoid the duplication of efforts, particularly in the field of home service, which ANRC had initiated during World War I to provide casework services to servicemen's families in the United States. In 1920, representatives of these two agencies joined an informal group of executives from other national agencies, all concerned essentially with the quality of social service on the local level. The monthly meetings led these executives to establish the discussion group more formally in 1923. These discussions led to the establishment in New York City in November 1923 of The National Assembly of National Voluntary Health and Social Welfare Organizations (NANVHSWO) as the National Social Work Council (NSWC).

Although the new NSWC adopted an organizational structure, its major focus continued to be the regular discussions among the national agency leaders. Beginning with the establishment of the NSWC in 1923, the executive director of the AAOFSW, David Holbrook, became the part-time, unpaid secretary of the new organization. Holbrook became the full-time secretary of the NSWC when he resigned his leadership of the AAOFSW in 1925. Remaining the head of the NSWC until 1945, Holbrook influenced significantly the early activities and orientation of the new group. In the 1920s, the NSWC did not conduct programs of its own, but it served as a major vehicle for increased coordination and improvement of social services by the leading national agencies. Monthly meetings dealt with a full range of important and timely topics in the field. In the early 1920s, for instance, when communitywide and other new fund-raising techniques were becoming popular in American communities, the discussion meetings of the NSWC focused on such issues as budgets and funds. Other meetings dealt with issues relating to the relationship between national agencies and their local affiliates, a perennial concern for national voluntary agencies. When economic conditions deteriorated in the late 1920s and early 1930s, national agencies discussed the depression and the problems of agency retrenchment at NSWC meetings. And, to deal with transiency, a problem which concerned a number of national agencies, such as the National Association of Travelers Aid Societies* and the Bureau for Jewish Social Research,* the NSCW helped to sponsor and generally aided, beginning in 1932, the Committee on Care of Transient and Homeless* (CCTH). Composed of representatives from different agencies, the CCTH presented a coordinated approach to a significant social problem, involving local and national, as well as public and private, agencies of all kinds.

The activities of the CCTH represented only one of the special projects— departures from and outgrowths of the monthly meetings—of the NSWC. Another important early activity began in 1923 when volunteer leader Holbrook invited many national agencies that conducted casework to meet in Milford, Pennsylvania, to discuss their specialties and to work to prevent duplication of services. The group continued to meet annually under the NSWC auspices as the Milford Conference until 1929, when the depression halted the gatherings. The meetings resumed, however, in 1933. In 1928, the American Association of Social Workers* (AASW) published the report of the Milford Conference as *Social Case Work, Generic and Specific*. Coupled with the continuing regular meetings, which featured guest specialists and pressing topics for discussion, these conferences kept the NSWC an important agency in the social service field.

Fulfilling further its initial purpose—to coordinate and thus improve social service in the country—the NSWC implemented its machinery to deal with the social problems related to defense mobilization for World War II. In 1943, five NSWC member agencies helped to form the American War-Community Services (AWCS) to raise funds and to develop programs jointly. Approved by the federal War Relief Control Board (see *Government Agencies*), the AWCS cooperated in and with health and welfare programs in areas with the most serious social problems created by the war efforts. The service cooperation committee of the AWCS conducted field studies and coordinated services in such communities. Along with the AWCS, the NSWC studied the social problems of Japanese-Americans being relocated; NSWC's committee on Japanese-Americans, for example, published bulletins on such problems as discrimination in employment and housing and on prejudice in general. After the demise of the AWCS in 1947, the service cooperation committee continued as part of the newly renamed National Social Welfare Assembly, Inc. (NSWA), which also developed coordinated programs to deal with the problems of the postwar resettlement of refugees, Japanese-Americans, and other people.

The need to confront a variety of postwar problems had led to a reorganization of the structure and function of the organization on December 7, 1945, when it became the NSWA. The real significance of the reorganization was the expanded functioning of the agency. A larger and more diverse committee and division structure conditioned the development of more programs, which still stressed the coordination of resources in the social service field nationally. Continually concerned with developing sound social services for migrants after the demise of both the federal Division of Transients in 1935 and the CCTH in the late 1930s, the social casework council, an important functioning division of the NSWA, met with the National Travelers Aid Association* (NTAA) in 1947, and together they published a pamphlet on the transient problem. To improve the field services of many national agencies—a continuing concern in the social service field nationally—two NSWA groups, one from the social case work council and another from the council on field service, worked cooperatively beginning in 1947. Also in 1947, the NSWA strengthened coordination with the American Council on Education, illustrated by their joint efforts on the Committee on a Federal Department of Health, Education, and Security, which influenced the establishment of a new cabinet-level department in 1953.

The NSWA worked closely with veterans' centers throughout the country and conducted as well a multifaceted youth division, which worked in 1947 with the American Jewish Committee to produce a film, *Youth for a Better Home Town*. A dramatic story utilizing documentary film techniques, and a joint product of twenty-one national youth agencies, the film was considered highly by experts. NSWA efforts to coordinate youth work culminated in 1948 with the establishment of the Young Adult Council (YAC), a group of twenty-eight national student and youth agencies concerned especially with eighteen to thirty-year-olds. The NSWA contributed directly to the field of social service, serving as the technical advisory committee of the National Conference on Family Life, held in 1948 at the invitation of President Harry Truman.

The NSWA ended its initial five-year existence in 1949 with a diverse array of activities and programs and with special activities that promoted long-range planning in social welfare and that suggested its emerging national leadership role. With the National Conference on Social Welfare* (NCSW), the NSWA developed the joint program planning committee to put together a long-range, comprehensive program for forums and discussions of social welfare issues. Late in the decade, in December 1947, the NSWA reached an important understanding with the Community Chests and Councils, Inc.* (CCC), recognizing the NSWA as the central planning organization for social welfare and the CCC as the national spokesman in the fund raising for social service.

In the 1950s, the NSWA solidified its leadership in the social service field and continued to conduct a wide range of services and to introduce new issues. In 1950, for instance, the NSWA helped to establish the National Committee on the Aging* (NCOA), which dealt with an increasingly important issue in social welfare. Years of activities by the NSWA culminated in 1953 with the creation of the federal Department of Health, Education, and Welfare (DHEW). In 1953, the NSWA also moved to new national headquarters in the Carnegie Peace Building in New York City. Demonstrating its long-time interest in professional social work trends, it published in 1955 the results of years of discussion as *Where Is Casework Going?* In the 1950s, the NSWA maintained its interest and activities relating to social work personnel, acting continually as the coordinating recruitment agency in the field, conducting in 1955 a workshop on popular attitudes toward social work as a hindrance to recruitment, collecting data on salaries in social work, and, with a group of federal agencies (including the Bureau of Labor Statistics), publishing *Salaries and Working Conditions in Social Welfare Manpower* in 1960. This study was presented first at the annual meeting of the NCSW and was subsequently revised and reissued as *Social Welfare as a Career.*

Fund raising in social service developed in the 1950s as an important NSWA issue. Working especially with the National Health Council* (NHC), the NSWA capped years of discussions with the publication in 1957 of *Standards of Fund Raising Practices for Social Welfare Organizations.*

Dealing with yet another vital issue in social service, the NSWA paid special attention to the role of the volunteer. In 1953, for example, the citizen participation committee, sponsored jointly by the now renamed Community Chests and Councils of America, Inc.* (CCCA), conducted a workshop for local volunteer bureaus at the annual meeting of the NCSW and, with the CCCA, a workshop on citizen participation and neighborhood planning. In 1955, cooperating similarly with the CCCA, the NSWA's field service analyzed the role of the volunteer in the programs of national social work agencies. The citizen participation committee conducted workshops for volunteer bureaus and published *Volunteer Viewpoint.* The NSWA worked with national magazines and other media forms to depict and interpret the role of volunteers in social service. Broadening its concern to include volunteers in service abroad, in 1961 the NSWA drafted a statement, *Goals and Principles Relating to Social Welfare and the Peace Corps,* which initiated discussions between the Peace Corps and the NSWA on the use abroad of the skills and resources of social welfare agencies.

The inauguration of John F. Kennedy as president in 1961 seemed to usher in a new phase of the NSWA. The most controversial events of the early 1960s related to the discussions of the role and importance of national voluntary social service agencies, culminating with the issuance of the so-called Hamlin report on fund raising in 1961. Assuming further national leadership in the field, the NSWA responded with the appointment of an ad hoc committee on the role of social welfare agencies. It issued in 1962 *The Role of Voluntary Social Welfare Agencies,* which agreed generally with five major criticisms of the Hamlin report. The agency thus called for the leading private organizations, the NHC, the recently renamed United Community Funds and Councils of America, Inc.* (UCFCA), and itself to promote changes in the field. The NSWA worked to improve accounting procedures of social service agencies, one of the comments of the Hamlin report. But, even before it responded to this controversial report, it had been developing a new orientation for itself. At the end of the year, the NSWA decided to take positions on legislative issues affecting welfare, breaking an agency tradition since its inception in 1923. Implementing this decision, the membership unanimously adopted a public statement on public welfare, developed by the NSWA committee on social issues and social policy. This action also helped the staff to develop a statement, *Needed Public Welfare Legislation,* a request initiated by Associate Executive Director George Rabinoff. The spring assembly in 1961 dealt with the problem of chronic unemployment, leading subsequently to discussions with the United States Department of Labor to determine the role of voluntary agencies to work with the government on this problem. This action fulfilled another point made in *The Role of Voluntary Social Welfare Agencies:* voluntary agencies should work with the government to improve services in social welfare.

These actions, which indicated a new thrust for the NSWA, developed clearly in the next few years. Illustrating the new direction and helping to fulfill a goal suggested in the NSWA response in 1962 to the Hamlin report were the following: a strong public statement supporting the proposed federal economic opportunity bill, the arrangement of meetings between top staff members of affiliate agencies with the staff of the community action program of the new federal Office of Economic Opportunity (OEO), and the sponsoring, with the UCFCA, of regional conferences where local leaders met appropriate OEO officials. Developing the suggested voluntary-government agency leadership further in 1966, the DHEW asked the NSWA to prepare a report on the role of voluntary agencies in child and family welfare planning. Consistent with the theme of the response in 1962, the NSWA committee on tax policy determined to oppose any policies, increasingly being discussed by lawmakers, that would reduce incentives for voluntary donations. In the field of civil rights, the NSWA sponsored a range of conferences, initiated a program in 1964 to send books to black colleges and to community centers in the South, and, in 1965, resolved formally to implement a long-standing agency policy of no racial discrimination. Most importantly for the future of the NSWA, the board of directors decided to begin a self-evaluation of the organization in 1965. It retained a consulting firm to study and to guide a reorganization, leading to a decision reached in 1966 to reconstitute the NSWA as a national citizens' organization that would emphasize social planning and social policy development. Discussions and negotiations culminated on December 5, 1967, when the agency became the National Assembly for Social Policy and Development (NASPD).

The inauguration of this new phase in the history of the organization prompted conscious new directions and activities, although the NASPD continued to pursue long-standing interests and issues. With a clear purpose to develop social welfare policies, the NASPD established in 1968 its council on social policy and program development, composed of leading professionals in economics, social welfare, social policy, and the like, to advise the organization. At the same time, it also contracted with the National Study Service, a unit created by leading national agencies, to establish a public welfare reporting center to collect, analyze, prepare, and distribute information on practices and policies. Pursuing the other clear goal of the new NASPD, the organization in 1968 brought together representatives from the Social and Rehabilitation Service of the DHEW and from private groups in the rehabilitation field to discuss how the voluntary agencies could help to implement public policy. The opening in April 1969 of the Washington, D.C., office of the NASPD—which other voluntary agencies utilized for their business in the capital—helped further to effect the NASPD goals. It also established a task force on youth for the White House Conference on Children and Youth, a task force on national priorities, various activities to develop projects relating to the federal model cities program, a statement in 1972 supporting the concept of income maintenance for the poor, support for the Dublino case in 1972 relating to work rules for welfare recipients, and its commitment to a national social report by a group of experts and agencies.

The NASPD continued its strong tradition of service to the field of social welfare. To bring the organization in closer contact with its constituency, it held five regional conferences for the field staffs of national social service agencies. These conferences focused on such issues as the role of voluntary social agencies in the urban crisis and how to deal with the confrontations occurring at annual and other meetings of many agencies, both important issues in the field. In 1968, the NASPD began efforts to fund a center to promote uniform accounting standards for social service agencies. To help vitalize the voluntary sector, the NASPD participated in the establishment of the national program for voluntary action, created by President Richard Nixon's executive order on April 30, 1969.

In the early 1970s, the NASPD worked to implement compulsory unemployment insurance coverage for employees of social service agencies. Still active in the campaign to protect and promote private social welfare, the NASPD continued efforts to prevent legislation concerning taxing and donating; in 1972, for instance, it testified before Congress advocating legislation to allow groups with 501(c)(3) status to lobby for or against issues affecting them, and it issued an official statement, *Voluntary Giving and Tax Policy: Charity Is Not a Loophole*. In 1972, the NASPD also began discussions that culminated in the decision in late 1973 to become the new National Assembly of National Voluntary Health and Social Welfare Organizations (NANVHSWO).

In its few years as the NANVHSWO, the organization fulfilled its major purposes: to serve as a coordinating agency, to provide services to its constituents, which remained about forty since the reorganization of November 1973, and in a direct difference with the NAPSD, not to take a stand on issues in the field. *Washington Notes* provided information and proved to be popular with the constituents. In December 1973, the NANVHSWO issued a timely publication on confidentiality in social welfare services. Social policy seminars focused on such issues as juvenile justice, an area in which the organization developed a task force, which in turn decided to develop a model program to deinstitutionalize status offenders, using a mix of community and national agencies. To serve its constituents and the field further, the NANVHSWO prepared materials to help national agencies and their affiliates adjust to changes enacted in Title XX of the Social Security Act in 1974, and it remained concerned with standard accounting, voluntary giving, and the activities of the 501(c)(3) group. The NCSW declined an offer to merge, but the NANVHSWO helped prepare many sessions at the NCSW forum in 1975. A limited full-time staff of five and an attempt to keep administration simple suggested the minimal but nevertheless important NANVHSWO role in the field of social service.

The Papers of the National Social Welfare Assembly, containing records of all phases of the agency's history, are filed at the Social Welfare History Archives Center at the University of Minnesota, Minneapolis. The published *Annual Reports* are detailed and therefore extremely valuable as a primary source. A host of agency publications also reveal various aspects of the organization's history.

The brief history of the NSWA in *Descriptive Inventories of Collections in the Social Welfare History Archives Center* (1970), 504–506, by Nancy M. Wiggins is a helpful study. There does not appear to be a scholarly history of the NAN-VHSWO, and even the standard works in social welfare history do not deal significantly with this important agency.

NATIONAL ASSOCIATION FOR HEARING AND SPEECH ACTION (NASHA). In the early twentieth century, the Nitchie School in New York City was promoting the lip reading method of teaching speech to the hard of hearing. In 1910, the Nitchie School Alumni Association (NSAA) was organized chiefly to provide a range of social services, such as employment advice and placement, for the hard of hearing. The NSAA expanded activities and became the New York League for the Hard of Hearing (NYLHH) in 1913, when Dr. Harold Fay, a leading otologist, argued in *The Volta Review* for the creation of a national organization in the field. A leading physician in New York City, Dr. Wendell C. Phillips, influenced the NYLHH to convene an organizing meeting in February 1919. At that meeting, the group chose a committee to present a plan of organization. Subsequently, the National Association for Hearing and Speech Action (NAHSA) was established as the American Association for the Hard of Hearing (AAHH) in New York City on April 3, 1919, when representatives from local organizations and schools for the hard of hearing met to establish a national organization and to adopt the plan of organization. At this meeting, another committee was appointed. This committee worked to incorporate the AAHH according to the laws of the state of New York, which was accomplished on June 23, 1919. The NYLHH gave the new national agency rooms in its offices to serve as the national headquarters, where volunteers conducted the entire early work of the AAHH.

The AAHH developed gradually. In March 1923, the agency, now called the American Federation of Organizations for the Hard of Hearing (AFOHH), moved its national headquarters to The Volta Bureau (VB) in Washington, D.C., the institution and school that promoted lip reading and that was associated with Alexander Graham Bell's work for the deaf and the hard of hearing.

While other national and local social welfare organizations languished in the 1920s, the AFOHH grew rapidly in its new home in the VB. Within a few months, it hired its first employee, a part-time field secretary, who lasted only a few months. The organization then hired Betty Wright, who served the group until 1955, influencing its development more than any other individual. Quickly the AFOHH became important nationally. In 1924, the United States Office of

Education published its report on hard-of-hearing children. The AFOHH itself, reflecting its earliest concern, published a survey of occupations and the placement of the hard of hearing. The number of affiliates grew steadily in the early 1920s, leading the organization in 1924 to divide its structure into four regions, each headed by a volunteer vice-president. To publicize both the organization and the needs of the hard of hearing, the AFOHH initiated the annual National Hearing Week in 1927. In the late 1920s, the AFOHH publicized the use of telephone amplifiers, setting the basis for Executive Secretary Wright's campaigns in communities to promote Federation Field Fones, a device to improve hearing. In 1930 alone, Wright traveled fifteen thousand miles to promote the new device and to establish local affiliated agencies, especially in the South. Riding high on its successes, in 1930, the organization began its own publication, *The Auditory Outlook,* and hired another eventual long-time staff worker, Ada M. Hill, as director of vocational advice and exhibits.

The Great Depression of the 1930s affected the organization negatively, but it recovered and even prospered after a few years of hardship. Budget reductions and staff cuts in the early 1930s forced the AFOHH to abolish its formal field service, and the much more economical, shorter *The Federation News* replaced *The Auditory Outlook,* which ceased publication in 1933. The staff and leaders appealed to the members for funds, but the response fell short of agency goals. The voluntary workers, however, contributed importantly to the functioning of the AFOHH, helping especially at the national office. In the field, regional vice-presidents, board members, and other volunteers traveled and spoke in behalf of the national organization. Publicity following a story in 1934 about the AFOHH in a syndicated national medical column and the national radio hookup for the annual convention of 1934 helped set the organization on its path of recovery.

Pursuing its interest for increasing the use of devices that aided the hard of hearing, the AFOHH began a campaign in the spring of 1934 to install special earphones in movie theaters. Unprecedented publicity for the organization, which became the American Society for the Hard of Hearing (ASHH) in 1935, resulted from an article in the *New York Herald-Tribune* and from a nationwide broadcast by ASHH and medical leaders. National Hearing Week grew during the 1930s; it received a boost when President Franklin D. Roosevelt endorsed it formally at the White House in 1936. Eleanor Roosevelt, herself hard of hearing, helped the organization, delivering a nationwide broadcast for the ASHH during National Hearing Week in 1937, when the agency also hired its first publicity expert. Representatives from local affiliates, which numbered 114 in June 1938, as well as Wright from the national office, testified at state legislative hearings and promoted legislation for the hard of hearing. Throughout the 1930s, the organization emphasized its traditional concerns of employing the hard of hearing and providing better services and audio devices for children.

The period of World War II and its aftermath, especially events relating to physical rehabilitation, prompted the growth of the organization as a more truly national social service agency. Suggesting an important field of activity and an area of major agency contributions, during the war, the ASHH released Executive Secretary Wright, at the request of the American National Red Cross,* to serve as a caseworker for the war deafened in military hospitals. An outstanding organizational achievement occurred in the early 1940s when the ASHH published a textbook, *New Aids and Materials for Teaching Lip Reading, with a Manual for Teaching.* By the early 1940s, the use of social work methods by affiliated agencies had spread widely, influenced by workshops conducted by Annetta W. Peck, who had been associated with the national agency since its inception. Peck also prepared a manual for volunteers, who continued to participate actively in the organization. In 1946, now receiving funds through local united funds and community chests, the ASHH changed its name once again, becoming now the American Hearing Society (AHS). Business procedures instituted at the national headquarters, which moved to a suite of offices in downtown Washington, D.C., in 1946, helped to triple the income of the AHS between 1945 and 1951. In the late 1940s, the AHS campaigned for improved service by the Veterans Administration for hard-of-hearing servicemen.

While federal officials did not develop sufficient hearing-related services for veterans, federal programs, particularly grants and contracts, influenced the AHS program profoundly in the 1950s. An amendment to the Hill-Burton Act provided federal funds to construct independent speech and hearing centers apart from general hospitals. This helped affiliates to expand their facilities and programs. In 1952, Mary Switzer, the director of the federal Office of Vocational Rehabilitation (OVR), joined the board of directors, cementing a relationship between the voluntary agency and the federal government to improve services for and the condition of the hard of hearing. In the 1960s, for instance, the AHS received from the successor agency of the OVR, the Vocational Rehabilitation Administration (VRA), a five-year grant for a demonstration project on establishing speech and hearing facilities in small communities. The OVR financed an AHS film, *The Glass Wall,* narrated by Paul Newman. In 1955, two major organizational events occurred: Executive Secretary Wright retired, and the agency published *Hearing Loss–A Community Loss,* which the OVR helped to fund.

Increased federal spending in the social service field, but more importantly, broad trends in social welfare, especially the so-called welfare rights movement, affected the course of the organization in the important decade of the 1960s. In 1963, the AHS broadened its bylaws to include activities in speech problems, even if they did not relate to hearing difficulties. In 1963, the appointment of a new staff member accelerated the education and training program, a long-time agency interest. In 1964, the board set up a self-study committee to determine the AHS's future. Presented in November 1965, its proposals led the board to act immediately: at a spontaneous late night meeting, leaders agreed to change the orientation of the organization. A consulting firm that had conducted fund-raising work began to manage the office, and its head, Tom Coleman, became acting director in March 1966. In July 1966, he closed his consulting company and became the executive director of the organization, which was renamed the National Association of Hearing and Speech Agencies (NASHA) in 1966. *The Hearing News* became the *Hearing and Speech News,* and the agency promoted the growth of facilities and services, as well as increased professional training and methods in the hearing and speech fields.

Concerned with the plight of the handicapped, in the early 1970s, the NAHSA commissioned a study of the needs and attitudes of patients, specialists, and the general public. A special study committee analyzed the report, as did the NAH-SA's policy and program review committee, and an important proposal resulted: to develop a consumer-oriented, grass-roots program emphasizing more fully than before legislative work and preventative programs, as well as long-standing, patient-related concerns, such as employment services. To implement its new advocacy role, the organization became the National Association for Hearing and Speech Action (NAHSA) in 1974.

The most helpful primary source for studying the NAHSA's history is the published *Proceedings*. They contain reports of agency activities and, occasionally, helpful contemporary summaries, such as Betty Wright, "Ten Years Growth in the History of the Federation," AFOHH, *Proceedings, 1929,* 580–584. The variously named *Hearing News* also prove helpful, as do agency materials, such as a letter sent in the early 1970s to members explaining the agency's goals and direction.

The NAHSA published a six-page "History" (c. 1970), a helpful outline. There do not appear to be any scholarly historical studies of this agency.

NATIONAL ASSOCIATION FOR MENTAL HEALTH, INC., THE (NAMH).

By the late 1940s, there were a number of national organizations working in the field of mental health and mental hygiene. This situation prompted three organizations to consolidate to become a strong, single national agency. The most important of the consolidating groups was The National Committee for Mental Hygiene* (NCMH), which was founded in 1909 by Clifford Beers, who had led the agency for many years. The two other groups were the National Mental Health Foundation* (MMHF), an organization that provided humane care to mentally ill patients in institutions, and The Psychiatric Foundation (PF), which promoted research in the field of mental illness. Pressure for a more unified national voluntary agency in mental health had been developing, and a bill passed by the New York State legislature and signed by Governor Thomas E. Dewey allowed the three groups to establish the NAMH in New York City on September 13, 1950.

The initial structure included a twenty-five-member board of directors chaired by Arthur M. Bunker. Others serving on the original board included Mrs. Henry

Ittleson and Mary Lasker, both important philanthropists in mental health, Dr. Marion E. Kenworthy, an influential social worker and teacher, and Dr. George Stevenson, who was important in the NCMH and who served the new NAMH also as medical director. The organizational structure also included a president, a treasurer, and an administrative staff of eleven.

Since experienced administrators and staff members from the three predecessor agencies joined the NAMH, the new agency began its activities immediately. The new NAMH represented a true mixture of the activities and functions of each of the predecessor organizations. For example, in its first year, the NAMH helped to finance a hospital rating project by the American Psychiatric Association (APA). Such ratings had been an activity of the former PF. The NAMH continued to publish and circulate about five thousand copies of *Psychiatric Aide,* a publication begun by the NMHF in 1946. Further absorbing programs for psychiatric aides, an activity of the former NMHF, the new NAMH held its first national workshop on psychiatric aide programs in the early 1950s. Continuing the sixteen-year research project of the former NCMH, the NAMH sponsored, from its inception in 1950, research in dementia praecox, or schizophrenia.

Other early activities suggested the national importance of this new agency. In 1951, it established a commerce and industry committee to develop plans in industry for mental health activities. The first chairman of this important committee was Walter D. Fuller, the board chairman of the Curtis Publishing Company. In its first year, the NAMH began a two-year study of state psychiatric services with a $32,000 grant from the United States Public Health Service (USPHS). With support from such organizations as the Rockefeller Foundation, the Carnegie Corporation, the Commonwealth Fund,* and the American Legion, the new NAMH received about $700,000 in its initial year. Joining the national social service community immediately, the NAMH had its budget for its second year approved by the National Budget Committee of the Community Chests and Councils of America, Inc.* In its first year, the new NAMH distributed about four million pamphlets and leaflets, and it continued to publish *Mental Hygiene* and *Understanding the Child,* journals formerly issued by the NCMH. In the vanguard of using dramatizations to convey the meaning of its work, the NAMH developed plays with a theater company. At the White House Conference on Children and Youth in 1950, around two thousand people saw such plays. The NAMH also sponsored the Mental Health Film Board. It served as a consultant for many groups, including federal agencies, and it surveyed the need for and then established a mental health plan in rural Hunterdon County, New Jersey, where other national agencies helped to develop a comprehensive health facility.

The NAMH continued its basic program and activities in the early 1950s. In 1953, it completed a study of laws and conditions in the states, a project funded by the federal National Institute for Mental Health (NIMH). The NAMH produced jointly *My Name is Legion,* a play based on Clifford Beers's autobiography; it began a tour in the fall of 1952, receiving national attention. In 1953, the organization created the so-called mental health bell. Iron for the bell came from mental hospitals' metal restraints formerly used to bind the mentally ill. The bell quickly provided a national symbol and a slogan, "Fight Mental Illness—Ring the Bell for Mental Health." With state and local associations in twenty-one states, the NAMH initiated a pilot mental health fund campaign, which yielded a little over $1 million. The National Mental Health Week in early May 1953 was the first proclaimed by a United States president. Continuing its nationwide services,the NAMH developed, with the Congress of Industrial Organizations' Community Services Committee, a leaflet, *The Worker's Stake in Mental Health*. And in the summer of 1952, the NAMH cosponsored a four-week training session for staff workers in state associations.

The year 1955, with the creation of the Joint Commission on Mental Illness representing eighteen national agencies, was an important one for the mental health field, and the NAMH was in the center of activity. In 1955, the NAMH reorganized its structure to develop a successful nationwide citizens' campaign to fight mental illness. A revision of the bylaws converted state associations into divisions, and local organizations became chapters. In 1955, there were thirty-five state associations, compared with eighteen in 1950, when there were 150 locals; in 1955, there were 470 chapters. Two large grants in 1955 enabled the NAMH to expand its field service, making the organization more nationwide than it had been. The NAMH developed a program to improve psychiatric aides, including orientation for youth workers from the American Friends Service Committee.* Two new plays were developed, and the organization received special help in publicity from Dr. Frank Stanton, the president of the Columbia Broadcasting System.

Despite some organizational problems, the NAMH continued its important activities in the late 1950s. For some years, a staff worker, Mike Gorman, had apparently been urging the agency to become more heavily involved in politics. The NAMH resisted, however, fearing the loss of its tax-free status. Philanthropist Mrs. Lasker agreed with Gorman, and, apparently tired of the NAMH's lack of political aggressiveness, she helped to establish and to support instead the National Committee Against Mental Illness. In June 1958, probably partly in response to these developments, the board of directors established a committee to coordinate federal legislative issues, and it began to press for increased funding for the federal NIMH. Also in June 1958, the NAMH held a significant conference on volunteers in mental health work. So important were the deliberations of the conference that not only the NAMH but other agencies agreed to sponsor the proceedings as a published report: the APA, the federal Veterans Administration, the American National Red Cross* (ANRC), and the American Hospital Association (AHA). Other important services in the field included the publication in 1957 of a booklet, *A Program of Vocational Rehabilitation,* by Assistant Executive Director Morris Klapper; the issuance, with the APA, beginning in 1957, of a statistical fact sheet on issues in the field; and the convening of the annual

National Conference on Mental Health, beginning in the mid-1950s. For 1957 and 1958, the NAMH arranged for Dr. Bertram Mandelbrote of England, a pioneer in advocating open hospitals, to tour the United States. The NAMH also publicized open hospitals in magazine articles and in a pamphlet. The NAMH cooperated with other leading agencies, drafting plans for the White House Conference on Children and Youth in 1960, advising a manual on health by the National Council of Jewish Women, working with the ANRC, the APA, and the AHA to expand volunteer services, and cooperating with an agency to establish halfway houses for discharged mental patients. Public recognition as a leading national agency increased steadily. In 1958, for instance, the organization raised about $5 million, 500 percent more money than in 1953 and 20 percent more than in 1957. Mental Health Week in May 1959 featured Operation Friendship, a project to have volunteers visit mental patients. Many different national agencies cooperated in this constructive project.

In the early 1960s, as the Joint Commission on Mental Illness continued to deliberate, the NAMH sustained its active leadership in the field. In 1960, the organization established its Research Foundation to promote better research in mental illness. The NAMH expanded its efforts to attract volunteers, holding the first nationwide institute for mental hospital directors of volunteers in Topeka, Kansas, in February 1960. After this institute, the NAMH published the first *Roster of Directors of Volunteers in State Mental Hospitals*. In early 1962, the NAMH held a national leadership conference on action for mental health, in Washington, D.C. About three hundred people, representing over a hundred national agencies, participated. The conference stressed the need to determine how national agencies should deal locally with the mentally ill. Five regional conferences in 1962 focused again on mobilization to deal with the problem. The NAMH also helped the American Medical Association (AMA) in the early 1960s to establish its program in the field.

By the early 1960s, the NAMH machinery was prepared for a comprehensive movement to utilize newly available federal funds in the field. NAMH representatives worked continuously with communities to develop their plans for federal funds, and by the end of 1966, nearly a hundred comprehensive mental health centers were approved for first-year federal support. The highlight of 1967 occurred when agency leaders agreed to a central role in efforts with other agencies to develop legislation for the construction and staffing of community mental health centers. Also in 1967, the organization conducted surveys to identify problems in the administration of community mental health centers. Mental health careers for youth, which the National Institute for Mental Health (NIMH) supported actively, and the mental health seminars for business and industry executives helped to expand public involvement in the problem of mental illness.

The NAMH performed another important service, publishing—mostly for police, who brought over one-half of the mental patients to hospitals—a booklet, *How to Recognize and Handle Abnormal People*. The organization also distributed a film, "Booked for Safekeeping," produced by the Louisiana Association for Mental Health. The NAMH's participation in the White House Conference on Children and Youth in 1960 stimulated state associations to begin studying the needs of mentally and emotionally disturbed children. The organization was rightfully proud when the Joint Commission's report in 1961 emphasized some basic NAMH tenets: that mental patients should not be treated in isolated institutions, that mental illness is a sickness that needs proper medical care, and that the problem of mental illness cannot be dealt with by making slight improvements in the conditions and care in mental hospitals. In the early 1960s, staff members worked to inform other national organizations that might encounter mentally ill people. The aged mentally ill emerged as an important concern, as the NAMH worked with many groups, including the National Council on the Aging.* In 1961, the NAMH publicized the disgraceful emergency care of patients. And, in the early 1960s, the organization cosponsored studies on including mental illness in health insurance; it acted as a consultant for many insurance companies on this issue.

As the Joint Commission's report suggested, the NAMH was concerned with the care of hospitalized mental patients. In the early 1960s, the organization pressed for better state laws for the protection of the mentally ill and promoted the acceptance of the Interstate Compact on Mental Illness, which assured full service to patients regardless of the length of residence in a state. As a result of local efforts, states adopted the compact in the early 1960s. To deal with the personnel problem in hospitals, the NAMH began by conducting a study of psychiatric aides, the first of its kind, cosponsored by the NIMH. The NAMH worked closely with representatives of the federal government to utilize the Manpower Development and Training Act of 1962 to train psychiatric aides, occupational therapists, and recreational therapists. The agency also promoted the development of youth volunteers in hospitals, publishing a guide for these programs.

Services for mentally ill children developed as a major activity for the NAMH in the early 1960s. Generally widespread inaction for such children led the organization to emphasize this activity beginning in the early 1960s. In February 1962, the NAMH absorbed the former National Organization for Mentally Ill Children and established the new childhood mental illness service at NAMH national headquarters in New York. The NAMH also created its advisory council on childhood mental illness, and many chapters developed similar organizations. The NAMH hired a staff consultant for this activity. With the National Child Welfare Commission of the American Legion,* the NAMH conducted a survey of the availability and adequacy of facilities for mentally ill children. The NAMH published *The Mentally Ill Child—A Guide for Parents,* and NAMH representatives on the Joint Commission on Mental Health of Children worked on a nationwide study begun in 1965. With this joint commission, the NAMH held a conference to develop a comprehensive program for children. In 1969, the agency influenced this commission to include among its priorities an emphasis on comprehensive services to mentally ill children. Chapters urged schools to utilize funds from the Secondary and Elementary Education Act of 1965, which allowed for special programs, for example, for mentally ill children. In the late 1960s, the NAMH published the widely acclaimed *A Directory of Facilities for Mentally Ill Children.* Also in the late 1960s, the organization prepared data for its participation in the White House Conference on Children and Youth in 1970.

The NAMH developed services for the aftercare and rehabilitation of patients in the 1960s. In May 1962, the organization held a conference of specialists, which recommended the establishment of aftercare and rehabilitation services. This was created in September 1962, and the NAMH appointed an advisory council on aftercare and rehabilitation. The service advised many divisions and chapters on proposed projects. With authorites in rehabilitation from other agencies, in 1962, the NAMH completed a study "The Psychiatric Patients and the State Vocational Rehabilitation Organization—A Nationwide Survey for State Agency Practices."

The NAMH developed its educational services to publicize the problem of mental illness and constructive measures in the field in the 1960s. Beginning in 1960, it developed a program for states to publicize careers in the field, issuing many guides and booklets on the subject. In 1962, with a grant from the NIMH, the NAMH began to prepare a color film on careers in mental health, and the agency produced films and publications for policemen on how to handle mentally ill people. In 1962, the NAMH published a revised, twentieth-anniversary edition of Edith Stern's *Mental Illness: A Guide for the Family,* of which over 300,000 copies had been distributed since 1942. Broadening the scope of its concerns, in 1967, the NAMH published, through the Joint Information Service with the APA, *The Treatment of Alcoholism.* In 1969, when the NAMH helped to influence the President's Commission on the Causes and Prevention of Violence to reverse its original emphasis on mental disturbances, the NAMH's board of directors authorized funds to study public attitudes toward mental illness. In the same year, the NAMH established a task force on public information.

Some important changes in the structure occurred in the late 1960s. The reorganization plan was developed in 1966, approved by the board of directors in November, and implemented in 1967. It streamlined the committee structure and broadened the representation of all levels, especially those relating to volunteers. The entire staff began to serve as a field staff, with the executive director filling also the position of director of field services. This restructuring attracted more volunteers than before. To bolster the organization further, in the fall of 1967, the NAMH formed its council on financial development, with the president of GENESCO as its chairman. The council created three committees to raise funds, and their members were recruited from the chapters and divisions, bringing people in communities closer to the national structure. In the late 1960s, the agency's journal, *Mental Hygiene,* began to appeal more to policy makers than to mental health professionals. During this period, the NAMH developed a legislative network, training volunteers in areas represented by influential congressmen.

The legislative network that the NAMH had developed in the late 1960s helped to make it, as the United Way of America* pointed out, a leading advocacy agency in the 1970s. Using its influence, the NAMH helped to affect a number of administration and other decisions favoring patients. The agency worked to include provisions for mental illness in a variety of national health insurance proposals, campaigned strongly against the Nixon administration's efforts to replace community mental health centers with essentially prepaid group plans, and, most importantly, helped in 1975 to override the veto of the Community Mental Health Act. Repeated actions, including lawsuits, forced federal officials to include patients employed in mental institutions in fair labor practices. The theme of the annual meeting of 1971 was "Mental Health Services for the Disadvantaged." In the early 1970s, the organization influenced amendments to the Community Mental Health Center Act to include preferential treatment for poverty areas. Concerns for children continued as the NAMH worked to include mentally ill children in developmental disabilities legislation in the 1970s. In 1975, to improve coordination within mental health systems, the NAMH established its committee on service delivery, and the agency worked to increase the role of minorities at all levels of the organizational structure. An important event occurred in 1971 when the NAMH moved its national headquarters from New York City to Rosslyn, Alexandria, Virginia. This move allowed staff and board members greater access to members of Congress and others in the federal government structure. Public information programs expanded to include new major films and to stimulate and support in 1975 an acclaimed television series, "The Thin Edge," on mental illness. Returning the focus once again to an initial agency concern—patients' rights—the NAMH participated in 1975 in the Donaldson case, giving expanded rights, including freedom, to in-patients who were not receiving adequate treatment.

The primary sources for studying the NAMH's history include the difficult-to-locate, published *Annual Reports,* which are more detailed for the earlier years than for recent ones. The unpublished "Annual Reports of the Board of Directors by the President," which I used for the late 1960s and 1970s, contain detailed information. In late 1976, some of the NAMH's files were shipped to the Oskar Diethelm Historical Library of Cornell University Medical College in New York City.

There does not appear to be a scholarly history of the NAMH.

NATIONAL ASSOCIATION FOR RETARDED CHILDREN: see NATIONAL ASSOCIATION FOR RETARDED CITIZENS.

NATIONAL ASSOCIATION FOR RETARDED CITIZENS (NARC). As in the histories of other national social service agencies, especially in the health

field, a group of parents and other laymen helped to form a national organization focusing on the care of mentally retarded children. Initial steps for the establishment of such an organization were taken in May 1950 at the annual meeting of the American Association on Mental Deficiency* (AAMD), held in Columbus, Ohio. The AAMD provided in its program for some parent sessions; following these, the parents got together and appointed a steering committee, giving them the directive to call a national meeting of the parent groups. During the summer of 1950, over a hundred local groups were identified. Consequently, in late September 1950, at an organizing meeting convened by parents in Minneapolis, Minnesota, the NARC was established as the National Association of Parents and Friends of Mentally Retarded Children (NAPFMRC). At this meeting, which lasted from September 28 to October 1, 1950, a constitution was drawn up with the broad purposes to promote the welfare of mentally retarded persons of all ages and to prevent mental retardation. These agency goals have remained constant.

The convention in Minneapolis in late 1950 elected the traditional officers, including two vice-presidents. All of the initial officers were parents of retarded persons. The constitution, however, provided that the national association would not come formally into existence until twenty local units had ratified this constitution and so signified by mail. This was accomplished on February 6, 1951. At the second convention held in Grand Rapids, Michigan, in October, 1951, fifty-seven charter member units were recognized. Several publications, produced by volunteers, were authorized.

Several factors appear to be responsible for the establishment of this organization: the widespread exclusion from school of children with IQs below fifty; an acute lack of community services for retarded persons; long waiting lists for admission to residential institutions; parental dissatisfaction with the conditions in many state institutions; the vision of leaders who believed that mutual assistance could bring major benefits in public relations, exchange of information, and political actions; and the assistance of a few key professionals.

A research advisory board was established in 1952 under the chairmanship of Grover Powers, a professor of pediatrics at Yale University. The association's official publication, *Children Limited,* was also initiated at that time, produced by a volunteer editor. It was later renamed *Mental Retardation News* and in 1976 was being issued ten times a year.

Dr. Salvator George DiMichael, the first executive director, was hired when the headquarters was opened in New York City on January 2, 1954. During 1954, the first National Retarded Children's Week was proclaimed by President Dwight D. Eisenhower. The association issued a variety of publications and stepped up its public information program. The following year, it produced its first film, *Tuesday's Child.*

By 1955, the membership reached 29,000 with 412 local units. A major survey of agency activities undertaken in 1955 reflected the kinds of programs NARC was sponsoring. There were over 1,000 activities or projects operated by

296 reporting member units. Some of the kinds of direct services offered by the units were 221 classes for trainable retarded; 124 classes for educable retarded; ninety-four nursery school classes; eighty-six recreational or social groups; seventy-nine counseling and guidance groups for parents; seventy-eight parent education classes; seventy-eight institutional services, such as providing special equipment; and sixty-three social welfare activities and information and referral services. In addition, some units were also providing other services to their members: special clinics, day care services, sheltered workshops, summer day camps, or home training programs. Indirect services provided by the units were conducting surveys of the mentally retarded in their area; establishing legislative or citizens' committees in their community or state to work for improved legislation; providing scholarships; conducting or sponsoring special training programs for professional persons; and supporting research projects. As a means of becoming more involved in the community organizational power structure, 163 units became affiliated with a local council of special health and welfare agencies or were affiliated with the local community chest or united fund agency.

Considering the fact that the NARC had begun to organize only about five years before the survey, the activities that had been undertaken at that time indicated the considerable vitality of this newly growing body. What was occurring in 1955 was simply a forerunner. The enthusiastic involvement of volunteers in program development had, by 1955, led to a perceived need for paid staff. By 1955, twenty-eight member units reported that they employed an executive director or secretary either full or part time.

By 1956, NARC's "Federal Program of Action for America's Retarded Children and Adults" was presented to Congress by Congressman John E. Fogarty of Rhode Island, chairman of the House Sub-Committee on Appropriations for the Department of Health, Education, and Welfare (DHEW). In addition, NARC provided congressional testimony on bills to expand teaching and research in the education of mentally retarded children. In 1957, it backed social security coverage for adults disabled in childhood and supported the reinterpretation of the Hill-Burton Act to include funding for medical facilities for the retarded. It urged Congress to increase appropriations for vocational rehabilitation programs and pointed out the need for additional grants to states for maternal and child health programs.

In 1958, the volume *Mental Subnormality,* was published. This book reported the findings of a three-year research survey sponsored by NARC and served as an important cornerstone in research literature in the field of mental retardation. Concurrently, NARC began to give support to research projects. Because it was greatly concerned about the quality of institutional care, it began to formulate policies relative to comprehensive programming in institutions. It collaborated with the AAMD in developing standards and was a charter member of the Accreditation Council of Facilities for the Mentally Retarded. In 1959, NARC published a landmark report, *A Decade of Decision.* It was presented to the

White House Conference on Children and Youth in 1960 and described the accomplishment and prospects of NARC with regard to meeting the service needs of the mentally retarded. A large number of NARC teachers participated in this conference as state and national delegates.

By 1960, the membership of NARC totaled sixty-two thousand; the organization had become nationally respected. It was accepted as one of the ten voluntary health organizations recognized by the President's Committee on Fund Raising in the Federal Service. Organizationally the association recognized the need for continued support from its local units, and in 1961, a constitutional amendment provided for mandatory financial support of NARC by its member units. The NARC also received the Distinguished Service Award from the President's Committee on Employment of the Handicapped that year for its meritorious contribution. It was later similarly recognized by the President's Committee on Mental Retardation (PCMR). NARC also made an impact on research funding by the federal government. Between 1956 and 1961, identifiable federal support for mental retardation services and research increased from $14 million to $94 million. In 1962, NARC received the International Award of the Joseph P. Kennedy, Jr., Foundation for "outstanding leadership in the field in mental retardation." The NARC leadership participated in the White House Conference on Mental Retardation in 1963 and provided considerable consultation and support to President John F. Kennedy's mental retardation legislative program.

Beginning in 1963, NARC focused on activities that supported the implementation of the recommendations of the President's Panel on Mental Retardation. This effort included not only support for the Mental Retardation Facilities Construction Act of 1963 and the planning amendments and maternity and infant care projects, but efforts to expand the Vocational Rehabilitation Act and to establish support for special education programs. NARC also fostered state level planning by encouraging its state leaders to participate in the provision of technical assistance. By 1964, NARC's membership reached 100,000. The association convened the first interorganization conference on mental retardation, which had representatives from twenty-eight national organizations. In addition, an important document, a *Manual of Information for Armed Forces Personnel with Mentally Retarded Dependents,* was issued.

With the impetus given by the Kennedy administration for comprehensive state planning programs for the mentally retarded, the state and local NARCs became active participants in the development and implementation of these state programs during 1965. NARC provided a million booklets on mental retardation information to the PCMR for distribution. The association became further involved in the area of employment and produced a film, *Selling One Guy Named Larry,* which launched its three-year campaign focusing on the value of employing mentally retarded persons. It also received funds from the Department of Labor for a program of on-the-job training of retarded persons capable of moving into competitive employment.

Recognizing that the local associations did not have a sufficient funding base to provide the needed spectrum of community-based services for the mentally retarded, NARC reaffirmed in 1965 an earlier policy that the member units should expend their efforts to obtain services for the mentally retarded rather than to provide them. NARC's efforts focused on educating and persuading the state and local public and private agencies to serve the mentally retarded as part of their social and public obligation.

Recognizing that there would be merit in involving younger people, particularly siblings, in its association, NARC launched the YOUTH—NARC in 1967, an organization of young people concerned with the welfare of the mentally retarded. These youthful volunteers decided their own priorities. They worked with mentally retarded individuals on a one-to-one basis, as well as with groups. One of the program's objectives was to encourage young people to seek careers in the field of mental retardation. In less than a decade, YOUTH—NARC had twenty thousand members.

As more and more concern was being expressed in the mid-1960s about the quality of care being offered in state institutions for the mentally retarded, NARC in 1968 took a definitive stand on the subject and stepped up its insistence on the immediate eradication of inhumane treatment and improvement in the quality of care in state institutions; it communicated this belief publicly. Beginning in the early 1970s, NARC and state associations assisted in the preparation of court suits to defend the rights of the mentally retarded in state institutions. It became a strong supporter of "deinstitutionalization" and "normalization."

NARC's role vis-à-vis the federal government has expanded and diversified steadily since the mid-1950s. A major component of its original strategy was to pressure for increased appropriations to relevant existing programs, particularly those involving grants in aid to the states, such as those of the United States Children's Bureau, with the understanding that these federal agencies would press more strongly for the rightful inclusion of retarded children and adults within their programs at the state and local level.

NARC also played a major role in the formation and passage of the Developmental Disabilities Services and Facilities Construction Act in 1970. Following this success, NARC spearheaded the formation of a Washington-based coordinating group, the Consortium Concerned with the Developmentally Disabled (CCDD). Its membership included some eighteen consumer and provider groups with common interests in a variety of federal programs. CCDD formed task forces around such issues as housing for the handicapped under the various sections of the Housing and Community Development Act, national health insurance, early and periodic screening, diagnosis and treatment of children with physical and mental handicaps under Medicaid, and the rapidly evolving legislation related to the education of the handicapped, rehabilitation, and civil rights.

Over the years, NARC's governmental affairs committee, with excellent leadership given by Dr. Elizabeth Boggs, has been involved in such diverse issues as immigration, benefits for dependents of service people, civil aeronautics authority regulations, fair labor standards as applied to mentally retarded workers, lead paint poisoning, and immunization programs. Between 1973 and 1976, it placed particular emphasis on the complex issues surrounding the use of human subjects in research, both medical and behavioral. The disclosure that retarded residents in some state institutions had been used as subjects for drug and vaccine trials without consent of parents created a wave of indignation within the organization, resulting in the passage of a convention resolution in 1973 calling for a moratorium on all biomedical research in state-operated or state-supported institutions. In 1975, this stance was revised to express a policy in support of certain limited studies, under detailed safeguards, and to those of therapeutic benefit to residents or directly related to mental retardation where no other subject population could be substituted. NARC made one of the major presentations to the National Commission on Research on Human Subjects in 1976. Policies in this, as in other areas, reflected active participation, often initiation, by the membership. No doubt the grass-roots character of the organization was a factor in its ability to influence public policy at the state and federal level.

The NARC has been so effective in its legislative and public education programs because of the nature of its grass-roots structure, the socioeconomic characteristics of its members, the kinds of social action strategies that were utilized, and the able professional leadership of its executive directors and staff.

NARC's continuing effectiveness stems from the fact that its local units are strong and have always had a vote in the policy development of the national and state associations. An examination of the history of voluntary organizations in the health and welfare field will show that rarely has a grass-roots organization, developed from the bottom up with continued independence of the local groups, achieved such phenomenal success as has NARC.

The socioeconomic characteristics of the membership of NARC insured the organization success in achieving its goals. In 1974, NARC undertook a survey of 15,043 persons to obtain a membership profile. The response indicated that 81 percent of the members were married; 60 percent had attended college; 44 percent were employed as administrators, professionals, and managers; 96 percent were white and 40 percent had an income of over $15,000. These statistics indicated that the membership had a middle-class background. The more active members involved in social policy development and social action tended to be upper middle class. They thus tend to have access to persons in decision-making positions in the community and are more knowledgeable and comfortable about contacting public officials or providing testimony at legislative hearings.

NARC's social action strategies focused on the use of public education, consultation, and persuasion. Change was effected through the existing social institutions and legislative channels rather than through demonstrations or marches, techniques used by other social service agencies.

NARC had had four executives in its history. DiMichael came from the field of vocational rehabilitation. Gunnar Dybwad came from the field of child welfare with a legal background. Luther Stringham, with basic training in economics, came out of the field of public administration with a federal career to which he returned on leaving NARC in 1968. Philip Roos moved from a background in clinical psychology to become superintendent of the Austin State School, a public facility in Texas for the mentally retarded. Those facts do not convey Roos's interest in management, change, and the uses of futurism to mold the present. Each of these men has left the imprint of his unique style on the organization. Although there has been a steady, and sometimes subtle, shift over the twenty-year span during which the organization has had staff at the national level, from reliance on motivated volunteers to reliance on staff, NARC today remains an organization in which decision making is decentralized and national policy is determined by board and committee members, many of whom are parents of mentally retarded persons.

NARC and its member units continued to function as advocates for the mentally retarded in the following ways: acted as a watchdog to determine that programs that have been funded are providing the kinds of services that are needed and that the money is being wisely spent; assisted in standard setting and evaluation of institutional and community-based programs; provided services in the community on an interim basis to fill the gaps in needed programs until such services are provided by the local or state governments; initiated demonstration projects for new and innovative programs as a means of testing new approaches to the care of the retarded; and implemented research projects to broaden the knowledge base in the areas of prevention and treatment.

By 1974, NARC had grown to include well over 225,000 members affiliated with more than 1,750 state and local member units. Because it did not wish to perpetuate the misconception that the mentally retarded person will always remain a child, NARC in 1974 changed the word "Children" in its title to "Citizens." NARC moved its headquarters from New York to Arlington, Texas, in 1970. In 1976, the staff consisted of fifty-five persons, of whom twenty-one were professionals. In addition, NARC had six regional offices, as well as its office in Washington, D.C.

The positive impact of NARC, both in its public education programs and its legislative program, indicates that social processes can be influenced by particular interest groups that have carefully and skillfully developed strategies and methods to effect social change.

The primary sources for studying the NARC's history include the difficult-to-locate published *Annual Reports* and such agency publications as *Decade of Decision* (1959).

Frank J. Menoloscine and Lair W. Healy, "The Role of the National Association for Retarded Children in Developing Research in Mental Retardation," in Richard Koch and Felix X. De La Crux, eds., *Down's Syndrome (Mongolism): Research Prevention and Management* (1974), 215–235, is one secondary study of the NARC. Robert Segal, "The Association for Retarded Children: A Force for Social Change" (Ph.D. diss., Brandeis University, 1969), provides a scholarly history of the organization.

Robert Segal

NATIONAL ASSOCIATION FOR THE STUDY AND PREVENTION OF TUBERCULOSIS: see AMERICAN LUNG ASSOCIATION.

NATIONAL ASSOCIATION FOR THE STUDY OF EPILEPSY AND THE CARE AND TREATMENT OF EPILEPTICS (NASECTE). In the late nineteenth century, social workers, charity officials, and reformers grew increasingly concerned about the conditions and the treatment of welfare cases in institutions, especially publicly run ones. One such individual was William P. Letchworth, a prominent figure in late nineteenth-century social service. After retiring from business and devoting his life to social service, Letchworth was a commissioner of the New York State Board of Charities, a founder in 1874 of the Conference of Boards of Public Charities,* and a specialist in the care of dependent children. Letchworth was concerned also with the plight of epileptics, and he was the most important founder and early leader of the National Association for the Study of Epilepsy and the Care and Treatment of Epileptics (NASECTE), which was established as the National Society for the Study of Epilepsy and the Care of Epileptics (NSSECE) at a meeting at the New York Academy of Medicine in New York City on May 24, 1898. Other well-known founders of the NSSECE included Professor William Osler and Dr. Abraham Jacobi, a prominent physician who was active in the movement in New York City for better treatment of foundlings. The constitution of the NSSECE provided for a president, two vice-presidents, a secretary, and a treasurer. It also stipulated that the president appoint the executive committee, on which he also served ex officio. The officers and members of the executive committee tried to stimulate interest in the care and treatment of epileptics, a neglected group of dependents. Through publications, especially in medical journals, the leaders of the NSSECE urged state boards of charity, state medical societies, and the like to adopt remedial legislation to improve the welfare of epileptics.

The short-lived and soon renamed NASECTE apparently did very little beyond publishing materials and meeting annually. Its first major activity, and perhaps its most important venture, was a compilation of data about epileptics, their treatment, and their institutions. Letchworth compiled this information as *The Care and Treatment of Epileptics* (1900). Because officials at institutions considered epileptics to be deviants, Letchworth and the organization urged that epileptics be segregated from both the insane and the feebleminded. Letchworth had argued that the organization elect a new president each year to provide fresh leadership. But, in 1900, he still served as president, and the executive committee numbered, aside from the president, five physicians.

In August 1900, the executive committee requested the Connecticut State Board of Charities and the Connecticut Medical Society to conduct a study of and to report the conditions of epileptics. The NASECTE published the report in its first *Proceedings,* in 1901. By 1906, the executive committee numbered nine physicians, including Dr. Adolf Meyer of The Johns Hopkins University, one of the founders of the National Committee for Mental Hygiene,* and a leading early psychiatrist. In 1906, the executive committee appointed a five-member committee to coordinate and to supervise the research and the work in the field. In the same year, the NASECTE voted to appoint a press agent to publicize the activities of the organization. During this period, like other national social service and reform agencies, the NASECTE had an exhibition of its work that was displayed in different cities. Also, by 1908, the organization had ambitious plans to develop an endowment fund to allow its members to conduct research. Ironically, in 1908, the NASECTE voted to discontinue publishing *Transactions* because of a lack of funds. The organization planned to abstract its meetings in widely read medical journals, a decision that suggested its increasing movement away from the social work community. The NASECTE apparently disbanded by about 1915, but it had sensitized both the social work and medical communities to the need for better service for epileptics, a class generally neglected by Progressive reformers.

The chief source for the history of the NASECTE is its published *Transactions at the Annual Meeting,* issued between 1901 and 1914. There does not appear to be any scholarly work on its history.

NATIONAL ASSOCIATION FOR TRAVELERS AID AND TRANSIENT SERVICE: see TRAVELERS AID ASSOCIATION OF AMERICA

NATIONAL ASSOCIATION OF DAY NURSERIES (NADN). In the late nineteenth century in the major industrial urban centers, settlement houses and other local social service agencies had been developing day nurseries to care for children, especially those of working mothers. Some day nurseries also cared for dependent and illegitimate babies, helping to make day nurseries a useful urban social service. Not surprisingly, a woman philanthropist close to the social work community, Josephine Jewell Dodge from a prominent New York family, founded one such early facility, the Virginia Day Nursery in the slums of the Lower East Side of Manhattan in 1878. Suggesting the ties between religion and social reform in this period, this nursery was under the auspices of the New York City Mission and Tract Society, which had helped earlier to organize the influential New York Association for the Improvement of the Condition of the Poor* (AICP) in the 1840s. Dodge helped to establish other such day nurseries in New York City, and she was instrumental in the development of citywide organizations of local day nurseries, which began to hold biennial conferences in 1892 to discuss common issues and problems. Dodge also organized the Chicago Day

Nursery Association in 1897, adding it to the group of similar citywide organizations in New York, Boston, and Philadelphia. Representatives from these citywide organizations met in Chicago for their biennial conference, and on April 20, 1898, they formed the National Association of Day Nurseries (NADN) as the Federation of Day Nurseries (FDN).

The founders established a formal organization, but the agency did not function full time. The founding meeting chose the officers, including Dodge as president. In 1900, she established headquarters in New York in a small office, guaranteeing the fifteen dollars per month rental fee herself. Dodge continued personally to promote day nurseries throughout the country, and she and her tiny organization of volunteers tried in many ways to strengthen existing ones. By 1905, growing closer to the national social work community, the FDN offices were at 105 East Twenty-second Street, in the Charities Building in New York City, which headquartered the leading national social service agencies.

The principal issue at the FDN annual business meeting in New York in April 1905 ended with the organization's authorizing the president to join the National Conference of Charities and Correction* (NCCC). In 1905, the president also appointed a three-member committee to draft changes in the constitution to adapt the FDN to its changing role. The committee worked with four other standing committees: nominations, publicity, arrangements, and program. The executive committee, which determined policies, consisted of the officers—which now included two vice-presidents and both a corresponding and a recording secretary—and representatives from eight or more centers of day nursery activities. Each day nursery belonging to the agency had an official representative at the conference.

In the 1920s, the FDN, which became the National Federation of Day Nurseries (NFDN) apparently in 1916, continued to meet biennially and to promote the day care movement. In 1919, for instance, it helped the local day nursery committee in Cleveland, Ohio, to obtain a city ordinance governing day nurseries. When Dodge died in 1908, the FDN had an executive secretary, H. Mary Sears. A change in the bylaws in the late 1920s reflected agency maturity: the NFDN admitted individuals as well as agencies to membership. Despite its professional executive secretary, the agency continued to rely heavily on volunteers. In 1928, for instance, the president, Mrs. Herman Biggs, the wife of the New York City commissioner of health and a prominent physician in the public health movement, raised money to help pay a traveling field worker. In 1928, the NFDN established an endowment fund and, reflecting its slow but steady growth, moved to larger quarters, lent to it by the National Tuberculosis Association* (NTA). In 1929, Sears resigned as executive secretary, and the agency named Mary F. Bogue as its director. An associate group of the National Conference of Social Work* (NCSW), the NFDN became incorporated on November 26, 1929, according to the laws of the state of New York.

With both its structure and its relationships with the social work community more crystallized than before, the NFDN expanded its activities further in the 1930s. In early 1930, the executive committee appointed a standards committee to represent not only the NFDN but also the day nursery movement. The executive committee appointed as chairman Helen Tyson of Pittsburgh, a pioneer worker in the field who had written *Essential Standards of a Day Nursery*.

The executive committee also appointed a subcommittee to work with the National Committee on Nursery Schools (see *Educational Institutions*). In late 1930, the growing NFDN appointed as assistant executive director, Helen Hart, the former head worker at the East Side House, a major New York settlement. In 1931, the agency moved its headquarters to the Russell Sage Building, where it shared offices with other national social service agencies, such as the Child Welfare League of America* (CWLA) and the Family Welfare Association of America.*

The NFDN prepared a survey of day nurseries for the White House Conference on Child Health and Protection of 1930, and in 1932 it published *Day Nursery Manual,* an important guide. The organization also worked on publications with such major agencies as the United States Children's Bureau and the National Committee for Mental Hygiene.* In 1933, the NFDN established an advisory board of figures in child welfare work, including Dr. Lois Hayden Meek of the Child Development Institute of Columbia University and Dr. Mary Dabney Davis of the United States Office of Education. Not everything the NFDN did succeded and prospered. In the early 1930s, the Great Depression and reduced income forced salary reductions and a strict limitation on field visits. Discussions at the NCSW in Philadelphia in 1933 focused on affiliating with other child welfare agencies. An important organizational event occurred in early 1934 when the board of directors established a system of seven districts with a national board member heading each region; this action to broaden the agency implemented a scheme Dodge had pursued during the last years of her life.

More important organizational activities occurred when the executive committee of the NFDN voted in September 1935 to affiliate with the CWLA for one year, 1936. The plan called for exchanging two board members from each agency, and Sophie Van Theis, a prominent child welfare specialist from the State Charities Aid Association* of New York, joined the NFDN as one of the CWLA representatives. The NFDN president became the third vice-president of the CWLA, and NFDN executive Amy M. Hostler joined the staff headed by CWLA Executive Director Carl Christian Carstens as part-time executive secretary of the NFDN. Cementing the relationship, on December 28, 1935, the NFDN moved to CWLA offices in the Russell Sage Building. The arrangement persisted beyond the initial one-year agreement as the CWLA became more heavily involved itself in activities relating to day nurseries.

Another major organizational development occurred in April 1938 when the NFDN merged with the Association of Day Nurseries of New York City to become the National Association of Day Nurseries (NADN). The new agency was incorporated according to the laws of the state of New York on May 19, 1938. The presidents of the two former organizations became honorary presidents, as the NADN elected Mrs. Ernest Frederick Eidlitz of New York as president. Amy Hostler became the executive secretary, and Carl Carstens served as chairman of the consultants' committee, which consisted of representatives from related professions, simlar to the advisory committee of the former NFDN. The new organization moved its headquarters to 122 East Twenty-second Street on May 1, 1938.

The NADN never seemed to attract great interest, and in late August 1942, the organization decided to dissolve and to become part of the CWLA before the end of the year. A series of discussions between leaders of the two organizations worked out the agreement: the CWLA executive director, Howard Hopkirk, became the director of programs for the NADN, which retained a reduced staff. In further negotiations, the CWLA agreed to accept individual day nurseries as members and to promote their interests. With the CWLA filling the NADN publication orders, in late 1942, the NADN, one of the oldest social service agencies, dating back to the nineteenth century, dissolved.

The primary sources for studying the NADN's history include some materials of its meetings for the late 1930s and early 1940s at the library of the CWLA in New York City. The Social Welfare History Archives Center at the University of Minnesota, Minneapolis, also has some primary materials in their papers of the CWLA. Other helpful sources are the variously named *Day Nursery Bulletin* and some issues of the *Bulletin* of the CWLA. The files of *The New York Times* also yield information about the NADN.

Popular studies of the day care movement, such as Ethel S. Beer, *Working Mothers and the Day Nursery* (1957), barely mention the NADN. There do not appear to be any scholarly works dealing with the NADN's history.

NATIONAL ASSOCIATION OF LEGAL AID ORGANIZATONS: see NATIONAL LEGAL AID AND DEFENDER ASSOCIATION.

NATIONAL ASSOCIATION OF SOCIAL WORKERS, INC. (NASW). In the late 1940s, there were several specialized professional organizations for social workers, such as The American Association of Medical Social Workers, Inc.* (AAMSW). During this period, the leading professional organization, the American Association of Social Workers* (ASSW), began to urge the consolidation of all the groups into a single, unified professional organization. Discussions about the proposal led to the establishment of the Temporary Inter-Association Council of Social Work Membership Organizations, in which the AASW had a leading role. Finally, after several years of discussions, the AASW, the AAMSW, the Association for the Study of Community Organization, the American Association of Group Workers, the National Association of School Social Workers, and the Social Work Research Group agreed in early 1955 to form a new organization.

Consequently, in 1955, in New York City, the NASW was created. It began to function on October 1, 1955. Joseph P. Anderson, the former executive secretary of the AASW, became the NASW's first executive secretary.

The new organization's structure, like its major predecessor agency's, the AASW, reflected the basic concerns and interests of the profession. The NASW initially preserved its predecessors' functions through five sections: group work, medical social work, school social work, social work research, and psychiatric social work. The new organization agreed to have a committee review the first five years of operation. These years represented a period of consolidation, as specialized as well as generic practice interests were continued. During this period, the NASW's commission on social work practice helped to coordinate and to integrate the various interests. It became clear, however, that not all fields were represented fully. For instance, there was no structure to study social work administration or to study casework generally. It also became evident that the five sections duplicated functions. At the delegate assembly—the agency's national meeting—in 1963, the NASW adopted the report and recommendations of the committee to review the first five years. This action led to the adoption of a new structure. The three major social work methods—casework, group work, and community organization—were given commission status. To be more representative, the structure also included seven councils which replaced and supplanted the former sections. The new councils were on social work in community planning and development, correctional services, family and children's services, group services, medical health services, mental health and psychiatric services, and schools. Two new councils were also created: research and administration. The division of practice and knowledge brought these groups together, coordinating and integrating their activities. The chairmen of the nine councils and five commissions composed a cabinet responsible for the NASW's practice-related programs.

In the late 1950s and early 1960s a new, restrictive certification and membership plan was introduced. First formulated by the Southern Minnesota Chapter, the NASW's restrictive practices were opposed by the big city chapters generally. Nevertheless, in the early 1960s, after considerable discussion within the organization, the proposal passed. The measure included the creation of a paper agency in 1962, the Academy of Certified Social Workers, which had the same board of directors as the NASW. Apparently, in NASW's first seven years, the Academy received the most enthusiastic support. In the first six months, nineteen thousand social workers joined it.

From the NASW's inception through the mid-1960s, its activities reflected a calm professionalism rather than an activist advocacy. In 1955, in the tradition of its chief predecessor, the AASW, the NASW supported the following issues relating to federal programs: contributory social insurance, benefits to disabled people under the age of sixty-five, and the lowering of the retirement age for women. Throughout that period, the NASW supported bills and plans for national health insurance. In 1959, the organization received a grant from the National Foundation-March of Dimes* to recruit students in medical social work. In 1961, like the former AASW, the NASW conducted a study of social workers' salaries, and in 1962, with the Council on Social Work Education,* it sponsored the National Commission for Social Work Careers. In 1962, the delegate assembly failed to support a means—or eligibility—test for welfare recipients that was being drawn up. According to critics, the NASW's inaction was significant because means tests would affect millions of clients, but too few members and chapters paid attention to the evaluation of means tests programs and policies.

In the mid-1960s, the NASW seemed to go beyond its narrow professional concerns and face the broader national issues. In May 1963, the board of directors backed the civil rights drive. In 1964, the organization's human rights assembly urged immediate passage of the civil rights bill, and an integrated group from the NASW met two important southern senators to gather support for the bill. At the delegate assembly in 1964, the NASW became the first professional organization to support the principle of a guaranteed income. In 1964, the NASW supported a new, innovative program based in the Lower East Side of New York City, Mobilization for Youth, and the NASW questioned federal officials about the legality of so-called midnight raids of welfare recipients' homes to determine if claims of their being fatherless families were fraudulent. In the 1964 presidential election, the NASW's social action committee felt it was a social worker's duty to oppose Barry Goldwater, but the board of directors refused to support this viewpoint. With the National Conference on Social Welfare* in 1965, the NASW discussed the role of the poor in administering social programs. In May 1966, the NASW held a seminar on social action, and in 1967, the agency backed federal and state support for birth control programs.

Despite these liberal stands and actions in the 1960s and early 1970s, the NASW generally seemed less innovative and less progressive than some of its chapters, especially those in the large cities. In early 1965, for example, a chapter in Colorado helped mothers on Aid to Families with Dependent Children—a federal welfare program—to form social action groups to protect their legal rights, and in the mid-1960s, the Washington, D.C., Chapter declined to pursue the NASW's study of implementing the 1962 amendments to the federal Social Security Act; it urged the national organization to study more actively alternative methods of income maintenance. In the mid- to late 1960s, the NASW even debated the precise role it should take in social action and advocacy. In 1971, the New York City Chapter, apparently ahead of the national organization, denounced the Nixon-Rockefeller concept of work for relief. In 1972, the New York City Chapter made public a letter to the federal Department of Health, Education, and Welfare charging that the city and state seemed determined to oppose a fair hearing for welfare recipients stricken from the rolls. In the mid-1970s, the New York City Chapter charged that chemotherapy was being used instead of professional help to treat the mentally ill, and it charged that social services at the majority of privately owned nursing homes were inadequate because the homes were "understaffed and inadequately programmed." The New Jersey Chapter attacked several aspects of the state's public welfare system; some of the outspoken members were dismissed from their state jobs.

Despite some chapters' activism, the national association fulfilled its purpose as spokesman for the social service field. In 1968, the board of directors established a task force on the urban crisis and public welfare to coordinate and redirect the NASW program so it would be more responsive than before to the then current national crises. The task force, in turn, created an ad hoc committee on advocacy. In 1969, this committee presented a definition of advocacy in line with the NASW's professional code of ethics stipulating that social workers were ethically bound to be advocates for their clients in order to fulfill their professional responsibilities. In 1970, with several other agencies, the NASW urged a liberalized national welfare plan, and in 1971, again in cooperation with several other social service, civil rights, and other groups, it tried to block Earl Butz's appointment as United States secretary of agriculture. In 1972, the NASW joined seventeen other national organizations to challenge legally a New York State work-relief law. And, in the agency's tradition of protecting the profession and supporting social workers generally, Executive Secretary Chauncey Alexander in the mid-1970s criticized the tactic of using social workers as scapegoats for problems in the welfare system, and he lauded what he felt was the constructive role of social workers.

The primary sources for studying the NASW's history include its papers, which have been deposited at the Social Welfare History Archives Center at the University of Minnesota, Minneapolis. *Social Work, The Social Service Review,* and *The New York Times* report highlights of the agency's activities. *The NASW Bulletin* also contains information about the agency.

Mary Jane Fout, "National Association of Social Workers," in *Descriptive Inventories of Collections in the Social Welfare History Archives Center* (1970), 232–233, is a very brief history, and there does not appear to be a full-length, scholarly history of this major professional organization.

NATIONAL ASSOCIATION OF SOCIETIES FOR ORGANIZING CHARITY: see FAMILY SERVICE ASSOCIATION OF AMERICA.

NATIONAL ASSOCIATION OF THE DEAF (NAD). In the late 1870s in the *Deaf-Mutes Journal,* Henry Rider of New York began to write about the possibility of holding a national conference of people interested in the welfare of the deaf. The idea gradually took shape, and some individuals began to organize such a gathering. Robert P. McGregor of Ohio, himself deaf, was known widely as an eloquent orator and was perhaps the most important person in the events leading to the conference. Subsequently, the first national deaf-mutes convention was held in Cincinnati, Ohio, in late August 1880. At this meeting, the NAD was established as the National Association of Deaf-Mutes (NADM). Important founders of the new NADM included McGregor, who became the organization's first president, Edwin Hodgson of New York, and Edmund Booth, deaf like McGregor and who had prospered during the gold rush in California and as a successful midwestern newspaper editor. The group quickly elected officers and established a five-member national executive committee. An early—and continuing—organizational concern was the trend toward paternalism and oralism in the field of teaching the deaf as opposed to the use of finger spelling and sign language.

The NADM's earliest activities concentrated on solidifying the structure, protecting the rights of the deaf, and promoting the sign language-oralism combination associated with Dr. Thomas Hopkins Gallaudet, a Frenchman who had migrated to the United States and had taught some of the NADM founders. Raising funds for and unveiling in 1889 Gallaudet's statue in Kendall Green in Washington, D.C., were two important early activities that helped to solidify the organization. The group's third convention, held in 1889, adopted a constitution, the bylaws, and the present name, the National Association of the Deaf (NAD). The NAD held a world congress of the deaf in Chicago in July 1893. On February 23, 1900, it incorporated itself in the city of Washington, D.C. In the 1880s, the group led movements calling for separate enumeration of the deaf in the federal censuses and objecting to the practice of states' assigning public schools and asylums for the deaf to departments of charities and correction. The organization called for an end to discrimination in the civil service. The NAD also promoted its methods within the field of deafness, working particularly against the growing influence of The Volta Bureau (VB) in Washington, D.C., which stressed oralism, and of its founder and benefactor, Alexander Graham Bell. The NAD convention in 1907 featured a confrontation between Gallaudet and Bell, who led eugenicists trying to prohibit the intermarriage among the deaf. The convention in 1907 also agreed upon a proposed $100,000 endowment fund.

Conflicts with the VB and with its emphasis on oralism continued, but the NAD focused more of its energies on programs benefiting the deaf. In 1917, for instance, it proposed a specialized bureau for the deaf in the United States Department of Labor, but World War I stalled its establishment. Like other national welfare organizations, the NAD helped to rehabilitate war-torn Europe; in 1920, for example, it provided financial aid to the Austrian and Belgian deaf. In the mid-1920s, NAD began its campaign for the full rights for deaf automobile drivers, a campaign that led to court cases in many states. The NAD's Impostor Bureau, apparently established in the 1920s, maintained its denunciation of hearing persons who solicited alms as deafs; in the 1940s, the NAD even asked the Federal Bureau of Investigation to help enact a bill making the interstate activities of peddlers posing as deaf persons a criminal offense. In 1926, the NAD president hoped that an increased endowment fund would allow the organization to establish national headquarters.

Although national headquarters were not established in Chicago until the fall of 1950, the NAD grew as a national social service agency. A special NAD Day, held on May 29, 1940, at the New York World's Fair, another such day at the Golden Gate Exposition in San Francisco in the same year, and Massachusetts Senator David Walsh's bill—admittedly given little chance—to establish a federal bureau for the welfare of the deaf all helped to give the agency national exposure. In the early 1940s, for example, the NAD began to determine seriously the extent and types of special services in the new vocational rehabilitation field. The NAD's victory fund, which supplied three American National Red Cross* clubmobiles for the men in the combat field, promoted the NAD's stature in the field; so did increased cooperation with the federal Office of Vocational Rehabilitation, which, in 1956, sponsored a survey for the NAD of the occupational conditions of the deaf. These developments also led to the NAD's conferring and cooperating with such government agencies as the United States Public Health Service and the Senate subcommittee on juvenile delinquency. NAD workshops dealing with the problems of deafness and promoting the development of vocational rehabilitation centers on a regional basis gave it prominence in the field by 1960.

Organizational developments also helped to strengthen the NAD, allowing it to conduct important activities. The national office in Chicago was situated next door to the American Bureau of Public Relations, which handled all the NAD publicity. Important discussions and sessions at Fulton, Missouri, in the summer of 1956 led to a reorganization in 1960. It gave more power to the twenty-seven state associations, which ratified the reorganization. In 1960, NAD also established Junior NAD, whose growth continued in the 1960s. Another important decision in 1960 was to move NAD's national headquarters to Washington, D.C., a move completed in September 1964.

The year 1964 represented a significant watershed in the NAD's history. An entirely new administration, the first since 1942, also promoted the new NAD thrust. It began with a cooperative project with the Deafness Research Foundation to develop a Temporal Bone Banks Program. In the mid-1960s, the NAD initiated its efforts to promote captioned films; and the circulation of its publication, *Deaf Americans,* jumped from 2,400 to 3,700 four years later. The 1964 convention also approved the employment of a full-time executive secretary, and the executive board agreed with the president's choice of Frederick C. Schreiber, former NAD secretary-treasurer.

Organizationally strong, the NAD developed an ever-expanding program. The organization began a feasibility study of admitting deaf youths to programs of the federal Job Corps or Office of Economic Opportunity. It conducted a workshop and other activities for the deaf through the Registry of Interpreters for the Deaf (RID), an enterprise leading the NAD to campaign successfully for a full-time RID executive officer. A grant in 1967 from the federal Rehabilitation Services Administration to conduct a three-week international research seminar on the vocational rehabilitation of deaf persons and another grant to publish its proceedings led to more NAD staff positions and strengthened its publishing program, which began in the late 1960s. In early 1968, the NAD hired a former faculty member from Gallaudet College to direct its manual communications program. Leadership training institutes, including some for members of Junior NAD, helped to professionalize the organization as a specialized agency in the field, as did an ad hoc committee to evaluate, advise, and strengthen teacher education programs for the deaf. These and other social service activities led the NAD to push for acceptance by the United Community Funds and Councils of America, Inc.,* and to develop cooperative ties with such organizations as the National Association of Hearing and Speech Agencies* and the National Advisory Committee on the Education of the Deaf.

Developments in the 1970s featured the move in 1972 to new headquarters in Silver Springs, Maryland, and some organizational changes in 1970: limiting the presidential term to two years and expanding the executive board to eight members with two from each of the four geographical areas of the country.

The primary sources for studying the NAD's history include its published *Proceedings.* In the library at Gallaudet College in Washington, D.C., there is a helpful history of the organization, Bert Shaposka, "The N.A.D. Story . . . A History of Enlightened Self-Interest" [1972]. There do not appear to be any scholarly studies of the agency's history.

NATIONAL ASSOCIATION OF TRAVELERS AID SOCIETIES: see TRAVELERS AID ASSOCIATION OF AMERICA.

NATIONAL ASSOCIATION ON SERVICES TO UNMARRIED PARENTS: see NATIONAL COUNCIL ON ILLEGITIMACY.

NATIONAL CATHOLIC COMMUNITY SERVICE (NCCS). During the early stages of what became World War II, American Catholics had begun to provide a variety of social services. While the United States prepared for war, for instance, the National Council of Catholic Women (NCCW) and the bureau of immigrants of the American bishops' National Catholic Welfare Conference (NCWC), as well as thousands of volunteers, helped to register aliens. The NCWC itself was chiefly concerned with the religious and moral welfare of the men in the armed forces and of the women and families in hard-pressed, defense-related industrial communities.

During this period, Catholic women's groups established centers for men and women in communities with heavy defense installations and industries. To meet the needs of these groups and to coordinate Catholic efforts, the bishops established the administrative board of the National Catholic Community Service (NCCS) at their meeting on November 13, 1940, in Washington, D.C. They designated the NCCS as the Catholic church's official war relief agency.

The new NCCS began to assemble a staff and to develop its programs. In response to invitations from the president of the NCCW, Mrs. J. W. McCollum, officers and leaders from various Catholic organizations (such as the Catholic Daughters of America and the Daughters of Isabella) met in Washington, D.C., on March 12, 1941, to discuss the relation between the NCCS and the United Services Organizations for National Defense, Inc.* (USO). In his address to the conference, the Most Reverend Edward Mooney, the archbishop of Detroit and chairman of the administrative boards of both the NCWC and the NCCS, expressed confidence in the abilities of Catholic women to provide such social services. At this conference, it was announced that former NCCW president, Anne Hooley, would serve as assistant director of the NCCS, in charge of the women's division.

In early April 1941, Hooley, who had a long and distinguished career with the NCCS, was the first staff member to arrive at NCCS headquarters in New York City. Two weeks later, she was joined by the NCCS director, Dr. Franklin Dunham, a music educator, and by his administrative assistant, James J. Morris, an experienced social worker. On March 17, 1941, the first NCCS-USO men's division club was dedicated in Spartanburg, South Carolina. Its director was Forrest Cotton, a former all-American football player at the University of Notre Dame and, for ten years ending in 1941, the assistant football and head basketball coach at The Catholic University of America.

In April 1941, the seven-member NCCS executive committee held its first meeting. The chairman was Francis Matthews, who was active nationally in the Knights of Columbus. Other members included John F. Hickey, a New York banker and active as well in the new USO, and Mrs. Henry Mannix, the vicepresident of the Brooklyn, New York, diocesan NCCS. The early NCCS structure also included a board of trustees, chaired by Archbishop Mooney, a secretary to the board of trustees, and a four-member governing committee, chaired also by Archbishop Mooney. For new personnel of the NCCS, the agency conducted training courses beginning in August 1941 at the National Catholic School for Social Service in Washington, D.C., where the NCCS was now headquartered. In early September 1941, the first club for Negroes in Fayetteville, North Carolina, and the first women's division club in Hartford, Connecticut, were opened. By October 1941, even before the United States entered the war, the administrative machinery was completed and ready for operation.

In the 1940s, the NCCS crystallized its structure and staff. On February 1, 1943, James Norris became the NCCS's new acting director. Since late 1941, Norris had been the NCCS's representative to the USO. In 1943, the first area training conference for directors of NCCS clubs was held in Jacksonville, Florida. The agency provided a variety of services for members of the armed forces. For instance, during this period, the NCCS's program department mailed Mother's Day greetings for the men. During the early and mid-1940s, the NCCS conducted about four hundred units or clubs for the servicemen.

As the war was winding down in the mid-1940s, the NCCS initiated discussions about participating in postwar rehabilitation and other programs. In early 1944, the NCCS proudly announced the opening of its New York club's veterans' advisory and rehabilitation department. The service dealt mostly with veterans who wanted to return to their former, or obtain better, jobs. The department also helped to place war-disabled men in certain jobs. A five-day conference in June 1944 at the agency's national headquarters in Washington, D.C., focused on community youth programs and on methods of dealing with the housing shortage, a pressing national issue. Sessions also dealt with volunteer training, community organization, and group religious activity. In 1945, the NCCS had departments of personnel, training, volunteers, statistics, and publicity. The women's division helped to coordinate local programs that assisted servicemen's families and tried to develop community spirit in hard-pressed, defense-related communities. The division also offered services in federal housing projects. Further meetings to discuss the NCCS's future were held in early 1946. At the National Conference on Social Welfare* in Buffalo, New York, in 1946, the NCCS had an exhibit of its activities, which included work in 6 continents, 17 foreign countries, 48 states and the District of Columbia, 115 dioceses in the United States, and 509 cities. During this period the NCCS began its shift toward volunteer work in hospitals of the Veterans Administration (VA) and community organization activities. In 1947, the archbishops and bishops designated the NCCS as the Catholic agency serving patients in VA hospitals.

From the 1950s on, the NCCS conducted its VA hospital work and its services to the armed forces through its clubs, which remained affiliated with the USO. The NCCS also helped servicemen's families and dependents. During the Korean War, the NCCS helped local groups to promote and to conduct preinduction programs for men about to enter the military. Many NCCS programs were recreational, but the agency retained its special interest in the spiritual welfare of those served. The NCCS participated actively in the VA's voluntary service advisory committee, and in 1952, it received an award from the VA for its work in VA hospitals. More than the other agencies that assisted servicemen—such as the National Jewish Welfare Board* and the National Council of the Young Men's Christian Association of the United States of America*—the NCCS participated in efforts during the Vietnam War. During this period, it conducted services in over 150 VA hospitals. The NCCS clubs remained part of the USO network, but in January 1976, the NCCS broke its ties with the USO. Nevertheless, in 1976, the NCCS's headquarters was in the USO Building in mid-Manhattan in New York City. The NCCS's executive director in 1976 was Alice C. Collins, an experienced social worker who had served in the agency's unit in Rome.

The primary sources for studying the NCCS's history are limited. For the early years, the variously named *NCCS Bulletin*, available at the New York Public Library and only a few other libraries, are helpful. *The New York Times* also reported the agency's activities during the early 1940s. For the later period, I relied on the *Social Work Year Books* and Catholic reference volumes. I obtained some information from a brief interview with Executive Director Alice Collins in late 1976. The NCCS's annual reports are not published, and they are apparently confidential.

NATIONAL CHILD LABOR COMMITTEE (NCLC). During the late nineteenth century, the widespread use of children in mines, manufacturing plants, street trades, and other occupations began to stir various reformers concerned with the health, morals, and education of children. The United States Census of 1890 showed that more than 1.5 million children between ten and fifteen years old were employed, nearly 20 percent of all children in that age group. Children were used extensively in the textile mills of the South as cheap labor. These were virtually all white children. In North Carolina, almost incredibly, 75 percent of the spinners were under fourteen years of age. By 1900, the United States Census showed that over 1.75 million children between the ages of ten and fifteen "were engaged in gainful occupations," 1 million more than in 1870. It seemed that as the nation progressed, the evil of child labor increased.

As early as the 1870s, reformers and others began efforts to enact legislation prohibiting certain especially odious types of child labor. In New York, for instance, The Children's Aid Society* (CAS) influenced such child labor laws in the 1870s. The organizational efforts culminating in the establishment of a national reform agency began, not surprisingly, in the South. The first such efforts to combat the practice developed in Alabama, where a clergyman, Edgar G. Murphy, began to denounce child labor in the late 1890s. Advocating legislation to improve children's working conditions, Murphy and other reformers faced fierce challenges from employers, particularly the Southern Textile Association (see *Business Associations*). Undaunted, in 1901, they created the Alabama Child Labor Committee, the first American organization of this kind. In the light of obviously strong opposition, in 1903, the reformers gained a victory through a compromise bill, which, although it had modest provisions, set some of the highest standards in the South.

In New York City in the spring of 1902, Florence Kelley, a former resident of Hull-House* (HH) in Chicago, the chief factory inspector in Illinois, and the head of the National Consumers' League* (NCL), and Lillian Wald, the founder and head of the Henry Street Settlement* in New York, influenced the local Association of Neighborhood Workers to appoint a child labor committee to study the problem in New York. Some of the most distinguished social reformers and social workers in New York and the nation served on this committee, including Robert Hunter, chief head resident at University Settlement in New York, whose study, *Poverty* (1904), was one of the most important and revealing documents of the social justice Progressive movement. Others on the committee included Lillian Wald and Mary Simkhovitch of Greenwich House, a major settlement. In November 1902, this committee became an independent organization known as the New York Child Labor Committee (NYCLC). Felix Adler, head of the Ethical Culture Society, Robert Hunter, and philanthropists Paul Warburg and Jacob Schiff provided early leadership. At the annual meeting of the National Conference of Charities and Correction* (NCCC), Edgar Murphy had appealed for a unified child labor campaign. In 1903, Murphy had become secretary of the Southern Education Board in New York City, and he was soon in contact with the NYCLC's leaders, especially with Felix Adler. Adler suggested that to try to form a national organization, the NYCLC establish a provisional committee of three, including himself, to negotiate with Murphy and other interested people. A plan was developed that called for a nationwide agency with an executive committee of people in the New York area. Invitations were issued to interested people throughout the country, urging them to attend a meeting in New York City in April 1904 to crystallize the new organization. Subsequently, on April 15, 1904, at Carnegie Hall in New York City, the National Child Labor Committee (NCLC) convened its first general meeting. Headquarters were soon established in New York City.

The leaders of the NCLC represented the major figures in twentieth-century social service. Dr. Samuel McCune Lindsay, an industrial relations expert, served as general secretary from 1904 to 1907. One of his two associates, Owen Lovejoy, coordinated the campaign against child labor in the northern states and served as general secretary from 1907 to 1926. His NCLC activities earned him the title of the Children's Statesman. The fifteen-member board of trustees initially included Felix Adler, Paul Warburg, Florence Kelley, Robert de Forest, president of the prestigious Charity Organization Society of the City of New York,* Edward Devine, general secretary of that society and editor of the important reform journal, *Charities,* and Homer Folks, an influential welfare administrator. Rabbi Stephen Wise, Jane Addams, Lillian Wald, Graham Taylor, and Benjamin Lindsey were also influential NCLC members.

The NCLC evolved not only as the largest and most important national child welfare organization, but also as one of the major twentieth-century social welfare societies. In February 1907, the NCLC was incorporated by a special federal charter. Two years later, it claimed twenty-seven state and local committees with more than five thousand members. From its inception, the NCLC and its constituent committees conducted a variety of activities designed to alleviate the plight of laboring children. It investigated working conditions in several states, drafted a model child labor law in 1904, testified before national, state, and local conferences and legislative committees, campaigned for compulsory school attendance laws, and commissioned Lewis Hine to photograph the horrid conditions under which children labored. The NCLC's *The Child Labor Bulletin,* which was first published in 1912 and which in 1919 was renamed *The American Child,* played a major part in convincing the American public of the infamy of child labor.

In addition, the NCLC served as a major lobbying organization, drafting, for instance, the federal child labor bill of 1907. It campaigned repeatedly, but unsuccessfully, for a constitutional amendment giving the Congress the "power to limit, regulate, and prohibit the labor of persons under eighteen years of age." The idea for a federal children's bureau was pursued energetically by the NCLC, and its activities led to the establishment of the United States Children's Bureau (USCB) (see *Government Agencies*) in 1910. The USCB focused initially on the problem of child labor and was, in fact, administratively part of the United States Department of Labor (USDL).

Consistent with the NCLC members' views that child labor reform was a means to create happy, useful lives, the agency became more involved than before in the full range of child welfare during and after World War I. Many NCLC members for example, were active in the Progressive education movement to make schools relevant to children's daily lives. As early as 1908, the NCLC began to participate in efforts to obtain federal aid to education, notably in promoting agricultural and industrial training—vocational education—in the schools. In early 1918, at the request of the Committee on National Aid for Education, which NCLC leaders had helped to organize in 1916, the NCLC initiated a campaign to have the federal government assist elementary education. The group hoped funds would go to aid rural schools chiefly, especially in the South. Later in 1918, the NCLC cooperated with the National Education Association to prepare a congressional bill that provided for a federal department of education and for aid to the states for improving rural education, physical education, teacher training, and health instruction. Beginning in Oklahoma in 1917, the NCLC investigated and then published accounts of child welfare laws and conditions in several states. The NCLC's historian, Professor Walter I. Trattner, argued that these "studies were responsible for improved child labor standards and compulsory school attendance laws, the appointment of children's code commissions, the creation of juvenile courts and boards of child welfare, and the licensing and state supervision of maternity homes." Studies of both the juvenile court movement in Oklahoma and the children's code movement in Missouri, however, suggested the indigenous origins of these reforms and the minimal role played by the NCLC. The NCLC did, however, help to create the Child Health Organization* in 1918 and gave it office space and clerical help.

From an early date, the organization suffered from differences between conservative and militant factions. Embittered by the NCLC draft of a federal child labor bill, which he argued threatened states' rights, Edgar Murphy resigned in 1906. When Lovejoy retired in 1926, the executive committee named Wiley Swift as his successor. Swift represented the conservatives and wanted to transform the NCLC from a crusading to a clearinghouse organization. Dissension followed. To conciliate the militants, Gertrude Folks Zimand, an activist, was appointed Swift's assistant. In 1930, the aggressive New York social worker Courtenay Dinwiddie became executive secretary, and when he died in 1943, Zimand assumed the position.

Despite the diminution of child labor problems following World War II,

Zimand kept the NCLC in the vanguard of social reform. The organization conducted pioneering studies and developed programs to deal with work-study projects and with school dropouts. In late 1955, it conducted a review of its future policies and programs, which led to the establishment of two separate committees, one on the employment of youth and the other on the education of migrant children. In the mid- and late 1950s, the NCLC was increasingly absorbed in the problems of youth. Since the 1920s, there had been pressures to change the fairly restricting name of the NCLC, and, as a result of its recent activities, in late 1957, the board of directors decided to call the agency the National Committee on Employment of Youth (NCEY). The group soon found that the change created problems with its federal charter and with bequests, so in December 1958, the board retained the NCLC as the corporate entity but for program purposes called the agency the NCEY of the NCLC, a name retained until apparently 1973. In the 1960s, the NCEY of the NCLC led the nation in establishing programs to help youths entering the labor market to chose, receive, and keep appropriate and satisfying jobs.

In the 1960s and 1970s, the NCEY of the NCLC conducted activities and studies that were at the core of the national social work community and its concerns. In 1963, the agency established its National Committee on the Education of Migrant Children. It also influenced aspects of the federal antipoverty programs of the mid-1960s, focusing especially on the training of paraprofessionals for child welfare agencies. In the late 1960s, with funds initially from the federal Office of Economic Opportunity and later from the USDL and the New York State Department of Labor, the NCEY of the NCLC conducted a demonstration project on the training of such paraprofessionals. In the field of youth employment, it studied and then published reports on employment practices and programs and on the education of migrant children. In the 1970s, it was the only national organization to testify and campaign successfully against the attempt by growers to lower the age limit of children picking potatoes, strawberries, and such in Maine and on the West Coast. In the mid-1970s—when it was renamed the NCLC—to deal with the problem of youth employment, the NCLC organized a loose coalition of interested agencies, such as the Boys' Clubs of America, Inc.,* the National Urban League,* the National Federation of Settlements and Neighborhood Centers,* and the National Association for the Advancement of Colored People.

Since 1973, the NCLC has moved away from its activities in training paraprofessionals but has retained its interests and activities in youth employment and migrant children. The agency presented proposals to President-elect Jimmy Carter in 1976 and 1977. Reminiscent of its earlier activities in the social justice movement of the Progressive era and the establishment of the USCB, the NCLC proposed in 1976 the creation of a presidential commission on youth. These activities demonstrated the NCLC's continuing concern for improving the lives of American children, a vital social issue.

The primary sources for studying the NCLC's history include the voluminous

NCLC Papers at the Library of Congress in Washington, D.C., and its published reports and surveys. The papers of leading figures and societies bearing on the NCLC include the Edgar Murphy Papers at the University of North Carolina, the Lillian Wald Papers at the New York Public Library, the Homer Folks Papers at the Columbia University Library, the Gertrude Zimand Papers at the Social Welfare History Archives Center at the University of Minnesota, Minneapolis, and the Alexander McKelway Papers and the NCLC Papers at the Library of Congress.

The best source for beginning any study of the NCLC or of child labor is Walter Trattner's full-scale study, *Crusade for the Children: A History of the NCLC and Child Labor Reform in America* (1970). His bibliography is extensive. Jeremy Felt, *Hostages of Fortune: Child Labor Reform in New York State* (1965), is largely a history of the NYCLC. Hugh C. Bailey, *Edgar Gardner Murphy: Gentle Progressive* (1968), treats the founder of the southern group. Other studies dealing with major NCLC figures and giving information on the NCLC include Allen Davis, *Spearheads for Reform: The Social Settlements and the Progressive Movement, 1890–1914* (1967), Josephine Goldmark, *Impatient Crusader: Florence Kelley's Life Story* (1953), and Walter Trattner, *Homer Folks: Pioneer Welfare Statesman* (1968). Clarke Chambers, *Seedtime for Reform: American Social Service and Social Action, 1919–1932* (1963), discusses the NCLC in the period between World War I and the New Deal. Stephen Wood, *Constitutional Politics in the Progressive Era* (1968), is a sociological history of the federal child labor laws of 1916 and 1919.

NATIONAL CHILD WELFARE COMMISSION OF THE AMERICAN LEGION: see AMERICAN LEGION, NATIONAL CHILDREN AND YOUTH DIVISION OF THE.

NATIONAL CHILDREN'S HOME AND WELFARE ASSOCIATION (NCHWA). Like many other nineteenth-century child welfare leaders, Martin Van Buren Van Arsdale was trained initially as a minister. While a student at the McCormick Theological Seminary in Chicago in the 1860s, Van Arsdale worked with homeless and destitute children, helping to organize the Newsboy's Home in that city. In the 1870s and early 1880s, he was a minister in various Protestant churches in Indiana and Illinois. Like Charles Loring Brace, the founder of The Children's Aid Society* (CAS) of New York, and Louisa Lee Schuyler, who established the State Charities Aid Association* (SCAA) of New York, visiting the almshouse—in Van Arsdale's case, in Hanover, Indiana, in 1882—influenced the establishment of this important nineteenth-century social service agency. In 1883, when he moved to Bloomington, Illinois, Van Arsdale cared for the first child in his own home and then found a foster family for the child. Concerned initially with educating destitute girls, Van Arsdale quickly established the National Children's Home and Welfare Association (NCHWA) as the

American Educational Aid Society (AEAS) in 1883 in Bloomington, Illinois. In 1885, the state of Illinois granted the organization a charter, allowing it to find foster family homes for destitute and dependent children. After 1885, the AEAS opened receiving homes throughout Illinois. In 1888, the organization started a state branch in Iowa, establishing more fully the organizational structure and home finding work.

The organization spread rapidly in the Midwest, where it remained strongest throughout its history. In 1889, a group in Minnesota became the third branch of the organization. Each state agency had a board of directors, comprised generally of church and community leaders and headed by a prominent individual; the first president of the Minnesota state group, for instance, was Dr. Cyrus Northrop, of the University of Minnesota. Perhaps more importantly, advisory boards of prominent citizens developed throughout each state in localities where the home-finding work took place. By 1892, the organization—now called the National Children's Home Society (NCHS)—had ten state boards, ten receiving homes, and about fifteen hundred local advisory boards. Many state organizations published prosperous newspapers; the Missouri newspaper, for example, went to about sixteen thousand contributors and members, who paid a dollar each per year to support the home finding work.

In the early phase of the organization, before founder Van Arsdale's death in 1893, agents of the society traveled to communities soliciting funds, searching for orphaned children and finding them foster family homes. The agents kept half of their solicitations as salaries. Such dubious practices as earning salaries through solicitations for a charity organization helped to influence both exaggerated and well-deserved criticisms of the NCHS throughout the late nineteenth century. Social workers, especially from the East, criticized these dubious practices and emphasized the need for specially trained agents, not wandering, marginal ministers, which many NCHS agents were.

In 1894, a special committee of the New York State Board of Charities rejected an application to establish a state society there. The committee objected to the commissions from solicitations paid to agents, feared a mix-up between New York and Illinois child placing laws, and argued, incorrectly, that placing-out work in New York State was already satisfactory. The New York committee was obviously influenced also by the complaint of Charles Loring Brace, who argued that the name of the petitioning agency coincided too closely with his Children's Aid Society* and might therefore confuse donors. Writing privately in early 1896, another important New York social worker, Homer Folks, called the NCHS ''reckless'' and ''a delusion and a snare.'' Unquestionably, as a New York investigating committee found in the late 1890s, the NCHS did not professionally supervise or follow up its placed-out children.

These criticisms—which emanated primarily from eastern social work circles—did not affect the prosperity of the NCHS as an organization. Despite Van Arsdale's death in 1893 and some dissatisfaction with his replacement as superintendent, George K. Hoover, memberships increased, and the work of placing children in family homes expanded. In Illinois, where state services did not include child placing, the NCHS affiliate conducted the major home finding work in the state, helping to keep children out of the almshouse, an important practice according to all child care workers.

By the mid-1890s, advances in the organization became evident. One of the leading advocates of increasingly professionalized work, Reverend Hastings Hart, supported the agency. In 1898, Hart became the superintendent of one of the NCHS's leading affiliates, the Illinois Children's Home and Aid Society (ICHAS). The brother of a famous American historian, Professor Albert Bushnell Hart of Harvard University, Reverend Hart became a major social reformer. Active in Minnesota state Indian work and public charities, Hart later held various positions in the Russell Sage Foundation* (RSF) and became a prominent penologist. In 1897, however, when the NCHS in Illinois merged with the Chicago Children's Aid Society to become the ICHAS, Hart became the leader of the NCHS, which still existed as a national organization with many affiliates throughout the country, but primarily in the Midwest and West. The offices of the NCHS had been located and its official newspaper, *The Children's Home Finder,* had been issued in Chicago; the merger in 1897 solidified Chicago as the center of the organization.

In the early twentieth century, the NCHS developed ties with the Progressive social work community in Chicago, helping to elevate the stature and importance of this important home-finding agency. University of Chicago Professor Charles Henderson, who was active in the settlement house and social reform movements in Chicago and nationally, became its president. Hart, the superintendent of the local affiliate, was secretary of the national organization.

In the first decade of the twentieth century, the NCHS supplied probation officers for the Juvenile Court of Chicago, the first in the nation. In 1904, the NCHS display won the grand prize at the Louisiana Purchase Exposition; one of the two judges was Edward T. Devine, the general secretary of The Charity Organization Society of the City of New York,* editor of the most important social work journal, *Charities and the Commons,* and a leader in New York and national social reform movements.

Other developments in the child welfare field helped also to improve the stature of the NCHS. Throughout the nineteenth century, social workers criticized the group-placing methods of the other home-finding agency, the CAS. By the early twentieth century, the individualized home-finding characteristic of NCHS work led such experts as Robert Hebberd of the New York State Board of Charities and others to favor the midwestern agency. A national specialist in child welfare, William H. Slingerland of the RSF, in an article in 1912, "Modern Agencies in Child Welfare Work," argued that the NCHS was the national leader in home-finding work. By the end of the first decade of the twentieth century, the NCHS had twenty-nine affiliated societies, was spending over $400,000 annually, and owned property valued at around $750,000, especially receiving homes for destitute and dependent children awaiting placement.

The organizational structure of the NCHS developed as a loose federation, with state affiliates publishing their own newspapers and conducting their own affairs but conforming generally to NCHS home-finding regulations and standards. In some midwestern states, such as Minnesota, Wisconsin, Missouri, and, of course, Illinois, state affiliates prompted child welfare reform legislation and worked in a variety of ways to improve child care practices. Annual meetings served as an important source of exchanging ideas and promoting group identity within the organization. By the early twentieth century, jealousies over the power of the national organization subsided significantly, and the NCHS—no longer suffering the often inordinate criticism of the late nineteenth century—became more tranquil. By 1917, thirty-four affiliates belonged to the NCHS, and more were seeking admission.

A combination of organizational changes and the emergence of child welfare as a professional specialization in social service combined to weaken the agency, which changed its name to the National Children's Home and Welfare Association (NCHWA) apparently in 1917. After World War I, professional child welfare workers debated more earnestly than before the establishment of a new national agency in the field. In 1915, the workers opened the Bureau for the Exchange of Information Among Child-Helping Agencies (BEI) to provide for discussions and for coordinating activities in the field. Suggesting the importance of the NCHWA, the Reverend William J. Maybee of the NCHS-affiliated Virginia Children's Home Society, headed the BEI. In 1920, the BEI became the new Child Welfare League of America* (CWLA), which quickly became an aggressive leader in the field. Many state societies joined the CWLA, but the NCHWA survived feebly as a national child care agency. Workers and superintendents continued to meet annually, usually at the gatherings of the CWLA or the National Conference of Social Work.* "Historical sentiment and social fellowship" characterized NCHWA meetings in the 1920s. Plagued by an increasing lack of funds and giving way to more professional child care services, the NCHWA ended apparently in the mid-1930s.

Very few primary materials relating to the history of the NCHWA have survived. There are some records relating to the later years in the Papers of the CWLA, which are on microfilm at the Social Welfare History Archives Center at the University of Minnesota, Minneapolis. Issues of the agency's journal, variously called *The Children's Home-Finder* and then *Children's Charities,* are difficult to locate. But the story of the NCHWA can be culled from sources as varied as the published *Proceedings* of the National Conference of Charities and Correction,* the Homer Folks Papers at Columbia University, and other contemporary reports and journals.

Henry Thurston, *The Dependent Child* (1930), is an important secondary source. Thurston corresponded with early associates of Van Arsdale, and he knew the organization operations firsthand, having worked with the organization for some years. Some of the interpretive statements in the text stem from the studies of Peter Romanofsky in the history of adoption practices and child welfare. There does not appear to be a complete, scholarly history of the NCHWA.

NATIONAL CHILDREN'S HOME SOCIETY: see NATIONAL CHILDREN'S HOME AND WELFARE ASSOCIATION.

NATIONAL COMMITTEE FOR CHILDREN AND YOUTH, INC. (NCCY). In 1909, President Theodore Roosevelt, at the urging of leaders in the field of child and social welfare, convened what became the first in a series of White House conferences on the care of children. The first one, the White House Conference on the Care of Dependent Children, featured a national meeting of child welfare workers and set the tradition of holding such national meetings every ten years, except in 1920. In late 1959, to plan and organize the conference proceedings in 1960, the National Commitee for Children and Youth, Inc. (NCCY), was established as the National Committee for the Golden Anniversary White House Conference on Children and Youth (NCGAWHCCY). With a mandate also to develop an agency to implement the conference's recommendations, the NCGAWHCCY was established apparently at the urgings of President Dwight Eisenhower. Officials of the conference included funds for follow-up work, and the NCGAWHCCY adopted a resolution that called on the new agency to develop other sources for funds. The NCGAWHCCY became the NCCY in 1960, and in November 1960, the organization initiated its services by opening its national headquarters in Washington, D.C.

The early structure of the NCCY became the basic structure for its fourteen-year history. A chairman, a vice-chairman, a secretary, and a treasurer constituted the major officers, and a small paid staff, headed by the executive director, conducted NCCY programs. A board of directors completed the rather fundamental administrative structure of this small but influential agency.

Like other national voluntary agencies in the 1960s—when huge governmental social welfare programs absorbed many traditional activities by voluntary organizations—the NCCY proved to be a creative and pioneering agency in its field. In its first few years, however, the agency did not develop creative programs and activities but focused rather on conferences and publications. In 1961, for example, it held a Conference on Unemployed, Out of School Youth in Urban Areas in various cities throughout the country. Considerable staff energies and the cooperation of such prominent national leaders as Winthrop Rockefeller of Arkansas and Dr. Paul A. Miller, president of West Virginia University, helped to develop another conference in September 1963, the National Conference on the Problems of Rural Youth in a Changing Environment. On July 1, 1962, the NCCY began its development program, essentially a nationwide appeal to raise funds. In 1962, cooperating with the Automotive Safety Foundation, the NCCY campaigned to bring driver education to previously unreached youth, such as school dropouts. In the early 1960s, the NCCY sponsored a traveling photographic exhibit, "These Are Our Children," given initially to the White House Conference in 1960 by the Eastman Kodak Company and published in 1964 as *The Joy of Children,* with a text by Pearl S. Buck.

More importantly, the NCCY began its demonstration projects in the mid-1960s. In early 1964, with a grant from the Office of Manpower Administration and Training of the United States Department of Labor, the NCCY initiated what became known as its Youth Services Program (YSP). Beginning with pilot programs in Washington, D.C., in February and in the Baltimore, Maryland, area in March, the YSP served youths rejected for the armed forces by conducting counseling, job training, testing, job placement, and other related services. The assistant director of NCCY became the full-time program director of YSP, and others, such as trained job counselors, joined the project staff. As *The Baltimore Evening Sun* pointed out, the YSP "gives [rejected and disadvantaged youth] what amounts to another chance." In 1965, a grant nearly three times larger than the initial one continued the project. In the spring of 1966, the NCCY began another program, funded by federal agencies, to teach staffs in five other cities the techniques and experiences of the initial YSP. This activity trained the personnel, who in turn developed similar programs in sixty-two other cities. The NCCY phased out the YSP in June 1967 and published a *Final Report* evaluating it. Specially NCCY-trained personnel, however, continued to staff the programs in cities throughout the country.

In July 1966, the NCCY began another project for disadvantaged youth, Project Challenge, to develop in seventeen- to twenty-five-year-old inmates of the Lornton, Virginia, Youth Center better attitudes toward work and to help make vocational training at the center more meaningful. The project offered a full range of services, such as job-oriented, basic remedial education. Leon G. Leiberg, who was the administrator of the Washington, D.C., office for the previous YSP, headed this program, which was funded by two federal agencies. Local industries cooperated energetically, and in April 1967, the Smithsonian Institution helped some project members exhibit their free-form welding sculptures in the lobby of the Office of Economic Opportunity building in Washington, D.C. When on June 20, 1967, Executive Director Isabella J. Jones met former President Eisenhower to report on the agency's six-year activities, she presented him a welded sculpture produced at Lornton. In the late 1960s, the NCCY completed its contract for Project Challenge and implemented an original project goal: the District of Columbia Department of Corrections, which ran the facility at Lornton, continued to conduct the project.

By the late 1960s, the NCCY had become known for its demonstration projects. Indeed, the successes of both Project Challenge and the YSP apparently led the USDL to request the NCCY to prepare two new pilot programs based on its experiences in the initial two. One was to assist state institutions throughout the country applying for federal funds for pilot projects to train prisoners. The other, which produced yet another NCCY program, hoped to provide a "sizable number" of first offenders in Washington, D.C., with intensive, pretrial rehabilitation services as a possible alternative to prosecution in criminal courts in the District of Columbia. NCCY staff member Leon Leiberg helped to inaugurate this Project Crossroads in the late summer of 1968. The Vera Institute of Justice conducted a similar program in New York City. On May 15, 1969, NCCY began the second phase of Project Crossroads with a larger grant from the federal Manpower Administration.

Before it dissolved in the mid-1970s, the NCCY continued its basic programs. In July 1970, the name of its journal changed to the *NCCY Reporter and White House Conference News*. Later in the year, the NCCY announced that Project Crossroads would be absorbed by the local court system in the District of Columbia. Early in 1971, the pretrial prevention pilot project became a service of the Superior Court of the District of Columbia. Still working to identify children's needs throughout the nation in the middle of 1971, the NCCY began, with funds from the President's Committee on Mental Retardation, a study to determine programs being operated and being planned by nationwide and state organizations in the field of mental retardation and birth defects. In what became a step toward its amalgamation with the Council of National Organizations for Children and Youth (CNOCY), the NCCY established, with the CNOCY, a nine-month Project Action Now for Children and Youth, Inc., a study and consultation program. Incorporated in the District of Columbia on August 17, 1972, this project had traditional officers, including a first and a second vice-president. Funded by the federal Office of Child Development, the project had also a fifteen-member steering committee. Mary Dublin Keyserling became the project director. In 1973, the two groups received a grant from the Foundation for Child Development* to conduct a conference of their members in the summer of 1973 and to help establish a new organization. In June 1973, the NCCY merged with the CNOCY to become the new National Council of Organizations for Children and Youth (NCOCY).

The difficult-to-locate, variously named *NCCY Follow-Up Reporter* provided generally full and detailed information about the NCCY. *The New York Times* covered some NCCY activities. Materials in the archives of the new NCOCY in Washington, D.C., provided information on the 1970s. There does not appear to be any scholarly work on the NCCY's history.

NATIONAL COMMITTEE FOR HOMEMAKER SERVICE: see NATIONAL COUNCIL FOR HOMEMAKER-HOME HEALTH AIDE SERVICES, INC.

NATIONAL COMMITTEE FOR MENTAL HYGIENE, INC., THE (NCMH). During the Progressive era, a number of reform and social service agencies were established to assist people with problems. As early as 1907, the acknowledged leader of psychiatry in the country, Dr. Adolf Meyer of New York City, and others from the New York Psychiatrical Society sponsored lectures in the hopes of developing a national organization for the mentally ill similar to the ill-fated, earlier National Association for the Protection of the Insane and the Prevention of Insanity, established in the 1880s. By the early twentieth century, as Dr. Barbara Sicherman has argued, psychiatry was increasingly acceptable as a legitimate field to the public and to professionals. The establishment of other national health agencies in the Progressive era, such as the contemporary National Association for the Study and Prevention of Tuberculosis* (NASPT), also set the stage for the development of an organization dealing with the mentally ill.

In the early twentieth century, Clifford Beers, a graduate of Yale University, was institutionalized in a mental asylum, where he observed what he thought were deplorable conditions and methods of treating patients. After his release, he published an account of his experiences in his autobiography, *A Mind That Found Itself* (1908). Continuing his efforts to improve the treatment of mental patients in institutions. Beers worked to establish on May 6, 1908, the Connecticut Society for Mental Hygiene (CSMH) as a trial organization to determine the feasibility of a national agency. The CSMH was established in the home in New Haven, Connecticut, of Reverend Anson Phelps-Stokes, a philanthropist and the secretary of Yale University. Other prominent professional and lay people who supported Beers's efforts included Dr. Adolf Meyer, Professor William James of Harvard University, who had both a personal interest and confidence in Beers's activities, and Dr. William Welch of The Johns Hopkins University Medical School, a prominent figure in public health.

As executive secretary of the CSMH, Beers developed some social services for patients, especially individual aftercare treatment, but he worked more energetically to establish a national organization. The CSMH experiment proved generally successful, and consequently, on February 19, 1909, The National Committee for Mental Hygiene (NCMH) was established in New York City by a group of twelve men and women who had been supporting Beers's efforts. Some of the people at the founding meeting were Julia Lathrop, a settlement house worker from Hull-House* (HH) in Chicago and later the first chief of the United States Children's Bureau (USCB), Jane Addams, the head of HH and the most respected national social welfare figure, and Horace Fletcher, a popular writer on health and nutrition.

The NCMH did not engage immediately in social service programs or in the social action that Beers had envisioned. Conflict, particularly between Beers and the NCMH president, Dr. Meyer, influenced the NCMH's early inaction. Beers wanted lay people—whom he felt could promote reform better than specialists could—to dominate the NCMH, but Dr. Meyer and his faction disagreed. By October 1909, Beers wanted nationwide activity to raise funds, but Meyer and his group wanted the NCMH to continue to develop such programs as the CSMH's aftercare services for patients. By early 1910, the differences between Meyer and Beers had become personal. The group that supported Beers, including Phelps-Stokes and others affiliated with Yale University—although none was a psychiatrist—decided to begin a fund-raising campaign despite Meyer, who resigned in May 1910, effective January 1911.

A reorganization of the executive occurred, and in January 1911, the NCMH decided to raise funds to secure a medical director. After Meyer's resignation, the NCMH developed a statement of goals, chiefly to protect the public's mental hygiene, but also to develop standards of care, to conduct studies of conditions, especially in mental institutions, to coordinate activities in the field, and to organize state societies similar to the one in Connecticut. In November 1911, Dr. Welch influenced philanthropist Henry Phipps, who had also contributed significantly to the NASPT, to give the NCMH $50,000. Consequently, in March 1912, the agency hired Dr. Thomas W. Salmon, who had a long and influential career with the NCMH, as director of special studies.

In 1912, Salmon initiated the wide-ranging activities of the NCMH. In the period before World War I, a series of NCMH studies showed that in some states, mental patients were still kept in jails and almshouses. This finding initiated a movement that by 1930 had removed patients from such facilities in all but five states. Made only upon request, state surveys influenced reform, for instance, in Wisconsin and Texas. In some states, the public enthusiasm generated led to the creation of state societies, which allied with the NCMH to promote further reforms in particular states.

To prevent mental illness, the NCMH developed prophylactic programs in prisons and in schools and, especially through Dr. Salmon, worked successfully for federal legislation to exclude mentally defective aliens from the country. An early, popular organizational activity was the mental health exhibit, which traveled to twelve cities in 1912 and 1913. In early 1917, the NCMH hired as associate medical director, Dr. Frederick W. Williams, who also became the editor of the agency's journal, *Mental Hygiene*. The journal was part of an expanded public education program that also included pamphlets and cooperation with established journals, such as the leading one in medicine, *The Journal of the American Medical Association*, and with *The Survey*, the leading, almost crusading, publication of the social justice Progressive movement. By 1917, when the United States entered World War I, the NCMH had already provided, from its surveys, useful information about conditions and problems relating to mental illness. It had also prompted a course in mental hygiene in the curriculum for public health officers at the Harvard University Medical School.

During the era of World War I and the 1920s, the NCMH began to achieve a national importance. In 1917, the agency began to publish annual statistics on inmates in mental institutions, a program that the United States Bureau of the Census took over in 1923. Working with federal officials, the NCMH influenced the development of neuropsychiatric services for men in the armed forces, and with the American Legion worked to establish psychiatric hospitals and services for veterans. More importantly, in 1921, with a grant from the Commonwealth Fund* (CF), the NCMH sponsored a conference to draft a program of establishing child guidance clinics, a nationwide, five-year demonstration project that the NCMH, with funds from the CF, began in 1922. In the early 1920s, the NCMH established its division on the prevention of delinquency, which conducted some demonstration projects itself, such as the one in Monmouth County, New Jersey, begun in 1922 with funds from the Laura Spelman Rockefeller Fund. The division also coordinated the drive to establish child guidance clinics in cities throughout the country. This program helped to establish a new national social service agency to deal with and to study juvenile delinquency: The American Orthopsychiatry Association* (AOA), which had its first headquarters in the NCMH offices in New York City. When this influential child guidance program ended in 1927, the NCMH's division on the prevention of delinquency became the division of community clinics and, as its new name implied, expanded its functions. With the CF and two social work schools, the NCMH established on July 1, 1927, the short-lived but important Institute for Child Guidance in New York City. The NCMH expanded its survey programs, which influenced the founding of the agency's division on hospital surveys in 1924. Also in the 1920s, the NCMH successfully encouraged colleges and universities to appoint psychiatrists to their staffs. An important organizational event occurred on May 24, 1928, when the NCMH established its American Foundation for Mental Hygiene (AFMH) as its funding and fund-raising arm, initiating an increasingly popular and important activity for national health agencies.

In the 1930s, the NCMH, as one historian suggested, became "a flourishing organization." In the early 1930s, to study medical school curriculums and to improve psychiatric training, the organization established its division of psychiatric education, which worked closely with the American Psychiatry Association (APA). With help from the CF, beginning in 1935, the division of community clinics awarded fellowships to psychiatrists to join child guidance clinics. In 1936, the NCMH joined with other groups to establish the Mental Hospital Survey Committee, carrying out a long-standing organizational activity. Also beginning in 1936, the NCMH inaugurated its research program on schizophrenia (dementia praecox). Funds from the Supreme Council, Thirty-third Degree Ancient Accepted Scottish Rites (Northern Masonic Jurisdiction)—Scottish Rites Masons (SRM)—initiated and continued this long-standing activity, still an important part of the NCMH's successor agency, The National Association for Mental Health.* (NAMH).

Consistent with its early interests in children, the NCMH began to publish in 1937 a new quarterly, *Understanding the Child,* and in the late 1930s, the agency started to sponsor regional conferences with representatives of teachers' colleges, focusing on children. In the early 1940s, with the National Education Association and the American Medical Association (AMA) and reminiscent of child hygiene campaigns in the Progressive era, the NCMH prepared *Mental Hygiene in the Classroom* for teachers. This was part of the NCMH's activities for mental hygiene, which also included cooperation with the National Congress of Parents and Teachers to coordinate mental hygiene aspects of parent-teacher programs.

In 1939, fulfilling an earlier organizational goal, the NCMH established its division on extension and field service to develop closer ties between the national agency and affiliates. In its initial year, the division focused on Delaware, where the state society quickly became a corporate member of the NCMH. In the late 1930s, with the APA, the United States Public Health Service (USPHS), and other agencies and with funds from the CF, the NCMH began a nationwide mental hospital survey.

During World War II era, the NCMH once again provided and influenced important services to the country and helped to shape important developments in rehabilitation. The NCMH continued to function generally through its divisions, which numbered seven in 1941. As the 1940s opened, the NCMH worked with the federal Selective Service to develop more effective psychiatric examinations for the armed forces. This culminated with the decision in October 1943 to have social workers and public health nurses record family and other social and psychological information. With other social service agencies, the NCMH began a study of four home communities of draftees to determine the social forces affecting the men. Early in the war preparation period, the NCMH put its educational service facilities at the disposal of Paul McNutt, the Federal Security administrator. An NCMH publication, *When He Comes Back,* was distributed widely, and it influenced growing interest in mental rehabilitation of the men in the armed forces and, consequently, other mental patients. In early 1944, the NCMH's division of rehabilitation published a directory of psychiatric resources in the country, and with funds from the Josiah Macy, Jr., Foundation, distributed it to all neuropsychiatrists in military hospitals. The NCMH had worked for years to include the psychiatric handicapped in state vocational rehabilitation services. The Borden-LaFollette Act of July 1944 made this group eligible for such services. NCMH personnel lectured widely on and promoted the development of rehabilitation facilities for the mentally handicapped, and the NCMH cooperated with many other agencies to help returning men. This concern for rehabilitating servicemen led to further NCMH activities, such as a pilot project begun in 1946 with funds from the CF to work with the federal Bureau of Vocational Rehabilitation and state bureaus in Connecticut, Michigan, and New York to develop vocational rehabilitation programs for the mentally or emotionally handicapped. The NCMH contributed in a variety of ways to cooperative work with the federal Veterans Administration (VA).

During the war, the NCMH also continued its basic programs and activities and even developed some new ones, aside from those relating to the war. In 1940, the NCMH inaugurated an aggressive plan to begin a nationwide campaign, state by state, to have its recommendations adopted and to improve conditions in the care of mental patients. The war emergency apparently delayed this activity, and as manpower in mental hospitals shifted to the war effort, some facilities deteriorated. Despite the enactment of the Hospital Survey and Construction Act of 1946, the NCMH decided in 1946 to renew this effort to improve conditions.

In 1942, it began a creative new activity to dramatize the problems and the social services of mental hygiene in play format, an idea that later became popular in the social service field, especially through Plays-for-Living, a program of the Family Service Association of America* (FSAA). Research into schizophrenia continued, and during the period, the NCMH continued its efforts, successfully, to establish what became in 1946 the federal National Institute of Mental Health (NIMH) (see *Government Agencies*).

Activities related to child guidance began to focus on rural needs. In 1946, the division on community clinics surveyed smaller and rural communities to determine how they could best use funds provided by the Mental Health Act of 1946 for mental health facilities. Also in 1946, the division helped to establish the American Association of Psychiatric Clinics for Children as an independent organization. The efforts to improve mental hygiene in the schools expanded. Beginning in 1940–1941, with funds from the Carnegie Corporation, the NCMH began experiments at three colleges to teach prospective teachers about the importance of mental hygiene. A project in Delaware tried to show the feasibility of promoting mental hygiene in the schools. Films, publications such as the NCMH's *Understanding the Child,* and other sources helped these efforts. In 1943, a demonstration project for the New York City Board of Education at Public School 33 tried similarly to show the benefits of teaching mental hygiene. Attempting to spread this program, beginning in 1944, the NCMH sent reports of this continuing program to interested social service agencies. Other activities during the war period included new and expanding efforts to attract more trained personnel to the field; serving as an adviser to the Social Work Vocational Bureau; establishing in 1946 an advisory committee on psychiatric social work, and in December 1945, a psychiatric personnel placement service, supported jointly by the APA, to place physicians in mental facilities; and, beginning in 1946, with funds from philanthropist Mary Lasker, research in psychosomatic medicine.

Some important organizational events occurred during the 1940s. On July 9, 1943, founder Beers died, depriving the NCMH of one of its most energetic workers. Also in 1943, psychiatric pioneer Dr. Meyer retired as president; he became honorary president. In 1945, the field staff was established formally, and it quickly organized groups in Ohio, Illinois, and Oklahoma. In 1948, the NCMH received a sizable grant, $500,000, from the Ittleson Family Foundation. The rise and development of other agencies in the field, such as the National Mental Health Foundation, Inc.* (NMHF), prompted discussions about forming a single, unified organization. Subsequently, in September 1950, the NCMH merged with the NMHF and The Psychiatric Foundation to form the new National Association for Mental Health (NAMH).

The sources for studying the NCMH's history are extensive. Throughout the Papers of Clifford Beers, deposited at the Oskar Diethelm Historical Library of Cornell University Medical College in New York City are correspondence, scrapbooks, minutes of meetings, and the like relating to the history of the organization. In the summer of 1976, that library had just received the first shipment of the NCMH's records, which include pamphlets of all types, histories of the mental hygiene movement and the NCMH, correspondence with and about state associations and with important individuals, and minutes of meetings. The papers were completely disorganized when I saw them. The Papers of Arnold Gesell at the Library of Congress in Washington, D.C., contain minutes and publications of the agency. More accessible are the NCMH's published *Annual Reports*. Founder Beers's *A Mind That Found Itself* (1953) contains a helpful history of the NCMH, as does an agency publication, *Twenty Years of Mental Hygiene, 1909–1929* (1929). Contemporary accounts of the agency's activities can be found in a host of sources.

Secondary studies of the agency include Barbara Sicherman, "The Quest for Mental Health in America, 1880–1917" (Ph.D. diss., Columbia University, 1967), and Nina Ridenour, *Mental Health in the United States: A Fifty-Year History* (1961). There does not appear to be a scholarly, full-length history of the NCMH.

NATIONAL COMMITTEE FOR THE PREVENTION OF BLINDNESS: see NATIONAL SOCIETY FOR THE PREVENTION OF BLINDNESS, INC.

NATIONAL COMMITTEE ON ALCOHOLISM: see NATIONAL COUNCIL ON ALCOHOLISM, INC.

NATIONAL COMMITTEE ON PRISONS AND PRISON LABOR (NCPPL).

The nineteenth-century practice of contract labor using convicts and road gangs prompted reformers' outcries. At its inception in the 1870s, for instance, the American Prison Association* (APA) denounced the exploitative contract system. The APA occasionally discussed this issue, and eventually there was some reform. In New York State in 1894, for example, a law was passed making such forms of contract labor illegal. The movement in New York also prompted the development of another system of labor in prisons. Prison reformers generally agreed that inmates should do constructive work in which they were not exploited and abused. Gradually prisoners began to produce various goods that were sold outside the prison. Organized labor generally opposed this practice because prison-made products were often substituted by buyers for union-made products. Consequently, laws were developed that required full and proper labeling on prison-made goods, which also were sold to state agencies, the so-called states' use system. Apparently in 1909, the chairman of the industry and child labor committee of the New York State Federation of Women's Clubs, Helen Varick Boswell, learned of a violation in the system, and, concerned that violations intefered with the legitimate occupations and work of women, she filed a complaint with the New York State Department of Labor (NYSDL). The commissioner of labor, L. John Williams, assigned this complaint to an investigator in the department, E. Stagg Whitin, who had been the secretary of the New York Welfare Commission of the National Civic Federation (NCF) in 1906 and 1907.

This complaint and reports of other abuses prompted Commissioner Williams to argue in late 1909 that violations in the prison labor system threatened free labor, and he called on "penologists, public officials, practical businessmen, publicists, and representatives of social reform" to meet and develop a nationwide policy on prison labor. Obviously aware of Commissioner Williams's suggestion, apparently in late 1910, such a group did form the National Committee on Prisons and Prison Labor (NCPPL) as the National Committee on Prison Labor (NCPL). The NCPL's founders and early leaders, led by Whitin, included Reverend Thomas R. Slicer of the All Souls' Church in New York City, who was long identified with prison labor reform, R. Montgomery Schell, an architect and philanthropist who served for many years as a general trustee of the George Junior Republic, a unique organization dealing with delinquent and tough boys, and, from the social reform group to which Commissioner Williams had referred in 1909, Joseph Byers, the secretary of the APA, who served on the NCPL's initial executive committee, as did Harry Soloman, president of the New York State Prison Commission.

In an ambitious attempt to develop a nationwide policy, the NCPL began immediately to determine prison labor conditions in each state. Collecting information through questionnaires and NCPL agents, the group even began to draft plans for particular states. In its first decade, the NCPL concerned itself with a variety of prison-related issues, but it focused on its initial concern, convict labor. Chiefly through the personal efforts of Secretary Whitin, who was also an assistant in social legislation at Columbia University, the NCPL helped to draft the labor plank in the platform of Eugene N. Foss, who was elected governor of Massachusetts in 1911. During this period, Whitin also addressed the Kentucky legislature and the annual meeting of the charity organization society in Lexington, where he organized reform groups to work in the state with the Kentucky Federation of Labor.

Governor Francis E. McGovern of Wisconsin sought the NCPL's assistance, assigning Whitin to a state board and giving him power and remuneration. At the Federal Aid Congress in Washington, D.C., Congressman Oscar W. Underwood of Alabama and Whitin spoke jointly about the need for a national movement to build roads with convict labor. This subject interested members of the women's department of the NCF, who organized a committee to promote local-level reform in prison labor. Whitin's national influence led him to serve with a distinguished committee steering a bill for a national jail commission. Others in this group included Hastings Hart of the Russell Sage Foundation,* Paul Kellogg, editor of *The Survey,* the most important journal in social service and social reform, Professor Charles Henderson of the University of Chicago and a noted reformer, and Bailey Burritt, the executive leader of the New York Association for Improving the Condition of the Poor.*

By 1912, the NCPL had established its lecture bureau, featuring Reverend Slicer. The agency's publication, *Penal Servitude* (1912), was distributed by the Charities Publication Committee, a national body. In 1912, the Thomas Edison Company prepared a motion picture of the NCPL's work, which was shown at the Conference of Hygiene and Demography in Washington, D.C., and at the opening ceremonies of the Educational Building in Albany, New York. In 1911–1912, the NCPL surveyed and published references to prison labor in party platforms. In 1912, the NCPL participated energetically in the campaign for a bill to restrict the interstate commerce of prison labor, and in New Jersey, the agency supported the movement for a states' use system there. The NCPL's legal committee challenged the use of convict labor in Rhode Island calling it slavery. Reverend Slicer spoke at the National Conference of Charities and Correction* in Cleveland, Ohio, in June 1912, and the agency made presentations to the governor's conferences in 1911 and 1912. The NCPL was forming local committees in Massachusetts, Ohio, Illinois, Pennsylvania, and Alabama, and in 1912, the NCPL moved its offices from Columbia University in New York to midtown Manhattan. At its headquarters, the agency maintained its bureau of information.

To reflect its broadening interests in the prison field, the NCPL changed its name to the National Committee on Prisons and Prison Labor (NCPPL) in about 1915. Its committee structure suggested its concerns and activities. There were committees on social hygiene of the prisoner, chaired by James Reynolds of the American Social Hygiene Association,* and on labor, headed by Collis Lovely, vice-president of the International Boot and Shoe Workers' Union. The jail committee, chaired by Hastings Hart, had members in thirty states who guided investigations in their respective states. One such study apparently exposed the scandalous conditions at the Oneida County, New York jail in Utica, promoting the removal and indictments of some officials. The NCPPL's committee on honor men promoted legislation to have prisoners work outside prisons, such as on roads. And the educational committee was developing a night school at Sing Sing prison in New York in cooperation with Teachers College of Columbia University.

In the 1920s, when other national reform agencies experienced difficulties, the NCPPL increased its activities, involving itself increasingly in the mechanics of a sound prison labor system. In the early years of the decade, the organization focused once again on the development of states' use methods of marketing prison-made products to state institutions and agencies and of selling the surplus to other states: the plan called for all ablebodied prisoners to work as a constructive activity. In 1924, the NCPPL helped four regional conferences on allocating products. The success of the first one led to a grant of $15,000 from the Bureau of Social Hygiene (BSH). NCPPL's standing committee on the allocation of prison industries sponsored these gatherings, which contributed significantly to the zone plan of marketing prison goods regionally. A notable achievement occurred in New York in 1925 when, through the efforts of Honorary President Adolph Lewisohn, officials created a board of prison industries and hired an experienced businessman as the superintendent of prison industries. The prejudice in some state institutions against prison-made products, however, led the NCPPL in the mid-1920s to lead in the development of Associates for Government Service, Inc., which acted as an agency to exchange surpluses among the states. Continuing to specialize in the field of prison labor, the NCPPL committee on the care and treatment of delinquent women and girls, with a special grant from the BSH, conducted a survey of industries suitable for women's institutions. Beginning in the early 1920s, the organization campaigned for federal legislation in the field, a movement culminating in a conference in December 1927 that crystallized NCPPL aims, and prepared briefs for impending federal legislation sponsored by Senator Harry B. Hawes of Missouri and Congressman John G. Cooper of Ohio, a former steel worker.

The enactment of the Hawes-Cooper Bill, signed on January 19, 1929, which facilitated the interstate distribution of prison-made products, highlighted the later years of the 1920s, which brought other accomplishments as well. A NCPPL suggestion apparently led to a study by the United States Children's Bureau, published in 1928 as *Welfare of Prisoners Families in Kentucky*. More trade associations, such as the Association of Cotton Textile Manufacturers, welcomed NCPPL presentations at their annual meetings to improve the contract system in prisons, and the United States secretary of commerce, Herbert Hoover, aided the reform movement when he convened the conference in December 1927 that worked on the Hawes-Cooper bill.

Such new activities led inevitably to organizational expansion. At its annual meeting in 1930, the NCPPL authorized the doubling of its board of directors from twelve to twenty-four members, and in 1931, the agency created its national advisory committee on institutional industries to help prison officials reorganize and develop industries and to prepare for the implementation of the Hawes-Cooper Act. At the annual meeting in 1913, the organization established a national council, composed initially of fifteen state prison, educational, and other leaders to carry out the work of the NCPPL in their respective states. In 1931, the board of directors created a finance committee to deal with an increasingly complex organizational issue: finances.

The NCPPL characteristically broadened its range of concerns and activities in the 1930s but continued its efforts in the labor field, for instance, by helping states to prepare for the implementation of the Hawes-Cooper Act in January 1934. At its meeting in December 1929, the board of directors reaffirmed its faith in inmate shop organization, despite misuses and the recent riots at the state prison in Auburn, New York.

During the 1930s, the NCPPL initiated studies of prison architecture. Articles appearing in 1931 in *The Survey* and the *Architectural Forum* and other analyses argued that fortress-type institutions were needed for only part of the prison population. NCPPL efforts led the New York State legislature to establish in August 1930 a Commission to Investigate Prison Administration and Construction, with which it cooperated.

In the summer of 1933, the NCPPL committee dealing with women prisoners established a six-week training course and internship at the New York State Training School for Girls in Hudson, New York. In the late 1930s, the NCPPL's interest in and concern for the handling of juvenile delinquents in New York City led the agency to urge Mayor Fiorello La Guardia to establish a committee to study this problem. Subsequently, the NCPPL was asked to help develop a plan to regulate the intake bureau, an adjunct of the Children's Court of the City of New York. The committee on slavery, which was part of the NCPPL, led the agency to protest in 1941 against German products because they were made, according to the agency, with slave labor. The death of Julia K. Jaffray in May 1941 deprived the NCPPL of one of its most important workers. In September 1941, a diminished income forced the agency to reduce its office staff and facilities further. The death of its leader, E. Stagg Whitin, in 1946 hurt the agency even more, and apparently in the late 1940s, the NCPPL disbanded.

The NCPPL's history can be traced through a variety of sources. For the 1920s and early 1930s, there are published and detailed *Annual Reports,* and for the earlier years, *The Prison Labor Bulletin* is helpful. Some contemporary publications, such as *The National Committee on Prisons and Prison Labor—Its Origin, Purpose, and Present Activity* (1915), and E. Stagg Whitin, *Penal Servitude* (1912), contain information about the agency. There are some materials in the Papers of Samuel McCune Lindsay at the Library of Columbia University in New York City.

There does not appear to be a scholarly historical study of the NCPPL.

NATIONAL COMMITTEE ON THE AGING: see NATIONAL COUNCIL ON THE AGING, INC., THE.

NATIONAL COMMITTEE ON VOLUNTEERS IN SOCIAL WORK: see ASSOCIATION OF VOLUNTEER BUREAUS, INC.

NATIONAL CONFERENCE OF CATHOLIC CHARITIES (NCCC). In 1845, in St. Louis, Missouri, a major Catholic social service agency in the United States, the Society of St. Vincent de Paul* (SSVP) was established. It was not a truly national agency but operated primarily on the diocesan level. The need for a national organization concerned with Catholic charities was recognized at the annual meeting of the SSVP at Louisville, Kentucky, in December 1897. Its leaders held another meeting to discuss the issue at Cliff Haven, New York, in August 1898, but nothing seems to have materialized from these talks.

Growing interest in a national conference became more evident at the SSVP's meeting in Richmond, Virginia, in 1908. At Richmond, Thomas Mulry of New York, a volunteer leader of the SSVP and known affectionately as the American Ozanam—after the SSVP founder in France—assembled the interested delegates. Others important in these organizing efforts in 1908–1910 were Monsignor William J. White, the director of Catholic charities in Brooklyn, New York, since 1899, and Monsignor Dennis J. McMahon, the supervisor of Catholic charities in New York City. Further discussions occurred at the annual National Conference on Charities and Correction* (NCCC) in 1909. The Catholic group designated Brother Barnabas, who had organized a home-finding bureau for dependent children at the New York Catholic Protectory, to approach Bishop Thomas Shahan, the rector of The Catholic University of America, about convening a meeting to establish a national organization for Catholic charities. Bishop Shahan issued an invitation to Catholic leaders throughout the country to attend such a meeting. Subsequently, on February 19, 1910, twenty-two representatives from Catholic social work founded the National Conference of Catholic Charities (NCCC) at a meeting at The Catholic University of America in Washington, D.C.

The organizing sessions took three days. At these meetings, the founders appointed a committee on the organization and chose a provisional executive committee to organize a conference in September 1910. The provisional officers included as president, Bishop Shahan; as vice-president, Mulry; as secretary, Monsignor William J. Kerby, a professor of sociology at the Catholic University of America; and a treasurer. With four other members of the executive committee, these men arranged the first national conference of Catholic charities in Washington, D.C., beginning on September 25, 1910. About four hundred delegates, largely lay volunteers and professional social workers from twenty-four states and thirty-eight cities attended. A permanent organization, with Bishop Shahan as president and Monsignor Kerby as secretary, was established.

In its early years, the NCCC fulfilled its initial purposes: to study the conditions of Catholic charities, to develop closer contacts between workers in the field, to develop a body of literature about Catholic social work, and to involve the clergy in social service activities. Another early goal, generally fulfilled by 1930, was to establish well-run charitable bureaus in every diocese in the United States. As early as 1916, diocesan directors of charity formed a group at the conference. This group became a constituent organization of the NCCC, providing a link between the national conference and local communities. In September 1916, the NCCC formally established *The Catholic Charities Review,* edited by

Reverend John Ryan, the long-time head of the Social Action Department* of the National Catholic Welfare Conference (NCWC). At this time, the earlier *St. Vincent de Paul Quarterly* ceased publication and merged with the *Review,* which first appeared in January 1917. In 1920, the religious orders formed the special conference of religious engaged in social and charitable work, known as the conference of religious, which also became a constituent member of the NCCC in 1920. Another important organizational event occurred in 1920 when Monsignor Kerby resigned as secretary and was replaced by Reverend John O'Grady, the former assistant secretary of the NCCC. During the period between 1910 and 1920, the NCCC met biennially, but it decided to meet annually beginning in 1921.

The year 1921 thus ushered in a new era for the NCCC. During this and the earlier period, the conference was organized, like the National Conference of Social Work* (NCSW), around topic committees: families, the sick, dependent children, social and civic activities, women's activities, and delinquency. Diocesan directors, the conference of religious, and the SSVP each continued to have separate sessions. During the 1920s, however, the SSVP became increasingly isolated as the NCCC stressed professionalism. In 1921, the executive committee of the NCCC reached an agreement with the NCWC, allowing the NCCC to focus on dependency and family relief. In 1922, fulfilling an initial goal, the NCCC published *A Directory of Catholic Charities,* and the organization conducted surveys of local areas. Concern with the problems of child care institutions prompted the appointment of a special study committee. The committee published *A Program for Catholic Child-Caring Homes* in 1923. Other publications of the NCCC in the 1920s included Monsignor Kerby's *The Social Mission of the Church* (1921), hailed as a "milestone" in Catholic social work, and Reverend Edward R. Moore, *The Case Against Birth Control* (1931), the result of a two-year study by the NCCC's committee on population decline and related problems. In 1926, the NCCC's committee on standards of family casework in diocesan agencies prepared *A Program for Family Service in Diocesan Agencies,* and the NCCC ended the decade with the publication of O'Grady's important *Catholic Charities in the United States* (1930).

In the 1930s and 1940s, there were some changes in the NCCC's structure and some other important developments. Amid the rise of government welfare services in the 1930s, the NCCC became a vigorous defender of the role of voluntary agencies. Despite the conservative Catholic laity, the NCCC worked for such progressive measures as old age security and improved housing, a movement in which Secretary O'Grady was especially active. Also in the 1930s, the conference leaders wanted some form of national health legislation. This identification of the NCCC with the social reform movement before about 1935 was, according to the historian of the NCCC, one of its greatest achievements. Beginning in late 1934, the continuing committee of diocesan directors of charity issued bulletins and, in late 1943, the NCCC began to publish informational bulletins for child care institutions. In the late 1930s, the NCCC began to hold regional conferences, which quickly became popular. After roughly 1935, the NCCC shifted from its emphasis on professionalism to a concern for and an emphasis on volunteers and the SSVP, publishing in 1942, *A Call to Service,* a manual for volunteers. In 1940, with the federal Bureau of Prisons, the NCCC held the Institute for Catholic Prison Chaplains in Washington, D.C. In 1943, it established its committee on neighborhood organization.

Toward the end of World War II, the NCCC once again studied local communities, and after the war, the NCCC served as an information center, issuing a new *Information Bulletin* in January 1947. In 1947, the standing committee for religious was established; it emphasized study and research. After soliciting suggestions about the program at the annual meeting, the executive committee appointed, in 1947, a committee on interpretation of the constitution to study and to explain the relation of the diocesan leaders and the religious, as well as the SSVP, to the conference. One of the committee's recommendations was to establish a nine-member program committee to take the place of the topic committees. The executive committee approved this proposal on November 18, 1949, and the membership did so the next day. Also in 1949, the executive committee was renamed the board of directors.

Professionalism, new forms of sessions, and high-caliber studies characterized the decade of the 1950s. A growing distaste for prepared papers and speeches prompted the conference of religious to use workshops successfully. By the mid-1950s, the conference emphasized "integration" of the laity, the religious, and the clergy. Sessions began with a keynote speaker and followed with small discussion groups. The participants then reassembled to hear reports from the discussion groups. The conference also stressed "subsidiarity," or the recognition of a hierarchy of social problems beginning with the family and continuing through the neighborhood and community before the government had the right to interfere. In 1954, the NCCC published a study sponsored by the conference of religious, *The Housemother,* by Sister M. Charles, R.S.M. Another important study was one by Beatrice M. Faivre on Gannondale, a children's home in Erie, Pennsylvania. In 1955, the NCCC sponsored the Work Conference of the Problems of Juveniles in Cleveland, Ohio, and in the late 1950s, the NCCC held conferences on ways to eliminate the odious features of the reactionary McCarran-Walter Act of 1952, which dealt with immigration. The golden anniversary meeting, held in New York City in late September 1960, was a gala event. President Dwight D. Eisenhower attended the conference.

In the 1960s, the NCCC received a grant from the United States Children's Bureau to develop a system of collecting data for agencies serving unwed mothers. This was a cooperative project with the Florence Crittenton Association of America, Inc.,* and The Salvation Army.* Continuing to serve its own constituents, the NCCC held institutes on administration in Catholic agencies and institutions during the 1960s. In the late 1960s, the associate secretary traveled around the country with others to raise funds for Biafran children. In the early 1970s, the NCCC went through a lengthy process of discussions and reorganization. Among other topics, it discussed the theological bases of charities and justice and renewed its emphasis on education, advocacy, and social planning.

The primary sources for studying the NCCC's history are the agency's files at its national headquarters in Washington, D.C., as well as the papers of Monsignors Kerby and John A. Ryan and Bishop Shahan, all at the archives of The Catholic University of America, in Washington, D.C. Published primary sources include the *Proceedings* and *The Catholic Charities Review*. Some papers delivered at conferences contain information about the NCCC's history.

Donald P. Gavin's *The National Conference of Catholic Charities, 1910–1960* (1962) is a helpful account.

NATIONAL CONFERENCE OF CHARITIES: see NATIONAL CONFERENCE ON SOCIAL WELFARE.

NATIONAL CONFERENCE OF CHARITIES AND CORRECTION: see NATIONAL CONFERENCE ON SOCIAL WELFARE.

NATIONAL CONFERENCE OF JEWISH CHARITIES: see NATIONAL CONFERENCE OF JEWISH COMMUNAL SERVICE.

NATIONAL CONFERENCE OF JEWISH COMMUNAL SERVICE (NCJCS). In the late nineteenth century, Jewish charities arose in cities throughout the country. To discuss common problems and programs, philanthropists and social workers from local Jewish charities founded the National Conference of Jewish Communal Service (NCJCS) as the National Conference of Jewish Charities in the United States (NCJC) at a meeting on June 11, 1900, in Chicago, Illinois. Max Senior, a Cincinnati businessman and philanthropist active in the Jewish federation movement, served as its first president, and Boris Bogen, a Russian-born social worker who during his career directed local, national, and international Jewish social service institutions, assumed the post of secretary. The NCJF met biennially until 1918 and annually thereafter. From the time of its inception the NCJCS has been the major forum at which Jewish agencies and social workers discuss their common problems and programs.

One of the first issues to confront the NCJC was the growing number of Jewish transients who moved from one city to another and requested aid at each stop. The transients demanded a significant share of Jewish relief funds from the member agencies and then abandoned each city before any constructive work could be accomplished with them. To meet this problem, the NCJC in 1900 worked out a set of "Rules for the Regulation of Transportation," which defined a transient's home city and placed on it primary responsibility for the relief and care of the mobile individual or family. The conference hoped to implement this program through the voluntary cooperation of Jewish social service bureaus across the country.

Early conferences also dealt with the highly visible problem of the Jewish poor who remained resident in the overcrowded slums of major American cities. Social workers read papers advocating the resettlement of a significant portion of Jewish ghetto dwellers in agricultural communities or in the midwestern United States. They described and supported endeavors such as the Galveston movement, directed by Morris D. Waldman, the Industrial Removal Office* (IRO), headed by David M. Bressler, and the Baron de Hirsch Fund's agricultural projects, the most prominent of which was at Woodbine, New Jersey, under the direction of H. L. Sabsovich. All of these agencies and programs aimed at redistributing the Jewish immigrant population from urban to rural areas. Though much effort and money went into these schemes, they failed fundamentally to alter Eastern European Jewish residence patterns in America.

Another issue discussed by the NCJC during the first two decades of its existence was the proper care of dependent or orphaned children. Although congregate facilities still had their proponents in the NCJC, the majority opinion gradually swung to a policy of foster care in cases of placement, small group homes where institutionalization was deemed necessary, and a new stress on keeping families of half orphans together so that the need for placement would be reduced. Ludwig B. Bernstein, superintendent of the Hebrew Sheltering Guardian Orphan Asylum, established himself early as an expert in the field.

In 1910, Morris D. Waldman, then head of the United Hebrew Charities of the City of New York* (UHC) and who later became executive vice-president of the American Jewish Committee, read a stunning paper to the conference on the pressing problem of desertion among Jewish families. In response to Waldman's and others' proposals, the NCJC established under its auspices the National Desertion Bureau* (NDB) to help locate deserting husbands and induce them to return or at least to support their families. Legal action was taken where appropriate. In September 1914, when the NDB was incorporated according to the laws of the State of New York, this influential agency broke its formal ties with the NCJC.

Reflecting the current trend toward professional social work and away from traditional charity, the NCJC changed its name in 1919 to the National Conference of Jewish Social Service (NCJSS). Workers discussed the latest methods of scientific and professional casework at their meetings and tried to apply them in practice. It became a point of pride among Jewish agencies to attain the highest professional standards then possible in the field of social service.

After earlier halting attempts to support an independent journal, the NCJSS founded the *Jewish Social Service Quarterly (JSSQ)* in 1924. As editor, the conference chose Dr. I. M. Rubinow, a nationally prominent expert on social insurance and executive director of the Jewish Welfare Society of Philadelphia.

Rubinow attempted to print articles of scholarly as well as social service interest in the *JSSQ,* although his efforts did not always succeed. He was particularly interested in the adequacy of relief given by the Jewish agencies and in having the family agency retain its place as the center of a city's federation of Jewish philanthropies.

In 1925, after much discussion of its scope and function, the NCJSS helped to found the Training (later Graduate) School for Jewish Social Work (TSJSW). Students at this school took courses in generic social work at the nearby New York School of Social Work while they received training in the Jewish aspects of their field at the TSJSW. Maurice E. Karpf, until then director of the Jewish Social Service Bureau of Chicago and later active in many national and international social work organizations, headed the school, which was closed in 1940. Among the professors of Jewish social and religious history and institutions was Mordecai M. Kaplan, who also taught at the Jewish Theological Seminary and founded the Reconstructionist Movement in Judaism. Kaplan maintained an enduring interest in Jewish social service and wrote frequently about the topic.

In the 1920s, the NCJSS, the *JSSQ,* and the Training School all concentrated their attention on establishing a scientific basis for their work. They strove to perfect their procedures for granting relief and to develop the nonrelief aspects of social casework. Topics prominent at this time included advocacy of birth control, the mental hygiene movement, helping families with personal problems, and the utilization of home economics.

When the Great Depression struck in 1929, the NCJSS responded in two ways. First, led by Rubinow, Harry L. Lurie, director of the Bureau for Jewish Social Research* and later of the Council of Jewish Federations and Welfare Funds* (CJFWF), Frances Taussig, executive director of the Jewish Social Service Association* of New York, and Dorothy Kahn, executive director of Philadelphia's Jewish Welfare Society, the NCJSS became a vocal and powerful advocate of government takeover of relief to the unemployed. The conference quickly recognized that its agencies could not continue their traditional role of caring for all Jewish dependent cases and called for public assistance measures to relieve private agencies of the burden of economic assistance. Second, NCJSS encouraged its members to maintain high standards of relief in cases they did aid. During this period, in 1937, the conference again changed its name to the National Conference of Jewish Social Welfare (NCJSW).

Just before and after World War II, Jewish social service agencies were called upon to care for refugees who fled from Nazi rule and survivors of the European holocaust. The community organized on national and local levels to aid refugees and displaced persons by getting them to the United States and helping them adjust to their new country. This process served as a constant topic for discussion at NCJSW conferences in the late 1930s, 1940s, and early 1950s.

Jewish social service, like the field of social work in general, took on new functions in the postdepression era. Having given over its relief responsibilities to the federal government, it now concentrated on personal and intensive work with its caseload. It adapted the techniques of psychology, psychiatry, and psychoanalysis to understand its clients better and to provide them with more skilled service. Numerous social workers and executives discussed the techniques and implications of the new directions in social work at NCJSW conferences.

In 1951, the NCJSW changed its name to the National Conference of Jewish Communal Service (NCJCS). Five years later, the *JSSQ* followed by altering its title to the *Journal of Jewish Communal Service (JJCS)*. These new designations reflected an expanding interest of the conference beyond traditional social welfare issues to the newer fields of community center work, educational matters, and communal relations. Discussants at the meetings now dealt with topics like the relationship of the community center to the synagogue, the responsibility of the social welfare network for the needs of the entire Jewish community, and the latest trends in helping techniques. These have remained the major interest of the NCJCS through the 1970s. Two recent concerns of the conference were the plight of the Jewish aged and the geographical distribution of the Jewish community and its implication for social service.

Throughout its existence the NCJSS struggled to defune the nature of the Jewish auspices of its work. In the 1920s, for example, NCJSS members often expressed the rationale that only Jewish social workers could fully understand the needs and values of Jewish immigrants, and therefore Jewish agencies were necessary to service this particular population. In the 1950s, with the emergence of personal casework on an intensive basis, the Jewish agencies argued that a Jew could discuss his problems more easily at a Jewish agency because of a primary ethnic bond between client and worker and that Jews desired to support Jewish casework agencies. This issue has never been satisfactorily resolved. Among those who have made outstanding contributions in addressing this topic are Harry L. Lurie, Harold Silver, director of the Jewish Social Service Bureau of Detroit, and Robert Morris, assistant director of the social planning department of the CJFWF and later professor of social planning at the Florence Heller Graduate School of Brandeis University.

An outstanding one-volume introduction to the NCJSC is Robert Morris and Michael Freund, eds., *Trends and Issues in Jewish Social Welfare in the United States, 1899–1958* (1966). Morris and Freund have reprinted the most important papers read at NCJCS conventions, covering all of its existence. They also provide lucid introductions to each section and an appendix containing lists of conference publications, meeting locations, presidents, secretaries, and selected documents. The reader who wants to go beyond a one-volume introduction will have to explore the *Proceedings* of each conference, which was published, with some interruptions, in book form until 1930 and as a section of the *JSSQ* and *JJCS* thereafter. The papers of the conference from the 1920s to the 1950s are located at the YIVO Institute for Jewish Research in New York. Papers of the

Graduate School for Jewish Social Work can be found at the American Jewish Historical Society in Waltham, Massachusetts. Secondary works that touch on the history of the NCJCS are Herman D. Stein, "Jewish Social Work in the United States, 1654–1954" (Ph.D. diss., Columbia University, 1958), which is abridged in the *American Jewish Year Book, 1956*, 1–98; Alfred J. Kutzik, "The Social Basis of American Jewish Philanthropy" (Ph.D. diss., Brandeis University, 1967); and Harry L. Lurie, *A Heritage Affirmed* (1961).

Gary E. Rubin

NATIONAL CONFERENCE OF JEWISH SOCIAL SERVICE: see NATIONAL CONFERENCE OF JEWISH COMMUNAL SERVICE.

NATIONAL CONFERENCE OF SOCIAL WORK: see NATIONAL CONFERENCE ON SOCIAL WELFARE.

NATIONAL CONFERENCE ON SOCIAL WELFARE (NCSW). In February 1872, the secretary of the Illinois Board of State Commissioners of Public Charities, Frederick H. Wines, and the president of the State Board of Charities and Reform of the State of Wisconsin, Andrew E. Elmore, spent a few days visiting welfare institutions in Wisconsin and discussing issues in their field. After these discussions and exchanges of ideas, the men decided to write to delegates from similar official charity boards from other states in the Upper Mississippi Valley. Subsequently, in May 1872, representatives from the boards of Illinois, Wisconsin, and Michigan held a two-day conference in Chicago. Delegates from these three states met again on April 15, 1873, in Milwaukee, Wisconsin. These conferences attracted national attention; they so impressed the American Social Science Association (ASSA) that it decided to expand its meetings to include representatives from all such state boards of charity and health in the United States. In 1874, the Massachusetts Board of State Charities and the ASSA's section on social economy sent invitations to these representatives to meet. Consequently, on May 20, 1874, delegates from the state boards of Massachusetts, Connecticut, New York, and Wisconsin met in New York City and founded the National Conference on Social Welfare (NCSW) as the Conference of Boards of Public Charities (CBPC).

The state boards of Rhode Island, Pennsylvania, Michigan, and Kansas soon approved of the venture in establishing a clearinghouse between the state agencies. The most important founders of the CBPC were Franklin B. Sanborn, the first secretary of the Massachusetts Board of State Charities, Wines, Elmore, and William P. Letchworth, a Quaker from Buffalo, New York, who had retired from business at the age of fifty and devoted his life to charities. Both Sanborn and Wines later credited Elmore with the idea for a national conference of charities. The CBPC, which changed its name to the Conference of Charities (CC) in 1875, began to hold sessions at the annual meetings of the ASSA. The range of people attending grew gradually. The CC's interest in such issues as immigration, child labor, and compulsory school attendance overlapped with those of the ASSA. In 1877, representatives from Wisconsin felt the CC should meet separately as an independent body. Wisconsin even refused to attend the meetings unless its wishes were met, but the CC did convene in 1878, without Wisconsin delegates. At the conference in 1878, the group voted to separate from its parent body, the ASSA.

The CC began to meet separately in 1879. In this early period, men in the field of medicine, mostly from state welfare institutions' staffs, were prominent in the organization. Early themes at the conferences included insanity, the prevention of pauperism, immigrants, and, as expected, public buildings for dependents and prisoners. Dependent, delinquent, and impoverished children were early concerns. Debates dealt with subjects such as whether state boards should be administrative or supervisory. After frequent name changes during this period, the organization became the National Conference of Charities and Correction (NCCC) in 1884. Discussions revealed interests in the accuracy of statistics in the field and in abolishing physical and other restraints in state institutions. The NCCC was close to the American Prison Association* during this period and shared many of its concerns. The NCCC, however, often clashed with the National Association of Superintendents and Members of Boards of Asylums for the Insane. One highlight was the paper in 1876 by Richard Dugdale on the study of the criminally insane Juke family. As expected, representatives from and the interests of public (rather than private) charities dominated the early phase of the organization's history.

The rise of private, voluntary organizations, especially charity organization societies, in the late nineteenth century influenced the NCCC's increasing concern with the field of charities and helped to add a new dimension to the organization. Representatives of state boards and public welfare had dominated the presidency during the NCCC's first twenty-odd years, but in the twenty-year period from 1896 to 1916, only six presidents were from this class. For the next thirty years, no representative from public charities served as president until 1945, when Dr. Ellen Potter, who was close to the national private social work community but who also worked for the New Jersey Department of Institutions and Agencies, became president. In 1891, the NCCC's committee on penology and reformatory systems conducted a comprehensive report that stressed the values of individualized treatment. It also emphasized that institutions should be strictly reformatory, not punitive.

Private charities began to exert a stronger influence than before. Discussions of child welfare at the NCCC in the 1890s generally opposed the system of state subsidies to private agencies caring for children, a movement spearheaded by the leaders of voluntary organizations, such as Josephine Shaw Lowell of the Charity Organization Society of the City of New York* (COS) and Homer Folks, the executive secretary of the State Charities Aid Association* (SCAA) of New York. The NCCC sponsored the session on child welfare at the Columbian

Exposition in Chicago in 1893 and published the proceedings of this conference as *History of Child Saving in the United States*. The volume's contents contributed importantly to the contemporary—and at the NCCC, occasionally bitter—debates on whether dependent children should be cared for in institutions or foster family homes. Apparently in the mid-1890s, the NCCC developed a plan whereby the president regularly appointed functional committees. With only slight changes, this system remained until 1934, when the bylaws began to provide for a program committee to handle the sessions. Although social settlements became an important factor in social work and social reform in the 1890s and beyond, in the period through the 1920s, they did not seem important at the NCCC. The settlements had their own sessions only eight times in the thirty-odd years between 1894 and 1923. Nevertheless, the NCCC dealt with some important issues in social welfare and social reform. In 1892, for instance, the NCCC's committee on nonresidents suggested that Congress establish an interstate migration commission for transients. A forward-looking idea that recognized the nationwide aspects of unemployment and poverty affecting migration patterns, such a federal agency did not come into existence until the period of the New Deal, in 1933. Around the turn of the century, the NCCC promoted and was in contact with state conferences on charities and correction, of which there were eight in 1901. Mary Richmond's paper in 1897, stressing the need for training in the field, had an almost immediate and deep-seated effect on the field, as agencies and schools responded by developing training courses and the like.

The NCCC opened the twentieth century with some administrative changes but it nevertheless soon developed as a leading organization in social service. In May 1901, General Secretary Hastings Hart, a child welfare specialist and a penologist, resigned. His replacement, Homer Folks, began his tenure in October 1901, but he resigned shortly after to become commissioner of public charities in New York City. Following an idea of Charles R. Henderson, a leading national figure, in 1902, the NCCC appointed a commission to investigate social insurance, an important subject for social reformers in the Progressive era. Another paper whose ideas were followed quickly was on the need for children's codes by Judge George S. Addams of the Juvenile Court of Cleveland, Ohio, in 1910. The NCCC's committee on children, especially in 1915, when it was chaired by Carl Christian Carstens, a leading child welfare worker, also stressed the need for such children's codes. Within a few years, such movements developed in states throughout the country. The NCCC and its publications also served as a forum for the mothers' pension movement. During this period, some of the leading national social service agencies, such as the Child Welfare League of America* and the National Association of Societies for Organizing Charity,* which later became the Family Service Association of America* (FSAA), were created at the NCCC. The first report on infant mortality by the United States Children's Bureau (USCB) was presented at the now named National Conference of Social Work (NCSW) in 1919. The period of reform also brought the only protest to the election of a NCSW president—in this case in 1919 of Owen Lovejoy, "the children's statesman," of the National Child Labor Committee.* Critics challenged Lovejoy because of his support of Eugene Debs's candidacy for president of the United States on the ticket of the Socialist party.

The organizational structure was crystallized and ran smoothly under the executive leadership of Howard Knight, who served in that post for twenty-one years beginning in 1926. By the mid-1920s, agencies that met with the NCSW were required to become an institutional member of and to have its program printed by the NCSW. During this period, the NCSW developed the practice of dealing with nine set topics each year; by 1926, as more topics were added, there were twelve sections reflecting the major subjects in the field. This organizational pattern continued until 1934 when the NCSW decided to have four permanent sections: social casework, social group work, social action, and community organization. The NCSW offered an advisory service to the state conferences, including an annual meeting of these conferences' secretaries to exchange ideas and such.

Since World War II, the NCSW—which became the National Conference on Social Welfare (NCSW) in 1956—continued to focus on the major issues in social service, interpreted broadly to include health care, economics, social planning, and the like. In the postwar rehabilitation period of the late 1940s, the NCSW characteristically dealt with foreign aid and international social welfare. In 1954, the annual meeting became known as the annual forum, the designation still used in 1976. In the late 1960s, the NCSW was forced to deal with welfare recipients' rights and with the question of minority participation in the conference and in social work itself. Like those of other national organizations, such as FSAA, the NCSW's proceedings were disrupted by welfare recipients in the late 1960s. At the NCSW in New York City in May 1969, members of the National Welfare Rights Organization* (NWRO) triggered a series of confrontations when they held about fifteen hundred delegates captive for nearly one hour while the NWRO presented its demands. The demands included paying the NWRO $35,000 from the conference registration fees to help organize welfare recipients. The group also called for welfare leaders to work for the complete restructuring of the welfare system, placing power in the hands of the poor. Further disruptions prompted the conference to appoint a four-member commission to raise funds for the NWRO, and the NCSW delegates voted to conduct a mail canvass of its nine thousand members to determine if the NCSW should raise the $35,000. The NCSW agreed also to have 250 welfare clients attend the meeting in 1970.

In the early 1970s, there were rumors that the NCSW was going to disband. But the NCSW's presenting a progressive document on social issues to the platform committee of both the Republican party and the Democratic party suggested that it was returning to its advocacy role of the Progressive era. Suggesting further Professor Clarke A. Chambers's point that at times the "democratic spirit . . . has characterized . . . the Conference," in 1974, the theme of the 101st annual forum was "mobilizing for a Just Society."

The annual *Proceedings* contain information about the NCSW. I also used *The New York Times* to gather information about the NCSW. The agency published a helpful *Bulletin* throughout much of its long history.

The most helpful secondary source for the NCSW's organizational history is Frank J. Bruno, with Louis Towley, *Trends in Social Work, 1874–1956: A History Based on the Proceedings of the National Conference of Social Work* (1957). The essays in Clarke A. Chambers, ed., *A Century of Concern, 1873–1973* [1973], unfortunately for my purposes, deal more with the field of social welfare than with the history of the NCSW itself. This suggested, as does Bruno's volume, the NCSW's centrality in the history of social welfare. There does not appear to be a full-length, scholarly history of the organization itself.

NATIONAL CONSUMERS' LEAGUE (NCL). The idea of a league of consumers organized to persuade retail merchants to improve working conditions of women and children had first been implemented by the short-lived Consumers' League of London, England, in 1890. When investigations by the Working Women's Society revealed the work conditions of women in New York City, Josephine Shaw Lowell, the noted charity worker and philanthropist, borrowed the English idea and became instrumental in forming the first consumers' league in the United States in New York City in 1891. During 1897 and 1898, leagues were formed in Philadelphia, Boston, and Chicago, and the nucleus of the national organization was complete. Consequently, on May 1, 1899, delegates from the four city consumers' leagues of Boston, New York, Philadelphia, and Chicago met in Boston and founded the National Consumers' League (NCL).

The rapid expansion of the leagues occurred after the national organization was founded in 1899. By World War I, there were sixty-four leagues in twenty different states. The consumers' leagues then spread to Europe where they were organized in France, Switzerland, Belgium, Germany, and the Netherlands with allied organizations existing in Spain and Italy by 1913. Two international conferences of consumers' leagues were held—the first in 1908 in Geneva, the second in 1913 in Antwerp. Delegates from twenty nations exchanged reform ideas and techniques of improving social welfare at the conference in Geneva; among them was a discussion of legislating minimum wage boards. Delegates from the NCL attended both conferences and reported on the growth of the NCL and its activities in eliminating homework and sweatshops through use of white lists and the NCL label awarded to approved manufacturers.

The NCL's organizational structure was relatively loose. City and state leagues completed their own investigations of local work conditions and labor legislation and lobbied for local and state laws, while the NCL coordinated national campaigns to educate the public and to promote social welfare legislation on the federal level. Annually delegates from city and state leagues met with the national leadership to formulate policy, and an executive council consisting of national officers and elected state delegates met quarterly to supervise the execution of policy. The membership of the executive council fluctuated in number from 1899 through 1975 between a low of six in 1901 to a high of twenty in 1975. The daily routine was executed from the office in New York City by the post of general secretary, a position held by the ardent reformer, Florence Kelley, from the inception of the NCL to her death in 1932. Among the general secretaries have been notable women as exemplified by Lucy Randolph Mason (1932–1938), important later for her efforts to organize southern laborers in the Congress of Industrial Organizations, and Elizabeth Stewart Magee (1943–1958), an authority on industrial social work and secretary of the Consumers' League of Ohio from 1925 to 1943.

The leadership of the NCL since 1899 mostly consisted of a directory of leaders in consumer reform, government officials, and legal minds. Notable among the directors and supporters were social reformers and government officials such as Frances Perkins, Louis Brandeis, Felix Frankfurter, John Graham Brooks, Josephine Goldmark, Mary Anderson, Eleanor Roosevelt, Mary W. Dewson, Alice Hamilton, Newton D. Baker, and Esther Peterson. Esther Peterson, president of the NCL in 1975, is the former director of the Women's Bureau of the federal Department of Labor and former assistant secretary of labor. Although the NCL was never a mass organization, the membership was drawn from the increasing numbers of middle-class professional social workers, academicians, lawyers, government officials, and businessmen and women who were concerned with the development of social welfare in the United States.

The initial objective of the NCL was to utilize the purchasing power of organized consumers to pressure merchants and manufacturers to provide adequate wages and working conditions for employees. "White lists" of retail stores conforming to NCL standards were issued in expectation that consumers would purchase only from approved stores, and the NCL issued a label to approved manufacturers to signify that their product was made under clean and healthful conditions. As economic pressure and persuasion were revealed as inadequate to assure better conditions, the NCL shifted to supporting legislation to abolish child labor (1903), to establish minimum wages (1909), to ensure pure food and drugs (1906), and many other acts designed to promote public health, consumer protection, and fair labor standards. At the outset, in 1899, a four-point program was developed in which the NCL leadership investigated work conditions, educated the public, promoted legislation to protect the public welfare, and engaged in inspection to ensure adequate enforcement of the law.

A major innovation occurred in 1908 when the NCL established a committee on the legal defense of labor legislation. The basic principle was to utilize the courts to defend the right of the state to restrict the interpretation of freedom of contract in the interests of public health and welfare. The staff, led by Florence Kelley and Josephine Goldmark under the direction of Louis D. Brandeis, compiled the sociological evidence utilized in the famous Brandeis brief presented in 1908 to the United States Supreme Court in *Muller* v. *Oregon*. The

Court accepted the evidence and sustained the right of the state to restrict the working hours of women. The NCL committee monitored laws, prepared legal briefs, and provided the staff for its counsel who argued state and federal court cases. Between 1908 and 1923, fifteen cases were argued, fourteen successfully. The notable failure was in *Adkins* v. *Children's Hospital* (1923) when the court declared state minimum-wage laws unconstitutional, a decision that set back the minimum-wage movement until the 1930s when the NCL was once again instrumental in the passage and defense of state legislation and the Fair Labor Standards Act of 1938.

In addition to introducing the idea of minimum-wage legislation to the United States, the NCL lobbied for a variety of reform laws. Women and children at work were of primary concern throughout NCL history. The NCL lobbied for the passage of child labor laws restricting hours and ages of child laborers from 1903 through 1938, and after federal legislation was declared unconstitutional in 1921, the NCL actively supported the unsuccessful child labor amendment during the 1920s. Laws restricting the hours of work for women, night work, and laboring conditions were also supported from 1905 through 1938 while, at the same time, the NCL urged the establishment of state bureaus of women in industry and the appointment of women factory inspectors to ensure adequate enforcement of laws pertaining to women and children in industry. Coincidental with their campaigns to improve work conditions, the NCL advocated the abolition of sweatshops and tenement house industries. The league also provided a wide range of information and support for the first Pure Food and Drug Act in 1906 and for occupational safety legislation, notably the La Follette Seamen's Act of 1915. Conditions of life, work, wages, and the welfare of migrant workers were also investigated as early as 1912, although the major NCL campaign for improving the conditions of migrant workers did not begin until the 1950s.

A great variety of methods were used by the NCL to obtain support for its program. Handbooks of legislation on minimum wage, child labor, and court decisions were published and periodically updated. Model bills were prepared and distributed to legislators and allied organizations. Exhibits illustrating the harmful effects of poor work conditions and wages were prepared and shown widely; some won prizes. Books, articles, pamphlets, and legal briefs were authored and distributed to libraries, lawyers, academicians, social workers, and legislators, while members of the NCL testified at legislative hearings, bringing their expertise in support of social welfare and consumer legislation. The NCL also coordinated campaigns of interested, allied organizations such as the American Association for Labor Legislation* in initiating, renewing, or extending the law. In the 1970s, the NCL promoted consumer action through publication of a monthly *Bulletin*, first published in 1939, which documents food, health, and other consumer news by reporting on legislation, regulatory agency action, and activities of other consumer organizations.

Partial credit must be granted to the NCL for the successful accomplishment of much of the social legislation in the United States in the twentieth century. The establishment of a federal Children's Bureau in 1912 and the Women's Bureau in 1920 was partly attributable to the NCL, as was the formation of the National Child Labor Committee* in 1904. Besides the minimum-wage, maximum-hour and child labor legislation, the NCL was important in the passage and sustaining of the Sheppard-Towner Maternity and Infancy Act of 1921 and the Fair Labor Standards Act of 1938. In revisions of the latter in 1946 and 1961, the NCL effectively lobbied for increasing the minimum wage, widening coverage, and strengthening the child labor provisions. A multiplicity of sociological investigations resulted in reports such as *Wage-Earning, Women in Wartime: The Textile Industry* (1919), used by legislators, lawyers, teachers, and the court to promote social welfare in the NCL's main areas of endeavor: labor legislation, social security, compulsory health insurance, occupational safety, and consumer protection.

In 1943, NCL headquarters was located in Cleveland, Ohio, where it remained until transferred in 1961 to Washington, D.C. During the 1940s and 1950s, the NCL worked to extend coverage of the minimum wage to agricultural workers, to increase the amount, and to guarantee the rights of agricultural migrant laborers as exemplified in the adoption in 1940 of the standards approved by the International Labor Organization for migratory workers. Also important was support for health care for the aged under social security. Through its *Bulletin,* the NCL waged opposition to the Kerr-Mills bill (1960) and support for Medicare, eventually enacted in 1965. At the same time, consumer protection legislation such as the truth-in-lending bills (1962), which would require statements of true annual interest for installment purchases and loans, were advocated, as was legislation for standard labeling of consumer products.

From 1960 to 1975, the NCL actively promoted the establishment of a consumers' bureau in the executive branch of the federal government through its publications, testimony in committee hearings of Congress, and close monitoring of amendments to legislation. Since 1973, the NCL has directed its efforts toward the development of a program to establish regional consumer centers to acquaint the public with action in the food marketing and health service areas. In 1974, the Health Service Information Center for metropolitan Washington, D.C., was developed as a centralized source of information on health services. The center was used as a model for other cities to follow. This activity was transferred in 1975 to the National Council of Senior Citizens. The NCL continues to promote action to protect the consuming and working public through research and publications, issuance of model bills, service on federal advisory councils, and monitoring new and revised legislation and the actions of regulatory agencies.

Primary sources for the NCL's history consist of the records of the NCL located in the Manuscripts Division of the Library of Congress. Intermittently published *Annual Reports* for the early years and the *Bulletin* since 1939 for the later years are indispensable, as are the hundreds of investigative reports of the NCL. For an introduction, see Maud Nathan, *The Story of an Epoch-Making Movement* (1926), and Josephine Goldmark, *Impatient Crusader: Florence Kelley's Life Story* (1953), both by important NCL members.

There is no published scholarly study of the organization, although Louis L. Athey, "The Consumers' Leagues and Social Reform, 1890–1923" (Ph.D. diss., University of Delaware, 1965), is useful, as are the analyses in William L. O'Neill, *Everyone Was Brave: The Rise and Fall of Feminism in America* (1969), and Clarke A. Chambers, *Seedtime of Reform: American Social Service and Social Action, 1918–1933* (1963).

Louis L. Athey

NATIONAL COORDINATING COMMITTEE FOR AID TO REFUGEES AND EMIGRANTS COMING FROM GERMANY (NCC).

In the early 1930s, as news of Adolf Hitler's atrocities reached the United States, American Jewish relief agencies especially began to develop a new specialization, caring for refugees. For instance, in early 1933, the Jewish Social Service Association* (JSSA) of New York decided to have one worker in its application bureau handle all such cases. In the summer of 1933, the American Jewish Joint Distribution Committee* proposed further coordination of the work with refugees and emigrants. To handle this work, a new Joint Clearing Bureau (JCB) was established. Mrs. Jonah J. Goldstein, the controller of the Federation for the Support of Jewish Philanthropic Societies of New York City, became the leader of the early JCB, and she later became chairman of its executive committee. Meanwhile, other reformers, social workers, and people concerned with the plight of German refugees began discussing the formation of an even larger group. The most important of these individuals was Professor Joseph Chamberlain of Columbia University, who was active in other social service organizations. Chamberlain and James G. MacDonald, the high commissioner for refugees coming from Germany of the League of Nations, decided to convene a meeting of interested people. Consequently, on March 9, 1934, in New York City, a number of individuals and representatives of social service agencies interested in refugee and emigration problems relating to Nazi Germany met and established the National Coordinating Committee for Aid to Refugees and Emigrants Coming from Germany, commonly called the National Coordinating Committee (NCC). Further organizational details were being worked out when the records and work of the JCB were turned over to the NCC on April 24, 1934. At another meeting, on June 7, 1934, the NCC was established formally. The new organization adopted a constitution and chose its officers.

The NCC hoped to stimulate non-Jewish interest and to involve non-Jews in its work. It began its work in a one-room headquarters at the Clara de Hirsch Home in New York City, and the National Council of Jewish Women (NCJW) lent the executive director of its Service to Foreign Born, Cecilia Razovsky, as executive secretary of the NCC. Razovsky was the most important individual in the establishment of the NCC, particularly in the early, crucial years. She traveled frequently to Washington, D.C., to defend deportation and other individual cases and to appeal State Department regulations often relating to individual cases.

Another important activity of the NCC was the long-established concept in Jewish social service of resettling immigrants in communities other than New York City. To conduct this activity in October 1936, the NCC established its resettlement division and hired as its director Jacob Billikopf, an important figure in Jewish social work who had experience in similar programs with the former Industrial Removal Office.* In the late 1930s, the NCC was in the center of the movement to allow refugee children into the United States. These efforts were formalized in the unsuccessful Wagner-Rogers children's bill of 1939. As nazism spread in Europe, the volume of refugees increased so heavily that by February 1, 1939, the NCC had a staff of 180 employees in addition to the 142 workers under the Greater New York Coordinating Committee (GNYCC), an affiliated agency specializing in activities in New York.

Largely because of the nature of the refugees, the NCC by the late 1930s became virtually an all-Jewish agency. In 1938, the great volume of work led to the founding of the National Coordinating Committee Fund, Inc., an entirely Jewish organization, to provide central financing for the NCC and to develop national support for its work. By the end of 1938, only one non-Jewish agency was represented on its twenty-five-member board of directors, the nonsectarian International Migration Service* (IMS), and only three Gentiles participated in the leadership of the agency: founders Chamberlain and MacDonald and George Warren, the international director of the IMS. Although the NCC developed new organizational structures and had a large staff, its work did not keep pace with the volume of refugees and emigrants. Following pogroms against Jews overseas in November 1938, Harry Greenstein of the Baltimore Jewish Community conducted a "Reorganizing Study of the NCC and Its Affiliated Agencies." Issued in May 1939, the evaluation pointed out both NCC inadequacies and the considerable confusion, overlapping, and duplication of such relief work among Jewish agencies. The report recommended the establishment of a new, more unified, and better-coordinated organization. Influenced by this analysis, the NCC helped to form the new organization to replace it. Subsequently, in June 1939, the NCC merged with its fund, the GNYCC, and the work of administering relief to refugees in New York conducted previously by the local JSSA, the Jewish Family Welfare Society of Brooklyn, and both the New York and Brooklyn Sections of the National Council of Jewish Women to form The National Refugee Service, Inc.*

The primary sources for studying the NCC's history include its records, which have been deposited at the YIVO Institute for Jewish Research in New York City. The Papers of Joseph Chamberlain relating to refugee work, on microfilm at YIVO, also contain NCC materials.

Lyman Cromwell White, *300,000 New Americans* (1957), contains a short history of the NCC, which is also dealt with briefly in Saul S. Freidman, *No Haven for the Oppressed* (1973).

NATIONAL COUNCIL FOR HOMEMAKER-HOME HEALTH AIDE SERVICES, INC. (NCHHHAS). In the early twentieth century, social service agencies recognized the need to provide a variety of direct services to families in trouble. In 1903, the New York Association for Improving the Condition of the Poor* (AICP) hired four "visiting cleaners," who cooked and cleaned in the homes of the sick and elderly, to supplement the work of AICP nurses in their clients' homes. In 1913, the advisory committee of the Associated Charities in Detroit, Michigan, began a visiting housekeeper service. But the first organized homemaker service began through the Jewish Welfare Society of Philadelphia (JWSP) in early 1923. This service was established to provide help to incapacitated mothers to prevent their children from going to institutions or foster homes.

The idea for the JWSP project came from Morris Kind, a layman who was the organization's president. In late 1924, Jacob Kepecs, a leading child welfare worker, initiated a homemaker program at the Jewish Home Finding Society (JHFS) in Chicago. Kepecs felt strongly that replacing the mother with a homemaker was better than placing children in foster homes. These agencies conducted no formal training of the women who served as homemakers. In 1927, the JHFS enlarged its homemaker service to care for the children of widowers, marking the beginning of homemaking as a long-term service. Publicly provided services began with the public welfare programs of the 1930s, such as through the Social Security Act of 1935, the Civil Works Administration (CWA), and the Works Project Administration (WPA). But, especially in the WPA, these programs emphasized providing work and salaries for needy women with secondary emphasis placed on benefits to the welfare of clients. In the late 1930s, a gradual shift in emphasis from short-term services to services for the chronically ill began. In 1935, in New York City, a large-scale project began exclusively for the chronically ill. This activity was initiated by the committee on chronic illness of the Welfare Council of New York and the Visiting Nurse Service of the Henry Street Settlement* (HSS). At about the same time, a homemaker service for old age assistance clients was established in New York, and in 1938, the two programs merged to become the Housekeeping Service for Chronic Patients.

In the late 1930s, efforts were made by the agencies providing homemaker services to form a coordinated network of services nationwide. On November 6, 1937, at the request of the Welfare Council of New York, the United States Children's Bureau (USCB) called the first national conference on homework service. Maud Morlock, a USCB agent who had considerable experience in professional social and child casework, represented the USCB. At this conference, the delegates recognized the wide range of services and decided on the need for a national organization to provide leadership. Consequently, a small steering committee was appointed. On April 7–8, 1939, the USCB held another conference on standards for housekeeping services. At this meeting, a small group of workers tried to define and clarify various types of services. Also at this meeting in April 1939, the steering committee became the National Committee on Supervised Homemaker-Housekeeper Service (NCSHHS). A group of twelve workers, eleven from family and children's agencies and one from a housekeeper agency, formed the initial group. The meeting in 1939 proved so valuable that the NCSHHS decided to hold another meeting in June 1939 at the National Conference of Social Work* (NCSW) in Buffalo.

A voluntary agency staffed and conducted by professionals in the field who had full-time jobs and duties with other agencies, the NCSHHS promoted homemaker services. It chose as its first chairman, Elinore R. Woldman of the Jewish Social Service Bureau of Cleveland, a specialist in child research, home economics, and homemaker services. The NCSHHS, which became an associate group of the NCSW, chose a vice-chairman to succeed the chairman annually. A subcommittee of workers in Cleveland aided the chairman, but the organization lacked a permanent central office and a paid executive officer. The group met again at the NCSW in 1940, when it appointed a small steering committee designed to invite other national social agencies providing homemaker services to participate in the NCSHHS. The organization also discussed establishing an advisory committee to act as a clearinghouse and a consultative body. At another meeting in Cleveland in October 1940, the NCSHHS decided both to prepare a directory of homemaker services and to issue an occasional rather than a regular newsletter. At this time, the NCSHHS also appointed its advisory committee. In 1942, the organization, apparently now called the Committee on Supervised Homemaker Service (CSHS), began to issue a directory of agencies which provided homemaker services.

The CSHS continued to sponsor meetings that featured professional papers and offered specialists an oppprtunity to discuss issues and exchange ideas. The existing committees in 1942 suggest the range of interests: research and evaluation, publication of a manual, personnel practices, wages and hours (of workers), interrelation and integration in the community, standards, and case record exhibit. Continuing its interest in child care work, the CSHS committee on standards prepared materials for a report on day care for the USCB. By late 1942, the CSHS was emphasizing the use of its speciality in the national war emergency, focusing on the problems of attracting skilled homemakers to serve during the war. The participation of social workers in the general war effort, however, eventually hurt the CSHS. In November 1945, its chairman resigned, and for nearly a year and one-half, the group, which had never functioned on a daily basis, was inactive.

Only the personal concern and commitment of its members reactivated the organization. At a meeting on February 15, 1946, in New York City, Frances

Preston of the Associated Charities of Cleveland presented a constitution and bylaws, and the nominating committee presented a slate of officers. Representatives from the Child Welfare League of America* (CWLA) and the Family Welfare Association of America* (FWAA), as well as Maud Morlock of the USCB, assured the cooperation of their agencies. The group agreed to reconstitute the organization and renamed it the National Committee on Homemaker Services (NCHS). Still without either a central office or a full-time executive, the NCHS continued to sponsor professional and other meetings, distribute literature, and correspond with interested parties throughout the country. In October 1946, the NCHS issued a definition of homemaker services and appointed a special committee to draft recommendations for supervision in homemaker services. The NCHS endorsed these recommendations at its annual meeting in New York City in November 1949.

By the mid-1950s, demands for materials about providing and promoting homemaker services grew far beyond the capacity of the group of volunteer professionals with full-time jobs who constituted and ran the NCHS. Despite the fact that NCHS members largely comprised a committee of the CWLA to develop standards for homemaker services for children, leaders of the NCHS agreed that their agency was unable to provide proper services in publicity and consultation. NCHS members began themselves to promote the development of a new national agency in the field with a full-time staff and permanent office. Meetings in the late 1950s and early 1960s focused on the financial problems, the burden of work, the lack of staff, and the need for a new national agency in the field. These discussions prompted actions by leaders in the health and social welfare fields.

Interest in establishing another national organization in the field in 1959 had prompted twenty-eight national health and welfare agencies and eight units of the United States Department of Health, Education, and Welfare (DHEW) to sponsor a conference. The next organizing step occurred in February 1960, when the National Health Council* (NHC) sponsored a conference on homemaker services at Arden House in Harriman, New York. Like the USCB's conference in the late 1930s, this one focused on the value of homemaker services in preventing the unnecessary institutionalization of patients. The chairman of the conference was Dr. John Ferree, the executive director of the National Society for the Prevention of Blindness.* In 1961, representatives from the conference in 1959 met to consider establishing a national organization; they then asked the NHC and the National Social Welfare Assembly, Inc.* (NSWA), to sponsor this independent national agency. The two organizations promptly appointed a board of directors for the new agency based on recommendations from thirty national organizations interested in the service. The executive director of the Family Service Association of America* (FSAA), Clark W. Blackburn, chaired the board, which drafted the structure of the new agency. Finally, at the invitation of the two sponsoring agencies, the NHC and the NSWA, the board of directors met in New York City in December 1962 and established the National Council on Homemaker Services (NCHS) as a five-year demonstration project. The board incorporated the NCHS in the state of New York that same month.

The board began immediately to activate the NCHS. The NHC gave the new organization office space and acted as its fiscal agent for the first few months. The board realized the need for a major fund-raising drive to enable it to establish an office and a staff. By October 1963, the board had raised enough money to hire an executive director and to lease an office in the same New York City building as the NHC and other national agencies. The National Committee on Homemaker Service disbanded in 1962, turning over its materials and assets to the new NCHS. The American Medical Association (AMA) gave the new agency funds from the national conference on homemaker services of 1959. Other national agencies helped the new NCHS to develop its programs in the early years. For instance, the NCHS commissioned a play dramatizing the value of homemaker services, *To Temper the Wind,* from Plays-for-Living, a division of FSAA. Along with the NSWA, FSAA helped the NCHS to sponsor sessions at the NCSW in 1963 and 1964. The major early activity of the NCHS focused on planning a national conference in Washington, D.C., in spring 1964. The contribution of staff services by the commissioner of welfare of HEW, Ellen Winston, enabled the NCHS to plan this conference. In its first year, 1963, the NCHS also issued its first publication, *New Horizons for an Essential Health and Welfare Service.*

In its initial years as a demonstration project, the NCHS developed a far-reaching and sophisticated range of programs. In July 1964, to serve agencies in the field and others, the NCHS established its library services. Like its predecessor agency, the NCHS relied heavily on the contributions of volunteers, both professionals from other agencies and laymen. Continuing its contacts with government agencies, in May 1965, the NCHS began work on its contract with the Office of Economic Opportunity (OEO) to produce what became the *Homemaker Home Health Aides Training Manual,* a government publication. With the extension of government medical benefits in 1966, the NCHS increased its professional staff to include a program director and a public information director. Playing an increasing role in the health and welfare field generally, the NCHS was one of ten national agencies invited to the Conference on Home Care of the AMA in December 1966. In 1967, the final year of the five-year demonstration period, the NCHS proved again its value in the field. In May 1967, it held the first forum, bringing together workers to discuss the impact of federal Medicaid programs on the homemaker field. The NCHS continued to participate in conferences and to issue publications. In 1967, it prepared publicity kits for local agencies that provided homemaker services. The new NCHS attracted considerable support from corporations and foundations, such as the Lois and Samuel Silberman Foundation. This foundation sponsored in 1967 two publication projects, a comprehensive reference volume and a teachers' resource book. When the representatives of government and private agencies met on December 13, 1967, to evaluate the NCHS and to determine its future, the success of its programs and activities virtually assured its continuance.

The next phase of the organization's history fully justified its existence, as the NCHS served the field well. It continued to issue publications in the field, including book-length studies, pamphlets, and serials. It participated increasingly in all kinds of conferences, including the White House conferences on children and on aging in the early 1970s. Annual forums for workers in the field focused on relevant issues, such as "A Clinic on Financing" in 1970 to discuss the problem of local fund raising. The communications committee of the NCHS replaced the former interpretation committee in 1968, and it developed more sophisticated publicity techniques and campaigns. On March 5, 1971, the agency changed its name to the National Council for Homemaker-Home Health Aide Service, Inc. (NCHHHAS).

The new name helped to symbolize the national leadership that the agency had assumed. An enlargement of its social policy and legislative committee to include representatives from national voluntary as well as government agencies helped to expand NCHHHAS testimony before government officials; a national policy statement, issued in a pamphlet, *Whereas . . . ,* for example, became the basic principles of the agency's testimony on national health insurance in 1971 to the Committee on Ways and Means of the United States House of Representatives. A statement on February 7, 1974, to the home health subcommittee of the Health Insurance Benefits Advisory Council led to the inclusion of some NCHHHAS recommendations for broadening Medicare to include homemaker services. Indicating further its leadership role, in 1972, the agency initiated discussions with private insurance companies to have homemaker service included in insurance plans.

In 1970, the board of directors assigned top priority to implementing standards in the field. Late in the year, the board had appointed an accreditation standards committee. Supported by two foundation grants—an anonymous donor and the Social and Rehabilitation Service of USDHEW—and chaired by Peter Meek, the executive director of the NHC, the accreditation standards committee developed an approval program in 1971. The responsibility for implementing the program rested in the agency approval review committee, chaired by Inez Haynes, a board member and the former general director of the National League for Nursing. In 1972, a three-year grant from the W. K. Kellogg Foundation and a one-year grant from the Field Foundation enabled the NCHHHAS to appoint a director, an assistant director, and other professionals to administer the agency approval program. The organization also added a part-time research consultant and a coordinator for a series of regional meetings on the program, three of which occurred in 1972. In the early 1970s, public service radio broadcasts and feature articles in national publications helped to publicize further the field of homemaker services.

The sources for studying the NCHHHAS's history are not widely available in libraries. The mimeographed proceedings of the annual meetings of the National Committee on Homemaker Service and the published *Annual Reports* of the NCHHHAS are difficult to locate but extremely useful. I found these sources in the agency's national headquarters in New York City, where there are also unpublished and uncataloged sources, such as minutes of meetings and correspondence, all of which proved extremely helpful. The variously named newsletters and other agency publications are other important primary sources. Contemporary articles, such as those in the *Social Work Year Books* and Elinore R. Woldman, "New Directions in Supervised Homemaker-Housekeeper Service," *Journal of Home Economics* 32 (April 1940), 237–239, provide some information. Maud Morlock, *Homemaker Services: History and Bibliography* (1964), contains a valuable history and a comprehensive bibliography. An interview in New York City in December 1976 with a long-time agency leader, Nora Johnson, also provided helpful information for this study.

There does not appear to be a scholarly history of the NCHHHAS.

NATIONAL COUNCIL OF JEWISH FEDERATIONS AND WELFARE FUNDS: see COUNCIL OF JEWISH FEDERATIONS AND WELFARE, INC.

NATIONAL COUNCIL OF THE CHURCHES OF CHRIST IN THE U.S.A., DIVISION OF CHURCH AND SOCIETY (DCS) OF THE. The social gospel movement in the late nineteenth and early twentieth centuries sensitized Protestant denominations and others to the great social issues of the day—poverty, industrialism, immigration, and so forth. Reform movements within virtually each of the churches prompted some to develop institutions and agencies to further such work. Gradually the denominations began to cooperate with one another. The earliest important activities bringing together denominational representatives in social reform were the great conferences of the Evangelical Alliance of the United States held in 1887, 1889, and 1893. These meetings made delegates aware of others' efforts and helped to set the stage for further interchurch cooperation.

In 1894, the Open Institutional Church League (OICL) was established by some of the leaders of reform in the churches, such as Frank Mason North of the Methodist Episcopal church, Josiah Strong, and Elias B. Sanford, who was the OICL's energetic secretary. The OICL's platform called for the alleviation of human suffering. The group, which had an impressive journal, *The Open Church*, was influential among social reformers in the churches by 1899.

During this period, church workers were also organizing across denominational lines. They formed local federations, such as the Federation of Churches and Christian Workers of New York City. Active also in this group, Sanford helped to establish in 1900 the National Federation of Churches and Christian

Social Workers (NFCCSW). Contemporaries and students alike viewed the NFCCSW as the forerunner of the Federal Council of Churches of Christ in America (FCC) (see *Religious Organizations*). Delegates from thirteen city or state federations organized the NFCCSW officially in Philadelphia in 1901. At its 1902 conference, plans were adopted for a significant national meeting in 1905.

After years of careful planning, five hundred delegates met at Carnegie Hall in New York City on November 15, 1905, and approved a further plan for federation. This conference dealt with such social issues as labor and laws and justice. In the interim between 1905 and the official establishment of the FCC in late 1908, a continuing commitee maintained interest in social issues. Its 1906 report, for instance, contained a statement by Reverend Charles Stelzle, a Presbyterian who led the Labor Temple in New York City, on the churches and organized labor, and its 1907 report drew attention to temperance, immigration, and child labor.

Suggesting the importance of social issues in the establishment of the FCC, at its founding meeting in Philadelphia in December 1908, the assemblage dealt with immigration, child labor, family life, and other social issues; a special meeting on the church and labor was also held. One labor official who attended said it was the largest gathering of workingmen in Philadelphia in his memory. In 1908, the continuing committee adopted a report, *The Church and Modern Industry*, prepared largely by Frank Mason North. This report contained the "Social Creed of the Churches"—almost verbatim from the Methodists' "The Church and Social Problems," also written by North. More importantly, *The Church and Modern Industry* (1908) recommended the establishment of a commission on social action. Subsequently, in December 1908, the Division of Church and Society (DCS) of the National Council of the Churches of Christ in the U.S.A. (NCC) was established as the Commission on the Church and Social Service (CCSS) of the FCC.

Under Stelzle's voluntary secretaryship, the CCSS began a wide correspondence with leading social workers and distributed pamphlets, especially *The Social Creed of the Churches* and *The Church's Appeal in Behalf of Labor*. Within a short time, the successful work of the CCSS led to its establishment in early 1911 as an FCC program on a budgetary basis. Reverend Charles S. Macfarland was called as the CCSS's secretary in May 1911. Under his leadership, the CCSS quickly grew; for instance, it developed a library of over a thousand volumes by 1912. In this very early period, the CCSS also sponsored three interdenominational conferences, one in Boston in June 1911, another in Chicago in November 1911, and a third in Chicago in December 1912. Perhaps its most important early activity was its investigation of the steel strike in South Bethlehem, Pennsylvania, in 1910. The three-member investigating committee consisted of Stelzle, Strong, and Paul U. Kellogg, the editor of *The Survey*, a leading social work and reform journal. Other early investigations of industrial conditions included the one in Muscatine, Iowa, by a committee that included social gospellers Henry F. Ward, Baptist Samuel Z. Batten, and Graham Taylor, a Congregationalist and the famous founder of Chicago Commons, a pioneering settlement house. The investigation of conditions in Colorado in 1914 was yet another important CCSS activity.

The CCSS's report in 1912 also contained the revised "Social Creed of the Churches." Its sixteen points included such mainstream issues of the social justice Progressive movement as providing full education and recreation for all children; abolishing child labor; protecting individuals from the liquor traffic; protecting workers from "dangerous machinery, occupational disease, and mortality"; and developing suitable provisions for old and injured workers forced to stop working.

The CCSS's activities for the next fifteen or so years showed that the agency tried to fulfill the ideas of the "Social Creed." In the middle of the second decade of the twentieth century, the CCSS was trying to establish ties with schools of theology to train people with distinctly spiritual viewpoints in social work. The CCSS also cooperated with other national social service agencies to implement its ideals. Such organizations included the Playground and Recreation Association of America* and, of course, the National Child Labor Committee* (NCLC). One of the most important issues to the CCSS was its participation, partly with the American Association for Labor Legislation* (AALL), in the nationwide campaign for rest for one-day-in-seven for industrial workers, and every year the CCSS publicized Labor Sunday and urged churches to observe it. Like other national agencies, the CCSS had an exhibition and gave lectures at the Panama-Pacific Exposition in San Francisco in 1915. The CCSS also continued its studies of industrial conditions in such well-known labor battlegrounds as Lawrence, Massachusetts, and Paterson, New Jersey. Serving its constituency, the CCSS did promote cooperation among the denominations. Each of the secretaries of the individual denomination's social service agencies served as an associate secretary of the FCC's agency.

Consistent with its heritage and the ideals of its "Social Creed," the CCSS emphasized labor-related issues in the 1920s. In May 1920, in Atlanta, Georgia, it held its first industrial conference on Christian ideals in industry. Other conferences followed quickly, such as the one in New York City in March 1921 between business, industrial, and church leaders. Following the President's Conference on Unemployment in New York City in 1921, the CCSS held a session with representatives from church boards, the church press, and experienced Christian social workers to determine its role in dealing with unemployment. The newly created CCSS research department focused on such issues in 1919 and 1920 as the tramway strike in Denver, Colorado, and deportation cases. Developed in response to the requests from the denominations, the research department continued to build up a library of Christian social work. In 1921, the CCSS issued a statement criticizing the open shop as a means of destroying organized labor. This statement, coupled with a similar one by the Social Action Department* (SAD) of the National Catholic Welfare Conference, generated considerable discussion and embarrassed the FCC. The research program, which focused initially on labor studies, proved so valuable that by 1924 it became the separate Department of Research and Education of the whole FCC. Another important activity in the early 1920s was the development of a program for community organization. An apparent interest of the new executive secretary, Worth M. Tippy, this enterprise led eventually to a national conference on community organization. Helen Ward Tippy—whose salary was raised by Executive Secretary Tippy from sources outside the FCC—served as secretary for community organization of the CCSS in 1921 and 1922. This work apparently led also to the CCSS's interest in prisons and jails in the mid-1920s.

In the field of child welfare, the CCSS developed a committee on child welfare in 1922 in response to urgent requests by the denominations. Henry Thurston of the New York School of Social Work and one of the leading specialists in this field chaired this committee, which tried to complete studies of church-related orphanages, a survey begun earlier by the Interchurch World Movement. After failing to get a foundation to support this venture, Thurston's committee arranged with the Child Welfare League of America* (CWLA) to cooperate together on this project. Disasters such as the hurricane in Florida in 1926 and the floods of the Mississippi River in the spring of 1927 prompted Executive Secretary Tippy to study disaster relief.

Although it worked in these other areas of social work—child welfare, community organization, and disaster relief, for instance—the CCSS still focused on industrial and economic conditions. In 1925, the agency hired an industrial secretary, a position made possible by a gift of $7,000 per year from the Golden Rule World Service Fund of the Universalist General Convention. Under James Myers, the former personnel director of an industrial company in upstate New York, the CCSS increased its industrial conferences and in 1927–1928 brought agricultural leaders and workers into the discussions. In 1926, the CCSS's staff collaborated with southern religious leaders to formulate and then issue an appeal to southern industrial leaders urging them to initiate reforms, especially shorter workdays, better protection for women and child laborers, higher salaries, and improvements of mill villages. The appeal was signed by Bishop James Cannon, Jr., a major southern religious leader, and forty-one other well-known individuals. The FCC's quadrennial meeting in Rochester, New York, in 1928 appointed a ten-member committee to review the "Social Creed of the Churches." Edward T. Devine, the widely respected leader of The Charity Organization Society of the City of New York* (COS), chaired this committee.

Characteristic interests and concerns continued as focuses of the CCSS in the depression years of the 1930s. The industrial committee helped to raise funds and clothing, especially for the children's relief work of the American Friends Service Committee* (AFSC) in the soft-coal fields. The CCSS's committee also promoted a study, "The Human Price of Coal." A long-contemplated church conference on social work finally took place in Boston in June 1930, with Tippy as its executive chairman. The conference became an associate group of the National Conference of Social Work* (NCSW) in 1931. The CCSS sponsored conferences throughout the country on the moral aspects of birth control. The American Social Hygiene Association* (ASHA) and the Committee on Maternal Health of the New York Academy of Medicine assisted these discussions. The CCSS, however, failed to obtain funds for a staff worker in the prison field, so this activity was not as strong as it could have been in the ensuing years.

The industrial committee cooperated with the President's Organization on Unemployment Relief in the early 1930s, and the industrial secretary helped to advise officials about unemployment relief programs. With the SAD and the Social Justice Commission of the Central Conference of America Rabbis, the CCSS held a conference on permanent preventives of unemployment in 1931, and the industrial secretary joined others for a public hearing and radio broadcast on federal relief measures from Washington, D.C., in June 1932. The "Social Creed" was revised in September 1932.

The renamed Department of Church and Social Service (DCSS) expanded its programs after 1932. A sizable donation from an individual benefactor to employ office workers who needed work helped to place about 360 workers in about forty religious agencies' headquarters in New York City, including the FCC's. In October 1934, Reverend H. Paul Douglass, the former project director of the Institute of Social and Religious Research, joined the staff part time to supervise social and other surveys, to counsel Protestant social work in cities, and to develop a temperance policy for the churches. The industrial secretary was still active, continuing to assist the AFSC relief work in the coal fields. For some years, he gave a two-week course at Vanderbilt University for a special church institute. Despite a lack of sufficient staff, in August 1933, the DCSS issued *The Chain Gang and Care of Prisoners in the South*. In 1934, the DCSS entered the campaign for decency in motion pictures, issued a statement on juvenile courts, and, at the request of the federal commissioner of prisoners, began a project to select and train chaplains for federal prisons. In the late 1930s, the DSCC participated in communal cooperatives and adult education programs. The industrial secretary was a speaker at the first protest meeting in Jersey City, New Jersey, publicly condemning the violation of civil liberties by Mayor Frank Hague. In 1936, the DSCC established its committee on prison chaplains, and according to a plan in cooperation with federal prison officials, the DSCC nominated five candidates for chaplaincies in federal prisons. The DSCC was publicly commended by the director of the Federal Bureau of Prisons and the American Prison Association's* (APA) congress in 1937.

Despite the illness of Industrial Secretary Myers, labor, the family, prisons, and some other new issues were the major interests and concerns in the 1940s. Industrial conferences continued to be held throughout the country in the early

1940s, when the DCSS was interested in workers' education and consumers' cooperatives movements. The DCSS prepared special issues of the FCC's *Information Bulletin* on social legislation in the 1940s. With the FCC's Race Relations Department and the Home Mission Council of Women for Home Missions, the DCSS began to focus on the plight of sharecroppers, devoting a special issue of *Information Service* to this subject. The DCSS continued its earlier concerns and interests in marriage and the family, holding discussions and institutes and cooperating with such other agencies as the ASHA and the Planned Parenthood Federation of America* (PPFA).

A significant event in church social welfare occurred in the early 1940s when the Episcopal Social Work Conference merged with the Church Conference on Social Work (CCSW) under the DSCC's auspices. In 1942 especially, the DCSS strengthened cooperative relations with Catholic and Jewish groups in the prison chaplaincy work. In 1945, the DCSS changed its name to the Department of Christian Social Relations (DCSR). In February 1946, in cooperation with the SAD and the Social Welfare Department of the Synagogue Council of America, the DCSR helped to sponsor the Interfaith Conference on Industrial Relations in Brooklyn, New York, in February 1946. During this period, the DCSR also held a conference on the problem of alcoholism. About thirty-five representatives from other agencies attended the session, which was held in New York City. Continuing to develop activities in the spirit of the "Social Creed," the DCSR distributed the FCC's important statement, "The Church and Economic Tensions," and a pamphlet, *How Labor and the Church Can Work Together,* prepared by Industrial Secretary Myers. Developing further its ties with the national social work and social reform communities, the DCSR became a member of both the National Social Welfare Assembly* (NSWA) and the National Public Housing Conference* (NPHC). The DCSR continued to sponsor the CCSW and such other conferences, for example, on Protestant homes for the aged.

When the FCC was reorganized as the NCC in 1950, the name of the social service agency was changed to the Department of Social Welfare (DSW) of the Division of Christian Life and Work (DCLW). In the 1950s, the DSW seemed to develop more fully than before as the coordinator and spokesman for Protestant denominational social welfare agencies. At the Mid-Century White House Conference on Children and Youth, the DSW was responsible for the large interdenominational exhibit. It continued to sponsor the CCSW, which absorbed the Association of Church Social Workers in the early 1950s and became the Christian Social Welfare Association (CCSW). At the CCSW in Chicago in 1952, Katharine Lenroot, chief of the United States Children's Bureau, spoke on spiritual resources and ethical goals in social work. DSW publications included one on narcotics. Done in conjunction with the NCC's Department of Pastoral Services, this pamphlet was ordered in quantities by such groups as the state Division of Correction and Parole in Trenton, New Jersey. Another manual in the early 1950s dealt with activities for the aging. In the summer of 1951, Beverly M. Boyd, who had headed the FCC's DCSR, resigned as executive director of the DSW. In August 1952, Catherine Wahlstrom, well known in the field of group work and a former national field secretary for the Camp Fire Girls,* became head of the DSW.

In the mid-1950s, seventeen denominations participated in a DSW-sponsored conference on natural disasters and relief. Later in the decade, the DSW began to develop a program in juvenile delinquency for its constituent agencies; it produced a background paper on the psychological and socioeconomic factors relating to juvenile delinquency. In September 1960, the DSW held a two-day conference to delineate the church's role in this field. Despite its own limited staff, at times, the DSW served as an adviser on social welfare issues to denominations lacking specialized staffs. The DSW also aided state and local councils of churches in their relations with the government and voluntary agencies. These and other activities helped to merit the statement by the social action secretary of the United Church of Christ that "the DSW . . . led the churches to think about programs and strategies."

In the 1960s and 1970s, the DSW—which became the Division of Church and Society (DCS) in 1973—continued to suggest strategies and programs to its constituents and to testify before Congress on a number of vital social issues, such as the public welfare amendments of 1962, education for migrants, the Youth Employment Act of 1963, health and educational services for migrants, minimum wage, the Food Stamp Act of 1969, and unemployment compensation for farm workers. The agency also filed a number of amicus curiae brief during this period, such as in cases involving the Aid to Dependent Children program and residency requirements for welfare benefits. In the 1970s, staff cuts reduced the program, but the DCS continued its basic activities, stimulating the interests and programs of its constituents—denominational social welfare agencies.

The primary sources for studying the DCS's history include its reports to the parent body, published biennially or quadrennially at different periods. Contemporary published sources, such as Frederick Ernest Johnson, ed., *The Social Work of the Churches* (1930), and *The Survey,* yield information about the agency. The organization's records from 1911 to 1967 are on microfilm at the Social Welfare History Archives Center at the University of Minnesota, Minneapolis. Documents relating to the agency can also be found in the papers of some of its leaders, such as those of Worth M. Tippy at DePauw University in Greencastle, Indiana.

Secondary sources, while extensive, generally provide only bits of information. For the DCS's origins, Charles H. Hopkins, *The Rise of the Social Gospel in American Protestantism, 1865–1915* (1940), is especially helpful. Such studies as Robert M. Miller, *American Protestantism and the Social Issues* (1958), and Donald Meyer, *The Protestant Search for Political Realism* (1960), also refer to the agency, as do some of the standard works in social welfare history, such as Clarke Chambers, *Seedtime of Reform* (1963). There does not, however, appear to be a full-length, scholarly history of the DSC.

NATIONAL COUNCIL OF THE CHURCH MISSION OF HELP: see EPISCOPAL SERVICE FOR YOUTH.

NATIONAL COUNCIL ON ALCOHOLISM, INC. (NCA). In early 1944, a reformed alcoholic, Marty Mann of New York, drafted a plan for an organization to help alcoholics, similar in some ways to other recently established and recently reorganized national health agencies. She and a colleague presented this plan to the staff of the section on alcohol of the Yale University Laboratory of Applied Physiology, which agreed to assist Mann and her proposed organization. Consequently, on October 2, 1944, in New York City, Mann announced that the National Committee for Education on Alcoholism (NCEA) had been established. When she made this announcement, she pointed out that the NCEA was sponsored by the Yale Plan for Alcohol Studies, which agreed to help the new NCEA publicize its work and educate the public.

Dr. E. M. Jellinek, the director of the section on alcohol of the Yale Laboratory, became the first chairman of the board of directors. The initial officers of the NCEA included as president, Dr. Howard W. Huggard, the director of the Yale Laboratory; as vice-president, Mann; a secretary; and a treasurer. Other important founders included Dr.Jellinek and Austin MacCormick, a noted penologist who headed The Osborne Association* and who was also active in Alcoholics Anonymous.* Also part of the NCEA's early structure was its women's organizing committee, which included Mrs. Sidney Borg, who was active in many charities, including the Big Brother and Big Sister Federation,* and Mrs. Albert D. Lasker, a noted philanthropist who was interested in mental health.

The NCEA quickly set up its initial headquarters in the New York Academy of Medicine Building in New York City. The women's organizing committee was designed to act as a liaison between the NCEA and local civic, social service, fraternal, and other groups. This committee also arranged speaking engagements for Mann throughout the United States. Mann planned to organize doctors, social workers, and others to form local committees, which she hoped would affiliate with the national organization, the NCEA. The NCEA hoped to enlighten professional and public opinion about the neglected subject of alcoholism and to distribute leaflets published by *The Quarterly Journal of Studies on Alcohol*.

The NCEA began its work energetically. In a period when alcoholism was not discussed publicly and remained clouded in mystery to the public, the NCEA quickly adopted three important principles to guide its work: that alcoholism is a disease; that the alcoholic can be helped and is worth helping; and that alcoholism is a public health problem and therefore a public responsibility. Between the establishment of the NCEA in early October 1944 and March 1945,

Executive Director Mann traveled about twelve thousand miles throughout the country, speaking and trying to organize local committees. Within a year, the large volume of requests for her to speak forced the board of directors to withdraw a leaflet publicizing a lecture service until the organization could provide a formal speakers' bureau.

The NCEA received considerable publicity almost from its inception. In the first year, through the efforts of the women's organizing committee, the NCEA sponsored two exhibits of its literature and services, including one at the American Prison Association's* annual congress of correction in New York City in October 1944. As early as its first year, as Mann had envisioned, the NCEA had become an information center for the general public and a consultant for professionals. By the end of its second year, the NCEA had fourteen local committees as affiliates. During this period, affiliates gave the national organization 10 percent of the funds they raised. Representatives from affiliates participated, with the NCEA staff, in conferences after the Yale summer school on alcohol. The NCEA had field representatives in various regions of the country who held the title of assistant to the executive director. In the summer of 1947, the NCEA tried an experiment in administration, bringing a field representative in the Midwest to New York City to be acting executive director. By 1947, it was clear to the board of directors that the NCEA was successful, and it planned to increase the staff, to develop greater specialization, and to improve services to affiliates. During this period, the NCEA established five major divisions, including research, publications, and a summer school of alcohol studies. Professor Selden D. Bacon of Yale University was elected secretary-treasurer, and he became the administrative secretary, maintaining a branch office in New Haven, Connecticut, in the hopes of relieving administrative burdens on the headquarters in New York City. By August 1949, there were over fifty local affiliates, including strong groups in Texas. Texas affiliates helped to promote the establishment of the Yale Institute of Alcohol Studies at Texas Christian University, under Dr. Jellinek. Many states turned to the NCEA for help with legislation, and in early 1949, the NCEA published a special *Bulletin on Legislation* and a digest of existing laws. In 1949, both the administrative officers of the Yale group and the NCEA's board of directors ofen considered the establishment of the NCEA as a separate agency.

On January 1, 1950, the NCEA became independent of the Yale Plan on Alcoholism, initiating a new phase in the organization's history. In early 1950, the board of directors changed the name of the agency to the National Committee on Alcoholism (NCA). In 1950, the NCA began to crystallize as a national organization. Suggesting the NCA's ties to the national social service community, it was now a member of the National Budget Committee of the Community Chests and Councils of America, Inc.,* which approved its budget. The NCA also became a member of the National Conference on Social Welfare* (NCSW). Services to affiliates and localities were strengthened. For instance, in 1950, the

NCA influenced the Welfare Council of New York City to determine the resources for alcoholics in the city. At the Welfare Council's request, the NCA then helped to prepare a report, "Problems and Needs in the Field of Alcoholism in New York City," which stimulated the creation of a new coordinating body in New York.

In the early 1950s, the NCA focused on educating both the public and appropriate professionals, such as social workers and physicians. Through an article by Mann in the *Journal of Rehabilitation,* the NCA helped the federal Office of Vocational Rehabilitation (OVR) to determine the best ways to interpret and to inform personnel in their field offices. There was also an emphasis on youth. For example, in 1951, the associate director traveled to West Virginia, where he held meetings with superintendents of schools, with county supervisors, and with deans and the faculty at West Virginia University and Fairmont Teacher's College. In 1951, the NCA collaborated with the Columbia University School of Public Health to conduct an all-day conference on alcoholism, and, to reach adults, it produced a radio series, "The Lonesome Road." In 1951, the NCA developed a New York City medical committee, which served as a model medical committee for affiliates. A new radio program, "This I Believe," was prepared in 1952, when the NCA opened its annual meeting to the public for the first time. In October 1952, the NCA and the National States' Conference on Alcoholism held a day-long conference for medical and psychiatric clinicians in Richmond, Virginia, and these two groups held a session at the NCSW in Cleveland in April 1953. The NCA created a second class of affiliation for state programs in alcoholism. And, because there was no local citizens' committee on alcoholism in New York City, the NCA, with its national headquarters there, developed special services for alcoholics, such as the alcoholic loan and relief fund.

By the mid-1950s, the organization had grown into a nationwide agency with affiliates throughout the country. In 1955, when the name of the agency was changed to the National Council on Alcoholism, Inc. (NCA), for the first time, the NCA created the positions of and hired both a public information director and the first field director to assist affiliates. It also hired a full-time secretary for the volunteers and a full-time bookkeeper. Activities and services expanded and diversified. In late 1955, it began to conduct a pilot project in New York City to counsel families with alcoholics. In the following year, further reflecting its national stature, the organization became an active member in both the National Health Council* (NHC) and the National Social Welfare Assembly* (NSWA). It also began to cooperate with other national agencies, such as with the AFL-CIO Department of Community Services* and with the National Tuberculosis Association* on a project for tubercular alcoholics. The homeless and institutional alcoholic committee had twenty-eight members, representing official welfare departments and personnel from The Salvation Army* and the Volunteers of America* (VOA) in cities throughout the country. Reflecting these nationwide activities, the organizational structure expanded. In June 1955, the board of directors voted to enlarge itself to sixty members and to institute three-year terms. The executive committee now began to conduct and to supervise the work of the agency between the quarterly meetings of the board of directors.

Activities in the late 1950s developed increasingly. The NCA proclaimed 1959 as the Year of Recognition. In 1957, implementing the initial NCA purpose of education, the General Federation of Women's Clubs (GFWC) adopted alcoholism as a project. In 1958, the NCA prepared the first comprehensive report on the *Homeless and Institutional Alcoholic,* worked with the National Council of Churches to prepare its important resolution joining the campaign against alcoholism, and joined with the National Industrial Conference Board to prepare the report, *The Alcoholic Worker,* Culminating the decade, the NCA business and industry committee conducted a symposium for industry in New York in 1959. The NCA also received two grants from the United States Department of Health, Education, and Welfare (DHEW). At its fifteenth-anniversary celebration on October 1, 1959, at the Waldorf-Astoria Hotel in New York City, the secretary of the DHEW, Arthur Fleming, called the NCA "America's agency for alcoholism."

Despite the expansion and proliferation of government-sponsored and government-conducted health and welfare programs in the 1960s, the NCA continued as the leading voluntary agency in the field of alcoholism, growing increasingly closer to the social service community. Beginning in the mid-1950s, the organization had sponsored a course at the Fordham University School of Social Service, and in 1960, it participated in a family research project under a professional social worker. An important organizational highlight occurred when President Dwight D. Eisenhower supported the agency's first Alcoholism Information Week. Staff members served schools of alcohol studies at various universities throughout the country, and they helped to produce issues featuring alcoholism of the *Ladies Home Journal* and *The Saturday Evening Post.* The NCA industrial advisory committee, established in 1961 and chaired by the former president of United States Steel, Clifford Hood, conducted successful programs on alcohol education in leading American businesses. At a widely publicized press conference on December 1, 1964, Hood inaugurated the "five year plan of action for industrial services," a major organizational activity. The NCA represented the alcohol field at the White House Conference on Health in November 1965, and the NCA continued to advise various federal agencies and groups.

To adjust to the increased importance of the NCA, further organizational expansion and changes occurred in the mid-1960s. Several years' work by the committee on affiliate relations resulted in 1963 in a new national structure, developing higher standards for affiliates and giving them greater influence over national policies and activities. Sixty-five of the seventy-five affiliates agreed to the plan, and five new ones joined in 1963, giving the NCA seventy affiliates. A grant from the Field Foundation allowed the NCA to hire the long-desired West

Coast fieldworker, which, together with the establishment of an affiliate in Los Angeles, represented important organizational expansion. *The Newsletter,* published since the mid-1950s, became a more important publication. Reorganization neared completion when William W. Moore, the former associate executive director of the American Heart Association,* became the executive director in 1968, replacing Mann, who then became the founder-consultant. To strengthen relations with affiliates further, thirteen new board members were elected in 1968 by affiliate councils.

As the NCA argued, the year 1969 brought new direction and life to the organization. The report in 1969 of the committee on program goals and priorities helped to shape the new trust. Early in 1969, the NCA moved its headquarters from the New York Academy of Medicine Building, in a deteriorating section of New York City, to Two Park Avenue, a move that not only helped the NCA to recruit and to hold better employees but also improved its image. In 1969, the NCA hired its first full-time medical director, and it established a new department of financial and administrative services to coordinate financial and administrative functions of the NCA. In the late 1960s, the program services' department was established and activated. The resource material center and program information exchange developed in 1969, and in 1970, the fund-raising and field operations' department merged to form the development and field services. The industrial services' department was reorganized and renamed the labor-management services' department. Major activities in 1969 included helping to establish an alcohol program and training course for the federal Office of Economic Opportunity (OEO) and issuing a statement and resolution about drug abuse. The message called for the NCA to continue its focus on alcoholism; it also prompted the appointment of a task force on alcohol and drug abuse. Another organizational highlight occurred on October 1, 1969, when the NCA celebrated its twenty-fifth anniversary with a gala event at the Americana Hotel in New York City. One of the clear challenges for the organization in the 1970s was to establish itself as the national spokesman in the field of alcoholism.

In the 1970s, the NCA became the national spokesman for voluntary agencies in the field. On August 1, 1972, it announced the completion of the Medical Criteria for the Diagnosis of Alcoholism, formulated by the NCA's criteria committee. The labor-management department held five regional conferences in 1971, and a grant from the National Institute on Alcohol Abuse and Alcoholism (NIAAA) (see *Government Agencies*) helped it to hold more in 1972. During this period, this department served as a consultant to the United States Army, Navy, and Air Force in developing programs for their personnel. The NCA helped to plan the National Parent Teachers Association's alcohol education program for youth in the early 1970s. In July 1972, with funds from the United States Department of Transportation (USDOT) the NCA began a research project on the effects of rehabilitation on the drunk driver. In April 1972, the NCA signed a memorandum of understanding with the USDOT whereby each agency agreed to exchange information and research. A year later, it absorbed the American Medical Society on Alcoholism. The NCA provided technical assistance to and monitored about eighty NIAAA community services poverty alcohol programs all over the country. The NCA helped to organize the National Nurses Society on Alcohol, which obtained provisional component status in the NCA in 1975. In the mid-1970s, the NCA promoted understanding within the medical community and other circles of the fetal alcohol syndrome, and suggesting its leadership role, in 1975, it led twenty-one organizations to establish the National Coalition for Adequate Alcohol Programs. Organizational highlights in the 1970s included the naming of actress Mercedes McCambridge in 1971 as the first national honorary chairman. She traveled throughout the country representing the NCA. In 1972, George C. Dimas, the former director of alcohol and drug section of the Oregon Mental Health Division, replaced Moore as executive director. Also in 1972, the organization held its first delegate assembly. This group determined overall policy and chose the board of directors. In the early 1970s, there was considerable discussion about state alcohol associations, and in April 1973, the delegate assembly resolved that the NCA emphasize establishing them. In the next fiscal year, 1973–1974, with a contract from the NIAAA, the NCA established five new state associations. In late 1973, the NCA founded an office in Washington, D.C. And in 1975, it established both a new office and a board committee on minority affairs.

The primary sources for studying the NCA's history include the fairly detailed, published *Annual Reports*. The early annual reports were published in *The Quarterly Journal of Studies on Alcohol*. The files of the NCA are deposited in the archives at Syracuse University. *The New York Times* and other contemporary publications covered the NCA. There does not seem to be a scholarly history of the NCA.

NATIONAL COUNCIL ON CRIME AND DELINQUENCY (NCCD). As probation developed as a service, probation officers began to develop a sense of common association. In 1907, a prominent attorney from Chicago who was active in agencies dealing with juvenile delinquents, Timothy Hurley, suggested that probation officers from around the country meet to discuss forming a national organization to promote their concerns and interests. Consequently, on June 17, 1907, in Minneapolis, Minnesota, at the annual meeting of the National Conference of Charities and Correction* (NCCC), the National Council on Crime and Delinquency (NCCD) was established as the National Association of Probation Officers (NAPO). The NAPO limited its membership to those in probation and juvenile court work. The group did not initially adopt a constitution or bylaws, but the NAPO elected four traditional officers, including a president, Timothy Hurley.

During its very early years, the NAPO remained primarily a conference to exchange ideas. The organization continued to meet during the annual NCCC sessions. At the one in June 1909 at Buffalo, New York, the NAPO adopted bylaws and established the organization more firmly, initiating year-round but still limited activities. The gradual expansion of the work and the organization stemmed from the enthusiasm of some important individuals. In 1909, for example, Chairman Homer Folks, a nationally famous social welfare leader, appointed the committee on forms, terminology, statistics, and reports. An attorney from Louisville, Kentucky, Bernard Flexner, chaired the committee, which included Maude Miner, the energetic and enterprising founder and leader of the New York Probation and Protective Association.* This committee became the committee on juvenile courts and probation, whose report in 1912 to the National Probation Association (NPA) was enlarged by Flexner and Roger Baldwin of the juvenile court in St. Louis and who later founded and led the American Civil Liberties Union. This report was issued in 1914 as *Juvenile Court Standards*. An early publication of the United States Children's Bureau (USCB), it became a standard work in the field. At the 1911 meeting, the NPA appointed a corresponding secretary in every state. The meeting in 1912 featured an elaborate program. The NPA, however, still lacked a board of directors and other features of a permanent agency. Its tenuous position became clear in 1915, when, at its lowest ebb with fewer than fifty members, the NPA even discussed disbanding.

Energetic leadership and a commitment to further activities, however, helped to revive the NPA almost immediately. Plans to publish the *Proceedings* of the sessions in 1915 materialized, inaugurating a long series of annual *Year Books*. In 1915, the organization established its first headquarters in the offices of the New York State Probation Commission in Albany, New York. NPA leaders also began to campaign for a federal probation law, testifying at hearings on the bill in the spring of 1916. The NPA gained confidence when the United States Congress passed the legislation in 1917 (which the president vetoed, however). In 1916, the USCB had asked the NPA to help it prepare what became *Courts in the United States Hearing Children's Cases* (1920). Apparently acting on the NPA suggestion, the USCB also asked Henry Thurston, chairman of NPA's committee on rural probation, to conduct a study of rural juvenile delinquency. Issued in 1918 as *Juvenile Delinquency in Rural New York,* this USCB publication added further prestige to the still developing agency. Joining in its appreciation of the NPA work, the National Child Labor Committee* (NCLC) asked the organization to prepare what quickly became the Juvenile Court Law of 1919 for North Carolina. Further organizational crystallization occurred in 1919 when the NPA added bylaws providing for a board of directors, and when Charles L. Chute, a penologist—who had been the secretary of the New York State Probation Commission—became the first permanent general secretary.

Chute shaped the NPA into a leading national social service agency in the penology field, directing and leading its organizational expansion and its activities in areas other than juvenile courts, its initial concern. Chute supervised the incorporation of the NPA in December 1921 when his position became executive secretary. In 1921, the NPA began what became annual fall conferences at the annual meeting of the American Prison Association.* In the spring of 1922, the NPA initiated its *Probation Bulletin*. Most importantly, however, Chute activated the important field service. In 1922, at the request of the local community chest of St. Paul, Minnesota, he studied the local juvenile court. In the next few years, similar local requests swamped the NPA, which began a new campaign for a federal probation law in the fall of 1923 and which, by 1924, had drafted both juvenile and adult probation laws for many states.

Unlike other national social service agencies, the NPA expanded dramatically in the 1920s, when it also developed or participated in creative new programs. In March 1924, there were 3,267 active members; a year later, nearly 1,000 more, approximately 33 percent increase. The board of directors of twenty members included such important figures as Herbert Parsons, an influential former Republican congressman from New York, Emma Lundberg, a leading child welfare worker, and Dr. Miriam Van Waters, an important pioneering and activist penologist. In 1925, when the NPA issued its Standard Juvenile Court Act, the board of directors established a thirty-four-member advisory committee, which included such prominent leaders in penology as United States Supreme Court Chief Justice Charles Evans Hughes, former United States Attorney General George Wickersham, former Harvard University President Dr. Charles W. Eliot, Adolph Lewisohn, the president of the National Committee of Prisons and Prison Labor,* and Mrs. Gifford Pinchot, wife of the reform governor of Pennsylvania and herself interested in reform. A grant from the Commonwealth Fund* (CF) in May 1926 allowed the NPA to increase its fieldwork staff, which participated— especially through Chute and Field Secretary Francis H. Hiller—in institutes, conferences, and, most important, community surveys. In many cases—such as the analysis of county probation work in New Jersey, which resulted in an NPA-initiated campaign to improve such activities in Bergen County—the NPA promoted reform. The publicity efforts of the NPA were succeeding, and in September 1928, *Probation* became a monthly publication. The agency ended this successful decade with a grant from the Bureau of Social Hygiene, which supported a project that alone employed a staff of five to study the problem of detaining children awaiting juvenile court trials.

The NPA began the 1930s still riding the crest of its diversified and locally conspicuous activities, culminating with the radio network coverage by the National Broadcasting Company of the annual luncheon in March 1931. The event featured a speech by New York Governor Franklin D. Roosevelt and generated considerable publicity. But, faced with increasing deficits and with problems raising funds, the NPA felt the first effects of the depression in July 1932 when it curtailed its work. The CF grant for the field services had ended in April 1932, and in July, the NPA released two field secretaries, including the energetic Hiller. *Probation* became bimonthly again, and the NPA did not publish a *Year Book* for 1932. Too firmly established to be hurt significantly, the NPA rebounded quickly. A grant from the Carnegie Corporation allowed the agency to rehire Hiller in January 1933. In the summer of 1932, the NPA dropped its publicity department, but the agency cooperated with the programs of the National Social Work Council,* which urged continued public support for social work. By early 1935, the NPA had returned to its normal activities, conducting fieldwork in Kentucky where it not only helped to enact an adult probation and parole bill but also implemented the appropriate state machinery. Further expansion of NPA concerns occurred in late 1938 when a special committee of the board of trustees resolved to conduct work in parole. Promoting the movement for neighborhood and community councils to prevent crime, the NPA nurtured in the late 1930s what became an important nationwide activity.

Some important activities occurred in the 1940s. In October 1940, the NPA released its first film, *A Boy in Court*. In March 1943, the NPA held its first regional conference. In 1947, it absorbed the American Parole Association and became the National Probation and Parole Association (NPPA). In 1948, the board of trustees released Chute from his executive duties, making him vice-president. Most importantly, in the 1940s, however, the agency developed ties with local and regional groups, which led to nationwide expansion. Early in the decade, the NPPA had developed a western advisory council to assist its regional director there, and the Western Probation and Parole Conference had voted to affiliate with the NPPA.

During the 1950s, organizational developments that reshaped the agency occurred. In April 1953, the NPAA invited twenty-five prominent judges to a conference; they subsequently organized themselves as the NPPA's advisory council of judges. The Mary Reynolds Babcock Foundation supported for nearly a decade the program of the advisory council of judges, which developed communications between the NPPA and other legal and judicial organizations. The judges' group also established a national citizens' council, composed of prominent citizens, such as the former president of the General Electric Company and former head of the federal Office of Defense Mobilization, Charles E. Wilson, who chaired the group. In 1955, this group inaugurated the Citizens Action Program (CAP) to improve crime control on the local level. A five-year grant of $600,000 from the Ford Foundation allowed the development of local affiliates, whose activities ranged from delinquency prevention programs to eliminating political patronage in state correction work. A second five-year grant of over $1 million extended the CAP to more states. Local committees increasingly dominated the activities of regional NPPA offices in the western, southern, and central areas of the country. By the early 1960s, the CAP had become the major action unit of the agency, broadening significantly its range of interests and concerns. Realizing that chiefly because of the CAP, the NPPA no longer focused only on juvenile courts, probation, and parole but on a broad range of issues, the members voted in 1960 to change the name appropriately to the NCCD.

Propelled by its broadened interests and nationwide network of diverse CAPs, the NCCD developed as a major national social service agency in the 1960s. Early in the decade, it reorganized its annual conferences as the national institute on crime and delinquency, conducted annually by one of the five different regional associations. Receiving a series of grants from major foundations such as the Rockefeller Brothers Fund and from government agencies, the NCCD cooperated with a new government agency to inaugurate the National Information Center on Crime and Delinquency in early 1964. Also, with major foundation support, the NCCD joined the Osborne Association* to begin a nationwide assessment of new ideas and programs for juvenile training schools and of possible alternatives to traditional institutional care for juvenile offenders. By cosponsoring a conference in 1964 that created the Joint Commission on Manpower and Training, the NCCD helped to enact the federal Correctional Rehabilitation Act of 1965. During the 1960s, a creative decade for social service generally, the NCCD crystallized ties with the social work community, participating in programs and surveys with nationally important agencies. In the early 1960s, for instance, with three other agencies concerned with state and community services to families and children—the Family Service Association of America,* the Child Welfare League of America,* and the National Travelers' Aid Association*—the NCCD formed the independent National Study Service.

The creativity and proliferation of NCCD activities characterizing the 1960s continued to prevail in the 1970s. Early in the decade, major projects included a program to divert delinquency-prone youths from justice systems to appropriate local social service agencies; educational and legislative campaigns to repeal victimless crime laws, which drained police time and energies; and a study to ensure that federal funds were spent properly to upgrade criminal justice systems. In 1972, a major policy statement urged that no more penal institutions be built until other alternatives were exhausted, and the NCCD promoted the practice of treating offenders in the community. By the mid-1970s, the NCCD was increasingly becoming a national leader in the field; in early 1972, it took over the publication of *Criminal Justice Newsletter* and, as a consultant to federal model cities programs in nearly thirty cities, it evaluated and planned local criminal and juvenile justice agencies and programs.

The basic primary source for studying the NCCD's history is the annual reports, published in variously named *Year Books* and *Proceedings* of the agency. For the recent period, the *Annual Reports* were published separately. The NCCD library at NCCD headquarters in Hackensack, New Jersey, has the agency's files. Contemporary agency publications, such as Charles L. Chute, "National Probation Association: Historical Sketch," NPA, *Proceedings, 1923,* 7–18, are helpful.

The standard works in social welfare history generally neglect the NCCD, and there does not appear to be a scholarly history of this veteran agency.

NATIONAL COUNCIL ON HOMEMAKER SERVICES: see NATIONAL COUNCIL FOR HOMEMAKER-HOME HEALTH AIDE SERVICES, INC.

NATIONAL COUNCIL ON ILLEGITIMACY (NCI). In the late nineteenth and early twentieth centuries there was considerable controversy over the care of unwed mothers and their illegitimate children. Many different local welfare agencies—humane societies, societies for the protection of cruelty to children, children's aid societies, and adoption agencies—dealt with illegitimacy, but not until the period of about World War I did a sense of community develop among the workers in this increasingly specialized field.

In the later years of the second decade of the twentieth century, basic casework principles in illegitimacy were beginning to crystallize. A group of professionals established the Inter-City Conference on Illegitimacy (ICCI) in 1918. As its name suggested, the ICCI had affiliates in major cities, especially in the East. Through these local groups, workers in the field met for discussions and presentations of professional papers about their work. Local constituent agencies differed in their structure. In Chicago, for instance, in the 1920s, the illegitimacy group was subsumed under the child welfare committee of the city's Council of Social Agencies. In Boston, however, despite a number of veteran and well-known children's agencies, the local Conference on Illegitimacy seemed to be independent and important. In 1928, it even thought of developing an adoption agency (there was none at that time in Boston). These local affiliates held national meetings annually, generally in connection with the National Conference of Social Work* (NCSW) in the spring of each year.

The ICCI appeared to be useful to the small circle of workers in illegitimacy. In the early 1920s, one leader called on the ICCI to initiate a general movement to have required investigations of adoption cases in the courts. In Boston, especially in the late 1920s, the local affiliate kept track of the increasing interest in adoption following the publication of a major study of adoption by one of its leaders, Ida Parker's *Fit and Proper? A Study of Legal Adoption in Massachusetts* (1927). Despite these features, the ICCI was, compared with other social service organizations, a generally ineffective national agency. A loosely organized national structure with local affiliates in a number of cities, led by full-time workers from other agencies and with a widely scattered executive committee, the ICCI was for some time in the late 1920s and early 1930s discussing its future. By 1931, agency leaders admitted it had "not been possible to accomplish much." Various unsuccessful attempts had been made to become part of the Child Welfare League of America* (CWLA). In 1931, the ICCI's officers considered the possibility of obtaining a foundation grant but were told that the early years of the Great Depression was not an opportune time for such favors. In the early 1930s, social workers in Cleveland led the ICCI. Maud Morlock, a specialist in the field who had worked for the Connecticut Children's

Aid Society and a former instructor of child welfare at Western Reserve University's social work school in Cleveland, was president; the three other traditional officers, including the nationally recognized Lawrence Cole of the Cleveland Children's Bureau, were all from Cleveland. The ICCI apparently dissolved in the mid-1930s.

Despite the ICCI's apparent demise, the field of illegitimacy casework grew in the 1930s. Interest in reestablishing an organization in the field became evident by the mid-1930s. In 1936, Maud Morlock was appointed a consultant on illegitimacy for the United States Children's Bureau (USCB), and in 1938, she apparently led in establishing the Committee on Unmarried Parenthood (CUP). In the late 1930s, Morlock brought together a group to prepare a program on illegitimacy for the NCSW. Also, the CUP held informal round table discussions at its annual meeting at the NCSW in 1939. These discussions proved so worthwhile that they were held again at the NCSW in 1940. The organization continued the basic functions and activities of its predecessor organization, participating in national conferences, educating the public about illegitimacy, promoting legislation in the field, providing referral services, and publishing a directory of maternity homes in the United States, a valuable guide for workers in the field.

In the early 1940s, a national advisory committee was apparently established, and in early 1945, Katharine Lenroot, the chief of the USCB, apparently strengthened this national advisory group of workers in the field to help deal with the increasing problem of illegitimacy, which was caused partly by the domestic effects of World War II, such as dislocations and family breakdowns. Lenroot brought to this committee workers from around the country involved in the field of illegitimacy. They included Josephine Deyo of The Salvation Army* (SA) in Chicago, Mary E. Sampson of the Children's Aid Society of Pennsylvania, and the supervisor of Child Welfare Services for the Massachusetts State Department of Public Welfare, Agnes M. Forman. Lenroot's leadership and affiliation with the CUP kept the group functioning largely within the social work community, sponsoring conferences, providing information, and the like. In 1946, the agency changed its name to the Committee on Unmarried Parents (CUP), and by 1949, it was called the Committee on Service to Unmarried Parents (CSUP). Apparently in the early 1950s, the CSUP became the National Committee on Service to Unmarried Parents, which became the National Association on Service to Unmarried Parents (NASUP) in about 1953.

Some changes occurred in the 1960s. Early in the decade, the NASUP became an independent organization, no longer under the aegis of the NCSW. It was now composed of over 200 agencies and of about 150 individual members. The chairman of the organization in these years was Edith Balmford, the executive secretary of the Episcopal Service for Youth* (ESY). For some time, the NASUP had been seeking ways to expand its activities and to become a full-fledged national agency. In 1964, however, the leaders agreed to the unlikelihood of such developments, and they agreed to affiliate with the CWLA and the Family Service Association of America,* both of which conducted services and were interested in the field of illegitimacy. A three-year grant from the Field Foundation sponsored the project, which the organization hoped would increase both its program and its membership. During the affiliation period with these two leading national social service agencies, the NASUP preserved its identity, but the CWLA furnished its services, such as distributing publications. The NASUP continued to publish its *Newsletter,* edited by a volunteer. In 1964, such prominent philanthropists and professionals as Mrs. Julius Rosenwald II of Philadelphia, and Vincent de Francis, the respected director of children's services of The American Humane Association, were serving the NASUP. The committee in Chicago continued as part of the NASUP's structure. In the middle of 1965, the forty-five-member advisory board initiated changing the name of the organization to the National Council on Illegitimacy (NCI). By this time, the organization had a paid director, Ruth Chaskel, who was an experienced worker in the field. In late 1965, the NCI established a new legislation and social issues committee and prepared a revised *Directory of Remedial Homes and Remedial Facilities for Unmarried Mothers.*

NCI's growing recognition in the field was evidenced when the agency agreed in the middle of 1966 to administer a research project to develop and to test a data-collecting system for the universal use of agencies serving unmarried mothers. The SA, the Florence Crittenton Association of America, Inc.,* and the National Conference on Catholic Charities* had begun this project in 1964. In the late 1960s, the NCI dealt with legislation in the field and issued policy statements, such as the ones in late 1966 declaring the right of clients to information about birth control and supporting continued public education for unmarried mothers. Fulfilling an important agency goal, new local organizations were developing throughout the United States, and in April 1969, the Minnesota Council on Illegitimacy, established in 1965, affiliated with the NCI. Also in April 1969, the NCI received a grant from the American Legion Child Welfare Foundation to strengthen its technical information and consultation center. At the end of the decade, Ruth Chaskel resigned in 1969 to become executive director of the SA foster home service in New York City. She was quickly replaced by Ruth V. Friedman, who had long-time experience with many agencies in the field.

In 1970, the legislation and social issues committee drafted a bill of legal rights for parents and children, and in April 1970, the NCI's director led an institute at the central regional conference of the CWLA. In March 1971, the NCI moved with the CWLA to new headquarters in New York City. And in 1971, the NCI developed a segment for "When Birth Control Fails" for the National Educational Radio Network. Despite these and other services and faced with the lack of funds, the constantly struggling, often tenuous organization— one of the few focusing exclusively on illegitimacy, a major subject in social welfare—dissolved in September 1971.

The primary sources for studying the NCI's history include issues of the agency's difficult-to-locate in libraries *Newsletter;* however, it is on file at the CWLA's library in New York City. Some materials in the NCI Papers, received by the Social Welfare History Archives Center in 1976, provide information. For the earliest period, the CWLA *Bulletin* is helpful. Some of the interpretive statements about casework in illegitimacy stem from Peter Romanofsky, "The Early History of Adoption Practices, 1870–1930" (Ph.D. diss., University of Missouri, 1969).

There does not appear to be a scholarly historical study of the NCI.

NATIONAL COUNCIL ON NATURALIZATION AND CITIZENSHIP (NCNC).

In 1929, the naturalization of alien residents was decreasing alarmingly because of a dramatic 400 percent increase in naturalization fees and stricter educational requirements. In that year, 44 percent of the foreign born in the United States were still aliens, and many feared the growth of a permanent alien class. The Council on Adult Education of the Foreign Born and its New York Committee on Naturalization, chaired by Ruth Z. Bernstein (later Murphy), actively opposed these measures. Encumbered by its localized scope, the New York Committee persuaded other voluntary social service organizations to join in the formation on January 17, 1930, of the National Council on Naturalization and Citizenship (NCNC) as a "clearinghouse for assembling information about naturalization and citizenship laws, procedures, organized naturalization aid and related matters and to further a coordination of effort to bring about improved conditions." Headquartered in New York City, membership in NCNC was open to national, statewide, and local social welfare, adult education, and civic organizations and to individual authorities in the field of naturalization, including representatives of the federal government. Membership dues and private contributions were the only sources of funding.

NCNC was not a direct service agency, but rather an association of organizations and individuals interested in studying nationality and naturalization and working for revisions of naturalization laws and regulations. Major policy decisions required the approval of 75 percent of the membership. The principal work of the NCNC was conducted by the legislative committee, charged with reviewing current and proposed naturalization legislation, and the administrative committee, charged with examining government policies in the administration of the naturalization laws. The organizational structure of NCNC consisted of a president, a first vice-president, four other vice-presidents, a treasurer, and a secretary, all of whom were elected annually. The twenty-four-member executive board held terms of three years, and the advisory board members served a one-year term.

Throughout its thirty-year history a group of dedicated individuals shared the NCNC's executive duties, in addition to pursuing their individual work in a variety of social service associations and organizations. Prominent among the NCNC executive officers were Read Lewis, director of the Foreign Language

Information Service* (FLIS), later Common Council for American Unity* (CCAU); then American Council for Nationalities Service* (ACNS); Donald R. Young, general director (1948–1955) and then president (1955–1963) of the Russell Sage Foundation*; Abram Orlow of Philadelphia, renowned immigration lawyer, professor of political science at the University of Pennsylvania, and president of the National Association of Nationality and Immigration Lawyers; and Frank Auerbach, a German émigré who became deputy director of the U.S. Department of State's (USDS) Bureau of Security and Consular Affairs and author of *Immigration Laws of the United States* (1955).

The prime mover of the NCNC from its inception in 1930 to its merger with the American Immigration Conference* (AIC) in 1960 was Ruth Z. Murphy who served as its secretary from 1930 to 1948 and as executive vice-president from 1948 to 1960. Murphy was also a member of the board of directors of the International Institute of New York City and a member of the executive committee of the Committee on Equality in Naturalization, as well as serving in executive positions on the CCAU and the AIC.

During the 1930s, NCNC sought the reduction of naturalization fees, a halt to rising educational requirements, and increased funding for the Works Projects Administration (WPA) adult education programs. More significantly during this decade of economic depression, the NCNC opposed the section of the National Recovery Act of 1933 and various state legislation that barred aliens from employment on national and state public works projects. Its first recommendation to the federal government NCNC urged in 1934 "that every effort be made to speed up the granting of declarations of intent and certificates of arrival in view of the great need for unemployed aliens to qualify for employment on public works." The exclusion of aliens from public relief provisions and old-age assistance programs was an additional concern of NCNC during this period. Arguing against discriminatory relief programs, the NCNC demonstrated that three of four aliens qualifying for some type of relief were members of a citizen family.

The advent of World War II further exacerbated the employment problems of aliens by requiring proof of citizenship for employment in many defense-related industries. In response, the NCNC administrative committee, chaired by Ruth Z. Murphy, submitted to the federal Immigration and Naturalization Service extensive recommendations to simplify the procedures for obtaining such proof. By 1945, NCNC could look back on a decade and a half of accomplishments: reduced naturalization fees, elimination of a certificate of arrival requirement for persons having entered the country before June 20, 1906, increased appropriations for naturalization administration, and the codification of nationality laws in the Nationality Act of 1940.

The immediate postwar years were ones in which problems associated with nationality captured the attention of the NCNC. War brides and their children, refugees, and displaced persons strained previous definitions of dual nationality, statelessness, and loss of nationality. Abram Orlow and his committee on expatriation studied the problem of naturalized United States citizens who had forfeited their citizenship because the war or conditions after the war made it impossible for them to return from visits overseas in time to fulfill residency requirements. A special committee on the nationality of children, chaired by Frank Auerbach, studied the Nationality Act of 1940 and recommended the simplification of complicated provisions.

In 1949, NCNC sponsored a Joint Conference on Alien Legislation, chaired by Read Lewis, whose purpose was to "bring together the representatives of national organizations in social work and related fields interested in promoting a similar legislative program dealing with immigration, naturalization, and allied questions, in order to obtain coordinated action and more effective results." Members of the Joint Conference included the International Migration Service,* National Travelers' Aid Association,* American Civil Liberties Union, and others. The report of the conference committee on immigration policy on the problems of unused quotas and selective immigration recommended a more flexible administration of the quota system; the pooling of unused quotas and their redistribution among various categories of immigrants; and the elimination of occupational selectivity.

The NCNC's twentieth annual conference in 1950 was a celebration reaffirming the principles of its founding. In an address before the conference, Frank Auerbach enumerated these principles: (1) every person should have a nationality; (2) dual citizenship and the conflicts resulting from it should so far as possible be eliminated; (3) acquisition of the same nationality by members of the same family should be facilitated; (4) aliens should not be disqualified from naturalization because of race; (5) administration procedures leading to the naturalization of aliens should be uniform, expeditious, and fair to the applicant without interfering with the government's obligation to withhold citizenship from individuals not qualified under the law; (6) the induction to citizenship should be dignified and should signify the importance of the act.

The McCarran-Walter Immigration and Naturalization Act of 1952 harkened to these principles. NCNC was particularly successful in gaining three concessions in the design of the act: first papers were no longer a prerequisite for naturalization; the waiting period for a spouse of a citizen to gain citizenship was reduced from five to three years; and any person denied an American passport abroad had the right to appeal the case in an American court. These provisions recognized an important change in the pattern of postwar immigration. In 1950, Ruth Z. Murphy described this change: "Formerly immigration was voluntary, today immigration is more often than not involuntary. Former immigrants represented farm and laboring people; today immigrants represent increasing numbers of skilled persons and white collar workers."

Two issues dominated NCNC activity in the early 1950s. The NCNC argued strenuously for the uniform application of the Internal Security Act of 1950, and it promoted efforts to hasten the assimilation of the foreign born into American life. To facilitate the latter goal, NCNC added two new committees to its operation. The education committee, chaired by Dr. Henry F. Nugent, prepared a bibliography of texts and films for teachers of the foreign born; the committee on dignifying naturalization ceremonies encouraged the solemnity of such proceedings and opposed efforts to remove them from the courts and delegate them to a strictly administrative office.

Membership in NCNC was at its height in 1952. Seventy nationally prominent organizations were members of the NCNC, including the American Friends Service Committee,* the National Council of the Churches of Christ in the U.S.A., the American Jewish Committee, International Social Service,* the National Lutheran Council, the National Board of the Young Women's Christian Association of the U.S.A.,* and of course, the CCAU. In subsequent years, organizational and individual membership declined steadily. The official incorporation of NCNC by the state of New York on April 13, 1954, did little to delay this decline.

Flagging membership did not detain NCNC leaders from contributing their skill to the formation of the American Immigration Conference* (AIC) on October 1, 1954. AIC was an association of over fifty organizations interested "in the need for an humanitarian, non-discriminatory immigration policy in keeping with the best tradition of the United States." While NCNC focused on naturalization legislation and administration, AIC was concerned with immigration policy and administration.

The two organizations shared more than a common interest in the immigrant. Many of the individuals involved in NCNC from its beginnings were actively engaged in the fledgling AIC—Read Lewis, Abram Orlow, and Ruth Z. Murphy, who served as AIC executive secretary. Both organizations shared the same office and clerical staff. By 1956, the work of the two organizations was sufficiently congruent for the formation of a joint committee on community integration of the foreign born. This committee encouraged the assimilation of resident aliens into community life with particular emphasis on the growing numbers of Mexican and, after 1956, Hungarian immigrants. A survey of twenty cities with large concentrations of Hungarian immigrants was undertaken by this committee in 1957; a similar study of Mexican immigrants was planned but never completed.

In 1959, after three years of informal discussion, NCNC presented a merger proposal to the AIC executive board. The merger was formalized on March 18, 1960, at the thirtieth anniversary celebration of the National Council. The combined new organization, the American Immigration and Citizenship Conference* (AICC), retained the basic AIC constitution, modified by the addition of the words "naturalization and citizenship" and "nationality" in the appropriate places. NCNC accepted the original AIC provision that policy decisions be contingent on the unanimous approval of the membership.

The NCNC's papers are held by the Social Welfare History Archives Center,

University of Minnesota, Minneapolis. These papers include the board of directors' minutes, 1944–1957, committee papers, 1940–1960, general correspondence, reports, speeches, and financial records. For additional information on the concerns of the NCNC see Ruth Z. Murphy, "Government Agencies Working with the Foreign Born," *Annals of the American Academy of Political and Social Science* 262 (March 1949): 131–138; and Frank L. Auerbach, "Principles Which Should Underlie Our Nationality Laws," *The Social Service Review* 24 (December 1950): 477–483.

Mary L. Ostling

NATIONAL COUNCIL ON REHABILITATION (NCR). By the late 1930s, the number of agencies in the field of rehabilitation prompted workers to become interested in an organization to coordinate their diverse activities. Subsequently, in the early 1940s, the American Physiotherapy Association (APA) initiated the movement to establish such an agency when it convened a preliminary meeting of interested parties in Wisconsin in the summer of 1942. Hazel Furscott of the APA called the preliminary meeting to order, and the group elected Dr. Louis M. Bauer of the American Medical Association as chairman. Dr. Bauer appointed a committee on organization, which included such important figures in the field as Harry Howett of the National Society for Crippled Children* (NSCC) and Colonel John N. Smith, Jr., the benefactor and leading spirit of the pioneering rehabilitation facility, the Institute for the Crippled and Disabled (ICD) in New York City. The committee on organization convened another meeting in New York City on August 15, 1942, when representatives from thirty-eight national agencies founded the National Council on Rehabilitation (NCR) as the Council on Rehabilitation (CR); it was designed to be a central exchange in the rehabilitation field. The new CR elected the traditional officers of chairman and vice-chairman as well as a nine-member executive committee.

Designed to promote research and discussions and to establish social service programs, the CR developed gradually. At its meeting on March 12, 1943, the executive committee elected Holland Hudson of the National Tuberculosis Association* (NTA) as secretary-treasurer of the CR. World War II, however, delayed the development of the organization as many workers in the rehabilitation field served in the armed forces and as social service agencies turned to more pressing defense-related problems. In September 1943, the CR became the NCR. By early 1944, the NCR was becoming more active than before. The NTA gave the NCR office space in its headquarters in New York City and allocated Hudson's services to the NCR, which employed an office secretary in early 1944. At the annual meeting in 1944, the nominating committee recommended and the NCR agreed that because the NCR was a new organization that the individual experienced officers—a president, two vice-presidents, and the secretary-treasurer—remain rather than electing new officers. The NCR also adopted its constitution at the annual meeting in 1944 when part of the discussion focused on how the voluntary NCR would help the federal Veterans Administration (VA) to obtain physicians trained in physical rehabilitation medicine.

As World War II was winding down and as the social service community generally prepared for the postwar rehabilitation of the country, the NCR grew. It presented a program on rehabilitation in the postwar era at the National Conference of Social Work,* bringing the NCR closer to the heart of the social service community. In late 1944, the Kellogg Foundation awarded it a grant, which it used to expand its staff and operations. In February 1945, David R. Salmon became the first paid executive director of the NCR; within a few months, Chauncey S. Truax replaced him. In June 1945, the NCR moved to permanent offices at 1790 Broadway in New York, a building that housed many major other agencies in the medical field. Like other organizations in rehabilitation, the NCR sent its leaders to testify before congressional committees on legislation affecting the field. In 1946, the NCR voted to publish its report on health and employment, sponsored another session at the National Conference on Social Welfare,* and approved Executive Secretary Truax's plan to expand the organization (for instance, by increasing the executive committee to fifteen members). Feeling strongly about its growing role in the field, the executive committee favored Colonel Smith's suggestion in 1946 that the NCR instead of the NSCC sponsor the developing committee on the Severely Handicapped.

With the dramatic postwar expansion of the rehabilitation field, from about 1947 until the demise of the NCR a few years later, the organization never seemed to clarify satisfactorily its purposes and never drew the kinds of funds that the leading agencies in the field did, some of which pioneered in massive fund-raising campaigns. Indicative of this inferiority feeling, in 1947, the NCR scheduled its annual meeting to coincide with the conference of the National Rehabilitation Association* (NRA), a more established and politically powerful organization. In 1947, the NCR stopped publishing its *News Letter* and reduced the agency budget considerably; members differed on whether the NCR should continue as an exchange or become involved in direct services. Some members, even of the executive committee, urged dissolution, but in late April 1947, the majority of the executive committee determined to maintain the NCR, with or without the dissenters. The executive committee nevertheless authorized the president to appoint a committee on finance to decide the issue of dissolution before October 1947. This interim advisory committee studied the future but recommended vigorously in September 1947 that the NCR continue.

In late 1947, the outlook brightened. Influenced by Colonel Smith, the ICD of New York agreed to finance the NCR *News Letter,* which resumed publication in June 1947. In March 1948, the NCR held a banquet to honor the retiring medical director of the VA, General Paul Hawley; virtually all the prominent people in the rehabilitation field, as well as government officials, such as United States Congressman Jacob K. Javits of New York, attended. Despite the glamour and publicity of the banquet, in 1948, the NCR stopped publishing the *News Letter* once again. Its activities increased briefly in March 1949 when the *News Letter* reappeared. In 1949, the NCR published a two-volume, 900-page bibliographical study, *The Rehabilitation of the Handicapped, 1940–1946,* by the new executive secretary, Maya Riviere. Nevertheless, the problems the NCR had been encountering since its origins persisted.

An ambitious agency that attracted some important leaders and tried to promote a coherent rehabilitation movement, the NCR apparently lacked effective leadership and was undercut by the major agencies already in the field. Facing these realities, the NCR—which had staved off dissolution before—yielded finally and terminated its activities apparently in late 1949.

I have not been able to locate the manuscripts of the defunct NCR, but some important primary materials, such as minutes and reports of meetings, can be found in the library of the ICD in New York City, which also has many copies of the hard-to-find *News Letter,* an important source for NCR activities. Other publications in the rehabilitation field, such as *The Crippled Child,* contain scattered materials about the NCR, and *The New York Times* reported agency highlights.

There does not appear to be a scholarly historical study of the NCR.

NATIONAL COUNCIL ON THE AGING, INC., THE (NCOA). By the late 1940s, the field of social work for the aged had become a definable one led by such prominent social workers as Ollie Randall, the staff consultant on services for the aged of the Community Service Society* of New York, and Dr. Ellen C. Potter of the Department of Institutions and Agencies of New Jersey and the former president of the National Conference of Social Work.* A number of groups and individuals, such as state and local government workers, commissions, and professional and civic organizations began to explicate the need for a national organization in the field of social work for the aged. In the late 1940s, requests for establishing such a body came from the Community Chests and Councils of America, Inc.,* and the Section on Aging of the National Conference on Social Welfare* (NCSW), which in 1948 and 1949 took formal action to request "the appropriate national organization" to assume leadership in the field. Most importantly, the Citizens Advisory Committee to the federal Bureau of Public Assistance drafted a statement of purpose for the proposed organization and presented it to the National Social Welfare Assembly, Inc.* (NSWA), the leading national coordinating and planning body in social work. Subsequently, at its meeting in January 1950, the NSWA established the National Committee on the Aging (NCOA) as a standing committee of the NSWA. Representatives from business, industry, labor, health and social work, education, and the clergy supported the new NCOA.

In its first decade, the NCOA developed the basic pattern of its activities and services. Its initial project, to formulate standards for sheltered care of the aged, was designed partly to implement recent legislation requiring states to establish procedures for setting and maintaining standards for institutions for the aged in which the people received old age assistance. Published in 1952 as *Standards for Sheltered Care* and revised periodically, the findings of this project initiated a continuing agency interest in institutions serving the aged. The NCOA's concern for the problems of retirement began with a national conference on retirement in 1952, when the agency initiated a two-year study on developing tools for retirement. Employment of the elderly, another sustained activity, developed in 1954 with the founding of a subcommittee of the organization. In 1955, the agency produced the first of many films, *A Place to Live,* which won more awards in 1956 than any other documentary. A major grant—$500,000 from the Ford Foundation—helped the NCOA to expand its publications, projects, and activities, as well as to initiate new work. Staff growth paralleled this expansion: one worker, for example, joined the staff in 1958 to direct a project on standards for old age club and center programs. As of May 1959, another worker joined as director of the project on dependency and guardianship.

The organization's structure also expanded throughout the 1950s. The executive committee grew to twenty-five members by 1958. Prominent lay and professional workers in the field, such as Ollie Randall, who served many years as vice-chairman, joined the executive committee, which in turn, chose the officers. An executive secretary headed the staff. A week-long, tenth anniversary celebration in October 1960 culminated the activities of the National Committee.

At the celebration, Chairman G. Warfield Hobbs, who had served since the NCOA was formed, announced that the group would become an independent organization. Incorporated with a New York State charter on November 17, 1960, as The National Council on the Aging, Inc. (NCOA), the new organization became operational on January 1, 1961. Hobbs became president, Randall became one of three vice-presidents, and the positions of secretary and treasurer were created. The former executive committee of the National Committee became the board of directors of the new NCOA. The new agency continued the basic activities of the old, expanding them only gradually. In early December 1961, NCOA moved to a larger headquarters in New York City. In 1962, the NCOA developed the first of many new organizations and institutes, the American Association of Homes for the Aging.

As a result of the federally sponsored social welfare programs of the mid-1960s through the early 1970s, the work of the NCOA expanded greatly. The agency increased its efforts in behalf of workers between fifty and sixty-five years of age with demonstration projects showing their employability. The Department of Labor supported what became the senior community service project of the NCOA to stimulate local welfare and health agencies to hire the aging as paraprofessionals and in other capacities. A host of NCOA committees and subcommittees dealt with the issues of training and retraining older workers, preparation for and criteria of retirement, and retirement income and activities. NCOA efforts for aging workers led to the development in 1968 of its Institute of Industrial Gerontology, which publishes a quarterly journal. Other federal funds, such as those from the United States Public Health Service, helped administer an NCOA project initiated in 1964, home-delivered meals for the ill, handicapped, and elderly. The federal Office of Economic Opportunity provided important contracts and funding for such major activities as Project FIND (Friendless, Isolated, Needy, and Disabled), initiated in 1967, which used primarily older people to find those who needed services, and the NCOA training institutes throughout the country for local community action programs. The United States Department of Housing and Urban Development funded the NCOA program to train workers dealing with the aged poor in local Model Cities programs.

The NCOA also strengthened federal activities for the aged, for example, through testimony to government officials and energetic participation in the White House Conference on the Aging in 1971. Largely because of these federal alliances, the NCOA moved its national headquarters from New York to Washington, D.C., in March 1970. As a headline in *NCOA Reports on the Aging* proclaimed in early 1971, federal support continued to "make NCOA hum."

With the shift in federal social philosophy and priorities in the early 1970s, the NCOA underwent significant changes. A financial crisis in 1972, which threatened the very existence of the organization, helped streamline the agency through reassignment and elimination of personnel. The crisis also prompted an aggressive membership drive, which, in 1973, resulted in a 30 percent increase. In addition, in 1972, the board of directors was increased to sixty-eight members to provide better geographical and ethnic minority representation. Even though the flush times of the 1960s were gone, the NCOA continued nevertheless as the leader and innovator in the field. In 1972, for instance, its research department evaluated the previous year's White House Conference on the Aging. NCOA's national institute for senior citizens, established in 1970, continued as a clearinghouse in that field, publishing a monthly *MEMO.* By the end of 1973, NOCA's senior community service project had over a thousand people working in a hundred agencies in eighteen areas of the country.

The primary sources for studying the NCOA's history consist largely of its own publications and mimeographed materials in the agency's library in the headquarters in Washington, D.C. The NSWA's *Annual Reports* contain information on the National Committee. Most helpful are the NCOA's *Annual Reports* and the existing issues of both the *NCOA Progress Report* and the *NCOA Journal,* which are not widely available in libraries. The NCOA has many of its files, but they are not part of the library and are not available generally to researchers. There is no full-length, scholarly history of the NCOA, but Henry J. Pratt, *The Gray Lobby* (1976), treats it.

NATIONAL DESERTION BUREAU: see FAMILY LOCATION SERVICE, INC.

NATIONAL EASTER SEAL SOCIETY FOR CRIPPLED CHILDREN AND ADULTS, THE (NESSCCA). In the second decade of the twentieth century, in Elyria, Ohio, Edgar Fiske Allen, a wealthy businessman, became interested in the problems of crippled children following the accidental death of his son. As a memorial to his son, Allen founded a hospital in Elyria. "Daddy" Allen not only established other philanthropies in the town but also urged a friend to fund the local Gates Hospital. One day, a crippled little boy came to Gates Hospital, and upon seeing his condition, Allen resolved to establish an organization to help crippled children. On May 8, 1919, Allen and a group of members of the Ohio Rotary Club founded the Ohio Society for Crippled Children (OSCC). The success of the OSCC-influenced, so-called Ohio plan for crippled children led Allen and others to discuss forming a national organization. Consequently, on October 14, 1921, in Toledo, Ohio, The National Easter Seal Society for Crippled Children and Adults (NESSCCA) was established as the National Society for Crippled Children (NSCC). Allen led the group of founders, which also included members of the OSCC, prominent leaders of the International Society of Rotary Clubs, such as Paul P. Harris of Chicago, president emeritus, and representatives from Rotary clubs in New York and Michigan. Allen became the president of the NSCC, a post he held until 1934. The NSCC established its initial headquarters in Elyria.

In its early years, the NSCC, which became the International Society for Crippled Children (ISCC) in 1922, concentrated on developing affiliate societies, on arousing local concern for crippled children, and on pressuring state legislatures to provide programs for such children. Within a few years, the basic organizational structure was crystallized. Allen remained president, and there were several vice-presidents, a treasurer, an eleven-member board of directors, chaired by one of the founders, Paul Harris, an advisory council of thirteen specialists in special education, rehabilitation medicine, and social work, and a publicity committee. An executive secretary headed the staff, which increasingly expanded. The organization began to publish its bimonthly journal, *The Crippled Child,* in August 1923. President Allen, an effective organizer, and the executive secretary, Harry M. Howett, stimulated local groups to organize as affiliates. In 1928, there were twenty-five state societies and one society in Canada. The national and local organizations worked closely with state commissions studying the condition of crippled children, such as the one in New York in the 1920s. ISCC leaders such as Harry Howett helped to mobilize state campaigns to promote legislation for such children. The successful experiences of the OSCC with its state legislature in the early 1920s served as a model for the other efforts. In 1929, the ISCC incorporated itself according to the laws of Ohio.

The ISCC also began, in the late 1920s, to work on the national level. It campaigned aggressively to have the White House Conference on Child Health and Protection of 1930 include discussions of crippled children. At its own convention in 1931 in Cleveland, the organization adopted the "Crippled Children's Bill of Rights," parts of which were adopted by the White House Conference. ISCC leaders, particularly its legislative committee, helped to shape the provisions of the Social Security Act of 1935 relating to the care of crippled children. In late 1933, the ISCC launched its cerebral palsy program, which became the most advanced coordinated program of its kind in the 1940s, when it featured medical specialists advising local programs, cerebral palsy parents' councils, and a Cerebral Palsy Fund, which provided scholarships to train qualified personnel in specialties related to cerebral palsy work. Most importantly, however, in early 1934, the ISCC inaugurated its fund-raising White Cross Seals to help fight crippling diseases. President Franklin Roosevelt quickly endorsed the seals, the ISCC hired a special staff member to direct the sales, and in 1935, the campaign became known as Easter Seals. Despite the Great Depression gripping the country, the Easter seal became an immediate success, helping to thrust the organization into national leadership in the field.

In 1940, the agency, now called the National Society for Crippled Children (NSCC), strengthened its structure, initiating the important counsellor plan of having specialists in a field head specific departments. These departments coordinated activities between the professional staff at national headquarters and volunteers at the affiliates. In 1942, there were counsellors for ten separate activities, such as the cerebral palsied child hospitals and institutions and curative and sheltered workshops. Such specialists as Dr. John J. Lee in special education and John A. Kratz, an experienced federal vocational rehabilitation official, became counsellors in their particular fields. The NSCC's activities indicated its increasing national importance: the publication of *A Primer on the Prevention of Deformity in Childhood* in the early 1940s; the continuation of area institutes for professionals, such as teachers, doctors, and social workers; NSCC-led campaigns to liberalize state workmen's compensation laws to permit handicapped workers' participation in defense-related industries; and a two-day conference in June 1942 in Wilmington, Delaware, to discuss the impact of American entry into the war on the rehabilitation field.

As reflected in the activities of the conference in Wilmington, the organization expanded its concerns to include the adult handicapped. A model bill, drafted by the NSCC in 1943 and 1944, contained benefits for both children and adults, and in 1943, the NSCC sponsored Federal Security administrator Paul McNutt's nationwide radio address on programs for the handicapped. The Easter seal campaign expanded steadily, and state affiliates—which relied heavily on their own local seal campaigns—continued the early trend of considerable autonomy. State affiliates, however, relied on the national offices for expert advice, program guidance, publications, and the like. The movement to change the name, appropriately, to The National Society for Crippled Children and Adults, Inc. (NSCCA), occurred officially in the fall of 1944. Founder Allen's death in September 1937, but more importantly, the society's national leadership in the field of handicapped, influenced the agency to move its headquarters from Elyria to Chicago in the fall of 1945. In the same year, some administrative streamlining and the establishment of a professional consultation service in the following fields geared the NSCCA for its leadership role after World War II: physical medicine, orthopedic and public health nursing, medical social service, rehabilitation, employment, and recreation of the handicapped.

The NSCCA became a leading national agency in the creative and significant postwar developments in the field of services to the handicapped. Disabled American veterans influenced the important developments in vocational and physical rehabilitation, social and psychological services, and medical advances. New programs and research sponsored by the Veterans Administration and other government agencies brought a new force into the field, but private agencies like the NSCCA continued to develop and implement important programs and activities. By its silver anniversary year, 1946, the organization had over two thousand affiliated societies, many of which were conducting important social services in their communities. The New York State Association for Crippled Children, Inc., for instance, sponsored at Lenox Hill Hospital in New York City a well-rounded cerebral palsy program utilizing local volunteers and medical specialists, as well as the services of the national organization. In 1945–1946, the NSCCA pioneered in the cerebral palsy field, authorizing new programs and structures, such as the National Parents Council on Cerebral Palsy. The medical advisory council to the cerebral palsy work of the NSCCA developed into the American Academy for Cerebral Palsy, a professional medical organization. During the steady growth of the rehabilitation field in the 1950s, the NSCCA strengthened its services to the handicapped, providing nearly nine hundred services and facilities for the crippled in the mid-1950s.

In the 1960s, as the federal government expanded its own services in the field of social welfare broadly and in the rehabilitation field specifically, the NSCCA demonstrated that private, voluntary agencies could develop creative and progressive programs. Project Earning Power (PEP), begun in 1964, worked to design competitively marketable products in sheltered workshops using the severely handicapped. A host of programs, such as developing a national personnel registry and other conferences and projects to attract professional workers in the rehabilitation field and special training programs to encourage volunteers, dealt effectively with the social work personnel shortage of the 1960s. A program begun in 1960 helped to eliminate all obstructions interfering with the access of the handicapped to new buildings. Culminating nearly twenty years' work, a law that all federally funded buildings provide access for the handicapped was signed by President Lyndon B. Johnson in August 1968. The NSCCA also continued its tradition of mobilizing support for greater federal appropriations in all aspects of rehabilitation.

The NSCAA completed a major administrative reorganization in the mid- to late 1960s, following several years of self-study and guidance by representatives of the Massachusetts Institute of Technology. In 1964, for example, the agency abolished its executive committee and created a new twenty-four-member board of directors, with varying numbers of ex officio members, to manage and direct its affairs. To represent all the state societies, the agency also established a house of delegates, which implemented procedures in the late 1960s whereby state and local societies streamlined their administrative and governing structures. In 1965, the NSCCA founded a National advisory council, composed of civic and other leaders, such as Senator Birch Bayh of Indiana. The NSCCA, which became The National Easter Seal Society for Crippled Children and Adults (NESSCCA) in 1967, joined other leading national voluntary agencies in adopting the uniform accounting system in the mid-1960s.

In the late 1960s and early 1970s, the organization became more heavily involved than before in community issues and in outreach inner-city programs. A project begun in the late 1960s of information, referral, and follow-up increased services in the field by nearly 50 percent by the end of the decade and led also in 1970 to a visiting homemaker program. Another program to train volunteers in the field and renewed commitments by professional advisers and the board of directors also prompted the growth of services, particularly in inner cities, such as the Easter Seal-Goodwill Industries Rehabilitation Center in New Haven, Connecticut. Programs in local rehabilitation centers emphasized increasingly such social-recreational activities as housing and camping. Largely because of amendments in 1971 to the Wagner-O'Day Act, allowing the federal government to purchase a wider range of products from sheltered workshops, the agency expanded its facilities and programs in this area. To continue its lobbying for federal funds in the rehabilitation field, the agency published, beginning in the early 1970s, *Washington Watchline* and opened an office in Washington, D.C., in January 1973.

The most helpful published primary sources for studying the NESSCCA's history are, for the earlier years, the issues of *The Crippled Child,* and in the 1950s and later, the published *Annual Reports.* All these materials, some of which are difficult to locate, are in the library of the organization at its Chicago headquarters. At the national headquarters there are full archival records, which are not part of the library but which are available to researchers.

Very few secondary studies mention the NESSCCA, and there is apparently no scholarly history of the agency.

NATIONAL FEDERATION OF REMEDIAL LOAN ASSOCIATIONS (NFRLA). During the late nineteenth and early twentieth centuries, especially in cities, immigrants, the poor, and laborers were subject to various forms of exploitation, including the practice of loansharking. Reformers denounced usurious interest rates. Not surprisingly, some of the earliest agencies to deal with this problem, the so-called remedial loan societies, were established by charitable organizations. The Charity Organization Society of the City of New York* (COS), for instance, appointed a committee to study loansharking and other exploitative practices, and this committee prompted the development of the Provident Loan Society of New York (PLSNY). Indeed, even though historians have neglected the problem of usurious loan practices engulfing the poor and the vulnerable, the campaign to deal with this problem seemed to be an aspect of the social justice Progressive movement.

During the Progressive era, writers pointed out the philanthropic nature of remedial loan societies. Leaders from these associations began in the early twentieth century to discuss forming a national group to promote their interests and concerns. Consequently, in 1909, W. N. Finley, the manager of The Chattel Loan Association of Baltimore, Maryland, issued an invitation to local leaders to meet at the upcoming meetings of the National Conference of Charities and Correction* (NCCC). Subsequently, the National Federation of Remedial Loan Associations (NFRLA) was established in Buffalo, New York, on June 10, 1909, at the local building of the Young Women's Christian Association by delegates attending the NCCC. Besides Finley, the other important figures in the convening of the founding meeting were Frank Tucker of the PLSNY and Hugh Cavanaugh, the manager of the Citizens' Mortgages Loan Company of Cincinnati, Ohio. The relation of this unique organization to the field of social service was suggested further in its early and continuing relationship, as an affiliate group, with the NCCC and in its close ties with the Russell Sage Foundation* (RSF), the most important financial supporter of social service agencies and movements in the Progressive and other periods.

The NFRLA's early structure included a chairman and a secretary, held by Finley and Cavanaugh, respectively. These two men joined one other representative of a loan society to form the initial executive committee. The major objectives, agreed upon at the organizing sessions, included stimulating the development of new societies and strengthening existing ones and providing advice on all aspects of these associations—financing, loans, and the like. From the beginning, membership was open to representatives of local loan societies and to individuals sympathetic with the reform movement to compel enforcement of laws regulating chattel, salary, and pawning loans and to protect borrowers from extortion. The new NFRLA had neither a full-time executive officer nor a formal headquarters, but Arthur H. Ham, an agent of the RSF, cooperated with the organization, answering its correspondence and providing other basic services. Ham also headed a department of the RSF dealing with such remedial loan societies.

The activities of the NFRLA consisted mostly of holding annual conferences, publishing its proceedings, and corresponding with local groups that were setting up such societies. By June 1911, there was a 61 percent increase in the membership since 1909. Also, by 1911, local affiliates had been fighting the evils of loansharks and conducting reform campaigns, including pressing for legislation in cities throughout the country. The local press, reform journals such as *The Survey,* and the local social service committees of the Men and Religion Forward Movement all aided local campaigns, especially in Chicago. In Jersey City, New Jersey, exploitation led to a grand jury investigation. The large attendance at the

NFRLA's annual conference in Cleveland, Ohio, in June 1912 prompted the agency to begin to publish the quarterly *Bulletin,* which carried news from the field, as well as the proceedings of the annual meetings. In 1913, the organization, like other national associations, drafted a model law for small loans. In 1915, serving its constituents in the field, the NFRLA prepared a model form for annual reports, which the organization wanted local affiliates to submit to. In 1914, when Ham argued before the delegates at the annual meeting that making small loans was as necessary as emergency relief provided by charitable institutions, the NFRLA had thirty-seven affiliate members, and its executive committee numbered seven. The maximum number of affiliates, forty, belonged in 1915, but within a few years, the organizations began to lose affiliates, most of which went out of existence. No new affiliates were established after 1918, and the organization seemed to die slowly.

The NFRLA apparently stopped publishing its annual proceedings in the mid-1920s, but it did continue to issue statistics on the work of its affiliates through the early 1940s. Ham served the organization until 1918, after which time the headquarters seemed to be wherever the chairman of the NFRLA was located. Membership declined from thirty-five affiliates in 1917 to twenty-six in 1931, and, apparently in the mid-1940s, the NFRLA disbanded.

The chief source for studying the NFRLA's history is the published *Proceedings of the Annual Meetings, 1909–1924.* Contemporary publications, such as Arthur Ham, "Remedial Loans as Factors in Family Rehabilitation," NCCC, *Proceedings* (1911), 305–311, and Frank Marshall White, "The Crusade Against the Loan-Shark," *Munsey's Magazine* (November 1913): 216–331, indicate the basic activities and purposes of the movement. John M. Glenn, Lilian Brandt, and F. Emerson Andrews, *Russell Sage Foundation, 1907–1946* (1947), contains some references to the NFRLA, which historians have neglected.

NATIONAL FEDERATION OF SETTLEMENTS: see NATIONAL FEDERATION OF SETTLEMENTS AND NEIGHBORHOOD CENTERS.

NATIONAL FEDERATION OF SETTLEMENTS AND NEIGHBORHOOD CENTERS (NFSNC). In the late nineteenth century, settlement houses developed in the major American cities, especially in Chicago, Boston, and New York. As early as 1892, when they began to meet informally, the leaders of the earliest settlements, such as Jane Addams of Hull-House* (HH) in Chicago, Robert A. Woods of the South End House in Boston, and Lillian Wald of the Henry Street Settlement* of New York, envisioned a national federation of settlements. In 1894, in Chicago, the existing settlements established the first citywide federation to promote cooperation and communication among their members. Settlements in other cities soon followed suit, establishing similar citywide organizations.

On the national level, only occasional gatherings of representatives from settlements were held until May 1908, when about twenty residents from settlements in New York, Boston, and Chicago met to discuss further cooperation. At the annual meeting of the National Conference of Charities and Correction* (NCCC) in 1908, a strong feeling that there be separate gatherings of people from the settlements became evident. The settlement group held a number of sessions at the NCCC in 1910, but a special meeting—to which representatives from nearly every known settlement were invited—crystallized the movement to establish a new organization. At these meetings in 1910, the group appointed a national committee of ten representatives to gather information about the experiences of individual settlements. This venture led quickly to the new National Federation of Settlement's (NFS) initial enterprise, the publication in 1911 of *Handbook of Settlements,* an amazingly detailed array of information about existing settlements. The national committee also drafted a platform, which it presented at the June 1911 meetings in Boston at the NCCC, for united action by settlements throughout the United States. Consequently, on June 11, 1911, in Boston, the National Federation of Settlements and Neighborhood Centers (NFSNC) was established as the NFS when, at the invitation of the organizers, some two hundred delegates attended this national gathering of settlement representatives. The leaders in the new NFS's establishment included Jane Addams, who became the first president, Robert Woods, who became the first secretary, and Graham R. Taylor of the Chicago Commons. The initial structure called for member settlements to contribute dues as members. It also provided for individuals interested in settlement work to enroll as corresponding members without voting privileges.

With a very small part-time staff, the early NFS, more than agencies with more formal structures, relied on the enthusiasm, ideals, and voluntary activities of its members. Consistent with the ideals of the early settlement house pioneers, an initial agency goal was to promote all phases of social action. The NFS also hoped to develop clear and strong policies on issues common to settlements, to publish the results of experiences, to attract college-educated men and women to become residents, to cooperate with other agencies in social work programs, and, consistent with the activities of the pioneer settlements, to promote the democratic organization of community life. Quickly fulfilling some of these principles, the NFS played an important role in the creation of the United States Children's Bureau (USCB) (see *Government Agencies*) in 1912.

Like the earliest settlements, the USCB conducted detailed surveys of conditions—focusing on those affecting children—and it promoted social action. In its very early period, as well as in its later history, an important service was to gather information about settlement activities and to publish the results. In its first cooperative study, the NFS analyzed work with adolescent girls. Published in 1913, *Young Working Girls* quickly became a source and a guide for local units developing and strengthening their youth programs. Robert Woods was the first secretary, but in 1914 Albert J. Kennedy, a resident and later head resident of South End House in Boston and who became known for his enthusiasm for cultural activities at settlements, became the chief administrator of the NFS.

The NFS, which maintained headquarters in Boston, began to take shape. In 1915, it resolved to have the seventeen-member executive committee study securing a field secretary and publishing a quarterly. It also endorsed the unemployment platform of the American Association for Labor Legislation.* Activities in 1916 included supporting the Smith-Hughes bill in Congress for federal support of vocational education, an early concern of settlements, urging local units to conduct concerted efforts with adolescent girls, and supporting the movement to establish a women's department of the National Bureau of Labor and Industry. In 1917, the NFS adopted a resolution supporting compulsory health insurance, an issue the organization kept alive. During the years of World War I, despite internal differences between pacifists and supporters of President Woodrow Wilson's efforts, the NFS helped the government by providing information about urban immigrant districts. The national agency helped to develop a few local units, sending specialists to these communities. The NFS also conducted a study of the war work of settlements, and to strengthen another activity of many settlements, it appointed a special committee on music, chaired by John Crolle, in 1919.

Like other reform-oriented agencies during the 1920s, the NFS was less interested in social action than it had been during the Progressive era, but signs of the pioneering spirit were still clear, especially toward the end of the decade. Early in the 1920s, the NFS developed a policy of organizing local and regional institutes to discuss issues of common concern. The NFS added a secretary to conduct activities in the Midwest and another to cooperate with European settlements, which led to efforts in the early 1920s to establish the International Federation of Settlements.

As historian Clarke Chambers has pointed out, the failure in 1926 by the NFS to create a committee on education in social relations to bring settlements closer to the labor movement suggests the conservatism of the organization in this period. Another activity of the 1920s—an exhibition of settlement arts and crafts, which traveled to ten cities in 1925—did not smack of the social justice reform spirit of the earlier days. The exception to this conservative trend was in the field of housing. The NFS's conference in 1920 focused on housing more than on any other issue. At this meeting, the organization appointed a committee, chaired by Lillian Wald, to promote public interest in better housing, which the NFS now felt was a matter of governmental responsibility. Two years of efforts resulted in a report calling housing a key community and social problem. The lofty resolution of 1922 also called for a model housing code and for coordinating housing commissions at all levels of government. Signs of change, however, were more discernible in 1926, when the NFS appointed Wald to head a committee to investigate the social effects of prohibition at a time when other agencies neglected this important subject. Martha S. Bruère, a writer and artist with ties to settlement work, directed the study, and the NFS helped to finance it. Published in 1927 as *Does Prohibition Work?* the study dealt with the impact of the Eighteenth Amendment to the Constitution on settlement neighborhoods in nearly one hundred cities. Also, in late May 1926, the NFS held a symposium at the Cleveland Museum of Art and published the first of its discussions as *Settlement Goals for the Next Third of a Century*. The most prominent idea was the need to transform charity into education for social action.

Perhaps more than any other national social service organization, the NFS first felt the effects of the depression in the late 1920s. These conditions prompted social action reminiscent of the earlier period. Responding to urgings that the NFS move away from "administrative minutiae," the NFS in 1928 appointed a committee headed by Helen Hall, then the director of the University Settlement in Philadelphia and later the head resident at the Henry Street Settlement, and Irene Hickok Nelson. The NFS authorized this committee to study the impact of the economic slump on families. Published as *Case Studies of Unemployment* (1931), the investigation showed clearly the deleterious effects of the growing depression. The material that the NFS had produced was also reported in popular form in *Some Folks Won't Work* (1930) by Clinch Calkins. Interest in group work developed in the late 1920s, and the NFS tried to help local settlements develop this social work technique, calling for local units to submit data for a study. To keep the settlement community informed, the NFS began to publish *Neighborhood* in 1929.

In the 1930s, the NFS returned to its earlier interest in social issues and social action. In 1930, of about 230 settlements in the country, only 160 belonged to the NFS. Many did not join because of the dues and because they were sectarian. Membership in the NFS remained stable even though the depression worsened. Once a unit joined, during the 1930s, the NFS generally ignored the dues payments requirement. Also, during the depression, the dozen or so music school settlements dropped from membership in the NFS. In 1930, the NFS began to support the old age pension movement. In 1932, it endorsed states' establishing compulsory unemployment insurance systems, and as the economic situation worsened, the NFS increasingly looked to federal involvement in unemployment insurance, an issue on which the NFS lagged behind its outspoken individual leaders and members. In 1934, the NFS endorsed the principles of the Tennessee Valley Authority, and in 1936, it became the first national organization to hold its convention at the site of the project, Norris, Tennessee. Beginning in 1934 and continuing through the late 1930s, the NFS supported workers' educational programs conducted by settlements, chiefly in New York and Chicago.

In 1935, the NFS still hoped to include, in the Social Security Act, provisions for nationwide minimum standards of relief, an issue in the national social work community. Almost immediately after the enactment of the Social Security Act of 1935, the settlements began to apply its provisions, which included minimum health services. After a series of labor strikes in 1937, the NFS held a symposium, "The Place of the Settlement in Industrial Relations." The NFS became involved in the movement for national health insurance. In 1938, it conducted a study in twenty-three cities of what neighbors of the settlements did when they were ill; a high number lacked medical services. In the late 1930s, the NFS helped Dr. Douglas W. Orr and his wife, Jean, to study the health insurance laws and general health conditions in England. In 1938, they published *Health Insurance with Medical Care* for the NFS. Grace Abbott, a major figure in social work, called it a "timeless" work. Although the NFS held a racially integrated convention in Tennessee in 1936, the NFS, in the words of a student of settlements in the 1930s, was "noticeably silent on racial matters." Neighborhood centers affiliated with the National Urban League* in seventeen cities did not even join the NFS, whose interracial committee remained inactive in the 1930s.

During the period of World War II and the 1950s, the NFS continued to participate in national social work movements and to provide field services and general leadership for local settlements, which numbered eighty in 1939. In the early 1940s, the organization decided that it should play a leading role in national postwar planning. In 1944 and 1945, the NFS analyzed case studies to determine the relation between family life and unemployment, and in 1945, it strongly supported the Employment Bill, which, when enacted in 1946, provided means for the federal government to monitor unemployment trends. National medical insurance continued to interest the NFS, which in 1954 studied some families and their medical insurance and sent a representative to England to observe its health plans.

The traditional NFS awareness of major trends affecting people in cities prompted a conference in 1958 at Arden House in Harriman, New York. Public figures and academicians, such as Wilbur Cohen, a professor at the University of Michigan's School of Social Work, the chief consultant of the conference, joined settlement leaders to discuss the implications of population expansion, race tensions, public service, alienation, the new mobility, and other effects of urbanization and industrialization. The report of the conference was *Neighborhood Goals in a Rapidly Changing World*. The conference helped to support an NFS project in the late 1950s—to study settlement activities, such as youth service, citizen participation, and services to multiproblem families in a changing society. Fieldwork in twenty-five cities, correspondence, and other sources provided materials for the report by Arthur Hillman, *Neighborhood Centers Today* (1960), which was studied at meetings and conferences throughout the country. It presented an informative picture of settlement and neighborhood center work. Recognizing the importance of the increasing number of neighborhood centers, the organization became the NFSNC in 1949.

Another important service to the settlement field was the realization that more continuing education was needed to train and to prepare staff members for settlement work. After a feasibility study, the NFSNC in 1960 established a national training center, initially at HH in Chicago and later in another part of the city.

The NFSNC was in the mainstream of social work and the excitement and controversy of the 1960s when it continued its leadership in the settlement field. Throughout the decade, the NFSNC training center, which closed in 1971, conducted programs and conferences, often focusing on specific issues or services. The center sponsored similar institutes and courses in other cities as well. The largest session dealt with youth workers involved with street gangs. Conferences often led to publications, prepared at the center itself. As the federal government developed its expanding social services in the 1960s, the NFSNC worked with officials, informing them about urban social services. In the late 1960s, with a grant from the federal Office of Economic Opportunity (OEO), the NFS conducted a study of federally supported poverty programs, such as Volunteers in Service to America (VISTA). The study was entitled *Making Democracy Work* (1968).

The NFSNC response to racial issues and civil rights was more effective in the 1960s than its earlier activities in these areas. Responding to the changing racial makeup of urban neighborhoods, to new, aggressive, minority staff members in local settlements, and to greater demands for community control over local agencies, the NFSNC commissioned a study not only to collate and to learn from local experiences but also to stimulate further actions in the settlement tradition. Aided by field workers, St. Clair Drake, a noted sociologist from Roosevelt University, headed the study. The report, published in 1966, provided guidelines for settlement boards and staff; the immediate relevance of the report, however, was diminished by the increasingly militant approaches being voiced. Dealing further with the issue of social services and race relations, the NFSNC began its Mississippi project in 1966, which promoted community organization, social action, and other traditional settlement activities there in the early 1970s.

Paralleling the experiences of such national social service agencies as the Family Service Association of America* and the Council of Southern Mountain Workers,* the NFSNC establishment faced an internal challenge initiated by black settlement workers in 1969. The movement broadened to include brown, red, and yellow people, becoming known as techniculture, which was the name of a conference held in February 1970 and attended by over six hundred people. Both the board of directors and the executive director, Margaret Berry, officially endorsed the ideals of the techniculture movement. In the board elections for 1970, the techniculture forces succeeded in electing representatives, and the percentage of minority representation in the NFSNC increased by 30 percent to over 60 percent.

The reduced federal government support of community-sponsored social service programs in the late 1960s and early 1970s helped to diminish the NFSNC as well as local settlement activities. In the early 1970s, the NFSNC had only three committees: international, social education and action—an important committee throughout—and civil rights. The agency, however, still continued to provide field services, to develop standards for local settlements, and, in the spirit of its founders, to conduct studies of health, housing unemployment, and other social problems, and to promote legislation to improve conditions for people in the inner cities.

The NFSNC began a new era in 1971 when Walter Smart replaced Margaret Berry as executive director, a position she had held since 1959. Under Smart, the NFSNC served its affiliates and was in the mainstream of progressive developments in the national social service community. Smart was the first black NFSNC executive director. In 1971, the agency amended its bylaws to ensure participation by those served by settlements and neighborhood centers. The NFSNC provided a service to help provide personnel for local units. In 1972, the agency established its committee on housing to coordinate the efforts of and to assist local affiliates in developing their housing programs. Illustrating the NFSNC's ties to national programs and its ways of serving affiliates, in the early 1970s, the agency emphasized economic development as a major priority. Executive Director Smart visited fourteen cities to study ways to increase economic opportunities for minorities, resulting in a funded proposal from the federal Office of Minority Business Enterprise, which provided grants to ten settlements and neighborhood centers. Finally, for its affiliates, the NFSNC held a week-long conference on economic development. Executive Director Smart frequently testified before a variety of government agencies in Washington, D.C., and one of the highlights of 1972 was the acceptance by the platform committees of both the Democrat and Republican parties of the agency's social policy platform.

During the mid-1970s, the NFSNC conducted a project to prepare teenagers for parenthood, with funds from the Office of Child Development of the Department of Health, Education, and Welfare. In 1975, the NFSNC, which was attempting to change its name to United Neighborhood Centers of America, adopted two major objectives: juvenile justice and delinquency prevention and full employment. In June 1975, Smart completed a juvenile justice program, and to implement it, the NFSNC established its emergency task force on juvenile delinquency prevention, cochaired by United States Senator Birch Bayh of Indiana and Mary Dublin Keyserling, a well-known figure in the national social work community who had been active in national children's and youth agencies. The NFSNC featured discussions of full employment at its annual meeting in 1976, and the agency began to provide data about unemployment for congressional hearings and legislation. This effort was similar to Helen Hall's in the late 1920s. Although an inadequate staff continued to plague the NFSNC, it was able to borrow staff from member agencies, such as the Henry Street Settlement* in

New York City and collaborate with other national agencies on a variety of issues.

The sources for studying the NFSNC's history are diverse. The Social Welfare History Archives Center at the University of Minnesota, Minneapolis, has the agency's records through the 1960s. At the headquarters in New York City are also the minutes of meetings and the agency's "bible," a chronological list of events, publications, meetings, and such. NFSNC materials can also be found in the collections of its leaders, such as the Jane Addams Papers at Swarthmore College. Published primary sources include the *Proceedings* of the earliest conferences, *Neighborhood,* the agency's journal in the late 1920s and early 1930s, and such contemporary publications as Robert A. Woods and Albert J. Kennedy, *The Settlement Horizon* (1922). For the recent period, there are published *Annual Reports.*

A host of scholarly publications in the field of social welfare history, including Clarke Chambers, *Seedtime for Reform* (1963), and Judith Ann Trolander, *Settlement Houses and The Great Depression* (1975), for that period, contain information about the organization. There does not appear to be a scholarly history of the agency itself.

NATIONAL FOUNDATION—MARCH OF DIMES, THE (NF-MD). The origins of this unique and important philanthropic agency relate to Franklin Delano Roosevelt, who contracted infantile paralysis—as polio was then called—at Campobello Island, New Brunswick, Canada, in August 1921. The former assistant secretary of the navy and scion of a wealthy and well-known New York family, he narrowly escaped death. In 1924, Roosevelt visited Warm Springs, Georgia, to see the effects of the resort's famous spas on his crippled body. So impressed with his own and others' improvements, Roosevelt decided to determine the effectiveness of the spa on a group of twenty-three patients who were then observed closely. All did well, helping to convince Roosevelt to establish a hydrotherapeutic center at the old resort. Roosevelt enlisted his law partner and friend, Basil O'Connor, in this venture. After lengthy negotiations, Roosevelt signed an agreement to purchase the entire complex on April 29, 1926. He then organized the Warm Springs Foundation (WSF), which was incorporated on July 8, 1927, to sponsor patient care and research in the field of infantile paralysis. When he was elected governor of New York in 1928, Roosevelt turned over the enterprise—to which he had contributed his own money—to O'Connor. By 1932, when Roosevelt was elected president of the United States, the WSF was nearly bankrupt. Like other philanthropies and charities, it suffered from the effects of the Great Depression.

Events beginning in 1933 shaped the redirection and further development of the venture and helped eventually to establish The National Foundation—March of Dimes (NF-MD) as The National Foundation for Infantile Paralysis (NFIP). In late 1933, O'Connor, Colonel Henry L. Dogherty, the wealthy utility owner and hotel and resort promoter, and public relations expert Carl Byoir decided to raise funds to fight infantile paralysis by a nationwide celebration of the president's birthday on January 30, 1934. They developed the idea to hold birthday balls throughout the country and drafted the slogan, "Dance so that a child may walk." The events, about six thousand of them, held in thirty-six hundred communities, "quickly stirred national enthusiasm." The committee working on the balls, chaired by Doherty, raised over $1 million. To encourage greater local support for the celebration in January 1935, the Birthday Ball Committee (BBC) determined that 70 percent of the receipts would stay for patient care and similar work in the communities in which the funds were raised and that 30 percent would go to the recently organized Commission on Infantile Paralysis Research (CIPR), headed also by Doherty. The WSF would not get any funds this time. Again, the events were successful in raising funds for the national organization, now called the President's Birthday Ball Commission for Infantile Paralysis Research (PBBCIPR). The appeal of the birthday ball celebrations gradually faded, and O'Connor and an aide, Keith Morgan, went ahead with their plans to establish a permanent, independent national polio fund-raising organization. Subsequently, on September 22, 1937, at his family home in Hyde Park, New York, President Franklin Delano Roosevelt announced the establishment of the NFIP to promote research, to find a cure for the disease, and to help patients.

The new NFIP, however, planned to continue the balls. It was decided, with Roosevelt's approval, that all the funds raised would go to the new NFIP and none to the WSF. The Committee for the Celebration of the President's Birthday for Fighting Infantile Paralysis (CPBFIP) was also created. A student of these developments, Professor Scott M. Cutlip, argued that these events in late 1937 signaled the beginning of the shift away from honoring Roosevelt to fighting infantile paralysis. NFIP headquarters was quickly established in midtown Manhattan in O'Connor's law office.

The NFIP began to operate officially in January 1938. From the birthday ball campaign in 1938, the NFIP kept half of the proceeds and allowed the other half to remain in the local communities, despite O'Connor's initial desire to have the NFIP keep all the funds raised. The NFIP and the committee conducting the birthday balls were kept as separate entities. In January 1938, a major organizational event for the NFIP occurred when two popular radio entertainers—singer Eddie Cantor and the adventure hero, the Lone Ranger—and other celebrities urged people to send dimes for polio to the White House, a campaign that yielded $2.68 million and indicated the popularity of the cause, the organization, and, it seems, President Roosevelt. In November 1938, a month of important decisions for the NFIP, the board of trustees approved a plan to establish local chapters, and the board allowed O'Connor to appoint a committee of three to prepare a manual for such chapters. The chapters, organized largely by the chairman of the local committee for the president's balls, provided early patient care and services, and they evolved gradually as the March of Dimes units of the organization, units that organized generally in the 1950s.

The NFIP developed one of the best national organizational structures; efficient and simple, it relied heavily on volunteers. The early national structure included the president, Basil O'Connor, three vice-presidents, and a treasurer. The board of trustees, which initially numbered thirty-five members, had overall authority within the organization, and a five-member executive committee conducted affairs regularly. Such well-known personalities as James W. Forrestal, Jr., as well as philanthropists Marshall Field of Chicago and Jeremiah Milbank, who had established the Milbank Fund to specialize in medical and public health, joined the first board of trustees; other prominent individuals served on the board throughout the agency's history. Prominent individuals in medicine also joined the organizational structure of the NFIP, helping to create respect for it. Suggesting strongly the future NFIP emphasis on research, the organization created a committee on scientific research in July 1938 to determine which research proposals the NFIP would support. Reflecting the constant changes and advances in research on polio, this committee went through several name changes: in 1940, it became the committee on virus research, in 1947 the committee on virus research and epidemology, and in 1959, when the NFIP had expanded its research goals, it became the committee on research in the basic sciences. In 1939, the NFIP established the position of medical director; fortunately for the organization, the medical statesman Dr. Thomas Rivers filled the post, which he maintained until his death in 1962. Dr. Rivers also chaired the committee on scientific research. Other prominent scientists and researchers served on a host of national committees, which related to various aspects of research and medical care.

The most unique aspect of the organizational structure of the NFIP, however, was the use of volunteers in the chapter structure. Beginning in the late 1930s, the various local chairmen of the birthday ball committees organized most of the local chapters. In the 1940s, chapters continued to retain 50 percent of the funds they raised, using this money for services to patients, rehabilitation facilities, hospitalization, aid to polio-stricken families, and the like. The national organization also helped patients, directly supporting institutions caring for victims, hiring nurses and doctors during epidemics in particular localities, sending chapters emergency patient-care equipment (such as iron lungs), and giving money directly to chapters that had exhausted their own funds. These services to local communities, coupled with the widespread fear of polio—partly induced by the propaganda campaigns of the NFIP itself—helped to generate support for the organization even before the development of the Mothers March of Dimes in the early 1950s.

The creation of the first such Mothers March of Dimes by volunteers in Wausau, Wisconsin, in 1950 initiated one of the most popular and successful fund-raising and publicity techniques in the history of American philanthropy, and it had an important effect on the NFIP itself. Because the marches—an idea that caught on dramatically—took place in a very short time span, their administration did not require an administrative bureaucracy. It also seemed to give all segments of the community an opportunity to participate in the fight against polio. March of Dimes units developed administratively separate from local chapters. A volunteer state March of Dimes chairman supervised the campaign generally, coordinating his work with county directors and also volunteers. There was no state organizational structure within the NFIP; each locality worked directly with the national headquarters, strengthening volunteer respect and admiration for the national staff. Because the March of Dimes campaign was temporary, open to all, and did not generally develop a bureaucracy of its own, the public apparently perceived the organization differently from, for instance, the American National Red Cross,* which developed a reputation for elitism in some communities. The unique organizational structure and its effects on volunteers in the NFIP served as the subject for a classic study in sociology, *The Volunteers: Means and Ends in a National Organization* (1957), by David L. Sills. Crucially important in the NFIP's activities and program, the March of Dimes helped to raise large amounts of funds for the organization.

Although the NFIP spent more funds for patient care than did all the other voluntary health agencies combined, it also spent vast amounts of money for research. Slowly and painstakingly, research in the field succeeded gradually, helped partly by the NFIP. As a historian of the disease of poliomyelitis suggested, the NFIP alone did not conquer polio, but NFIP funds helped to develop the dramatic Sabin and Salk vaccines, as well as to develop a typing project which determined the immunological characteristics of polio viruses in the 1940s. Some scientists felt that the latter was the most important work. The NFIP can nevertheless take credit for the work of Dr. Jonas Salk, an NFIP grantee at the University of Pittsburgh. Characteristically, the NFIP had created in 1953 a committee of scientific experts to supervise the Salk vaccine's trial inoculations. The NFIP constantly sponsored scientific seminars on polio and publications, including bibliographies, in the field, contributions that are difficult to evaluate. In the late 1950s, the NFIP sponsored mass Salk vaccine inoculations all over the country. One agency claim is sound: the NFIP did help significantly to conquer the dreaded disease of polio.

The virtual elimination of polio, as David Sills predicted in *The Volunteers* (1957), did not terminate the activities of the NFIP. A classic example of how American social service agencies have shifted their emphases to attack new problems, the NFIP, as early as 1958—when it was renamed the NF-MD—determined to focus now on congenital disorders and arthritis. In the field of patient care, the agency shifted from widespread, community-level activities to demonstration projects on a limited scale. In 1959, the first full year of its new emphases, the NF-MD operated four centers for research in arthritis, as well as the first unit for congenital defects at the Children's Hospital in Columbus, Ohio. Chapters (rather than NF national offices) sponsored centers to promote the exemplary care of the disabled, continuing the organization's concern for people afflicted with polio. In February 1960, funds from three chapters in northern New Jersey developed a special pilot treatment center for rheumatic arthritis at the Seton Hall College of Medicine in New Jersey, and in early 1961, the NF-MD established the first treatment, as opposed to a strictly research, center for congenital defects in children.

Continuing its tradition of services in the scientific and medical fields, the NF-MD sponsored conferences and seminars, such as the first international conference on congenital malformations, in London in July 1960, and published monthly, annotated bibliographies, still on poliomyelitis but also one each on arthritis and related diseases and on congenital defects. Most importantly in the area of research, the NF-MD in 1961 announced ambitious plans to establish and to finance the new Salk Institute of Biological Studies, campaigning initially for $15 million for this enterprise. By 1964, the NF-MD had become the largest single private source supporting research in arthritis, but it nevertheless worked with the Arthritis and Rheumatism Foundation (see *Foundations and Research Associations*) and another organization to create the new Arthritis Foundation (see *Foundations and Research Associations*) in 1964, enabling the NF-MD to focus on birth defects.

The NF-MD continued its tradition of sponsoring medical and scientific research, focusing after 1965 on birth defects. By the end of May 1965, there were forty-five birth defects centers throughout the country. Grants to scientists and medical researchers resulted in new findings and dramatic methods of treatment, such as injecting the bone marrow of siblings into deformed babies at birth and operating on spinal defects in early infancy. In 1962, construction on the Salk Institute in La Jolla, California, began; its facilities opened gradually in the mid-1960s, and by 1970, the NF-MD had invested $22 million in it.

In the mid-1960s, the NF-MD moved into the broad area of patient services relating to birth defects. Beginning in 1964, some chapters began to provide prenatal care for women. In 1966, noting that many birth defects were environmentally caused, the NF-MD expanded its audiences, previously largely medical and scientific researchers and allied professionals. To educate the public about birth defects, it promoted reprints of scientific articles, literature for science teachers, discussions about birth defects with youth groups in local communities, and the publication and distribution of *Be Good To Your Baby Before It Is Born* (1966), including some copies in Spanish. In January 1968, the NF-MD sponsored a two-year pilot project in Boston to create birth defects medical service centers for parents and pregnant women. Increasingly, chapters supported these centers, sometimes part of a local medical center with an NF-MD-related research and/or treatment facility. These centers acted as clearinghouses of information about social services available and how to obtain them.

Increasingly concerned with the socioeconomic factors in infant mortality and birth defects, the NF-MD sponsored various medical social services, such as nurse-midwife programs and prenatal clinics in rural and poverty areas. In 1971, the NF-MD moved its national headquarters from New York to White Plains, New York. By the early 1970s, the NF-MD activities had helped to create and expand a new branch of medicine, perinatology. Characteristically, the NF-MD established a committee on prenatal health in 1972. As much concerned with preventive medicine and with medical and social services for children and families with birth defects as with research, the NF-MD demonstrated the best traditions in American social service: prevention and relief.

The most convenient primary source for studying the NF-MD's history is its published *Annual Reports*. The *National Foundation News* also provides information about the agency, as do some agency publications, such as *Twentieth Anniversary* (1958). The accessible and indexed *The New York Times* generally covers the agency's highlights. The NF-MD maintains complete files pertaining to all aspects of its operations and program as a national voluntary health organization at its national headquarters in White Plains, New York. This material is available only to accredited and qualified researchers, subject to the right of the agency, because of confidentiality, to determine which materials will be made available to these researchers. There are also some primary materials at the Franklin D. Roosevelt Library at Hyde Park, New York.

There are several helpful secondary studies. A chapter in Scott M. Cutlip, *Fund Raising in the United States: Its Role in America's Philanthropy* (1965) concerns the NFIP's origins. There is a brief organizational history in Richard Carter, *The Gentle Legions* (1961). David L. Sills, *The Volunteers: Means and Ends in a National Organization* (1957), is an important study that contains some organizational history although its emphasis is sociological. Dr. John R. Paul, *A History of Poliomyelitis* (1971), also has a brief history of the organization. A full-scale, scholarly history of the organization has apparently been started, but in the mid-1970s, it was at a ''standstill.'' There is clearly more room for serious historical studies of this unique and important agency, which historians have neglected.

NATIONAL FOUNDATION FOR INFANTILE PARALYSIS: see NATIONAL FOUNDATION—MARCH OF DIMES, THE.

NATIONAL HEALTH COUNCIL, INC. (NHC). Around the turn of the twentieth century, some major national health agencies were founded, such as the United States Society for the Study of Tuberculosis* and the National Committee for Mental Hygiene.* The first suggestion for a cooperative effort among health agencies apparently came from Dr. F. R. Green, the secretary of the Council on Health and Public Instruction of the American Medical Association (see *Political and Civic Organizations*). In April 1913, the council convened representatives from thirty-nine health organizations to discuss the issue. Professor Selskar Gunn of the Massachusetts Institute of Technology conducted a survey of existing health agencies, but World War I suspended the movement to form a major general health agency. Just after the armistice in December 1918, the president of the Rockefeller Foundation, George E. Vincent, suggested publicly that the American Public Health Association* (APHA) reopen discussions; the APHA did, resulting in a temporary council of seventeen agencies. Only the efforts of Dr. Livingston Farrand, the chairman of the American National Red Cross* (ANRC), resulted in meaningful activity. His organization financed an intensive study of the possibilities, a study that led to two conferences held in Washington, D.C., in late 1920, one in October and the one at which the National Health Council (NHC) was created in December 1920. The new NHC began to operate officially on January 1, 1921.

Comprised initially of ten private national health agencies and one governmental advisory member, the NHC had its headquarters in Washington and administrative office in New York City. Its early leaders were the most prominent contemporary figures in health and welfare work. Dr. Livingston Farrand was the chairman of the NHC in 1921 and 1922, and Lee K. Frankel, a prominent Jewish social worker and statistician, succeeded him, holding the chairmanship between 1923 and 1926. Dr. C.-E. A. Winslow, a leading figure in the public health movement, was active in the NHC and was its recording secretary in 1927 and 1928. The other important positions in the early years were the manager and the Washington representative.

In the early 1920s, the NHC conducted a variety of functions: it promoted health legislation generally, published a monthly digest of health information, established the important national health library in its offices in New York, organized a series of national health congresses to discuss major issues in the field, and published a list of about three hundred health films. It also published a distinguished national health series on various topics. Dr. Donald B. Armstrong, the first executive officer, left in 1923, and the NHC began to decline. By 1926, open dissatisfaction was evident. Chairman Frankel had urged a five-year program to enlarge and broaden the organization, but his proposals went unheeded. In the 1930s, the NHC lacked an executive officer, and it drifted meaninglessly, doing little but maintaining services for its constituent agencies, which included accounting, letter, telephone, exhibition, publication, and convention services.

Only in the early 1940s did the NHC become revitalized. A three-year study published in 1945, again by Dr. Gunn, stirred interest and generated discussion and controversy in the national health field. Finding large gaps in health care services, Dr. Gunn urged the NHC to broaden its board of directors to include both lay and professional representatives, to develop strong executive leadership, to cooperate more actively with welfare agencies, to develop an "all compelling dynamic project," and to lead the local health council movement.

The NHC followed Gunn's recommendations. Bailey B. Burritt, a former executive of the Community Service Society* (CSS) of New York became the acting executive director. In June 1948, he announced major groups of activities to promote local health institutes and councils and cooperation with health councils to act as a clearinghouse and to recruit and train personnel to staff local health councils. The movement to promote local health councils throughout the country proved to be the kind of "dynamic project" that Dr. Gunn had envisioned. In mid-October 1948, Dr. Thomas D. Dublin, former professor and head of the Department of Preventive Medicine and Community Health at the Long Island College of Medicine, became executive director. Two other high-placed NHC staff members, Dr. John Ferree and S. S. Lifson, helped to develop the vigorous NHC program. By 1949, the board of directors, which included health leaders such as philanthropist Mrs. Albert Lasker and Basil O'Connor, founder and leader of the National Foundation for Infantile Paralysis,* had been expanded to sixty members. The board and eight delegates-at-large, including Dr. Thomas Parran, the former surgeon-general of the United States Public Health Service (USPHS), and Dr. Howard Rusk, the pioneer and leader in rehabilitative medicine, helped to guide the work of the revitalized NHC. The year 1949 also brought the largest increase in membership—from twenty-four to thirty constituent member organizations. The NHC continued to promote the development of local health boards and councils and also reorganized its common services. Effective January 1, 1950, the NHC adopted a model retirement program for its fifty employees.

A few years later, however, the NHC faced another organizational crisis when the loss of key staff members proved difficult to overcome. Despite its successful programs, the NHC did not seem to be fulfilling its promise. Following an extended study of potential funds and its program, the board of directors recommended to the delegates that the NHC disband on the last day of 1953. At a special meeting on May 12, 1953, the delegates, however, refused to accept this course, voting rather to curtail activities immediately. At the urging of the delegates, the board of directors named a special committee on program and finance, which on October 13, 1953, influenced the board to agree to continue only programs such as the national health forums, the national advisory committee, the local health council projects, and the national citizens' committee of the World Health Organization. The board also established a committee on health education to promote health careers, a project that developed as a major one. A new and important executive director, Philip E. Ryan, an experienced welfare administrator, began his duties on October 1, 1953.

As executive director, Ryan revitalized the NHC, shaping it as a leading social service agency in the country. Beginning in 1955, the NHC cosponsored, with the United States Junior Chamber of Commerce, the successful National Health Weeks throughout the country. The Health Careers Horizons Project attracted many young people to the growing field of health care. These two functions alone gave the NHC more national recognition than all of its previous projects and publications.

The NHC recovered remarkably well from the organizational crisis of the 1950s to become, even by the late 1950s, an important national social service organization. In the late 1940s, for example, foundations contributed most of the budget of the NHC, but signaling the NHC's independence, by the late 1950s, the agency raised its funds largely through contributions from constituent agencies. The health careers project, an outgrowth of the national health forum of 1954, progressed well, contributing to manpower needs in the health services field. Even by the late 1950s, the NHC-led movement to promote state and local health councils and health departments was spreading. To improve efficiency, the organization reduced the size of both its board of directors and executive committee in 1957. Suggesting the NHC's national scope, it held its first national health forum away from New York City in 1957. The project to develop uniform accounting systems in the private agency field, however, progressed little, chiefly because the staff lacked time to coordinate it. The NHC ended the decade in 1959 still promoting successfully the development of local health councils and working, at the request of the USPHS, with other national health organizations to vaccinate children with the Salk vaccine against polio. In 1959, the NHC also showed its national leadership by sponsoring and leading events that led ultimately to the establishment of a new national agency, the National Council on Homemaker Service,* in 1962.

In the early 1960s, the NHC continued to strengthen its health career, community health, and uniform accounting programs, and it developed new forms of its increasingly national leadership. In July 1961, an ad hoc citizens' committee established by the Rockefeller Foundation published a study of voluntary health and welfare agencies that emphasized the importance of the NHC. The NHC demonstrated its national leadership in 1961 when it began to supervise the development of a single, unified national organization in the field of epilepsy. In the following year, the board of directors approved the uniform accounting code, and in May 1962, the NHC published *Voluntaryism and Health,* a strong statement on the significance of volunteer agencies in light of expanding government programs. In the early 1960s, with the APHA, the NHC established the National Commission on Community Health Services, which published *Health Is A Community Affair* in 1966. The publication recommended a program to promote community health facilities, which the NHC and the APHA implemented as Community Health, Inc. (CH), in late 1966. With a board composed of representatives from each national agency, CH received a grant of over $1 million from the Kellogg Foundation, which it used to fulfill a consistent NHC concern—improving community health. After studies in 1962 and 1963, the NHC in 1963 established its committee on continuing education to train staff members from constituent agencies in new methods in delivering health services. This program became a major one. Pursing its earlier activity, the NHC published a pamphlet in late 1962 on accounting procedures, launching at the same time a program to get agencies to comply with them. Assuming a role in the campaign to preserve the tax-exempt status of voluntary social service agencies, in May 1963, the NHC established a committee to deal with all levels of laws that regulated donations and solicitations.

These programs laid the basis for important activities of the late 1960s, when the NHC continued to emphasize solicitations, health careers, and professional staff training and also developed some new programs. In 1967, with the National Assembly for Social Welfare, the NHC formalized the campaign for improved accounting procedures, establishing the National Center for the Promotion of Uniform Accounting Standards. The NHC also became active in the 501(c)(3) group of national agencies concerned with preserving the tax-exempt status of nonprofit agencies. Grants in the late 1960s from the federal Bureau of Health Manpower Education (BHME), for instance, helped the NHC to strengthen its health careers program, and in 1969, the NHC renewed its continuing education program, which received funding for another five years from the KF. Becoming active in new areas, the NHC focused the forum in 1969 on the timely subject of health care problems of the inner city, which influenced the board of directors' decision in June 1969 to involve more representatives of and spokesmen for inner-city minorities. Acting on a recommendation made in late 1968, the board established a committee to plan and to promote the use of its meetings as a forum at which constituents could debate major health issues. The NHC supervised the participation of member agencies in the establishment of President Richard Nixon's National Program for Voluntary Action in 1969. But, most importantly, feeling that the 1970s might call for more action in national health issues than in the 1950s, the board in 1969 reversed a fifteen-year-old policy of not involving the agency directly in legislative issues concerning the health or any other field.

Further development of long-standing concerns and programs and the realization of principles established in the late 1960s characterized the activities of the NHC in the 1970s. In 1972, for instance, for the first time the NHC presented arguments to a congressional committee, dealing with Congressman Al Ullmann's proposal of permissible activities for tax-exempt agencies. NHC relations with the federal government developed further in mid-1974 when the organization created a new government relations program, including the establishment of an office in Washington, D.C., which opened in October 1974. To implement its concern with health consumers, especially minorities, the NHC committee on consumer concerns collected evidence and then developed a brochure, published in December 1971, on the value of consumer input in health-related issues. An analysis of the NHC constituent agencies' attitudes and activities relating to health consumers, especially minorities, and their contribution to decision making showed receptivity to such practices, and the NHC launched a program to develop such activities, planning an information kit on involving consumers and hiring in 1973 a specialist to work with member agencies on this project. Previous NHC activities expanded. Grants from the BHME enabled the NHC to continue as the liaison between professional organizations and youths interested in health careers. Another grant from the same agency in June 1972 initiated an NHC study and recommendations of the acknowledged maldistribution of health services in the country. In 1972, fulfilling a variety of NHC concerns, the organization began to involve black colleges in health manpower programs. A host of conferences, the publication of *Health Manpower Memo,* and other campaigns, such as the nationwide Put Your Talent to Work in the Health Field in 1974 indicated the NHC commitment to this continuing program. The NHC completed the development of its participating agency review. In January 1975, it conducted the first study of an agency, the Epilepsy Foundation of America. Revisions of publications such as *Viewpoints* and the one on standard accounting indicated other continuing NHC programs and concerns.

The sources for studying the NHC's history include the published and detailed *Annual Reports.* In the 1920s and 1930s, *Statements* served as reports of NHC activities. Other contemporary publications, such as *The National Health Council* (1925) and *A Good Look At Your National Health Council* (1952), provide information about the agency. The papers of the NHC have been deposited at the Social Welfare History Archives Center at the University of Minnesota, Minneapolis.

Historians have generally neglected the NHC, and there does not appear to be a scholarly history of this important national agency.

NATIONAL HOUSING ASSOCIATION (NHA). In the nineteenth century, social reformers such as Jacob Riis viewed solving the housing problem as the key to eliminating or dealing effectively with poverty. An important nineteenth-century group, the tenement house committee of The Charity Organization Society of The City of New York* (COS), created a nationally recognized successful housing reform movement in New York. Lawrence Veiller, the secretary and director of the group, emerged as the central figure in the COS committee and in the housing movement. Veiller stimulated movements in other cities in the 1890s and in the next decade. Increasingly, the volume of inquiries to the New York group led its leaders to consider establishing a specialized national agency to handle the myriad problems and issues. In 1907, Veiller initiated such discussions with Robert de Forest, president of the COS and himself active in its tenement house committee. In July 1909, Veiller again proposed a national association to de Forest, who in 1909 had helped to establish and had become a leader in the Russell Sage Foundation* (RSF), an important reform organization in the Progressive era and beyond. De Forest influenced the RSF to support the expenses of a new national housing reform agency in its first year. Consequently, to institutionalize the nationwide housing reform movement—a major campaign of the Progressive era—the National Housing Association (NHA) was organized in January 1910 in New York City. At its formal organizing meeting, representatives from about twenty cities throughout the country elected the officers, all of whom lived then in New York: Robert de Forest as president, John H. Glenn, the general director of the RSF, as treasurer, and Lawrence Veiller as secretary and director. The initial board of directors had thirty-seven members; it expanded in 1916 to forty-seven members.

The NHA devoted its initial energies to crystallizing its organizational structure. The board of directors had an eleven-member executive committee, chaired by de Forest, which included such reformers as Frederick Almy, the founder of the first charity organization society, in Buffalo in 1877, and Alfred T. White of Brooklyn, the promoter of famous model tenements for workers. The numerous honorary vice-presidents included Jane Addams of Hull-House,* Frederick Law Olmsted, a city planner and designer of Central Park in New York, and Mrs. Russell Sage, founder of the philanthropic foundation bearing her name. In December 1913, the board of directors established one of many committees reflecting NHA activities, the committee on construction and management. The NHA had from its inception three classes of membership: annual, sustaining, and life. It quickly established national headquarters at the Charities Building at 105 East Twenty-second Street in New York City.

Veiller's pattern of leadership in the housing reform field since the 1890s of promoting local campaigns established the basic operational mode of the NHA. After solidifying its organizational structure, the NHA undertook as its purpose "to improve housing conditions . . . in every practicable way." The organization hired John Ihlder as field secretary to aid Veiller. In March 1910, the NHA initiated its publication series of numbered monographs, largely reprints of articles and speeches by such reformers as Alfred T. White and Mary Richmond. The NHA journal, *Housing Betterment,* appeared initially in 1912, and in May 1916, Veiller took over editorial responsibilities. In March 1928, it became a substantial publication, *Housing.* The NHA produced bibliographies in the housing reform field, and its office in the Charities Building became known as the best reference source for the texts of housing laws, reports, and the like. Annual conferences held between 1911 and 1920, except two years, attracted housing and other welfare reformers and agents. Along with the publications and Veiller's and staff field visits, these annual conferences stimulated local housing campaigns. The NHA sponsored seminars and institutes either alone or with other organizations. In June 1916, for example, with the Pittsburgh Housing Conference and the Pennsylvania Housing and Town Conference, the NHA held a housing institute in Pittsburgh, the city whose housing and other social problems drew national attention in the famous *Pittsburgh Survey* of the Progressive era.

The NHA operated throughout its first decade with a serious financial shortage, compounded in 1915 when its leading source of income, the RSF, cut its annual appropriation by one-third. Despite staff and budget limitations, Veiller made the NHA, according to a student of the housing movement, "a vigorous instrument of reform." By 1916, eighty-five of the hundred cities with more than fifty thousand people had working groups, and in the other fifteen, there were some indications of interest in housing reform. When the United States entered World War I, however, the first phase, the "stimulating" phase, of the history of the NHA ended.

Neither the NHA nor the local housing reform campaigns that it fostered recovered fully from the shift away from reform that occurred during the war and postwar years, but the organization continued to promote activities of high caliber. During World War I, the agency helped the federal government to adopt housing standards for permanent construction, and, as the war concluded, when officials threatened to halt all war-related housing construction, the NHA and others campaigned successfully for the United States Housing Corporation (see *Government Agencies*) to complete jobs already begun. Secretary and Director Veiller's report on British housing for the United States Senate Committee on Reconstruction and Practice, published in the summer of 1920 as *How England Is Meeting the Housing Shortage,* attracted widespread attention. The NHA partly initiated the postwar considerations of the relation of housing to labor turnover. Despite these activities, due largely to Veiller's perseverance, the energy of the organization, like other social welfare groups, dissipated in the 1920s. In early 1923, there was no field secretary, as Veiller pushed himself toward ill health from overwork. National conferences, so popular in the Progressive era, were held only in 1920, 1923, and 1929, and the NHA discontinued its monograph series in 1930 after publishing sixty-two books. Membership declined throughout the 1920s.

There was some activity in the early 1930s. The issue of *Housing* for June 1931 contained important articles describing slum conditions in other countries. Chiefly through the personal efforts of Veiller, the NHA influenced the White House Conference on Child Health and Protection of 1930 to adopt standards for the homes of American children, and in late 1931, for the President's Conference on Home Building and Home Ownership, Veiller prepared a statement, which the President's Conference presented to the country as "a housing bill of rights."

The New Deal ushered in the final phase of the NHA. Still its leading figure, Director and Secretary Veiller opposed the trend toward governmental construction and ownership of housing, yet his journal continued to view the movement objectively. The organization realized the futility of opposing the trend because of its apparent popularity. The issue of *Housing* for October 1935 was the last. The NHA leaders discussed the NHA's future, turned over its valuable library and files to the Central Housing Committee in Washington, D.C., and disbanded the NHA on December 31, 1936.

The primary sources for studying the NHA's history are the brief reports of the organization, published in the NHA, *Proceedings,* and in its journal, variously named. Also, contemporary accounts of the NHA appeared in reform journals; see especially, Veiller, "The NHA," *The Survey* 23 (March 5, 1910): 841–848. The Veiller Papers and his Reminiscences, both at Columbia University, deal more with the housing and reform movements than with the NHA itself. I have not been able to locate the official files of the NHA.

There is no scholarly history of the NHA, but it is mentioned in secondary studies of both the Progressive era and housing reforms. See, for example, Roy Lubove, *Progressives and the Slums: Tenement House Reform in New York City 1890–1917* (1962), the standard account of the housing reform movement of the Progressive era, and John Glenn, et al., *The Russell Sage Foundation, 1907–1946* (1947), 2 vols.

NATIONAL HOUSING CONFERENCE, INC. (NHC). In 1930, the City Affairs Committee (CAC) of New York, a nonpartisan group, was founded to work for a better city through research and education. One of the CAC's activities was its housing committee, whose members and supporters initiated the founding of the National Housing Conference, Inc. (NHC), as the Public Housing Conference (PHC) in New York City on March 22, 1932. The PHC's chief founders were Mary Kingsbury Simkhovitch, since 1902 the director of the Greenwich House settlement; Helen Alfred, a social worker who had served as secretary of the CAC; and Edith Elmer Wood, an author and consultant to the housing division of the federal Public Works Administration. Also participating in the organizing of the PHC were Louis H. Pink, a member of the New York State Board of Housing, and Ira S. Robbins, an attorney who served as counsel to the State Board of Housing. Among the vice-chairmen were Paul Blanshard, an ordained Congregationalist minister, who served as field secretary of the League for Industrial Democracy (LID) and as executive director of the CAC, and Father John O'Grady, secretary of the National Conference of Catholic Charities.*

The PHC was created as a pressure group to bring together social workers and housing experts to lobby on the state and federal level for housing legislation. As the original letterhead on the stationary of the organization explained, its goal was "To Promote Slum Clearance and Low Rent Housing through an Established Federal-Local Service." Specifically, at the state level, they wanted an extension of the New York State housing laws that would permit the financing of cooperative or limited dividend building projects through the issuance of state bonds. On the federal level, the PHC sought to have provisions for housing to be constructed as part of the public-works program incorporated into the Federal Relief and Reconstruction Act of 1932. Although unsuccessful in its first lobbying effort in 1932, the group did succeed in having housing constructed as part of the public works program through the National Industrial Recovery Act (NIRA) of 1933.

The long-range goal of the organization was the establishment of a permanent program of housing and slum clearance with the federal government supplying the money and local government constructing and managing the housing projects. To accomplish that goal, the organization supported the plan, first proposed by Louis H. Pink, a member of its special legislative committee, to have local housing authorities be substitutes for regular housing commissions or city housing departments. That plan was introduced into the New York State legislature in the regular session of 1933 and was adopted with slight revisions in January 1934. The New York Municipal Housing Authorities Law of 1934 thus created the NYCHA and led to the development of a public housing program in New York City.

Up to that time all that social reformers who wanted to improve housing conditions could do was ask the city's Tenement House Department for strict code enforcement of the Tenement House Law of 1901 and of the Multiple Dwelling Law of 1929. Dilapidated houses could be condemned and torn down, and new housing could be built in their place by the city. The government at the local level was now empowered by the law to clear away slums and to provide low-rent housing. Simkhovitch was appointed by Mayor Fiorello H. La Guardia as one of the first commissioners of the NYCHA.

The PHC changed its name to the National Public Housing Conference (NPHC) in July 1933 to meet the need for a national housing program that was being formulated by Senator Robert Wagner of New York in Washington. By July 1933, the NPHC had clearly defined its long-range goal as the construction of low-cost housing through slum clearance. Two chairmen resigned on May 24, 1933, because of their dissatisfaction with that aim of the organization. Harry W. Laidler, executive director of the LID, and Loula D. Lasker, the editor of *The Survey,* the leading social service magazine, replaced the two dissidents.

The conference quickly began mobilizing support for a federal housing program and joined the Labor Housing Conference (LHC) led by Catherine Bauer, an architect and planner, and the National Association of Housing Officials (NAHO) in supporting the program put forth by Senator Wagner and Congressman Henry Ellenbogen of Pittsburgh, Pennsylvania. Indeed, the PHC worked very closely with Leon Keyserling, Senator Wagner's legislative assistant, throughout the three-year fight for the passage of the Wagner-Steagall Housing Act of 1937. They had to overcome not only a persistent Republican opposition to the concept of the government's building housing for people in competition with private industry but also President Franklin D. Roosevelt's preference for single-family home ownership and his opposition to families living in large, multiunit dwelling projects.

Helen Alfred, a social worker who had written the pamphlet *Municipal Housing* published by the LID in 1932, served as the NPH's secretary and executive director from its founding until June 1941, when she left to take up peace work. During her ten years as the chief administrative officer, the headquarters at 112 East Nineteenth Street served as a rallying point for all ''public housers'' in the lobbying effort for the passage of the Wagner-Steagall Housing Act of 1937. She also edited the monthly newsletter, *Public Housing Progress,* from its inception in November 1934, and through its pages she coordinated the efforts of all pressure groups and social service agencies that were interested in slum clearance and public housing. Once the Wagner-Steagall Act was passed, she also helped achieve the passage of the housing amendment to the New York State constitution in 1938. That housing amendment authorized the contracting of a state debt up to $300 million for housing loans, the expansion of the debt limit of cities by 2 percent, and the granting of state subsidies to local housing authorities.

After the passage of the Wagner-Steagall Act of 1937 and the housing amendment to the New York State constitution in 1938, the nature of the organization changed. As an organized pressure group, it had accomplished its goal, and in order to survive it had adapted to changed circumstances. It became concerned with the implementation of the Wagner-Steagall Act and with the carrying out of its provisions in New York. The organization, however, seemed to be uncertain about its purposes and goals.

The transformation of the group from an organized pressure group into an organized lobby occurred when Helen Alfred left in June 1941 and was replaced as executive director by Alexander L. Crosby. Crosby was an experienced newspaperman, and he realized that the organization would have to broaden its constituency if it was to survive. In June 1944, Crosby moved to make the organization truly national by effecting a closer alliance with labor unions and local housing authorities throughout the nation. Labor leaders and local authority representatives were added to the board of directors. When Simkhovitch resigned as president in February 1943, she was replaced by Dr. Byrn J. Hovde, who was chairman of the Pittsburgh Housing Authority. What Crosby had done was to merge the constituency of the NPHC with those served by the Labor Housing Conference (LHC) and the National Association of Housing Officials (NAHO) during the lobbying effort for the passage of the Wagner-Steagall Housing Act of 1937.

The creation of a truly national lobby was confirmed by the closing of the New York City office and the opening of an office in Washington, D.C., in February 1944 under the direction of Lee F. Johnson. The office in Washington was located at 414 Bond Building on Fourteenth Street and New York Avenue, N.W., only a few blocks from the National Housing Association (NHA) and the Federal Housing Administration (see *Government Agencies*) offices in Washington. It was equally accessible to the headquarters of both the Congress of Industrial Organizations (CIO) and the American Federation of Labor (AFL). The opening of the office in Washington was accompanied by Crosby's resignation, effective July 1, 1944, and the appointment of Lee F. Johnson as executive vice-president.

The selection of Johnson indicated the shift that had occurred within NPHC. Johnson was an experienced newspaperman who had served as secretary to

Senator Edward P. Costigan of Colorado and later as a special assistant to Nathan Straus in the United States Housing Authority. At the time of his appointment to the NPHC executive vice-presidency, he was assistant administrator for management in the Federal Public Housing Authority. He understood the federal housing bureaucracy and how it worked. The move to Washington and the appointment of Johnson brought the NPHC into direct contact with the federal housing bureaucracy as an organized housing lobby.

The major goals of the NPHC were then adapted to meet a national program for postwar housing. The organization became the principal lobbyist for the Taft-Ellender-Wagner bill, which became the United States Housing Act of 1949. That act created urban renewal programs in line with the long-range slum clearance goals of the NPHC.

The effectiveness of the NPHC in the campaign for the passage of the Taft-Ellender-Wagner bill was in sharp contrast to its previous effort on behalf of the Wagner-Steagall Act, however. In the 1930s, the "public housers" had been able to sell public housing as part of a public works program that would create jobs. Public housing was promoted as an economic program, not as a social philosophy. In the period after World War II, the Taft-Ellender-Wagner bill was tied up for four years in the Congress because of its avowedly public-housing aspects.

Another element to explain the ineffectiveness of the NPHC after the war was its own internal weakness. As Richard O. Davies has pointed out in *Housing Reform During the Truman Administration* (1966), the NPHC "suffered from shaky finances, small membership, limited purpose, and inability to develop grassroots support." The NPHC had become a spokesman for organized pressure groups, but it had lost touch with its original base in the social settlements.

A generational change had also occurred in the leadership of the public housing movement. Simkhovitch had retired, Wood was dead, and Alfred had left the movement. According to Professor Davies "Housing reform desperately needed a prominent national figure to revive national interest, but none was forthcoming. . . . Poor health had forced the retirement of the one man who could have provided the necessary leadership—Senator Robert F. Wagner. His departure from politics left a vacuum in the movement, and no person of his abilities or stature emerged to take his place. Consequently, within a year after the passage of the Housing Act of 1949, the entire housing reform movement had become stagnant."

Evidence to support Professor Davies's thesis can be found in the fact that the publication of the monthly newsletter *Public Housing,* which originated in November 1934 as *Public Housing Progress,* stopped in February 1948 because of a lack of financial support. A recognition of the weakness of the organization and the narrowness of its base was confirmed in May 1949 when the NPHC changed its name to the National Housing Conference, Inc. (NHC). The reason for dropping "public" was to signify that the organization was not limited to public housing and to expand the membership to include planning professionals as well as members of the housing bureaucracy. That change in the structure of the organization allowed it to survive the financial difficulties of the postwar years. The name change signified that the public-housing emphasis was being broadened to include urban redevelopment and community planning. It was the outward manifestation of a change that had already taken place within the organization.

In the face of a united real estate lobby that could reach into every community in the nation and hinder the development of public-housing projects, the conference was forced to focus its attention upon Washington and to redefine its goals in terms of urban redevelopment. It sought a greater centralization of power at the federal level because it could not compete with the decentralized real estate industry at the community level. At the same time it sought to become a spokesman for the municipal housing authorities that came into existence around the country.

Lee F. Johnson served as executive vice-president between 1944 and 1959. Just as Helen Alfred dominated the early years of the conference, Johnson handled the formation of policy in its middle years. As a succession of presidents replaced Dr. Hovde, Johnson took overall responsibility for keeping the various components of the conference informed of activities on the housing front. He was ably assisted during that period by Ira S. Robbins, one of the original founders of the organization, who took over as chairman of the board of directors in 1951 and who served as president in 1954.

Under Johnson's stewardship in the 1950s, the conference lobbied for a new department of housing with cabinet-level status and finally achieved that goal with the creation of the federal Department of Housing and Urban Development (HUD) in 1965. The NHC also pressed for more public-housing construction, more liberal occupancy rules to allow over-income families who could not find decent private shelter to remain in public housing, the purchase of private housing by local housing authorities, loans for middle-income families through a proposed federal mortgage bank, and various urban redevelopment changes.

The man who came to dominate the organization in its later years was Nathaniel S. Keith, the first director of federal urban renewal as the head of the division of slum clearance and urban development in the Housing and Home Finance Agency from 1949 to 1953. Keith served as a consultant to NHC in 1957 and became its president in 1959. He served as president of NHC from 1959 to 1972 and at the time of his death in 1973 was chairman of the board of directors.

The program that the NHC lobbied for in the 1960s and through the 1970s was originally spelled out in a paper written by Keith in 1957, "Blueprint for Full Community Development, 1957–1975." Although never published, the paper was influential in shaping the concepts that were incorporated into housing legislation over the next two decades. The paper recommended the establishment of a new federal department of housing and urban development to coordinate and consolidate state and local initiatives in the housing field; the repeal of the requirements for eviction of tenants whose incomes rose above fixed limits; and the use of the open land and predominantly open land provisions of the federal redevelopment statute in suburban and metropolitan locations to provide housing to meet relocation needs and to accommodate the increasing urban population.

While some of Keith's proposals of 1957 were later adopted by the federal government through the creation of HUD in 1965 and the passage of the Housing and Community Development Acts of 1968 and 1974, many provisions of the program remained unattained. For instance, not until April 1976 did the United States Supreme Court order the Chicago Housing Authority (in the case of *Hills* v. *Gautreaux*) to promote low-income housing for minorities in the suburbs.

The NHC's history falls into three distinct phases. The first was the so-called New York phase dominated by Helen Alfred, who served as secretary and executive director from 1932 to 1941, and centered around the struggle for the passage of the Wagner-Steagall Housing Act of 1937. The second was the shift to a truly national organization by making an alliance between the conference, which consisted mainly of social workers and "good housing" advocates, and the national labor unions and local housing authorities that were coming into existence around the country under the provisions of the Wagner-Steagall Act. Alexander L. Crosby engineered the transition in the character of the group, and Lee F. Johnson carried it to fruition. Johnson served as executive vice-president and editor of the monthly membership newsletter from 1944 to 1959, and he lobbied extensively for the Housing Act of 1949 and for the implementation of the urban renewal program, despite the financial difficulties that plagued the conference after the war. The third phase came with the ascension of Nathaniel S. Keith to the presidency of the NHC in 1959. That phase symbolized the growing alliance between the NHC and the federal housing bureaucracy. Formerly a pressure group lobbying for reform, the NHC became a valuable ally in the budget battles of the federal housing bureaucracy. During Keith's presidency, the NHC became the major spokesman for the interests of the municipal housing authorities throughout the country.

In the 1970s, the NHC became a coalition of builders, construction unions, and real estate developers. In 1976, the president of the conference was Leon N. Weiner, a builder and real estate developer from Wilmington, Delaware, and the executive director was Gene R. Schaefer, another developer. The membership in 1976 consisted roughly of two thousand members, most of them representatives of groups conducting business with the government. The NHC has shifted away from the social concerns that brought it into existence and, in 1976, was mainly concerned with continuing a housing program that supported the needs of the housing industry.

Information on the establishment of the NHC can be found in the correspondence between Helen Alfred and Edith Elmer Wood in the Edith Elmer Wood Collection, Avery Library, School of Architecture and Planning, Columbia University. The conference published its own monthly newsletter, *Public Housing Progress,* from November 1934 to February 1948; it was called *Public Housing* after March 1943. That publication was replaced by a membership newsletter, which has appeared monthly since April 1949. Between 1934 and 1973 the *Proceedings* of the annual convention were published. The conference published its first *Yearbook* in 1954 and continued doing so annually until 1973. Since 1973, the NHC has published a *Convention Journal and Directory* at the time of the annual convention in March of each year. Anyone interested in the NHC's historical development will find these sources useful.

The best account of the agency's lobbying activities in behalf of the Wagner-Steagall Housing Act of 1937 is provided in Timothy L. McDonnell, *The Wagner Housing Act: A Case Study of the Legislative Process* (1959). A favorable account of the activities of the organization in later years can be found in Nathaniel S. Keith's *Politics and the Housing Crisis Since 1930* (1973). Keith served as president of the organization from 1959 to 1973. A more critical account of its activities can be found in Richard O. Davies, *Housing Reform During the Truman Administration* (1966).

John J. McLoughlin

NATIONAL INDUSTRIES FOR THE BLIND, INC. (NIB). In the late nineteenth century, workshops for the blind began operating, especially as adjuncts to training schools for the blind. The Perkins Institution for the Blind in Watertown, Massachusetts, established the first such workshop. The workshop at the Industrial Home for the Blind (IHB) in Brooklyn, New York, established in 1893, was a leading innovator in the rehabilitation of the blind. These workshops produced simple articles, such as baskets and brooms.

Early in the twentieth century, similar industries arose in prisons and threatened the market of the workshops for the blind. A movement to have only the states and not private industry use prison-made products was supported by both organized labor and workshops for the blind, and the movement culminated in the Hawes-Cooper Act of 1929, a federal law providing for so-called states' use of prison-made products. Realizing that the demands of governments for basic goods provided an opportune market for their products, representatives of workshops for the blind began in the late 1920s to create legislation favorable to their interests. Peter Salmon of the IHB, a graduate in 1917 of the Perkins Institution for the Blind, became a prominent worker in the field and promoted this movement. He testified before the congressional interstate commerce committee in the early 1930s and later persuaded the National Broom Manufacturers Association (see *Business Associations*) to endorse a policy that brooms for state and federal government agencies be purchased only from workshops for the blind. It was also through Salmon's influence that the American Association of Workers for the Blind* and the American Foundation for the Blind* (AFB) became active in this campaign.

Philanthropist and AFB President M. C. Migel persuaded Senator Robert Wagner and Congresswoman Caroline O'Day, both of New York, to introduce legislation supporting the government's purchasing of products made by the blind. AFB Executive Director Robert Irwin, himself blind, urged legislators to adopt what became the Wagner-O'Day Act of 1938, which created a presidentially appointed Committee on Purchases of Blind-Made Products (CPBMP). Composed of representatives from government agencies using such supplies, the CPBMP met initially in late July 1938 to discuss the implementation of the purchasing program, and in the summer of 1938, the AFB moved to create an independent, nonprofit organization of workshops to coordinate the sales. Consequently, on August 10, 1938, in New York City, an AFB advisory committee of workshops managers founded the National Industries for the Blind, Inc. (NIB), to administer and to coordinate the sale of products made in workshops for the blind to the federal government.

At first, the NIB concentrated on developing a structure to provide government agencies with the products made in workshops. The first director of the NIB was Chester C. Kebler, who had earlier directed the production of talking books for the blind, an AFB project, and who had been the secretary of the advisory committee of workshop managers, serving as the committee's liaison with the AFB. The AFB played a crucial role in the establishment and early history of the NIB, providing space for the new organization in the AFB building in New York. in the early NIB, Migel was president; Irwin executive vice-president; Salmon vice-president; and William Ziegler, Jr., a New York businessman who headed another foundation for the blind, secretary-treasurer.

In the first year of operation, thirty-six workshops participated in the NIB program, which featured sales of about $220,000 to the federal government. In mid-1939, the NIB added the first group of new products to its line, cocoa mats and pillowcases. In 1940, forty-four agencies in twenty-six states participated, and in September, thirty-two representatives met at the AFB to develop a better distribution system and established a General Committee on Sheltered Workshops for the Blind. This group evolved into the executive committee of the NIB. In the early 1940s, the NIB instituted a service to help affiliated workshops market their products commercially in their localities. The increased demands of the defense industries during World War II enabled the NIB to expand its program and brought the affiliated workshops closer together as they shared common practices and problems.

After World War II, the NIB reduced its production slightly, but then rebounded and expanded its program and services, moving further into nongovernmental markets. A freeze on production of government orders, instituted the day after V-J Day in 1945, led the NIB to evaluate government catalogs and adjust workshop programs so as to produce needed articles, not just those that were produced easily. In 1948, seeking to broaden its sales, the NIB initiated its efforts to sell products through military commissary stores. The appointment to the committee on purchase of blind-made products in 1954 of an officer supporting these efforts, Major General Kester L. Hastings, helped to create the NIB military sale program in 1955.

The reorganization of the federal government in the late 1940s created NIB fears that the agencies it dealt with were being absorbed. As a result, a prewar idea to open an NIB office in Washington, D.C., was renewed. Opened in the fall of 1950, this office supervised sales to the government, including those to the military commissaries. The office also conducted research to determine the government's product needs, thereby helping workshops to adjust their production schedules. To facilitate the distribution of articles to military commissaries, the NIB developed five appropriately located affiliated workshops as distribution centers in the mid-1950s. In the late 1950s and early 1960s, the NIB began using sophisticated marketing practices and created the trademark of Skilcraft for its commissary as well as commercial sales markets. A consumer sales division coordinated these markets and trained and supervised NIB salesmen. In the fall of 1960, General Manager Kleber died, and Robert C. Goodpasture replaced him.

Under Goodpasture, the NIB continued to expand its business programs. By 1964, it had sixty-seven affiliated workshops, both public and private, provided nearly five million hours of work, and distributed about $6 million in wages. Continuing to develop aggressive marketing techniques, it implemented a successful worldwide military sales program in 1969. During this period, the NIB also developed a rehabilitation program for the blind and, increasingly, the multihandicapped blind. In the late 1960s, it converted a regular operating plant in Hazlehurst, Mississippi, into Royal Maid, Inc., its new model rehabilitation facility.

In the 1970s, the NIB adjusted to changing situations in rehabilitation work for the blind. General business conditions prompted reduced operating costs, and new products in diversified areas kept sales high. In 1971, a grant from The Seeing-Eye, Inc.,* helped the NIB to hold the first of a series of seminars and conferences for workshop managers. The NIB also initiated a program to develop stable commercial markets because of the unpredictable government procurement program. In 1971 the Wagner-O'Day Act was amended to include about seventeen hundred additional workshops in the government purchasing program, and the amendment prompted the NIB to provide field service and professional consultations to its affiliates to help them adjust to this important change. With a grant from the Charles E. Merrill Trust, the NIB established a pilot project in which smaller workshops developed subcontracts with private industries. In the early 1970s, the NIB completed a demonstration project—supported partly by a grant from the Social and Rehabilitation Service of the federal Department of Health, Education, and Welfare—showing that new products and services could be developed to utilize the work of even multihandicapped blind persons.

Continuing business problems related to inflation, supply shortages, and other problems common even to private industry led the NIB in 1974 to establish a continuing workshop board orientation program. In 1974, the NIB stopped using brokers in its program, replacing them with NIB staff and representatives from NIB-affiliated workshops. These numbered eighty-three in 1974. Searching continually to provide employment opportunities for the blind and multihandicapped, the research and development staff of the NIB completed feasiblity studies for new products, including several in the health care field, in 1974.

The primary sources for studying the NIB's history are the published *Annual Reports* and publications such as *Outlook for the Blind,* the AFB journal.

The NIB has not been studied by historians, but the brief *The Story of the Wagner-O'Day Act* (1966) by Robert LeFevre, who participated in some NIB activities, is helpful.

NATIONAL JEWISH WELFARE BOARD, THE (JWB). Just as other religiously based national welfare agencies, particularly The International Committee of the Young Men's Christian Associations* (YMCA), assisted and served men in the armed forces, a Jewish Agency—the Council of Young Men's Hebrew and Kindred Associations (YMHKA)—aided Jewish men in the service. Founded in 1913, the YMHKA grew from the locally oriented Jewish community centers, the first of which developed in Boston in 1875. Its headquarters was a room in the Boston City Hall set aside for its use by the mayor. In the late nineteenth century and later, however, the leading such Young Men's Hebrew Association (YMHA) was the center on Ninety-second Street in New York City. Its leaders had in fact helped to organize the YMHKA. As American entry into what became World War I appeared imminent, Jewish leaders began to discuss developing a separate agency to assist Jewish servicemen, a function that the YMHKA had been providing. Subsequently, the YMHKA's general secretary, Samuel A. Goldsmith, initiated a meeting on April 9, 1917, in New York City attended by representatives from five national Jewish religious organizations: the United Synagogue; the Union of American Hebrew Congregations; the Reform, Central Conference of American Rabbis; the Union of Orthodox Congregations; and Agadath Harabbanim. This meeting, which included also representatives of the Jewish Publication Society and the YMHA, decided to establish such a new organization. Consequently, the National Jewish Welfare Board (JWB) was established in New York City on April 15, 1917, as the Jewish Board for Welfare Work in the United States Army and Navy (JBWWUSAN). As its name suggested, the JBWWUSAN hoped initially to provide welfare services, particularly chaplain and other religious services, to the men.

Representatives of the YMHKA dominated the early JBWWUSAN. The first chairman was Dr. Cyrus Adler of Philadelphia, an important Jewish cultural leader, who was active in other national Jewish charities and was a leader in the YMHKA. Samuel Goldsmith, the YMHKA's general secretary who had moved to found the new organization, became its first secretary. To broaden the representation of the JBWWUSAN among Jewish groups, in 1917, Adler yielded the chairmanship to Colonel Harry Cutler of Providence, Rhode Island. The JBWWUSAN also agreed to increase the board of directors but to centralize control in a small, three- to five-member committee. These proposals did not satisfy Mortimer Schiff, the son of prominent philanthropist, banker, and community leader, Jacob Schiff, and whose efforts led to a broader reorganization on November 15, 1917. The board was expanded to between twenty-five and one hundred members, and a seventeen-member executive committee was given complete control of the organization's activities. The executive committee worked through committees, which originally numbered five: finance, publicity and propaganda, secular activities, religious activities, and, reflecting its ties to the YMHKA, buildings. The JBWWUSAN, however, strove to break its links with the YMHKA, no longer sharing its executive director but having its own, Chester G. Teller. The JBWWUSAN also employed field secretaries in late 1917 to conduct its program.

The JBWWUSAN's initial activities related to Jewish men in the armed forces. An early problem for the JBWWUSAN was to obtain federal government recognition as the official agency for Jewish soldiers. Only in September 1917, following a letter to President Woodrow Wilson, did the JBWWUSAN become part of the seven-member Commission on Training Camp Activities (CTCA) of the War Department (see *Government Agencies*), headed by penal expert and Progressive reformer, Raymond Fosdick, and known popularly as the Fosdick commission. Other members of this group, all of which conducted similar war welfare work, included the National Board of the Young Women's Christian Association of the U.S.A.,* the YMCA, the Salvation Army* (SA), and the American Library Association.

Like other agencies, the JBWWUSAN provided social and recreational facilities, counseled the men, visited the sick and wounded, conducted religious activities, and, in the spirit of the social justice Progressive movement and along with other agencies in the CTCA, strove to reduce the incidence of venereal disease and to promote abstinence from alcohol among both men and women in and around military encampments. The JBWWUSAN welfare workers were known popularly as "Star of David Men."

In the spring of 1917, the JBWWUSAN began to recruit rabbis to serve as chaplains, and in October 1917, working especially through Cyrus Adler, the agency influenced special legislation to appoint Jewish chaplains for the men. The JBWWUSAN quickly showed its influence in the diverse American Jewish community. In January 1918, the chairman of the committee on religious activity, Irving Lehman, the president of the YMHA of Manhattan, decided to mitigate conflicting claims by competing rabbinical groups by establishing a rabbinical advisory committee, composed of the heads of the five rabbinical organizations that had helped to establish the JBWWUSAN in April 1917. On March 13, 1918, the organization changed its name officially to the Jewish Welfare Board,

United States Army and Navy (JWB), but the abbreviated JWB quickly became the common usage.

The leaders of the JWB had been striving to make theirs a truly representative agency in American Jewish organizational life. In the spring of 1918, after considerable negotiations, it won the cooperation of the B'nai B'rith (BB), an important, nationwide fraternal organization. In another attempt to make the JWB more representative, it decided in the summer of 1918 that the board should be composed of the heads of all affiliated agencies, such as the BB, the present executive and all other committees, and the heads of local JWB branches throughout the country. Influenced by Louis Marshall, perhaps the most important figure in Jewish communal life and who had helped to found the JWB in 1917, the organization appointed an advisory committee of twenty members. By 1919, many national organizations, such as the BB and the National Council of Jewish Women, and 182 local community groups functioned as JWB branches, aiding the men in the armed forces and, in some cases, their families as well. Indeed, as the historian of the JWB argued, it was a major achievement to mobilize the heterogeneous American Jewish community for this particular welfare, or for any other, activity.

Some important changes in structure and in activities occurred after World War I. In the spring of 1920, leaders of the organization began to discuss its future. On April 12, 1920, as a result of these discussions, Judge Irving Lehman of New York presented a plan to focus on American Jewish community centers. Efforts were being made in 1920 to merge the community centers with the JWB, and in 1921, the JWB absorbed the YMHKA, thrusting itself into the Jewish community center movement, as Judge Lehman had urged. The community centers in localities throughout the country had been synonymous with the YMHKA. In the 1880s and 1890s, such centers had generally stressed, as did some Jewish settlement houses—from which they differed but yet were similar—Americanizing Jewish immigrants. During and immediately after the war, local agencies that had developed to aid Jewish servicemen converted themselves into Jewish community centers. By 1921, there were nearly four hundred such loosely defined centers. During the consolidation in 1921, some centers did not affiliate with the JWB and others dissolved, but after the amalgamation in 1921, there were 207 Jewish community centers. Only seventy-five of these actually had buildings, and to improve this situation, the JWB established a building service in 1922, which aided construction in local communities. By 1939, as a result of this program, there were 238 Jewish community centers in buildings. In 1922, to serve the centers, the JWB established its Lecture and Concert Bureau, which increased the intellectual activities in some centers.

The JWB compiled manuals on administering community centers, assisted in developing center work as a professional service, and encouraged the National Association of Jewish Center Workers (NAJCW), an organization founded in 1918 before the JWB became heavily involved in Jewish community center work. Even though they were not clearly social welfare institutions, in the sense that settlement houses were, local centers began in the late 1920s to receive financial support from local Jewish federations and welfare funds, the equivalents of Jewish community chests, a fund-raising activity. Other activities of the JWB in the 1920s relating to community centers included the undertaking of surveys in communities and the initiation of courses for Jewish community center workers in 1921, subsequently abandoned in 1922, probably because of the lack of funds. Between 1921 and 1946, the JWB conducted 181 such surveys in seventy-six communities; the most thorough and famous one was the five-volume analysis of Los Angeles, published in 1942. In the 1930s, the JWB focused on youth programs, camping, services to Veterans' Administration hospitals, and community organizations, becoming recognized in the national social work community as the Jewish agency in group work. As students of the JWB admitted, however, the influence of the organization during these decades was not important. Hampered by a generally inactive lay leadership and a diffused and varied constituency, the JWB did not emerge as a truly national social service agency until the late 1930s and early 1940s.

The group of skillful new leaders and aggressive activities during World War II shaped the JWB as an important national social service agency. In 1938, Louis Kraft, former head of the Jewish community center division, became the acting executive director and, in 1939, the executive director. In 1940, founder Lehman stepped aside as president; Frank Weil, a lawyer from New York who was active in YMHA and other Jewish philanthropies, replaced him. In the late 1930s, the JWB enlarged its staff and established a national health advisory board of medical specialists to help local centers begin and improve their health activities. In 1940 and 1941, Kraft became an important organizer of the United Service Organizations for National Defense* (USOND), serving as the acting secretary during its formative period. President Weil was one of the USOND's founders and directors. In the summer of 1940, there were fifteen national Jewish agencies affiliated with the JWB's army and navy committee; after the expansion Kraft and Weil initiated, thirty-five were affiliated by December 1942. Following a conference of the heads of Jewish seminaries in December 1941, the JWB reorganized in early 1942 its important committee on chaplains as the committee on army and navy religious activities. In April 1942, the JWB began to organize its women's division, which coordinated local service; this division supervised as many as 106 local committees during this period. The JWB formed its committee on personal service, which supervised the field staff and which promoted cooperation with Jewish social service agencies to aid the men. During the war, the JWB sent ten field representatives, through the American National Red Cross,* to Europe to help establish religious hospitality centers there. Twenty-four Jewish community centers affiliated with the JWB became USOND clubs under the JWB. Other war-related services included the compilation of Jewish war records, an activity dissolved at the end of 1946. Highlights not related directly to wartime activities included the establishment in 1943 of the Jewish community center divisions, which later became Jewish community center services, to coordinate work in this field. In 1943 the JWB received funds from the United Jewish Appeal of Greater New York.

In many ways, the *JWB Survey,* authorized in March 1945, directed by sociologist Oscar Janowsky, and published in 1948, set the tone for activities during and after the postwar period. It helped to crystallize such important aspects of the recent history of the JWB as leadership in the Jewish community center field, services to the military, and interest in Jewish life in America. In 1947, the JWB published its two-volume *American Jews in World War II.* Following a recommendation of Janowsky's *Survey,* in 1948, the delegates to the convention approved a statement of principles on Jewish community centers' purposes, emphasizing the Jewish content of their program. In 1949, the experimental research department conducted a study to help centers make their Jewish programs more meaningful, especially to Jewish youths. Important organizational changes occurred when Kraft retired as executive director in 1947 and when Weil left the presidency in 1950. Replacing Kraft was Samuel D. Gershovitz, a center worker with long-time experience in the JWB.

The 1950s and 1960s brought more examples of the national leadership of the JWB. For instance, when the USOND dissolved in the early 1950s, the JWB helped to create the Associated Services for the armed forces as a temporary group awaiting the reorganization of the USOND. Despite the USOND's dissolution, the JWB maintained its contacts with the growing number of hospitalized veterans. The JWB helped to organize the National Jewish Youth Conference (NJYC), and it continued to conduct such activities as the Jewish Book Council. The JWB participated in the White House Conference on Children and Youth at the end of the 1950s. Despite establishing its JWB Associates in 1956, the JWB struggled financially; it was forced to abandon its sponsorship of the NJYC and the American Jewish Historical Society, close the service center in Germany, implement staff cuts, and dissolve the research department.

Successful financial developments helped the JWB to expand its services in the 1960s. The adoption of the community fair share plan in 1960, which brought funds to the JWB, helped to bring the national office and its constituent Jewish community centers closer than before. Also, the annual review of the JWB finances by the Large City Budgeting Conference of the Council of Jewish Federations and Welfare Funds,* helped to set the basis for long-range financial planning. In 1963, the JWB cosponsored the Lakewood conference, at which social scientists, rabbis, center workers, and JWB staff discussed Jewish living in America.

Local centers were especially active in the civil rights movement and the War on Poverty, and in 1963, the JWB held a conference on the center and civil rights. Also in 1963, with the cooperation of the NAJCW, the JWB reestablished its research center. During the 1960s, the JWB conducted exchange programs to bring Israeli social workers to the United States and send center workers to Israel; established its national public affairs committee, helping the JWB to take public positions on issues affecting its work; and encouraged Jewish centers to provide services for senior citizens.

The JWB served its constituents well, holding the first national training institute for center teenage workers in 1965 and initiating intensive in-service training for experienced workers in the mid-1960s. "A Reappraisal," a study completed in early 1962, emphasized the integration of JWB services to the men in the armed forces with those to and by Jewish community centers. The plan was not fully implemented at first, but the national staff helped to fulfill this goal. In 1964, the JWB merged its center and armed forces field staffs into single regional consultation services. In the fall of 1966, a study committee began another inquiry. At the biennial meeting in 1970, the JWB adopted the study committee's findings, which were used to develop priorities for and to measure the effectiveness of centers' services to Jewish communities. Another committee, planning and evaluation, studied the programs and recommended changes. Yet another important activity of the late 1960s and early 1970s was the development and use of the program development and research services, which took the lead in determining new directions for centers, especially increasing the Jewish content of their programs. This new emphasis on Jewish content helped to implement a major part of the Janowsky study of the late 1940s. Also, the JWB established the Solomon and Mary Litt JWB headquarters in Israel.

In the mid-1970s, through the National Jewish Music Council and the Jewish Book Council of America—both of which the JWB served as secretariat—and through such programs as a three-day conference on the Jewish cultural arts in 1976, the JWB continued to strengthen Jewish cultural identities. A three-year study by the health and physical education committee, completed in 1976 and adopted by the board, called for changes in the health, physical education, and recreational programs in centers. Continually serving its constituents and helping to strengthen the Jewish community center movement, in the mid-1970s, the JWB was working on a standard-setting project for its affiliates.

The primary sources for studying the JWB's history consist of a host of agency publications, such as *The Jewish Welfare Board* (1918) and the serial publication, *The JWB Circle,* which is not widely available in libraries. The JWB archives at its national headquarters in New York City contain the agency's files. These records are available to properly identified and qualified scholars, who can generally gain access by contacting the national headquarters staff.

The secondary sources, mostly published by the JWB itself, are diverse. The most helpful are the writings of Professor Oscar Janowsky, such as, with Louis Kraft and Bernard Postal, *Change and Challenge: A History of 50 Years of the JWB* (1966), and his earlier *The JWB Survey* (1948). Janowsky also authored the entry on the JWB in the *Encyclopedia Judaica* (1971), 12: 872–878, which deals more with Jewish community centers than with organizational details. There does not, however, appear to be a full-length, scholarly history of the JWB, which historians have generally neglected.

NATIONAL LEAGUE OF ASSOCIATIONS OF WORKING WOMEN'S CLUBS: see NATIONAL LEAGUE OF GIRLS CLUBS.

NATIONAL LEAGUE OF GIRLS CLUBS (NLGC).   In American industrial cities in the late nineteenth century, working women's clubs developed to protect single women from bad urban influences. The earliest clubs were organized in the industrial Northeast of the United States. The first was established in New York City in the early 1880s by Grace Hoadley Dodge, a social worker, philanthropist, and educator, who helped to found the National Board of the Young Women's Christian Association of the U.S.A.* (YWCA) in 1906 and Teachers College of Columbia University. Dodge helped to arrange the first National Convention of the Association of Working Girls Societies in New York City in 1890. Two other conventions followed, one in Boston in 1894 and one in Philadelphia in April 1897, at which delegates discussed the idea of establishing a national organization to promote the clubs' interests. Dodge was the chief organizer of these efforts; she was aided by Mrs. Henry Ollesheimer of New York City.

During this period, state associations of working women's clubs developed. Girls' club leaders continued to discuss forming a national organization, and in November 1897, in Mrs. Ollesheimer's rooms at The Savoy in New York City, delegates from five of the state associations established the National League of Girls Clubs (NLGC) as The National League of Associations of Working Women's Clubs (NLAWWC), a federation of such clubs. The founding group established itself as a temporary executive committee, represented by one delegate from each of the five state associations. The temporary secretary of this committee was L. N. Platt, the secretary of the Pennsylvania Association.

With the organization established in November 1897, the structure began to take shape. The earliest months of the agency's history were focused on developing the organization. In April 1898, Mary Richmond of Baltimore, Maryland, who later became one of the most important social workers nationally, joined the executive committee as a member at large. The primary activities of the executive committee in these early months were to appoint the organization's officers and to find a paid secretary. The first president was Edith M. Howes of Boston's Shawmut Club, and there were a vice-president, a secretary, and a treasurer. The executive committee also discussed plans to hire Charlotte C. Wilkinson of Syracuse, New York, who began a two-year term as a paid secretary in October 1898.

With the beginning of Wilkinson's term, the organization initiated its activities. In 1899, the NLAWWC changed its name to the National League of Women Workers (NLWW). The early activities of the NLWW fulfilled and even exceeded the founders' visions. In the first year of operation, 1898–1899, Secretary Wilkinson traveled for nearly twenty weeks to visit local clubs, going as far west as Louisville, Kentucky. In February 1899, the NLWW began to publish *The Club Worker,* a bimonthly magazine, which soon became monthly. The NLWW leaders wrote personal letters to newspapers to publicize the organization. The idea of the movement spread, and in the spring of 1900, the president and Secretary Wilkinson traveled to Milwaukee, Wisconsin, to speak at the biennial national meeting of the General Federation of Women's Clubs (GFWC).

In August 1901, the NLWW held its first general convention in Buffalo, New York, the site of the Pan-American Exposition. Over five hundred members attended, and the NLWW published the papers as its *Fourth Convention Report.* Wilkinson resigned there as secretary, but she remained as a member at large on the executive board. Jean Hamilton of Oswego, New York, a recent graduate of Vassar College, became the new secretary, and she traveled for five months during the winter of 1901–1902, speaking and organizing clubs. She also spoke at the biennial meeting of the GFWC in 1902. In 1901, the executive board decided to conduct a study of working women. After consulting with the United States Department of Labor (DL), the NLWW began to study the value of public school education for working women generally, with the hope of improving their educational services. The DL could not, as planned initially, tabulate the statistics the NLWW culled from its affiliates, and the clubs had to spend so much time answering the questionnaires developed by the DL that club activities suffered. But the Massachusetts Bureau of Labor generously tabulated and published the results of the survey in 1905. The NLWW's volume of activity increased so much that the agency hired an assistant secretary who handled correspondence and the magazine, *The Club Worker.* In 1902 and 1903, *The Club Worker* featured a regular column by the National Consumers' League* (NCL).

During the early years, the executive board met each spring. In 1903, the Massachusetts Association invited two members from each club, and the spring meeting quickly became a league-wide rather than an executive board meeting. In 1903–1904, the organization began a publicity campaign especially with state federations of women's clubs. In 1904, it won a gold medal for its exhibit of its work at the St. Louis World's Fair; this exhibit was also shown at the National Conference of Charities and Correction* (NCCC) in Portland, Oregon, in 1904. During this period, the NLWW revised its constitution, which provided that officers be elected for two years, and increased the executive board once again, this time from fourteen to twenty-one members. In 1906, the organization adopted an official seal and a motto, "to have and to share."

The decision in 1906 to emphasize expansion and to establish an extension committee to organize clubs in industrial towns near large cities helped to infuse new life into the NLWW. With help from the New York and Pennsylvania associations, the NLWW added a secretary for extension work. After studying the situation, the NLWW decided to focus on establishing new clubs in northern

New Jersey, where there was no state association. The NLWW president sent a letter about the clubs to all companies employing women, and the NLWW then sent a field representative to the companies. Interestingly, at the Johnson and Johnson Company in New Brunswick, New Jersey, the NLWW established one club for Hungarian and another for American women.

At the biennial meeting in Philadelphia in 1906, Owen Lovejoy, the general secretary of the National Child Labor Committee* (NCLC) who developed a reputation as the "children's statesman," delivered a stirring address about child labor. Lovejoy's speech influenced local clubs to become active in the child labor movement. Beginning in the winter of 1907–1908, each local club had a chance to feature itself in *The Club Worker*. This stimulated further interest in the movement. In 1908, the extension service succeeded in organizing three new clubs, and in the spring, the NLWW held its biennial convention in Washington, D.C. The highlight of the convention occurred when President Theodore Roosevelt held a reception for and then spoke to the convention in the White House. After a study by the organization, the NLWW concluded that immigrant girls could be reached by the clubs only after they had a sound working knowledge of English. This principle helped to shape future NLWW programs in adult education.

In the next decade, 1910–1920, the NLWW continued its basic endeavors and developed special activities to aid the war effort late in the decade. In 1910, in response to questions from club members, the secretary investigated the methods of insurance for working women. This activity led to an agreement in 1911 by which the NLWW wrote insurance for its members in cooperation with a private insurance company. In 1911, the spring meeting of the executive board featured a discussion of the NLWW's work in relation to the so-called social center movement in public schools, YWCAs, and settlement houses, and in the Playground Association of America.*

In 1912, the NLWW established its correspondence bureau, with a separate secretary, in New York City. This bureau served affiliates, for instance, by keeping a file on the best methods for conducting local activities, such as vacation houses, lunch rooms, dances, boardinghouses, and the like. When Secretary Hamilton took a one-year leave of absence in 1913, *The Club Worker* suspended publication because it lacked an editor. In 1914, however, the magazine resumed publication, and the publication office relocated from Philadelphia to New York City. A highlight of 1914 included the participation of about six hundred girls in a pageant, "The Romance of Work," staged at the Sixty-ninth Regiment Armory on May 15, 1914, in New York City during the spring meeting of the executive board. Hoping to bring the national organization closer to local clubs, in 1915, the executive board decided to establish auxiliary boards in six different parts of the country. The NLWW had a committee on instruction and cooperation, headed by the first NLWW president, Edith Howes, of the Massachusetts Association. The committee tried to keep club members informed of laws affecting women and children. In 1917, for instance, the NLWW sent a telegram to New York Governor Charles S. Whitman urging him to reject a bill that tried to break down restrictions on working hours.

An important organizational development occurred in 1917 when the executive board authorized the president to appoint an executive committee of experienced women in the organization to advise the board from a national, as opposed to a local, viewpoint. The need for this executive committee, which initially had six members, stemmed from the failure of board members to contribute meaningfully to national policies and from their tendency to emphasize regional interests rather than those of the national organization. The NLWW secretaries were generally social workers rather than labor organizers. For example, in early 1918, the NLWW hired another assistant secretary, Ruth C. Reed. Like Jean Hamilton, a graduate of Vassar College, Reed had studied at both the Chicago School of Civics and Philanthropy and the School for Community Center Workers in New York City under John Collier, who was a founder of the Camp Fire Girls.* She had also worked for two years as a social worker in Waterloo, Iowa.

In 1918, the structure of the NLWW included an executive board, composed of the four officers, General Secretary Hamilton, two associate secretaries, a correspondence secretary, and an active staff of seven field workers in different localities and fields of specialization. The NLWW also had an eleven-member advisory staff, which included Owen Lovejoy, Juliette Low, the founder and leader of the Girl Scouts, Inc.* (GS), Mary Richmond, now of the Russell Sage Foundation,* Robert Woods, the secretary of the National Federation of Settlements,* and Orin C. Baker, the general secretary of the National Travelers Aid Association.*

War work on the home front included taking Red Cross classes, selling Liberty bonds, and sewing and knitting materials for French and Belgian children. Late in the decade, the NLWW began to sponsor training courses for prospective workers, both professionals and volunteers. General Secretary Hamilton, sometimes aided by other leaders, conducted these courses at Columbia University in New York City.

In the 1920s, the organization—which became the National League of Girls' Clubs (NLGC) in 1920—focused on adult education, a field in which it made some important contributions. The interest in organized recreation for women during World War I to offset the fast pace of work in munitions factories and elsewhere created renewed interest in the club movement. In April 1920, to try to spread the movement, the organization established the Ohio division of the national executive committee, headquartered in Columbus, Ohio. In the summer of 1921, the NLGC opened its summer school for women workers in industry at Bryn Mawr College in Pennsylvania. The NLGC explicitly did not want teachers, office workers, saleswomen, and waitresses, for instance, to attend the initial sessions, since the organization did not consider them industrial workers. In 1921, *The Club Worker* ceased publication, but the eighteen-thousand-member NLGC apparently had six well-organized state associations and a strong national organization. The NLGC had an education committee, which encouraged the establishment of local evening classes and which even helped to select teachers. The national office provided course outlines in such subjects as literature and social history. In 1926, to deal with the problem of lack of following up interests stimulated at the summer school, the NLGC created the position of traveling teacher, who demonstrated educational programs throughout areas with girls clubs. Aided by funds from the Carnegie Corporation, this project was especially successful in parts of Pennsylvania and in the Berkshire Mountains area. The activities of the national organization stimulated many state leagues to establish special education departments with paid, trained secretaries. In the 1920s, certain trends influenced the decline of girls' clubs and of the NLGC: the development of better facilities in YWCAs, settlements, and such; the improvement of other evening schools and extension courses; the development of modern transportation, allowing women to live farther away from congested urban areas; the greater availability of commercial recreation; and the glamour of volunteering during World War I, which made it difficult to keep volunteer workers and to attract new ones for the clubs. Consequently, at the regular biennial convention in 1928, the NLGC voted to disband on the basis that its work was completed and that there were sound state associations to carry on.

The primary sources for studying the NLGC's history include its journal, *The Club Worker,* and a published *Annual Report* for the very early years. Agency publications, such as *The National League of Women Workers* (1908) and *History of the National League of Women Workers* (1914), contain helpful histories.

Secondary sources, such as Abbie Graham, *Grace Hoadley Dodge* (1926), mention the NLGC, as does Robert Cross in his entry for "Grace Hoadley Dodge" in *Notable American Women, 1607–1950* (1971), 1: 489–492. There does not appear to be a scholarly history of this agency.

NATIONAL LEGAL AID AND DEFENDER ASSOCIATION (NLADA). One of the problems facing immigrants and poor people in late nineteenth-century urban America was access to the legal system. In 1876, to provide legal assistance to the German poor of New York City, the Der Deutsche-Rechtsschutz-Verein (DDRV), an immigrant aid organization, was established. The DDRV was, in fact, the predecessor of the New York Legal Aid Society (NYLAS). Although the New York society attracted the support of such prominent attorneys and reformers as Elihu Root, Jacob Riis, Joseph H. Choate, who was active in the State Charities Aid Association* of New York, and Robert W. de Forest, the long-time president of The Charity Organization Society of the City of New York,* it was not until 1911 that Arthur V. Briesen, the president of the NYLAS, and Mark W. Acheson, Jr., of the Pittsburgh society, were able to unite the fifteen existing legal aid societies into a loosely organized national alliance. Their efforts led to the establishment of the NLADA as the National Alliance of Legal Aid Societies (NALAS) on November 10, 1911, in Pittsburgh, Pennsylvania.

During its early years, the NALAS barely managed to fulfill its limited objectives of stimulating publicity, cooperation, and new recruits for legal aid. Lacking adequate funds and organization, the NALAS was totally dependent upon its autonomous local chapters. In *Justice and the Poor* (1919), Reginald Heber Smith surveyed legal aid nationwide and concluded that, in spite of the NALAS, the movement was desperately lacking in centralized responsibility and authority. In 1921, acting on Smith's recommendations, the American Bar Association (ABA) (see *Political and Civic Organizations*) created a standing committee on legal aid work. One year later, a convention of legal aid organizations met in Philadelphia to reorganize the NALAS.

Under the leadership of Roscoe Pound of Harvard University's Law School, Moorfield Storey of the ABA, and William Draper Lewis of the University of Pennsylvania Law School, a constitution was drafted and ratified in 1923 creating the National Association of Legal Aid Organizations (NALAO). Albert F. Bigelow, president of the Boston Legal Aid Society, was elected the first president but the moving force proved to be John S. Bradway, the first salaried national secretary who served in that post until 1940. An executive committee of seven persons was established, as was a system of dues. A generous grant from the Carnegie Foundation in 1923 helped launch the new organization.

Progress over the next two decades was painfully slow. Hampered by inadequate funding, the NALAO was forced to serve primarily as a clearinghouse for the dissemination of information. Decisions of the United States Supreme Court reaffirming the right of the accused to counsel in criminal prosecutions in *Powell* v. *Alabama* (1932) and *Johnson* v. *Zerbst* (1938) renewed the NALAO's commitment to "equal justice under law" and stimulated the organization of additional local chapters across the country. By the late 1930s, the NALAO had achieved significant advances in its own internal administration, financial accounting, and standards and practices. Stimulated by the mass unemployment and poverty created by the Great Depression, local legal aid societies were active in enacting legislation covering relief and protection for debtors and the establishment of small claims and domestic relations courts, as well as its providing evidence of violation of the laws against usury. The NALAO strengthened contacts with local bar associations, social welfare agencies such as the National Conference of Social Work,* and later, with law schools in an effort to broaden the scope of legal aid. As confidence grew in the efficiency of legal aid chapters, so too did contributions. In 1923, the public donated $328,000 for legal aid, and by 1938, the sum reached $687,540. In the same years, the number of applicants assisted by NALAO-affiliated chapters rose from 130,000 to 306,000.

The outbreak of World War II underscored the importance of legal aid. The NALAO found itself involved in areas concerning the draft, naturalization laws, aid to dependents, common law marriages, and the confinement of Japanese-Americans. During this crucial period, Emery A. Brownell replaced John Bradway as national secretary and initiated publication of the NALAO's first newsletter, *The Legal Aid Brief Case*. Additional changes came in 1949 when the NALAO was reorganized as the National Legal Aid Association (NLAA) and incorporated in the District of Columbia. The executive committee was expanded to thirty-nine directors representing trial lawyers, the bench, and local legal aid societies. Harrison Tweed, former chairman of the ABA standing committee on legal aid work, was elected president, and a permanent staff headed by Executive Director Brownell was created.

Throughout the 1950s, the NLAA depended for support on its dues-paying chapters, individual members, and community chests. Legal aid officials repeatedly emphasized the importance of maintaining private funding rather than government subsidies. Indeed, the association was able to grow primarily by grants from John D. Rockefeller, Jr., and the Ford Foundation (FF). Increased financial assistance enabled the NLAA under the leadership of President Orison S. Marden to transfer its national headquarters in 1956 from Rochester, New York, to the American Bar Center in Chicago, broaden its promotional work through the launching in 1953 of a television series, "Justice," publish a revised survey of legal aid, *Equal Justice for The Accused* (1959), establish fifty new legal aid and defender offices, draft a model defender act, and create a semiautonomous defender section for criminal cases. The increasing importance of the defender sector was reflected in October 1958 when the NLAA changed its name to the National Legal Aid and Defender Association (NLADA).

The NLADA had experienced a 250 percent rate of growth between 1950 and 1960, when there were 210 local legal aid offices operating nationally, handling almost half a million cases per year and spending over $4 million annually. Yet the next decade was to transform both the structure and philosophy of the NLADA. A grant from the FF of $800,000 in 1960 for training law students was followed by additional stipends of $2.3 million in 1962 and $3.8 million in 1964–1965 for the establishment of the national defender project. This tremendous expansion of interest in legal aid reflected the impact of Supreme Court decisions in *Gideon* v. *Wainwright* (1963), *Escobedo* v. *Illinois* (1964), and *Miranda* v. *Arizona* (1966), which greatly expanded the right to counsel under the Sixth and Fourteenth amendments. The concomitant entry of the federal government into the War on Poverty and the Office of Economic Opportunity's (OEO) legal services program suddenly made millions of dollars available for legal assistance.

Though some conservative members of the legal profession questioned the efficacy of "judicare," the NLADA, under the direction of Executive Director Junius L. Allison, adapted its philosophy to embrace federal assistance. Attention was devoted to reforming laws that perpetuated poverty, ameliorating those conditions most susceptible to legal treatment, and developing an acceptable means for evaluating free legal services of all kinds. By the end of the 1960s, most of the funds obtained by the NLADA came from OEO, with significant though lesser amounts from local community chests and united funds.

Structural changes accompanied the NLADA's expansion. New demands on the association's staff in 1966–1967 necessitated establishing the offices of director of research and publication, as well as the director of defender services and development. The civil legal aid committee was also created in 1966 as the matching arm of the defender branch. Another grant from the FF enabled the NLADA to establish a national law office to work solely with federal agencies. By 1971, the NLADA's board of directors numbered seventy-two, and the executive committee was expanded from fifteen to thirty.

Early in the 1970s, after the diminution of federal assistance, the NLADA returned to a philosophy that viewed legal aid as a direct personal response to legal problems rather than an impersonal, massive frontal assault by government. Yet by 1973, the NLADA was itself a product of bureaucratic growth, with 790 chapters representing 6,000 attorneys and 4,000 individual members in fifty states, in addition to Canada, Puerto Rico, and the Philippines. The NLADA continued to cooperate with the federal government by providing technical assistance and training through its sponsorship in 1973 of the National Defender College and through support of the Legal Services Corporation Act, signed into law by President Richard M. Nixon in July 1974.

The most helpful primary sources for studying the history of the NLADA consist largely of its own *Annual Reports,* handbooks, the *Brief Case,* and especially the personal papers of former legal aid officials such as Reginald Heber Smith, John S. Bradway, Emery A. Brownell, and Junius L. Allison. Students should also consult Reginald H. Smith, *Justice and the Poor* (1919); John S. Bradway, "National Aspects of Legal Aid," *Annals of The American Academy of Political and Social Science* 205 (September 1939): 101–107; Emery A. Brownell, *Legal Aid in the United States* (1951); Harrison Tweed, *The Legal Aid Society of New York City, 1876–1951* (1951); NLADA's *Equal Justice for the Accused* (1959); and J. J. Graham, *Enemies of The Poor* (1970).

Eugene M. Tobin

NATIONAL MENTAL HEALTH FOUNDATION, INC. (NMHF). During World War II, conscientious objectors were allowed to perform alternative public service instead of serving in the armed forces. Conscientious objectors came during this period largely from the so-called peace churches, the Church of the Brethren, the Society of Friends, and the various Mennonite bodies, and they performed such services generally through their respective church social service agencies, the Brethren Service Committee* (BSC), the American Friends Service Committee* (AFSC), and the Mennonite Central Committee* (MCC). One of the projects such conscientious objectors conducted was serving as psychiatric aides and in other jobs in mental hospitals throughout the country. Reacting to the generally poor conditions and treatment of patients in such facilities, a number of these young men became increasingly interested in the problems of the mentally ill. Consequently, in early 1946, in Philadelphia, Pennsylvania, representatives from the peace churches and from the BSC, the AFSC, and the MCC established the National Foundation for Mental Health (NFMH).

The group hoped to work to improve conditions in mental facilities and to interpret the nature of mental illness to the public. The original sponsors of the NMHF not from the church groups included Eleanor Roosevelt and Bess Truman, the novelist Pearl Buck, well-known clergyman and reformer Dr. Harry Emerson Fosdick, and Dr. Thomas Parran, the surgeon-general of the United States Public Health Service. The most important founder and early leader of the NMHF was Owen J. Roberts, a former justice of the United States Supreme Court. By the time that Roberts announced the establishment of the organization on May 5, 1946, representatives of the group had already collected over fourteen hundred reports on conditions and treatment and from employees of mental institutions. The NMHF also began to prepare teaching pamphlets, pamphlets interpreting the nature of mental illness, and other such publications. The AFSC, the BSC, and the MCC contributed the early funds for the new organization.

In its first years, the NMHF focused on its initial concerns—to improve conditions and to enlighten the public—while also shaping its organizational structure. In October 1946, for instance, the NMHF named a group of nineteen leaders in American society to its board of directors. The board, which held its organizing session in Philadelphia on October 12, 1946, included Roger Baldwin, the founder and executive director of the American Civil Liberties Union, Clarence Pickett, the executive secretary of the AFSC, and Mary McLeod Bethune, the founder-president of the National Council of Negro Women, Inc.

With headquarters established in Philadelphia, the NMHF published some early important pamphlets, such as *If Your Child Is Slow* and *Forgotten Children*. Fulfilling an initial concern to provide materials for psychiatric aides working in institutions, the agency published *Psychiatric Aid,* which superseded the earlier publication, *The Attendant. Psychiatric Aid,* as well as the easy to use and helpful *Handbook for Psychiatric Aides* (1946), served as guides for such workers. By early 1947, the NMHF was also conducting an educational campaign that focused on the need for the early detection of mental illness. In 1948, while Harold Barton served as executive secretary of the NMHF, Dr. Fosdick became the chairman of the national sponsors, and Dr. Frederick H. Allen of Philadelphia, a widely known authority on child psychiatry, joined the board of directors. Fulfilling its goal of trying to enlighten the public about mental illness, in the late 1940s, the NMHF, its legal division, and the National Committee for Mental Hygiene* (NCMH) published summaries of mental health laws in some states in simple and direct form. Another publication, *Admission to Mental*

Institutions: Legal Requirements for Treatment, Detention and Release in Louisiana (1950), provided further insight into conditions and treatment.

In its last year, 1950, the NMHF continued to provide important and enlightening services. In January, for instance, with radio station WNYC in New York City, the agency began to sponsor a weekly series, "Hi, Neighbor," dealing with the problems of family life and narrated by Eddie Albert. Another project used comic books to interpret mental illness to patients' relatives; by 1950, the NMHF had sold about thirty thousand illustrated booklets to hospitals and to state departments of mental hygiene. Apparently in 1950, the NMHF moved its headquarters to New York City in the building with other national health agencies at 1790 Broadway. The NMHF in 1950 developed a pilot project to improve commitment and discharge practices in Berks County, Pennsylvania. The agency also examined hospital, court, police, and jail records, a pioneering, intensive study. The NMHF had been awarding the Psychiatric Aide of the Year, a project attracting national attention, and in 1950, it initiated awards for best attendants in training schools for mental deficients. The NMHF concluded its short but influential history on September 13, 1950, when it joined with the NCMH and The Psychiatric Foundation to become the new National Association for Mental Health, Inc.,* a major national organization.

The primary sources for studying the NMHF are diverse. For the later years, there are some published *Annual Reports.* There are a few published pamphlets, minutes of meetings, and correspondence in a group of unorganized materials, still in boxes in August 1976 at the Oskar Diethelm Historical Library of the Cornell University Medical College in New York City. A few publications at the New York Public Library are helpful, and *The New York Times* provided information about the NMHF, which has not been written about by historians.

NATIONAL MULTIPLE SCLEROSIS SOCIETY (NMSS). In the early 1940s, the fact that physicians knew so little about multiple sclerosis concerned Sylvia Lawry of New York, whose brother had the disease. In 1946, she placed advertisements and notices in the local press about possibly forming an organization to promote research in the disease. Many people responded, and in October 1946, a group met in New York City and formed the National Multiple Sclerosis Society (NMSS) as the Association for Advancement of Research in Multiple Sclerosis (AARMS). The AARMS's organizers included Mrs. Wendell Willkie, William J. Norton, the secretary of the Children's Fund of Michigan, Senator Brien McMahon of Connecticut, and eight other business and professional leaders. The founders of the AARMS supported the budget for the first two years, allowing the organization to open headquarters in a single room in the New York Academy of Medicine. The original objectives of the new society were to determine the number of multiple sclerosis sufferers and to publicize doctors' and others' efforts in the field.

In its early years, the organization focused on establishing its organizational structure and on publicizing theirs and others' activities and concerns. To supervise the AARMS's activities, the agency established a board of directors, chaired initially by a prominent New York attorney, Carl W. Owen. A medical advisory board of twenty members included Dr. Roger L. Lee, the retiring president of the American Medical Association. AARMS's honorary chairman was Dr. Tracy Jackson Putnam, the director of neurology and neurological surgery of the Neurological Institute in New York City. The participation of prominent physicians in the initial affairs and activities of the organization—which became the NMSS in 1947—helped to establish its early reputation as a scientifically oriented health agency, confirmed in the early 1950s by a survey by the Lasker Foundation showing that, compared with all other voluntary health agencies, the NMSS spent the highest percentage of its funds for research. In 1950, the National Health Council* (NHC) elevated the NMSS from associate to full-fledged active membership status. Suggesting the implementation of an initial organizational goal, in 1950, Congress enacted Public Law 692 to establish the National Institute for Neurological Diseases and Blindness (see *Government Agencies*); four of the eight physicians appointed to the new government agency's first advisory council served on the medical advisory board of the NMSS. By 1951, forty-one physicians served on the NMSS medical advisory board, and the NMSS established an international fifty-six-member committee of corresponding neurologists representing twenty-six countries. In 1950, the agency hired its first national field director to organize the work of the chapters, which, along with the NMSS, conducted multiple sclerosis clinics in the late 1940s.

The agency had similar success in its nonmedical activities. Fulfilling an original organizational aim, the NMSS helped to influence increasing press coverage of the field generally, such as in the *The New York Times,* and it issued a quarterly, *AARMS Forward,* which publicized organizational activities. The NMSS developed early as a national information center, and it had close ties with the United States Employment Services, helping afflicted people find jobs. In 1949, to raise funds the NMSS established its Lou Gehrig Memorial Fund, but discontinued it the next year because, unlike other organizational activities, it proved ineffective.

As it argued in the mid-1950s, the NMSS spent the first ten years establishing itself as a national organization, like industry, "tooling up" for production. In less than ten years, the agency spent over $1 million for research, initiating fifty-five new projects. In the same period, NMSS grew structurally to nearly seventy-five thousand members and eighty-four local affiliates in thirty-six states; by 1955, there were twenty-seven clinics and evaluation centers throughout the country. In 1955, the First Lady, Mamie Eisenhower, again served the multiple sclerosis fund campaign, and actress Grace Kelly and prominent businessman Robert Sarnoff cochaired the event. Also in 1955, the NMSS appointed its first director of public relations. Most importantly, however, the third annual chapter conference, held in Chicago in October 1955, adopted the MS Hope Chest as the fund-raising technique of the NMSS.

Finally established as a national agency in the mid-1950s, in the late 1950s, the NMSS demonstrated leadership in the health and welfare fields, focusing, of course, on multiple sclerosis. A thirty-minute film, narrated by Joan Crawford, *In Sickness and in Health,* further educated the public about this affliction. Its national fund-raising campaign, the MS Hope Chest, continued to attract top personalities, such as Senator John F. Kennedy, the national chairman in 1958, and Joan Crawford, the chairman of women's activities. The volunteer public relations committee brought the NMSS into the mainstream of national voluntary health agencies, relying creatively on volunteers throughout the country. In 1959, the leading organizational highlight occurred when the American Broadcasting Company national radio network covered a thirty-five-minute panel discussion on multiple sclerosis, moderated by the NMSS Father of the Year.

The NMSS entered the important decade for social service generally of the 1960s with 175 chapters in forty-nine states in 1960 and as a full member of both the NHC and the National Conference on Social Welfare.* The policy of returning 60 percent of their collections to the chapters and using 40 percent of the funds collected nationally for research was well established and helped to improve appreciably services to patients and research. At the chapter conference in Kansas City in October 1960, the NMSS introduced its "Patient Service Guide" to improve services, and in the following year, regional chapter conferences focused on patient services. In 1961, the NMSS created six regional offices, each headed by a field representative who functioned also as area campaign director. In 1961, the drive yielded about $3.3 million, and the NMSS became one of ten national voluntary health agencies receiving funds through the President's Committee on Fund Raising within the Federal Service. The NMSS consistently improved service to patients, for instance, cooperating in 1963 with both the American National Red Cross* (ANRC) and the National Recreation Association* to develop projects in recreation and in home nursing instruction. In late 1963, the organization approved a major five-year growth plan calling for, among other things, eighty-five new chapters, which would have made over two hundred of them by the end of 1968.

The NMSS succeeded at least in having 210 chapters at the end of the period and in many other activities as well. Enshrined as a national event, the Hope Chest in 1964 was inaugurated by President Lyndon B. Johnson at the White House flower garden in May. In what the medical leader in the rehabilitation field, Dr. Howard Rusk, called an excellent example of cooperation between the federal government and a voluntary health agency, the NMSS began a three-year collaborative study to determine the value of ACTH and other steroid drugs in multiple sclerosis medicine. At the twentieth anniversary conference in 1966, the NMSS established the International Federation of Multiple Sclerosis Societies (IFMSS), a worldwide group, and the conference delegates paid an emotional tribute to founder Sylvia Lawry for her years of dedicated service. Also in 1966, the NMSS strengthened a major organizational activity, research. The brilliant and successful former research director for the National Foundation for Infantile

Paralysis,* Dr. Harry Weaver, became the consultant for all NMSS research programs. In 1967, the agency guided the incorporation and other organizational details functionally establishing the IFMSS, and in the same year, the NMSS completed agreements with the graduate school of the New York Medical College to establish the NMSS as the placement agency for neurological nurses. At the end of the five-year plan, the forty-seven-member board of directors went ahead vigorously, approving a program to raise $10 million for research in the next five years. The NMSS developed an important research technique in 1968 when it established a tissue and fluid storage bank for multiple sclerosis patients, which provided researchers access to previously unavailable, but vital, sources. In the same year, a record income of more than $6.5 million suggested the success of the first five-year plan and firmly established the NMSS as a strong voluntary health agency. Its national advisory council had in 1968 thirty-seven members, including such prominent American personalities as Bing Crosby, Earl Warren, Arthur Fiedler, and Hubert Humphrey.

The 1970s brought a further strengthening of NMSS activities. Through the IFMSS, the NMSS held the first seminar on the home care of multiple sclerosis patients in 1971. Demonstrating once again its commitment to research, the research development fund, allowing donors to give money only for research, developed in 1969 and grew steadily in the early 1970s. The twenty-fifth anniversary celebration in October 1971 featured the most prominent scientific researcher of the era, Dr. Jonas Salk. As the NMSS argued, the year 1973 was one of its most significant in its history. In 1973, for instance, Ralph I. Straus of New York City established the single, largest prize for medical research in American medical history, $100,000 for multiple sclerosis research. The establishment of the federal National Advisory Commission on Multiple Sclerosis ranked high on the list of NMSS achievements. Under the personal direction of Mrs. Charles W. Goodyear, Jr., the NMSS established its national youth leadership council. So successful were its efforts that in 1975, the federal commissioner of youth development for the Department of Health, Education, and Welfare (DHEW) claimed that the "National Multiple Sclerosis Society is setting the pace for youth involvement for other national organizations." The most notable event of the year was the establishment of the Athletes vs. MS Program, designed by Mary Wells Lawrence and the advertising agency in New York City, that she headed. Attracting major popular sports figures, this activity gained greater nationwide publicity for the NMSS. In 1975, Ray A. Kroc, the founder of McDonald's restaurants, gave the NMSS and its Chicago chapter $1 million. The still important patient services included counseling and recreational and other services by local chapters. In 1973, the NMSS completed a socioeconomic study of the impact of multiple sclerosis on patients and their families in the Rochester, New York, area. One-to-one, garden-related activities for local chapters were conducted through the cooperation of the National Council of State Garden Clubs. In 1975, in cooperation with the ANRC, the NMSS developed another home care course for patients. The NMSS published the helpful *Independent Living for the Handicapped*, and it continued its efforts for affirmative action to hire the handicapped, for public funds for homemaker health services for the chronically ill, and for national health insurance. Demonstrating the NMSS's leadership in the field, an ad hoc committee from the board of directors met with federal officials in 1975 to press for the full implementation of the recommendations of the National Advisory Commission on Multiple Sclerosis. As the NMSS entered its thirtieth year in 1976, founder Sylvia Lawry continued to serve as the agency's only executive director in its history.

The primary sources for studying the NMSS's history include the published *Annual Reports,* which are available from the society upon request and are sent to all major public and medical school libraries for reference availability as they may determine. *The New York Times* has reported on major NMSS activities through the years. The society maintains a reference library at its headquarters in New York City, which contains material on its history. Other files (except for confidential material) are available to properly qualified and identified scholars; but the NMSS reserves the right, because of confidentiality, to determine which material researchers can use. Historians have neglected this organization, and there does not appear to be a scholarly history of the NMSS.

NATIONAL ORGANIZATION FOR PUBLIC HEALTH NURSING (NOPHN). Since the late nineteenth century, visiting nurse agencies had been conducting important social services. The link between social work and nursing in such visiting nurse services was illustrated especially in the activities of the Henry Street Settlement* (HSS) in New York City. HSS's founder and leader, Lillian Wald, developed one of the most prominent visiting nurse services in the country. Gradually such services developed throughout the country, especially in cities. By about 1910, correspondence among public health nurses increasingly concerned not only the need to establish standards in this specialized field but also the desire for an appropriate forum for workers in this branch of nursing. Opinions differed on whether a new organization should be independent or a committee of the Associated Alumnae of the United States, which became the American Nurses Association (ANA) (see *Political and Civic Organizations*) in 1911. Some leaders of the National League of Nursing Education (NLNE)—formerly called the American Association of Superintendents of Training Schools for Nurses (AASTSN)—and especially Lillian Wald and Adelaide Nutting, a leader in nursing education, were encouraging an independent national organization to promote the interests of what was becoming called public health nursing.

In 1911, a group of public health nurses, acting through the recently established committee on visiting nursing of the ANA, asked both the ANA and the AASTSN to appoint a joint committee to study the possibility of a new, specialized agency. Wald became chairman of this committee, which included three representatives from each of the two agencies. Mary Gardner of the Providence, Rhode Island, District Nursing Association was the secretary of this committee, which met four times in New York in early 1912 to discuss plans for a national organization. The committee corresponded with over a thousand organizations, forty-eight of which agreed to send delegates to a special meeting in Chicago on June 7, 1912, during the annual meeting there of the ANA. The joint committee had prepared the constitution, and at this meeting on June 7 the delegates—mostly public health nurses—founded the National Organization for Public Health Nursing (NOPHN).

The founders elected the first officers, which included as president, Lillian Wald, a vice-president, a treasurer, and a secretary, Edna P. Crandall, who became an important figure in the NOPHN. The initial board of directors numbered fourteen, including Mary Gardner and Julia C. Stimson of the social service department of the Washington University Hospital in St. Louis, Missouri. The new agency was created as an affiliate of the ANA, which increased its executive committee by two members, both from the NOPHN. The initial plan called for the NOPHN board to meet jointly with the boards of the ANA and the NLNE. At the ANA convention in 1912, the new NOPHN received two benefits from the lay board of directors of the Cleveland Visiting Nurse Association, the *Visiting Nurse Quarterly* and an official seal, designed by the sculptor Herman Matzen.

The new agency began its work in the spirit of the contemporary urban social justice Progressive movement. In November 1912, the group established headquarters in New York City, where it remained throughout its history. Yssabella Waters, Crandall's secretary, began her important work in statistics, reminiscent of the statistical work of the settlement houses in the urban Progressive movement. Within a few years, she completed five statistical studies and prepared a list of all public health agencies involved in child welfare work, a list she made available to the United States Children's Bureau. Waters's work helped to make the NOPHN a visible national agency. In January 1913, the magazine changed its name to the *Public Health Nurse Quarterly*. Despite its limited means, from the beginning, the NOPHN fulfilled an initial purpose, to provide direct help to local service agencies. The new NOPHN quickly established ties with other social service and medical social service agencies, being invited to corporate membership in both the American Public Health Association* (APHA) and the American Association for the Study and Prevention of Infant Mortality.*

In the tradition of the social justice movement, the first convention demonstrated an almost religious fervor. At the convention, Gardner was elected president, a position she held through 1916; Wald became honorary president. In its early years, with the help of a prominent social worker, Dr. Lee K. Frankel, then an executive of the Metropolitan Life Insurance Company, the NOPHN prepared a standard patient record form for the use of all public health nurses. Other services and efforts brought the agency close to the social work community. With two other nursing agencies, the NOPHN pressed for better attendants in the home care of the sick. The new agency was viewed increasingly as an authoritative body. Two national social service agencies asked Secretary Crandall to serve on their committees as a representative of public health nursing. An early publication discussed nursing for tuberculars, and, always close to education in the field, the NOPHN prepared standardized courses in public health nursing. Before American entry into World War I, the NOPHN, with the American National Red Cross* (ANRC), issued a statement clarifying the confusion between it and the town and country nursing service of the ANRC. One organizational problem in the early years was the lack of interest by lay women in New York; the group in Cleveland, however, remained staunch supporters. Partly because of this situation and in response to some advice from the Rockefeller Foundation (RF), in early 1915, the NOPHN established an eight-member advisory council of well-known people, such as Dr. Frankel, Julia Lathrop, the first chief of the USCB, and public health physicians and advocates Drs. Herman Biggs, William Welch, and C.-E. A. Winslow.

During World War I, the NOPHN cooperated energetically with health and social welfare movements on the home front. Immediately following the convention in 1917, the board of directors initiated contacts with the National Council of Defense (NCD) to promote public health nursing as a war service. In June 1917, the NOPHN made an unusual sacrifice, allowing Executive Secretary Crandall to work for the nursing groups under the NCD. Also to help maintain public health nursing during the war, the NOPHN tried to prevent public health nurses from joining the ANRC. As the war progressed, greater demands were placed on the NOPHN. In 1918, the federal government, for instance, asked its advice and help in establishing the new Division of Venereal Disease in the United States Public Health Service (USPHS). At the beginning of the Children's Year—which began on April 6, 1918, as a war-related movement—USCB Chief Lathrop asked the NOPHN to serve as a consultant and to distribute public health information through its library loans. The NOPHN helped to supervise nurses and also gave aid to expectant mothers in the three important Children's Year rural demonstration projects. The agency contributed further to the war-related hygiene movement, participating in an important demonstration project in New York City, the Morningside Health Center. Later in the war period, as a service to the new state directors of public health nursing—positions influenced by the war—the NOPHN held a special conference in Cincinnati. Most of the war-related work was coordinated by a six lay-member war program committee, which was initially called the war emergency committee.

War activities increased the general program of the NOPHN, which continued to move closer to the national social service community. In 1917, major changes in the bylaws resulted in a new structure, using councils, sections, and standing committees. The sections, for example, represented various specialties in public health nursing. Other national organizations, particularly in the health field, had similar structures. In 1917, the NOPHN established a committee to determine an appropriate role in the new mental hygiene movement. An important event for the agency occurred in December 1917, when the RF approved a three-year grant to support the agency's general operations. These funds led to the expansion of the library service, the hiring of a permanent education secretary to advise local agencies, and the opening of a branch office at the Chicago School of Civics and Philanthropy, an important training ground for social service workers. In 1919, the NOPHN opened a branch office in Portland, Oregon. In December 1918, the agency amended its bylaws to provide for the election of lay members to the board of directors, but the lay members' voting privileges were limited to non-technical nursing matters.

The 1920s began with some organizational problems. In 1921, the NOPHN faced its first financial crisis. The budget, which had grown to $100,000 a year, was cut substantially. Recently hired staff members were fired, and the agency closed its offices in Chicago and Portland. In response to these developments, the agency established Friends of Public Health Nursing, a lay group, to raise funds. This effort was not successful, but a long-time friend of the NOPHN, Frances Payne Bolton, paid the entire debt, allowing the organization to begin 1922 on a sound basis. The NOPHN decided that state organizations for public health nursing should be branches of the agency. But the NOPHN never pursued the establishment of such branches energetically. Another financial crisis, caused largely by the lack of support at the local level, occurred in 1924 when the NOPHN asked local associations to contribute 1 percent of their annual budgets to the national organization. This so-called percentage plan worked well during the history of the agency.

There were many staff changes in the 1920s, highlighted by the resignation of Crandall as executive secretary in October 1920. At the tenth anniversary celebration in 1922, the organization made Mary Gardner honorary president; only she and Lillian Wald received this honor from the NOPHN. An evaluation by Gardner in 1926 suggested strengthening the chief executive position, now called general director, continuing the percentage plan, and providing a more decentralized structure. The involvement of lay members in the conduct of the NOPHN increased with the creation of the board and committee members section in 1928, the year in which the NOPHN was incorporated according to the laws of the state of New York.

Despite some organizational problems in the 1920s, the NOPHN developed an active program, keeping the earlier Progressive spirit alive in a decade when other national social service agencies reduced their programs. In 1920, the NOPHN established an industrial nursing section to stimulate interest in this branch of public health nursing. A formal agreement with the ANRC in 1920, also signed by the National Tuberculosis Association* (NTA), clarified public health nursing functions, with the NOPHN supervising educational matters. Although the NOPHN still held joint board meetings and conventions with the two other nursing groups, it moved steadily closer to non-nursing social service agencies. It was one of the earliest groups to join the National Health Council* (NHC), and it remained the only nursing group in the NHC. In 1922, the NOPHN helped the APHA to establish its public health nursing section. Beginning in 1922, the American Child Hygiene Association* (ACHA) paid the salary of a nurse to work for the NOPHN, to conduct a full-time study of school nursing practices, and to provide a school nursing advisory service. Even after the ACHA stopped supporting this position in 1927, the NOPHN continued the service at its own expense. In 1924, another staff member completed an extensive survey of public health nursing in the country, and she began a detailed yearly salary survey of all public health nursing agencies. This later became the *Yearly Review,* providing important information for the field. Since its very early years, the NOPHN had operated an informal occupational bureau, and in 1926 with the American Association of Social Workers* (AASW), the NOPHN helped to establish what became, in January 1927, the Joint Vocational Service, an agency to help social service workers find jobs. An important activity in the 1920s was the extensive study of visiting nursing in the country, a project suggested by Lee Frankel and funded by the Metropolitan Life Insurance Company. In 1926, the NOPHN published the *Public Health Nurse Manual,* which served the field.

In the 1930s, the NOPHN responded to the Great Depression like other social service agencies, continued cooperative ventures with other organizations, and, especially later in the decade, moved closer to the other nursing groups. In the early 1930s, the NOPHN established a committee on the economic emergency. During part of the decade, the NOPHN employed an industrial nurse secretary at headquarters in New York. General Director Katherine Tucker helped to influence her friend Harry Hopkins to include medical care for the poor as legitimate public relief work. After the enactment of the Social Security Act of 1935, which provided services for crippled children, the NOPHN hired a staff consultant to direct a special project, financed by the National Foundation for Infantile Paralysis* (NFIP), to help nurses to provide better care for orthopedic patients. In 1941, this project became the Joint Orthopedic Advisory Service, a cooperative venture of the NOPHN and the NLNE. In 1935, a $10,000 grant from The Commonwealth Fund,* followed by other grants in 1936 and 1937, helped the NOPHN to broaden its support basis. By 1939, there were over ten thousand members, and 854 agencies had full membership. Less active at the beginning of the decade, the board and committee members section were revitalized by 1935. The twenty-fifth anniversary celebration, held at a New York City hotel, was broadcast over network radio. A study of the agency's accomplishments prepared for the anniversary declared, "If in 1962 there is no NOPHN, it will be because our goals have been accomplished." Suggesting the future course of the agency, in January 1939, the ANA appointed a special committee to consider its consolidation with the NLNE and the NOPHN.

The decade of the 1940s, which was filled with activities, showed the desirability of consolidating the nursing organizations. Cooperation between the groups became clear during the World War II period. In the early 1940s, the NOPHN worked with the Nursing Council on National Defense, a cooperative venture of all nurses. In 1940, the NOPHN moved its headquarters in New York to the building at 1790 Broadway that housed other national medical social service agencies. A major project of the early 1940s was a joint survey with the USPHS to study the public health nursing content in university programs. In 1944, a major change occurred when the NOPHN removed previous eligibility restrictions for nurse members. Increasingly recognized nationally as the leading group in the public health nursing field, the NOPHN was given funds by the NTA for a staff consultant to assist voluntary agencies in helping their nurses to improve skills in caring for tuberculars. With other major national groups, the NOPHN participated in the American War-Community Service. Between July 1943 and January 1945, the NOPHN's special project was the war consultant project to stimulate the development of public health nursing in communities especially hard hit by defense mobilization. Increased national interest in midwifery led the NOPHN to establish its midwifery section in 1944. Demonstrating the traditional NOPHN concern for education, this section had an important committee to study and evaluate standards for schools of midwifery. During the war, the NOPHN conducted a study of public health nursing services in clinics. In 1945–1946, the agency sponsored Public Health Nursing Day and Public Health Nursing Week, public relations campaigns to acquaint the public with community nursing services.

During the immediate postwar years, the NOPHN participated in some major developments in the field of social service, while it, paradoxically, moved closer to formal consolidation with other nursing groups. The postwar planning committee, comprised of all committee chairmen, worked with other agencies, especially promoting the inclusion of home nursing benefits in health insurance plans, participating with the ANA in vocational counseling programs, stimulating research to determine local nursing needs, and promoting a plan to utilize public health nurses in family welfare services. In 1946, the NOPHN supported President Harry Truman's national health program. An important aspect of the educational activities in the field was the curriculum guide for public health nursing courses in universities, which the agency developed. Organizational highlights included the so-called Raymond Rich Report in 1946 calling for either one or two national nursing organizations and the vote by the board of directors in January 1947 to support only a consolidation plan that allowed lay members to serve on the governing boards.

Consolidation efforts dominated the agency in the early 1950s, but important services in the field continued. In January 1950, the NOPHN began seriously to discuss its future structure, and in May 1950, the members voted for the two-organization plan, setting the basis for the dissolution of the NOPHN. Toward the goal of consolidation, also in 1950, the NOPHN moved its headquarters not with the NHC but with other nursing organizations. Continuing its service in the field, the agency, acting through the midwifery section, studied relevant curriculums in schools, and the NOPHN conducted an important cost analysis study, which prompted the NOPHN to sponsor special cost study institutes to test the new system. In early 1951, the NOPHN published statements on public health nursing and national security. The year 1952, however, brought the end of the NOPHN. In January, the nursing groups formed the new National League for Nursing (NLN), although the NOPHN continued to publish its journal until the end of the year. Finally, at the convention on June 19, 1952, at the last meeting of the agency, the members voted to dissolve the NOPHN and to transfer its resources to the new NLN.

The primary sources for studying the NOPHN's history include the important but not fully extant agency materials, such as memoranda, minutes of meetings, and other manuscripts, on microfilm at the NLN Library in New York City. Other relevant manuscripts are in such collections as the Lillian Wald Papers at Columbia University in New York and the Mary Gardner Papers at the Schlesinger Library at Radcliffe College in Cambridge, Massachusetts. The NOPHN's published *Proceedings* and *Annual Reports, 1912–1918,* which became *Proceedings and Biennial Reports* in 1920, also provide materials, as do other published books and pamphlets at the Sophia Palmer Library of the American Journal of Nursing Company in New York. *Public Health Nurse Quarterly,* which went through some name changes, indicates the interests and activities of the organization.

The best history of the agency is M. Louise Fitzpatrick, *The National Organization for Public Health Nursing, 1912–1952: Development of a Practice Field* (1975), a detailed and comprehensive organizational study.

NATIONAL PROBATION AND PAROLE ASSOCIATION: see NATIONAL COUNCIL ON CRIME AND DELINQUENCY.

NATIONAL PROBATION ASSOCIATION: see NATIONAL COUNCIL ON CRIME AND DELINQUENCY.

NATIONAL PUBLIC HOUSING CONFERENCE: see NATIONAL HOUSING CONFERENCE.

NATIONAL RECREATION AND PARK ASSOCIATION (NRPA). Although the United States remained primarily rural and small town in the early twentieth century, the significance of the city and factory loomed large in the national consciousness. The development of municipal recreation was but one of a number of related social reforms of the Progressive movement in response to industrialization and urbanization. Municipal recreation was intimately connected with attempted corrections of adequacies in parks, housing, education, and health, as well as other ills arising from the squalor of the slums.

These reforms were intellectually united by an increasing emphasis by reformers on the important effects of the environment on individuals. Progressives came to believe that improvement of the city's environment would foster constructive citizenship. One such improvement was the development of supervised playgrounds and recreation, which could provide outlets for leisure time that might otherwise be spent in misguided ways. Several congested industrial cities throughout the United States followed the pattern set in Boston, where private philanthropic agencies had initiated the first organized playgrounds in America in 1885 as a social service for slum children.

True to the Progressive impulse to move from the local to the national level to launch reform groups dedicated to voluntary action for nationwide improvement of specific social ailments, the Playground Association of America (PAA) was founded in Washington, D.C., in 1906. The originators of the PAA, New York City Progressive educators Dr. Luther Gulick and Henry S. Curtis, had little trouble persuading the leaders of the playground movement to band together as a promotional organization.

The playground advocates who met in Washington, D.C., included educators, social workers, physical education specialists, settlement workers, and laymen. The group created the PAA to provide national coordination, guidance, and promotion of the spreading local movements for public recreation then found in about forty cities. After a White House reception with President Theodore Roosevelt, who was named honorary PAA president, the organizers selected their officers: Luther Gulick, president; Jane Addams of the famous American settlement house, Hull-House* in Chicago, and Boston philanthropist Joseph Lee, vice-presidents; Henry Curtis, secretary; and New York School Superintendent Seth Stewart, chairman of the executive committee.

Gulick and Curtis, the active forces in the association's early years, recognized that public recreation had three great needs to meet if it was to become widely accepted: adequate, permanent financing by municipal tax dollars; trained professional leaders to administer organized recreation; and a broad, popular concept of recreation and creative leisure time to include varied, year-round activities for all citizens.

Confronted with the increasingly rapid spread of public playgrounds in the United States after 1906, the PAA had only meager resources to accomplish its self-appointed goal of coordinating national development while at the same time building an effective organization. After its first year, the PAA had 408 members and $2,000 in funds. Despite the lack of financial support, the PAA published the first issue of its monthly periodical, *The Playground* (later renamed *Recreation*), and also held its first annual play congress, in Chicago.

The PAA did not accept funds from the federal government because of the association leaders' commitment to local responsibility and individual freedom. Instead, they depended upon private support and volunteers until the newly established Russell Sage Foundation* (RSF) decided to fund the playground movement. This new stability enabled the PAA to undertake systematic fund raising, to recruit a paid, professional staff, to open a headquarters in New York City, and to pioneer more effective methods of operation, such as field services, which were to become permanent. Howard Braucher, a social worker, was selected as the first full-time professional executive secretary for the PAA, a position he held for forty years.

By 1910, Gulick had succeeded in implementing most of his initial plans and policies. The PAA upgraded existing playgrounds, fostered organized local support in a few pilot cities, held several short training institutes, and published manuals. While the spread of American public recreation accelerated significantly in the first years of the PAA, the organization itself soon developed serious problems. Internal dissension and tight control of funds by the RSF led to the resignation of both Gulick and Curtis and finally to the withdrawal of the foundation's support. Boston philanthropist and social worker Joseph Lee succeeded Gulick as president in 1910, and he remained in that position for almost thirty years. The withdrawal of foundation support greatly endangered the PAA's future, but the new leaders, Lee and Braucher, molded the association into a stable institution. Within a few years, the PAA budget topped $100,000.

In 1911, the association changed its name to the Playground and Recreation Association of America (PRAA), which symbolized the growing and broadening role of the association. The former name seemed to connote no more than children's play, while the new name accorded more readily to the increasingly dynamic conception of recreation held by the PRAA's new leaders, Lee and Braucher.

Like many other Progressives, the two leaders had great confidence in expertise and fully expected the PRAA to use that quality in guiding the development of municipal recreation. The most effective method to achieve this aim, they believed, was to expand the field service of the PRAA. This would provide short-term, expert assistance to individual cities. Always wary of standardization, the PRAA expected their fieldworkers to provide individual solutions to the recreation problems encountered in local communities. By 1916, the PRAA staff numbered about forty people who visited 174 cities. In addition to field work, the PRAA continued to publish the monthly *Recreation,* and other, more specialized manuals and pamphlets, and it held regional training institutes and annual recreation congresses. The actions undertaken by the PRAA to broaden the scope and definition of recreation included the introduction of new activities: providing more varied recreation for more people than before, such as folk dancing, community pageants, arts and crafts, athletic events, social centers, and rural recreation; initiating industrial recreation; considering the problems of commercial recreation; discussing the need and significance of recreation; and increasing the public recognition of rising leisure time.

Besides broadening the concept of recreation, Lee and Braucher also desired to make local governments recognize their responsibility for providing at least basic recreation facilities. That local governments were accepting these responsibilities is reflected in the figures in 1916, which showed that municipal funds supported two-thirds of the approximately three thousand playgrounds and neighborhood centers found in four hundred cities, a huge increase in local support for recreation since the founding of the PRAA a decade earlier.

In 1917, the mobilization for World War I unexpectedly presented the PRAA with an opportunity to expand the organization greatly. Lee and Braucher transformed the association into an institution to coordinate off-post social services for millions of troops stationed in training camps throughout the nation. The PRAA formed the War Camp Community Service (WCCS) ''to create a massive settlement house around each camp'' to foster voluntary community cooperation in towns near military bases. This enlarged function of the PRAA succeeded primarily because of the fervent patriotism and civic cooperation of wartime. When peace arrived, Braucher and Lee overestimated the permanence of this cooperation and attempted to continue a movement for peacetime community service that would center on the creative use of leisure. This ill-planned operation quickly faded in the unfavorable postwar atmosphere, and the PRAA returned to the narrower work of the association.

Wartime revelations of a lack of physical fitness among Americans created an opportunity for the PRAA to strengthen physical education in public schools. Braucher and Lee established the National Physical Education Service, which lobbied throughout the nation for legislation requiring physical education in schools. This new vehicle for PRAA proved successful, as twenty-eight states passed new laws for mandatory physical education.

Another significant new PRAA service, which grew out of its wartime experiences, concerned recreation opportunities for blacks, which developed out of the WCCS programs for black soldiers. Braucher was anxious to broaden even further the recreation possibilities for Negroes. In 1920, he selected Ernest T. Attwell to head the bureau of colored work for the PRAA, a position he held until his death three decades later. The bureau was successful from the beginning, and within six years, almost a hundred cities had established recreation facilities for blacks. Realistically appraising the segregationist attitudes of many Americans, Attwell and Braucher decided that separate yet equal facilities were more desirable than no facilities.

The postwar decade was a time of marked growth for leisure activities, as well as a period of substantial expansion for municipal recreation. The PRAA received record contributions during the 1920s and embarked on several new ventures to broaden its services. They formed programs to train thousands of volunteer leaders for rural, organized recreation, founded the first school for systematic training of professional recreation leaders (the National Recreation School), and funded several projects for scholarly research and publications in the field of recreation. The rising budget of the PRAA, which reached a peak in 1929, did not keep pace with soaring local budgets for public recreation, and Braucher and

Lee were unable to extend the PRAA list of contributors. Fortunately for the association, the Laura Spelman Memorial appropriated $500,000 to the PRAA to be used for twelve years beginning in 1929.

In mid-1930, the PRAA again took several steps to gain wider support for a broad definition of recreation and leisure. The most significant change was adopting the name National Recreation Association (NRA) to replace PRAA with the restrictive term "playground" in its title. Mounting unemployment brought forced leisure time to the American people, and the officers of NRA created a national leisure time committee to explain to the nation the importance of training for the wise use of idle hours. In 1932, an Olympic year, the NRA hosted the first international recreation congress in Los Angeles.

As the depression wore on, declining contributions forced the NRA to curtail its programs. In addition, aging leadership lacked the strength to cope with the challenge to the NRA's position as the leading recreation organization by the proliferation of professional groups interested in various aspects of recreation. Even more fateful to the NRA position of leadership was the entry of the federal government into the field of recreation on a massive scale, primarily through the Works Progress Administration. A cardinal virtue of the NRA had always been local control of recreational work, guided, of course, by NRA expertise, but free from the spirit of a centralized bureaucracy. At this crucial point in the NRA's history, Joseph Lee died in 1937, after twenty-seven years as president, and Braucher assumed even more responsibilities in the organization.

Following on the heels of the depression, World War II further solidified the centralizing thrusts in the field of recreation. The powerful factions forming the United Service Organizations for National Defense, Inc.* defeated Braucher's plans to restore the NRA's WCCS and displaced the NRA as the leading private recreation organization.

In the postwar years, Braucher's health continued to fail, and the NRA was in need of new, top-level leadership. The NRA had promoted local governmental responsibility, a broad concept of recreation, and professionalism so successfully over the years that budgets for local public recreation were increasing faster than ever before. Yet the ideas promoted by the NRA had obviously outgrown the organization. Braucher died in 1949, leaving no capable executive secretary to replace him. Despite its substantial achievements, the NRA was seemingly doomed to failure in its hope to be the primary representative of public recreation in America. Insofar as they believed in local control and initiative, a relatively weak national association was inevitable and ill equipped to fend off federal bureaucracies that showed increased interest in recreation.

Since the war, the NRA has continued to act as a clearinghouse for information on recreation problems. It conducted studies, published literature, trained leaders, and provided field services for local communities. In 1965, the NRA merged with several of the professional groups in the field of recreation to form the new National Recreation and Park Association (NRPA). The groups included the

American Institute of Park Executives (founded in 1898), the American Recreation Society (1938), the National Conference of State Parks (1921), and the American Association of Zoological Parks and Aquariums (1924). This last group again became an independent association in 1971. The NRPA described itself in the mid-1970s as a "public interest organization dedicated to improving the human environment through improved park, recreation and leisure opportunity."

The primary sources for studying the NRPA's history consist largely of the association's papers deposited at the Social Welfare History Archives at the University of Minnesota, Minneapolis. Also helpful are the organization's periodicals, *The Playground, Recreation,* and *Parks and Recreation.* Richard F. Knapp, "Play for America: The National Recreation Association, 1906–1950" (Ph.D. diss., Duke University, 1971), is a history of the NRA. K. Gerald Marsden, "Philanthropy and the Boston Playground Movement, 1885–1907," *The Social Service Review* 35 (March 1961): 48–58, deals more with the early movement than with the association.

William Wallach

NATIONAL RECREATION ASSOCIATION: see NATIONAL RECREATION AND PARK ASSOCIATION.

NATIONAL REFUGEE SERVICE, INC., THE (NRS). During the 1930s, as news of Adolf Hitler's atrocities against European Jews became known in the United States, immigrant aid and relief agencies were established, such as the National Coordinating Committee for Aid to Refugees and Emigrants Coming from Germany*—commonly called the National Coordinating Committee (NCC). Following pogroms against Jews abroad, in November 1938, Harry Greenstein of the Baltimore Jewish Community conducted a study of available social services for emigrants and refugees in the United States. Focusing on the NCC, the report, the "Reorganization Study of the National Coordinating Committee and its Affiliated Agencies," pointed out the inadequacies of the NCC and the considerable confusion, overlapping, and duplication of relief work among Jewish agencies. Issued in May 1939, the study recommended the establishment of a new, more unified, and better-coordinated organization. To implement these recommendations, the leaders of the following groups and activities agreed to merge into a new national agency: the NCC, its fund, the Greater New York Coordinating Committee, and the work of administering relief to refugees in New York conducted previously by the local Jewish Social Service Association* (JSSA), the Jewish Family Welfare Society of Brooklyn, and both the New York and Brooklyn Sections of the National Council of Jewish Women (NCJW). Consequently, in June 1939, representatives from a number of agencies concerned with the plight of Jewish refugees founded The National Refugee Service,

Inc. (NRS). The president of the new NRS was William Rosenwald, who had been active in the NCC.

The new agency adapted quickly to the increasingly threatening circumstances affecting Jewish refugees. At its inception, the NRS had a small staff, no departmental structure, and no headquarters. But within three months, during which time war broke out in Europe, the NRS responded to increased demands. By July 1939, the NRS had 428 employees. Its departments suggested the nature of its work: migration, resettlement, employment, special categories (for instance, physicians), relief and casework, information and research, comptroller, and central office management. Also in 1939, with the help of over seven hundred local agencies, the NRS established its resettlement activities. In 1939, the employment department found nearly 5,000 opportunities for work for refugees in America and provided over two hundred loans to refugees to begin businesses. The agency also provided temporary cash assistance. In its first year, when it began to receive funds from the United Jewish Appeal, the NRS helped to sponsor classes in English and in American government and history, as well as to administer the German-Jewish Children's Aid (GJCA), an agency established in 1934 to help refugee children. With the NCJW, the NRS placed 460 refugee children in American foster homes by the end of 1939. William Haber, an economist and a professor and administrator at the University of Michigan, served as the first executive director of the NRS.

The dizzying pace of activity during the first year continued into the early 1940s, resulting in quick praise of the NRS by President Franklin Delano Roosevelt in March 1940. In 1939, the NRS founded a branch in Miami, Florida, to receive and resettle immigrants from Cuba. The chief service of the NRS was providing, through its field staff, basic standards for work with refugees by local committees in communities throughout the country, but it also retained responsibility for refugees in the New York City area. Some local agencies helped the NRS considerably in these endeavors in New York. Also in 1940, to help the refugees adjust to America, the NRS began to study job retraining, experimenting with this service in New York in 1940. The agency also began agricultural training and farm settlement for the refugees. An agricultural consultant, who worked closely with the Jewish Agricultural Society,* aided this program. Responding to the immigration through West Coast ports, in July 1940, the NRS held an emergency meeting in San Francisco, working out agreements between it and refugee relief agencies in those cities. Some organizational changes occurred in early 1941 when Haber resigned and in July 1941 when the NRS moved to new headquarters. Professor Albert Abrahamson became the new executive director, but the most important individual continued to be Professor Joseph Chamberlain of Columbia University, who was active in a number of other social service agencies. In the early 1940s, in light of the federal enemy alien program, the NRS kept refugees posted on changes in their status, serving frequently as a liaison between Washington, D.C., and local communities. In 1941, the NRS sponsored the Committee for the Summer Placement of Refugee Children. Early in the year, the GJCA had voted to have the NRS administer it. In 1941, the NRS established its department of family service. In late October, partly at the request of the NRS, the federal Office of Procurement and Assignment, issued a much-needed statement on the status of alien physicians, a group with which the NRS was concerned. The NRS continued to find work for many elderly refugees who were on the relief rolls of social service agencies. By 1942, the social adjustment program had provided over ten thousand services for refugees. To strengthen its services, in 1942, the NRS founded its technical advisory committee, which included the leaders of the principal family service agencies. to advise the staff and executives about various technical problems of organization. In early 1943, Joseph E. Beck replaced Professor Abrahamson as executive director. In 1943, the NRS helped to pressure the United States Department of Justice to free fifty-four refugee families from Camp Algiers in Louisiana who were held under "internment at large." The NRS continued to interpret alien regulations to local agencies and, with the American Jewish Joint Distribution Committee* and other organizations, helped to reunite families. Field staff visits continued to advise and to help local agencies dealing with refugees. In 1943, the NRS issued a survey of the manpower of the refugees.

American participation in World War II did not change significantly the nature of NRS activities in the mid-1940s. Its resettlement department, known as "America on Display," operated in a room filled with maps, guidebooks, photographs, and the like. In May 1944, the NRS established a large-scale service to search for friends and relatives, operating its location and search services. In 1945, the NRS took over the administration of its affiliate, now called European-Jewish Children's Aid. The NRS was the only agency consulted in the planning of President Harry Truman's directive in December 1945 relating to displaced persons. NRS officials suggested the use of corporate affidavits for refugees, a provision of the directive. Although it developed a comprehensive migration program through the trying World War II period, on August 1, 1946, the NRS merged with the service to foreign-born program of the NCJW to form the more consolidated United Service for New Americans* (USNA).

The primary sources for studying the history of this short-lived but important agency are extensive. The files and papers of the NRS, which comprise over fourteen hundred folders, are on microfilm at the YIVO Institute for Jewish Research in New York City. An unpublished finding aid at YIVO facilitates the use of this collection. The published *Annual Reports* provide helpful details about the agency, as do the files of the *NRS Community Bulletin* and *The New York Times*.

Lyman C. White, *300,000 New Americans* (1957), discusses the NRS's history briefly. More recent and scholarly studies, such as David Wyman, *Paper Walls* (1968), and Henry L. Feingold, *The Politics of Rescue* (1970), mention it briefly, but there does not appear to be a full-length, scholarly history of the NRS.

NATIONAL REHABILITATION ASSOCIATION, INC. (NRA). In the period after World War I, largely because of veterans' wartime injuries, the federal government began to develop programs for the physical rehabilitation of the disabled and wounded. As with other federally supported welfare programs, grants to the states provided funding for rehabilitation services during the early 1920s. Workers in the field of rehabilitation began to discuss forming a national organization to promote their field and interests. The idea for such a group was conceived more formally at the meeting of the National Society for Vocational Education (NSVE) in Buffalo, New York, in 1923. The NSVE agreed to establish the National Civilian Rehabilitation Conference (NCRC), which met annually. At the NCRC in Cleveland, Ohio, in 1926, a group of professionals in the federal-state rehabilitation program set up the structure for a national organization. Following the meeting in Cleveland, the NCRC's executive committee met in New York City in 1926, amended the NCRC's constitution, and changed the group's name to the National Rehabilitation Association (NRA).

The members at the next NCRC, held in Memphis, Tennessee, in 1927, approved of these developments and officially established the NRA. The ninety professionals who attended the conference in Cleveland in 1926 became the charter members. The important organizers of the NRS included Dr. Fred Albee of New York City who had founded the American Rehabilitation Committee* in 1922; Tracy Copp, a regional representative of the United States Office of Education (USOE); John A. Kratz, the chief of vocational rehabilitation of the USOE; R. L. Bynum, the supervisor of vocational rehabilitation in Nashville, Tennessee; Mrs. Alexander Kerr of Los Angeles; and Marlow B. Perrin, chief of vocational rehabilitation for the state of Ohio. The goal of the NRS was to make permanent and to increase the funding of the Industrial Rehabilitation Act of 1920 and of other federally funded programs in rehabilitation.

Organizationally, the NRA has been headed by a president, who, except for a very few years, has been a professional worker in a federally funded state rehabilitation program. The president determined important organizational decisions only after conferring with the board of directors. Since the 1930s, state associations, often comprised of representatives from local chapters, have been part of the NRA structure. In late 1940, state associations became affiliated with one of nine regional offices, and in December of 1948, the NRA changed these regions to conform to the social security regions. The rather elaborate and complex organizational structure of 1948 became the overriding plan. Each of the regions elected one member to the NRA's board of directors.

From its inception through the years of the New Deal, the NRA promoted legislation for the handicapped, concerned itself with improved standards of work in the rehabilitation field, and emerged as a leading private organization in the field. At the NRA's convention in Louisville, Kentucky, in 1934, for instance, the organization resolved itself in favor of tenure for all state rehabilitation staffs, urging that this job security be written into all federal-state legislation. The NRA promoted the inclusion of rehabilitation in the Social Security Bill and Act of 1935, and in 1935, influential Congressman John Bankhead, the majority leader in the House of Representatives, became the vice-president of the group, representing the NRA's lay members.

In the years following the New Deal, the NRA broadened its concentration on federal-state rehabilitation programs and began to represent more earnestly the interests of the handicapped and the diverse workers in the field. In February 1940, for example, the board of directors created a new committee, planning and promotion, to promote a national conference for the disabled and to act as a clearinghouse for all defense-related issues concerning the handicapped, particularly the granting of defense contracts to sheltered workshops. In 1942, the NRA changed its constitution, broadening its membership to include more lay people and not just those in federal-state programs. Total membership in the organization grew quickly, with over fifteen thousand by 1950, including physicians, nurses, social workers, and teachers involved in rehabilitation work. Demonstrating its leadership in the field, in 1947, the NRA offered its first annual award for distinguished service in rehabilitation, which has remained a valued citation. In 1948, the NRA further demonstrated its position as a leading agency in the field when it opened its national office in Washington, D.C., to focus on federal legislation. This office was the first of its kind established by a rehabilitation organization. Initially temporary, the office became permanent later in 1948 and was headed by the NRA's executive director.

The NRA continued in the mainstream of the rehabilitation field, as it began to cooperate with other organizations in the 1950s and 1960s to develop new programs. In 1958, for example, it worked with the National Association of Sheltered Workshops for the Homebound Programs to sponsor the National Institute on the Role of the Workshop in Rehabilitation, which established standards for both the classification and evaluation of workshops. In 1960, one of three co-sponsored programs developed a seminar on international rehabilitation. In 1962, at the request of other groups in the field, the NRA, with the help of two other organizations, developed standards for rehabilitation facilities. Demonstrating the broadening of its interests, the NRA joined in 1962 with the Council on Exceptional Children and The National Society for Crippled Children and Adults* to develop the National Institute on Services to Handicapped Children and Youth.

In the 1970s, the NRA remained in the vanguard of new trends in the rehabilitation field. In the early 1970s, for example, it conducted a survey on the proper utilization of substitute preprofessionals in rehabilitation work. Reflecting increased community and citizen involvement in social service, by the early 1970s, the NRA envisioned itself not as a professional organization but rather as "a primary citizen interest group."

The primary sources relating to the NRA's history include a few published *Annual Reports,* which are not available widely, its serial publications, especially the *National Rehabilitation News,* the *Newsletter,* and, since 1951, *The Journal of Rehabilitation,* which contains some organizational details. The NRA files in the ICD Library in New York City hold some documents relating to the NRA's history.

John G. Hill and Richard E. Hardy, *Vocational Rehabilitation* (1972), mentions the NRA briefly. There do not appear to be any scholarly historical studies of the NRA.

NATIONAL SHUT-IN SOCIETY, THE. (NSS). In the 1870s, Jennie M. Drinkwater of Convent, New Jersey, an invalid and apparently homebound, read about other invalids in the pages of the *Advocate and Family Guardian,* a religious paper published in New York City by the American Female Guardian Society and the Home for the Friendless, a local charitable institution. Drinkwater decided to write to two of the invalids, Alice Ball of Yonkers, New York, and Susie Hewitt of New York City. The circle of correspondents grew gradually, and in January 1877, the group of invalids met in New York City and founded The National Shut-In Society (NSS) as the Shut-in Society (SS). The editor of the paper, Helen E. Brown, helped to found the SS, and she became active in it. The SS gradually gained public attention. Other groups developed in New York, New Jersey, Brooklyn, and Connecticut in the early 1880s. By May 1881, there were about three hundred invalid members and forty associates who corresponded with the shut-ins.

Representatives from the constituent groups assembled in New York City on December 2, 1884, the first annual meeting of the SS. Although Mary Hamilton Hadley of New Haven, Connecticut, was the first secretary-treasurer, Helen E. Brown was the chief organizer of the national group. Other local organizations, such as those in Missouri and Massachusetts, developed themselves and affiliated with the national agency. The SS's monthly journal, *Open Window,* began publication in January 1885. By 1928, there were shut-in societies in all of the states except Utah and Nevada and in some foreign countries, including Canada and England.

From its inception, the SS had two classifications of membership. Associates, who paid slightly higher dues, corresponded with and visited the invalids, who constituted the group of regular members. Throughout the history of the organization, there were far more regular, or invalid, members than there were associates. This phenomenon became critical during the Great Depression of the 1930s when the number of associates dropped precipitously, hampering the functioning of the SS in some of the far western states, which lacked sufficient numbers of associate members.

Although associates aided and comforted the invalids, one rule of the SS was that they should never give any alms. The society wanted invalids to follow the self-help principle, urging them to conduct minor chores such as weaving and repairing clothes, just as did one of the founders, Susie Hewitt, who taught her neighbors' children the fundamentals of reading, writing, and arithmetic five days a week.

The members of the SS elected the board of direction, the planning and administrative group. This board, which consisted initially of fifteen but was raised to twenty-one members in 1940, elected the SS's officers annually. The major officials were the president, vice-president, and secretary-treasurer. Standing committees, which reflected the activities of the SS, included wheelchair, library, correspondence, and helping hand, which supplied such items as hot water bags, stationery, and stamps to invalids. In 1926, when one of the earliest members, the chairman of the library committee, died, the board of direction decided to discontinue the operation of that committee. In 1932, a minister from Boston helped to introduce a committee for the blind, which sent braille books and letters to this group of invalids. The SS also had a men's department, a girls' department, and an invalids' auxiliary. The agency corresponded with lonely seamen and with prisoners. The SS was proud that while most other welfare agencies had become professionalized by the mid-1930s, it remained a strictly voluntary organization.

During some of the depression years of the 1930s, the SS actually lost members, but in 1942, the organization enlarged its membership to include physically handicapped people who were able to leave their homes and thus were not true shut-ins. In the same year, the organization established a department of occupational therapy, and the SS's secretary, Mrs. Thomas D. Rambaut, attended the National Conference of Social Work,* particularly the sessions relating to the handicapped. In the mid-1940s, some members, particularly from the Massachusetts branch, campaigned for absentee voting rights for shut-ins, a proposal endorsed by the annual convention of the national organization in 1945. The SS continued to sponsor and publicize Shut-in Day, held the first Sunday in June. Prominent personalities, such as Dr. Norman Vincent Peale in 1943 and Lawrence Welk in 1964, spoke at the annual convention, always held in New York City. A series of articles in the 1960s, such as those in *The New York Times* and in *Coronet Magazine* in 1965, stimulated interest in the group.

Throughout its history, few organizational changes occurred, but an important event was the change of national headquarters in 1967 to a "more desirable and pleasant" location at 30 East Forty-second Street in New York City. In the 1970s, the organization still had a twenty-one-member executive committee.

The chief primary source for studying the NSS's history is its journal, *The Open Window,* which contains annual reports, as well as news of the national and local organizations.

There does not appear to be a scholarly history of this veteran agency.

NATIONAL SOCIAL WELFARE ASSEMBLY: see NATIONAL ASSEMBLY OF NATIONAL VOLUNTARY HEALTH AND SOCIAL WELFARE ORGANIZATIONS, INC., THE.

NATIONAL SOCIAL WORK COUNCIL: see NATIONAL ASSEMBLY OF NATIONAL VOLUNTARY HEALTH AND SOCIAL WELFARE ORGANIZATIONS, INC., THE.

NATIONAL SOCIETY FOR CRIPPLED CHILDREN: see NATIONAL EASTER SEAL SOCIETY FOR CRIPPLED CHILDREN AND ADULTS, THE.

NATIONAL SOCIETY FOR CRIPPLED CHILDREN AND ADULTS, THE: see NATIONAL EASTER SEAL SOCIETY FOR CRIPPLED CHILDREN AND ADULTS, THE.

NATIONAL SOCIETY FOR THE PREVENTION OF BLINDNESS, INC. (NSPB). In the early years of the twentieth century, the conservation of eyesight developed as a characteristically social justice Progressive issue and reform movement. The problem of ophthalmia neonatorum—popularly called "babies sore eyes"—an eye inflammation usually caused by gonorrheal infection in the mother's birth canal, occurred largely in children in institutions, such as orphan asylums and hospitals, and stirred the social conscience of workers in medicine, social work, and services for the blind. In 1903, New York Governor Benjamin B. Odell, Jr., appointed the New York State Commission to Investigate the Condition of the Blind (NYSCICB). The NYSCICB dealt with this problem of babies' sore eyes. In 1907, the president of the American Medical Association (AMA) appointed a special committee to study this problem; the committee's scope was enlarged in 1910. Meanwhile, on April 10, 1907, the NYSCICB issued its report, which contained touching photographs of babies whose sight could have been saved. Louisa Lee Schuyler, the founder of the famous State Charities Aid Association* (SCAA) of New York and leader in New York charities, read this report, which moved her to action. In April 1908, Schuyler influenced the Russell Sage Foundation* (RSF), the great supporter of social work agencies and projects, to help her establish a group to deal with the prevention of blindness, especially of ophthalmia neonatorum.

On April 27, 1908, the RSF appointed two of its members—John Glenn, a major figure in the RSF and in other charitable organizations, and Gertrude Rice, a leading philanthropist—to serve with Schuyler as a three-member committee of the RSF on the prevention of blindness. Later in June 1908, Schuyler summoned to her home leaders in the field in New York, including Dr. F. Park Lewis of Buffalo, the chairman of the NYSCICB, and Winifred Holt, a "dynamic woman" who, with her sister Edith, dedicated herself to assisting the blind and who established the Lighthouse in 1906 in New York City, which later became the New York Association for the Blind (NYAB). These new people, the RSF committee, and others soon formed the New York Committee for the Prevention of Blindness (NYCPB), which established relations with and functioned as a special committee of the NYAB. With support from the RSF, the Schuyler group expanded to work on the national level in 1910. Within one year, there were state associations affiliated with the NYCPB in Kentucky, Missouri, and Arkansas.

Plans were developing and maturing to form a new national organization in the field. In 1911, the Schuyler group helped to create the new American Association for the Conservation of Vision (AACV). Schuyler's RSF committee obtained funds for the AACV, but it proved to be a disappointing venture. The AACV was soon in debt and its activities were suspended. Some AACV directors and people from the RSF, however, revived the group in 1914. With two equal five-year grants from the RSF and the Rockefeller Foundation, the AAVC started again at an opportune time. Edward M. Van Cleve of Ohio, who was an active promoter of a national movement, came to New York City as the principal of the New York Institution for the Education of the Blind. An effective administrator, Van Cleve fortunately agreed to become the AACV's managing director, giving the new enterprise a sound beginning. The NYCPB of the NYAB had changed its name to the New York State Committee for the Prevention of Blindness (NYSCPB) in 1913, and it now affiliated with the revitalized AACV, becoming one of its standing committees. On January 1, 1915, the National Society for the Prevention of Blindness (NSPB) was founded when the NYSCPB and the AACV merged to form the new National Committee for the Prevention of Blindness (NCPB).

The new national agency, the NCPB, began its work immediately. The NCPB's initial structure included a thirty-member board of directors, with an executive committee that supervised the managing director, the chief administrative officer of the staff. The NCPB also had a secretary and a field secretary. The new agency began almost immediately to issue and distribute a multigraphed "News Letter." Still led by Schuyler, the NYSCPB maintained its separate identity, even in the new NCPB. In its very first year, the NCPB cooperated with the United States Children's Bureau (USCB), which helped to publicize the new society's work. The NCPB itself publicized the need to prevent blindness through articles in *The Survey,* the leading social work journal, and one on the dangers of wood alcohol in the *American Journal of Nursing.* The NCPB's traveling exhibit was lent to individual workers and organizations in ten states. The NCPB's secretary, Carolyn Van Blarcom, served as an editor for *Modern Hospital,* and she chaired the National Organization for Public Health Nursing's* (NOPHN) committee on midwives and the prevention of blindness. The NCPB almost immediately began a nationwide program of conducting surveys and studies of trachoma in Kentucky. Cooperating with the National Medical Association, a black physicians' organization, the NCPB made studies of conditions in Tennessee and North Carolina. In these early years before 1920, the NCPB emphasized each year one particular aspect of the field of preventing blindness. For instance, in 1917, it stressed accidents to eyes in industry. The agency conducted an extensive study, which resulted in a 145-page publication, *Eye Hazards in Industrial Occupations,* by Field Secretary Gordon Berry, who also lectured to soldiers in army camps under the authority of the United States surgeon-general. Recalling the episode that motivated founder Schuyler, the agency had prominent exhibits during so-called baby week campaigns, and at the National Conference of Charities and Correction,* its exhibit on eye accidents was popular. The NCPB—which was legally incorporated in 1917 and was then called the National Committee on the Prevention of Blindness, Inc. (NCPB)—participated in such diverse programs as the third annual industrial safety exposition of Ohio in Columbus, the Iowa State Fair in Des Moines, and the American Museum of Safety (AMS) in New York City. Articles by Field Secretary Berry and others alerted the public to the necessity of preventing blindness.

Working in the early 1920s, particularly with state movements to have physicians place medicinal drops in newborns' eyes to prevent ophthalmia neonatorum, the organization began important research, surveys, and publications in the field of children's eyesight. The organization and its New York affiliate, for example, spearheaded the drive there for eye-saving classes and classrooms. In 1921, the NCPB produced a pioneering educational motion picture, *Saving the Eyes of Youth*. In 1926, it conducted the first preschool vision screening testing using volunteers, and in 1932, it published the first study of the causes of blindness in schoolchildren. In the thirty years since its inception, largely because of the work of the group, the percentage of schoolchildren blinded by ophthalmia neonatorum was reduced from 26 to 7 percent.

Fulfilling founder Schuyler's visions of helping to prevent blindness in children, the NCPB expanded its activities, beginning in the mid-1920s, to reduce industrial eye hazards. Beginning with pioneering studies of the number of eye-related accidents and promoting eye safety in industry with the AMS, the organization launched a major educational campaign, hoping to reach five million workers. Cooperating with the American Federation of Labor, five representatives lectured to state and local conventions and distributed pamphlets and other information. On January 1, 1928, the agency changed its name to the NSPB. In 1930, the NSPB conducted the first broad survey of industrial eye safety in over 580 plants and factories. As war production accelerated in the United States, in 1940, the group established its industrial advisory committee with representatives from the major industries. Under the auspices of the federal War Production Board, in 1943, the NSPB established an advisory service on eye safety for some twenty-eight hundred war production plants. The NSPB also worked in campaigns to reduce syphilis, which caused blindness; publicized the need for safe July Fourth celebrations; and cooperated with medical social workers, training them beginning in 1930. In 1940, when the NSPB became an associate group of the National Conference of Social Work,* the NSPB presented a program dealing with eyesight.

By the period of World War II, some important administrative and structural changes had occurred within the NSPB. In 1923, founder Edward M. Van Cleve retired as the managing director; Lewis H. Carris, who had come to the organization as field secretary in 1921, replaced him. In September 1940, the first vice-president of the NSPB, founder Dr. Park Lewis, died, and President William Fellowes Morgan, a businessman, philanthropist, and civic leader, retired in December 1940 after serving for twenty-five years. By 1940, the organization, which had one paid worker when it began, had a staff of thirty-eight working in its headquarters at Radio City in New York City. Members of the NSPB still elected a thirty-member board of directors, which in turn vested administrative authority in its executive committee, composed of nine board members.

In the postwar period, the NSPB continued its leadership and pioneering in the field, turning increasingly to research. In 1946, for instance, it sponsored a study of the relation between German measles, or rubella, and congenital cataracts. In 1950, NSPB supported the first research project linking retrolental fibroplasia (RLF), the leading cause of blindness in school children in the 1940s, to the high levels of oxygen administered to premature infants. Beginning in the 1960s, the NSPB cosponsored annually, with the Association for Research in Ophthalmology, a scientific glaucoma symposium. In 1971, NSPB held an important symposium on diabetic retinopathy, which attacks diabetics and which has, in the 1970s, challenged both cataract and glaucoma as the leading cause of blindness in America.

Other programs continued the prevention campaigns of the earlier periods. An expanded industrial eye safety program, developed through the NSPB-sponsored Wise Owl Club of America (WOCA), grew rapidly. Founded in 1948, by 1953, the WOCA had almost five thousand members in nearly nine hundred plants. The program offered protection to over 1.1 million workers in 1953. The NSPB's fifteen-year campaign for impact-resistant eyeglasses resulted in federal regulation in 1971. The agency's nationally publicized eye safety campaign relating to the eclipse of the sun in March 1970 reduced damage compared with that caused by the 1963 eclipse. The NSPB's documentary on industrial accidents made in 1967, *Don't Push Your Luck,* won national awards, including the Safety Film of the Year from the National Safety Council.

In 1974, the NSPB had an expanded seventy-six-member board of directors, which still chose its now twenty-one-member executive committee. The structure in 1974 also included an executive staff of thirteen and eight advisory committees composed of physicians, social workers, union and industrial representatives, and others. In 1977, there were twenty-two state affiliates of this important national agency, still headquartered in New York City.

The best accessible primary source for studying the NSPB's history is the published and helpful *Annual Reports.* For much of its history, the agency published its *News Letter,* which contains helpful information about the organization. *The New York Times* reported the agency's important activities. The agency files, which are not part of its library in New York City, are available only to properly qualified and identified scholars. These files contain minutes of board and other meetings, correspondence, and the like. Contemporary publications, such as a memorial volume honoring the agency's founder, *Louisa Lee Schuyler, 1837–1926* (n.d. [1926]), also provide information.

Secondary studies are not as rich as the primary materials. John Glenn, Lilian Brandt, and F. Emerson Andrews, *Russell Sage Foundation, 1907–1946* (1947), mentions the organization briefly, and Harold M. Cavins, *National Health Agencies, A Survey with Especial Reference to Voluntary Associations* (1945), contains a little information about the NSPB. Even a standard specialized work, Frances Koestler, *The Unseen Majority, A Social History of Blindness in America* (1976), mentions the agency only briefly. Standard histories in social work, such as Clarke A. Chambers, *Seedtime of Reform* (1963), Walter Trattner, *From Poor Law to Welfare State* (1974), and June Axin and Herman Levin, *Social Welfare: A History of the American Response to Need* (1975), fail to mention the NSPB. There does not appear to be a full-length scholarly history of the NSPB.

NATIONAL SOCIETY OF PENAL INFORMATION (NSPI). In 1913, Thomas Mott Osborne, the chairman of the newly created state commission for prison reform in New York State, entered the Auburn, New York, State Prison under the pseudonym of Tom Brown to learn firsthand of prison conditions. This episode and his chairmanship of the state commission helped to launch Osborne, a colorful and wealthy figure who had served as mayor of Auburn, into the prison reform movement nationally. During the period from 1914 to 1920, Osborne founded and led the Mutual Welfare Leagues, which were self-governing units of prisoners in prisons. In 1920, in New York City, Osborne brought together a group of individuals concerned about prisons and then formed the National Society of Penal Information (NSPI) to publicize and to work to improve conditions in the entire criminal justice system. The NSPI attracted some of the most important social reformers and penologists of the period. In 1922, an eighteen-member general committee included Felix Adler, the founder and leader of the Ethical Culture movement and a noted influential reformer, Dr. Albert Shaw, who had been the editor of the liberal *Review of Reviews,* and Dr. Anson Phelps-Stokes, a philanthropist and educator. The seven-member executive committee included the chairman of the NSPI, Samuel A. Eliot, a well-known Unitarian minister, Spencer Miller, Jr., who was active in labor reform, George W. Kirchwey, a lawyer, penologist, former New York State commissioner of prisons, and a member of the department of criminology at the New York School of Social Work, and Elmer S. Forbes, the secretary of the Department of Community Service* of the American Unitarian Association. The NSPI's first executive secretary was Paul W. Garrett.

In the 1920s, the NSPI developed some activities that were important in the penal reform field. In the early 1920s, the NSPI began to publish *The Prison Yearbook,* which described major topics in the field, such as prison labor, as well as the state prison systems and prisons. NSPI also published, beginning in 1925, several editions of the *Handbook of American Prisons and Reformatories.* In 1922, the NSPI initiated its *Bulletin,* which became a helpful source of information about the criminal justice field. By June 1923, societies were being organized in Pennsylvania, Ohio, and North Carolina, and there was a strong reform movement in Massachusetts. In New York, the NSPI worked closely with another prison reform organization Osborne had established, the Welfare League Association (WLA).

The activities of the NSPI increased in the late 1920s, when some more influential people became active in the organization. The eight-member executive committee, chaired by Osborne and including George Kirchwey and Dr. Thomas W. Salmon of the National Committee for Mental Hygiene,* conducted most of the active work of the NSPI. An important recognition of the agency came in the spring of 1927 when, on the advice of the American Association for Adult Education, the Carnegie Corporation granted funds to the NSPI to conduct a study of the educational and library work in American prisons and reformatories. The NSPI hired a leading penologist, Austin MacCormick, to conduct the study. This episode began MacCormick's long affiliation with the NSPI and its successor agency, The Osborne Association* (OA).

Before the study began, the NSPI appointed an impressive advisory committee, including Professor Harry Elmer Barnes, a student of American prisons. George Kirchwey, and Spencer Miller, Jr., then the secretary of the Workers Education Bureau of America. Between November 1927 and August 1928, MacCormick visited all but three of the prisons and reformatories for men and women in the United States. In addition to completing the MacCormick study in 1928, the NSPI conducted three other important projects: the publication of the third edition of the *Handbook of American Prisons,* a careful study of state prison reform in five southern states, and a study of health and hospital work in prisons and reformatories by Dr. Frank Leslie Rector, which was made possible by a grant from the Laura Spelman Rockefeller Fund. Field Secretary William B. Cox, formerly of Hiram House, a settlement in Cleveland, conducted a study of thirty-eight prisons in five states, and he reported his findings to sessions at the National Conference of Social Work* and the American Prison Congress, which held a dinner discussion session on this topic with state prison officials. So impressed were the officials that they asked Cox to conduct a similar study in the South of county-controlled prisons and to help them reorganize prison systems in the South. Cox agreed, and he spent November and December 1928 in the South, returning to his duties with the NSPI in New York in early 1929. In the late 1920s, as this episode suggested, state prison officials recognized the NSPI as a respectable organization. In 1928, the thirty-three-member general committee included such prominent Americans as New York Governor Franklin Delano Roosevelt; the president of Stanford University, David Starr Jordan; prominent penologist Hastings Hart; Bronson M. Cutting, a journalist and United States senator from New York; former secretary of the navy and editor, Josephus

Daniels; Felix Adler; and the most famous social worker, Jane Addams. In 1929, the NSPI moved to new headquarters in New York City in the Osborne Memorial House, established by the Trustees of the Thomas Mott Osborne Memorial Fund.

In the early 1930s, until it merged with the WLA to become the OA in 1932, the NSPI continued to provide relevant services in the penal reform field. In the early 1930s, noted reformer Dr. F. Lovell Bixby, a psychologist who had implemented in 1929 the pioneering classification system in New Jersey prisons, served as field and research secretary of the NSPI. Bixby helped in the study begun in 1931 of over sixty institutions to determine the extent of such conditions as overcrowding and idleness. In 1931, with a grant from the Carl Schurz Memorial Foundation, the NSPI sponsored lectures in America by Dr. Clara Maria Klepmann. The lectures discussed German law and social work in prisons in the United States and Germany. The *News Bulletin,* whose circulation averaged around five thousand copies in the early 1930s, was a continuing success. In 1932, the NSPI successfully opposed legislation in New Jersey that would have impaired the progressive prison program of the state Department of Institutions and Agencies. In 1932, the executive secretary, William B. Cox, testified about conditions in prison camps in Georgia at extradition hearings in New Jersey. The NSPI shared its New York headquarters with the WLA, with which it functioned almost jointly in the early 1930s. Dwindling finances in the early 1930s led each agency to meet with representatives of the Thomas Mott Osborne Memorial Fund; together they worked out the merger in November 1932 of the two organizations to form the OA.

The primary sources for studying the NSPI's history include the *Bulletin* for the early period and the variously named published *Annual Reports* for the later period. *The New York Times* occasionally reported the NSPI's activities. There are minutes and other materials relating to the NSPI in the papers of Thomas Mott Osborne at The George Arents Research Library at Syracuse University in Syracuse, New York.

Standard works in prison history, including Frank Tannenbaum, *Osborne of Sing Sing* (1933), either neglect the NSPI or mention it very briefly. There does not appear to be a scholarly history of the NSPI.

NATIONAL TRAVELERS AID ASSOCIATION: see TRAVELERS AID ASSOCIATION OF AMERICA.

NATIONAL TUBERCULOSIS ASSOCIATION: see AMERICAN LUNG ASSOCIATION.

NATIONAL URBAN LEAGUE (NUL).   In the early twentieth century, urban reformers began to build an institutional structure to bring social services to blacks in American cities. To expand employment opportunities for New York City's Negroes, a black school principal, William L. Bulkley, founded the Committee for Improving the Industrial Condition of Negroes in New York

(CIICN), in 1906. At the same time, Frances Kellor, a white social worker concerned about the exploitation of black women new to the city, established the National League for the Protection of Colored Women (NLPCW) in the interests of providing suitable employment, safe recreation,and decent, low-cost housing. In 1910, a black sociologist, George Edmund Haynes, and a white philanthropist-reformer, Ruth Standish Baldwin, joined to create the Committee on Urban Conditions Among Negroes (CUCAN). Much of the CUCAN's plan of work was by that time conventional—seeking improved housing, health and sanitary services, and recreational facilities in black neighborhoods, protecting black women from exploitation, and helping blacks to improve their skills and to find better jobs. But the CUCAN, reflecting the influence of Haynes and other professional sociologists and economists among its leaders, went beyond the scope of the CIICN and the NLPCW in at least three respects: its practical activities were to be based on research about urban life, it would seek to train black social workers, and it would place trained workers in welfare agencies and induce those agencies to include blacks in their programs.

In order to avoid duplication of effort and to make possible a coordinated national attack on the problems of blacks in American cities, the three organizations in New York City consolidated on October 16, 1911, to form the National League on Urban Conditions Among Negores (NLUCAN), which later shortened its name to the National Urban League (NUL). The NLUCAN divided with the National Association for the Advancement of Colored People (NAACP) (see *Political and Civic Organizations*) the great work of the struggle for racial advancement. Both organizations shared a concern that blacks be accorded the full responsibilities and opportunities of first-class citizenship. But while the NAACP believed that ensuring recognition and free exercise of legal rights was the most important task at hand, the NLUCAN wanted to make certain that blacks would be prepared, through having a stake in the nation's economy and a mastery of the perils of city life, to assume the burdens and rewards of being a citizen. The league's emphasis on economic opportunity and social welfare as the route to racial advancement reflected the ideological imprint of Booker T. Washington. Reflecting, too, its roots in the Progressive era, the NUL relied historically on tools of negotiation, persuasion, education, and investigation to accomplish its economic and social goals.

Like the social settlements of the Progressive era, the NUL conducted scientific investigations of conditions among urban blacks as a basis for practical reform. Its studies—some published independently, some reported in the NUL's magazine, *Opportunity: Journal of Negro Life* (1923–1929)—contributed importantly to the development of a body of reliable literature on aspects of black urban life. Usually the surveys were conducted at the request of social agencies interested in inaugurating programs for blacks. Interracial councils in Trenton, New Jersey, Denver, and Worcester, Massachusetts were among those that requested comprehensive studies of their black communities; social agencies in

Pittsburgh and Fort Wayne, recognizing the existence of problems in their black neighborhoods but uncertain how to respond, asked the NUL to investigate. The resulting studies generally began with a sketch of the history of the city's black population and the circumstances under which migrants had come there. They drew a detailed portrait of the way blacks lived—the sections of the city, type and cost of housing, numbers in each household, and the proportion of home owners to renters. An economic profile showed where blacks worked, how much money they made, and how local unions treated them. Interviews revealed why employers refused to hire blacks, or, if they did hire them, what their experiences had been. Statistics summed up comparative rates of disease and mortality, crime and delinquency. The studies surveyed educational and recreational opportunities in the city and described the social and civic organizations active in the black community.

Often the surveys were a first step toward the establishment of an NUL affiliate. Sometimes they aided existing affiliates in reevaluating their programs and services. Often, too, they responded to specific requests from outside agencies. The Metropolitan Life Insurance Company, for example, wanted to know how many blacks were employed in industrial concerns having pension plans. The National Commission on Law Observance and Enforcement requested information on law observance and enforcement among Negores; the White House Conference on Child Health and Protection of 1930 asked for a study of dependency problems among blacks; as the depression deepened in 1930, the President's Research Committee on Social Trends enlisted the NUL's aid in examining the industrial status of blacks in New York, New Jersey, and Pennsylvania. Major surveys of such areas as black membership in labor unions, the status of black workers, black unemployment and underemployment in times of depression and recession, and housing conditions among blacks have been noted as pioneering works in their field and have been used by the NUL in its efforts to shape public and private employment and social policies with respect to race.

The NLUCAN pioneered professional social service training for blacks. George Haynes opened a training center for black social workers in Nashville in 1914 under the NLUCAN'S auspices, Fisk University, and the Women's Missionary Council, Methodist Episcopal church, South; the NLUCAN encouraged black colleges to incorporate instruction in economics, sociology, and urban problems in their curriculums; and a league fellowship program from the 1910s to the 1960s enabled promising young blacks to pursue advanced studies in designated schools of social work while gaining some practical experience at local leagues or similar agencies. The result was the first corps of professional black social workers, whom the NUL placed in community service positions as staff members for Urban Leagues and other social service agencies, family caseworkers, probation officers, settlement house workers, supervisors of day nurseries and boys' and girls' clubs, travelers' aid workers, and others.

The NUL adapted for blacks the welfare services already offered foreign- and native-born whites by settlement houses, charitable agencies, and immigrant aid societies. Principally through a network of affiliates in cities around the country (more than two dozen by the end of its first decade, more than one hundred a half-century later), the NUL sponsored community centers with clubs, classes, recreational, and cultural activities; summer camps; clinics; kindergartens and day nurseries; pageants, contests, lectures, and demonstrations to dramatize proper health care; community clean-up and beautification projects; travelers' aid; probation, tutoring, adoption, and foster home services; and, occasionally, even direct relief. Local league staff members engaged in casework to deal with individual problems, including juvenile delinquency, truancy, and marital adjustment, and, in the interests of improving manners and morals, counseled blacks new to the city on behavior, dress, sanitation, health, and homemaking.

Encouraging public agencies to assume responsibility for the pilot projects it started was typical of the NUL's social service efforts. The NUL envisioned itself as an administrative or coordinating agency; it engaged in practical social service programs because no one else would, and it eagerly turned them over to more appropriate sponsors. In St. Louis, for example, the league ran a dental clinic for blacks from 1920 until 1929, when the local health department agreed to take it on. Since blacks were barred from public playgrounds, the league set up three of its own in 1928 to persuade the city to provide public recreational facilities. In 1929, Atlanta established an infant welfare station that was taken over by the city health department. Seeing to it that municipal agencies added blacks to their staffs was another part of this effort. At the urging of the Detroit Urban League, for example, the probation department of the municipal court hired a black worker who had previously been on the league's payroll. The league was also responsible for the appointments of a black policewoman, a black physician in the health department, and a black worker in the girls' protective league, in the recreation commission, and in the welfare department. In Philadelphia, the board of education hired the league affiliate's long-time home and school visitor. Columbus secured the appointment of a black policewoman to work with newcomers to the city. In Newark, the Social Service Bureau hired four black caseworkers to take over the family casework formerly conducted by the league affiliate there. The Jacksonville Urban League was responsible for the appointment of a black supervisor for the city's black public schools.

In addition to its social service efforts, the NUL has been concerned primarily with gaining jobs for blacks. Its work in this area has followed a number of paths: placing workers in private industry, attacking the color line in organized labor, and sponsoring programs of vocational guidance and job training. While the NUL first concentrated principally on changing discriminatory employment practices in the private sector, it became increasingly involved in trying to influence the development of public policy. During the Great Depression, for example, it lobbied for the inclusion of blacks in federal relief and recovery programs; in the 1940s, it pressed for an end to discrimination in defense industries and for the desegregation of the armed forces. It strove to commit the federal government to policies of equal employment opportunity, and once those policies were adopted with respect to defense industries in 1941 and more broadly in the early 1960s, to see that they were enforced consistently and evenhandedly.

In the 1960s, the NUL supplemented its traditional social service approach with a more activist commitment to civil rights: it embraced direct action and community organization, helped to organize the march on Washington of 1963 and the poor people's campaign of 1968, called for a domestic Marshall Plan, and began to concentrate on building ghetto power as a means to social change. Its program reflected a combination of new activism and historical NUL concerns. Together with the Child Study Association of America and the Family Service Association of America,* for example, the NUL participated in Project ENABLE (Education and Neighborhood Action for Better Living Environment), financed by the federal Office of Economic Opportunity. ENABLE recruited and trained social work aides in sixty-one cities to serve as a bridge between slum families and community services, especially in the areas of child rearing, employment, and education. In 1966, a grant from the Ford Foundation allowed the NUL to undertake Operation Equality, a project to attack segregated housing patterns and expand fair housing programs in eight cities. In the wake of the race riots of 1967, the NUL and the Urban Coalition pushed the nation's insurance industry to commit a billion dollars to the reconstruction of black ghettos. In Washington, Project Alert hired youth leaders in tense neighborhoods to put community residents in touch with the local league and other agencies. A grant from the Rockefeller Foundation enabled the NUL to initiate a leadership development program in thirty-one cities, whereby local trainees were educated in the workings of their city and organized in important community action efforts with respect to police brutality, educational discrimination, violations of housing codes, and discrimination in employment, among others. The NUL continued its employment efforts with its national skills bank, launched in 1962, a clearinghouse for skilled positions for blacks. In 1964, the United States Department of Labor (USDL) awarded the NUL a contract under the Manpower and Development Training Act to train unemployed blacks for industrial employment. Urban League street academies prepared teenaged public school dropouts in black ghettos for college entrance. And voter education and registration projects added significant numbers of blacks to the voting rolls and brought them to the polls in more than fifty cities in 1964 and 1968.

First guided by George Haynes, the NLUCAN in 1917 came under the direction of his assistant, Eugene Kinckle Jones, a former high school teacher with a master's degree in sociology from Cornell University. When Jones retired because of ill health in 1941, he was succeeded as executive secretary by Lester B. Granger, educated at Dartmouth and the New York School of Social Work, previously secretary of the NUL's depression-era workers' bureau. Granger stepped down in 1961, turning the NUL's leadership over to Whitney M. Young,

Jr., formerly dean of the Atlanta School of Social Work. Following Young's unexpected death, the executive secretaryship passed in 1972 to Vernon E. Jordan, Jr., a lawyer then serving as executive director of the United Negro College Fund. While the league's executive secretaries have always been black and its executive staff predominantly black, its presidents have always been white, and its executive board has always been interracial, dominated by educators, social workers, lawyers, doctors, and philanthropist-reformers.

The NUL has depended for its financial support chiefly on private philanthropy, with an emphasis on major gifts from foundations, such as various Rockefeller funds and the Carnegie Corporation (CC). From time to time, special gifts have allowed the NUL to develop new program areas; a gift in 1921 from the CC, for example, funded the establishment of the department of research and investigations. Increasingly in the 1960s, federal grants supported some league activities; money from the USDL, for instance, made possible league development and administration of on-the-job training programs for unemployed and underemployed blacks. Local Urban Leagues have derived their financial support mainly from community chests.

The NUL's papers are housed in the Manuscript Division of the Library of Congress. Two books treat the NUL history. Guichard Parris and Lester Brooks, *Blacks in the City: A History of the National Urban League* (1971), an in-house history prepared for the NUL's sixtieth anniversary, is the only full survey. Nancy J. Weiss, *The National Urban League, 1910–1940* (1974), is a scholarly study that sets the NUL's efforts in its early decades in the context of the struggle for racial advancement and larger social and political developments. Arvarh E. Strickland, *History of the Chicago Urban League* (1966), is the only book about an NUL affiliate. *Opportunity* is a rich respository of information about Urban League activities, especially its social welfare projects. While the existing studies of the agency are comprehensive in scope, they have focused especially on the NUL as a vehicle for racial advancement, so that more work can profitably be done in this area by students of social welfare.

Nancy J. Weiss

NATIONAL WELFARE RIGHTS ORGANIZATION (NWRO). In the early 1960s, the so-called welfare-rights movement originated. Perhaps the first indigenous organization of welfare recipients developed in the Watts section of Los Angeles in 1963. The leader of this movement was Mrs. Johnnie Tillmon, who became the first national chairman of the National Welfare Rights Organization (NWRO). The most important founder, however, was Dr. George Wiley, who had a doctorate in organic chemistry and who had taught briefly. Dr. Wiley had also worked for a year as an associate national director of the Congress of Racial Equality (CORE), where he developed important contacts with the leaders of the civil-rights movement. For about three months, Dr. Wiley had also worked for the Citizens Crusade Against Poverty (CCAP), an organization founded by the United Auto Workers in 1965. Wiley tried unsuccessfully to convince the CCAP to become an action center such as the Poverty/Rights Actions Center (PRAC) he opened in Washington, D.C., in late May 1966. A mixture of events and ideologies in the spring and summer of 1966 led consequently to the growth of welfare recipients' consciousness and to the further development of the welfare-rights movement. In the May 2, 1966, issue of *The Nation,* Columbia University professors of social work, Frances Fox Piven and Richard Cloward, outlined a strategy whereby welfare recipients could demand so much from centers as to immobilize the welfare system, which they viewed as clearly inadequate. Wiley knew Professor Cloward through his experiences at CORE. Discussions with both Professors Piven and Cloward helped to influence Wiley to enter the field of welfare rights.

In many ways, Piven and Cloward were the ideologues of the welfare-rights movement and of the early NWRO itself. Perhaps reacting to the publicity surrounding the article in *The Nation,* welfare recipients in Cleveland, Ohio, planned to march 155 miles to the state capital in Columbus, hoping to arrive there on June 30, 1966. Wiley heard of this project, and he began to organize rallies for June 30 in about twenty other cities. Following the successful demonstrations in August 1966, about one hundred representatives from seventy-five welfare recipients' organizations in twenty-three cities met in Chicago and established the National Coordinating Committee of Welfare Rights Groups. This group then chose Wiley's PRAC to lead the welfare-rights movement. The NWRO was officially established in the summer of 1967 in Washington, D.C., when a group of poor people and welfare recipients held a conference and organized a formal national agency. Capitalizing on the experiences of the earlier civil-rights movement, the welfare-rights campaign utilized representatives from social work groups and from the civil rights and labor movements, as well as support from church and social work groups.

The NWRO began its activities spiritedly, coordinating local groups and their demonstrations throughout the country. In late 1966, for instance, the NWRO demonstrated against the inaction by the United States Congress on welfare legislation, and in early 1967, leader Wiley criticized the establishment of a two-year commission to study the issue of a guaranteed minimum income as a purposeful delaying tactic. The NRWO quickly became the national spokesman for welfare clients' rights. In early 1968, the organization went to court to challenge the state of Mississippi for stopping welfare payments without a proper hearing for the affected individual. Trying to establish itself as the nation's conscience for welfare issues, the NWRO, through George Wiley, argued, in late 1968 that thirty million Americans below the poverty level should be on the federal welfare rolls.

The year 1969 marked the beginning of the NWRO's national prominence. With growing influence and a nationwide constituency, the organization had, through Director Wiley, a voice in Washington, D.C. Membership was doubling every six months, and in early 1969, there were thirty thousand members, with chapters in about one hundred cities. Although membership was open to all races, most were black. The agency received nationwide attention in May 1969 when some members in New York City disrupted the proceedings of the National Conference on Social Welfare* (NCSW), holding about fifteen hundred delegates captive for nearly an hour while the NWRO presented its demands. The demands included paying the NWRO $35,000 from the conference registration fees to help organize welfare recipients. The demands also called for welfare leaders to work for the complete restructuring of the welfare system, placing power in the hands of the poor. Further disruptions prompted the conference to appoint a four-member commission to raise funds for the NWRO, and the delegates voted to conduct a mail canvass of all nine thousand members of the NCSW to determine if the organization should raise the $35,000. The NCSW agreed to have 250 welfare clients attend the proceedings in 1970.

Also in 1969, the increasingly vocal NWRO was critical of welfare policies and practices, notably those of President Richard M. Nixon. In a speech in August 1969, Dr. Wiley attacked the president's welfare plan. In testimony before Congress in October, the agency threatened widespread disruptions if President Nixon's plan to force welfare mothers with school-age children to work were implemented. In December 1969, the NWRO demanded that the president order that free food stamps be given to all poor people, and a full-page advertisement in *The New York Times* a few weeks later urged President Nixon to declare a hunger emergency. President Nixon, characteristically, implemented neither of these plans. The NWRO was also active in opposing the practices and plans of New York State Governor Nelson Rockefeller and of New York City officials. In August 1969, the NWRO sponsored demonstrations that helped to influence the New York City Board of Education resolution restoring clothing and other benefits to poor families. In April, the NWRO denounced the state welfare cuts. Director Wiley himself led a demonstration in Central Park opposing the plan. In July, he led another one in New York City welfare offices. In November, the NWRO held a New York State Conference of the Welfare Rights Organization, in Syracuse. About a hundred delegates attended the sessions, held simultaneously with the New York State Welfare Conference. Both groups agreed to campaign against Governor Rockefeller and to press for further benefits.

The NWRO not only criticized practices, but it also initiated some important programs for welfare recipients and developed some projects to enlighten public policy. In March 1969, the NWRO threatened to boycott Sears-Roebuck stores unless the company gave credit to welfare recipients. The company did not cooperate, and demonstrations at the New York City store, led by Director Wiley, highlighted the boycott. Another chain store, Montgomery Ward, however, agreed to give $100 credit to three thousand welfare recipients who belonged to the NWRO. The NWRO chose the people, and Montgomery Ward screened them according to normal procedures in this one-year pilot project. Suggesting the respect the NWRO had gained, in late February 1969, Wiley and organization leaders met with the secretary of the United States Department of Health, Education, and Welfare (DHEW), Robert H. Finch, who called the welfare mothers of the NWRO an important constituency of the DHEW. In the summer of 1969, the NWRO sponsored an experiment for congressmen and their families to live for one week on a welfare budget. After a few months, the NWRO received from a group of ministers the money they had saved by following the welfare diet themselves. In December, the NWRO announced that it planned to lobby for its proposed $5,500 minimum income at the forthcoming White House Conference on Food, Nutrition, and Health.

The NWRO acted and spoke aggressively, but there was some dissension within the organization itself. In late May 1969, for instance, the Philadelphia chapter denounced the NWRO for accepting a nearly $435,000 contract from the United States Department of Labor to help implement a new federal work incentive program for welfare recipients. At the biennial convention in August 1969, Wiley and Chairman Mrs. Johnnie Tillmon, both black themselves, were accused of collusion with the federal government and of dismissing about ten black staff members at the NWRO's national headquarters in Washington, D.C. Dissenting members staged a demonstration critical of Wiley, and further disturbances occurred when the displeased faction denounced the cafeteria of Wayne State University in Detroit because of the apparently poor quality of the breakfast. The delegates, however, later unified to approve of an aggressive program for the next two years. The results included promoting the so-called spend-the-rent project to force landlords, including public housing developments, to consider changes in public welfare policies. The NWRO also resolved, at the convention, to begin a nationwide movement to obtain wage supplements for the working poor.

In the early 1970s, the NWRO continued to use militant tactics to support welfare recipients rights, and the organization also utilized other means to help its constituency. In April 1970, with President Nixon attending the ceremonies honoring astronaut Thomas Paine, members of the NWRO caused a disruption to protest the federal government's spending practices. At an anti-Vietnam War rally in May 1970, NWRO Vice-President Beulah Sanders urged men to burn their draft cards. A few days later, members of the NWRO demonstrated in Secretary Finch's office, demanding a $5,500 minimum income guarantee and calling on the government to shift funds being spent for the war to help the poor at home. In a characteristic act of defiance in 1971, NWRO cochairman James Branscome threw into a wastebasket the list of participants in the forthcoming White House Conference on Children and Youth because Director Wiley was not included. He also charged that the delegates represented such establishment and antiwelfare agencies as the chambers of commerce and the American Bankers Association. In April 1972, the NWRO staged a week-long protest in Nevada because that state had eliminated clients from the welfare rolls.

In the early 1970s, the NWRO increasingly used the courts and lobbying techniques to support the rights and interests of welfare recipients. In January 1970, for instance, the NWRO attorney filed suit in a United States circuit court to allow welfare recipients to participate in hearings to determine if a particular state's welfare program conformed to federal laws and regulations. In April 1970, the NWRO urged the DHEW to enforce its ruling that thirty-nine states did not meet federal standards. In 1972, there were more lawsuits, including one to bar possible cancer-causing hormones in beef. Other lawsuits successfully forbid states from keeping confidential applications for exemptions from welfare rules and challenged the DHEW from withholding public information about state applications for changes in their welfare systems. The NWRO charged, correctly, that this tactic of keeping plans secret hindered the NWRO's organizing and protest activities. The NRWO campaigned against unfriendly officials. In 1971, for example, with other groups, the NWRO unsuccessfully opposed the appointment of Earl Butz as United States secretary of agriculture. A NWRO suit attacking new welfare laws in New Jersey was dismissed in July 1971. But at the convention in the summer of 1971, the NWRO drafted plans to become involved in state and national politics. Director Wiley began to talk of a welfare caucus at the Democratic party's national convention in 1972. Although the NWRO conducted demonstrations at the convention in the summer of 1972, the Democratic party defeated the agency's guaranteed minimum income plan for its platform. In 1972, Wiley charged that the DHEW intentionally refused to give children Medicare forms for medical care due to them under the Social Security Act of 1967. The NWRO's influence in the nationwide black community became clear when the agency's poor peoples' platform was included in the national black political agenda, which itself reflected the major concerns and interests of blacks in 1972. The NWRO suffered a major loss when founder and Director Wiley announced his resignation as of December 31, 1972. He hoped to start a new group, Movement for Economic Justice. More damaging to the NWRO and the welfare-rights movement was the loss of its guiding figure in the summer of 1973, when George Wiley drowned.

Associate Director Tillmon replaced Wiley as executive director in early 1974, but the NWRO did not recover from its loss of Wiley. In 1974, there were reports of a leadership battle within the organization. The NWRO continued to attack, verbally and legally, the welfare system, but the agency seemed to lack the kind of clout and drama it had during Wiley's tenure. The NWRO was critical of President Gerald Ford's welfare policies and practices. The agency participated in a suit charging that officials viewed work relief as cheap labor, and in early 1974, the NWRO was invited by the Symbionese Liberation Army to help in the food distribution in California, which was part of the ransom for the kidnapping of Patty Hearst. But, unable to pay its rent or phone bill, the NWRO closed its office in the spring of 1975 and disbanded.

The primary sources for studying the NWRO's history include *The Welfare Fighter,* a monthly publication, which is difficult to locate in libraries, and *The*

New York Times, which covered the agency extensively. Joseph E. Paull, ''Recipients Aroused,'' *Social Work* 12 (April 1967): 101–106, helps to explain the NWRO's origins.

NAVY RELIEF SOCIETY (NRS). The idea for a welfare agency to provide assistance to needy families of men in the United States Navy and Marines and to the dependents of deceased men had been recognized in navy circles around the turn of the twentieth century. When a physician from Philadelphia, Dr. J. William White, suggested that about $9,000 in proceeds from the army-navy football game of 1903 be utilized for such a purpose, top naval officers, including Admiral George Dewey, approved enthusiastically. Consequently, on January 23, 1904, a group of nineteen people, including Anna Roosevelt Cowles, Admiral Dewey, and other naval leaders, incorporated the Navy Relief Society (NRS) in Washington, D.C., to provide charitable assistance to families and children of the men in the navy and marines.

The bylaws of the new NRS provided that the board of incorporators—which always had nineteen members—choose the fifteen-member executive board of managers, which in turn conducted the NRS's business. The board, which always included navy officers, chose from among its own members an executive committee to conduct the daily work in the summer months. The other committees established in 1904, the NRS's first year, included finance, organization, and education. The relief and employment committee of the board of managers conducted the central activities of dispensing funds to needy men and their families. The first headquarters was apparently in Washington, D.C. The early structure of officers was more complex than other similar relief agencies and included three vice-presidents, fifteen honorary vice-presidents, both a recording and a corresponding secretary, and three trustees, two of whom were John L. Cadawalder of New York, an attorney and civic leader, and the NRS's originator, Dr. J. William White of Philadelphia. The first president was a prominent Washington woman, Mrs. F. J. Higginson. In 1905, Admiral Dewey became the NRS's president.

In these first few years, the basic structure and functions of the NRS crystallized. Auxiliaries around major naval bases devloped quickly to help implement the process of providing funds to eligible persons. In 1906, the NRS began obtaining reports of deaths and disabilities directly from the Bureau of Medicine and Surgery to facilitate the process of relief, handled as often as possible through the auxiliaries. In that same year, the NRS began what later developed as a full-scale activity: it paid board and tuition at school for two young girls. In 1907, signs of a recurrent theme emerged: sluggish contributors from the fleet itself. President Dewey urged strongly that the organization committee implement its plan of having ship captains explain the NRS verbally rather than relying so heavily on what he thought were ineffective written appeals. An amendment to the bylaws in 1909, making the mothers of navy-marine personnel eligible for relief, broadened the basis of the work, as did other changes in the bylaws in later years.

The era of World War I expanded and clarified the activities of the NRS. The war-related activities of both the American National Red Cross* (ANRC) and the NRS led to conflicts between the two groups and even the fear that the ANRC would absorb the NRS. But the personal intervention of Eleanor Roosevelt, the wife of the assistant secretary of the navy and who then served on the board of incorporators, allayed the fears and helped to clarify the activities of each agency. Also, the establishment of a government-sponsored insurance plan questioned briefly the need for the NRS. The NRS, however, proved its value by getting funds to the needy much more promptly than did the government insurance bureau. The incorporators in 1920 expanded the list of eligible recipients to include the dependents of disabled—in addition to those of deceased—naval-marine personnel. In 1920, an amendment of the bylaws allowed the auxiliaries to elect five members to the board of managers.

In the period between the two world wars, the NRS continued its basic activities but expanded as situations dictated. Beginning in 1921, the NRS urged Congress to provide proper hospital care for the families and dependents of naval-marine men. The continued failure of Congress to provide proper hospital care for these men led the NRS, as in 1927, to begin endowing beds or rooms for dependents in particular private hospitals near naval bases. Also, in the late 1920s, auxiliaries began to hire home service nurses to assist families, a service that volunteers from local auxiliaires and branches also conducted. When the Great Lakes Auxiliary ended its affairs in 1921, it left $20,000 to the Chicago Lying-In Hospital to care for naval-marine men's wives. As economic conditions deteriorated in the mid-1920s, the NRS began a loan program, which became controversial within the organization. By 1930, the program occupied three-fourths of the time of the secretary's office. In mid-September 1932, the volume of requests forced the board of managers to reduce allotments by five dollars as some banks carrying NRS funds foreclosed. By 1939, economic conditions were such that the board favored renting rather than endowing hospital beds.

A vigorous fund-raising campaign changed the gloomy status of the NRS. Chaired by prominent New York City banker Clarence Dillon, the campaign of the national citizens' committee began in 1942. It netted over $10 million, which became the NRS's reserve fund. Also in 1942, the board of control of the Naval Institute allotted funds to the NRS. A sound investment policy, guided by a finance committee of the board of managers, coupled with significant donations like the $1 million Selfridge Fund, made the NRS comfortable financially. The interest from the reserve fund alone still pays for all the administrative costs, including those of the auxiliaries and branches. Despite occasional criticism within the navy that the NRS was well financed, the annual drive among the navy continued, which also served to publicize the agency.

The important fund-raising successes of the World War II period and the executive leadership of Vice-Admiral Vincent Murphy, who served from 1947 to 1963, strengthened the NRS services. Beginning in 1945, the field visiting service facilitated relations between the Washington area headquarters and the auxiliaries around the country. Initially called the special assistant to the executive vice-president, in January 1948, field visitors became field representatives, whose numbers grew steadily to five in 1971. Beginning in 1948, field representatives taught courses in social work to volunteer women in the auxiliaries. Increasingly, executive secretaries of auxiliaries were trained social workers, and in 1966, the board of managers established the Myrle James Scholarship Fund to train naval dependents in professional social work. In 1964, the board established the NRS education fund, providing interest-free loans for naval dependents' educations. Regional and national conferences of executive secretaries further enriched the NRS professional social work.

Throughout its history, the NRS has had comparatively little organizational changes. Apparently in 1924, the board of incorporators dissolved itself. In May 1942, the NRS created the post of executive vice-president as the chief administrative officer, and in November 1946, the board of managers decided that a retired naval officer should always fill the post, which became the president in 1963. The number of auxiliaries has fluctuated as naval installations closed and opened and as personnel shifted, but in 1973, there were fifty-five auxiliaries, including a number abroad.

Government-sponsored benefits for the armed forces continually replaced NRS services, but the society adapted well. It still supplemented federal allotments in needy cases, and in August 1969, for instance, it conducted disaster relief for victims of Hurricane Camille in Mississippi.

The principal primary source for studying the NRS's history is its detailed published *Annual Reports*. There does not appear to be a scholarly history of the NRS.

NEAR EAST RELIEF (NER). During World War I, a number of relief agencies developed in the United States to aid people in war-torn countries abroad. The Persian War Relief Fund (PWRF), for instance, was founded in March 1915 under the sponsorship of the Presbyterian Board of Missions (PBM). In the spring of 1915, the PBM also helped to organize the Syria-Palestine Committee (SPC). Later in 1915, in September, the Committee on Armenian Atrocities (CAA) was established. Responding to a call from Henry Morgenthau, Sr., the American ambassador to Turkey, these three agencies—the SPC, PWRF, and CAA—merged to form the American Committee for Armenian and Syrian Relief (ACASR) in November 1915. American colleges in Turkey and Syria and the American Board of Commissioners for Foreign Missions (ABCFM) also sponsored the ACASR. The chairman was Dr. James L. Barton of the ABCFM. Day-to-day direction was provided by Charles Vernon Vickrey of the Laymen's Mission Movement. Most important of the lay leaders was Cleveland Hoadley Dodge, a philanthropist from New York who had close ties to both missionary and educational activities in the Near East.

During the war, relief workers—missionaries and educators—provided temporary shelter, first aid, and food. In Persia, missionaries lent seed grain and distributed farm implements in order to restore food production. Families in the United States sent remittances to relatives in Syria. In Anatolia, the principal area of need, mission hospitals and schools housed the ill along with thousands of children.

By publicizing the "Terrible Turk" and the "Starving Armenians," the ACASR reached a wide public through *The New York Times* and the *Literary Digest,* as well as through nationally known speakers such as Henry Morgenthau, Sr., Oscar Straus, and Abram Elkus, both former ministers to Turkey, Charles Evans Hughes, and William Howard Taft. By 1917, a nationwide, fund-raising organization was functioning. ACASR receipts in 1915 amounted to $176,000 and reached $19 million in 1919. While the war in Europe was over by 1919, turmoil continued in the Near East. Consequently, to establish more permanent relief there, the United States Congress incorporated the ACASR as the Near East Relief (NER) in August 1919. Congress charged NER with providing relief and assisting in the "repatriation, rehabilitation and re-establishment of suffering and dependent peoples of the Near East." The principal sponsors were the ABCFM, the PBM, and the independent colleges.

By the end of 1920, the new NER had over five hundred relief workers abroad, ministering to some four million refugees including 400,000 children. Concentrating on the children, NER gathered them into mission stations in Turkey and into army barracks in Alexandropol, Soviet Armenia. Because thousands of the children had trachoma, scabies, or favus, NER undertook a massive prophylaxis program. The youngsters were taught trades such as shoemaking, baking, tinsmithing, and tailoring. In Constantinople, NER operated day nurseries for the children of working mothers and treatment centers for victims of tuberculosis and trachoma. Destitute adults were fed and clothed. The American Relief Administration* (ARA), the United States Grain Corporation, and The Commonwealth Fund* provided NER with funds and foodstuffs.

As turmoil continued, NER officials sought political solutions, choosing first an American mandate for Armenia. While President Woodrow Wilson approved, Congress did not, whereupon Barton and Dodge persuaded President Wilson to ask Congress to loan funds to the Armenian republic; Congress declined. Next, NER sought to replace Admiral Bristol, the pro-Turkish American high commissioner. In the aftermath of Mustapha Kemal's victory, Barton, recognizing the need to reach an accommodation with Turkey, became a leading proponent of ratification of the Lausanne Treaty, which abrogated the capitulations, established most-favored-nation commercial relations, and guaranteed American religious, educational, and medical institutions treatment equal to that enjoyed by similar Turkish institutions.

Mustapha Kemal's victory in 1922 created a crisis of major proportions, although paradoxically it brought peace. The burning of Smyrna (Izmir) in September 1922 left 260,000 homeless refugees, mostly Greeks. Supported by the American Women's Hospitals, NER provided food, shelter, and medical care. The League of Nations negotiated an exchange of populations, bringing some 300,000 Turks living in Greece to Asia Minor, while transporting the remaining Greek and Armenian residents of Turkey to Greece. Although a League of Nations operation, NER fed and housed the refugees until they were placed aboard ships for repatriation. Most of this work was completed in 1923.

As a result of Kemal's victory, NER evacuated its orphan charges from Anatolia to Syria or the Greek island of Syra where facilities for twenty-five thousand children were constructed. Children were taught various trades until they were about sixteen. In cities, where their former wards tended to congregate, NER sponsored low-cost shelter, recreation and social programs, and night school classes.

In the Caucasus, NER operated a seventeen-thousand-acre farm school that combined classes and work. Once a youth had mastered farming skills, he was assigned a tract of land and became self-supporting. Difficulties with Soviet authorities led NER to withdraw from this project in 1924, although orphanages at Alexandropol (Leninakan) continued until 1930.

The most significant postwar activity of NER was its effort to design programs that would enable the local populations to provide for themselves better. In conjunction with other groups interested in the Near East, NER commissioned a systematic survey of economic and social conditions in the Near East, resulting in *The Near East and American Philanthropy* (1929). Accordingly, in 1928, NER initiated an experimental program of agricultural technical assistance and community development work in Macedonia. Then in 1920, as it concluded its orphan relief work, NER reorganized as the Near East Foundation to support a program of agricultural extension services, home demonstration work, public health projects, recreation, and adult education work. This new program became a precursor of Point Four.

By 1930, NER had raised $91,146,000, exclusive of aid-in-kind. Only the American National Red Cross* and the ARA had functioned on a larger scale.

James L. Barton, *The Story of Near East Relief* (1915–1930) (1930), is by far the guiding spirit of NER. The *Annual Reports* of NER were published privately or as Senate documents from 1920 through 1928. The organization's files have been destroyed, but correspondence relating to the ACASR and NER is found in the ABCFM papers, Houghton Library, Cambridge, Massachusetts. Minutes of the PWRF and Syria-Palestine Relief are held by the Presbyterian Mission Library, New York City. The *News Bulletin of the ACASR* (1917–1919) and the *New Near East* (1920–1927) are official publications. Robert L. Daniel, *American Philan-*

thropy in the Near East 1820–1960 (1970), details the work of NER; the bibliography should be consulted.

Robert L. Daniel

NEEDLEWORK GUILD OF AMERICA, INC., THE (NGA). In 1882, a serious mine accident in Wales left many orphans who became wards of an asylum run and financed by Lady Giana Wolverton of Iwerne, Dorsetshire, England. Lady Wolverton subsequently asked each of her friends to bring two sets of new clothes for the children. Publicity of this work appeared in the London, England, press. Mrs. Alanson Hartpence of Philadelphia, Pennsylvania, read about these developments on her trip to England in early 1885. In the spring of 1885, in Philadelphia, Hartpence described Lady Wolverton's work for the children at a prayer meeting of six young women, one of whom was Hartpence's niece, Laura Stafford. The young women recognized this simple activity as an answer to their prayers to do constructive work, and they promptly founded The Needlework Guild of America, Inc. (NGA), when they organized themselves as the Needlework Guild of Philadelphia (NGP) in June 1885. They quickly elected traditional officers and adopted fundamental rules. The women did not plan initially to expand their work of receiving garments and distributing them to local charities, but the interests of other women in Philadelphia led the group to describe its activities in a publication appearing in June 1885. The pamphlet led quickly to the expansion of the parent group, or guild, as it came to be called, and to the establishment of other branches in the Philadelphia area. In its first year of operation, the NGP and its branches collected and distributed nearly a thousand garments to charitable institutions and agencies. An important organizational activity and feature, the "ingathering," developed in the first year when, in late October 1885, a large group of women assembled to sew and repair over nine hundred pieces of garments.

During the early years of the organization, its national structure developed gradually. Locally, in Philadelphia, the work had religious overtones; the local Women's Bible Reading Society, for example, helped to distribute garments. Notices of the work in several religious papers, such as *The National Baptist* in October 1888, attracted new members of the original guild and led to the founding of two new branches within a few months. In 1888, when the founder, Laura Safford, now Laura Stewart, lived in New Jersey, she organized and led branches in Montclair and Glen Ridge. Other branches in New York, New Jersey, Pennsylvania, and even California were organized by the early 1890s. In 1891, the NGP changed its name to The Needlework Guild of America (NGA) to reflect its nationwide organization. In the next year, the NGA opened its national office, a desk in the offices of the Philadelphia Ladies' Depository and Exchange for Women's Work. Also, in 1892, sections—or subdivisions of a branch with at least 110 garments—were developed. In the spring of the 1896, the six original organizers incorporated the NGA in Philadelphia. By 1900, the national organization had 311 branches in forty states, and the NGA collected nearly 330,000 garments in 1900.

In the early twentieth century, the NGA crystallized its structure, expanded its activities, and moved to larger headquarters in Philadelphia. The major officers changed titles frequently, but early in the century they were established as honorary president, national president, national secretary, national treasurer, and national corresponding secretary. The board of directors, which included the four national officers, numbered fifteen in 1904. In the late nineteenth and early twentieth centuries, the NGA published *The Altruist,* which described its and similar organizations' work and helped to increase membership in the NGA. In 1907, the NGA became affiliated with the American National Red Cross* (ANRC), in 1909 with the General Federation of Women's Clubs, and in 1917 with the Camp Fire Girls.* Between 1906 and 1920, over a hundred branches were organized. The NGA developed its work nationwide. For example, in 1903 and 1904, it helped the victims of floods in Topeka, Kansas, and of floods and fires in Baltimore, Maryland. In 1906, it aided earthquake victims in San Francisco, sending them repaired and recycled clothing.

With the outbreak of World War I in 1914, the NGA established services abroad. To honor former President Theodore Roosevelt's son, Quentin, who was killed in the war, the NGA concentrated on aiding St. Quentin in France, and in 1914, the NGA opened a workshop in Lyons, France, to aid the community. In May 1916, the NGA established its war relief department in New York City, which operated until August 1931. The death of its chairman, founder Stewart, in June 1931, prompted the demise of the war relief department. During World War I, branches throughout the country enlarged NGA activities, caring for over 230 war orphans. To recognize and to honor these and other NGA wartime services, the French government conferred on Stewart "la Décoration de Chevalier de l'Orde Nationale de la Légion d'honneur" on July 16, 1928.

At home, the NGA became more widely known in the United States because it participated in the home service work of the ANRC throughout the country in the 1920s. In 1927, the NGA distributed materials to victims of the flooding of the Mississippi River. By the late 1920s, the NGA was also a member of the National Conference of Social Work* and the National Council of Women of the United States. Despite such charitable and almost patriotic activities, in the 1920s, many ultraconservative organizations and individuals implicated the NGA in the right-wing "spider web" of dangerous, subsersive groups. Although the NGA had had younger members since its inception, the appointment in 1925 of a director for junior work shaped and made this particular organizational activity more important. In 1925, to honor the fortieth anniversary, the branches initiated a "thanking offer," or fund-raising drive, which the leaders decided to use to promote extension activities.

During the Great Depression of the 1930s, the NGA concerned itself primarily with organizational rather than national problems. One depression-related development—the practice of many branches collecting items other than clothing for their local charitable institutions and hospitals—came under heavy and repeated criticism from the board of directors and from the secretary in national headquarters. Sloppy collections and distributions of legitimate items, along with the failure of many branch officials to report their specific work to national headquarters, also drew repeated criticism during the decade. Late in the 1930s, the NGA, which consistently borrowed and quickly returned cash from the endowment fund to finance the functioning of the national office, instituted such economies as sending only one convention invitation per branch and reducing the size of the *Biennial Report,* which formerly contained detailed lists and addresses of members.

An important organizational event occurred when long-time president, Mrs. Thomas J. Preston of Princeton, New Jersey, resigned in May 1938. In the late 1930s, the board of directors approved, effective in 1940, a rotating board, with each member elected for four rather than two years. More importantly, in 1939, the board instituted changes in the national office, reducing the executive secretary's salary, appointing an energetic volunteer, Alma Desbraugh, as her assistant, and, after completing an inventory, discarding all unnecessary papers and records. In December 1939, because the building in which the NGA had its headquarters was slated for demolition, the agency moved once again to another location in downtown Philadelphia. Highlights of social services in the 1930s included the increased volume of work by the branches and the NGA's cooperating actively with the President's Organization on Unemployment Relief in the early 1930s.

During World War II and through the early 1950s, branches continued to send money instead of garments to the national office, but NGA leaders, especially because of war-related shortages, could do little to prevent this practice. By the late 1940s, traditional activities returned, but public relations activities grew in importance. In 1946, the NGA began to publish *Verbal Snapshots,* a journal describing the work of the branches. The organizational highlight of 1948 was being placed on the list of the Radio Advertising Council, and the annual meeting in Philadelphia in May 1949 was broadcast nationally on radio for the first time. In 1948, the board of directors approved an experiment in publicity, which featured the development of a "ragged boy" poster to publicize NGA work. Characteristically for this agency—which relied on volunteers rather than professional help more than did other social service organizations—the executive secretary's grandson posed for the photograph on which the different-sized posters were based. When in 1949, the Massachusetts state chairman agreed to pay half the expenses, an expert in public relations and publicity was hired to work at the national offices. In the early 1950s, the NGA produced a film depicting its work and rented it to branches to help them publicize their activities locally. Because analyses by the NGA showed that National Membership Week was more effective in the fall than in the spring, the NGA shifted the week to early October. In the 1950s, the NGA apparently established its national headquarters for flood relief, which was centered at the national headquarters in Philadelphia.

In the 1960s and 1970s, the NGA remained much the same type of organization with limited changes and developments. Economizing to help make the diamond jubilee annual convention in 1960 a success, the NGA cancelled the annual convention in 1959. In the early 1960s, it launched a new publication, *NGA News.* In 1961 and 1962, the NGA modernized its national office. By 1965, when a little less than half its income came from branches and the rest from interest, investments, sales of publications, pins, and the like, the NGA had a small staff of four workers. In 1966, the organization published a manual in public relations to assist branch publicity chairmen. The NGA was not part of the major developments in social welfare in the 1960s. While more significant and even dramatic issues were developing in American social service, in 1967, for instance, an organizational highlight for the NGA occurred when the executive committee engaged an advisory service to handle investments. In the late 1960s, the NGA's national president noted perceptively that since World War II, especially in light of increased federal activity in social service, voluntary service had changed. But, she argued, the NGA adjusted and found there was still a function for the personalized service it offered. No significant developments occurred in the 1970s, as the NGA maintained its structure and its traditional function of providing garments and linens to the needy. In 1975, there were over three hundred branches in thirty states collecting almost a million pieces of garments each year. The national headquarters had a full-time staff of three workers.

The primary sources used in preparing this brief history include the *Annual* and *Biennial Reports,* as well as the *Reports of the Proceedings of the Annual Convention.* Miscellaneous publications at the New York Public Library, such as *Queries and Answers Concerning the NGA, 1912* (1912), also helped, as did some information from *The New York Times.* Arthur Burks, *United Littles: The Story of the NGA* (1955), is a popular and helpful history of the organization. There do not appear to be any scholarly historical studies of this veteran agency.

NEW YORK ASSOCIATION FOR IMPROVING THE CONDITION OF THE POOR (AICP). In the mid-nineteenth century, urban missionaries were becoming conscious of the plight of the urban poor as they traveled around cities promoting the Gospel. In New York City in the early 1840s, leaders of the New York City Tract Society (NYCTC) (see *Religious Organizations*) became aware of poverty, and during the depression of the late 1830s and the 1840s, four of the wealthiest leaders of the NYCTS began to discuss and then proposed, in July 1843, the establishment of a society for the relief of the worthy poor. The four men were James Boorman, a merchant and banker, Robert Minturn, a merchant and philanthropist, Apollos R. Westmore, and James Brown, who became president of the New York Association for Improving the Condition of the Poor (AICP), a position he retained until 1875. These men developed a constitution, which the NYCTS's executive committee promptly approved.

The group hired a professional agent, Robert M. Hartley, to visit other cities to learn about similar societies to help organize the New York group. A New York merchant, Hartley had strong ties with religious organizations in nineteenth-century New York. After hearing Hartley's reports, in January 1844, the group issued an "address to the public," which announced the establishment of the AICP as the New-York Association for the Improvement of the Condition of the Poor (AICP). In early 1845, the group of founders and supporters met and adopted the group's constitution. It provided for a president, five vice-presidents, a treasurer, a secretary, and a general agent. The agency also had a hundred-member board of managers. The AICP adapted the NYCTS scheme of dividing the city into districts conforming to the wards; each district was subdivided into sections, each with the same estimated number of poor people. Each district had an advisory committee and each section a visitor. All the members and workers were initially men, some of whom were paid.

In 1847, the organization changed its name to the New-York Association for Improving the Condition of the Poor (AICP). A certificate of incorporation, approved on April 12, 1848, reduced the board of managers to twenty members—the sixteen district advisory committee chairmen and four elected members. In 1848, the agency established its supervisory council, a large group composed of the board of managers, the members of all the district advisory committees, and some elected members. The board of managers functioned as its own executive committee until 1883, when it created a five-member executive committee, a finance committee, a tenement house committee, a committee on supplies, a committee on nominations, and an auditing committee.

The AICP plunged into the activities that made it one of the leading nineteenth-century social service agencies. In its first year of operation, it loaned coal stoves and collected and distributed old clothes and scraps of food for the impoverished. In 1846, it formally began its long and important activities in housing reform, establishing a committee to study the housing of the city's poor. A new committee, appointed in 1853, conducted a study and produced a report that remained, for many years, the model for housing and public health reformers in nineteenth-century urban America. Another early study in October 1845 produced a plan to develop health facilities in the city, and in 1851, the AICP opened its Demelt Dispensary, followed in 1869 by another, The Northern Dispensary. The AICP's first tract, *The Economist,* published in 1847, stressed the basics of nutrition, another field in which the agency pioneered. General Agent Hartley led a campaign in the city against swill milk. This effort resulted in an official state investigation in 1858. In 1852, the AICP opened the first people's public bath, and in 1862, it founded the Society of the Ruptured and Crippled, which operated a hospital dealing largely with injured workers. Even before the

Progressive era reformers, this pioneering social welfare agency saw that occupational injuries caused poverty and were preventable. Consistently concerned with the relationship between the social environment and the condition of life, the AICP opened, in 1855, its Workingmen's Home, a model tenement in Lower Manhattan. In the vanguard of the reform movement, which saw housing as the key to social improvement, the AICP appointed, in the late 1870s, a tenement house committee, which had paid investigators. This provided another early example of paid specialists in a social welfare agency. In this early period of AICP history, in 1847, it appointed a nursing committee, which visited and reported on conditions in the children's institutions on Randall's Island. The AICP helped to found the New York Juvenile Asylum as a pioneering reformatory in 1851.

The retirements, first of President James Brown in 1875 and then of the only general agent, Robert Hartley, in 1876, inaugurated another phase in the AICP's history. In the late 1870s, paid staff workers, particularly women, began to replace the previously all-male friendly visitors. In 1880, suggesting a decline in its ties with the urban missionary movement of earlier nineteenth-century New York, the agency moved its headquarters from the Bible House, where it had been since the early 1850s, to its own building on Fourth Avenue. In the early 1880s, the tenement house work changed from an "incidental labor" to a recognized department, and the public health work became more institutionalized in 1884, when the AICP created its sanitary department, a merger of the independent Sanitary Reform Society and the AICP tenement house inspection service. In 1883, the AICP inaugurated its long-standing program of sending poor mothers and their children on outings to the New York area seashores. The 1890s brought the expansion of these fresh air programs and such activities as peoples' baths and housing and nutrition work. The AICP cooperated in 1895 with a dietary study conducted and published by the United States Department of Agriculture. In 1894, it participated in an increasing concern of social reformers: urban congestion. It appointed a committee in April to study extensively the abandonment of rural New York State and its relation to urbanization. A contribution of $10,000 to the University Settlement for the striking cloakmakers in 1895 and implementing J. G. Phelps Stokes's urgings to establish a settlement, Hartley House, brought the AICP even closer to the social justice settlement movement. A reorganization in November 1892 created six departments, reflecting AICP activities and increasing the board of managers to thirty. The board in turn furnished five members for each department. This reorganization helped to establish another phase of the AICP's history.

The AICP was not committed enthusiastically to its settlement house and separated from Hartley House in 1903. The organization nevertheless spearheaded many Progressive programs and movements in New York City, some of which served as national models. In 1907, for instance, it assigned the first prenatal nurses in the nation to Caroline Rest, its home for convalescent mothers and their babies. In 1915, the AICP established one of its many pioneering work relief programs, this time employing Harry L. Hopkins as supervisor. The AICP also initiated programs that later became, or clearly should have become, Progressive public programs. Cooperating with the State Charities Aid Association* (SCAA) of New York, it created a program demonstrating that foundlings should be cared for in family homes rather than in institutions, where they died at incredibly high rates. The AICP campaign, begun in 1904, to establish a fresh air hospital for tuberculars eventually became the public Neponsit Beach Hospital, and the AICP committee on the physical welfare of schoolchildren conducted important studies that influenced the development of urban America's first public bureau of child hygiene. The AICP's city institution for sick babies, established adjacent to the Rockefeller Institute in 1906, influenced the proliferation, by around 1911, of baby health stations run by the New York City Department of Health. The AICP also developed, alone or with other agencies, programs for the unemployed and the homeless. In April 1913, the AICP consolidated the work of its departments into two departments: family welfare, directed by reformer William Mathews, and social welfare, which focused on public health and child welfare. The AICP continued to deal with pressing social problems up to American entry in the world war, studying venereal disease and expanding its health facilities. In 1917, the AICP inaugurated health facilities for black families in one of the most congested areas of the city, Columbus Hill.

As in its earlier history, in the Progressive and later years, some of the most influential philanthropists as well as some of the most respected agents in social work were affiliated with the AICP. AICP president for twenty years, R. Fulton Cutting was an important financier, civic leader, and philanthropist. J. G. Phelps Stokes and George Wickersham, the future United States attorney general, served the agency. Elizabeth Milbank Anderson, who established the Milbank Fund, supported many AICP projects. John Kingsbury, an important reformer close to the settlement movement who became New York City commissioner of charities in 1903, served as general agent. Harry Hopkins, who became a leading New Deal figure, joined the AICP staff, and William Mathews, who had important ties with the settlement movement and the New Deal, was on the staff for many years. Also William Allen, who had a distinguished career in New York public and social service, was an agent for the AICP.

AICP experiences during and after World War I, particularly in the health field, support the thesis that the war promoted rather than retarded social reform. Strikingly aware of the physical weaknesses revealed in draft board studies, the AICP, in 1918, established a community health center in the Italian section of New York, which functioned effectively until April 1939, when it and the AICP disbanded. The AICP organized its nutrition bureau in 1920, campaigned against rickets with the city Department of Health in 1921, extended its tuberculosis work in the 1920s, and continued to conduct public health activities in poor districts, especially in Negro areas like East Harlem. While other national and local agencies languished in the 1920s, the AICP established its vocational guidance bureau in 1926, opened the Tompkins Square Apartments for the aged in 1929, and with the National Committee for Mental Hygiene* established an experimental family welfare clinic in 1924.

The AICP also developed programs that showed the link between the Progressive reforms and the New Deal social welfare programs. In the mid-1920s, the AICP created the independent emergency work bureau, which demonstrated effectively the value of public works programs. The director of the project, William Mathews, brought Harry Hopkins to his staff at the AICP in the second decade of the twentieth century. While Franklin Delano Roosevelt was governor of New York, Mathews served on many state commissions where he consistently urged public works programs. The AICP's consistent attention to the social problems of unemployment resulted in a study in 1933 showing the relationship between unemployment and illness.

Despite the ongoing depression and the expansion of public welfare programs, the AICP continued to show the value of voluntary social service agencies in the 1930s. Focusing on a major agency activity since its inception, the AICP expanded its health work, establishing the Robert R. Moton Health Service in Harlem in 1939. As an institutional member of the American National Red Cross* since 1909, the AICP participated in the emergency flood relief in western Pennsylvania in 1937, demonstrating a national activity in which it had participated for many years. In light of national trends in social service, its program was obviously limited, and in 1936, the AICP appropriately simplified its structure. It created four services in traditional and new fields—family, fresh air and recreation, health, and old age. In 1938, the AICP began seriously to consider unifying with The Charity Organization Society of the City of New York* (COS). On February 1, 1939, the AICP decided officially to merge. Subsequently, on April 12, 1939, the AICP disbanded, joining with the COS to form the new Community Service Society* (CSS).

The sources for studying the AICP are voluminous and diverse. The *Annual Reports* and a host of publications are convenient primary sources. The local press covered the agency well, and the published and widely available *Index to The New York Times* facilitates primary research. The unpublished minutes of the NYCTS at the archives of the New York City Mission Society in the Charities Building in New York show the AICP origins. Most importantly, however, in the Archives of the CSS are the unpublished materials of the agency. The John A. Kingsbury Papers at the Library of Congress and the William Allen Reminiscences at the Oral History Project of Columbia University are two of the many other collections with AICP materials.

A host of scholars and others have used these materials to reconstruct various phases of AICP history, but there is no scholarly organizational history. Lilian Brandt, *Growth and Development of AICP and COS* (1942), is a generally sound and detailed account of this history. Roy Lubove, "The New York Association for Improving the Condition of the Poor: The Formative Years," *New-York Historical Society Quarterly* 42 (July 1959): 307–327, is helpful, but the chapter on the AICP in Carroll Smith Rosenberg, *Religion and the Rise of the City: The New York City Mission Movement, 1812–1870* (1971), shows more properly the religious origins of the AICP. John Duffy, *A History of Public Health in New York* (1968 and 1974), 2 vols., shows the influence of the AICP on public health, and Paul T. Ringenbach, *Tramps and Reformers, 1873–1916: The Discovery of Unemployment in New York* (1973), shows its concern in this area. Peter Romanofsky, " 'To Save the Lives of the City's Foundlings': The Joint Committee and New York City Child Care Practices, 1850–1907," *New-York Historical Society Quarterly,* 61 (January-April 1977), 49–68, reveals part of the AICP's concerns for children. Dorothy Becker's doctoral dissertation, "The Visitor to the New York City Poor, 1843–1920" (Columbia University, 1960), and, more conveniently, her "The Visitor to the New York City Poor, 1843–1920," *Social Service Review* 35 (December 1961): 382–396, point out the workings of the district system and the visitors' activities. Arnold S. Rosenberg, "John Adams Kingsbury and the Struggle for Social Justice in New York, 1906–1918" (Ph.D. diss., New York University, 1968), sketches his subject's years with the AICP.

NEW YORK PROBATION AND PROTECTIVE ASSOCIATION: see GIRLS AND BOYS SERVICE LEAGUE.

NEW YORK SOCIETY FOR THE PREVENTION OF CRUELTY TO CHILDREN, THE (NYSPCC). In New York City in the mid-nineteenth century, amid the grinding poverty plaguing many of its residents, child abandonment, desertion, cruelty toward children, and even, especially earlier in the century, infanticide were not uncommon. In June 1871, Henry Bergh, the founder and leader of the American Society for the Prevention of Cruelty to Animals (ASPCA) and a popular humanitarian, was asked to intervene in the case of a beaten child. After the court of general sessions found her foster mother guilty of child beating, the child was sent to live with her grandmother in Philadelphia. Bergh arranged these events.

The depression of 1873 apparently helped to increase incidences of child neglect, and in early 1874, Etta Wheeler, a volunteer worker at St. Luke's Mission in New York City, discovered a case of child beating. The police, social agencies, and missions that Wheeler approached each refused to act, so she finally went to Bergh, a recognized humanitarian. Bergh directed his attorney, Elbridge Gerry, and two agents of the ASPCA to invade the tenement flat of Mary Connolly, who had received the child, Mary Ellen, in 1866 from city charity officials. The three men took Mary Ellen, who then appeared in court on April 9, 1874. The judge sent Mary Ellen to a local institution, The Sheltering

Arms. This episode led Wheeler to ask Bergh to form an organization to protect children. Bergh realized that his own agency could not handle cases of child abuse adequately so he asked Gerry and the president of the ASPCA, a wealthy Quaker, John D. Wright, to help him form a new agency. Subsequently, these men sponsored a meeting on December 15, 1874, at Association Hall in New York City. At this meeting, The New York Society for the Prevention of Cruelty to Children (NYSPCC) was founded. As its name indicated clearly, the purpose of the NYSPCC was to act in the interests of the neglected and abused children of New York City. The founders urged interested people to sign up for the organization at the ASPCA headquarters and to attend the first meeting of the new organization on December 28, 1874.

Bergh and his ASPCA work were well known, and at the meeting on December 28, Gerry noted that some critics—of which the NYSPCC had many during its history—charged that the NYSPCC was founded by Protestants to interfere with Catholic children and to convert them. This religious issue was a constant theme in the care of dependent and other children in New York City in the nineteenth century. Gerry declared that the new organization would place Catholic children in Catholic institutions. At the meeting, Bergh pointed out the existence of so-called baby farms, whereby destitute women took in unwanted babies and often killed them. Bergh also stated the need for constructive efforts to end this abuse. Bergh himself could not spare time for the new organization, but he gave it office space in the ASPCA's headquarters. Wright went to Albany, New York, to lobby for incorporation, but the legislature, as well as much of the press of New York City, feared an expansion of Bergh's activities because of the religious issue and because of the authority such expansion would give him over "naughty" children. After weeks of efforts by Wright, however, the legislature granted the NYSPCC a charter on April 21, 1875. Formal incorporation was completed on April 27, 1875. President Wright then began the work of the NYSPCC in a temporary office at Broadway and Nineteenth Street in Manhattan.

The new NYSPCC began its work energetically. In late 1874, the agency worked on the case of a child placed in a heated stove who died. In a well-publicized episode, the society rescued a child acrobat, "Prince Leo," from his employers in late 1875 and then urged the public to boycott places using such children. Although many early activities involved saving other children from similar cases of abuse and neglect, the agency helped to influence constructive legislation as early as 1877, when a state law was enacted to prevent cruelty to children, apparently the first of its kind in the nation. An attorney for the NYSPCC, Lewis L. Delafield, wrote the bill. An early activity, Delafield's compilation of the laws relating to children initiated a continuing concern for legislation in the state. The press, which had been hostile, began gradually to support the NYSPCC's work. At the agency's first annual meeting on January 4, 1876, many prominent figures, such as William Cullen Bryant, the poet and the editor of the New York *Evening Post,* Reverend Henry W. Bellows, the leader of the Civil War–era United States Sanitary Commission,* a pioneering voluntary philanthropic organization, and Joseph H. Choate, the acknowledged leader of the New York City bar and a founder and long-time leader of the State Charities Aid Association* (SCAA) of New York, a leading social service agency—each praised the new NYSPCC.

The care of a four-year-old child indentured to a circus, discovered by agents from the NYSPCC in California, focused national attention on the agency in 1877. The episode also inspired the establishment of a society for the prevention of cruelty to children in San Francisco, modeled after the one in New York. In 1878, just three years after the agency began its work, its agents had visited over three thousand homes, suggesting the NYSPCC's zeal. As early as 1878, working through its agents, the United States commissioners of emigration in New York City and the acting Italian consul-general, the NYSPCC rescued children from the so-called padrone (or contract labor) system popular among certain immigrant groups, such as Italians and Greeks. Within a few years, the NYSPCC's efforts reduced substantially the number of children working through this exploitative system.

In the first of many sensationalized cases, in 1879, the NYSPCC exposed a shady institution in New York, the Shepherd's Fold, which was run by an Episcopalian clergyman, Reverend Dr. Edward Crowley. The case began when NYSPCC agents learned of an emaciated child in a local hospital. The society influenced a grand jury to probe the Shepherd's Fold, and a trial revealed how horribly children were treated there. By 1879, the NYSPCC had influenced the establishment of four similar societies for the prevention of cruelty to children in New York and sixteen in other states. On August 21, 1879, President John Wright died, depriving the agency of one of its most active supporters. Consequently, on September 4, 1879, the members unanimously elected Gerry as president, a position he held until 1900. Gerry moved the society to new offices in its own building and justified the widely used appellation as the Gerry Society.

In the 1880s and 1890s, the NYSPCC aggressively pursued its mission to protect children, attracting some criticisms for its zeal. The agency, nevertheless, influenced some important developments to protect children. In 1880, the NYSPCC acquired its own building, allowing it to maintain its services around the clock. In 1881, the agency cooperated with the New York State Medical Society to improve medical care for the poor, enforcing health rules and regulations as the agents conducted their normal duties. In the early 1880s, working through police magistrates, the NYSPCC forced certain parents to support their children in institutions, helping to reduce slightly the number of institutionalized children. In 1882, the organization, especially through its counsel, John B. Pine, forced the closing of a baby farm, the so-called Van Etten infant asylum, run by a reputedly notorious woman. In 1883, the NYSPCC influenced the enactment of state legislation against baby farming, and, in New York City, it moved to close a disreputable infant asylum. In 1883, the society won the right to inspect and to enforce the laws against baby farms. Consistently concerned with the morals of children and the seedy environment of the city, the NYSPCC influenced officials to refuse to grant licenses to notorious establishments in the city.

Because of its work with children in the courts, the NYSPCC began to advocate what became the children's court in New York. In 1892, for instance, the agency influenced legislation establishing separate children's trials, which formed the basis of the state children's court laws. During the 1890s, the NYSPCC increased its interest in establishing a children's court, which opened in 1902. In 1893, the NYSPCC moved to its own building. By around the middle of the 1890s, the NYSPCC was known as "the children's friend," and its unique building, at Twenty-third Street and Fourth Avenue in Manhattan, opened all the time and providing a range of services, became known as the "children's building."

The agency noted the criticism of its work, which flowered later in the decade. Conflicts with other charities in the city deepened in 1895 when an amendment to the state constitution expanded the powers of the State Board of Charities (SBC) to inspect and regulate societies for the prevention of cruelty to children as charities, which agency officials, especially Gerry, argued the NYSPCC was not. In 1899, a court of appeals held that the SBC could not control the NYSPCC as a charity. The court ruled that the NYSPCC was in effect a government agency to enforce laws affecting children. Press attacks on the organization forced it to appoint a special three-member committee to study charges against it. Part of the attacks charged, probably correctly, that the NYSPCC's zeal in taking children away from parents increased the number of children placed in institutions.

Controversy over the NYSPCC continued into the twentieth century, but the agency nevertheless conducted some constructive work in saving children from abuses. Early in the new century, the state supreme court completed its investigation of the organization, declaring that the press criticisms were generally unsound. The decision of the court of appeals that the NYSPCC could not be supervised by the SBC continued to please the agency, as did the defeat in the legislature in 1900 of an attempt to include the NYSPCC as an institution to be visited by the SBC. But, in the early years of the twentieth century, Homer Folks, a leader in the social work community who served as New York City commissioner of public charities in 1902 and 1903, rekindled the debate over the NYSPCC. In *The Care of Destitute, Dependent and Delinquent Children* (1902), Folks charged, exaggeratedly, that in the nineteenth century, the NYSPCC did more to strengthen and perpetuate the so-called New York system of institutionalizing children than any other single factor. Calling the agency "feeders of institutions," Folks nevertheless recognized that the fear of "the Cruelty"—a common name of the NYSPCC—caused a large number of parents to restrain their anger against their children. An era ended for the organization at the end of 1900 when Gerry resigned as president. He remained with the agency, however, as counsel and on the board of directors. His replacement, Vernon M. Davis, was an assistant district attorney, suggesting the agency's ties with the criminal justice system in New York City. Indeed, an act of the state legislature made the society the only one whose officers could serve as peace officers with the right to arrest. When Davis was elected to the state supreme court in 1902, John D. Lindsay replaced him.

By 1905, the NYSPCC was counseling every child arrested in New York City. The agency also conducted such child welfare services as its lost children's department. The NYSPCC was active in the new children's court, and in 1905, it agreed to establish a training school for agents in child saving and protective work, which opened in the society's building in 1908. The agency developed what later became known as probation. Superintendent E. Fellows Jenkins was, in fact, the chief probation officer for Manhattan and the Bronx, the areas in which the NYSPCC operated. Concerned that children learned stealing techniques from pernicious movies, the NYSPCC campaigned successfully to exclude unaccompanied children from theaters and dens showing such movies. Much of the credit for the state legislation in 1909 was due to Assemblyman Charles F. Murphy of Brooklyn, the skillful leader of Tammany Hall, the Democratic party of New York City. In 1909, Jenkins resigned as secretary and superintendent.

In the period before 1920, the NYSPCC remained controversial in the social work community, and it continued to strive for the decent treatment of children in New York. As early as 1909, President Lindsay opposed the creation of a federal children's bureau because he feared federal intervention in the activity of the society, a point he reiterated in 1913, a year after the United States Children's Bureau (USCB) was established. In 1912, *The New York Times* reported that Gerry and other societies for the prevention of cruelty to children opposed the proposed children's bureau on similar grounds, but Lillian Wald, an important national social worker and head of the Henry Street Settlement* in New York City, declared publicly that only Gerry, not the NYSPCC and other societies, opposed it. In 1910 alone, the NYSPCC agents investigated over nineteen hundred cases for possible baby farming, a practice they had helped to control through a law they helped to enact in 1883. Ever mindful of the ways of youngsters, by 1912, the society again campaigned against cheap and degrading movies, pointing out that children evaded the law by waiting for other children to enter, thus "accompanied," as the legislation of 1909 had stipulated. In 1913, the board of directors established an auxiliary committee of volunteer women to feed and clothe children in the NYSPCC's custody. In 1915, the board appointed a special three-member committee to assist the auxiliary committee on all matters relating to the shelter and general care of children in the society's custody. Also, by 1913, the NYSPCC had collected for the city almost $500,000 from parents paying for their children's stay in institutions. This activity and similar aggressive techniques influenced a former assistant district attorney in the county of New York, Lloyd P. Stryker, to praise the "Gerry Society" at a speech at the famous Labor Temple in New York City in July 1912. Stryker heralded the society as a "militant power for good," declaring that the district attorney welcomed the NYSPCC because "he knows that it means business." During this period, the NYSPCC helped to establish the Bronx SPCC, which quickly handled a number of cases for the NYSPCC. In 1915, a visitor who studied baby farms and the general traffic in babies praised the NYSPCC as the greatest friend of New York City's babies.

In the 1920s, the NYSPCC matured as a leading social service agency. Through the efforts and contributions of philanthropists Mr. and Mrs. August Heckscher, prominent New Yorkers, the NYSPCC moved to expand facilities on 105th Street just off Fifth Avenue in August 1922, the year in which the organization established its annual gold medal award for the most distinguished service by an individual in child protective work. While it continued primarily to rescue children and prosecute their tormentors, the NYSPCC continued in the 1920s to investigate complaints about boarding infants, some of which were reminiscent of the baby farms of the earlier period. By 1929, experts agreed that its shelter department was a model of its kind. Such developments, facilities, and programs prompted Carl Christian Carstens, a prominent child care worker who had experience in child protection services and was the executive director of the Child Welfare League of America,* to view in 1930 the NYSPCC as a pioneer in the field of child protection.

The NYSPCC continued its basic activities and functions in the 1930s and 1940s, but it still occasionally became embroiled in local controversy. In 1931, the agency established a clearinghouse for wayward Protestant Negro children, paralleling the efforts of The Children's Aid Society* during this period for these truly needy and neglected children. In 1933, the NYSPCC characteristically opposed a state bill to remove restrictions on children attending movies unaccompanied by an adult. Reminiscent of its nineteenth-century campaign against the padrone system, in 1933, the agency assailed employment agencies that were sending children from nearby states to New York as domestic servants. An important organizational event occurred in 1935 when Colonel Ernest K. Coulter retired as general manager. He was then appointed assistant to the president. John F. Smithers replaced him as general manager. In 1936, a city commissioner who investigated the NYSPCC and similar societies in the other boroughs urged that its agents be chosen by civil service because he found many were not trained for their work. He also charged that the NYSPCC was spending too much money for its executive staff. Controversy erupted again in 1943 when Mayor Fiorello La Guardia ordered an investigation of the apparently overcrowded and lax shelters. "If I had my way," the mayor exclaimed in October 1943, "I would abolish . . . the SPCC, but [it is] certainly entrenched in the laws." Arguing that the NYSPCC had outlived its usefulness, La Guardia took steps to remove children who were supported by the city from the agency's shelter and placed them in other facilities. In 1946, however, Mayor William O'Dwyer worked to restore funds for the agency to operate its shelters. A chapter in the agency's history ended in 1948 when New York City purchased the NYSPCC's building it had received from the Heckscher Foundation. Property owners and other residents opposed the NYSPCC's occupying its new headquarters on East Seventy-first Street in Manhattan, but officials ruled in the agency's favor.

In the years since the end of World War II, as public welfare services began increasingly to replace traditional agency activities, the NYSPCC appeared to be less publicized—and perhaps less controversial—than before, but it occasionally still rose to the level of controversy of the old days. In early 1952, after reporting that the increasing use of children on television presented new problems, the NYSPCC filed a complaint against the improper use of children on television. In early April 1952, a court ruled that the "Sam Levenson Show" had in fact used child laborers. In 1954, perhaps reflecting the NYSPCC's apparently conservative politics, the agency charged publicly that the children of Ethel and Julius Rosenberg, the accused spies killed by electrocution, were being cared for improperly. In 1965, the agency, as well as Mayor Robert Wagner, Jr., were sued by parents to allow their six and one-half-year-old child to appear on television. In 1966, the NYSPCC initiated a court case that ruled that parents can be declared guilty of child abuse based on the child's condition, an important decision. On April 27, 1975, the NYSPCC celebrated its hundred years of service to the community. In the 1970s, the agency continued to initiate child protection proceedings in courts to prevent abuse and/or neglect, and the agency remained "concerned with children under the age of sixteen who are professional entertainers on radio, [television], films, theater, opera, and ballet."

The primary sources for studying the NYSPCC's early history are diverse and full, but for the period since about 1930, there appears to be considerably less material available publicly. The published *Annual Reports* for the early period prove helpful and detailed. The accessible and indexed *The New York Times* also covered the agency's highlights. Some relevant documents for the early period are reproduced in Robert Bremner et al., *Children and Youth in America: A Documentary History* (1971), vol. 2. There are some NYSPCC papers at the Municipal Archives of the City of New York and in other collections, such as the William Rhinelander Stewart Papers at the New York Public Library. Contemporary publications, such as Homer Folks, *The Care of Destitute, Dependent and Delinquent Children* (1902), Lloyd P. Stryker, *The "Gerry" Society–A Militant Power for Good* (1912), and NYSPCC, *75 Years of Protecting Defenseless Children 1875–1950* (1950), a self-serving agency publication, describe the NYSPCC. For the recent period, *The New York Times* is helpful. Efforts to gain access to organizational materials held by the NYSPCC proved unsuccessful. Zulma Steele's biography of Bergh, *Angel in Top Hat* (1942), discusses the NYSPCC's origins and early history. Some of the interpretive statements in the text stem from Peter Romanofsky's research on the care and condition of dependent children in New York in the nineteenth and twentieth centuries. There is no full-length, scholarly history of the agency, and historians have generally neglected to study the NYSPCC's rich and long history.

NORTH AMERICAN CIVIC LEAGUE (NACL). In February 1907 in New York City, The International Committee of the Young Men's Christian Associations* held a conference on philanthropists, social workers, employers, and others interested in the question of immigration. Participants in this conference decided to organize a voluntary agency to deal with the issue of immigration, and they consequently formed the North American Civic League for Immigrants (NACLI) in 1908. The founders of the NACLI came largely from conservative economic interests, especially from employer associations, large manufacturing companies, and chambers of commerce in cities in the industrial Northeast. The NACLI's initial goal was to provide skills and an education for untutored and unskilled immigrants. The agency's charter also called for it "to strike at the cause of poverty," but according to a student of the agency and the so-called Americanization movement of which it was very much a part, the NACLI reflected fears that immigrants threatened the fabric of American life. The agency established headquarters in Boston and elected a slate of officers, including, as president, D. Chauncey Brewer, lawyer and civic leader and active in the Boston Chamber of Commerce, a vice-president, a treasurer, and a clerk. The initial board of managers, which apparently had thirty members, included, from Baltimore, James Cardinal Gibbons, an active reformer, and Professor Jacob H. Hollander, who was active in Jewish charities, and from New York, social reformer Jacob Riis and Thomas Mulry, an important figure in Catholic charities locally and nationally. The organization hired a small staff, including a recent graduate from the Harvard University School of Law and the secretary to the Massachusetts State Board of Charity, Robert Kelso, an acting general secretary. The NACLI also hired as Italian and Jewish secretaries, respectively, Joseph Bianco and Jacob de Haas, an associate of Louis D. Brandeis, the reform-conscious attorney.

Like other immigrant aid agencies, the NACLI helped newcomers in a variety of ways. Its first major activity was to investigate the conditions of immigrants in the United States. The study revealed what agency leaders wanted to show—that immigrants were influenced by radicals and that they had an inherited distrust of government. The NACLI decided to use Boston as the city in which to implement its program. With immigration patterns similar to New York City, Boston lacked the bigger city's problems and proved to be ideal for the NACLI. In Boston, as in Philadelphia and New York, the NACLI quickly assembled staffs to greet immigrants at the port and to assist them generally. In Boston, the NACLI conducted similar services, including the distribution of helpful pamphlets. The group worked at the railroad terminal and was even given special space at the new immigration station in Boston. In Boston, the NACLI conducted its work in cooperation with such local agencies as The Society of St. Vincent de

Paul,* the Young Travelers' Aid Society, the Associated Charities, and the Italian Immigrant Aid Society. In Boston and throughout the Northeast, the NACLI tried to influence local officials to increase their educational facilities and programs for the newcomers.

The NACLI conducted over forty lectures on civics and such for evening schools in its very first year of operation, 1909–1910; in the next year, it gave over 150 such lectures. The agency used advertisements in the foreign-language press to publicize its educational activities. The board of managers gradually developed ties with foreign-born community leaders. From its inception, the NACLI tried to organize committees in other cities. By the end of its first year, there were such groups in thirty-six cities in nine different states. NACLI secretaries and representatives gained the confidence of commissioners of immigration in virtually every port in the Northeast.

An important early event occurred on March 19, 1910, when the board of managers sponsored a dinner in Boston that attracted leading New England industrialists and featured the United States secretary of commerce and labor, Charles Nagel, and the president of the Boston Chamber of Commerce, Bernard J. Rothwill, a NACLI founder and its first vice-president. This gathering led to the appointment in 1910 of a fifteen-member industrial committee composed of prominent industrialists in New England. The industrial committee began immediately to persuade the public of the values of Americanization as a bulwark against alien industrial radicalism and as a means to maintain stable communities. Nevertheless, during its first year, the NACLI won praise from *The Outlook* and *The Survey,* the most important journal of the social justice Progressive movement and the national social work community.

The most important branch of the NACLI developed in the New York metropolitan area. In 1908, Governor Charles Evans Hughes of New York appointed a New York State Immigration Commission (NYSIC), which conducted an impressively thorough study of immigrants' conditions. The NYSIC recommendations to the state legislature, presented in the spring of 1909, arrived too late for consideration. Led by the NYSIC's secretary, Frances Kellor, a local settlement worker who became involved in a number of Progressive reforms, the members of the commission wanted to establish a new voluntary agency to help immigrants. Learning of the NACLI's work, they decided to become the New York City Committee (NYCC) of the NACLI, and Kellor and others arranged the founding of the group formally in December 1909. Kellor became the NYCC's secretary, and the group also had a chairman, a vice-chairman, and a treasurer. Other important organizers included Thomas Mulry, a layman who was active in local Catholic charities, and philanthropist Paul Warburg. The NYCC began its work early in 1910 by meeting immigrants at Ellis Island and assisting them generally. The group also began to promote the NYSIC's recommendations.

The NYCC emerged as an important reform organization. It began an experimental camp school in Valhalla, New York, in cooperation with the Society of

Italian Immigrants. In 1910, it helped to influence the passage of four immigration bills in the New York State legislature. In January 1911, the NYCC was expanded to include representatives from New Jersey, including such social reformers as settlement house worker Cornelia Bradford of Jersey City and Caroline Alexander, an important charity worker in the state. The expanded agency became the New York-New Jersey Committee (NYNJC) of the NACLI in January 1911.

The NYNJC continued its basic program of innovative education but also developed traditional social services for immigrants. In 1911, for instance, the group opened a special hall in Valhalla to serve as a day school for children and as English classes for adults in the evening. The group also taught household economics and other helpful courses. In February 1911, the NYNJC took over the work of the former Bureau of Promotion and Information of Foreigners in Rochester, New York. At Morristown, New Jersey, the NYNJC conducted experimental classes in English for Italians and at Raritan and Passaic, New Jersey, general adult education courses. A survey of the ways in which local agencies in Rochester, New York, dealt with immigrants showed there was no public school in a heavily populated Polish immigrant district. Consequently, in June 1912, the NYNJC opened the Polish Institute in small, rented quarters. The group cooperated with the Rochester Public Library and the Polish National Alliance, which furnished books. In Buffalo, New York, the NYNJC was chiefly responsible for the establishment of the immigration bureau of the Legal Aid Society of Buffalo, and it was instrumental in organizing a Legal Aid Bureau there in 1912. In June 1912, the New York–based group began an experiment in education in a railroad camp at Campbell Hall, New York, using a discarded freight car as a center. The NYNJC also prepared a bill authorizing the New York State Department of Education to establish schools in labor camps. By 1914, the NYNJC was so successful that it decided to work on the national level. Consequently, it changed its name to the Committee for Immigrants in America (CIA). It assisted other agencies and eventually became the consulting headquarters for immigration and Americanization work throughout the United States.

The Progressive social welfare activities characterizing the group from New York and New Jersey also developed in the parent organization. In 1910, the NACLI began to work in Massachusetts for a workmen's compensation law applicable to aliens. In 1912, it investigated the abuses of the padrone system, an exploitative labor system practiced by Italians and Greeks. The league distributed in many cities a pamphlet, *Messages for Newcomers,* warning of unscrupulous practices that could affect immigrants.

The year of the great strike in Lawrence, Massachusetts, 1912, proved to be a pivotal one for the NACLI. Stung by the radicalism of the strike, the league increasingly condemned immigrants as troublemakers, now stressing Americanization as social control rather than a means of helping newcomers adjust to the country. In 1916, the Boston-based NACLI countered organizing activities of the

International Workers of the World (see *Labor Organizations*) in New Haven, Connecticut, and it participated vigorously in liberty loan campaigns. In August 1917, the NACLI requested that major military installations classify immigrant soldiers racially; many complied. As it reported to the Department of Justice, the NACLI conducted various activities to reduce the threat of civil disorder, infiltrating immigrant labor organizations and the like.

The NACLI allied with regressive forces in what historian John Higham, in *Strangers in the Land* (1955), called the "Tribal Twenties." The NACLI subsidiary, the Order and Liberty Alliance (OLA)—which chiefly raised money from immigrant communities for scholarships—helped the NACLI to protest against what it considered unwise naturalization. The OLA spread to sixty-eight cities by early January 1929, and it claimed over thirty-seven thousand members, including a thousand immigrant community leaders. Throughout the 1920s, the NACLI was proud that the restrictive federal immigration laws embodied its principles.

During the 1930s and 1940s, the organization continued to maintain bureaus of information for non-English-speaking immigrants in industrial communities in New England. Reflecting the significant reduction in immigration to the United States in the 1920s and early 1930s, the NACLI changed its name to the North American Civic League (NACL) in 1934. Seemingly in line with its new name's emphasis on "civic" rather than "immigrants," the agency's services during this period remained "protective, educational, and patriotic." Headquarters continued to be in Boston. Having outlived the conditions responsible for its creation and early existence—bewildered immigrants and immigrant radicalism—the NACL apparently dissolved in the late 1940s.

The primary sources for studying the NACL's history include the published and variously named *Annual Reports* for the period through about the 1920s.

Edward George Hartmann, *The Movement to Americanize the Immigrant* (1948), devotes much of one chapter to the early history of the NACLI, which is also mentioned briefly in John Higham, *Strangers in the Land: Patterns of American Nativism, 1860–1925* (1955). There does not, however, appear to be a full-length historical study of the NACL.

O

ORT: see AMERICAN ORGANIZATION FOR REHABILITATION THROUGH TRAINING FEDERATION.

OSBORNE ASSOCIATION, INC., THE (OA). In the late 1920s, two penal reform groups—the National Society of Penal Information* (NSPI), which had been established in 1920, and the Welfare League Association (WLA), founded around 1915—began to share headquarters in New York City and to function jointly. Both agencies had been established and led by Thomas Mott Osborne. A well-to-do and well-educated business leader, Osborne served between 1903 and 1906 as the mayor of his native city, Auburn, New York. In a well-known episode to learn firsthand of the conditions in prisons, Osborne had entered the Auburn State Prison under the pseudonym of Tom Brown. These experiences helped to shape Osborne as an enthusiastic and often colorful penal reformer. His trust in the inmates led him to establish, around 1915, so-called welfare leagues for the men in prisons. These leagues were self-governing groups that tried to shape certain practices and policies in prisons, especially those at which Osborne himself served as warden, such as Sing Sing, in Ossining, New York. The WLA was an association of such leagues and it also functioned as an aid society for discharged prisoners.

During the Great Depression, dwindling finances in the early 1930s forced the WLA and the NSPI closer together than before. Subsequently, representatives from each group—several individuals interested in penal reform had served each group—met with representatives from the Thomas Mott Osborne Memorial Fund (TMOMF), which had been established after Osborne's death in 1926. The TMOMF agreed to donate about $32,000 to help amalgamate these two organizations. Consequently, in November 1932, in New York City, the WLA and the NSPI merged to form the new The Osborne Association, Inc. (OA).

The new OA continued the basic work of the two agencies and attracted, like its predecessors, eminent reformers. Its organizational structure included the president, the treasurer, and the executive secretary, as well as the field and research secretary, an important position, filled initially by a noted prison reformer, Dr. F. Lovell Bixby, a psychologist who had implemented the pioneering classification system in New Jersey prisons in 1929. The first board of directors, which numbered sixteen, included Dr. Richard Cabot, an eminent reform physician from Boston, Dr. Samuel Eliot, a well-known Unitarian minister, and George W. Kirchwey, a lawyer and penologist who held official prison-related positions and who was a member of the department of criminology at the New York School of Social Work. In 1933, its first year, the OA conducted surveys of prisons in Virginia and Michigan, and the employment and relief secretary found jobs for nearly eighty men, despite the harsh depression. As with other social service organizations, the depression forced the reduction in the staff of the OA from eleven in late 1929 to eight in 1933.

Although the Great Depression affected the staff, the OA weathered the bad conditions and expanded its activities from 1934 on. The addition to the board of directors of such prominent individuals in the field as Stanford Bates, the director of the United States Bureau of Prisons (USBP), and Arthur T. Lyman, commissioner of corrections in Massachusetts, strengthened the organization. The OA continued to conduct and to participate in surveys of prison conditions. In March 1934, the agency also distributed free food tickets in New York and cooperated with the local social service unit of Bellevue Hospital to provide social services in New York for some former prisoners. In March 1936, in cooperation with prison officials in New York City, the OA began a new vocational demonstration project, which the board of trustees discontinued in April 1937 because of a lack of funds. In 1937, the OA began a new venture, surveying institutions for juvenile delinquents, in this case in the North Central states. Throughout the 1930s, friends and supporters of the OA gave presents and food at Christmas to the families of prisoners.

Some important staff changes occurred late in the decade. In December 1938, Bixby, who had served intermittently as field and research director, resigned once again to become chairman of probation and parole of the USPB. More importantly, on January 16, 1940, Austin H. MacCormick, former president of the American Prison Association* (APA) and a federal and local prison official, became the executive director, replacing William B. Cox, who had joined the predecessor agency, the NSPI, as field director in 1925.

In the 1940s and 1950s, the OA's activities seemed to revolve around the personal efforts of Executive Director MacCormick. In the 1940s, MacCormick helped to develop and strengthen the federal prison system. Beginning in 1941, he served as consultant to the United States secretary of war and as special assistant to the under secretary of war on military prisons and prisoners. Through these positions, MacCormick played an important role in the army's program of screening, retraining, and returning to service general court-martialed prisoners. After the end of World War II, Executive Director MacCormick served as vice-chairman of the Army's Advisory Board of Clemency. For his significant contributions, he received the Presidential Medal of Merit in 1947, when it was the highest award a civilian could receive for war services.

In the 1950s, MacCormick was a professor of criminology at the University of California at Berkeley and, late in the decade, served as acting dean of the School of Criminology. During this time, he opened the OA's western office in San Francisco, and he conducted a number of studies of prisons, prisoners, and prison systems in several states. In 1953, he hired Kenyon Scudder, a recognized worker in the field, as head of the OA's field service, based in California.

During the twenty or so years that executive Director MacCormick was away from New York City, the chief OA staff worker at headquarters was Robert Hannum, who served as head of the OA's Bureau of Vocational Placement (BVP), which continued as a major agency function. Hannum began his career as a counselor and later codirector of the Boys' Club of New York, and from 1930 to 1940, he was director of placement at Children's Village in Dobbs Ferry, New York, a famous facility.

In the 1960s, the OA continued to provide services to former prisoners, and it still influenced events nationwide. In 1960, after he retired from teaching at the University of California, MacCormick returned to New York City to serve full time as executive director at the headquarters. In 1961, the OA received two grants, one of $25,000 from the Vincent Astor Foundation and another from a member of the board of directors to allow the agency to find a qualified assistant for Robert Hannum, who was carrying an especially heavy work load. In the early 1960s, the OA cooperated so closely with the National Council on Crime and Delinquency* (NCCD) that there were apparently serious feelings that the two agencies might merge. The OA was honored in 1962 when Executive Director MacCormick was appointed by President John F. Kennedy to serve on the seven-member President's Advisory Commission on Narcotic and Drug Abuse. In early 1963, with the NCCD, the OA began a major survey of juvenile institutions throughout the country. Continuing its efforts to improve prison conditions, notably in the South, the OA contributed further to the development of the state system in Mississippi through the personal efforts of MacCormick. MacCormick also volunteered his personal help as well as the OA's assistance in 1966 to Governor Winthrop Rockefeller of Arkansas to reform prison conditions there. During this period, the OA conducted, on a regular two-year basis, studies of the Texas Youth Council's juvenile training schools and their parole programs. In late December 1967, the OA suffered a great loss with the death of Robert Hannum. To replace him, the board of directors quickly appointed an experienced worker in the field of vocational counseling, Joseph M. Callan, the former assistant director of the BVP. Under Callan in the late 1960s and 1970s, the BVP began increasingly to deal with the problems of drug addiction. The BVP services were also expanded, as it began to cooperate with the Fellowship Center in Manhattan to deal with alcohol-related problems of former inmates. Organizational highlights of the 1960s included the amendment to the agency's bylaws in February 1967, which increased the executive committee from five to seven members.

Basic services and programs continued in the 1970s. Visits and assistance to southern prison systems, especially by Executive Director MacCormick, continued. Callan spoke, in the early 1970s, on drug addiction to groups of adolescents, as well as to professional workers, and he still gave prerelease talks to prisoners at the New Jersey State Prison at Trenton. In the early 1970s, the OA administered a nonresidential drug abuse program under a contract with the USBP. The OA also received foundation and other grants for a residential drug treatment center, a so-called halfway house for probationers, parolees, and prereleases. After some problems in finding a suitable location, the project began in early March 1973. The facility started with a staff of fifteen administrative personnel and counselors. Callan also directed this project. The OA's Community Residential Treatment Center was officially dedicated in November 1973 and named Hannum House. It provided a full range of vocational and social services and even conducted bus trips and picnics and Christmas and Thanksgiving parties for current and former residents and their families. In 1974, the OA decided to end the nonresidential drug treatment program, which it felt should be implemented by a federal agency rather than by a private organization. In April

1975, the OA sponsored a workshop/conference for the International Halfway House Association. Also in April 1975, the OA's nonresidential drug treatment program was terminated. At its BVP, the OA continued to find jobs for and provide other services for some of the most hardened criminals. In 1976, a chapter in the OA's history ended when Joseph Callan replaced MacCormick as executive director. Austin MacCormick, the notable prison authority, however, remained as a consultant for this small but dedicated organization.

The primary sources for studying the OA's history consist chiefly of its published and mimeographed *Annual Reports,* which do not seem to be available widely in libraries, and the Papers of Thomas Mott Osborne at the archives in The George Arents Research Library at Syracuse University in Syracuse, New York.

Historians have generally neglected the OA, and there does not appear to be a full-length history of the agency.

P

PLANNED PARENTHOOD FEDERATION OF AMERICA, INC. PPFA).
In the early years of the twentieth century, Margaret Sanger served as a visiting obstetrical nurse on New York's Lower East Side. There she witnessed the plight of immigrant women denied access to reliable and safe contraceptive methods because of federal and state statutes that defined contraception as obscene and prohibited its lawful advocacy. Sanger was moved to action when a young patient, Sadie Sachs, died of a septic self-induced abortion. Announcing that she was tired of piecemeal palliative reforms, Sanger gave up her nursing career in 1912 and launched a campaign to repeal the detestable Comstock laws, so-named for the self-proclaimed arbiter of Victorian morality, Anthony Comstock. Under a banner of radical feminism, she proceeded to defy laws in an effort to publish scientific information about family limitation and to open a contraceptive clinic for women. Her pioneering battles to educate the public about sexuality and birth control, a phrase she coined, won her international recognition and widespread support, particularly from middle-class women. They expressed more sympathy for her cause than had many of her colleagues in the socialist and labor movements, and they were able to provide the volunteer and financial support for an organized birth control reform movement.

The supporters of birth control thus came to represent a broad spectrum of concerns, including social welfare, women's rights, and eugenics, a popular ideology that embraced, at one extreme, a Progressive interest in the scientific cure of hereditary defect and disease, but at the other, an unfortunate conservative sympathy for racial purification through the controlled breeding of the socially undesirable. The official rhetoric of the young birth control movement was consciously ambiguous and calculated to secure a broad ideological and financial base. Sanger sought the endorsement of business, professional, and scholarly elites. Her cause, however, always remained suspect in the eyes of the male establishment because of its identification with feminism. Volunteer and professional women organized birth control leagues and clinics, although men sat on advisory boards and provided meager financial support.

Formal organization at the national level followed nearly a decade of agitation against public prudery and restrictive birth control laws. The Planned Parenthood Federation of America, Inc. (PPFA), was founded as the American Birth Control League (ABCL) at a conference Sanger called in New York City on November 11, 1921. With headquarters in New York, the ABCL acted as a clearinghouse for public education and moral suasion, but it left policy decisions and the actual provision of contraceptive services to affiliated agencies that were chartered, administered, and, in part, financed at a local or state level. In 1976, PPFA remains a loosely federated structure consisting of a national umbrella organization and 189 affiliates, such as Planned Parenthood of New York City, Inc. (PP-NYC), and similar groups around the country that operated seven hundred clinical facilities with some twenty thousand volunteers and three thousand professional staff workers.

Under Margaret Sanger's direction and with funds provided by her second husband, businessman J. Noah Slee, and by others, the ABCL opened its first medically administered clinic in New York City in 1923. The Birth Control Clinic Research Bureau (BCCRB), as its name implied, experimented in new contraceptive techniques for women, principally the rubber-spring diaphragm that Sanger smuggled into the United States from Germany, where it had been invented in the 1880s. Various pessaries were known as contraceptive agents in the United States, although douches, condoms, withdrawal, and other primitive methods enjoyed greatest use. The diaphragm-jelly regimen, introduced by the Sanger clinic, however, quickly won confidence, and by 1930, fifty-five affiliated birth control clinics had opened in the United States, all of them fitting diaphragms. The Bureau, renamed the Margaret Sanger Bureau in 1940, continued operations in its brownstone quarters in New York's Chelsea district until 1973, when it merged with a nearby clinic under the auspices of PP-NYC.

The depression decade of the 1930s fostered the growth of the birth control movement. Sanger had resigned from the ABCL in 1928 in a personality and policy dispute and had taken the New York clinic with her. In 1931, she also founded the National Committee on Federal Legislation for Birth Control (NCFLBC), a Washington lobby that resumed the fight for free dissemination of birth control through the public mails that had been carried on in the 1920s by Sanger's principal rival for leadership in the movement, Mary Ware Dennett.

Sanger, however, called for a modification of the Comstock laws to allow for the transportation of contraceptive materials for the lawful use of physicians only, and not for outright repeal. She abandoned this fight in 1936 when a judicial decision achieved her goal. The case—*United States* v. *One Package*—was brought by Dr. Hannah Meyer Stone, the medical director of Sanger's BCCRB.

Throughout the 1930s, Sanger competed with rivals in the ABCL to stimulate continued establishment of birth control clinics, to broaden the acceptance of contraception by physicians, demographers, and other professional elites, and to promote the extension of birth control to public health programs. By the decade's end the birth controllers had witnessed endorsement by the prestigious American Medical Association, by hundreds of other professional, civic, and women's organizations, and by the governing bodies of the country's major religious denominations, with the exception of the highly vocal and critical Catholic church. Official acceptance into the community of established social welfare institutions continued to elude them, however, because of the moral controversy that surrounded birth control, despite its widespread use. The influence of Catholic voluntary agencies in many localities kept Planned Parenthood out of such networks as the community councils or community chests.

In 1939, claiming the combined affiliation of 417 birth control agencies, the ABCL and the BBCRB reconciled to form The Birth Control Federation of America (BCFA). In 1942, the BCFA adopted the family planning banner and became the PPFA at the urging of a public relations conscious staff that sought to emphasize the positive social utility of contraception—family planning rather than family limitation. Preparation in the United States for World War II heightened national concern about the birthrate, which had reached an all-time low during the Great Depression.

After a decade of substantial growth, PPFA consolidated and declined in the 1940s and 1950s. Despite public support for the principle of family planning, if not outright birth control, the diaphragm technique was available only by prescription through clinics or private physicians. Moreover, it was costly, cumbersome, and acceptable to only about half of the women who tried it. Most American families continued to rely on conventional drugstore contraceptive devices sold widely under the euphemism of personal hygiene. A number of Planned Parenthood physicians turned their attention to the psychological aspects of fertility regulation and pioneered in the field of marriage counseling. The American Association of Marriage Counselors, now the American Association of Marriage and Family Counselors, was founded in 1941, with Dr. Abraham Stone as its president. Stone, the husband of Hannah Stone, had taken over the Margaret Sanger clinic upon his wife's death that same year.

Further democratization of scientific contraception awaited improvements in technology and changes in the political climate allowing for federal funding of family planning facilities. PPFA, in the early 1950s, sponsored a small portion of the research that culminated in the development of the anovulent birth control pill and acted as a conduit for additional research funds. Professionals in demography and medicine, however, criticized the PPFA for devoting too much attention to clinical services and not enough to research. PPFA also supported legislative and judicial efforts in Massachusetts and Connecticut, where Catholic hegemony kept birth control illegal until the 1965 Supreme Court decision in *Griswold* v. *Connecticut* overruled restrictive state statutes. The PPFA also worked publicly and behind the scenes in such cities as New York where prescribing birth control devices was outlawed in all municipal hospitals until 1958.

The development and marketing of oral and intrauterine contraception in the early 1960s revolutionized birth control practice in the United States and abroad. Increased demand brought about a major expansion of Planned Parenthood facilities. In the past decade, the movement's clientele has expanded by 20 percent per year from several hundred thousand per year to nearly a million, much of it since 1969, subsidized by the federal antipoverty program. Since the Supreme Court decision on abortion in 1973, PPFA has provided abortion counseling and, in a number of its largest clinics, operates abortion facilities. Eligibility requirements that formerly existed at its clinics have been dropped. In 1976, PPFA endorsed contraception and sex education programs for teenagers.

The post–World War II recognition of a world population crisis has provided family planning with a compelling social justification and broadened the base of its support. Margaret Sanger had for years decried the evils of unchecked population growth and supported neo-Malthusian efforts to check population growth. In 1928, she sponsored the first World Population Conference in Geneva, Switzerland. In 1952, after a decade of semiretirement, she founded the International Planned Parenthood Federation. The desire to capitalize on growing private and governmental support for population control was evidenced by PPFA's decision in 1960 to sponsor a World Population Emergency Campaign and, thereafter, to adopt the "Planned Parenthood–World Population" trademark for much of its publicity and fund raising. In 1960, the PPFA gained further stature among business and scientific elites by appointing a male president, a post traditionally held by a woman who had risen from the ranks of its affiliates. In 1962, an internationally known obstetrician and sex educator, Dr. Alan Guttmacher, assumed that post and held it until his death in 1974.

The primary sources for studying the PPFA's history consist of its printed reports and publications, available in the library of PPFA headquarters at 810 Seventh Avenue in New York City and in libraries elsewhere. Relevant archival collections include the Margaret Sanger Papers at Smith College, Northampton, Massachusetts, and at The Library of Congress in Washington, D.C.; the PPFA Papers at Smith College; the Papers of Gregory Pincus, M.D., at The Library of Congress; the Papers of Alan Guttmacher, M.D., Robert L. Dickinson, M.D., Clarence Gamble, M.D., Abraham Stone, M.D., and Hannah Stone, M.D., all at the Countway Library of the Harvard University Medical School in Boston, Massachusetts; and the Papers of Mary Calderone, M.D., at The Schlesinger

Library of Radcliffe College in Cambridge, Massachusetts. The Schlesinger Library has also just completed an oral history project on women in the family planning movement.

Margaret Sanger, *An Autobiography* (1938), contains materials about the ABCL and its successor agencies, as do David Kennedy, *Birth Control in America: The Career of Margaret Sanger* (1970), Linda Gordon, *Women's Body, Women's Right: A Social History of Birth Control in America* (1976), and James W. Reed, "Birth Control and the Americans: 1930–1970" (Ph.D. diss., Harvard University, 1974), scheduled for publication in 1978. Ellen Chesler is preparing a thesis at Columbia University, "Women and Family Planning in America, 1912–1970," which focuses on the organizational history of PPFA and its affiliates.   Ellen Chesler

PLAYGROUND AND RECREATION ASSOCIATION OF AMERICA: see NATIONAL RECREATION AND PARK ASSOCIATION.

PLAYGROUND ASSOCIATION OF AMERICA: see NATIONAL RECREATION AND PARK ASSOCIATION.

PRESBYTERIAN CHURCH IN THE UNITED STATES OF AMERICA, CHURCH AND SOCIETY (CS) OF THE UNITED. The social gospel movement of the turn of the twentieth century influenced the establishment, in 1908, of the Department of Church and Labor (DCL) of the Board of Home Missions of the Presbyterian Church in the United States of America (PC) (see *Religious Organizations*). The leader of the DCL was Reverend Charles Stelze, who in 1910 opened the famous Labor Temple in New York City. Operating in an abandoned church in a congested area, the Labor Temple, which featured a night school, became associated with the urban labor and social justice movements. Further organizational development occurred in 1911 when the PC's general assembly directed the Board of Home Missions to establish the Bureau of Social Service (BSS), which included Stelze's DCL. The BSS helped, for instance, to establish a two-year graduate course in church social work at Teachers College of Columbia University in New York. In 1923, the general assembly created the new Board of National Missions (BNM) with a clear mandate to involve the church in social justice movements. Subsequently, in the early 1930s, the BNM established a Standing Committee on Social and Industrial Relations. The Department of Social and Industrial Relations of the BNM was soon formed. At the PC's general assembly in 1936 in Syracuse, New York, from these organizational precedents, Church and Society (CS) of The United Presbyterian Church in the United States of America (UPC) was established as the Department of Social Education (DSE) of the Presbyterian Church in the United States of America's Board of Christian Education (BCE), an important church agency. In 1937, the DSE was renamed the Department of Social Education and Action (DSEA). Headquarters were soon established in the PC's Witherspoon Building in Philadelphia, Pennsylvania.

The DSEA began its activities by focusing primarily on the issues of temperance, war, and peace. In early 1936, it began to publish *Social Progress,* which devoted many articles to peace and related subjects. By 1938, a series of *The Social Progress Pamphlets,* featuring discussions of temperance, gambling, and peace, indicated a continuing DSEA activity: to help educate the church on social issues. Beginning in the mid-1930s, the agency cooperated with the Federal Council of the Churches of Christ in America (FCC) to sponsor the first prison chaplaincy in federal institutions. In the 1930s, the DSEA encouraged local committees to participate in housing conferences, and the agency campaigned for the Wagner-Van Nuys antilynching bill. In 1939, the DSEA continued its normal activities, participating in the National Peace Conference and supporting the efforts of the National Temperance and Prohibition Council to enact federal legislation to ban liquor advertising.

As the war approached, the DSEA maintained its usual activities but expanded into some important progressive movements, especially civil rights. In 1941, the DSEA urged the church to priase the United States Supreme Court ruling that granted blacks the same travel accommodations as whites, and it spoke out against lynching, the poll tax, and racial discrimination in military and defense industries. It opposed segregation in military camps, and it urged President Franklin D. Roosevelt to remove liquor from these and from Civilian Conservation Corps camps. Throughout the war, the DSEA remained concerned with prohibition, but in the mid-1940s, with the Women's Committee of the PC's BCE, the DSEA sponsored a study of church women and household employees, trying to stir the church's social conscience on this thorny issue.

In the postwar years, the DSEA, except for its continuing stand against alcohol, participated in the mainstream of American liberalism and even pioneered in some activities, such as civil rights. In the fall of 1947, the DSEA participated in the Seminar on World Order. It lagged behind other, smaller denominations in international relations, but it participated in the Washington seminar in Washington, D.C., "Inflation and World Relief." In March 1948, the DSEA supported both the United Nations (UN) and the European recovery program, the Marshall Plan, and vigorously opposed universal military training. In apparently the late 1940s, the agency became the Division of Social Education and Action, which it remained until 1955, when it again became the DSEA. Suggesting the agency's concern for the emerging social issue of racial justice were the following: its interracial vocation schools, its institute on racial and cultural relations, begun in February 1948, and its three-year study of human rights and race relations, reported to the general assembly in 1951. The agency participated in housing conferences and, with other groups, in conferences dealing with the church and migrant labor.

The 1950s were generally quiet years for the agency, as it continued its peace, alcohol, and international work. In 1953, it prepared programs on freedom and on alcohol for the television series, "Lamp Unto My Feet." In the mid-1950s, the DSEA joined other church denominations, sending a representative to the Washington, D.C., office of the National Council of the Churches of Christ in the U.S.A. (NCC). In 1956, the DSEA began to publish *SEA Agenda,* a bimonthly journal for chairmen of local committees, and it continued to publish pamphlets on peace and on alcohol. In the late 1950s, the agency increased its activities in civil rights, for example, cooperating with the church's BNM to begin a program that assisted churches and ministers dealing with the problems of racial segregation. On July 2, 1958, the DSEA was incorporated in Pennsylvania as the social service group of the new UPC.

The general activities of the DSEA of the new UPC remained basically the same. Its most innovative work began in 1959 when it hired two field agents, headquartered in Nashville, Tennessee, to deal with racially tense areas. In 1960, amid the reorganization of the BCE, the agency became the Office of Church and Society (OCS). Suggesting the lack of importance the generally conservative UPC placed on the OCS and its work, in 1962, it received only 3 percent of the budget of its administrative agency, the BCE. Nevertheless, in the early 1960s, the OCS completed a compilation of general assembly pronouncements on race relations since 1954, enlarged its office in Washington, D.C., and opened its office of international affairs at the UN in New York City. In 1963, advisory committees composed of Presbyterian specialists in particular areas began to function; one was the advisory committee on the problems of a metropolitan society, which began a study of urban renewal and planning.

As the field of social service expanded dramatically in the mid-1960s, the OCS diversified its concerns and activities. In 1963, for instance, its advisory committee on community problems began a two-year study of migrant labor, and the OCS worked closely with the President's Committee on Migratory Labor and with the United States Department of Agriculture and Labor. In 1963, it also sponsored seminars on "The Church and Released Offenders," the first in conjunction with the annual meeting of the National Council on Crime and Delinquency* and then with the American Correctional Association.* In 1964, the OCS's secretary for national affairs in Washington, D.C., Dr. H. Ben Sissel, wrote articles and held discussions on the federal antipoverty bill, and with other agencies of the UPC, the OCS held a conference on the aging in October 1964. In 1966, the agency conducted seminars on such issues as crime and law, international aid, homosexuality, narcotics addiction, poverty and the laws, and racism. The office of international affairs cooperated closely with the progressive China Relations Project of the NCC. In 1967, CS created a new post, secretary for racial affairs, and by 1968, the agency was increasingly involved in draft counseling. In 1969, it began to help the poverty-stricken Mexican-Americans in Rio Ariba County, New Mexico. The BCE, under which the CS had functioned, was phased out in 1972, but the basic CS activities in race and international relations, for instance, remained under Unit II of the Program Agency of the UPC.

The primary sources for studying the CS's history include the agency's annual reports in the published *Minutes* of the church's general assembly. Some of the agency's files for the period from about 1944 through 1952 are in the Presbyterian Historical Society in Philadelphia, Pennsylvania.

Theodore E. Bachmann, ed., *Churches and Social Welfare* (1955), vol. 1, and Robert Moats Miller, *American Protestantism and the Social Issues* (1958), contain a little information about the agency, but there does not appear to be a scholarly history of the CS.

R

RED CROSS: see AMERICAN NATIONAL RED CROSS.

RUSSELL SAGE FOUNDATION (RSF). On July 22, 1906, Russell Sage of New York, a congressman and financier, died. He left virtually all of his large fortune of about $65 million to his wife, Margaret Olivia Sage, without any restrictions. An apparently kind and generous woman, Mrs. Sage began to give away some of her money to individuals, charitable institutions, and such. Although she occasionally acted impulsively, she considered her larger grants more carefully. She began to seek advice about establishing a philanthropic foundation from her attorneys, Henry De Forest and his brother, Robert, an important local New York and national charity leader, who served as president of the prestigious The Charity Organization Society of the City of New York* (COS) since 1888 and as president of the National Conference of Charities and Correction* (NCCC) in 1903. De Forest corresponded about the proposed project with leading figures in social work and social reform, such as John M. Glenn, active in Baltimore, Maryland, charities and the president of the NCCC in 1901, and The Johns Hopkins University president, Daniel Coit Gilman, who later joined Glenn on the first board of trustees of the Russell Sage Foundation (RSF). Following a series of correspondence between Robert De Forest and other charity leaders, such as Jeffrey Brackett of Boston, the RSF was incorporated in New York City according to the laws of the state of New York on April 11, 1907. Its purpose was to improve "social and living conditions in the United States of America."

The incorporators and the first board of trustees included some of Mrs. Sage's friends, such as Cleveland Dodge, an officer in both the New York chapter of the American National Red Cross* (ANRC) and the International Young Men's Christian Association, the philanthropist Helen M. Gould, Gertrude Rice, one of the founders of the COS and active in the State Charities Aid Association* (SCAA) of New York, and Louisa Lee Schuyler, another important figure in American social work. Schuyler was prominent as the founder of the SCAA in 1872, the National Committee for the Prevention of Blindness* (NCPB) around 1910, and the Bellevue Hospital Training School for Nurses in the late nineteenth century, the first institution of its kind.

Eight days after the act of incorporation, the incorporators met, adopted a constitution, elected themselves the first board of trustees, convened the first meeting of the board of trustees, elected Mrs. Sage as president and De Forest as vice-president, and chose Gilman, Gould, and Rice to serve with them on the executive committee of five members. On May 10, 1907, the executive committee appointed John Glenn as RSF director and as secretary of the board of trustees.

The individuals associated with the RSF since its inception helped to develop the organization as a leading force in American social service, helping it to fulfill one of its initial aims: to improve social and economic conditions in the United States. The RSF's first grant was to assist the publication of *Charities and The Commons,* the most important social work journal. It was issued by the COS. Other organizations assisted by initial grants, awarded on May 1, 1907, included the COS, the International Tuberculosis Congress, and the SCAA. Other Progressive social developments, agencies, and projects in which the RSF participated in its initial years included tenement house work, a reform movement close to the core of the social justice Progressive movement and to Robert De Forest and his COS as well; the consumer leagues; the playground movement; the Forest Hills Garden project; and most importantly, the so-called Pittsburgh Survey, an intensive study by leading social workers of social and economic conditions in that depressed city. As social welfare historian Professor Robert Bremner argued, this survey had a profound and far-reaching influence on social work and social reform. Among other things, it prompted the then named *Charities and the Commons* to change its name to *The Survey* in 1909.

The formal establishment of the departments, through which the RSF's activities functioned, occurred in 1909. Particular departments developed as very crucial not only in the RSF's history but also in American social welfare history. The recreation committee, for instance, had close ties with the new Playground Association of America* (PAA), which was founded in 1906 to institutionalize the important social justice Progressive movement for the development of playgrounds and open spaces in congested cities; the remedial loan department of the RSF helped to establish the National Federation of Remedial Loan Associations* (NFRLA) in 1909; and the southern highlands department, under John and Olive Campbell, founded the Conference of Southern Mountain Workers* in 1913. Conducting influential studies in their respective fields were the child-helping department, directed by Hastings Hart, the former superintendent of the National

Children's Home Society* (NCHS), and the women's work department, which later became the important industrial studies department. For example, such publications of the child-helping department as *Child Welfare Work in Idaho* (1920) by William Slingerland and *Child Welfare in the District of Columbia* (1924) by Hastings Hart described conditions and recommended reforms, some of which were followed. This department also published timely studies of illegitimacy, child hygiene, and infant mortality. Publications of the women's work department included *Wages in the Millinery Trade* (1914) by Mary Van Kleeck, an important social worker. The most significant of the RSF's departments, the charity organization department, became virtually the center of the American social work community, publishing studies on casework and on other important issues. Most outstanding and notable was the publication of the influential *Social Diagnosis* (1917) by Mary Richmond, a former social worker in Baltimore. Richmond headed the charity organization department from 1908 until 1928.

The RFS's activities during the 1920s lend support to the notion that the excitement and vitality of the earlier social justice Progressive movement had been dampened by the war and by the cynicism it had aroused. The RSF still continued to support some of the major national social service agencies and specific programs, but its most important activity in the 1920s was its sponsoring of the so-called New York regional plan, a project in which social workers and social reformers played a role.

RSF studies and surveys contributed to an understanding of the social and economic aspects of the Great Depression, and, as the federal, state, and local governments became increasingly involved in the development and delivery of social services, many RSF personnel joined government agencies in the 1930s and early 1940s. In 1949, the RSF broke up its fine collection of annual reports, miscellaneous publications, and such, and divided its library holdings between the School of Social Work of Columbia University and the City College of New York's Library.

In the period since the end of World War II, the RSF has continued to support some important research and programs in social work economics, social planning, and social welfare research. Individual executive leaders have in recent years shaped the direction of the RSF. In the 1960s and 1970s, the RSF focused on particular problems, such as mental health and education, and it conducted studies of the economy and of issues relating to civil liberties.

The RSF's history can be studied in the massive and detailed two-volume *Russell Sage Foundation, 1907–1946* (1947) by John M. Glenn, Lilian Brandt, and F. Emerson Andrews. This source is both primary and secondary because some of its authors played leading roles in the RSF's history. The detailed published *Annual Reports* are also available. Serious students might also wish to consult a number of RSF publications, which are available in several major libraries.

Suggesting the centrality of the RSF in the national social work community, it is mentioned in the standard histories in the field, such as Clarke Chambers, *Seedtime of Reform* (1963), Walter Trattner, *From Poor Law to Social Welfare* (1974), and Allen F. Davis, *Spearheads for Reform: The Social Settlements and the Progressive Movement, 1890–1914* (1967). The RSF is also dealt with in such specialized studies as Paul T. Ringenbach, *Tramps and Reformers, 1873–1916: The Discovery of Unemployment in New York* (1973), and Clarke Chambers, *Paul U. Kellogg and the Survey: Voices for Social Welfare and Social Justice* (1971). Nevertheless, there seems to be room for serious historical studies of this veteran agency, particularly in the more recent period.

S

ST. VINCENT DE PAUL SOCIETY: see SOCIETY OF ST. VINCENT DE PAUL, SUPERIOR COUNCIL OF THE U.S., INC.

SALVATION ARMY, THE (SA). Reacting to the widespread poverty in England, in 1865, William Booth began a Christian mission in Whitechapel, an impoverished section of London. In 1878, Booth's work in aiding the poor became known as The Salvation Army (SA). It was created to assist impoverished, homeless, and other needy people in several ways. The SA grew in England, and General Booth decided to expand his enterprise to the United States. In the early 1870s, he sent a representative to develop missionary work in Cleveland, Ohio, This venture failed after its organizer left. The SA, however, was established in the United States on March 10, 1880, when a group of eight uniformed SA workers from England, led by Commissioner George Scott Railton, arrived in New York City from England. The group was greeted by Reverend and Mrs. James E. Irvine of Jersey City, New Jersey, two of several Americans who had met Booth and observed his activities in England. The SA group soon established temporary headquarters at the Pickwick Lodging House in Lower Manhattan. The SA group hoped to convert downtrodden slum dwellers and derelicts to their mission of religious salvation through social service. The SA workers paraded through the streets seeking converts and performed at an infamous variety theater to attract souls. Their early meetings in a rented hall were successful, but New York City officials did not permit them to conduct outdoor meetings. This prompted Railton to leave, in late March 1880, for Philadelphia, where a local family—the Shirleys—who had worked with the British group before they migrated to America, was conducting similar parades and meetings.

Railton's trip to Philadelphia heralded the expansion of the fledgling organization. On his way, he organized a group in Newark, New Jersey. In Philadelphia, he established national headquarters. In the summer of 1880, he left for St. Louis, where he faced similar abuses and denials from the public, as well as from city officials. Denied the right to hold open meetings, he decided to meet on the ice on the Illinois side of the frozen Mississippi River; only by January 1881 did officials allow him to rent a hall for his missionary work. On January 15, 1881, in St. Louis, Railton published the first American edition of *The War Cry,* the SA's newspaper. A devoted and loyal aide of founder William Booth, Railton returned to England in 1881. He was replaced as national commander by Major Thomas E. Moore. Moore, who became a naturalized American citizen, precipitated a conflict with the British leader when, following an incompetent administration that alienated many followers, he incorporated the organization in 1884 under his rather than Booth's name.

Moore's dismissal and the arrival in November 1884 of a new commander loyal to Booth, Major Frank Smith, weakened but did not eliminate Moore. The pro-Booth forces, the Smith "World-Wide" organization, as it came to be known, struggled initially with a small headquarters in New York City while Moore's "Incorporated" group retained national headquarters at Brooklyn. The personal dedication of important American workers to the dynamic leadership of Booth, however, increasingly strengthened the Smith-Booth forces. The establishment of new groups in eastern cities, the development of groups loyal to Booth in the San Francisco area in the early 1880s, and the triumphant visit to the United States of founder Booth in 1886 all helped to strengthen the "World-Wide" faction, which was loyal to Booth.

On his American trip, General Booth, who exercised complete control over the international organization, decided to replace Smith with his son and daughter-in-law, Ballington and Maud Booth. They arrived in New York in April 1887 and began immediately to promote the organization. In October 1889, Ballington Booth formalized agreements bringing the Moore faction back to the SA. Maud conducted meetings in the homes of prominent people throughout the country, particularly in New York City. An expanded auxiliary league, which developed initially in the 1880s, attracted increased lay membership in the SA. The Ballington-Maud Booth administration expanded the social work of the organization, opening the "Cottage" for prostitutes in New York City in October 1886. Similar work on the Pacific Coast, begun in 1887, led members to visit women's prisons, a continuing SA activity. The first day nursery in 1890, the initial food and shelter depot in 1891, and the salvage corps, which featured a woodyard similar to that of The Charity Organization Society of the City of New York,* all began under the leadership of these two important national commanders, Maud and Ballington Booth.

SA services—the salvage junk shop, the labor bureau, inexpensive lodges for homeless men, a slum maternity nursing system, an orphan asylum, and the salvage brigade, which became industrial homes and the men's social service centers—were all influenced by these two leaders. In a dramatic development, in January 1896, founder Booth removed Ballington and Maud, but rather than undertake another SA post, they stayed in New York and founded, in 1896, The Volunteers of America* (VOA) to conduct the social welfare activities that interested them.

Replacing Ballington and Maud in 1896 were Frederick St. George de Lautour Booth-Tucker and his wife, Emma, a daughter of founder William Booth. Their administration supervised the moral, temperance, and spiritual work of the SA among the American troops in the Spanish-American War. They also incorporated the organization in New York State on April 28, 1899. Frederick Booth-Tucker lectured and published widely about the social service work of the SA, becoming particularly interested in the agricultural colonization work, a philanthropic venture other agencies undertook for oppressed urban dwellers in turn-of-the-century America. By 1897, the SA had developed three such colonies in California, Colorado, and Ohio. His wife's death in 1903, other family deaths, and the demise of his close friend and SA supporter, United States Senator Mark Hanna of Ohio, forced a depressed Booth-Tucker to abandon his commandership in 1904.

His replacement, another Booth—the founder's daughter, Evangeline—helped to consolidate and to expand the work in America. Temperance activities featured the annual Boozers' Convention, which was held until the enactment of the Eighteenth Amendment. War work, begun in 1914 with the old linen campaign to prepare bandages, continued with canteen and other personal and spiritual services to the soldiers and ended with hospital visiting and nursing aid in postwar France and even Germany. The war work significantly promoted the popularity of the SA, helping to make its national fund-raising drives in 1919 and 1920 very successful. An important organizational development occurred in October 1920 when the SA created three regional territories—eastern, central and western. In January 1927, the Southern Territory began to function. The leaders of the territories reported not to the national commander but to international offices in London. This development further decentralized the American organization, a trend Evangeline Booth encouraged. On May 18, 1930, during the fiftieth anniversary celebrations in New York, the SA dedicated its new national headquarters on West Fourteenth Street in New York City, still the national office in 1977.

In the period since the 1930s, the organization has solidified and expanded its social service activities. In October 1930, its emergency relief program responded to the problems of unemployment and the Great Depression. In 1936, the SA became an associate group of the National Conference of Social Work,* and it cooperated increasingly with many private and public, national and local welfare agencies.

The era of World War II and its aftermath brought signs of increasing professionalism in the delivery of social services by the SA. Its program to aid men in the armed services did not gain the publicity of efforts during World War I. Even before the events that brought the United States into what became World War II, the SA organized its war service department under the national commander and the four territorial supervisors. In early 1941, the SA became one of five national agencies helping to establish the United Service Organizations for National Defense, Inc.* (USOND), to aid defense-related communities and servicemen. The SA conducted servicemen's clubs that were shortly absorbed by the USOND. But by the spring of 1942, for instance, the SA was operating sixty-four men's club houses as part of the USOND structure. Although social services to families had always been a function of local corps, World War II activities helped to crystallize the service under the family welfare department on the territorial level.

The creation of the family welfare department on the national level, located at the national headquarters in New York City, suggested the characteristic manner in which the SA provided organizational structures for its services. Generally, local units developed their own programs and activities, based on community needs. As corps in other cities learned of these new developments—one of the functions of the general, two-day sessions of the SA, held before the convening of the National Conference on Social Welfare,* was to inform the national structure of these trends—similar activities developed in a number of localities, thus creating the need for coordinated and policy-making decisions by a territory-level group. For example, as corps developed formal family service programs in the 1940s and 1950s, they created the need for territory-level positions and structures to coordinate these activities. Thus, by 1955, each of the four territories had both women's and children's and men's social service departments. Only two territories, however, had territory-level departments in prison work, an activity that was not as well developed professionally as were other services, such as those for unwed mothers. The professional growth of SA services for unwed mothers resulted largely from the individual leadership of Lieutenant-Colonel Jane Wrieden, a professionally trained social worker and an important specialist in casework with unmarried parents. Nationwide, there seemed to be more professional standards and more specially trained social workers in child welfare, illegitimacy, and the like than, for example, in the care of transient and homeless men, a continuing function of the men's social service departments. The emphasis on the local origins of social services, however, remained a consistent principle in the SA. In the 1970s, for instance, when homes for unwed mothers were losing residents at significant rates, the organization allowed each individual institution to determine its new function or functions. Also in the 1950s, the SA had begun to cooperate more fully than before with other national social service agencies, for instance, participating in the conference in Chicago in 1959 that led to the establishment of the National Council on Homemaker Services.*

During the innovative and exciting period of the 1960s, the SA became more progressive and experimental than it had been. It participated in the White House Conference on Children and Youth in 1960, and the staff at the national headquarters in New York and the four territorial commissioners continued the follow-up work of the conference. For example, they participated in the conference on out-of-school unemployed youths in urban areas, held in Washington, D.C., in March 1961. With other national organizations, the SA supported and closely watched legislation affecting children, always one of its primary concerns. Disaster relief persisted, such as after earthquakes in Chile in 1960 and in Alaska in 1964. On the local level, as early as 1961, even before the term ''community control'' became popular in the late 1960s, the agency established a Spanish-oriented corps in the Bronx, New York, especially to assist migrants from Puerto Rico. In the mid-1960s, local programs began to utilize group therapy for alcoholics. And, in 1965, the SA helped to produce a television program, shown across the nation, on the hardships of poverty in Appalachia; after receiving clothes, food, toys, and such in response to the program, the network asked the SA to distribute these donations.

The death of Lieutenant-Colonel Wrieden in 1970 ended an era in the history of social services in the SA. Widely known and respected in the national social work community, she had helped to elevate the SA to the center, and even to the forefront, of the national social service community. Her replacement, Colonel Mary Verner, continued and even expanded SA social services in the early 1970s, when she served as the national consultant for social services. A professional social worker who had served and administered maternity homes and hospitals in Cleveland, Ohio, Colonel Verner coordinated the development of projects and services throughout the organization, and she also represented the SA on a host of national agencies and programs, such as committees and coalitions of The National Assembly of National Voluntary Health and Social Welfare Organizations, Inc.* In the early 1970s, programs functioning throughout the SA structure included Meals-on-Wheels for older people. The organization was one of seven national agencies to receive grants from the federal Office of Education for a project to educate selected clients for parenthood. One corps developed Project LINK-UP, a special activity focusing on families affected by the increasing problem of unemployment. Corps in Cleveland, Detroit, and elsewhere developed innovative Harborlight Projects to help alcoholics, a continuing social service of this major and veteran national agency.

The primary sources for studying the SA's history are diverse. A wide range of agency publications describing particular social services are helpful. *The Salvation Army Year Book* issued annually, contains information about the organization in the United States for a large part of its history. The SA has a small archives at its national headquarters in New York City. Files of *The War Cry* and other publications are preserved there.

Students are fortunate to have a fine history of the SA, Herbert A. Wisbey, Jr., *Soldiers Without Swords: A History of the Salvation Army in the United States*

(1955), which displays his enthusiasm for the organization. Wisbey's doctoral dissertation "Religion in Action: A History of the Salvation Army in the United States" (Columbia University, 1951), is more documented than his book. Standard histories in the field of social welfare, such as Walter Trattner, *From Poor Law to Welfare State* (1974), and Clarke A. Chambers, *Seedtime of Reform* (1963), neglect the SA, which is discussed in Paul T. Ringenbach, *Tramps and Reformers, 1873–1916: The Discovery of Unemployment in New York* (1973). There is room for more scholarly studies of the history of this veteran and leading social welfare agency.

SAVE THE CHILDREN FEDERATION (SCF). As high unemployment and economic depression began in the late 1920s, conditions were especially bad in the coal mining areas of Appalachia. A strike in the early 1930s and concomitant violence, especially in Harlan County, Kentucky, acerbated an already deteriorated situation for the children. In response to these problems, the American Friends Service Committee* (AFSC) began to conduct such social services as providing food, clothing, and medical care to the children of unemployed miners. Funds from the American Relief Administration* (ARA) assisted the AFSC's efforts, which were led and coordinated by Clarence Pickett. Conditions in the region grew worse in the fall and winter of 1931 and in early 1932. The local Harlan County Relief Committee (HCRC) tried to provide food, supplies, and medical relief to families and children in Harlan County. Social and church workers in Appalachia and New York grew so concerned about the plight of the children that in late 1931, they established the Save the Children Federation (SCF) as the Save the Children Fund (SCF). The most important figure in the founding of the SCF was John Voris, an experienced social work administrator. Other founders included such prominent figures as Carl Christian Carstens, the head of the Child Welfare League of America* (CWLA), Clarence Pickett of the AFSC, Dr. Charles H. Johnson, the commissioner of social welfare of New York state and the SCF's first chairman, Dr. Arthur J. Brown, of the Board of Foreign Missions of the Presbyterian Church in the United States of America (PC), and Professor Robert Lynd of Columbia University and coauthor of the classic, *Middletown* (1929).

The SCF developed ties with the Save the Children International Union, which had been established in England in 1920 primarily to aid children in war-torn Eastern Europe. Incorporated according to the laws of the state of New York on January 7, 1932, the American chapter minimized assistance abroad and emphasized the immediate and primary agency concern of helping the children of unemployed miners in Kentucky, West Virginia, Illinois, and other states where the AFSC had been operating. Citing the lack of a national child welfare agency to deliver social services and noting that even organizations concerned with rural life, such as the Farm Bureau, generally neglected child welfare, the SCF's founders hoped to concentrate on Appalachia. Suggesting the SCF's ties to the church social welfare community, it established headquarters in the PC Building at 156 Fifth Avenue in New York City.

With its structure established, the SCF began to function and to develop in 1932. The group of founders became the first board of directors. John Voris, the executive vice-president, directed the staff of two full-time and two part-time workers. Primarily because of Voris's enthusiasm and interest, the SCF initiated a project to develop a child hygiene center in Harlan County, the locale of not only bloody labor strife and high unemployment, but also a place with very high rates of infant mortality and malnutrition among the children. To determine conditions and to decide on services, Carstens conducted a survey of Bell and Harlan counties in Kentucky. Following the survey, the SCF sent a child health specialist who had experience with the United States Public Health Service and in China, Dr. Iva M. Miller, to conduct a more detailed, two-month study of the health and sanitary situations in Harlan County. This survey helped to establish a local welfare committee, headed by Reverend C. E. Vogel.

Conditions continued to deteriorate. In late May 1932, Reverend Vogel of the HCRC wrote, "from Wednesday to Saturday we starve." At its board of directors meeting in July 1932, the SCF authorized the establishment of the child hygiene unit. Dr. Miller was in charge of the unit, which also had a public health nurse and a sanitation inspector, both from the Kentucky State Board of Health. The health unit held clinics all over the county, in camps, schools, restaurants, and such. It analyzed the water supply, prompting either chlorination or condemnation. Local people helped build sanitary toilets and other facilities, and they were paid in clothing and shoes for the children. This pioneering SCF project initiated the agency's principle of self-help. The SCF realized that this type of work needed to be expanded.

In 1932, the SCF conducted a study of two counties in Tennessee reputed to be especially depressed, Overton and Campbell counties. The poor conditions there led to a meeting in late September 1932 at Pineville, Bell County, Kentucky, another hard-hit area. At this meeting, Dr. Miller developed a plan of cooperation among social workers, ministers, and others in these counties to provide immediate relief for the children. Interestingly, the personnel Dr. Miller selected to coordinate the work in Overton and Campbell counties were agents with service abroad, respectively, Belinda Bass, who had served with the Near East Relief,* Miss Ruth Louise Parker, who had served with the Young Women's Christian Association* (YWCA) in China and with the Presbyterian missions to American Indian children. Because these programs involved representatives from his department, the head of the Kentucky State Board of Health, Dr. A. T. McCormack, became interested in the agency's work. He soon joined both the state committee, which was participating in an SCF appeal, and the board of directors of the SCF itself.

Beginning in early 1932, the SCF began an appeal for clothes, shoes, and other supplies for the children of Appalachia. Prominent church leaders, such as Reverend Dr. Charles D. Texler, the president of the Greater New York Federation of Churches, were active in this campaign. Along with the AFSC, the Conference of Southern Mountain Workers,* and some important individuals in Appalachian social service, the SCF began a hot lunch program for Appalachian schoolchildren. This program was the forerunner of the hot lunch program of the early New Deal. In 1933, the SCF developed the first of many local committees to inaugurate child health work in other selected rural counties. The county committees—which typically consisted of about twenty members, including such local figures as ministers, the county farm agent, the county supervisor, and representatives of service and women's clubs—developed as the most important SCF structure. Stressing the self-help principle, county committees conducted such activities as distributing clothing and, beginning in 1938, developing demonstration schools. In the mid-1930s, the SCF expanded its activities, establishing services in the Imperial Valley of California, in the Pine Barrens of New Jersey, and in the coal fields of Williamson County in southern Illinois. In 1941, the organization sent a representative to develop a child care program in the Missouri Ozarks. Apparently in 1939, the agency was renamed the Save the Children Federation (SCF).

The most important single domestic activity of the SCF became the American Indian child welfare project. Initiated in 1948 following a cruel blizzard that left thousands of Navajo Indians homeless and hungry, the program characteristically developed the self-help principle. By 1972, there were over two hundred such locally conducted programs among fifty-three tribes in twenty states. American Indian children represented over one-half of the approximately twenty-five thousand child sponsorships in 1972.

The clothing program for Appalachian children also developed as a major SCF activity. Begun in the late 1930s, the program was conducted by schoolchildren throughout the United States who donated used clothing, which the organization then distributed free to Appalachian parents. In 1943, parents began to pay minimally for the clothing. The contributed clothing program was consolidated in 1951, with all processing now conducted in one building, in Knoxville, Tennessee. To evaluate and update its used clothing program, in the late 1950s, the SCF commissioned specialists in sociology from the University of Tennessee and from Berea College in Kentucky to analyze it in their respective states. Welfare workers from the Tennessee and Kentucky state welfare departments evaluated the program as well. All four sources strongly recommended continuing the service. The aid in 1960 of Benjamin Freedman, a member of the board of directors who was a textile executive, helped to strengthen the program further. In the mid-1960s, the agency approved of and then began construction of a new clothing center in Knoxville. By 1972, annual "bundle days" in some ten thousand American schools yielded tons of clothing, which were sent to the SCF's center in Knoxville. From there, the clothing was sorted and distributed to over 110 clothing centers in five Appalachian states, where parents still purchased clothing cheaply.

The SCF shifted its focus to activities abroad by the early 1940s, beginning in

1940 with the program of Americans supporting British day care centers and of "adopting" British children. The SCF sent Henry J. Allen, a former Kansas governor and United States senator, to survey conditions and to develop the British work further. These efforts resulted in the establishment of sponsoring groups in Detroit and in Savannah, Georgia, for instance, and at American colleges and universities. The SCF's overseas program quickly became a major activity. Cooperating with Stuyvesant High School in New York City, the SCF sponsored the Amiens Lycée in France. Conflicts within the organization developed over the percentage of foreign work undertaken, but the only policy was the SCF assessment of the promise of local self-help. The SCF continued to sponsor schools in France, Belgium, and eventually West Germany. The agency aided children in such war-torn and disaster-plagued countries as South Korea, South Vietnam, Peru, and Bangladesh. In 1959, SCF established its Community Development Foundation to promote the self-help principle abroad.

The refusal of the National Information Bureau (NIB) to recognize its legitimacy frustrated the SCF greatly. Even though it was endorsed by community chests in two states and despite repeated attempts at recognition, the SCF did not win NIB approval until 1970. One apparent charge by the NIB—that the structure and the leadership were unsound—was simply not true. Since its inception in 1932, the SCF had enjoyed the cooperation and endorsement of respected social welfare, church, and public leaders. Dr. Alva W. Taylor, a major figure in church and social welfare circles in the South, worked for the SCF. Eleanor Roosevelt spoke at the SCF's first annual meeting and continued to endorse enthusiastically the organization's work. Its board of directors, which numbered nineteen in 1952, has included such prominent figures as Dr. Wilbur J. Cohen, the former secretary of the Department of Health, Education, and Welfare.

In the period from the late 1940s through the 1960s, SCF continued its basic activities and consistently helped to develop new programs at home and abroad. With encouragement and assistance from the United States Bureau of Indian Affairs, for instance, the SCF developed a new program for Navajo children in 1948, the same year in which the National Congress of Parents and Teachers inaugurated its teacher package project to improve education abroad. The project supplied teachers overseas with necessary personal and classroom materials, through the auspices of the SCF. In the fall of 1951, the SCF hired an experienced business manager, who promptly streamlined the agency's administrative structure. By 1952, the SCF had programs in about 750 rural schools, concentrated in the Southeast. In the early 1950s, President Richard P. Saunders conducted extensive personal field observations at home and abroad, leading to new programs, including one in Yugoslavia. Characteristically, after he visited a school in Patrick County, Virginia, a SCF area consultant initiated a dental hygiene program at the school. Following the end of the Korean War, the SCF immediately began rehabilitation work in Korea. In this period, the agency introduced its school sponsorship program in Israel. Although not a traditional relief agency, the SCF helped victims of floods in France and Holland and of an earthquake in the Greek Ionian Islands. During the 1950s, the annual doll contests by *Seventeen Magazine* helped to publicize the SCF, for the dolls made by the contestants were sent to children abroad as Christmas presents.

Suggesting its increasingly important role, in 1953, the SCF moved from its national headquarters in downtown New York City to new offices at the Carnegie Endowment International Center. In 1957, however, the SCF moved its headquarters to Norwalk, Connecticut, to a building constructed initially to house the destitute children of Fairfield County. The organization continued to maintain an office in New York City. It developed programs of self-help for families and villages, and after about six years, these programs began to take shape. At a conference with representatives from Indian tribes in the American Southwest, the SCF offered to extend its community self-help program to them. A number accepted within a few years. Cooperating with the Community Development Trust Fund of Tanzania, in 1962, the SCF began a program there that helped students finish high school. In the mid-1960s, the SCF began a pilot project of providing interest-free loans to families in chronically poor Appalachia. The agency provided assistance to children and families after a blizzard on an Indian reservation in December 1967 and for refugees following the Tet offensive in Vietnam in March 1968. The agency's twenty-fifth anniversary in October 1967 was highlighted by a tribute from President Lyndon B. Johnson, a proclamation by governors of twenty-nine states, and a celebration dinner at the Carnegie International Center in New York City.

Community development and self-help projects continued to be emphasized in the 1970s. In the early 1970s, SCF adopted SAVE Impact, a program that pooled all the resources of a community to improve conditions for the children. Examples of such programs included the development of communitywide improvements in Syedbari, Bangladesh, a medical center in Hipolito Billini, Dominican Republic, and, reminiscent of the domestic origins of this famous humanitarian agency, a child care center in another American poverty-stricken area, the Bedford-Stuyvesant section of Brooklyn, New York.

The sources for studying the SCF's history are varied. The published *Annual Reports* are helpful, and articles appearing in *Mountain Life and Work* describe the SCF's origins and activities in Appalachia. The SCF archives at its national headquarters contain the files of the agency, which are available to properly qualified and identified researchers. There are four containers in the Henry J. Allen Papers at the Library of Congress in Washington, D.C., relating primarily to his fieldwork for the SCF in the 1940s, and the Dr. Alva W. Taylor Papers at the Disciples of Christ Historical Society in Nashville, Tennessee, contain materials relating to the SCF. E. George Payne, *Guideposts to Modern Child Service: A Survey of the SCF* (1951), is a contemporary analysis of SCF's operations.

A pamphlet, Alvin F. Harlow, *A Decade of Saving the Children* (1942), is helpful, as is an eight-page press release, "Save the Children Federation Anniversary Background'' (c. 1972), which the SCF headquarters gave to me. There does not appear to be a scholarly history of the SCF.

SAVE THE CHILDREN FUND: see SAVE THE CHILDREN FEDERA-TION.

SEEING EYE, INC., THE (SE). In the early 1920s, Dorothy Harrison Eustis, who came from a prominent family in Philadelphia, began to work at a laboratory at her home, "Fortunate Fields," in Vevey, Switzerland, with an American geneticist, Elliott S. Humphrey, to develop training dogs that were used to protect Swiss borders, by the Italian Metropolitan Police, in the Swiss Army, in helping to find missing persons, and in other types of civilian activities. In 1926, Eustis visited a school in Potsdam, Germany, where dogs were being trained for use by the blind. This experience prompted her to write an article on this subject, which appeared in the issue of *The Saturday Evening Post* for November 5, 1927. In Nashville, Tennessee, a young blind insurance agent, Morris R. Frank, had a friend read him the article. This led the aggressive Frank to correspond with Eustis about establishing such a program for the blind in the United States. This correspondence led eventually to Frank's being trained at Fortunate Fields in Switzerland to use the dog to help him get around.

Eustis and Humphrey, the dog trainer and instructor at Fortunate Fields, insisted that Frank and the dog function in the dangerous, automobile-plagued streets in the United States before certifying the value of this program for blind individuals. Amid considerable publicity in the press, Frank returned to Nashville, where, after functioning successfully, he determined to establish an organization to so help other blind people with trained seeing eye dogs.

Eustis returned to the United States in early 1928 to promote such an organization. She first asked Robert Irwin, the head of the American Foundation for the Blind* (AFB), if his organization would be interested in assisting this work, but the AFB declined. She then spoke of the proposed organization to the Colony Club, an organization of elite New York City women. When this venture failed to raise funds, Eustis convinced three of her friends each to subscribe $2,500 per year for three years, enough funds to help begin an organization in the United States. Eustis then went to Nashville, conferred with Frank and some other local people, and agreed, in 1929, to establish The Seeing Eye, Inc. (SE). The group then drafted a charter and drew up articles of incorporation. The term "seeing eye" came from Proverbs 20:12, "The hearing ear, and the seeing eye, the Lord hath made even both of them."

The SE grew slowly at first. Founder Frank opened the organization headquarters in a room next to his insurance office in Nashville. To develop what became one of the most important activities of the SE—to train instructors—the organization opened a school with three pupils in Lausanne, Switzerland, in June 1929. To implement the direct social service activity of the SE, it began classes in

Nashville for the blind in late 1928. The climate and its heat, however, quickly proved to be too taxing on the blind students. When Willi Ebeling, a wealthy businessman who had retired in 1918 and then raised and bred shepherd dogs, proposed that the organization move to his estate in New Jersey, the SE accepted his offer. The school operated with a small staff and a few students, and the SE continued to shy away from publicity and from organizational development and largesse. In October 1931, Eustis, still the SE's guiding figure, obtained a large tract of country property in Whippany, New Jersey. Fearing that the SE dogs would threaten their own domesticated pets, some home owners in the area complained, but a lawsuit upheld the right of the SE to move to the complex. In 1932, in Whippany, the SE established its first full headquarters and a school for twenty-two blind students.

With the school and administrative offices settled near Morristown, Eustis decided in the early 1930s to develop the organizational structure more fully. With some professional advice, she interested an outstanding person in the New York area to help her efforts for the blind, Herbert A. Satterlee, a former member of the New York State Commission for the Blind and a brother-in-law of banker J. P. Morgan. Eustis met Satterlee at the Cosmopolitan Club, an elite New York club, and convinced him to invite a few of his colleagues as possible supporters of the organization. The group met subsequently at the Downtown Association, another elite New York City club, which broke a long-standing tradition and allowed one of the training dogs in. Satterlee agreed to chair an advisory council and to act officially as the public sponsor of the SE.

Pleased with these beginning organizational developments, Eustis returned to Europe, leaving the affairs of the SE in the hands of Gretchen Green, a social events writer in New York. Green publicized the organization quietly through parlor teas with women's groups, while Satterlee and the advisory council moved quickly, organizing themselves as a functioning executive committee. The organization then sponsored, in November 1933, a dinner party attended by a surprising number (247) of wealthy people interested in the organization. The affair featured a film of the SE. The dinner helped to promote publicity about the SE, which still claimed to shy away from publicity in the press and the like. Next, an SE costume party for patrons and people interested in the work led to a report of the organization and its activities in the New York City press. Literary critic Alexander Woollcot developed as the organization's chief raconteur, relating its history and activities at various fund-raising functions. Beginning in this period, Booth Tarkington, the famous writer, served for many years as the honorary chairman of the national membership committee of the SE. An important organizational event occurred in 1936 when Eustis and Frank won the coveted National Institute for Social Science award for "distinguished service to humanity."

While the SE developed as a philanthropic organization on one level, its most important activity continued to be training blind people to use seeing eye dogs.

Still faced with the problem of attracting instructors, in 1938, in a determined effort to attract enrollees in its training program, the SE published a booklet, *Career Jobs for Five Men.* At the school in New Jersey, blind students practiced using the seeing eye dogs, and generally after one month, a student returned home with a dog. The SE did not allow benefactors to give dogs to students; it encouraged students to work to pay minimally for their social services, in this case, a seeing eye dog. This ideology coincided with the self-help notion then prevalent in social welfare, and it related also to the long-standing criticism in the work with blind people and of impostors begging for money.

The SE continued to provide a range of social services for the blind, for example, cooperating, in the early 1930s, with the Pennsylvania State Council for the Blind to help individuals recently blinded in accidents readjust to life and work by using the seeing eye dogs. By the mid-1930s, the SE had trained over 125 blind people, about 80 percent of whom returned to functioning, independent lives despite their handicaps.

The organization and its services continued to grow after 1940. Eustis died in 1946, but the SE strengthened its organization, attracting around fifteen thousand active and supporting members by the 1940s. At one point, in the late 1950s, the SE even stopped asking for yearly donations. The agency moved steadily in the social service field. At the request of the United States surgeon-general in the early 1950s, the SE published a pamphlet, *If Blindness Occurs,* a helpful guide for physicians, personnel in the field, and the families of blind individuals. In the early 1960s, the organization established a dog breeding farm in Mendham, New Jersey. A television production in 1966 of the story and activities of the SE helped to promote the organization, as did a Walt Disney production and a book by Peter Putnam, *The Triumph of the Seeing Eye.*

In the mid-1960s, some significant organizational developments changed the basic nature of the SE. A grant program had been operating informally since the late 1950s, but by 1966, it was crystallized further. To help direct this program, the SE brought together a group of specialists, led by Dr. R. Townley Paton, a representative of ophthalmologists. The first such grant had gone in 1958 to help construct desperately needed facilities for conducting research in ophthalmology. Also in 1958, the SE received the results of a three-year study by the research center of Columbia University's School of Social Work. Published as *Guide Dogs Training for Blind People,* the study argued that because only 1 percent of the blind people in the country used such dogs, there was no need for the SE to expand its facilities significantly. Coupled with an almost abundance of funds, this situation apparently prompted the SE to provide other such grants. In 1965, the SE's trustees moved to broaden its charter to allow relief services, education and vocational training, research and training with mobility devices, and training and rehabilitation for visually handicapped persons. One factor influencing the decision to broaden the SE was the perceived disparity between the minimal funds spent generally to prevent blindness and the funds given almost freely, it seemed, to relieve those already blind. A study done at this time also showed that not all ophthalmologists encouraged blind people to participate in rehabilitation programs, and this shift by the SE also represented an effort to educate these doctors. In 1966, the SE appointed a director of grants, and in 1967, the grants advisory council was established. By the end of 1972, the SE had dispensed nearly $6 million to 128 different institutions. By 1972, the organization had trained about sixty-three hundred dogs, which served over thirty-eight hundred people. The organizational structure in the early 1970s included a twenty-member board of trustees, including the SE's treasurer and its president, who served as the chairman of the board of trustees. The now renamed grants advisory coordinating committee had six members, including the president, who served as ex officio. Indicative of the SE's relatively new emphasis, in the early 1970s, it provided funds to preserve the functioning of the rehabilitation programs of the National Industries for the Blind, Inc.*

Libraries do not have many primary sources relating to the SE's history. Primary information, however, can be culled from such contemporary articles as "The Seeing Eye," *Time Magazine* 27 (May 18, 1936): 79–80, Horace B. Sodt, "The Seeing Eye, Inc. Is Unique Among American Philanthropies," *National Humane Review* 38 (October 1950), and an agency publication, *Here Is Freedom* (n.d. [1934]).

The secondary sources, however, are abundant. There is a helpful but not scholarly history of the SE, Dickson Hartwell, *Dogs Against Darkness: The Story of the Seeing Eye* (1942), and Frances A. Koestler, *The Unseen Majority: A Social History of Blindness in America* (1976), discusses the agency.

SHUT-IN SOCIETY: see NATIONAL SHUT-IN SOCIETY, THE.

SOCIAL ACTION DEPARTMENT OF NATIONAL CATHOLIC WEL-FARE CONFERENCE: see UNITED STATES CATHOLIC CONFER-ENCE, DEPARTMENT OF SOCIAL DEVELOPMENT AND WORLD PEACE OF THE.

SOCIETY OF ST. VINCENT DE PAUL, SUPERIOR COUNCIL OF THE U.S., INC. (SSVP). Around 1830, in Paris, France, a group of students at The Sorbonne, led by Bailly de Surcy, the editor of the *Tribune Catholique,* participated in a seminar to examine historical issues from the Catholic viewpoint. Among the students was Antoine Frederic Ozanam, a brilliant young scholar, who argued that the failure of Catholic laymen and clergy to do "good works" among the less advantaged elements of society both jeopardized the salvation of their own souls and threatened to drive lower-class Catholics out of the church and into the arms of secular social reformers. Under Ozanam's guidance, there-fore, the seminar was quickly transformed into an organization aimed at the "spiritual welfare" of its members through service to the poor and needy. At the suggestion of Monsignor de Surcy, the organization in 1834 adopted the name of the Society of St. Vincent de Paul, in honor of the seventeenth-century French priest who had devoted his ministry to charitable works.

Beginning with a core of one hundred students, the SSVP grew steadily within France, so that by 1840 there were two thousand members in fifteen centers throughout the country. Members included professionals, merchants, and even nobility, as well as students. The next two decades saw the movement taking root on virtually every continent, a fortunate development since the society was suppressed in France during the 1860s. After 1870 the society's expansion continued, slowly but steadily, and by 1933, its centennial year, it could claim thirteen thousand local conferences (chapters) with 200,000 members. Throughout its history, the SSVP has been under the control of the Catholic laity, a fact recognized and approved by Pope Gregory XVI in 1845 and reaffirmed by every succeeding pontiff. The society has, however, maintained close and cordial relations with the clergy, and since the papacy of Pius IX in the mid-nineteenth century, has operated under the general auspices of a "Cardinal Protector."

The first American conference of the SSVP was organized at the Cathedral parish of St. Louis, Missouri, in 1845 by Father John Timon, a second-generation Irish-American, who had become active in society affairs while studying in Europe. Within two years, conferences were established in both New York City and Buffalo, New York, and thereafter in many other American cities. The basic organizational structure of the American branch of the society resembled that of other countries. The principal unit was the conference, almost always organized by members of a local parish. Conferences in a given area were then brought together into a Particular Council, the first of which was New York City's, established in 1857. Above the particular councils were the central (diocesan) council, the superior council, and the worldwide council general, headquartered in Paris and presided over by the president-general.

In most countries throughout the nineteenth century, the superior council was the national-level organization of the SSVP, but in the United States, which was slow to organize on a nationwide basis, there arose several independent superior councils centered in major regional cities. Among the most important of these were the superior councils of New York City (the first to organize in 1860), Brooklyn, St. Louis, and New Orleans. Despite the calling of five national assemblies by the New York Superior Council, it was not until 1915 that a single American Superior Council was finally created with headquarters at Catholic University in Washington, D.C. At that point, the regional superior councils were transformed into metropolitan councils, adding a new stratum to the society's organizational structure.

In keeping with its mission to aid the needy in every possible way, the SSVP has been active in a wide range of social welfare services. During the nineteenth and early twentieth centuries, the society in the United States devoted its energies primarily to aiding the masses of Catholic immigrants who were crowding into America's cities. Because most of these were subject to the twin evils of economic hardship and religious prejudice, the SSVP sought to serve both their physical and spiritual needs, and thus to counteract the seeming proselytizing influence of the established, Protestant-dominated charity organizations.

Broadly, the SSVP's work fell into three major—and often overlapping—categories: emergency aid to the poor, sick, and disaster struck; family services; and aid to women and children. Among their work for those in distress, local conferences made home and hospital visits to the poor and sick; collected and distributed used clothing, furniture, and household goods; provided free food and fuel; and even arranged for the burial of the indigent dead. Although the society emphasized the importance of home visitations, its efforts extended to public institutions (such as mental hospitals and prisons), where it offered both physical relief and spiritual solace through personal counseling, religious services, and Sunday school classes. In every natural or economic disaster, the SSVP could be found at the forefront of relief agencies, providing such needed services as soup kitchens, emergency lodgings, and employment bureaus, without regard to the religious affiliations of the suffering.

Recognizing the importance of the family unit, the SSVP also worked to improve and strengthen family life. Among other activities in this area, it conducted regular parish surveys and censuses, offered visiting housekeeper services and sewing schools for housewives, and sponsored the construction of inexpensive housing for the working classes. In 1907, the Baltimore Particular Council inaugurated the SSVP's first family welfare program, which sent social workers into the homes of the needy to study their problems firsthand. Adopting the casework techniques of the emerging social work profession, this program was soon copied by other branches of the SSVP, as well as by other private welfare agencies.

The SSVP's work in behalf of women and children was a natural outgrowth of its interest in maintaining a stable family structure. Besides their services for working mothers—including day care centers first established in the 1890s—local conferences showed great concern for homeless and destitute women. Many followed the lead of the conferences of St. Peter's parish in Jersey City, New Jersey, which, as early as 1858, had a lodging house for them.

But it was in its services for children—especially orphans—that the SSVP made its most noteworthy contribution. Of major concern in the late nineteenth century was the fact that many Catholic orphans, as wards of the state, were often given into the care of private, Protestant-dominated agencies, which ignored, and in some cases undermined, their religious heritage. The SSVP took a leading role in the struggle to bring Catholic sacraments and instruction to these children. To ensure that they were placed with Catholic foster families, furthermore, various branches of the SSVP set up Catholic home bureaus, the first of which was organized in New York in 1898 by Thomas Mulry, often called the "American Ozanam."

Juvenile delinquents and children too old for orphanages were cared for by the

Catholic protectory movement, formed with the help of the SSVP, which maintained homes and schools in major American cities; and working "street orphans" could find refuge in facilities like Father Dunne's Newsboys' Home, established in St. Louis in 1905. The continuing efforts of SSVP leaders such as Timothy D. Hurley of Illinois to remove youthful offenders from adult criminal court proceedings were ultimately rewarded when Illinois became the first of many states to establish a juvenile court system.

Other services of the SSVP for children included the enrollment of Catholic students in parochial schools, in many of which it also instituted hot lunch programs, and the support of dozens of medical facilities like the New York Foundling Hospital. In most of these programs, the New York Superior Council, under the leadership of Thomas Mulry, was perhaps the most active in the nation. It was the New York Council, for example, that first noted in the 1890s that most of the city's boys' clubs offering recreational programs were controlled by Protestants. As a result, in 1896, the New York Catholic Boys' Association was formed to sponsor the creation of local Catholic boys' clubs and summer camps. After several organizational changes, this association emerged in 1920 as the Catholic Boys' Clubs of the Archdiocese of New York.

Although the SSVP was a Catholic organization, the outlook of its leaders was never parochial. To advance the cause of social welfare, Society members eagerly cooperated with non-Catholic relief agencies, especially the many charity organization societies so active in American cities. This interaction fostered both a mutual respect and a mutual interest in the need for professionally trained social workers. Thomas Mulry, himself a long-time member of The Charity Organization Society of the City of New York,* consistently supported the idea of professionalization, and he was largely responsible for the establishment in 1916 of the Fordham University School of Social Service, on whose board of directors sat several SSVP members.

Among Catholic charities, too, the SSVP was a leader. As its welfare activities became increasingly diverse, the society was among the first Catholic agencies to create diocesan bureaus of social welfare, beginning about 1898, to coordinate and act as a clearinghouse for its many services. *The St. Vincent de Paul Quarterly,* first published in 1895, quickly became the most important journal of the American Catholic welfare movement; and the society's occasional national meetings became the basis for the National Conference of Catholic Charities* (NCCC), which first met in 1910. Vincentians assumed a major role in the direction of the NCCC, and in 1916 the SSVP's journal was transformed into the NCCC's official publication, *The Catholic Charities Review.* Since 1920, the annual meetings of the SSVP have been held in conjunction with those of the NCCC.

Although many of the SSVP's early welfare functions have been absorbed by government agencies since the 1930s, the society remains an active provider of private services. In the 1950s, many councils began to establish schools to inform their members better of the aims and methods of the SSVP and to acquaint them with the most effective uses of community resources. The American branch of the organization also achieved a growing significance in the worldwide movement, and in the 1960s, it began to offer its expertise to the society in less-developed nations. Always among the most financially efficient welfare bodies, the SSVP gains its funds through contributions, especially from parish "poor boxes," and through the community chest (the SSVP has never imposed a membership fee). By 1960, the American SSVP had 37,000 members, organized into more than 4,300 conferences and 233 particular and central councils.

Besides *The St. Vincent de Paul Quarterly* and *The Catholic Charities Review,* information can be found in the *Proceedings* of the NCCC, especially those for 1933, which contain a section on the observance of the society's centenary. The best secondary source is Reverend Daniel T. McColgan, *A Century of Charity: The First Hundred Years of the Society of St. Vincent de Paul in the United States* (1951), 2 vols. Other useful works include Reverend J. W. Helmes, *Thomas M. Mulry* (1938); Charles K. Murphy, *The Spirit of the Society of St. Vincent de Paul* (1940); and Kathleen O'Meara, *Frederic Ozanam* (1883). To varying extents, the SSVP's work is treated in many works on Catholic history, including John O'Grady, *Catholic Charities in the United States* (1930); Donald P. Gavin, *The National Conference of Catholic Charities, 1910–1960* (1962); and Robert D. Cross, *The Emergence of Liberal Catholicism in America* (1967). There is a worthwhile article on the society in the *New Catholic Encyclopedia* (1967), vol. 12.

Philip De Vencentes

SPEEDWELL SERVICES FOR CHILDREN, INC., THE (SSC). During the late nineteenth and early twentieth centuries, babies in New York City and in other cities around the country died at exceedingly high rates. Around the turn of the century, for example, foundlings and other dependent babies in public institutions in New York City died at rates often reaching 90 percent. A New York City pediatrician, Dr. Henry Dwight Chapin, became interested in infant mortality while working in the city's tenement districts and, beginning in 1890, developed two new preventative programs while he was head of the Babies' Ward (BW) of the New York Post-Graduate Hospital. In one program, doctors sent children treated at the BW to a country home in upstate New York to recuperate. The mortality rate among these children was significantly lower than among those returned to their tenement homes. The second program, friendly visits, was derived from a social work technique. Aware of developments in the charity organization society movement and in social work, Chapin organized the Sunbeam Committee, a group of volunteer women affiliated with the BW. The committee visited homes in impoverished districts, explained child hygiene, and distributed pamphlets on baby care in Yiddish, German, Italian, and English. The emphases placed on proper environment and on systematic home visiting were carried over when Dr. Chapin joined with other philanthropic men and women in New York, such as Reverend and Mrs. Donald Sage Mackay, to establish the Speedwell Services for Children, Inc. (SSC), as the Speedwell Country Homes Society for Convalescent and Abandoned Children (SCHSCAC).

Initially concerned more with foundlings and illegitimate babies than with convalescing babies with families, the society opened its first unit in Morristown, New Jersey, in 1902. Chosen for its healthful, rural environment, yet close enough to maintain contact with the Post-Graduate Hospital, Morristown proved a good location. Carefully selected families were paid to board children, and prominent women in the community volunteered to inspect the boarding homes, thereby helping to promote hygienic conditions. A superintendent, a full-time nurse, and a local physician comprised the regular staff.

Although the Morristown organization disbanded in 1926 "because of difficulties arising from inter-state regulations" relating to child care, similar units were developed throughout the New York area. In 1915, volunteer women from the Free Synagogue of New York, headed by the famous rabbi, Stephen Wise, opened a unit in New Rochelle, New York. Prominent women in Yonkers cooperated with Chapin in founding a group there in 1917. By 1926, three other units, all managed by locally prominent women, were in operation: the Junior League Unit of Oyster Bay, the Easthampton, Long Island, Summer Unit, and a unit in Manhattan, managed by the graduates of a fashionable private girls' school, the Spence Alumnae Society.

In the late 1920s, as the number of foundlings decreased and as infant care improved, the society shifted its focus to convalescing babies. It cooperated with a number of New York hospitals and with the New York City Department of Public Welfare to care for sick and recuperating children.

Although it operated primarily in New York, as early as the 1920s, when the organization simplified its name to The Speedwell Society (SS), the society had influenced child care practices throughout the nation. Its success in reducing infant mortality helped convince child welfare workers and their agencies that family home care was healthier than institutionalization. Some social welfare organizations modeled their child care programs on the Speedwell technique, and the SS's principles influenced the establishment of the Louise Wise Services, the major Jewish adoption agency in New York and the nation.

Despite the Great Depression of the 1930s, the SS continued to provide social services for children in New York City. In 1930, suggesting its origins as a health and social service agency, the SS established an annual conference of doctors and nurses. In 1932, a unit on Long Island began to accept children with cardiac problems as an experiment; this effort was so successful that the SS established a special cardiac service in 1938 in cooperation with the New York Heart Association. In 1934, the SS closed its Harlem Unit because the low demand for convalescent care for Negro children did not seem to justify the expense. Other units took over the Harlem group's cases. In 1937, the SS began to implement a long-standing goal: to follow up cases by sending a worker to visit the children's homes and to educate mothers. Reminiscent of the friendly visiting at the BW in the 1890s, the program also began as an experiment. Two exhibits in 1939 resulted in some nationwide publicity for this technically local but influential agency. Exhibits for the American Academy of Pediatrics (AAP) in New York and another at the AAP's national conference in Cincinnati both resulted in correspondence and inquiries.

Basic Speedwell convalescent services continued in the 1940s. In 1940, the SS assisted public medical officials to combat an epidemic of scarlet fever. In 1944, the agency noted a problem: the scarcity of foster homes to care for convalescent children. In 1945, the loss of foster homes forced the closing of a postcontagious unit, an important group. In 1945, because of the problem of not enough foster homes, the North County Unit closed, but it reopened in 1947. In 1947, an SS exhibit at the Fifth International Congress on Pediatrics resulted in further publicity for the agency.

A basic shift in the SS's emphasis began in the late 1940s and early 1950s. In 1949, the North County Unit established a program to care for dependent and neglected children referred by the city's Department of Welfare, as opposed to convalescent children referred by health officials and agencies. A newly created central welfare committee became increasingly involved in child care policies and practices, and it began to emerge as a clearinghouse for social and medical services. A significant reorganization, studied and planned for about two years, took place in 1952. Foster care was now concentrated in two enlarged units, each served by the central office in Manhattan. Changes in the bylaws brought closer ties between units and the central society. Suggesting the new emphasis on services for dependent and neglected children, in 1953, the SS affiliated with the local Federation of Protestant Welfare Agencies. In 1955, a professionally trained social worker, Etta Steele, became the new executive director, a position she held until the dissolution of the agency in 1976. In the mid-1950s, the SS became eligible for partial reimbursements for staff expenditures through the Department of Welfare. In early 1956, the agency received a report on its operations, prepared by the Child Welfare League of America, Inc.* The study stressed the need to centralize administrative procedures, to coordinate medical, nursing, and casework services, and to simplify its financial structure. In the late 1950s, the SS increased the number of its foster homes and expanded its services to care for minority and physically and emotionally handicapped children.

In the 1960s and 1970s, the agency—which apparently became the SSC in about 1960—crystallized as a general child care agency. Foster homes and adoption continued to be emphasized, but the SSC became involved also in remedial, psychological, and psychiatric services. In 1968, the SSC stressed services to families to prevent the removal of the child. In the late 1960s and early 1970s, the SSC experimented with group homes and expanded group counseling. Beginning in 1970, agency-operated foster homes began to care for children with special needs who needed an understanding environment. School readiness and remedial education programs assisted agency children who attended school. By 1973, the SSC had seven group and agency-operated homes, and, reminiscent of the friendly visiting and counseling during the society's early history, thirty caseworkers dealt with the children on a one-to-one basis. Plagued by continuing financial problems, however, the SSC dissolved in 1976. The children for whom it was responsible were transferred to the auspices of the Sheltering Arms, another veteran child care organization in New York City.

The primary sources for studying the SSC's history include its published *Annual Reports,* which, for the most part, are available at both the New York Public Library and in the Russell Sage Collection at the Cohen Library of the City College of New York. *The New York Times* and other New York newspapers covered the activities of the agency. A host of articles by Dr. Chapin and his colleague in Morristown describe the agency. They include Chapin, "Convalescent Care for Hospital Babies," *Journal of the American Medical Association* 98 (January 2, 1932): 40–42; "Family Versus Institution," *The Survey* 55 (January 15, 1926): 458–488; and "A Plan of Dealing in Weak Infants and Children," *Charities and The Commons* 21 (March 27, 1909), 1267–1270. Dr. Francis Glazebrook, "A Method of Dealing with Illy-Nourished Infants," *Archives of Pediatrics* 28 (February 1911): 127–134, describes the unit in Morristown.

Peter Romanofsky, "Infant Mortality, Dr. Henry Dwight Chapin, and the Speedwell Society, 1890–1920," *Journal of the Medical Society of New Jersey* 73 (January 1976): 33–38, is apparently the only secondary study of the society.

STATE CHARITIES AID ASSOCIATION: see STATE COMMUNITIES AID ASSOCIATION.

STATE COMMUNITIES AID ASSOCIATION (SCAA). During the American Civil War, while she served with the United States Sanitary Commission,* Louisa Lee Schuyler, scion of a prominent New York family, became increasingly interested in charities. In the early 1870s, she heard of the horrible conditions inside the public welfare institutions of New York City and New York State. On January 9, 1872, Schuyler formed a committee in Westchester County to visit charitable institutions there. More importantly, on January 26, 1872, she founded the Visiting Committee for Bellevue and Other New York City Public Hospitals. These committees set up the need for a central association to coordinate these and other county committees in the state. Consequently, on May 11, 1872, Schuyler helped to organize the State Communities Aid Association (SCAA) as the State Charities Aid Association (SCAA) to organize and to supervise existing county visiting committees.

The SCAA also developed three initial standing committees—on children, on adult paupers, and on hospital patients. As the biographer of the SCAA's most important executive, Homer Folks, suggests, the founders were the best and most influential philanthropic and civic-minded people in New York. Charles Loring Brace, the founder of The Children's Aid Society,* prominent public health physicians, Dr. Stephen Smith and Dr. Abraham Jacobi, and Josephine Shaw Lowell were the best social welfare workers in the city. The benevolence, wealth, and influence of founders such as Joseph Choate, a leading attorney, and philanthropist Mrs. William B. Rice, a friend of Schuyler, assured the success of the new agency.

The SCAA quickly became a highly respected organization. State welfare officials valued its observations. The agency was concerned about removing children from the almshouses, influencing the 1875 law doing so for most children. A major late nineteenth-century achievement, the law unintentionally stimulated the growth of children's institutions. The SCAA campaigned vigorously against the institutionalization of children, contributing importantly to the national debate on the merits of family homes, as opposed to asylums, for dependent children. In its early period, the SCAA—whose rights to inspect almshouses were broadened in 1881—also worked to improve the care of the insane, a field in which, like child welfare, it remained constantly in the vanguard of state and even national developments.

A major turning point in the history of the SCAA occurred in February 1893, when a social worker from the Children's Aid Society of Pennsylvania, Homer Folks, became the executive secretary. Folks transformed the SCAA from a respectable voluntary agency with a paid staff of three workers into a model organization with a trained staff of specialists, involved in virtually all aspects of welfare in the state and having an impact in the field nationally. The New York City commissioner of public charities under reform mayor Seth Low and adviser to New York State governors and to President Franklin D. Roosevelt, Folks remained with the SCAA for the rest of his long and eminent career, influencing nearly all of its activities.

Although Folks's influence on the SCAA was extensive, a group of specialists in child welfare, independent of Folks, developed the most comprehensive voluntary child welfare programs in the state and, for a while, in the country. Folks did promote the establishment, in 1893, of the subcommittee on providing situations for mothers and babies, which found rural homes and jobs for single mothers and their infants, attempting to keep both off the welfare rolls. This work established the basis for the county agent system for dependent children, a widely used twentieth-century procedure. Emerging from the years of SCAA work in this field, first Mary Vida Clark and then Ida Curry became leading state and national child welfare specialists. The child-placing committee, established in June 1898, which had many different names, produced the most respected early adoption specialist, Sophie Theis, who worked from 1907 until her retirement in 1952. In 1898, the SCAA prompted the founding, with the New York Association for Improving the Condition of the Poor,* of the Joint Committee on the Care of Motherless Infants to convince public authorities that foundlings could be cared for better in family homes than institutions.

The SCAA pioneered not only in child welfare but also in the care of the mentally ill. In 1908, the SCAA established a subcommittee on the after care of the insane, whose agents became psychiatric social workers long before the term applied to professionals in the 1920s. After many name changes, it became the committee on mental hygiene, which aided the development of The National Committee for Mental Hygiene* in 1909 and which spearheaded a statewide educational campaign in 1910. As early as 1915, the SCAA committee campaigned for a bond issue to provide more and better state mental hospitals, and it helped enact the provision in 1917 for special school classes for mentally handicapped children. A committee on provision for the feebleminded published studies linking the SCAA to this important Progressive-era movement. In 1914, the secretary of the state committee on mental hygiene, Katherine Ecob, worked to assist local selective service boards to deal with mentally deficient men; by the end of 1942, the SCAA had enlisted about seven hundred volunteer social workers, assisting every board in the state.

The SCAA involved itself in another important Progressive reform issue: tuberculosis, the disease of the slum tenements and of urban congestion. In 1907, Executive Secretary Folks secured financial support from the Russell Sage Foundation,* created the SCAA Committee on the Prevention of Tuberculosis, and then hired social worker John A. Kingsbury as its agent. The committee quickly became the affiliated state agency, outside of the city, of the National Tuberculosis Association.* In 1907, the committee initiated a statewide tuberculosis campaign, as SCAA county committees throughout the state created subcommittees of their own; for this work, the SCAA won the coveted gold medal of the International Tuberculosis Congress in 1908. The committee influenced legislation allowing counties to build tuberculosis hospitals and helped convince county boards of supervisors to do so. In February 1920, it became the committee on tuberculosis and public health and continued to work in the field of public health, being chosen, for example, by the Milbank Fund in 1922 as the primary demonstration agency for public health demonstrations in upstate New York and conducting, in the late 1920s, a statewide diphtheria campaign. In 1963, it became the New York State Tuberculosis and Respiratory Disease Association, Inc., emphasizing the elimination of all respiratory diseases.

The SCAA also initiated some public welfare measures in the era of the Great Depression. The work of a special committee, created in 1925, to advise a state commission working to reform the public laws, led to modern, progressive legislation, enacted in 1929. Maintaining close alliances with state welfare officials, the SCAA urged Governor Franklin D. Roosevelt to deal with unemployment through public works programs in 1931, when it also published an influential pamphlet, *Work Relief.* Many SCAA staff agents were loaned to the state Temporary Emergency Relief Administration, and Executive Secretary Folks frequently advised its head, Harry Hopkins. The SCAA also developed a campaign to support an unemployment emergency relief bond issue, and in January 1933, the board of managers urged a program of federal relief for the unemployed.

In the post–World War II era, the SCAA remained in the vanguard of social welfare, creating new programs and strengthening others. Continuing its statewide leadership in the field, the SCAA in 1949 helped to organize the State Association of Councils of Social Agencies, for which the SCAA served the secretariat for many years. Well ahead of the later trend reviving the creative use of volunteers, the agency developed a program for them in city and state hospitals, prompting both the New York City Department of Hospitals in 1949 and the Hudson River State Hospital in 1955 to employ directors for volunteers. In 1949, the SCAA state committee on tuberculosis and public health established the New York Heart Assembly, which incorporated itself independently in 1957 and became part of the American Heart Association.* This continued the SCAA experience of having close ties with leading national social service organizations. SCAA preventive work had helped to reduce significantly the number of tuberculosis cases in New York State by the early 1950s.

In the mid-1950s, the organization noted that the solution of some problems, for instance, the plague of tuberculosis, led to new concerns, such as the care of the aged. Stressing that a creative voluntary agency moves in new directions, the board of managers established a program study committee in 1955 to assess the SCAA's work and to help it coordinate its diverse activities. By the 1950s, adoption had become popular, but the problem of placing minority, older, and handicapped children remained. With other agencies in the New York area, the SCAA helped to create the Adopt-a-Child campaign to publicize the issue, while the SCAA child adoption service continued on its own in a variety of ways to deal with this problem. In 1959, the SCAA established its social research service, which worked in the 1960s to coordinate programs better.

The SCAA entered the issue-filled and important decade of the 1960s in the midst of a major program dealing with the chronically ill, begun in 1957. An example will demonstrate the multiple ways in which the SCAA dealt with this nagging social problem: a survey of the problem in upstate Niagara County, the determination of proper services, grants from foundations and the United States Public Health Service (USPHS), the appointment of a project director—first a public health physician and then a community organizer—and a detailed report to the USPHS in 1969 and its digestion, distributed widely in 1970. In the mid- to late 1960s, a similar pilot project dealing with the multiproblem family resulted in *The Multi-Problems Dilemma* (1968), welcomed and discussed widely by the national social work community. As public assistance became a dramatic political issue in the early 1960s, the SCAA strengthened its traditional alliance with public officials, campaigning vigorously against a bill requiring long-term residence for public assistance. Governor Nelson Rockefeller, who vetoed the bill in

1960, praised the "exceptional" help of the SCAA in this important issue. In 1962, the agency responded to the heavily publicized "get tough" welfare policy in Newburgh, New York. A widely distributed publication explained the controversy. Attempting to create further understanding of the issue of public assistance, in 1962, the SCAA developed a project of having civic, business, and other community leaders in seven upstate counties view practices and visit and talk with welfare recipients. Groups in communities throughout the country adopted this practice, showing the nationwide influence of the SCAA, technically a statewide agency. In January 1964, the SCAA child adoption service incorporated separately as the Child Care and Adoption Service, Inc., disengaging the SCAA from its one remaining direct social service and completing its new function as a social catalyst agency. Indicating more accurately its role, the agency changed its name to State Communities Aid Association (SCAA) on May 19, 1967.

The name change reflected only one aspect of the SCAA's commitment to remain creative, to be "restless," as SCAA President D. Nelson Adams put it in 1962. More conscious of its catalytic role, in 1964, the SCAA led in founding the Citizens Committee for Clean Water. In the mid-1960s, the SCAA pushed for officials to provide family planning information to recipients of public assistance, and, in 1967, it pressed for expanded Medicaid service. In the late 1960s, the SCAA strove for a more liberal state abortion law, and it acted with other agencies to implement it. The drive for new service, the "restlessness" to which President Adams had referred, took shape in the SCAA activities to establish the New York State Council for Homemaker-Health Aid Services, Inc., the direct outgrowth of the chronic disability project and a reflection of greater SCAA coordination of programs. Continuing its leadership role, in 1971, the agency held a two-day seminar in the state capital, "The Making of Public Policy." The SCAA also contracted with the Temporary State Commission to Revise the Social Service Laws, organized a statewide survey of voluntary agency programs, and opened an office in Syracuse. In 1973, the SCAA received a special award from the New York State Welfare Council, symbolizing the SCAA's state and even national leadership in the social service field.

The primary sources for studying the SCAA's long history are diverse. Its widely available *Annual Reports* contain detailed information, which can be supplemented by other agency publications, such as the numbered *Publications, The SCAA News, Milestones in Health and Welfare, 1872–1929* (1930), a convenient summary of activities, and many others. At SCAA headquarters there are minutes of various meetings. The Homer Folks Papers and Folks's Reminiscences at the Oral History Project, both at Columbia University, describe his activities with the SCAA. Because of its diverse activities, SCAA's materials appear in other collections, such as the Archives of the Community Service Society* in New York City, the John Kingsbury Papers at the Library of Congress in

Washington, D.C., and the Louisa Lee Schuyler Papers at the New-York Historical Society.

SCAA activities have been described chiefly by Walter Trattner, especially in his *Homer Folks: Pioneer in Social Welfare* (1968), an important biography, "Louisa Lee Schuyler and the Founding of the SCAA," *New York Historical Society Quarterly* 51 (July 1967): 233–248, and "Social Statesman: Homer Folks, 1867–1947" (Ph.D. diss., University of Wisconsin, 1964). The material on SCAA child welfare programs came from the following by Peter Romanofsky: "The Early History of Adoption Practices, 1870–1930" (Ph.D. diss., University of Missouri, Columbia, 1969), "'To Save the City's Foundlings': The Joint Committee and New York City Child Care Practices," *The New-York Historical Society Quarterly,* 61 (January–April 1977): 49–68, and an extended study of the condition and care of dependent children in New York City in the nineteenth and twentieth centuries. There is no full-length, scholarly history of the SCAA.

SURVEY ASSOCIATES, INC. (SA). Nineteenth-century industrialization and urbanization brought to American society the benefits of accumulation of capital, increased manufacture of goods, availability of education, and the promise of a rising standard of living. With this progress, however, also came crowded tenements, a lack of adequate water and sewage systems in growing towns and cities, workers killed and maimed in industrial accidents, cyclic unemployment, and a wave of new immigrants who seemed ill-equipped to participate in representative democracy. Accustomed to treating dependence, whether temporary or permanent, through families, churches, and small communities, Americans discovered that a growing number of the "dependent, defective, and delinquent" had no access to these traditional sources of support. In response, concerned citizens formed groups and established institutions to provide services: children's aid societies, female moral reform groups, temperance societies, asylums, orphanages, hospitals, almsgiving and relief groups, playground associations, social settlements, and charity organization societies.

Following the Civil War, as problems escalated, voluntary associations embarked on a series of crusades to provide adequate living conditions, sanitation and health measures, social insurance, education and recreation facilities, and cultural and social benefits to those with needs. From the Progressive era to the mid-twentieth century, *The Survey* magazine chronicled these efforts and served as a link between and among reform groups and the emerging social work profession. It was, in the words of historian Clarke Chambers, the great national journal of record for twentieth century social work and social reform.

The Survey had its roots in several other journals published by philanthropic and social reform groups, most notably those of The Charity Organization Society of the City of New York* (COS). One of a number of societies formed in the late nineteenth century to substitute scientific charity for indiscriminate almsgiving, the New York COS, which was founded in 1882, investigated applications for assistance, coordinated relief efforts, and through friendly visiting attempted to reform character, as well as provide for physical needs. In 1891, using funds provided by attorney and businessman Robert W. De Forest, the COS president, the society established *Charities Review,* a monthly forum for the discussion of trends and ideas in the philanthropic field. In December 1897, the COS established a second publication, *Charities,* edited by COS General Secretary Edward T. Devine, to serve as a ''local news organ'' for charitable work in Greater New York and to provide an ''effective means of communication among the Society, its members, and the general public.''

In March 1901, *Charities* absorbed *Charities Review,* which itself had merged, in March 1897, with the Boston charities newsletter, *Lend a Hand,* founded in 1886 and edited by a clergyman and writer, Edward Everett Hale. At the time of the merger, the editors announced that *Charities* would continue to feature a monthly ''charities review'' issue in order to bring together, ''in readable form, the best thought and experience of the hour concerning men and women who cannot get through life alone.''

In 1905, *Charities* merged with *The Commons,* which had been founded in 1895 as a magazine of the Chicago Commons Settlement and edited by John Palmer Gavit and later by Graham Taylor, founder of the settlement. Although the new journal, *Charities and The Commons,* continued to be published by the COS, responsibility for it was assumed by a national Charities Publication Committee (CPC), formed by Devine to consider the possibility of making *Charities* a national journal for social work and reform. Among the members of the CPC were Jane Addams; Jacob Riis; Russell Sage Foundation* (RSF) officer John M. Glenn; and De Forest, chairman. In 1906, The CPC moved further toward making *Charities and The Commons* a national journal by absorbing *Jewish Charity,* the house organ of the United Hebrew Charities of the City of New York.* Both Taylor and Lee K. Frankel, the editor of *Jewish Charity,* became associate editors of *Charities and The Commons.*

In 1909, *Charities and The Commons* took the name *The Survey,* explaining in its first issue that ''charity,'' besides alienating many readers and supporters who objected to the term, no longer described accurately those movements the journal and the COS represented; the new name was drawn from the Pittsburgh Survey, an investigation in 1907 and 1908 of life and labor in the Pittsburgh steel district funded by the RSF and conducted by the CPC. For financial reasons and in order to assure editorial independence, the CPC broke its ties with COS in 1912 and formed an independent publishing organization, Survey Associates (SA), which published *The Survey* until its demise in 1952.

SA was incorporated in New York on October 31, 1912, as a cooperative publishing society to ''advance the cause of constructive philanthropy'' by publishing books, pamphlets, and periodicals and by ''conducting any investigations useful or necessary for the preparation thereof.'' A nonpartisan, nonprofit enterprise, SA had no capital endowment and relied on contributions from its members (anyone contributing ten dollars or more each year) to meet deficits not covered by publishing revenue; in the first year there were six hundred ''associates'' drawn primarily from social work, business, and the professions. SA officers, elected at annual meetings, were a president, chairman of the board (after 1938), vice-presidents, secretary, treasurer, and editor. Presidents of SA were De Forest from 1912 until his death in 1931, businessman Lucius R. Eastman from 1931 to 1938, and attorney Richard B. Scandrett from 1938 to 1948. Chairmen of the board of directors were Julian W. Mack, a circuit court of appeals justice, 1938–1943, and Joseph P. Chamberlain, a professor of public law at Columbia University, 1943–1952, who was active in several immigrant aid organizations.

Central to the creation and work of the SA was Paul Underwood Kellogg, who edited *The Survey* from 1912 until 1952. Born in Kalamazoo, Michigan, on September 30, 1879, Kellogg served as an editor of the Kalamazoo *Daily Telegraph* before coming to New York in 1901 to continue his education at Columbia University. He joined the staff of *Charities* in 1902 as an assistant editor and became managing editor in 1905 when *Charities* merged with *The Commons*. Kellogg was selected by the CPC to direct the Pittsburgh Survey and to edit its findings, *The Pittsburgh Survey,* published in six volumes by the RSF between 1909 and 1914.

In its first years of publication, *Charities* had been a conventional house organ devoted primarily to publishing calendars and lists of applicants and reporting legislation, disbursements, and events of interest to its members. In tones sometimes strident, with language characteristic of nineteenth-century attitudes toward poverty, it had deplored the pauperizing effects of relief and stressed that building character was the best means to end dependence. With the merger of the *Charities Review* in 1901 and perhaps because of the addition of Paul Kellogg and his brother Arthur Kellogg to the staff in 1902, *Charities* began to address individual problems in a larger social context. It studied the migration of Negroes to the cities of the North, for example, and the assets and liabilities the new Slavic immigrants brought to American life. Less emphasis was placed on reformation of character—the image of the woodpile receded—and more emphasis was on the impact of the industrial environment on individuals. The new orientation was reinforced in 1905 by the merger with *The Commons,* whose editors had argued, on the basis of firsthand observation of settlement workers living in industrial neighborhoods across the country, that weakness of character played less a role in dependency than did industrial accidents, fluctuations in the business cycle, and the cumulative effects of long hours, low wages, lack of education, and deprivation of social and cultural opportunities.

Finally it was the Pittsburgh Survey, the first social survey in the United States, which confirmed the journal in this path and gave *The Survey* not only its name but the methods and metaphors that were to govern its course for the next forty years. As the editors explained in a March 7, 1908, article introducing the first reports on the Pittsburgh Survey, groups had been formed to investigate and remedy particular social problems, such as child labor or the conditions of women in industry, but no one previously had examined and treated an industrial community, with all its interrelated social problems, as an organic whole. The significance of this approach to an entire community, the editors noted, was that it was part of the widening of the focus of social concern. The charity organization movement had begun by shifting philanthropy's focus on individuals and their problems to the family "in all its relations." In turn, the settlement movement expanded its concern from families to entire neighborhoods without sacrificing an interest in individuals and "personal relations." The social survey, the editors hoped, would finally extend the focus to entire communities while retaining an interest in personal relations and consequences for individuals of urbanization and industrialization.

Kellogg and the staff of the Pittsburgh Survey proceeded from the Progressive assumption that if the facts of social injustice were presented to an enlightened citizenry, citizens would act to correct the injustice. To this assumption, however, Kellogg added the writer's conviction that for people to be impelled to act, facts and statistics must be made real; readers must not see only wage schedules and accident statistics but the "piled up actuality" of those living in the new industrial order. In the published report of the Pittsburgh Survey and in the journal he edited for the next forty years, Kellogg worked to portray human and social problems truthfully and graphically. Although over the years he shifted *The Survey*'s emphases and came to define it as a broadly educational enterprise "operating along the borders of research, journalism, and the general welfare," Kellogg retained the conviction that firsthand investigation and inquiry had to be interpreted and presented in compelling fashion.

From its first days as *Charities* and *Charities Review* the magazine served multiple audiences: those working in philanthropy (who eventually called themselves social workers), executives and administrators of welfare agencies and reform groups, volunteers and agency board members, and "a leaven of people who . . . have a gleam of a better day." The early distinction between the newsletter and the monthly "charities review" issue, which eventually became the "graphic number," was formalized in June 1922 when *The Survey* shifted from the weekly publication schedule it had followed since 1898 to bimonthly publication. A graphic number was published on the first of the month and a midmonthly on the fifteenth. *The Survey Graphic,* as it was formally titled after 1933, was a magazine of "social interpretation" that addressed an audience of intelligent laymen concerned with the social and economic problems underlying the headlines. The *Survey Midmonthly* was a "modern service periodical," which served as a digest of social work and experience for practitioners, board members, and others in the fields of social work, health, recreation, and human welfare. The separation of the journals continued until financial crisis required their merger in 1949; the journal was then published monthly until the last issue in May 1952.

Through the forum of the graphic number, *The Survey* staff explored every significant social trend and problem of the twentieth century. Beginning in 1904 as *Charities,* it studied the creation of Slavic and Italian communities in the United States. It covered the Negro in the cities of the North (October 7, 1905) and, perhaps for the first time in print, the "Great Black Plague" of syphilis (June 24, 1905). In March 1906, in anticipation of the more systematic Pittsburgh Survey, the graphic number surveyed the District of Columbia, focusing on housing conditions, child labor, and social services.

The Survey's definition of social concerns always extended beyond the obvious issues of child labor, tenements, and the eight-hour day, all of which it campaigned to correct for years. In 1914, for example, the staff assembled "When Disaster Comes: The Red Cross in Time of Peace," featuring articles on the human and institutional consequences of earthquakes, mine explosions, shipwrecks, tornadoes, famine, floods, and other natural disasters. In special numbers, *The Survey* studied coal mining (April 1922), Mexico (May 1924), heart disease (November 1924), the "new Negro" (March 1925), regional planning (May 1925), city health (November 1925), the crime wave (March 1926), fascism (March 1927), and juvenile delinquency (March 1944). In other articles it provided extensive accounts of unemployment, medical care, social insurance, and such issues as women's suffrage, the high cost of dying, and the role of science in social progress. The social and human cost of war preoccupied the staff during the two world wars.

In the 1930s and 1940s, Kellogg conceived of the "Calling America" series, "variants of books" built around special themes. He began with "Calling America: the Challenge to Democracy Reaches Over Here" in February 1939. Edited by Raymond Gram Swing, the issue carried articles on the implications of fascism for American institutions by Archibald MacLeish, Thomas Mann, John Masefield, Bertrand Russell, Dorothy Thompson, Hendrik Willem Van Loon, and William Allen White. The issue went into three editions and sold more than ninety thousand copies. Subsequent issues in the series, though less successful, addressed major concerns: education, homes, the Americas, industrial relations and defense, physical fitness, full employment in the postwar period, Russian-American relations, the right to know, and world hunger. Two issues dealt with race: "Color: Unfinished Business of Democracy" (November 1942), edited by Alain Locke, who had also edited the "New Negro" issue in 1925, and "Segregation: Color Pattern from the Past" (January 1947), edited by Thomas Sancton.

While the *Survey Graphic* assayed to "see around corners," as one friend described it, the *Survey Midmonthly* served the social work and related human service professions. Beginning after World War I, other social work journals addressed special areas of practice such as medical social work or child welfare; only the *Midmonthly* attempted to cover the rapidly specializing profession of social work in its entirety by trying, as the editors stated, to be "social work plus—the art and practice of dealing with people." Less money and time was invested in producing the *Midmonthly,* but despite the resultant drab appearance, it was the "bible" of many social workers.

From the time the *Midmonthly* appeared in the early 1920s and reflecting its heritage as the *Charities* newsletter, the *Midmonthly* featured a few articles and devoted much of its space to regular departments: industry, communities, health, social practice, education, book reviews, letters, and a "shop talk" or "gossip" section. This format continued until January 1936 when the *Midmonthly* increased the number of articles and reduced its regular departments to the common welfare, the social front, books, and letters. Its contributors covered social work ethics and practices, the emergence of state and federal government programs, infantile paralysis, youth gangs, corrections, health care, and shifts in social work emphases resulting from depression, war, and inflation. A typical issue included, for example, articles on probation, the work of dealing with unemployment, problem children and their parents, and a psychiatric social worker's study of literature.

That *The Survey* made such substantial contributions to the field of social service and reform resulted in large part from Kellogg's ability to enlist leaders of social work and reform movements as expert advisers, editors, and members of the SA board; while paying modestly for contributions to the *Survey Graphic* and rarely anything for *Midmonthly* articles, he drew contributions from every major figure in social service and reform. Major contributors from the settlement and reform movements included Jane Addams, Lillian Wald, Emily Greene Balch, Florence Kelley, Alice Hamilton, Helen Hall, Graham Taylor, Robert Woods, Isaac M. Rubinow, John M. Andrews, Mary Van Kleeck, and others. Social work profession authors included Edward T. Devine, Alexander Johnson, Richard C. Cabot, Porter Lee, Eduard Lindeman, Grace Abbott, and Fred K. Hoehler. Kellogg elicited articles, advice, and contributions from foundation and business leaders, among them Robert W. De Forest, John M. Glenn, Shelby M. Harrison, John A. Kingsbury, Samuel S. Fels, E. A. Filene, and Harold Swift. Supreme Court Justices Felix Frankfurter and Louis Brandeis, whose estate provided an endowment for SA, were supporters, as were numerous other public officials—Frances Perkins, Harry Hopkins, Herbert Lehman, Eleanor and Franklin Roosevelt, A. A. Berle, and others. *The Survey* carried the work of little-known, young artists and photographers, as well as those of such major figures as artist Joseph Stella, cartoonist Henrik Willem Van Loon, and photographer Lewis Hine. Staff members Beulah Amidon, John Fitch, Mary Ross, Kathryn Close, Gertrude Springer—whose "Miss Bailey" series for new relief workers was a mainstay of the *Midmonthly* in the 1930s—and others acquired national reputations from their knowledge of their fields and their ability to predict and interpret trends.

Because of Kellogg's association with national leaders and because of the central place *The Survey* occupied in social welfare, Kellogg inevitably was involved in major reform efforts. Kellogg worked with Jane Addams and others to create a social insurance plank for the Progressive party platform in 1912 and was instrumental in forming the American Union Against Militarism in 1914, from which the American Civil Liberties Union emerged. He was one of the founders of the Foreign Policy Association in 1921 and mobilized efforts to prevent the execution of Sacco and Vanzetti in 1927. Kellogg served as a member of an advisory council to Franklin Roosevelt's Committee on Economic Security, which helped formulate social security legislation in 1934–1935 and was president of the National Conference of Social Work* in 1939.

The demise of *The Survey* resulted in large part from post–World War II financial problems and increased difficulty in defining how large its audience would be. Special issues often had circulation figures of fifty thousand to ninety thousand, but the number of regular subscriptions never exceeded twenty thousand, with additional newsstand sales of five thousand. While publication costs rose in the 1940s and subscription revenues did not, the number of Survey ''associates,'' whose contributions covered publishing deficits, barely held constant. *The Survey* had relied on foundations, especially the RSF, the Twentieth Century Fund, and the Julius Rosenwald Fund, for financial support, but this diminished or was withdrawn by World War II. Wealthy patrons had contributed hundreds of thousands of dollars between 1912 and 1952, but many of them— Agnes Brown Leach, Samuel Fels, Mr. and Mrs. Thomas Lamont, Harold Swift—retired, died, or stopped their contributions.

Other journals cut into *The Survey*'s mandate and audience: *The New Republic* and *The Nation* addressed reform issues, while *The Social Service Review, Family, Child Welfare,* and others may have reduced the number of subscribers from social work and related service professions. That *The Survey* had an aging editor—Kellogg was sixty-two and ill when World War II began—and a staff that for financial reasons was no longer able to undertake firsthand investigations in the field, inevitably had an effect on the quality of the magazine. Finally, the major social issues that were *The Survey*'s rallying cry—social insurance, industrial conditions, sanitation and public health—became the province of federal and state programs, increasingly militant labor unions, and welfare and health bureaucracies. Although poverty and deprivation persisted, although much of the nation was ill fed and poorly housed, *The Survey* had difficulty generating the enthusiasm for reform that had been its characteristic during the 1920s and 1930s. Indeed, in its last years *The Survey*'s graphic stories of hunger, poverty, and human misery described conditions in other countries, primarily in Asia and the Middle East. Concluding that the difficulties were insurmountable, the board of directors stopped publication with the May 1952 issue.

Clarke A. Chambers's *Paul U. Kellogg and The Survey: Voices for Social Welfare and Social Justice* (1971) is the major history of *The Survey*. The SA's records and the Papers of Paul Kellogg are held by the Social Welfare History

Archives, University of Minnesota, Minneapolis. Related collections in the Welfare Archives include personal papers of board and staff members George Britt, Mary Katz Golden, Agnes Brown Leach, and Janet Sabloff. Additional material about *The Survey* and its predecessors can be found in the archives of the Community Service Society* of New York.

Andrea Hinding

— *T*

TRAVELERS AID ASSOCIATION OF AMERICA (TAAA). In the mid-nineteenth century, many young, single women began to migrate to prospering American industrial centers in search of employment. Concerned with protecting these vulnerable young travelers from the vagaries of city life, the newly formed Young Women's Christian Association (YWCA) in Boston developed the first travelers' aid program in 1866. With direct focus on transient working girls who were seemingly ''ignorant of the dangers and snares in which cities abound,'' YWCA chapters in Boston and in many other urban areas after 1866 began to supervise guidance and protective services for young women at points of entry into the city, particularly at train stations and wharves. These activities gradually became directed from an official travelers' aid department within the local YWCA chapter, the first of which was shaped in Boston in 1887. The Boston YWCA also hired the first salaried travelers' aid station worker in 1887, Mary E. Blodgett of Mount Holyoke College, in order to provide service to working women at the docks and train terminal on a regular basis. Although the New York Society of Friends deserves credit for sponsoring the first American station worker two years earlier, in 1885, the Boston YWCA operation generated more acceptance for the practice among social service organizations.

By 1900, travelers' aid service had become a popular benevolent activity for many organizations in the United States, including local affiliates of the Catholic Women's League, the Deaconesses of the Methodist Church; the General Federation of Women's Clubs, the Girls' Friendly Society in America, the Hebrew Sheltering and Immigrant Aid Society,* the International Order of King's Daughters, the National Council of Jewish Women, the national Women's Christian Temperance Union, the YWCA, and many women's missionary associations. Travelers' aid workers and volunteers continued to help young women at the terminals and wharves, but services expanded in many cities to meet the needs of all moving people in distress. Immigrants, black migrant families, and the elderly were among those who benefited the most from these enlarged programs of assistance. Yet the existing multiplicity of local travelers' aid operations, whether sectarian or independently run, produced confusion and duplicated effort in large urban centers. Travelers' aid workers could not provide complete referral information and intercity follow-up assistance to all moving people until a network of cooperation was established between all travelers' aid offices.

Much of the initiative for building a cooperative travelers' aid network in America between 1905 and 1917 came from New York travelers' aid leadership. Grace Hoadley Dodge, a New York philanthropist and a national figure in the YWCA movement, played a key role in developing noncommercial, nonsectarian guidelines for executive planning in that direction, committed as she was to the idea of a national travelers' aid coordinating agency. In 1905, Dodge founded the Non-Sectarian Committee for Travelers Aid, which successfully combined the station work programs of several New York benevolent societies and clearly demonstrated the effectiveness of cooperative travelers' aid service. In 1907, the Non-Sectarian Committee was expanded and fused into the newly incorporated New York Travelers Aid Society (NYTAS), with Dodge serving as its first president. National unity continued to be a top priority for the organization, and in 1911 the NYTAS's department of national cooperation was established to accomplish that goal.

Working closely with representatives from travelers' aid organizations around the country, the department of national cooperation in New York designed an eleven-point program, the blueprints for what emerged in 1917 as a national organization. On April 26, 1917, the Travelers Aid Association of America (TAAA) was established as the National Travelers Aid Association (NTAA) when the NYTAS hosted a national gathering of independent and sectarian travelers' aid representatives in New York City. At that meeting, plans to develop a more professional, systematic service to moving people throughout the United States culminated in support for the new, noncommercial, nonsectarian protective and preventive NTAA organization.

During its first decade, the fledgling NTAA organization pursued several basic objectives: development of professional casework techniques and standardization of service to people who were moving; the creation of a sound financial program based on contributions from local member agencies and public endowments; cultivation of continued good relations with other national social service organizations; and the building of mutually supportive, productive relations between the national agency and the field of local travelers' aid workers. In 1917, this field consisted of twenty-five independent travelers' aid societies; seventy-four travelers' aid departments or committees under YWCA auspices; twenty-seven travelers' aid departments within other agencies; and 502 localities covered by "cooperating representatives" from several business and social service organizations.

NTAA executive leadership from 1917 to 1919 reflected continued dependence on New York members, although the Boston, Chicago, and Philadelphia Travelers Aid Societies became increasingly more influential in national policy matters. Orin C. Baker, the executive of the NYTAS from 1911 to 1917, presided over the NTAA thirty-member board of directors during the difficult war years, when money for social service agencies was scarce and experienced travelers' aid workers were in short supply. Important decisions made by the NTAA board under Baker's guidance included early endorsement of the NYTAS's publication, *Directory of Travelers Aid Work in the United States and Canada and Cooperating Organizations in Other Countries* (1917), and plans to issue a revised directory annually. NTAA's official news publication, *The Bulletin,* also began to appear at this time. In 1918, the board voted to make the NTAA an associate member of the National Conference of Social Work* (NCSW) and scheduled the yearly travelers' aid conventions to coincide with the meetings of that larger body.

Serious financial problems plagued the NTAA in 1919, when executive board members could no longer absorb the deficits of the organization themselves and member societies failed to contribute the necessary funds. As a result, Orin Baker hired consultants to study the money crisis and advise the board. NTAA's only major accomplishment in 1919 was the sponsorship of a new training school for travelers' aid workers, set up by a professional caseworker, Margaret Wead.

In 1920, the NTAA was renamed the National Association of Travelers Aid Societies (NATAS) and ushered in a period of reorganization, growth, and professionalized service to people who were moving. Virgil Johnson replaced Orin Baker as general secretary of the NATAS, bringing Philadelphia Travelers Aid Society casework experience to that executive position. On July 15, 1921, Johnson initiated a six-month investigation of NATAS financial and administrative problems, known as the Fosdick-Jones survey. According to the survey, the relationship between the local travelers' aid societies and the national agency needed clarification; the NATAS national staff was not large enough to sustain close field contact and also handle national planning responsibilities; and the local travelers' aid network did not provide uniformly professional assistance from coast to coast. The survey recommended expansion of the NATAS national staff to meet these challenges, as opposed to a merger with the American National Red Cross* (ANRC) or any other protective social service agency. The report also reiterated the nonsectarian principle to encourage the recruitment of more independent travelers' aid branches and urged better use of trained volunteers in the local agencies.

The NATAS national board implemented the suggestions of the Fosdick-Jones survey report in 1922–1923. John R. Shillady became general secretary— renamed general director—following Virgil Johnson's resignation early in 1922. Shillady earlier had been secretary of the National Association for the Advancement of Colored People from 1918 to 1920 and had served as executive director of the National Consumers' League* from 1920 to 1922. Assisting Shillady was

Virginia Kelley, the new NATAS director of field service and an experienced caseworker. She also supervised the four regional fieldworkers hired in 1923 to visit and teach at local travelers' aid offices throughout the United States. Four NATAS standing committees were established for more effective national planning: operations, coordinating, business, and finance. The finance committee was given top priority in efforts to develop a secure, operable money program for the organization. As prescribed by the Fosdick report, the NATAS national board agreed to keep expenditures below or at the level of income; work for a wider travelers' aid constituency; use volunteer assistance whenever possible; and urge member societies to assume responsibility for 50 percent of NATAS operation costs. In 1922–1923, the new finance committee also worked for foundation support, resulting in NATAS grants from the Laura Spelman Rockefeller Memorial and The Commonwealth Fund.*

Cooperation with other social service organizations remained a serious concern of NATAS leadership at this time. The national offices of the YWCA and the ANRC were quite friendly with travelers' aid executives, both committing themselves to helping NATAS develop a stronger network of local services. In 1923, the NATAS became one of five sustaining member agencies of the Committee on Transportation of Allied National Agencies.* This led to improved relations between travelers' aid workers and American railroad interests. The NATAS also became a member of the National Social Work Council* (NSWC) in 1928, reaffirming its commitment to professional casework techniques in short-term contacts with moving people.

Marcus L. Bell, general counsel and vice-president of the Rock Island Railroad, became the elected president of NATAS in 1925. Under Bell's guidance, the national travelers' aid staff sponsored an increasing number of regional and state training conferences; established a special committee to study immigrant problems in America after assisting a reported seventy thousand aliens in 1926; and began to develop closer contacts with social service agencies abroad.

The NATAS faced unprecedented challenges in the depression era when the widespread problem of transient men, women, and children forced the federal government and many voluntary agencies to concentrate on cooperative relief programs. In spite of staff reductions and severely limited budgets, the NATAS provided active leadership for both national service projects and local community planning operations. In June 1931, United States President Herbert Hoover's Emergency Committee on Employment asked the NATAS to prepare a study on transient families, which resulted in an unpublished report, "Transient Families in the United States." That same year, the council on travelers' aid service problems was created at NATAS headquarters, comprised of representatives from the Family Welfare Association of America* (FWAA), the national board of the YWCA, the Child Welfare League of America,* the National Catholic Welfare Conference, the National Recreation Association,* the International Migration Service, later called the International Social Service* (ISS), and the

NATAS. The council devoted much time to a study on transient youth, published in 1931 as *Study of Children Under Sixteen Traveling Alone*. By the summer of 1932, the critical transient situation required the formation of the national Committee on Care of Transient and Homeless* (CCTH), created under the auspices of the National Social Work Council* (NSWC) but masterminded by the NATAS and the FWAA. The NATAS was the only participating agency to have two representatives on the CCTH, Bertha McCall and Ella M. Weinfurther, and both exercised power in that body. When Harry Hopkins of the Federal Relief Administration announced plans in 1933 for federal aid to transients—the Federal Transient Program—the CCTH provided the ncessary organizational machinery to implement the program. At the local level, the travelers' aid network of services played a key role in allocating the federal transient assistance.

From 1930 to 1933, the NATAS staff had been reduced to the general director, an assistant director, two field representatives, and a small office crew. J. Rogers Flannery of Pittsburgh was elected NATAS president in 1930 to replace Marcus Bell, but the president did not manage the operations of the national office on a routine basis. At a time when many social service organizations were helping transients, the NATAS struggled to preserve its own identity and raison d'être as an indispensable casework agency. The national office also resisted the efforts of the community chests to merge local travelers' aid services with other organizations. However, many travelers' aid branches disappeared in the early 1930s because local communities could not afford to support more than one or two social service organizations in their area. Under these pressures, NATAS leadership resolved to lower the contribution requirements for member travelers' aid offices from 6 percent to 3 percent of their total budgets. In addition, NATAS President Flannery and General Director Sherrard Ewing resigned at the annual convention of travelers' aid societies in 1932 to allow for the reorganization of administrative power at NATAS headquarters. In their places an active board planning committee of six members was set up to direct and advise the NATAS office staff.

NATAS activity peaked in 1934, supported by large grants from the Carnegie Corporation ($5,000) and the Markle Foundation ($100,000), one year earlier. Publications flourished, including an expanded travelers' aid directory for transient camp use, *1934 Directory of Travelers Aid and Transient Service;* a new travelers' aid house organ, *The Transient,* to replace *The Bulletin;* and two studies, *Individual Service for Transients* and *Group Treatment for Transients*. At the annual convention of travelers' aid societies in 1934, the NATAS was renamed the National Association for Travelers Aid and Transient Service (NATATS) to reflect the agency's wider responsibilities and goals.

The organizational structure of the NATATS in 1934 also expanded to accommodate the heightened office activity. General Director Bertha McCall supervised three staff associates: the consultant on community plans for transients; the consultant on finance, and one office manager. McCall also helped to establish the new executives' council, made up of local travelers' aid executives from many American cities. Newly elected NATATS President Donald Stevens of the Baltimore-Ohio Railroad served with the treasurer, secretary, and four vice-presidents at the highest level of the NATATS organization, along with a twenty-one-member board of directors.

From 1935 to 1939, the NATATS concentrated on maintaining good relations with other social service agencies; developing stronger travelers' aid programs in local communities; and securing greater financial commitment from travelers' aid branches for the national office budget. The NATATS celebrated its twentieth anniversary in 1937, highlighted by record attendance at the annual convention of travelers' aid societies, which focused on the theme, "The Challenge of the Future." In the same year General Director Bertha McCall chaired a committee created by the NSWC to study the problem of support for national social service agencies. This effort resulted in a publication, *Support for National Agencies* (1938). In 1938, several major revisions of the NATATS bylaws were passed, including a return to National Travelers Aid Association (NTAA) as the official name of the organization; a decision to hold biennial, not annual, national convention meetings, and scheduling these meetings apart from the NCSW for the first time; election of executives' council members at each biennial convention after 1938, rather than appointment of members by the NTAA national board; and a decision to give the national board the power to create fluctuating dues quotas for member societies, although 3 percent was still considered the minimum quota. NTAA activity in 1939 seemed productive at the administrative planning level—four new members were added to the national board and three highly successful regional conferences were held—but the national agency did not recruit a single new travelers' aid society that year nor did it reduce the problem of inadequate member agency contributions to the national headquarters.

The NTAA moved into a new phase of service in 1940 when the United States prepared for war. Unlike their weak efforts in 1917, travelers' aid administrators were determined to assume active responsibility for the needs of traveling American servicemen, their families, and refugees from Europe. Accomplishing that goal required a stronger travelers' aid network of service, as well as a stronger public image of the national organization. Thus it hired the Harold F. Strong Corporation in January 1940 to study the matter and to recommend changes. The Strong report, which appeared in February 1940, urged the NTAA to build a new public relations program based on more fieldwork activity and more publications. Soon after, the NTAA hired E. W. Robothan and Company to consult on public relations strategies; one new staff associate was added to the national office for field service; and *Shifting Scenes* replaced *The Transient* as the NTAA official publication on a bimonthly basis.

The travelers' aid defense plan began on February 8, 1940, to facilitate the movement of United States military personnel from base to base. Toward that goal, the NTAA joined with four other voluntary agencies to create the Social Casework Council of National Agencies. This body set up a recruiting and training program for service volunteers. The NTAA also cooperated with the Health and Welfare Services organization, directed by President Franklin D. Roosevelt's appointee, Paul V. McNutt, in 1940. In March 1941, the NTAA became a member agency of the United Service Organizations for National Defense, Inc.* (USO), and quickly assumed a major role in the functioning of that body at American military installations. By December 15, 1941, the NTAA had made operational thirty-five of fifty-one designated USO-travelers' aid units, each employing qualified social caseworkers and assisted by volunteers. On December 16, 1941, the USO national board voted to give the NTAA control over troops in transit lounge program, a plan to establish recreational lounges for servicemen in many urban centers.

The NTAA headquarters staff enlarged its ranks in 1941 to manage the new wartime responsibilities. A new field department with six regional supervisors kept the national office in touch with local travelers' aid branches; the director of information and studies arranged training programs for travelers' aid volunteers; and a new personnel department and business office tackled employee and financial problems. According to General Director Bertha McCall's NTAA report for December 31, 1941, the national agency had responsibility for 98 travelers' aid societies, 43 operational USO-travelers' aid units, 89 USO personnel, and 308 volunteers in USO units, and it served forty-six thousand persons at the USO units.

By December of 1943, the NTAA managed a record total of 153 USO-travelers' aid units, as well as 134 troops-in-transit lounges. The NTAA office staff continued to expand with the needs of the USO operations, but a committee on postwar planning was also created in 1943 to begin preparing for demobilization. From that time until the end of the war, NTAA leadership debated about ways in which the USO-travelers' aid units established during the war might be transformed into new travelers' aid agencies for peacetime. The national office wanted to build strong governmental trust in the travelers' aid service network after the war so that the NTAA would remain a vital, autonomous agency of service to people who were moving.

From 1945 to 1950, the NTAA reorganized its administrative structure to handle postwar budget problems and gave special attention to strengthening local travelers' aid commitments to the national office in New York City. In 1946, Hobart McPherson replaced Randall L. LeBoeuf as president of the NTAA, the latter having served the agency throughout the war years. Under McPherson's direction, the NTAA ways and means committee was created in 1946 to plan a workable finance program. The lay council was also established that year in an effort to build rapport between the national office and the member agencies and consisted of local travelers' aid board members from around the United States. The activities of the lay council led to NTAA approval for six new regional vice-presidents in 1948. Representing each travelers' aid region as designated by the national office, these local vice-presidents were encouraged to become involved in NTAA planning operations; the national office, in turn, was given greater access to local administrative leadership and became more aware of member agency needs. The NTAA continued publication activity throughout this period as well. A textbook, *Intercity Service in Travelers Aid,* was prepared in 1948.

The NTAA continued to cultivate good relations with other national social service organizations in the postwar period. The National Social Welfare Assembly,* formerly the NSWC, received active NTAA support from the office of General Director McCall. When Defense Secretary James Forrestal coordinated plans for a peacetime USO operation in 1947, the NTAA again helped to serve military personnel in recreational-referral assistance capacities. The NTAA also became a member agency of the United Community Defense Services* (UCDS) body, incorporated in 1950 to help communities solve social problems related to crowded conditions and transiency in defense industry areas.

Throughout the 1950s, the NTAA concentrated on developing professional standards for training travelers' aid caseworkers and tried to maintain a cooperative "chain of service" between local travelers' aid offices. Migrant workers and refugees became an important concern of the national agency and remained target groups for travelers' aid services for two decades. Perhaps the most significant NTAA project relative to those groups in the 1950s was the effort to remove residency requirements for welfare relief from transient persons in many American communities. The NTAA biennial convention in 1956 devoted its entire program to this controversial issue, culminating in plans to work with other social service agencies toward eliminating those restrictions.

Federal financial assistance in the 1960s allowed the NTAA—renamed the Travelers Aid Association of America (TAAA) in 1966—to undertake several noteworthy casework programs involving migrant workers and their families. Under two contracts with the United States Department of Labor, from 1966 to 1968, TAAA branch agencies developed counseling, financial assistance, and special services for about twenty-five hundred migrant families in Virginia and West Virginia. The TAAA also faced the challenge of runaway juveniles in the context of the drug-oriented culture of the 1960s, although runaway youths had always been a concern of travelers' aid workers in the twentieth century. Travelers' aid branches provided casework emergency assistance for many such individuals from San Francisco to New York City.

After five years of negotiation and planning, as well as shrinking financial support from faltering local member agencies, the TAAA merged with the American Branch of the ISS in 1972 to form Travelers Aid-International Social Service of America (TAISSA). In this way, travelers' aid service was expanded to provide protective care and emergency assistance to people throughout the world. The most recent project directed by TAISSA's travelers' aid member agencies involved resettlement of Vietnamese refugees in 1975. TAISSA is a member organization of the United Service Organizations and cooperates with the National Information Bureau, the National Association of Social Workers,* The Advertising Council, and the committee for national agency support of the United Way of America.*

The primary sources for studying the TAAA consist mainly of that agency's own publications, staff reports, organizational studies, and biennial convention materials, which exist on microfilm at the University of Minnesota's Social Welfare History Archives Center. Also valuable on microfilm at the Social Welfare History Archives Center is Bertha McCall's unpublished "History of the Travelers Aid Association, 1911-1948" (1950), which provides detailed information about TAAA's development from the perspective of a former general director (1933-1949) of that agency. Grace E. Kimble's *Social Work with Travelers and Transients* (1935) describes travelers' aid activity before and during the depression; her study originally formed the background for the NATAS report to President Herbert Hoover's Emergency Committee on Employment. *Citizens in Service, Volunteers in Social Welfare During the Depression, 1929-1941* (1976), by John F. Jones and John M. Herrick, briefly describes the NTAA in the context of other social service agency activity in the 1930s.

Doris L. Lunden

___ U ___

UNITARIAN ASSOCIATION, DEPARTMENT OF SOCIAL RELATIONS (DSR) OF THE AMERICAN. The social gospel reform movement of the late nineteenth century influenced the American Unitarian Association (AUA) (see *Religious Organizations*). AUA leaders, in fact, helped to shape the social gospel movement. Some of them began to discuss forming an agency to institutionalize the church's social conscience. In early 1908, they developed a resolution, which AUA president, Samuel A. Eliot—the president of Harvard University—proposed at the business session of the annual convention on May 27, 1908. The convention passed this resolution, which established a new Department of Social and Public Service (DSPS). This was the origin of the Department of Social Relations (DSR). The DSPS organized itself during the summer of 1908, and it began to function officially on October 1, 1908, when the secretary, Reverend Elmer S. Forbes, began his work. The DSPS's initial mandate was to develop social service committees in Unitarian churches and to prepare a body of literature on social issues and social service. On November 23, 1908, the social ethics department of Harvard University sponsored a reception to honor the DSPS, initiating cordial relations between the new group and Boston and national social reformers, such as Professor Francis Peabody, who aided the early work of the DSPS.

The DSPS began its work energetically, making early and important contributions to the general field of social work. Forbes's first task, to study existing Unitarian social work, resulted in what one scholar called, correctly, a "long and distinguished" series of bulletins. Between 1909 and 1915, the DSPS published pamphlets in the *Unitarian Social Service Series* by such prominent national social workers as Mary Richmond of the Russell Sage Foundation,* Francis Peabody, and E. Stagg Whitin, one of the founders of the National Committee on Prisons and Prison Labor.* The pamphlets dealt with such topics as child labor, housing, prison reform, and tuberculosis. In 1913, the DSPS sponsored a conference in Boston to consider current social problems and the role of the church. Frederick Almy, who founded the first charity organization society in Buffalo, Anna Garlin Spencer, an important local reformer, Forbes, and many socially concerned Unitarian ministers delivered papers, which the department published as *The Social Ideas of a Free Church,* a timely contribution.

The agency, which changed its name to the Department of Community Service (DCS) in 1917, continued in the forefront of Progressive movements. Active in the housing reform movement almost since its inception, the department campaigned successfully for a Massachusetts housing reform law. It continued to sponsor various conferences and seminars with churches and other liberal groups throughout New England. Anna Spencer lectured for the department, helping to increase the number of local social service committees to thirty in 1913. Beginning in the summer of 1915, the DSPS developed the annual Meadville Social Service Institute at the Meadville Theological School in Chicago. The institutes featured lectures and discussions on topics such as "the church and public health" and "the church and dependent classes" by such prominent social welfare figures as Elmer Forbes, Professor Anna Spencer, and Alexander Johnson, who served as general secretary of the National Conference of Charities and Correction.* The zeal of the department and its staff dissipated significantly during World War I, when Secretary Forbes devoted most of his energies to war-related activities. Shortly after the Unitarian Laymen's League announced plans to develop a social reform program, the DCS disbanded in the mid-1920s.

In the spring of 1927, the board of directors of the AUA reestablished the agency as the Department of Social Relations (DSR). Dr. Robert C. Dexter reactivated the department when he began serving as secretary on July 1, 1927. Like Forbes, Dexter lectured and traveled widely, immersing the DSR in the pressing domestic and international issues. He allied the DSR with the Federal Council of the Churches of Christ in America (FCC), serving on its committee to investigate the Pennsylvania coal strike of 1927–1928. In its first year of new service, the DSR aided strikers in New Bedford, Massachusetts, and began a study of the aged. It developed the work of promoting social service in Unitarian churches, as Dexter and his wife traveled widely, addressing and counseling various groups. Special services to ministers, such as the Minister's Institute at Andover-Harvard Theological School on "The Minister and Family Problems" in the early 1930s and the subsequent publication of a manual on this subject, in addition to sending its publication, *Social Action,* to all ministers, helped to communicate social service ideals to this important segment of the church. Working pieces for *The Christian Register,* a major Unitarian publication, brought the DSR closer to the AUA. Beginning around the mid-1930s, the DSR cooperated increasingly with the AUA's Religious Education Department (RED), for instance, establishing, in the mid-1930s, the joint adult education committee to study the meaning of social service.

The DSR also became active in social service programs in the late 1920s and the depression-ridden 1930s. Executive Secretary Dexter and his wife taught a course in sociology at the Tuckerman School in Boston. A publication in 1931 on the socioeconomic conditions in the New England textile communities continued the tradition initiated in the Progressive era, and in the same year, cooperating with the American National Red Cross,* the DSR aided drought victims in the American Southwest. Like other liberal organizations, the DSR became involved in social justice movements in the South in the 1930s. It cooperated with other churches in the Delta Cooperative Farm in Mississippi. Dexter's investigation of conditions in Mississippi, "Light Along Tobacco Road," urged better medical care for the cooperators, and in the late 1930s, the DSR supplied a physician for the community. A significant activity was the DSR work in 1931–1932 with the American Friends Service Committee* (AFSC) to relieve the particularly depressed mining communities in West Virginia and Kentucky, mobilizing church resources for relief.

As Dexter hoped, the cooperative venture with the AFSC initiated joint activities with other progressive church agencies. A youth peace caravan traveled throughout the country in the early 1930s, forging closer links with the Quakers. The work in the coal areas declined as federal relief programs gradually extended aid, but the DSR still worked with the AFSC. Beginning in September 1934, the DSR launched other cooperative programs, joining with the Universalist General Convention and the Department of Social Action* of the Congregational Christian churches to publish a journal, *Church and Society.* In 1935, this publication became *Social Action,* which the DSR continued to send to all Unitarian ministers. In the late 1930s, the DSR cooperated with the AFSC to help Republicans in Spain.

While the DSR worked effectively with similar agencies of other liberal churches, it caused some controversy within the AUA. In 1935, the DSR presented the AUA's general convention with its program of social action, calling for such reforms as government ownership of all utilities, the abolition of the profit motive, a more equitable distribution of the wealth, and greater support for organized labor. The program caused immediate controversy, and while accepting it, the AUA did not implement it. The increasing alliance with the AUA's RED led the AUA's board of directors, in 1939, to recommend the amalgamation of the two departments in a new Division of Education. The DSR also started to phase itself out in January 1940, when Dexter began to study possible Unitarian service abroad, an activity that led to the establishment of the new Unitarian Service Committee* (USC). By 1941, with the new USC active, the DSR had been merged with the AUA's former Department of Adult Education to create the new Department of Adult Education and Social Relations.

The primary sources for studying the DSR's history include its annual reports in the AUA *Year Books*. The agency's papers are at the Unitarian Universalist Association's headquarters in Boston, Massachusetts.

Both Charles H. Hopkins, *The Rise of the Social Gospel in American Protestantism, 1865–1915* (1940), and Robert M. Miller, *American Protestantism and the Social Issues* (1958), mention the DSR and its predecessors. There is no full-length, scholarly history of this agency.

UNITARIAN SERVICE COMMITTEE: see UNITARIAN UNIVERSALIST SERVICE COMMITTEE.

UNITARIAN UNIVERSALIST SERVICE COMMITTEE (UUSC). As news of Adolf Hitler's atrocities reached the United States in the 1930s, a number of liberal organizations and individuals began to discuss developing services abroad for oppressed peoples. In the late 1930s, Dr. Robert Dexter, the executive secretary of the Department of Social Relations* (DSR) of the American Unitarian Association (AUA), conducted investigations of possible service abroad by his church. In October 1939, to further this activity, the DSR established the Commission for Service in Czechoslovakia (CSC), a joint venture with the American Friends Service Committee* (AFSC). The CSC rescued intellectuals in Prague scheduled for annihilation by the approaching Nazis. As a result of this early work with refugees, the Unitarian Universalist Service Committee (UUSC) was established as the Unitarian Service Committee (USC) in May 1940. The new USC was a committee of the AUA. The style of the early refugee work set the tone for the war relief efforts of the USC in its early years.

The USC, which in May 1941 became a standing committee of the AUA's board of directors, worked energetically to develop creative and effective war relief measures. As European refugees poured into France in 1940, the USC provided a carload of milk for sick babies in Bosses Pyrenees. Later in the year, the agency helped refugee children of six different nationalities escape to the United States; this episode initiated consistent USC cooperation with the United States Committee for the Care of European Children.* In 1941, the USC began its continued program of medical services for refugees at internment camps. The USC also founded its clinic at Marseilles, France, an important early activity. Also at Marseilles, the agency established its European office, headed by Dr.

Charles R. Joy. On April 1, 1941, the agency adopted its official seal, which had been designed by a European war refugee.

In the early 1940s, the USC initiated its domestic work, addressing itself to the most pressing social problems and issues at home. Its home service section worked with local church leaders to stimulate community action throughout the country. The first project, work camps for youth volunteers who served at home and abroad, developed as an important activity, which ended only in 1968. In another early project, volunteers aided communities in the Boston area, foreshadowing the work of Volunteers in Service to America (VISTA) in the late 1960s. USC projects also provided social services for minority defense workers, such as Japanese-Americans, and for minorities in the armed forces. A program in Detroit, established in 1941, evolved into USC support for the People's Institute of Applied Religion, whose director, Claude Williams, trained leaders, particularly ministers, in toleration and understanding in this racially tense area. These projects initiated a series of USC programs to support local minority groups.

In the early years as later, the administrative structure of the agency remained basically simple. A committee of leaders, generally Unitarian, including a chairman, a vice-chairman, a treasurer, and a recording secretary, led the agency. An executive secretary, initially Dr. Robert C. Dexter, the former executive secretary of the DSR of the AUA, headed staff personnel at home and abroad. The first USC headquarters was in New York City, but the agency soon moved its headquarters to Boston.

The importance of the USC, however, remained its activities and programs abroad in the 1940s and early 1950s. In the early 1940s, its headquarters staff at Marseilles helped to centralize the medical relief activities of the USC itself and of other progressive agencies working abroad, such as the AFSC and the International Migration Service.* In 1942, the USC initiated a children's camp and established a kindergarten in Rive-Saltes, France. Other medical relief projects in France led to a medical mission in Italy in 1945, the most significant project by a private relief agency, according to the United Nations Relief and Rehabilitation Administration. Cosponsored with the Congregational Christian Service Committee, the project sent medical personnel from outstanding American universities to deal with such problems as malnutrition and disease. In the late 1940s, the USC conducted similar medical teaching missions abroad at the request of both the World Health Organization and the United States Department of State. Summer medical missions abroad, initially in Czechoslovakia in 1946, led ultimately to USC's educational and child care institute in Germany, established in 1949. The institute continued as an annual activity, chaired and staffed by such American social service leaders as Lea D. Taylor, head resident of the famous settlement house, Chicago Commons, her sister Katherine, and some American academicians. In 1948, the USC was incorporated as an independent agency, but it maintained its relations with the AUA.

USC projects stressed educational and community-building skills rather than relief. For instance, in the early 1950s, the USC organized the first social work school in Korea to help the people deal with their own problems. Similarly, the Awo Omamma, Nigeria, community development and leadership training, inaugurated in 1958, like other programs in Africa, strove for self-development. Since its inception in 1945, the Universalist Service Committee had conducted similar community-based projects. In 1953, for instance, at the request of local Universalists and the Chicago Housing Authority, the Universalist Service Committee established a community center in the Le Claire Court Housing Project; increasingly enlarged, the facility became the Clarence Darrow Community Center.

The merger of the two agencies—the USC and the Universalist Service Committee—in May 1963 to form the new Unitarian Universalist Service Committee (UUSC) strengthened and expanded programs abroad. In 1966, for example, the UUSC developed in Port-au-Prince, Haiti, a family planning program, which broadened in the early 1970s into a more comprehensive sociomedical plan that organized health centers in surrounding villages. Similarly, the agency conducted a multidiscipline program in education, nutrition, and the like in elementary schools in Maudeville, Jamaica. To select, survey, and aid similarly people in Vietnam, the UUSC developed a social service program in the late 1960s.

Like UUSC activities abroad, the domestic program paralleled the best contemporary American social services. The Willow Run Project in Detroit, begun in 1945, illustrated its long involvement in community development activities. In the vanguard of the civil-rights movement, in the 1950s, the USC helped to establish local human relations councils in Atlanta, Georgia, and Knoxville, Tennessee, and worked to integrate a boys' club in Washington, D.C. Such concerns for urban minorities led to the Home Opportunities Made Equal project in Chicago in the mid-1960s, a wide range of services in housing, medical care, employment, and nutrition, which the UUSC developed for urban minorities in the 1960s and 1970s. The agency also sponsored Head Start summer programs, begun in the mid-1960s in Suffolk, Virginia. This developed from the UUSC kindergarten classes at the Jordan Neighborhood House, itself founded in the 1880s by a black Universalist minister. Perhaps the most widely recognized UUSC domestic activity, the Gallup, New Mexico, Indian Community Center served a neglected group; in the late 1960s, in the tradition of promoting community self-help, the UUSC turned the center over completely to an indigenous board representing the Navajo tribe, the town, and the county.

UUSC activities continued in the vanguard of American social service, both at home and abroad in the 1970s. A project dealing with food distribution and nutrition in Zambia, in the self-help tradition, was phased out in January 1972. During this period, the agency sponsored the United States Committee for Justice for Political Prisoners in Latin America. The UUSC began to explore experimental projects in certain South American countries, utilizing new adult education techniques based on the writings, for example, of Paolo Freire. Domestically, an antidrug abuse "rap-session," youth-oriented program serving Chicanos in Houston, Texas, and the United Urban Project stressing housing construction in the Watts section of Los Angeles, indicated continuing UUSC concerns. From a pilot program in justice administration in Chester, Pennsylvania, the UUSC developed a broader project, initiated in January 1973, to monitor courts, focusing on tenant rights in public housing and the like. To help implement an explicit UUSC goal—to provide information to help people change existing social conditions—another program began in 1972: the Mississippi Audio Visual Rural Information Center, a three-year pilot project with over one-half million dollars, and the Community Video Access Center, which helped communities participate in cable television programs. Both projects used modern techniques to help educate and empower rural and urban low-income groups.

The sources for studying the UUSC's history are diverse. The variously named annual reports appeared in the AUA's *Year Books* in the 1940s. Later, the *Annual Reports* were published separately. The agency's files have been deposited at the Wessell Library at Tufts University in Medford, Massachusetts. Reports of USC activities abroad in the 1940s are in the Papers of the Department of State, Record Group 59, at the National Archives in Washington, D.C. Information about UUSC activities can also be found in contemporary publications, such as *The Social Service Review*.

A brief agency publication, *A New Opportunity for Service* (1961), contains some historical materials, and Merle Curti, *American Philanthropy Abroad* (1963), mentions the USC. There does not appear to be a full-length, scholarly history of the UUSC.

UNITED CEREBRAL PALSY ASSOCIATIONS, INC. (UCPA). In 1942, in California, a group of parents of children with cerebral palsy met to discuss their common concerns and to form an association. Three years later, another parents' group developed spontaneously in New York City. By 1946, there were enough local groups of such parents in New York to form a state association. Some had organized the National Foundation for Cerebral Palsy. In February 1947, Alvin Boretz, another parent, wrote a radio show, "Love Is a Doctor." The nationwide audience responded so warmly to the broadcast that its sponsor produced a pamphlet describing cerebral palsy, written by the editors of *Science Illustrated*. The publication's circulation prompted other local groups to organize in the late 1940s. The leaders of these parents' organizations began to develop plans for a national organization. In August 1948, these leaders, including apparently Leonard Goldenson, a vice-president of Paramount Pictures, Inc., and the father of a cerebral palsied child, took out a certificate of incorporation for a new organization. On February 6, 1949, at a mass meeting in New York City of twelve hundred people interested in the problems of cerebral palsy, Goldenson announced publicly the creation of the new national society.

In the spring of 1949, a small group of women in New York, led by Isabelle Goldenson, began to raise funds and, by July 1949, they had raised enough to organize fully a national agency. Consequently, on August 12, 1949, the United Cerebral Palsy Associations, Inc. (UCPA), officially came into being under the membership laws of the state of New York. Other leaders in the UCPA's founding included such prominent individuals as Leonard Goldenson, William Clay Ford, vice-president of the Ford Motor Company, and Roger S. Firestone, president of the Firestone Plastics Company. Each was the father of a cerebral palsied child. The new UCPA adopted the following purposes: to publicize the disease, to promote employment, rehabilitation, and scholarships for the cerebral palsied, to cooperate with other health and welfare agencies, to promote research, to circulate information, to raise money, and to establish local chapters.

Fulfilling an original agency goal, the UCPA began immediately to promote research. Two physicians who had begun their research during the polio epidemic of 1916 joined the research organization of the group. Dr. Winthrop Morgan Phelps became chairman of the medical advisory committee, which supervised research and developed programs for local clinics, and Dr. Bronson Crothers joined the research advisory board, which determined research projects to be funded. Dr. Sidney Farber, a distinguished professor of pathology at the Harvard University Medical School's Children's Hospital, headed the research advisory board. Representatives from three other UCPA voluntary boards— clinical, educational, and adult vocational—each composed of professionals in the field, combined to form the medical-professional executive board. This board supervised all the research and patient-related programs of the UCPA until the establishment of the UCPA's Research and Educational Foundation (REF) in 1955.

The purpose of the REF was to study the causes and prevention of cerebral palsy and to improve, develop, and train new workers to apply new forms of treatment. The REF maintained a rigorous research program, providing scholarships to both promising medical students and to postdoctoral scholars in cerebral palsy–related research. The REF also funded research projects throughout the country, particularly the research that isolated the rubella virus that caused many cases of cerebral palsy. This research led to a German measles vaccine and free immunization programs, which the UCPA affiliates helped to organize and publicize. To help overcome the shortage of teachers trained to work with cerebral palsied children, the REF continued and expanded significantly grants to such educational facilities as the universities of Pittsburgh, Cincinnati, and Alabama to develop special education programs. These UCPA-funded programs led, in the late 1960s, to a large-scale, federally financed program.

The UCPA attracted not only distinguished educators, physicians, and researchers, but also popular personalities to help in the various fund-raising and publicity campaigns. Bob Hope, Danny Thomas, Pat and Richard M. Nixon, and Dwight and Mamie Eisenhower, for example, led the highly successful fund-raising campaigns of the 1950s, when the first series of telethons was inaugurated. The National Association of Letter Carriers, through its "postmen's walks," or house-to-house solicitations, in communities throughout the country, also helped to raise money, as did the fifty-three-minute marches begun in 1952. These marches symbolized the fact that cerebral palsy struck every fifty-three minutes.

Fulfilling yet another announced goal, the UCPA organized cerebral palsy societies throughout the country. From its inception, the organization had an affiliation committee, and in 1953, it appointed an affiliation director to stimulate growth. After only five years, there were affiliates in all states and in the District of Columbia. One of the first activities of a local affiliate—the Pennsylvania organization—was the establishment of the first cerebral palsy center at Chestnut Hill, Pennsylvania. Featuring the teamwork approach, which used doctors, therapists, and social workers, the Chestnut Hill facility became a model for other centers sponsored or conducted by local affiliates.

The national association not only organized local societies, but also provided important services to them. An important development in 1954 was the establishment of a program division to help set up local programs, such as operating rehabilitation clinics and providing recreational facilities for the handicapped. The UCPA's program division prepared a manual for affiliates, worked closely with staff professionals to develop standards of clinic equipment and procedures, and sponsored, beginning in 1954, program institutes, where representatives from local societies discussed organization and problems with staff professionals. The national organization also published *Program News* and *Campaign News* for affiliates and, in 1955, began *Guideposts,* which contained program information and suggestions for affiliates. In 1954, the UCPA's national campaign department organized an advisory community campaign section to aid locals. The national legislative department prepared charts, compilations of relevant state laws, and leaflets for the use of local societies in their legislative work. By 1958, forty issues of the *Legislative Bulletin* had been issued, and the national organization maintained a legislative reporting service, which kept affiliates informed of legislative developments in their respective states.

On the national level, the legislative department issued weekly information bulletins, prepared a booklet detailing lawmaking, campaigned for an extra federal income tax deduction for the handicapped, and, with other organizations, worked effectively for additional congressional funding for the federal National Institute for Neurological Disease and Blindness. In 1969, the legislative department began publishing a monthly newsletter, *Word from Washington,* informing affiliates of relevant national legislation. The UCPA's representatives in Washington also testified frequently before congressional committees and kept affiliates informed of federal programs, helping the New York City affiliate to win, in the fall of 1968, a sizable grant under the Handicapped Children's Early Educational Assistance Act.

In the late 1960s and early 1970s, the UCPA created new and innovative programs. In 1968, for example, it developed the IHF plan—Individual with Cerebral Palsy and His Family. This program provided psychological, vocational, educational, and other such services to families. In 1970, to expand services further to the cerebral palsied, the UCPA developed a youth activities department to coordinate young volunteers and, with a grant from the Department of Health, Education, and Welfare, sponsored a three-day conference, "The Life Enrichment Needs of Persons with Multiple Handicaps," under the UCPA's national task force on teenagers and adults.

The primary sources for preparing this history of the UCPA consisted of the agency's published *Annual Reports,* which are not available widely in libraries. *The New York Times* occasionally covered the agency.

Richard Carter, *The Gentle Legions* (1961), contains a brief section on the UCPA. There is no scholarly history of this agency.

UNITED CHURCH OF CHRIST, OFFICE FOR CHURCH IN SOCIETY OF THE (OCS). In the mid-1950s, the social service and social action agencies of two churches—the Commission on Christian Social Action* (CCSA) of the Evangelical and Reformed church (ERC) and the Council on Christian Social Action* (CCSA) of the Congregational Christian Churches (CCC)—became increasingly close. After some cooperative projects between the two agencies and a series of discussions, it became clear that the two would lead their respective parent denominations to merge officially. On June 27, 1957, four years before the CCC and the ERC merged to form the United Church of Christ (UCC), the two welfare organizations joined to establish the Office for Church in Society (OCS) as the Council for Christian Social Action (CCSA).

In the period between 1957 and 1961, each of the predecessor social service agencies maintained its separate headquarters—the ERC group in that denomination's headquarters in Cleveland, Ohio, and the CCC's agency in New York City. In this interim, the two agencies planned training institutes and other forums, considered opening an office of the new CCSA in Washington, D.C., and met jointly in late October 1957. The agency elected as its chairman Reverend Henry D. Koch of Washington, D.C. The early structure also included a vice-chairman, a recording secretary, and a treasurer. These four officers and four other elected members of the council formed the executive committee of the CCSA. The director, Reverend Ray Gibbons, former head of the Congregational agency, and Associate Director Reverend Huber F. Klemme from the ERC's organization headed the staff, which initially included also a secretary in each of the following three areas: international relations, field relations, and racial and cultural relations.

The newly created CCSA began to develop its programs quickly. In February 1958, it conducted the churchmen's Washington seminar and added an after-Easter Washington seminar to discuss important social legislation for the proposed new denomination, the UCC. The CCSA continued to publish the original Congregational *Social Action,* as well as the Evangelical and Reformed *Christian Community,* but it also published a new manual for leaders of local social action programs. One of the early study-discussion packets of the CCSA, *Racial Integration in the Church and in Housing,* suggested its strong involvement in this social area. The CCSA sponsored a number of regular workshops, each with a representative from the two predecessor agencies, but it soon realized that one representative from either group was equally acceptable. One consultation, as the denomination called these various workshops and seminars, focused on race relations in churches in North Carolina and Virginia. A long-time ERC activity, work with conscientious objectors, became part of the CCSA program, appropriately supervised by Reverend Klemme, who had conducted this activity for years. The international relations program suggested the CCSA's philosophical orientation when, in the fall of 1958, its secretary participated in the discussions of the Church Peace Union concerning possible American recognition of The People's Republic of China.

In the early 1960s, the CCSA was involved in three major areas: race relations, poverty, and international relations. Each area was broadly defined, and in each, the CCSA developed programs and conducted activities that were consistently in the vanguard of progressive movements. In the field of poverty and social welfare, the organization conducted a conscientious program. It participated in the White House Conference on the Aging in the early 1960s, and it published study packets for the church on this issue. In March 1961, it testified before a House of Representatives subcommittee on migrant labor, and in April, it reported to a similar subcommittee of the Senate. The CCSA developed a fair housing program in Minneapolis, Minnesota, in the early 1960s. In 1964, some consultations dealt with the subject of the government and community poverty programs, and in 1965, to implement a church statement to overcome poverty, the CCSA developed an antipoverty program, directed by Reverend Forrest N. Johnson in cooperation with another UCC agency. In the mid-1960s, the CCSA promoted the church's participation in the March on Washington for Jobs and Freedom. The CCSA's economic life committee, in the early 1960s, was concerned with actions against poverty.

The CCSA developed a progressive position on the issue of race relations in the early 1960s. To promote better understanding, it encouraged church members to attend the Fisk University institute on race relations. Around 1963, the CCSA began to devote most of its attention to the Racial Justice Now project of the church, shifting two full-time staff members to work for and with it. The CCSA sponsored voter registration drives in Mississippi, and in March 1964, it arranged for influential individuals from the eighteen states whose senators were blocking civil-rights legislation to travel to Washington, D.C., to work to change their senators' minds and votes. During this period, the CCSA held a mission in understanding on race for pastors in the East.

Paralleling federal economic and civil-rights actions and programs, CCSA activities increasingly linked racial justice and poverty together in the late 1960s. For instance, the task force on antipoverty of the church familiarized itself with the program of the federal Office of Economic Opportunity (OEO) and then began to study both the use of nonprofessionals in projects and the relation of education to poverty. In the mid-1960s, the CCSA helped projects in Harlem in New York City in voter registration, housing, employment, education, and community organization. In early 1966, the CCSA began operating experimental, middle-income housing projects in New London, Connecticut, and in White Plains, New York. During this period, the CCSA published occasional bulletins and antipoverty action notes, especially for pastors near Jobs Corps centers. Concerns with poverty spilled over to the field of international relations. In July 1966, the CCSA participated in the Conference on Church and Society of the World Council of Churches in Geneva, Switzerland, to publicize poverty in other nations. In January 1967, a consultation focused on strategies for school desegregation, and in 1967, the new director for urban education, Reverend L. Alexander Harper, helped to defeat potentially crippling anti-integration amendments to the School Funding Act in the United States Senate in 1967. Indeed, as the organization itself claimed, the CCSA was in the vanguard of the church-related actions for justice in the schools. The agency also cooperated with local citizens working to integrate racially schools in Lancaster, Pennsylvania, and Springfield, Massachusetts. Fulfilling a mandate of the UCC's fifth general synod to investigate poverty, the CCSA began programs in eastern Kentucky, which resulted in the establishment of some community action organizations. In 1968, the CCSA helped to prevent the termination of community action projects in Alabama and in Appalachia. The agency also worked with the UCC's antipoverty task force, acting as a consultant on the guaranteed income plan, a major issue in social welfare circles.

There were many important organizational highlights during the active 1960s. In July 1961, the CCSA added another staff member, Dr. Lewis I. Maddocks, to its office in Washington, D.C. Reverend Gibbons retired as executive director at the end of 1968, after serving for twenty-five years. Beginning in 1969, however, Gibbons served the CCSA as a consultant in housing. Reverend Klemme, the former associate executive director, became director of publications, editor of the principal publication, *Social Action,* and coordinator of draft counseling services, an activity in which he had considerable experience.

In the 1970s, when some important organizational changes occurred, the CCSA was active in efforts to end the war in Vietnam, but it continued some domestic programs. In 1971, the agency established its center for the study of power and peace, and two full-time staff members spent considerable time in 1972 working on legislation to end the war. The CCSA also cooperated with the peace priority team of the church. Domestically, in 1972, the CCSA helped a group to secure water rights for Chicanos in the Rio Grand Valley, supported legal services for American Indians in South Dakota who were suing in the United States Supreme Court over United States Army surveillance, and aided urban legal centers and students in this field. In 1972, the journal, *Social Action,* merged with the similar publication of the United Methodist church's Board of Christian Social Outreach to become *Engage/Social Action.* The former editor of *Social Action,* Reverend Klemme, became a contributing editor of the new journal. In April 1973, Reverend Larold K. Schultz became the CCSA's new executive director. The executive council of the UCC agreed with members of the CCSA that the organization change its name to the Center for Social Action (CSA), which it did in 1974. In the early 1970s, however, agency and church leaders had realized that the CCSA was duplicating programs conducted by other UCC agencies, a bothersome situation aggravated by dwindling finances and inflation. Consequently, following a recommendation from the executive council of the UCC, the general synod meeting in St. Louis in 1973 established an agency—the Office for Church in Society (OCS)—to conduct a two-year study of the future of social action in the church and to report back to the tenth general synod in 1975. As a result of these developments, the new OCS was established officially at the tenth general synod in the summer of 1975, and it was charged broadly with supervising the social action programs of the UCC.

The primary sources for studying the OCS's history include the annual reports, which appeared in the biennial UCC *Minutes* of the *General Synod* and in the UCC, *Advance Reports,* which were prepared before the general synod. Douglas Horton, *The United Church of Christ: Its Origins, Organization, and Role in the World Today* (1962), contains a brief section on the OCS. There does not appear to be a scholarly history of this agency.

UNITED COMMUNITY DEFENSE SERVICES (UCDS). In 1950, during the mobilization for American participation in the Korean War, various social problems developed in communities suddenly overwhelmed by new or expanding defense industries. Some leading national social agencies and others became concerned about dealing with these problems. Consequently, on December 18, 1950, in New York City, the National Social Welfare Assembly, Inc.* (NSWA), and the Community Chests and Councils of America, Inc.* (CCCA), established the United Community Defense Services (UCDS) to solve these social problems. The UCDS was founded also to counterbalance the United Service Organizations* (USO), which assisted men in the armed services and their families: UCDS solved civilian problems of defense-congested communities, while USO dealt directly with the welfare of and recreation for servicemen. UCDS was one of six major organizations whose budgets were established, coordinated, and supervised by the newly formed United Defense Fund (UDF). The other five were the USO, American Relief for Korea (ARK), the National Recreation Association* (NRA), United Seamen's Service* (USS), and American Social Hygiene Association* (ASHA).

UDF planned to finance budgets chiefly by inclusion in local community chest drives. The UCDC's fifty-nine-member board of directors was comprised of two members from each of the fifteen participating agencies, which also included such major national social service agencies as ASHA, NRA, Child Welfare League of America, Inc.,* National Catholic Community Service,* National Federation of Settlements and Neighborhood Centers* (NFSNC), National Travelers Aid Association* (NTAA), the National Urban League,* Family Service Association of America,* National Organization for Public Health Nursing,* National Board of the Young Women's Christian Association of the U.S.A.,* National Probation and Parole Association,* and the National Congress of Industrial Organizations' Community Services Committee. In addition, there were twenty-nine members at large, representative of various geographic areas and public organizations. The entertainment field, for example, furnished two members at large, Bob Hope, the radio, television, and film comedian, and Edward G. Robinson, another film star.

In addition to Executive Director John H. Moore, other UCDS leaders included Louis B. Seltzer, the editor of the *Cleveland Press,* who served as president from 1951 to 1954. In February 1954, he became the first chairman of the board of directors of UCDS—a new post created that year. The president after Seltzer was Donald Stralem, already a member of the UCDS board of directors and chairman of the UCDS finance committee.

Headquartered at 129 East Fifty-second Street in New York City, UCDS did not have even an active public relations unit in its first year of operation. Its first such group met for a brief organizational meeting in December 1951 and held its first full-scale meeting to plan a public relations program on January 30, 1952. Henry Weber, the public relations director of both CCCA and UDF, was a member of this new UCDS committee, thereby furnishing further liaison with UDF.

The chief publication of UCDS was the monthly *Newsletter.* UDF provided further publicity for UCDS in the weekly UDF *Newsletter.* These supplemented the fifteen member agencies' own information materials. For example, the CWLA published *Child Welfare* monthly, except in August and September.

At the time of UCDS's inception, UCDS and UDF signed an agreement that all financial support for UCDS was to come through UDF. There was to be no separate campaign. UCDS submitted its budget requests to the National Budget Committee (NBC) and the National Quota Committee (NQC). The supervision of the NBC guaranteed scrupulous honesty and efficiency. The NQC determined the amount of inclusion for the UDF in community chest fund drives and, in turn, the UCDS share of the UDF budget. Set up to check and approve appeals of all funds raising money through local community chests, the NBC approved the UCDS budget.

UCDS had its own finance committee with representatives from all its agencies included. It received and reviewed proposed budgets before submitting annual requests to the NBC. Agencies submitted interim reports each month, showing actual expenditures for the previous month, proposed budgets for the coming month, and a running report of their present services.

The basic purpose of UCDS was to help communities solve problems arising from congestions of population in areas of defense industry. In order to achieve this goal, it furnished consultant and advisory services and encouraged and trained leadership to establish, finance, and operate their own programs. During the Korean War, eight million people in the United States moved for reasons related to defense—some to vacant muddy fields, like the Savannah River, Georgia, and Paducah, Kentucky, project areas; or to towns near new military bases like Warner-Robins, Georgia, which grew from 25 to 16,500; or to small industrial towns like Vallejo, California (population 23,000), whose shipyard workers increased from 9,000 to 15,000 in only two months and whose arsenal workers increased from 1,500 to 5,000.

The defense worker and his family in a cramped trailer house might need child care to free the mother to work, help in budgeting and management, financial aid until the first paycheck arrived, recreation facilities to help prevent juvenile delinquency, and adult social activities outside the home. UCDS surveyed such problems and then coordinated the efforts of a variety of volunteer services to attack all of them. This team approach was the key service that UDF, NSWA, CCCA, and two ''self-study'' committees agreed was so important that it should be retained in the ongoing stream of social service after the UCDS's demise. Yet, UDF terminated UCDS without making any provision whatever for such service.

The most important innovation of UCDS in social work was its team approach—the efforts of several agencies working together to solve the multiple problems of the individual, the family, or the community as a whole. Agencies of the UCDS provided services for transients, for working mothers, for child protection, for recreation, for promotion of better race relations, for housing, for social protection, for family counseling, for maximum use of nursing and health facilities, for development of community sanitation and political systems, and for surveys and planning to integrate local and national resources into effective use for defense areas.

UCDS had two fundamental policies regarding its services to communities: to encourage local leadership in every possible way to develop, operate, and to make maximum use of existing facilities and services in order to achieve the utmost efficiency and economy.

In contrast to USO, which tended to operate in larger communities, UCDS worked mostly in the desperately overtaxed smaller communities, which lacked sufficient resources, facilities, and planning personnel to handle adequately the military and defense impact. This vital decision—to base priority on need rather than on expediency—cost the UCDS the kind of visibility that USO later claimed.

UCDS in turn coordinated the efforts of its own fifteen member organizations. Five UCDS members had been members of the American War-Community Services of World War II. The labor committees of the American Federation of Labor (AFL) and the CIO financed their own extensive participation in UCDS services to communities. Their inclusion further guaranteed that labor would support UDF-CCCA fund drives rather than run competitive campaigns. One UCDS member, the NTAA, had a long history of working with people who were moving. UCDS was able to coordinate this experience into the work of all its agencies.

The United States, however, was not ready for a permanent united community service. Opposition came from both the CCCA and the largest partner of UDF, the USO. As soon as the Korean War ended, in 1953, both insisted upon termination of financing for UCDS.

After the Korean War stalemated, local community chests drastically reduced support for war-related service agencies. Forced by the necessity of shrinking budgets and the demands of the largest member, USO, to eliminate other agencies, the UDF set up a self-study committee in 1953 to evaluate the functions and future of all six member organizations. This study led to the establishment, early in 1954, of two further committees, the Ingraham and Craigie committees, to study the UCDS. Pressed by a widening deficit between shrinking income and greatly expanded wartime programs, USO demanded that UDF abandon percentage formulas in budgeting for its agencies. Noting that UCDS had little public acceptance in contrast to USO's widespread visibility, USO demanded an increasing percentage of the funds. Partly because of a fear that UCDS would become another national bureaucracy overlapping the functions of its two parents, NSWA and CCCA, and partly because of increasing pressure from USO, UDF set a single deadline—December 31, 1955—for both the termination of UCDS and a plan on how its vital functions could be incorporated into the continuing programs of other agencies.

Although no plan was ready by the deadline, both ARK and UCDS were terminated on December 31, 1955. But the debates of UDF members over shrinking income were not ended. USO and some CCCA members had insisted that neither the second largest member, UCDS, nor UDF itself had any real public visibility for fund raising. The debate culminated in an acrimonious meeting between leaders of UDF and USO, from which all secretaries and staff were dismissed by these leaders.

USO and CCCA refused to consider continued financing of UCDS, which then shut down quickly, in order to conserve all possible funds for the programs of remaining members. But the fund-raising public had the last word: USO collections dropped sharply in the next community chest campaigns.

UCDS had demonstrated the effectiveness and efficiency of the cooperation of national agencies through the team approach to local communities. Its influence lingered on past its final demise at the end of 1957. During its brief history, it had developed a pattern for the future cooperation of national agencies in serving local communities; educated leaders for the joint planning of government, industry, and voluntary agencies; developed further the labor participation committees of the AFL and CIO; and, in many pathetically disorganized or unorganized communities, it had developed united funds, community chests, and councils to carry on their own local programs—often with hardly a backward glance at this wartime agency to which they owed their very existence.

The major primary bibliography source for the UCDS is in the UDF files located in the Social Welfare History Archives at the University of Minnesota, Minneapolis. The archives also house the papers of several of the UCDS members—NFSNC, CWLA, AFL-CIO Department of Community Services,* microfilm of the NTAA—as well as papers of fellow UDF members NRA and ASHA. In addition, UCDS put out its own bulletins and *Newsletter,* which are not widely available. Reginald Robinson, the UCDS research director, wrote a bulletin-length history of UCDS, using only a small fraction of materials in the UDF files.

The only balanced secondary account is Marvin Palecek, "United Community Defense Services," chap. 12 of *Battle of the Bureaucracies: The United Defense Fund* (1972). This book includes an account of all six member agencies of UDF.

Marvin Palecek

UNITED COMMUNITY FUNDS AND COUNCILS OF AMERICA, INC.: see UNITED WAY OF AMERICA.

UNITED HEBREW CHARITIES OF THE CITY OF NEW YORK: see JEWISH FAMILY SERVICE.

UNITED HIAS SERVICE (UHS). In response to the unique problems of Jews during World War II and in the postwar period of resettlement and rehabilitation, a number of American relief agencies were created, and existing ones were expanded to assist needy Jews. By the early 1950s, a number of agencies were conducting strikingly similar work. To avoid duplication and to make work for refugee and displaced persons more efficient, the United Service for New Americans,* the migration services of the American Jewish Joint Distribution Committee,* and the Hebrew Sheltering and Immigrant Aid Society* (HIAS) signed an agreement to merge on December 23, 1953. Lengthy discussions between representatives of these agencies produced painful compromises, especially HIAS's insistence on preserving its name, methods, and fund raising.

Nevertheless, on August 30, 1954, HIAS's board of directors voted to join with the others to establish the new United HIAS Service (UHS).

The new UHS continued the basic work of its predecessors, expanding and shifting its services as the constantly changing factors that affected Jews developed. For instance, on November 12, 1954, the sixty-two-year old immigration and naturalization office on Ellis Island in New York City closed, signaling formally the end of an era in American Jewish history; the staff of the service, however, transferred to the New York office of the federal Immigration and Naturalization Service, where the former staff continued to help Jewish immigrants. During the Hungarian revolution and crisis of the mid-1950s, the UHS reacted characteristically. Abroad, it sent experienced workers from all over Europe to Austria, the country to which fleeing Hungarian Jews were migrating. In the United States, it worked with official agencies, especially the United States Hungarian Escapee Program, to settle Hungarian Jews in the United States. As it had for an earlier generation of immigrants, the UHS again provided kosher food services, this time at Camp Kilmer in New Jersey, the reception center. Still relying heavily on interior Jewish communities to absorb immigrants, the UHS sponsored a special workshop in January 1957 on the Hungarian Escapee Program, and, throughout the 1950s, field staff from the New York headquarters traveled to interior Jewish communities. In 1957, to help immigrants applying for naturalization and other statuses requiring specific personal information and to facilitate the increasingly bureaucratic processes, the UHS reorganized its vast record of arrival file, which dated back to the early twentieth century. The UHS, which had previously relied solely on its chief predecessor's own fund-raising campaigns, ended its drives in 1957 when it agreed to receive a portion of the receipts from the New York United Jewish Appeal, a communitywide effort. In the late 1950s, the UHS worked out details of bringing oppressed Egyptian Jews to America and continued to promote better services, for example, by arranging conferences for staffs involved in increasingly complex sociolegal matters to hear explanations of regulations from proper government officials.

In the 1960s, true to its tradition, the UHS responded to the plight of oppressed world Jewry. Beginning in 1960, for example, the organization helped to settle Cuban Jews fleeing government changes there. Still relying on but sensitive to interior Jewish communities, the UHS continued to sponsor discussions at such meetings as the National Conference of Jewish Communal Service,* allowing both groups—the UHS and the communities—to express their problems and goals. *Notes on Immigrant Care,* a UHS journal, dealt with casework and community organization problems. Following a trend in social service agencies, in 1961, the UHS initiated a program to collect reimbursements from former migrants for their transportation. The UHS continued to influence official decisions and regulations that affected immigrants, prompting the Department of State

(DS) to allow the federal Immigration and Naturalization Service to waive visa and passport requirements for Cuban Jews, who could not obtain such documents after the closing of the American consulate in Havana in early 1961. Rescue activity increased significantly in the mid-1960s as the condition of Jews in North Africa and the Middle East deteriorated. In 1965, the UHS sold its headquarters in a landmark building in Lower Manhattan and moved to its new world headquarters in New York City. By 1969, after fifteen years as the UHS, the agency had helped resettle nearly 117,000 refugees.

In the 1970s, the UHS continued its basic services, although changing international developments influenced some new activities. In 1972, for instance, the agency was asked by federal officials to help non-Jewish refugees, a group of Moslem and Hindu Ugandan Asians. In 1973, focusing this time on Jews, the UHS alerted Jewish communities throughout the United States on possible reunions with Russian relatives, a development made possible by Attorney General Elliot Richardson's use of his parole authority for those waiting in Rome to come to the United States. The UHS negotiated a contract with the DS, which provided a $300 per capita grant for each Russian immigrant to the United States beginning in January 1974; the agency passed the funds on to the appropriate participating organization. Also, in 1973, the UHS held workshops in New York and in New Orleans to encourage professional social workers to exchange ideas and discuss problems relating to immigrants in their communities. Addressing itself to an old issue in American Jewish resettlement programs—the interior reluctance to take immigrants—UHS invited executives from local agencies to plan resettlement activities through its national technical advisory committee.

The primary sources for studying UHS's history include the agency's papers, through the 1960s, deposited at the YIVO Institute for Jewish Research in New York City. These papers consist of organizational materials, correspondence, cables, monthly reports of activities, and the like. There is a guide to these materials at YIVO. The more accessible published and detailed *Annual Reports* are especially helpful.

There do not appear to be any scholarly historical studies of the UHS.

UNITED SEAMEN'S SERVICE (USS). The outbreak of the hostilities that became World War II, the generally turbulent life-styles of seafarers, and the inability of existing institutions for merchant seamen in port cities to keep up with the men's demands and special interests necessitated by the war prompted the need for well-organized social services for merchant seamen in the early 1940s. As an indication of these needs, in 1942, for instance, casualties among the civilian merchant marines were 400 percent higher than the combined casualties of the United States Army, Navy, and Marine Corps.

In May 1942, the federal War Shipping Administration (WSA) created its Recruitment and Manning Office (RMO) to supervise the wartime shipping needs of the country. Concerned also with the seamen's welfare, the RMO began to discuss establishing a nonprofit social service organization. Coupled with a series of conferences and investigations of seamen's conditions in New York City, these ideas influenced Admiral Emory S. Land, the federal war shipping administrator and the head of the WSA, to submit to President Franklin Delano Roosevelt a memorandum on July 10, 1942, concerning the needs of merchant seamen and proposing such an organization. These developments led quickly to the incorporation, according to the laws of the state of New York on August 8, 1942, of the United Seamen's Service (USS) to promote the men's welfare.

A group of five men representing diverse interests in the merchant marine industry incorporated the USS: Admiral Land and his deputy, Captain Edward Macauley; Basil Harris of the United States Lines, a private corporation; and, representing organized labor, Harry Lundeberg of the Sailor's Union of the Pacific (SUP) and Joseph Curran of the National Maritime Union (NMU). The five incorporators and twelve other men representing similar groups and interests comprised a temporary board of directors, which engaged as medical director Dr. Daniel Blain, a retired senior surgeon of the United States Public Health Service, (USPHS) and as executive director, Douglas P. Falconer, a well-known, reputable social worker in New York City who was active in community chest work.

The organizational development of the USS occurred rapidly. The board met officially for the first time in early September 1942. At the meeting, the group chose as president, Henry J. Kaiser, an industrialist from Oakland, California, and as chairman of the executive committee, philanthropist Albert D. Lasker. The group also adopted bylaws, providing for 125 trustees to meet annually, chiefly to elect a thirty-member board of directors; in turn, the board elected from its own group between three and fifteen men as the executive committee, the central and most important group of the USS. Within a few days of the meeting, on September 14, 1942, the USS opened its national headquarters at 39 Broadway in New York City. More importantly in terms of the services of the USS, it opened two convalescent centers in September 1942—one in Bay Ridge, Maryland, and the other in Oyster Bay, Long Island. Also in September 1942, the USS took over the former Dartmouth Club in New York City, refurbishing it and renaming it the Furuseth Club, after a pioneering labor leader. In early October 1942, the USS included the men's dependents in the relief and assistance program.

The USS developed its program even further, including a medical division, which it conducted jointly with the RMO, a social work service centered in the national headquarters, and both domestic and overseas divisions. From mid-November 1942 through January 1943, the most heated controversy in the USS's history developed: some people charged that the agency was expanding too feverishly. In late November, Falconer reduced the staff, dismissing forty-six employees, but the controversy continued. On February 10, 1943, in an open letter to Admiral Land, carried by the Associated Press wire services, founder Harry Lundeberg of the SUP denounced the USS, charging it with overstaffing, excessive salaries, extremely high administrative costs, and providing easy jobs for social workers. Lundeberg's position of influence in the American Federation of Labor (AFL) dampened AFL maritime union support for the USS, which thrived nevertheless. In 1943, the USS decided to purchase rather than to rent facilities, and another important organizational event occurred in the same year when the National War Fund, a joint fund-raising organization during World War II, agreed to include the USS. This freed the USS to focus on its primary purpose: to provide basic welfare and medical services to seamen.

The USS's service program expanded as the war progressed. Hotels and medical services opened in many American port cities, some in new structures and others affiliated with local institutions for seamen, such as in Savannah, Georgia, and Galveston, Texas. The domestic activities developed into the following regions: Northeast, New York, Southeast, and Gulf and Pacific coasts. By June 1944, there were 115 facilities in the United States. Cooperation with the American National Red Cross* (ANRC) emerged gradually. A memorandum in 1944 formalized functions: the USS would use the ANRC to get access to social service for the men inland, and the ANRC would refer appropriate seamen to the USS. USS policies allowed wives to stay with their husbands in port hotels. Throughout the war period, the USS sold beer but not hard liquor, and the agency declined an offer from the Alcoholics Anonymous* (AA) to work to rehabilitate heavy drinkers in the larger centers. The USS had a Negro advisory committee to counsel the headquarters staff and the executive committee on Negro issues. The USS also hired an expert on Negro issues for the national staff, but the USS let local customs and traditions in the South nullify the official agency policy of no racial discrimination.

The two unique and most important services of the USS were the medical program and the personal service, or social work. Supported jointly by the WSA, the medical program aimed to comfort and to care for seamen, but keeping them fit for the essential shipping work was also a clear objective. Seven rest centers constituted the core of the medical program, which also stressed prevention. In July 1943, Dr. Florence Powdermaker joined the staff as director of health education, a program that used posters, films, and the like to stress hygiene. In the early 1940s, the health education program issued a pamphlet, *Safety for Seamen*. The USS sponsored the month of October 1946 as Seamen's Safety Month, campaigning against carelessness and industrial accidents on ships. By the end of 1947, when the USS had closed all domestic rest centers and medical offices, the medical program ended. By providing psychotherapeutic services to seafarers who led turbulent and traumatic lives, the program returned about ten thousand men to work, fulfilling a major agency goal. The medical services also helped to open new areas in the pathology of maritime labor; as early as January 1943, at the New York Academy of Medicine, the USS sponsored a conference on this specialized medicine, a symposium supported by funds from the Josiah Macy, Jr., Foundation.

The personal service division developed a new kind of social work. Professional social workers functioned skillfully in the society of the seamen, with its unique customs and life-style. The director of the division was Charles Nison. Social workers participated in this work in each of the port cities. In New York, Baltimore, New Orleans, and Los Angeles, they provided services in the local hiring halls of the NMU, in addition to working at the regular facilities of the USS. By June 1944, there were twenty personal service units in the United States, each staffed by professional social workers. As in other service-related social welfare agencies, financial assistance to the men became a controversial aspect of the work. Social workers in the USS generally viewed financial assistance as one aspect of their services, but in 1946, a stipulation that social workers use their better judgment in disbursing funds spelled the end of this practice, which came officially in February 1947. The entire domestic program dissolved finally at the end of 1947 when the New York social workers from the USS wrote *Understanding Merchant Seamen*. This publication proved useful to social service agencies that continued to work with the men, such as the ANRC and the National Travelers Aid Association.*

The overseas division of the USS was organized officially in October 1943, although the initial hotel and service center had opened in Glasgow, Scotland, in November 1942. Similar to the facilities in the United States, the units overseas provided sleeping quarters, recreational facilities, and other types of services, often spontaneous according to the men's needs. For example, professional social workers in the units provided emergency medical care and helped seafarers who had missed their departing vessels. As the war progressed and as the scope of the work broadened and the number of units increased, the USS developed regional divisions in the overseas programs. The end of the war, however, brought a rapid closing of overseas units.

The end of the war drastically affected the entire USS, but unlike the United Service Organizations for National Defense, Inc.,* the USS did not close entirely. In 1945, two internal reports by the USS revealed differences over the future of the agency, born in the war crisis but obviously fulfilling a continuing need of serving the merchant marine. Authored by the regional directors of the USS Gulf Coast division, the Bancroft report saw the need to continue the organization and outlined a future program, but the report by Philip Reed of the General Electric Company was skeptical and indifferent about the future of the USS. A questionnaire answered by the men in early 1946 showed that about 98 percent of them wanted the organization to continue in 1947. But, viewing the USS as a wartime emergency, local community chests generally refused to support it in the 1940 campaign. In February 1946, Otho J. Hicks became the executive director, replacing Falconer, who had guided and developed the USS since its inception. The USS was weakened in the postwar period by a series of strikes in the maritime industry, which embittered relations between workers and the owners who had supported the USS, factionalism in the NMU, and a split between the NMU and the USS when the latter closed its services in NMU halls. Subsequently, on June 26, 1947, the USS issued a public statement abandoning its fund-raising efforts and planning to dissolve when present funds expired. But the report of President Harry Truman's Advisory Committee on the Merchant Marines, issued on November 1, 1947, and which praised the USS, presaged the revival of the agency.

The benefit to the USS by the companies relying on seamen and the beginning of the Korean War resuscitated the USS. On December 4, 1947, the Croele Petroleum Corporation announced that for the first half of 1948, it would support the USS facility in Caripito, Venezuela, where the company conducted much of its business. This episode supported the contention of the historian of the early USS, Professor Elmo Hohman, that the organization was a fine example of industrial welfare, as well as a beneficial social service.

In the 1950s, the USS continued its basic services to the men, opening and closing facilities as conditions warranted. During the period of the Korean War in the early 1950s, the United Defense Fund (UDF), a joint fund-raising agency, supported USS operations in ports deemed necessary for the national defense. The USS had abolished its regional structures, placing additional burdens on the national office in New York City. In January 1952, each port began to contribute equally to help maintain the national office. During this period, because the executive committee met less frequently than in the earlier years, the USS's planning and budget committee conducted the managerial affairs, as well as the financial matters of the agency. In 1955, Mike Freeland, the head of the UDF, agreed to lead an independent USS fund-raising campaign. USS leaders appeared before the National Budget Committee of the Community Chests and Councils of America, Inc.* (CCCA), attempting to be included in united fund campaigns throughout the country. An important event occurred in the mid-1950s when founder Joseph Curran influenced the American Federation of Labor-Congress of Industrial Organizations (AFL-CIO) and its agencies to endorse the USS fund-raising campaigns. The bulk of USS funds, however, still came from the operations rather than from outside sources. In 1955, for instance, only one-sixth of the USS income came from outside sources. In the late 1950s, in response to a resolution by the NMU, the USS began a study of the need for shipboard educational and recreational activities. With other national agencies, the USS sponsored a session at the National Conference on Social Welfare* in 1958, and the board of directors approved the transfer of a staff member, Edward Sette, from the field to national headquarters as assistant director to work with community chests and united funds. Late in the decade, the USS approved the establishment of an international council, to include some members of the council of trustees and others around the world interested in the USS.

During the 1960s, the agency continued to provide services to seamen throughout the world, including Vietnam, where the United States was building an American presence in the early 1960s. The USS initiated efforts during this period to develop social services for sailors in the St. Lawrence Seaway and Great Lakes area of the United States. Partly because the National Social Welfare Assembly* (NSWA) had failed to implement its earlier agreement to organize a conference of national agencies located in New York City to discuss services on the St. Lawrence Seaway and the Great Lakes, the USS voiced dissatisfaction with the NSWA. At the end of 1963, the USS maintained sixteen units overseas and provided service in thirty-three ports, and the agency pointed out that 85 percent of its funds came from the men's use of USS services and facilities, indicating that the men wanted and used the USS. In the mid-1960s, in cooperation with Project HOPE, the USS had a service in Conakry, Guinea. Also in the mid-1960s, the executive committee approved establishing a facility in South Vietnam, and because of this increase of service, the national budget and consultation service of the CCCA approved its revised request for united funds. An important organizational event developed in late 1967, when Edward Sette replaced Otho Hicks as executive director. In appreciation of the USS's work, New York City Mayor John Lindsay declared September 25, 1967, as USS Day. During this period, the organization established its Betty Land committee to provide local women opportunities to serve the USS in communities throughout the country. An important step occurred in late 1967 when the maritime industry, which still provided funds for the USS, accepted the principle of a ship's fee for service. Also in 1967, the USS held a well-attended twenty-fifth anniversary celebration at a pier in New York City. And, in the late 1960s, the USS began to participate as an official observer at the Maritime Conference of the International Labor Organization.

War-related activities overshadowed other USS programs in the 1970s. New facilities in South Vietnam developed consistently in the early 1970s, without any financial support from the federal government. In December 1970, the enactment by the United States Congress of Public Law 91-603 provided government recognition of and cooperation with the USS. In December 1972, the American Merchant Marine Library Association (AMMLA) affiliated with the USS, and in 1974, the USS absorbed the AMMLA. In 1973, the USS amended its bylaws to increase the number of trustees from 120 to 130 to provide for the merger with the AMMLA. In March 1973, the USS held an important seminar at Arden House in Harriman, New York. And in May 1974, the USS moved to new headquarters in the World Trade Center in New York City, providing space for the AMMLA's books. The only social service organization to have spent its own funds for facilities in Vietnam, the USS participated in the Vietnam Sealift, which evacuated American personnel in 1975.

The primary sources for studying the USS's history include the unpublished minutes of annual and other meetings, located in the USS's files at its national headquarters in New York City. Douglas Falconer and others, "World-Wide Service for American Merchant Seamen," National Conference of Social Work, *Proceedings 1944*, 181–192, provide some first-hand information, as does Bertha C. Reynolds, *An Unchartered Journey: Fifty Years of Growth in Social Work* (1963), a staff member's autobiography.

For the USS's early history, students should read Elmo P. Hohman, *Sea Men Ashore: A Study of the United Seamen's Service and of Merchant Seamen in Port* (1952), vol. 2, a model of organizational history. There does not appear, however, to be a full-length, scholarly history of this agency.

UNITED SERVICE FOR NEW AMERICANS, INC. (USNA). Responding to the plight of European Jews afflicted by Adolf Hitler's atrocities, a number of American-Jewish relief agencies developed and expanded by the mid-1940s. To provide more unified and better-coordinated services than before, the leaders of two such social service agencies conducting similar work agreed to consolidate. The two agencies were the service to foreign born of the National Council of Jewish Women (NCJW) and the National Refugee Service* (NRS), which itself had grown from the relief work of yet another agency, the National Coordinating Committee for Aid to Refugees and Emigrants Coming from Germany* (NCC). Subsequently, in New York City, on August 1, 1946, the two groups merged to form the new United Service for New Americans, Inc. (USNA). The leaders in the founding of the USNA were Edwin Rosenberg, a New York City businessman who became its first president, and Mrs. Irving M. Engel from the NCJW, who became the first chairman of the board of directors. European-Jewish Children's Aid remained a subsidiary of the USNA, just as it had been of the NRS.

A very large and diverse administrative structure reflected the nature of the USNA's early work. At the end of 1947, the USNA had a staff of over six hundred people, making it then apparently second in size only to the American National Red Cross* among American social service agencies. The USNA had a personnel and procedures department and a community relations department, composed of the field staff and publicity divisions. The director of national services supervised the following activities and programs: port and dock service, which utilized well-trained volunteers, the shelter division, the national intake division, the resettlement division, the group care of religious functionaries division, a migration department, location services, and a corporate affidavit reporting service. The director of rehabilitation services supervised these activities in the New York area: family service department and vocational adjustment department. Continuing a long-time activity in Jewish social service, especially in New York, the director of rehabilitation also supervised a business and loan division. The comptroller conducted the financial apparatus of the USNA. The USNA had a national and local program for refugees, aiding Catholics and Protestants but concentrating on Jews. In May 1947, the United Jewish Appeal began an evaluation of USNA, leading to organizational changes by August 1948.

The establishment in early July 1949 of the New York Association for New

Americans brought three major changes to the USNA: it ceased as primarily a relief-granting agency; it developed as an agency facilitating immigration and resettlement; and it developed stronger field services to local communities and committees outside of New York. By the end of 1952, these administrative changes and the reduction in the volume of immigration prompted staff reductions and further organizational changes designed for maximum flexibility.

Reduced in size, the USNA continued nevertheless to adapt to changing situations, developing new programs as conditions merited. For instance, it held a number of conferences and seminars dealing with the procedural changes brought by the McCarran-Walter Act of 1952. It remained one of the most active agencies under the displaced persons program, for example, participating in the Joint Council on Resettlement of Displaced Persons. With Church World Service,* the National Lutheran Council, and the National Catholic Welfare Conference, USNA prompted the establishment, in the early 1950s, of the National Committee for Resettlement of Displaced Professionals. In the late 1940s, USNA published *Finding Jobs for Newcomers, A Manual for Community Job Placement Programs,* and it played an active role in the committee on the refugee program of the American Council of Voluntary Agencies for Foreign Service.* The USNA disbanded on August 26, 1954, when it helped to form United HIAS Service,* a further consolidation of Jewish refugee and immigrant aid work.

The primary sources for studying the USNA's history are extensive. The papers of the agency, deposited at the YIVO Institute for Jewish Research, contain relatively full files, including committee reports, minutes of meetings, and such. There is an unpublished guide to this collection at YIVO. The agency's publications, such as *New Neighbors,* are also helpful.

A history of the USNA, based on its files, can be found in Lyman C. White, *300,000 New Americans* (1957).

UNITED SERVICE ORGANIZATIONS, INC. (USO). During World War I, a number of the leading social service agencies conducted special services for men in the armed forces, as well as for families and individuals at home. As the United States mobilized for what became World War II in the early 1940s, communities with defense industries grew suddenly and quickly developed a host of social problems. As American entry into the war became imminent, letters from the general public to the National Jewish Welfare Board* (JWB), The Salvation Army* (SA), the National Board of the Young Women's Christian Association of the United States of America* (NB-YWCA), the National Council of the Young Men's Christian Associations of the United States of America* (YMCA), and the National Travelers Aid Association* (NTAA)—each of which had developed social service programs during World War I—stressed the need for a similar effort for the military. In 1940, General George Marshall also called for the development of social services for the military.

Marshall's appeal helped to initiate discussions by the leaders of these national agencies. These discussions resulted subsequently in the establishment of the USO, Inc. as the United Service Organizations for National Defense, Inc. (USOND) in New York City on February 4, 1941. Representatives from the JWB, NB-YWCA, YMCA, SA, and the National Catholic Community Service* (NCCC) founded the USOND, and in March 1941, the NTAA joined the new organization, completing the participation of the so-called big six. Walter Hoving, the president of Lord and Taylor stores and the first USOND president, Federal Security administrator Paul McNutt, and Louis Kraft of the JWB were important founders of the USOND.

The USOND quickly established an administrative structure, which changed frequently throughout its history but which remained generally patterned after the original one. The executive committee met every Monday and Thursday mornings for several months to help inaugurate a national fund-raising drive and develop a program. The need for social services in hard-pressed industrial defense communities was particularly strong in the spring of 1941. Local community chests and their national organization, Community Chests and Councils, Inc.* (CCC), worked with USOND representatives to determine local needs. President Franklin D. Roosevelt, as other presidents who followed him, supported the drive enthusiastically. So did prominent Republican, Wendell Willkie, whose wife served on the board of governors. The drive raised funds, which helped the organization to implement its programs, for instance, establishing service clubs and centers beginning in the summer of 1941 and incorporating USO Camp Shows, Inc. (USOCS), in November 1941. When the United States entered the war in December 1941, the USO seemed generally solidified and ready.

The war naturally stimulated USOND's growth. Within a year ending July 1942, the staff had expanded from six to around forty workers. Enjoying the cooperation of many governmental agencies, such as the War and Navy Departments, the Federal Security Administration (FSA), and the President's War Relief Control Board, the USOND had eighty-eight facilities abroad at the beginning of 1943, when nearly one hundred clubs served industrial communities in the United States, the original group with which the USOND was initially concerned. In early 1942, USOND began to deal with women defense workers, and when the Women's Auxiliary Army Corps was established, the USO served it. The year 1943—which marked the inauguration of the interagency training courses for new professional workers and the establishment of volunteer training institutes—also brought the peak number of USOND volunteer workers in World War II—739,000 in June. In March 1944, USOND reached its highest number of clubs, 3,035. The number of travelers' aid service units to help the armed forces in transit peaked at 136, serving about 661,000 cases in July 1944. In the spring of 1944, the USOND began its hospital programs of artists sketching wounded patients and of USOND camp shows entertaining at Veterans Administration hospitals. Also in 1944, with increasing numbers of clubs near hospitals,

USOND established eight regional offices, as well as its national council of volunteers, which served local advisory groups of business and professional leaders who knew their community needs.

As the war came to an end in 1945, the reduction in USOND services paralleled the armed forces' demobilization. On December 31, 1947, all USOND operations ceased, and at the annual meeting on February 4, 1948, the corporate structure was simplified greatly: the number of members of the corporation was reduced from sixty to six, with one representative from each of the member agencies; the number of directors was reduced from fifty to twelve; many leadership and staff positions as well as the executive committee, were abolished, and at the end of 1947, USO Camp Shows disbanded (although the new Veterans' Hospital Camp Shows, Inc., continued this most famous USOND service). Finally in early January 1948, the USOND dissolved; in February, overseas operations ceased.

The dissolution of such an important organization as the USOND, however, was short-lived. In the summer of 1948, just a few months after the disbanding, Secretary of Defense James Forrestal approved of the reactivation of the service organization. Events moved quickly. In January 1949, a committee of civilians developed plans and prepared a charter for the revised USOND. In February, President Harry S Truman formally reactivated the organization. At the USOND elections in April 1949, Harvey S. Firestone, Jr., became president. By the summer of 1949, the agency was serving over 72,000 daily. Because it could not attract suitable funding, however, the agency closed down again in early 1950. The USOND agreed to have the NCCC, JWB, and YMCA take over existing funds and to continue the work of serving the men.

The Korean War, however, prompted the reestablishment of a permanent USO. Government defense officials and the National Social Welfare Assembly* (NSWA) stimulated the big six—joined this time by USO-affiliate but the now independent Camp Shows, Inc.—to reorganize the USO on March 27, 1951. The agreement between USO and the government provided that the board of directors be responsible to the president of the United States, the secretary of defense, and the American people. The new USO joined the United Defense Fund, Inc., to raise funds, and it developed a program advisory committee, headed by Dean Kenneth Johnson of the New York School of Social Work. The reorganized structure had a seventy-five-member board of directors, chaired by Harvey Firestone, Jr., the head of a leading tire manufacturing firm. The board had an executive committee; a president, seven vice-presidents in 1951, a secretary, and a treasurer completed the leadership. Executive Director Edwin E. Bond headed the staff at national headquarters in New York City. By the end of 1951, the USO had 236 units. As in World War II, the USO established mobile and maneuver programs, as well as overseas units.

The peace accords of the summer of 1953 did not, as in the previous war, signal the demise of the USO; rather, the agency expanded significantly in the

1950s and early 1960s. It was brought into the national spotlight in 1953 by well-publicized anniversary celebrations in February, National Golf Day, the first USO Letter Week during which Americans sent letters to servicemen, and the second annual Pal Day, established at the White House by President and Mrs. Dwight Eisenhower in November 1953. In 1954, USO won the Meritorious Service Award—only the fourth of its kind—from the Department of Defense (DD). The next year became, as its executive secretary called it, a "year of decision," as USO changed its structure to adapt to nationwide participation in community chests and united funds. In 1955, a board of governors with fifty-seven members replaced the board of directors. The executive committee was expanded to broaden representation. Four newly established committees advised the board of governors: finance, operations, public relations, and campaign. USO initiated its national council with some four hundred members from communities all over the country. Helping to make USO a widely known agency were USO Month, a movie in 1958, *A Long Way from Home,* a USO overseas building fund campaign begun in 1959, a television show in 1961, "USO— Wherever They Go," a twentieth anniversary celebration at clubs at home and abroad in 1961, and a host of articles in the national press.

While public relations and fund raising strengthened the USO, it developed better social services. A unit in Japan, established in 1954, fulfilled the needs of numerous servicemen in this major area of activity. The personnel department, created in 1958, set up a USO training program for professionals. Counseling services and a housing bureau continued to be features of programs in local USO units.

With the military buildup in Southeast Asia in the early 1960s, USO entered a new phase. In 1962, to evaluate the agency, an outside ad hoc survey committee was established. Chaired by the president of Michigan State University, Dr. John A. Hannah, the committee presented its findings and recommendations in December 1962 to the executive committee, which studied the proposals intensively with other USO committees. USO officials accepted the Hannah recommendations, which stressed drastic USO curtailments, including having no units in the United States except in heavy military areas and having local facilities operated fully by local councils. Proud that no other national agency seemed to have agreed so fully with an independent survey, the USO implemented these changes in early 1964. Another USO milestone occurred in 1963 when the board of governors integrated all facilities. USO local councils participated actively in community united fund drives but in major cities, like New York and Chicago, independent USO fund-raising campaigns expanded.

While USO streamlined its domestic operations, its expansion in Southeast Asia continued steadily. As early as 1962, USO leased enlarged spaces for an expanded unit in Saigon, and in the same year, it appointed an executive for operations in the area, headquartered at Tokyo. Maintaining excellent relations with the DD, USO responded to the call for enlarging services in the region. In

1966 alone, six new units were established in Vietnam, as the USO raised an emergency fund of about $600,000; in the following year, it opened a facility in Thailand, and the number of USO shows doubled. Implementing again a request from the DD, USO organized a Pacific hospital circuit for wounded soldiers and those on leave. Special telephones in Asian units facilitated contacts with soldiers' families. In 1969, the Manpower and Reserve Affairs Section of the DD invited USO headquarter staff to a conference at the Pentagon to delineate ways in which the military could aid the agency. USO shows, highlighted by Bob Hope's Christmas shows, continued to be extremely popular on the front, as well as at home. USO also sponsored Letters to Servicemen by the public to demonstrate that many people supported the fighting men.

As the American participation in the war decreased and eventually ended, USO adapted well to the situations confronting it. In 1971, for instance, it cooperated with a nonprofit organization in New York in Operation Hire for returning soldiers, and along with the National College Education and Admissions Foundation, it helped servicemen enroll in colleges. USO established its domestic action program to involve returning men in big brother, golden age, environmental, and other such programs in their home communities. By the end of 1972, there were no units in Vietnam, but a much-publicized incident involving corruption reminded some Americans of the decadence of the Vietnam War years. In 1972, USO not only established a training school for Asian brides in Seoul, Korea, to help reduce the high divorce rate among Korean-American couples but also continued to deal with the persisting housing problems of servicemen, handling over twenty-five thousand such requests in 1972. As Vietnam-related problems such as drug abuse continued to surface and as the armed services became voluntary, USO strengthened its family drug and alcohol abuse counseling services, established a minority services program, and helped to implement the DD's human goals program.

The sources for studying the USO's history are extensive. The variously named published *Annual Reports* provide details of the agency's activities, as do a number of agency and other publications, such as *The USO Bulletin* for the early years and *Defense Morale* (1941). The New York Public Library has a good collection of these early publications, and the USO files relating to camp shows are on file at the Performing Arts Research Center of the New York Public Library at Lincoln Center. The conveniently accessible and indexed *The New York Times* reported the agency's important activities. The USO's files, such as minutes of meetings and correspondence, are kept at the national headquarters in New York City. These unpublished records are available only to properly qualified and identified researchers. Because it worked so closely with other national social service agencies, documents relating to the USO appear in such other collections as the Papers of the NSWA at the Social Welfare History Archives Center at the University of Minnesota, Minneapolis, and in the Bowne Historical Library of the YMCA in New York City.

Despite this wealth of materials, there does not appear to be a scholarly history of the USO.

UNITED SERVICE ORGANIZATIONS FOR NATIONAL DEFENSE, INC.: see UNITED SERVICE ORGANIZATIONS, INC.

UNITED STATES CATHOLIC CONFERENCE, DEPARTMENT OF SOCIAL DEVELOPMENT AND WORLD PEACE OF THE (DSDWP). During the early years of American participation in World War I, American Catholics had been conducting a wide range of activities to assist the war effort. Groups such as the Chaplains' Aid Association (CAA), directed by John Burke, and the Knights of Columbus (KC) were among the agencies conducting general welfare work. Group leaders soon realized the need to coordinate these Catholic activities, and John Burke approached James Cardinal Gibbons of Baltimore about establishing such an organization. Gibbons and other cardinals liked the idea. Burke then worked to have 115 Catholics, including forty-two bishops and representatives from twenty-seven societies, as well as the Catholic press, attend a gathering to discuss a new coordinating agency. Some representatives feared that the new agency would dominate and even take over the work of existing societies, but this notion was dispelled, and the delegates then formed the United States Catholic Conference (USCC) (see *Religious Organizations*) as the National Catholic War Council (NCWC). It was agreed that an administrative board of bishops would direct the new NCWC. In December 1917, the first such board was appointed. Bishop (later Cardinal) Patrick Hayes of New York was one of the initial board members. He was chosen to head the NCWC and to work with the government to lend Catholic assistance. In this early period, for instance, one NCWC committee of women went to France immediately after the war to serve the troops. These efforts were strikingly similar to those of other national social service agencies, such as the International Committee of the Young Men's Christian Association,* and the Jewish Welfare Board, United States Army and Navy* (JWB).

The nature of this temporary wartime work clouded the future of the NCWC, but the intervention of Pope Benedict XV assured its existence. In early 1919, the pope asked the American hierarchy to help promote social justice. Consequently, on September 24, 1919, the American bishops resolved to establish the National Catholic Welfare Council (NCWC), a new organization. With an administrative committee of seven members of the hierarchy, the group chose Cardinal Gibbons as its honorary chairman and Archbishop Edward J. Hanna of San Francisco, California, as its chairman. Realizing the immensity of the task, in December 1919, the administrative committee took over the National Catholic War Council and its staff. The new NCWC then unanimously elected John Burke as its executive secretary. Headquarters were soon established in Washington, D.C.

The new NCWC worked in its first few months to solidify its structure. It formed several departments to conduct its multifarious activities. Consequently, in early 1920, the Department of Social Development and World Peace (DSDWP) of the USCC was established in Washington, D.C., as the Department of Social Action (DSA) of the NCWC.

The first chairman of the DSA was Right Reverend Peter J. Muldoon, the bishop of Rockford, Illinois, and a member of the NCWC's administrative committee. Reverend Muldoon convened the meeting at which the SDA was created. The new SDA quickly chose its initial executive committee of nine members, which included Reverend William J. Kerby, professor of sociology at The Catholic University of America and an important founder in 1910 of the National Conference of Catholic Charities* (NCCC), Reverend Edwin V. O'Hara, the former chairman of the Oregon Minimum Wage Commission, and George J. Gillespie, a layman from New York City who was president of the Superior Council of the Society of St. Vincent de Paul of the U.S.* (SVDP). One of the DSA's first directors was Dr. John A. Lapp, who had been appointed by President Woodrow Wilson to the federal Board for Vocational Education in 1914 and who had served for two years as director of the Ohio State Board of Social Insurance. Dr. Lapp had just completed directing the extensive survey of the Catholic charities of New York, the report of which led directly to the founding of The Catholic Charities of the Archdiocese of New York* (CCANY) in 1920. The other director, whose name was for years virtually synonymous with the quickly renamed Social Action Department (SAD), was Reverend John A. Ryan, a professor of moral theology at The Catholic University of America and the author of *A Living Wage* (1906).

The SAD's initial announced purposes were to develop programs in citizenship, in industrial relations, and with Catholic charitable organizations. The SAD also planned to assist in diocesan surveys of charities and to furnish the Catholic press with information about industrial and labor movements and conditions. The naturalization and Americanization of immigrants also developed as an early and major agency concern. In August 1920, for instance, the SAD helped to organize an Americanization conference in Gary, Indiana. Apparently in late 1920, the SAD institutionalized its work with immigrants, establishing its bureau of immigrants under Bruce Mohler of Minneapolis, Minnesota, a former deputy commissioner of the American National Red Cross* in Poland.

Immigrant-related problems were a primary SAD concern in the 1920s. Reminiscent of some of the earliest immigrant aid work, such as those activities conducted by the Immigrants' Protective League* (IPL) of Chicago and the Hebrew Sheltering and Immigrant Aid Society,* the SAD hired personnel to assist immigrants at both ports of entry and embarkation and to help them to reach their American destinations. The SAD worked to mitigate abuses before legal restrictions on immigrants set precedents, and, in the spirit of other immigrant aid organizations, it defended immigrants unjustly denied entry to the United States. The SAD also worked, as it did at the conference in Gary,

Indiana, in 1920, to Americanize immigrants. It published texts stressing Americanization and advised local social service, civic, and fraternal organizations and parochial schools, which conducted Americanization programs, classes, and schools.

A more important activity than immigrant-related issues in the 1920s was the SAD's work in the fields of industrial relations and labor. As a recently published essay suggests, the SAD promoted the teachings of Pope Leo XIII on labor and social justice. These activities were conducted generally by the industrial relations department (IRD), administered by Reverend John A. Ryan. In 1921, the progressive stance of the SAD was suggested when the agency issued a statement, echoed by the Commission on the Church and Social Service* (CCSS) of the Federal Council of the Churches of Christ in America (FCC), which criticized the open shop because it destroyed organized labor. During the 1920s, guided by its labor leader Ryan and his IRD, the agency published books and pamphlets explaining the Catholic church's (CC) prolabor attitudes. Department leaders prepared prolabor articles for journals, especially for Catholic periodicals. Ryan and other IRD leaders spoke on such topics as child welfare and labor relations. To promote workers' interests, the SAD also held weekly news conferences on industrial issues. These conferences often voiced support for such labor reforms as minimum wage legislation. Beginning in 1922, the SAD held conferences on industrial questions and labor, which often brought together capital, labor, and outside experts to discuss labor-management issues in relation to Catholic principles. These sessions were similar to those conducted by the CCSS in the 1920s. With other church agencies, especially Protestant ones, the SAD participated in investigations of major labor strikes in the 1920s, especially in coal mining, textiles, and railroad industries. These reports generally favored labor over management. To help improve diocesan welfare programs throughout the country, the SAD conducted surveys of social and economic conditions.

While most of these programs in immigrant aid, labor relations, and charities seemed to benefit urban Catholics, the SAD also had a rural life bureau, directed by Reverend O'Hara, one of the agency's early leaders. Perhaps because of his service as a public official in Oregon, Reverend O'Hara conducted a survey of Lane County, Oregon, in the early 1920s.

The SAD's positions on basic social and economic issues became more emphatic in the 1930s. For example, the SAD urged the creation of a major public works program and unemployment insurance. Acting both alone and with similar agencies and personnel from the Protestant and Jewish communities, the SAD issued statements supporting the National Recovery Administration, the Wagner Labor Act of 1935, higher income taxes for the rich, organized labor, particular unions during specific strikes, and the merger of the American Federation of Labor (AFL) and the Congress of Industrial Organizations (CIO). The SAD also supported such key progressive issues and programs as large-scale public works projects, social insurance, cooperative economic planning, and a shorter work week.

In the 1940s, the SAD continued its basic concerns with industrial relations, but it seemed to expand its peace, international, and race relations activities. For instance, it held a special conference on the Negro in industry in 1940, when it also convened a series of one-day, regional priests' conferences, which dealt with the means by which priests could spread the teachings of encyclicals. The SAD continued also to sponsor industrial institutes in collaboration with the National Council of Catholic Women (NCCW) at the National Catholic School of Social Service in Washington, D.C. Its concern for minorities was evidenced in the conference on Spanish-speaking people of the Southwest and the West in late 1943. The SAD played an active role in the renewal of the United States Fair Employment Practice Committee in 1943, and the social service agency assisted the Negro Catholic Federation in the economic aspects of its work. In the early 1940s, the SAD began to develop its peace programs, and it cooperated with the Catholic Association for International Peace. Throughout the decade, the SAD sent monthly newsletters on social legislation to about a thousand priests. Consistent with its prolabor orientation, the SAD denounced the Taft-Hartley Act in the late 1940s. Fulfilling its role in the church, the agency also worked as a consultant to the NCWC's Youth Department and in 1949 published the pamphlet "Human Relations in Modern Business."

Like other church-affiliated social agencies, the SAD strengthened its international relations programs, especially those relating to the United Nations (UN), but it also continued its basic activities in the 1950s. Beginning in the late 1940s, the SAD dealt increasingly with labor issues on the international level, and it served as the secretariat of the Inter-American Catholic Social Action Confederation. Sensitizing the church to social issues, in 1951, the SAD held two week-long institutes for wage-earning women and for the social action chairmen of the NCCW. Race relations in the 1950s were conducted primarily through the race relations office of the Catholic Conference on Industrial Problems. By the mid-1950s, the SAD maintained close ties to major labor unions and employer associations. During this period, reflecting an initial interest and activity, the SAD conducted an intensive study of immigration and related problems.

In the 1960s, especially, SAD activities were supplemented by several other Catholic social action type institutions and agencies. This situation resulted in a diminishing role for the SAD. In the 1960s, especially after 1962, virtually every diocese established social action programs, as did councils of priests and many fraternal orders and lay groups. Religious orders also added important and formal social reform groups. In 1966, when the NCWC was reorganized as the United States Catholic Conference, the SAD was reorganized and expanded as the Department of Social Development (DSD). John E. Cosgrove, a layman, now headed the new social action agency. This reorganization did not indicate that social reform had failed but rather that Catholic activity and commitment grew greater than the initial SAD structure and format anticipated. In 1972, reflecting its peace work and international concerns, the DSD was renamed the Department of Social Development and World Peace (DSDWP).

The primary sources for studying the DSDWP's history consist of the agency's papers, available at the headquarters in Washington, D.C. Annual and other reports of the agency can be found in the variously named *Social Action* through 1953, when the publication ceased. John Ryan's Papers at The Catholic University of America in Washington, D.C., contain materials relating to the SAD. *The New York Times* occasionally reported some of the agency's activities.

Secondary sources relating to the agency include Francis Broderick, *Right Reverend New Dealer* (1963), and Neil Betten, "John Ryan and the Social Action Department," *Thought* (June 1971): 227–246.

UNITED STATES CHRISTIAN COMMISSION FOR THE ARMY AND NAVY (USCC).

During the very early phases of the American Civil War, some religious persons grew concerned with what they thought was the vagueness of military chaplains' duties, and they began to undertake efforts to aid the men. For instance, a bookseller affiliated with the Young Men's Christian Association* (YMCA) of Washington, D.C., William Ballantyne, distributed religious tracts to soldiers passing through his city. Concerned similarly with the men's welfare, the YMCA of New York established its army committee in late May 1861. Vincent Colyer of the New York YMCA left his business soon after the war began in order to help the men, and he initiated correspondence to form an organization to aid the men spiritually and physically. Colyer wrote to George H. Stuart, a merchant in Philadelphia and the secretary of the national committee of the YMCA. Subsequently, the United States Christian Commission for the Army and Navy (USCC) was organized at the Bible House of the YMCA of New York on November 14, 1861, to aid, both spiritually and physically, Union soldiers in the Civil War.

Stuart chaired the meeting, which representatives from seven states and the District of Columbia attended. The group established a commission of twelve members, headquartered in New York City, to conduct the work of ministering to the men in the military. This commission, the USCC, adopted rules for its delegates in the field and established a policy of not interfering with military authorities. Immediately after its founding, the USCC sent its plan to federal officials, including President Abraham Lincoln and Secretary of War Edwin Stanton, both of whom failed to recognize the agency officially. Not until 1863 did General Ulysses S. Grant, head of the army's Department of the Mississippi, recognize the USCC, allowing delegates free access to the troops and free passage for their supplies.

The USCC was spirited in its work, but the lack of official recognition and early popular support meant that it conducted little fruitful activity until about mid-1862. The USCC's central body—the general commission of twelve men—had a five-member executive committee, but the delegates ministering to the troops were the real heart of the USCC. Official delegates had to be members of an evangelical church and to have a recommendation from a minister, preferably one known personally to USCC leaders. Clergymen constituted the largest group of delegates. The first official commission was issued to an Episcopalian minister from Germantown, Pennsylvania, on May 14, 1862. The founders envisioned delegates as aiding the men spiritually, distributing religious literature, assisting military chaplains, leading prayer meetings, and ministering to the sick and wounded. With delegates free to perform whatever function they wanted to, the early line of command was very loose. The USCC had tried to structure the system, authorizing the hiring of a general agent in December 1861, but it was August 1862 before John C. Cole became the first to fill the position.

With the general agent directing the work, the USCC developed its administrative structure, which it based on earlier experiences in the field. The general commission had established its first headquarters in New York City in late 1861, but by the summer of 1862, it had become evident that the real center was George Stuart's store in Philadelphia. Stuart, who had chaired the initial organizational meeting, was the only chairman in the USCC's history. On January 29, 1863, the USCC moved its headquarters to his store, where it remained for the rest of the agency's life.

To administer the work, the USCC established six field areas, which did not always correspond to Union military areas. To aid the men on ships leaving New York and other coastal cities, the USCC created a separate organization, an auxiliary, the New York Branch. About one-fourth of all the men in the Union forces came under its jurisdiction. In 1863, the executive committee established four subcommittees to carry out USCC functions: home organization and finance, field organization and work, publications, and stores and stock. The executive committee supervised the activities, working through a general secretary, a general home secretary, and a general field secretary. A number of general field agents supervised delegates who were in the field and with the troops. Branch commissions developed throughout the country to stimulate public interest in the work and to raise funds, as did ladies' commissions, which performed similar functions and also prepared food and clothing for the men. There were 226 ladies' commissions.

As the war progressed and delegates came in contact with human suffering, the USCC became a true social welfare agency. Despite earlier, strained relations between doctors and the evangelics, the delegates' most important social service was to aid surgeons and to minister to the wounded. A woman from the Iowa Commission developed and initiated a special diet kitchen program, through which the hospitalized men received specially prepared meals prescribed by medical officials. Developed initially in only certain areas, the USCC decided to extend this project through the Union army in January 1865. In April 1864, the

USCC began to distribute secular magazines to the Army of the Cumberland, and like other military aid agencies, it developed a library loan system. In 1864, the USCC maintained twenty-five hospital libraries, as well as reading rooms in many cities. Delegates also visited military prisoners, relieving some of their suffering. The USCC also established bureaus of information and employment. Although contemporaries, such as the United States Sanitary Commission* (USSC) and historians, criticized the USCC as religiously fanatical and undisciplined, others agreed that through its help to the starving wounded, the USCC performed a benevolent social service.

The USCC continued to function for several months after the war ended in April 1865. At a meeting in July 1865, however, the executive committee, which had been expanded in 1864 and now numbered fifty, heard reports from agents suggesting disbandment. On December 1, 1865, the executive committee decided to cease operations, and the USCC approved this action at a mass meeting held on February 10, 1866, in Washington, D.C. The final meeting of the USCC was held on the evening of February 11, in the Hall of the House of Representatives, with the Speaker of the House, Schuyler Colfax, presiding.

The materials for studying the USCC are plentiful. The National Archives in Washington, D.C., hold the minutes, correspondence, reports, and even scrapbooks of the USCC. Many other primary sources, such as newspapers, contain further materials.

The agency has been studied widely. Many studies of the Civil War mention it. Robert Bremner's publications on Civil War era philanthropy, such as ''The Impact of the Civil War on Philanthropy and Social Welfare,'' *Civil War History* 12 (December 1966): 293–303, ''The Prelude: Philanthropic Rivalries in the Civil War Era,'' *Social Casework* 49 (February 1968): 77–81, and chap. 5 of *American Philanthropy* (1960), compare the USCC to the USSC. M. Hamlin Cannon, ''The United States Christian Commission,'' *Mississippi Valley Historical Review* 38 (June 1951): 61–80, James O'Henry, ''The United Christian Commission in the Civil War,'' *Civil War History* 6 (October 1960): 374–88, and his dissertation, ''History of the United States Christian Commission'' (University of Maryland, 1959), are accounts generally favorable to the organization.

UNITED STATES COMMITTEE FOR REFUGEES (USCR). In the United States by the late 1950s, most of the official and even some of the voluntary efforts to assist refugees had been terminated or reduced severely. A few persisted, however. In 1957, for instance, Dean Francis B. Sayre of the Washington Cathedral in Washington, D.C., conducted two months of resettlement work in Europe for the Intergovernmental Committee for European Migration (ICEM). In 1958, Dean Sayre called a conference of representatives from agencies dealing with refugees abroad, such as the American National Red Cross* (ANRC), the Cooperative for American Remittances to Everywhere* (CARE), and the ICEM, to discuss American participation in dealing with the problems of refugees. This meeting was held at the headquarters of the United States Department of State (USDS) in Washington, D.C., on October 17, 1958. Subsequently, in late January 1959, the United States Committee for Refugees (USCR) was established in New York City to promote American interest in the plight of refugees and to advise federal agencies about their programs relating to refugees.

An immediate USCR organizational goal was to help plan the program of the United States for World Refugee Year, beginning July 1, 1959, under the sponsorship of the United Nations (UN). The initial officers, chosen at the organizational meeting in late January 1959, included the president, Harper Sibley of Rochester, New York, a former president of the United States Chamber of Commerce, five vice-presidents, including former governor of and United States senator from New York, Herbert Lehman, and George Meany, the president of the American Federation of Labor-Congress of Industrial Organizations, a treasurer, and the executive director, Edward B. Marks, a former ICEM official. Dean Sayre, who had an important influence on the early history of the USCR, was the first chairman, a position he held until September 1962.

Although established for a single purpose—to promote American participation and interest in World Refugee Year—the USCR developed quickly as a broader agency, creating a number of social services in the field. In the early spring of 1959, Dean Sayre asked President Dwight D. Eisenhower to have the White House cooperate in the planning for World Refugee Year. President Eisenhower agreed to hold a conference in May 1959, which, among other things, agreed that the USCR would coordinate the American program for the event.

On May 22, 1959, after the conference closed, the USCR selected a fifty-eight-member national council. In 1959, its first year, it strove to raise $55 million to help refugees throughout the world. This activity used the mass media and helped the USCR to publicize the plight of refugees and thus to keep the aims of World Refugee Year before the American public. The publicity also strove to improve reception centers for refugees throughout the United States. As conditions and events affecting refugees unfolded, the USCR became actively engaged in serving refugees. In December 1960, for instance, Executive Director Marks went to Miami, Florida, to view the condition of Cuban refugees there. Soon thereafter, the USCR initiated one of its earliest activities, cooperating with three other agencies to provide charter flights to other cities for the Cuban refugees in Miami. In its very early years, the USCR conducted a job-referral service for refugees in the United States, and the organization began its long-time service of donating funds to other agencies that were engaged more actively than the USCR in direct relief and rehabilitation services.

Aside from a few direct social services, the USCR became generally an advisory, clearinghouse, coordinating agency in the field of refugee relief. Characteristic of its role and activity, in January 1961, the USCR sponsored Dean Sayre's investigation of refugee conditions in the Middle East. At the third annual meeting, held in May 1961 in Washington, D.C., the USCR passed many resolutions, such as one supporting the Escape Program of the United Nations Relief and Rehabilitation Administration (UNRRA), and then conducted a discussion of "refugees and the public interest." Another major activity in 1961 was promoting a drive to celebrate the centennial birthday of Fridtjof Nansen, who had been the first high commissioner for refugees of the League of Nations. The USCR also sold gift wrappings, an activity that developed as a consistent fund-raising technique. In 1961, the structure of the USCR, which was headquartered in New York City, included the president, four vice-presidents, one of whom was Herbert Lehman, a treasurer, and a secretary. There was also a forty-five-member board of directors, chaired by Dean Sayre, which included some prominent Americans. In early 1962, R. Norris Wilson, a minister and the former executive director of Church World Service* from 1955 to 1961, became the executive director of the USCR.

Under Wilson, the USCR developed its most ambitious programs and activities in its brief history. At the annual meeting in May 1962, President John Fitzgerald Kennedy spoke, and the USCR later passed resolutions asking the administration to help Chinese refugees and voted funds to the American Friends Service Committee* (AFSC) to work with Algerian refugees. The meeting also approved the USCR's plan to conduct a preliminary survey concerning possible USCR activities in Africa. The USCR's advisory nature was revealed again in late December 1962 when the board appointed two advisory subcommittees, one to work closely with the UN high commissioner for refugees and another to work with the UN Relief and Works Agency for Palestine Refugees. In 1963, the USCR sponsored a traveling art exhibit of refugee themes by West German children. At its April meeting that year, the board appointed a subcommittee on program development. The board's meeting in October 1963 observed the USCR's fifth anniversary, featuring USCR citations to three individuals for distinguished service to immigrants, including one to Hal B. Cook, the publisher of *Billboard* magazine, who had helped the USCR to publicize "The All Star Festival," a long-playing record album issued by the office of the UN high commissioner for refugees. For the fiscal year beginning July 1, 1963, the USCR raised $53,000 in contributions and $13,000 through the Christmas gift wrap paper sale, an important organizational activity, which had a separate committee, composed partly of celebrities.

In the late 1960s, the USCR continued its basic activities, mostly responding to new conditions and developments. In 1967, at the urging of a foundation, the USCR began a study of the refugee problem in Africa, a project absorbing a great deal of staff time. Responding in 1967 to the war in the Middle East, an ambitious USCR-sponsored conference of scholars in New York City in July 1967 discussed solutions in that troubled area of the world. Financial problems in 1967 threatened the primary USCR publication, *The World Refugee Report,* which included an annual compilation of statistics and conditions of refugees, but individual contributions by the agency's friends saved the journal. In 1969, the USCR characteristically aided Czech refugees and provided emergency funds for a refugee children's hostel in Dharmsala, India. Conferences on refugees sponsored by the USCR, such as one in 1969 in Washington, D.C., continued to be another important organizational activity.

Activities in the 1970s declined from the exciting days of the 1960s, but some basic USCR projects continued. The USCR issued annual reports on the status and numbers of refugees, and the agency contributed minimally to such social services for refugees as a counseling service in Ethiopia, to a research assistant to deal with trachoma problems among Palestinian refugees, and in 1974, to refugee students, mostly from Chile, to study in Europe. In 1975, the USCR merged with the American Freedom from Hunger Foundation,* but in 1976 it continued to maintain its small headquarters in New York City, while leaders of both agencies worked out the details of the merger.

The primary sources for studying the USCC's brief history include the *Newsletter* for the early years and the *World Refugee Report*. *The New York Times* occasionally reported the agency's activities.

Merle Curti, *American Philanthropy Abroad* (1963), mentions the USCR briefly. There does not appear, however, to be a scholarly history of the agency.

UNITED STATES COMMITTEE FOR THE CARE OF EUROPEAN CHILDREN, INC. (USCCEC). During the mid-to-late 1930s, as Americans learned of Adolf Hitler's atrocities abroad, some individuals and organizations became concerned with the plight of refugee children. In the mid-1930s, the National Non-Sectarian Committee for German Jewish Refugee Children (NNSC) was formed to bring large numbers of child refugees from Hitler's Germany to the United States. Influenced heavily by the Nazi domination of Norway, Holland, Denmark, Belgium, and France, in 1939–1940, American public opinion demonstrated grave concern for the plight of British children. Capitalizing on this popular concern, the NNSC met in New York City in May 1940 to develop a new organization. Eleanor Roosevelt, who attended the meeting in May 1940, subsequently invited a large group of citizens interested in protecting war-threatened European children to a meeting in New York in early June 1940. Her meeting led directly to the establishment of the United States Committee for the Care of European Children (USCCEC) in New York City on June 20, 1940. The new agency absorbed the NNSC, which left a successor, the Non-Sectarian Foundation, to focus entirely on the possibilities of rescuing children from the European continent. Marshall Field III of the Chicago department store family, chaired the USCCEC initially and continued as president until its demise in 1953. Eleanor Roosevelt remained the honorary president. Other important founders included Dr. Clarence Pickett, the executive secretary of the American Friends Service Committee* (AFSC), Dr. Marion Kenworthy, an influential social worker, and Rabbi Stephen Wise, a prominent Jewish leader.

Influential business, civic, and social work leaders helped the USCCEC to establish itself quickly and to begin its work, despite numerous obstacles. The agency quickly established its national office in New York City, staffed initially by volunteers and by professionals lent by other local and national social welfare agencies. Within a few weeks, nearly two hundred local committees throughout the country had affiliated with the USCCEC both to channel offers of American family homes to the national office and to interpret the emerging program to local communities. While the USCCEC established its administrative network, members met almost daily with representatives of the United States Children's Bureau, (USCB) the United States Department of State (USDS), and the attorney general of the United States to find a legal way to allow the British children to come to the United States. In mid-July 1940, the attorney general announced the use of "corporate affidavits," allowing nonprofit organizations to sponsor children, and the USDS immediately issued a thousand visas for the children. The USCCEC asked the USCB to verify each local cooperating agency, and the USCCEC hope for sound child care practices was strengthened when the USDS ruled that each agency taking children must comply with USCB's standards. To ensure high standards of its work, the USCCEC established its child care advisory committee, comprised of child specialists, to help determine policies and practices.

The initial activity of having British children sent to American foster families proceeded smoothly through the summer of 1940, despite British fears, articulated in mid-July, that the exodus weakened British morale at home. The USCCEC prepared for more evacuations, but following the Nazi's destruction of a ship with some refugee British children, the British government ended the project on October 3, 1940. Having just begun a national fund-raising campaign and having almost completed its network of cooperating agencies, the USCCEC cut back its staff, shifted its plans, and decided to concentrate on serving the children in the United States rather than evacuating more British children. Despite difficulties with some children, the British children remained in the United States for the duration of the war and returned generally without incident to their British families as the war ended. By V-E Day, about half of the children had returned, and in 1946, the responsibilities of the USCCEC for them ended.

The British phase of the USCCEC program helped to establish the agency's methods. In England, the London Branch, an outgrowth of the American Committee for the Evacuation of Children, helped to determine and generally served the children in England who were awaiting embarkation or returning home. When the children arrived in New York, they stayed in reception centers until they left for their American foster homes, which were located throughout the country. Particularly the Gould Foundation in the Bronx, a privately run children's village, and the Seamen's Church Institute in Lower Manhattan served as such reception centers. Volunteers in the New York area, in addition to professional child care agents, provided the children with services and activities.

From the beginning, the philosophy of the USCCEC stressed that all children be placed in families rather than in institutions. There were exceptions, however; some British children stayed at American boarding schools.

While the work with British children initiated USCCEC activities, its work with the refugee children from the European continent proved more trying and lasted longer. As the Nazi threat to all European Jews swept across the continent, some Americans worked to rescue Jewish children. In particular, the German-Jewish Children's Aid, which broadened its scope and name to European-Jewish Children's Aid (EJCA), brought nearly 450 children to the United States by early 1940. In late 1940, however, the USDS declared that the visas applicable to British children would not apply to continental children. Despite the ban, the Unitarian Service Committee* cooperated with the USCCEC in 1940 to smuggle a group of twenty-five children out of occupied France, through Spain and Portugal, to America. In 1941 and 1942, cooperating with the AFSC in France and the EJCA in other countries, the USCCEC placed a limited number of children in American homes. During much of the war period, the organization received money from the National War Fund and local community chests, and some cooperating agencies, especially the EJCA, paid some USCCEC administrative costs.

The USCCEC participated fully in the trying postwar rehabilitation of children refugees. Within months of President Harry Truman's directive of December 22, 1945, establishing that American consulates in Germany and Austria issue visas to displaced persons, including orphaned children, the USCCEC established its European headquarters at Frankfurt, Germany. Three other district offices in Germany and one in Salzburg, Austria, administered the program of finding and processing children for American homes. The agency worked abroad through the United Nations Rehabilitation and Relief Administration (UNRRA), and when the UNRRA expired at the end of June 1947, the USCCEC took over many of its responsibilities for children. With other American agencies, the USCCEC helped the United Nations Preparatory Commission for the International Refugee Organization raise its child welfare standards. The USCCEC assumed fuller responsibilities when it worked through the United States Displaced Persons Commission (USDPC), which was created in 1948. The USCCEC undertook the difficult job of dealing with war-ravaged children, some of whose parents were difficult to locate. Determining if the children were full orphans or obtaining far-flung parents' permission for their children to go to the United States proved to be difficult tasks, which the agency handled successfully. The USCCEC also helped and cooperated with the USDPC, and with the American Hellenic Educational Progress Alliance, it helped over two hundred Greek children come to American family homes.

With the gradual easing of the refugee problem in general, the USCCEC began to wind up its work. In March 1952, it closed its only remaining European office, in Munich. The International Social Service* agreed to help the refugee children eligible for immigration. In mid-1953, the USCCEC itself disbanded, having helped nearly three thousand children find American homes since V-E Day.

The sources for studying the USCCEC's history are diverse. Agency publications, such as *We Are Standing By* (1941), provide helpful information, as does *The New York Times*. Information about its work can also be found in contemporary publications, such as "European Children Brought to America," *The Social Service Review* 21 (June 1947): 239–240. There are four boxes of materials relating to the USCCEC's very early history in the Papers of the USCB, Record Group 102, at the National Archives in Washington, D.C., and there are some documentary materials in the Eleanor Roosevelt Papers at the Franklin Roosevelt Presidential Library in Hyde Park, New York.

Kathryn Close, *Transplanted Children* (1953), is a helpful history. Merle Curti, *American Philanthropy Abroad* (1963), mentions the USCCEC briefly, but there does not appear to be a scholarly history of the agency.

UNITED STATES COMMITTEE FOR UNICEF (USCUNICEF). In the aftermath of World War II, there developed a special concern for the plight of children from the war-torn countries, especially of Europe. During the period of postwar planning and reconstruction and in the early days of the United Nations (UN), it was logical that a special program for such children be developed. On December 11, 1946, by resolution of the UN's general assembly, the International Children's Emergency Fund (ICEF) was established. Member nations of the UN, including the United States, contributed to this special fund. Katharine Lenroot, the chief of the United States Children's Bureau, who represented the United States on the ICEF, realized that the ICEF needed strong American support. Probably in the halls of the early UN, which met in Lake Success, New York, before it moved to its present site in New York City in the early 1950s, Helenka Pantaleoni and Maurice Pate, the founder of the ICEF itself, recognized the same need. Lenroot, Pate, and Pantaleoni began to discuss the idea of an American organization to support the ICEF, and they formed the core of the group that incorporated the United States Committee for the ICEF (USCICEF) on December 23, 1947, according to the laws of the state of New York.

The new organization began immediately to develop its structure and to try to interest Americans in its work. Less than a month after its incorporation, on January 19, 1948, the USCICEF held a meeting in the East Room of the White House. Early members attending this meeting were Katharine Lenroot, Mary Bethune, the founder of the National Council of Negro Women (NCNW), who called for an interracial campaign at the grass roots and in American schools, and Mrs. Oswald B. Lord, a prominent New Yorker who was elected the first president of the fledgling organization. At the meeting, the group also elected five vice-presidents, one of whom was Mary Bethune. The group decided that its first task was to procure gifts and contributions to the American Overseas Aid-UN Appeal for Children, a special fund-raising organization established by the members of the American Council of Voluntary Agencies for Foreign Service* (ACVAFS) with the approval of the United States Department of State (USDS). By 1949, the USDS had placed responsibility for the fund-raising campaign with the organization, now apparently called the United States Committee for the Children's Fund (USCCF). Despite the support of such important people as Lenroot and despite its ties to the USDS, the USCCF became so inactive that it almost disbanded in the early 1950s.

In the early 1950s, the future of the UN's international children's organization, now known simply as UNICEF, appeared threatened by the Eisenhower administration's apparent wishes to end official American contributions to UNICEF. On Halloween 1952, American children in some cities, as they had since about 1950, collected pennies, nickels, and dimes to support UNICEF. The success of this effort encouraged Pantaleoni to work to revive the American organization to support UNICEF. Her efforts led to the "newly reestablished" United States Committee for UNICEF (USCUNICEF) in February 1953. In a memorandum dated April 21, 1953, from the United States representative to the UN, Henry Cabot Lodge, to the UN's general secretary, the USCUNICEF was officially reconstituted. In May, the group sent telegrams to American leaders urging them to support the international agency generously. Led by Pantaleoni, on October 21, 1954, the revived group filed an official certificate to change its name officially to the USCUNICEF, with the purposes of informing the United States about the international agency's work and of participating in coordinated planning with the American voluntary agencies involved in children's relief abroad. By March 1953, there was a nucleus of five members of the board of directors; by February 1954, when the agency had an executive secretary and a small but competent professional staff, the board had thirteen active members. Setting the pattern of operation, volunteers in the headquarters in New York and in local communities worked for the USCUNICEF. In its first year as a reorganized group, the agency raised about $90,000.

In the 1950s, the USCUNICEF grew gradually, developing and expanding some of its well-known and important activities. In October of 1953, for example, about two hundred communities participated in the Halloween fund-raising campaign. The USCUNICEF began its long association with *Seventeen Magazine,* cosponsoring, with Save the Children Federation* (SCF), a nationwide doll dressing contest. The executive secretary contacted both the National Advertising Council and the Public Relations Society of America, both of which helped to initiate the publicity techniques that the USCUNICEF developed so well. The agency worked with other national social service and other organizations, such as the National Association of Social Workers* (NASW) and Women United for the UN, to pressure Congress for American contributions to UNICEF. The sixty corporate members, which grew to seventy in the 1960s, included such prominent humanitarians and civic leaders as Katharine Lenroot and Clarence Pickett, the executive secretary of the American Friends Service Committee*

(AFSC) and one of the founders of the SCF. By 1955, Danny Kaye, the actor who publicized the USCUNICEF and UNICEF so forcefully, became involved.

Other features of the activities and policies of the USCUNICEF developed in the first decade of its existence. The organization conducted and earned the proceeds from the annual UN Art Exhibit, where celebrities sold their works of art. The agency also sold UNICEF postcards, developed films to publicize the work, established a few state committees, and became a participating organization in the National Social Welfare Assembly* (NSWA). The USCUNICEF also initiated UNICEF city committees throughout urban America, most of which only conducted the Halloween trick or treat events, but some of which worked on a year-round basis. The USCUNICEF continued to cooperate with nationwide publications, especially *Seventeen Magazine,* and it published its own *News of the World's Children.* In the mid-1950s, the USCUNICEF prepared the first in a distinguished series of Understanding our Neighbors children's books.

Compared with the admittedly "steady, slow ascent of the preceding ten years," 1965 was indeed a year of a "great leap forward." At the New York World's Fair, the USCUNICEF exhibit, "It's a Small World—A Salute to UNICEF," attracted great publicity and increased funds. Built by Walt Disney Productions and paid for by the Pepsi-Cola Company, the exhibit was one of the four most popular attractions at the fair, far outdistancing the other exhibits in attendance. In 1965, *News of the World's Children* increased its circulation by one-third, the first national workshop for state representatives was held, and the postmaster general of the United States authorized volunteers to sell UNICEF postcards in the United States Post Offices. In 1965, a leading public relations firm developed a new look for the UNICEF's publicity efforts, including innovative public service spots on television. All these developments, coupled with the expansion of other activities, gave the USCUNICEF its largest collection of funds in 1965.

Capitalizing on the events of 1965, the USCUNICEF continued to expand. Symbolizing efforts to improve education in the developing world, in 1966, the White House received a twelve-year-old Bolivian boy, and in 1967, President Lyndon B. Johnson proclaimed October 31 as National UNICEF Day. The USCUNICEF developed new techniques of publicity and fund raising; one was instituting a "food for India fast," whereby students at some 145 colleges and universities raised $43,000 in one day in 1967. In November 1967, the USCUNICEF opened, at its headquarters, the information center on children's culture, a unique library collection relating to children throughout the world. Despite structural changes at the headquarters offices in 1968, the agency worked to bring relief to children on both sides in the Nigerian-Biafran crisis. A good response from college and university students bolstered this effort. The agency also strengthened its nationwide volunteer structure, appointing new state representatives and organizing metropolitan UNICEF committees in nine cities. An enlarged communications and development department produced and distributed films and other information.

In the 1970s, the USCUNICEF strengthened existing activities and developed new ones, resulting in increased fund raising despite the unstable economy at home and a troubled world. In 1970, the first year of significant coverage for UNICEF on network television, the Halloween program netted a record $3.35 million. The communications highlight of 1970 was a cluster of three national television productions, including two specials in late November, "To All the World's Children." During this period, the headquarters was reorganized and relocated in a large suite of offices and rooms near the UN. The headquarters staff provided briefings for UNICEF's work to groups visiting the UN, and the public information staff expended considerable energies refuting charges, made by anti-UN, right-wing groups, that UNICEF was pro-communist and therefore anti-American.

Another highlight of 1970 was a field trip to Ecuador for metropolitan chairmen, local leaders, and staff to see the children's needs and to observe programs assisted by UNICEF. A two-day training session concluded the week's visit. The USCUNICEF discovered that the very young and adults were the major participants in the agency's activities. To bridge this gap, it established a committee on youth participation. During this period, the agency established a program that brought young adults to work with the staff. The USCUNICEF also welcomed college students to its board of directors. The agency changed the name of its trick or treat department to youth activities to reflect the increased support from young adults. In the early 1970s, the field service launched *Views and Reviews,* a newsletter to disseminate program information. In conjunction with a meeting of the executive board in 1972, the agency held a national training workshop for about sixty volunteer leaders.

The USCUNICEF developed a number of new ways to solicit and to raise funds, including direct mailings, special appeals to corporations, a "treat of life" label, and, with the cooperation of Pan American Airlines, a solicitation of unspent foreign money from international passengers. In the summer of 1972, the USCUNICEF opened its West Coast regional office in California to develop a full program there. The retired former director of public information, Paul Edwards, initially headed this office. A southeastern regional office in Atlanta, Georgia, which had an advisory board of prominent civic leaders in the South, and extensive field visits strengthened the nationwide network of fund-raising and promotional activities. In 1974, the agency inaugurated its development office, which prepared corporation proposals and established a deferred giving program. Suggesting the USCUNICEF's continued commitment to improving child life throughout the world, in 1974–1975, the communications department, through print and broadcast materials, focused on the world child emergency declared officially by the executive board of UNICEF, and throughout the period, the USCUNICEF conducted special appeals for children, including those in Bangladesh, Indo-China, and earthquake-stricken Peru.

The primary sources for studying the USCUNICEF's history include its published and variously named *Annual Reports* and its *News of the World's Chil-*

dren. Neither is widely available. The agency has its files at its headquarters in New York. *The New York Times* covered the ICEF and the controversies surrounding it, but paid little attention to the USCUNICEF and its predecessor agencies in the 1940s and early 1950s. The agency also provided me with some publications that helped to reconstruct its history. There are some materials about the agency in the Papers of the Department of State, at the National Archives, in Washington, D.C.

There does not appear to be a scholarly history of the USCUNICEF.

UNITED STATES SANITARY COMMISSION (USSC). Soon after the American Civil War began in 1861, President Abraham Lincoln called for voluntary societies to aid soldiers, and a number of them developed quickly in the North. On April 25, 1861, Reverend Dr. Henry Bellows of All Souls' Church in New York City and Dr. Elisha Harris, a pioneer in public health who belonged to such early social welfare agencies as the New York Association for Improving the Condition of the Poor,* met with some sixty women at the New York Infirmary for Women to discuss ways in which New Yorkers could aid soldiers. Four days later, at a meeting convened by Bellows at Cooper Institute, this group established the Woman's Central Association of Relief* (WCAR), itself an important aid society. Early plans to have this and other New York agencies cooperate with the government failed, so the WCAR and other New York organizations appointed a four-member joint committee to approach government officials in Washington, D.C. Bellows and Harris represented the WCAR, while Dr. W. H. Van Buren came from the Physicians and Surgeons of the New York Hospitals, and Dr. Jacob Hansen represented the Lint and Bandage Association. The men left for Washington on May 15, and Bellows later claimed that the idea for the United States Sanitary Commission (USSC) came to the group on the train between Philadelphia and Baltimore.

The group influenced Acting Surgeon-General Dr. R. C. Wood to recommend the establishment of the commission to the secretary of war, Simon Cameron, who drafted an executive order creating it on June 9. The four men returned to New York, and on June 12, 1861, they established the USSC as the Commission of Inquiry and Advice in respect of the Sanitary Interests of the United States Forces (CIASI). At this organizing meeting, the group elected Bellows as president. The agency elected as vice-president Alexander D. Bache of Philadelphia, a noted scientist and educator, and as treasurer, the famous New York diarist, George Templeton Strong. Other initial members of the CIASI included Dr. Harris and Samuel Gridley Howe, a noted social reformer from Massachusetts. On the next day, June 13, 1861, President Lincoln signed the executive order recognizing the new agency. Despite his earlier appeal, however, President Lincoln remained officially indifferent to this pioneering organization. The CIASI appointed as its first general secretary Frederick Law Olmsted, who later gained fame as the architect of Central Park in New York City.

General Secretary Olmsted supervised the activities of the CIASI, which consisted largely of dispensing supplies to soldiers and providing first aid in the battlefield, as well as transporting the wounded and sick to hospitals, arranging for nurses, and generally helping the government's Medical Bureau (see *Government Agencies*). Initially, the CIASI intended to conduct scientific studies of hygienic conditions, but the demands of war prompted the organization's shift, early in its history, to a supply and relief agency rather than a supplier of scientific evidence. It did, however, publish monographs for surgeons. As early as August 1861, the CIASI was supplying almost all the items needed by wounded and sick soldiers. For the entire period of the Civil War, the value of its stores approximated $15 million. Although it never received funds from the government but relied entirely on voluntary contributions, the organization hired a group of surgeons, called inspectors, to supplement the efforts of official agencies.

An early national social service agency, the CIASI not only aided the efforts in the battlefield but also, despite its short history, influenced official practices and policies. Early in the war, it influenced the establishment of a nursing bureau headquartered in Washington, D.C., where General Secretary Olmsted maintained a major CIASI office. The agency also worked closely with Surgeon-General William A. Hammond to solve problems relating to an ambulance corps and transportation generally. Generally Secretary Olmsted's *Report to the Secretary of war,* which appeared in 1862, commented constructively on problems in the Union army, called for higher standards of medical care, and consequently won praise both at home and abroad. Because the organization emphasized the need for national unity—its leaders led in establishing and then joined Union League clubs throughout the Union—the agency contributed to the government's war efforts.

The organizational structure reflected the agency's concern for unified national relief and war efforts. The board of commissioners met every six weeks in Washington, D.C., during its first year in sessions that generally lasted four to five days. The complexity of the growing activities led to the appointment of a standing committee of six members who became the real leaders of the CIASI. This committee included Bellows, Strong, and Charles Stillé, who later wrote a history of the USSC. Displaying an energetic commitment rarely matched by any other national voluntary social service agency, the standing committee met daily, except Sunday, for four years. By late 1862, this committee became important within the organization, and it opened permanent headquarters at 823 Broadway in New York, while General Secretary Olmsted maintained the Washington office. The USCC's western headquarters was in Louisville, Kentucky, under a western secretary whose precise relation to the general secretary was left unclear. The national structure dominated local branches, which increasingly served as supply shipping agencies and which contributed funds and supplies to the national organization. Women's councils, so important in developing and maintaining popular support for the USSC, convened nationally for the first time in Washington, D.C., in November 1862. In late 1863, the USSC inaugurated its *Sanitary Commission Bulletin,* partly to keep branches informed of national activities. Also in late 1863, on November 5, supporters in Chicago held the first sanitary fair, which attracted funds and supplies for the agency. Another important one, the New York metropolitan fair, held on August 14, 1864, helped these fairs to double the amount of supplies and to raise over $2.7 million. After April 1865, when the war ended, office staffs in New York, Washington, and Louisville diminished significantly, and in December 1865, the Washington office closed entirely.

The USSC conducted an impressive array of both medical and social services for soldiers. An important innovative service was the auxiliary relief corps, organized in Chelsea, Massachusetts. Composed initially of fifty volunteer men but having two hundred by July 1864, members of this group administered first aid in the battlefields, became nurses in hospitals, and established temporary hospitals to care for the men. A central claim agency, which collected government payments for the men and their families, operated throughout the country. During its history, the USSC supported forty homes and lodges for men. Sensitive to the men's needs after the war, one of the agency's leaders, Dr. Frederick Knapp, helped to establish employment offices. In September 1862, the agency established what its historian called perhaps its most humane activity—the hospital directory to help families and government officials keep track of hospitalized soldiers. In the tradition of humane social service, the USSC organized a group of clergymen as hospital visitors.

While some clergymen, notably Bellows, worked with the USSC, many more became part of the United States Christian Commission* (USCC), a rival organization that became a source of irritation and conflict for the USSC. Founded in 1861, the USCC enjoyed greater popular support than did the USSC in rural areas and in towns. Because it did not require requisitions for supplies and because it delivered supplies and services simply and humanely, the USCC gained perhaps greater favor among the men on the battlefields. Although the two agencies agreed in late 1862 and early 1863 to cooperate, suspicion and jealousy continued to characterize their relations.

Another rival agency, the Western Sanitary Commission (WSC), organized in St. Louis in late 1861 to conduct similar functions, threatened the national unity stressed by USSC leaders, who continued to criticize the independent WSC. Not all anxieties were external, however. General Secretary Olmsted's demands for greater powers for his office and his reorganization plans in June 1863 to give local branches greater autonomy antagonized the commissioners, leading finally to his resignation in August 1863. The USSC then lost much of its effectiveness; neither of Olmsted's two successors was as capable as he.

The experiences and influences of the USSC, an early national social service agency, prompted some important developments in the field of social welfare.

During its short history, it helped to establish over seven thousand local aid societies. The first national agency to mobilize volunteer women, the USSC had some of its workers, such as Louisa Lee Schuyler, a friend of Bellows and the founder in 1872 of the important State Charities Aid Association* of New York, pursue further activities in relief and social service. Indeed, as the historian of the USSC argued, because the USSC solved the problems of citizen volunteers working with medical officials, it provided the experiences necessary for establishing the International Committee of the Red Cross. Some of the USSC leaders promoted efforts to have the United States sign the Geneva Treaty of 1864, which agreed to allow volunteer assistance to the sick and wounded of armies. Others from the USSC, notably Dr. Elisha Harris, became active in the American Public Health Association,* which evolved as a major agency in the field. The USSC's experiences influenced the establishment of a similar French Commission in 1865. Like later social service agencies, the USSC developed an exhibit, which won the gold medal at the Paris Fair of 1867. Finally, while the nation was abandoning Reconstruction, on May 8, 1878, Dr. Bellows concluded the existence of the USSC, an important and pioneering social service agency.

The primary sources for studying the USSC's history consist of the unpublished agency files at the New York Public Library and the papers of its leaders, especially the Bellows Papers at the Massachusetts Historical Society in Boston and the Olmsted Papers at the Library of Congress in Washington, D.C. The library of Columbia University has a microfilm set of the important papers relating to the USSC. The published *Minutes of the USSC, 1861–1865,* covering twenty-two sessions, like the volumes of the *Sanitary Commission Bulletin,* are also helpful.

The USSC has been well studied by historians. The standard history of the USSC is William A. Maxwell, *Lincoln's Fifth Wheel* (1956), which is broader than a strict organization history. George M. Fredrickson, *The Inner Civil War* (1965), interprets the USSC as trying to instill stern discipline rather than offering humane social services. The agency is the focus of some of social welfare historian Robert M. Bremner's writings, such as "The Prelude: Philanthropic Rivalries in the Civil War," *Social Casework* 49 (February 1968): 77–81, and "The Impact of the Civil War on Philanthropy and Social Welfare," *Civil War History* 12 (December 1966): 293–303.

UNITED STATES SOCIETY FOR THE STUDY OF TUBERCULOSIS: see AMERICAN LUNG ASSOCIATION.

UNITED WAY OF AMERICA (UWA). Efforts to organize local charities on a communitywide basis began in the 1870s with the establishment of such organizations as the United Hebrew Charities of the City of New York* in 1874, and more importantly, the Charity Organization Society of Buffalo, New York, in 1877. As a result of the work of two ministers, a priest, and a rabbi, the first local communitywide organization to coordinate social services and to combine fund raising was established in Denver, Colorado. In the late nineteenth and early twentieth centuries, as local social welfare and health agencies realized the need to cooperate rather than to compete vigorously with each other to gain contributions, such coordinating, planning, and fund-raising agencies developed in several American cities.

The first modern United Way fund-raising organization was formed in Cleveland, Ohio, in 1913. The Cleveland Federation for Charity and Philanthropy (CFCP) featured the development of a budget program to allot funds to participating agencies. Other communities learned of the budget program in Cleveland and began to emulate it. By 1917, about twenty-five communities had attempted to develop what were becoming known as community chests, and about twenty were actually functioning. The united fund-raising organization also contributed to and paralleled the development of community councils, which attempted to coordinate the projects and programs of various social service and health agencies in a given city.

United Way of America (UWA) was established in Chicago in early 1918 when twelve representatives from centralized fund-raising agencies met and formed a national organization to exchange ideas and experiences. They called the new organization the American Association for Community Organization (AACO). Its initial purpose was ''to encourage and stimulate collective community planning, and the development of better standards of community organization for social work.'' The most important founders, both of whom initiated the meeting in Chicago in February 1918, were William J. Norton of the Associated Charities of Detroit, who had pioneered in federated financing in Cincinnati, and his successor in Cincinnati, C. M. Bookman. Norton became the first president of the AACO.

The agency began early to fulfill its initial purpose of improving the standards of fund raising in social work. In 1919, for instance, the AACO initiated, with the cooperation of the Ohio State University, a short course in the summer to train executives for community chest work. This course was repeated over many summers in the 1920s, and around 1930, it became a graduate course at the university. In this very early period, when volunteers such as Bookman in Cincinnati, Norton in Detroit, and others in Louisville and Chicago conducted the affairs of the agency, the AACO helped to place well-trained professionals in local positions. The AACO's annual income in these early years was about $1,000, which represented the $25 annual fee from the forty local community chests and councils which belonged to the national organization. At the AACO's annual meeting in June 1922, the delegates became convinced that the movement and its organization needed more effective organizational management. Subsequently, at the annual business meeting on June 23, 1922, the AACO formally invited the National Information Bureau (NIB), which determined the soundness and legitimacy of agencies, to serve as its secretary and treasurer for a year, 1923.

To conduct the work of the AACO, in 1923, the NIB added a new staff member, Pierce Williams. In 1923, the AACO elected its first layman as president, beginning the national lay leadership—overwhelmingly from the business community—in the community chest and council movements. The AACO continued to use the NIB as its secretary in 1924 and 1925, but in 1926, the agency became independent, finally getting its own separate staff. In January 1926, meeting in Cincinnati, the executive committee of the AACO appointed Allen Tibblas Burns, a former director of the NIB, as executive director. Two other initial staff workers were Pierce Williams of the NIB and Fred Evans. The AACO rented space in the NIB offices in New York City as its headquarters for 1926. The leaders of the AACO wanted to have the headquarters outside of New York City, preferably in a midwestern city with a community chest. New York City was not then a member of the AACO. At the meeting in January 1926, the executive committee voted to contribute $3,000 per year to the NIB, which would then provide reports about agencies to the members of the AACO.

The newly independent organization gradually developed programs that generally improved the field of social welfare. The staff of the AACO, even in 1926, the first year of independent operation, traveled to cities throughout the country, conducting studies of social welfare needs of individual communities and helping to organize councils and coordinate fund-raising machinery. In 1926, with the cooperation of the American Association for Organizing Family Social Work,* the AACO began a study of the problem of increasing relief funds and the budget problems of family welfare societies in local community chests in light of increasing relief expenditures. The social service exchange sagged in the mid-1920s, but the organization revived it as a major activity. To reflect more accurately the fund-raising focus of the organization, in 1927, it changed its name to the Association of Community Chests and Councils (ACCC).

Another agency activity, perhaps more important than coordinating social services, was the alliance with the business community that the AACO forged in the 1920s. Partly because of the appeals of local charities, hospitals, and such, businessmen began to develop an interest in charitable contributions. As a reflection of this, between 1920 and 1926, the United States Chamber of Commerce (USCC) conducted studies of social welfare organizations to help its members evaluate their contributions to charities. Businessmen, it seems, were especially interested in the effective, orderly operation of agencies to which they donated funds. Close to the business community since its inception, the AAOC was also fortunate to have Allen T. Burns, a professional social worker who had earlier helped to establish the CFCP, as its chief executive officer in 1923. Throughout the 1920s, the national office under Burns closely monitored court and administrative decisions dealing with the legality of corporations giving away funds that seemed to belong to stockholders. Attorneys who served on the AAOC's board of directors, especially Frederic R. Kellogg of New York, helped in this project. Burns quickly showed that he could deal with and could attract support from businessmen. Another issue affecting corporate giving was the problem of national corporations with branches in communities throughout the country, such as five-and-ten cents stores, which contributed to so many local campaigns.

In late 1926, the executive committee authorized a conference in Washington, D.C., in early 1928, to deal with the problems of the chest movement, and Burns added to the agenda sessions dealing with this sensitive and controversial issue. At the annual meeting in May 1927, the AAOC decided to call it the National Conference on Community Responsibility for Human Welfare. Anxious to have prominent businessmen and individuals associated with the conference, Burns helped to establish a national citizens' committee; among its members were United States Senator James Couzens of Michigan, and Harvey Firestone, the president of the rubber company bearing his name. The conference, finally called the Citizens Conference on Community Responsibility for Human Welfare, was held in late February 1928. The chairman of the gathering argued that business support was crucial to such "community responsibilities," and small group discussions emphasized this theme to participating businessmen. The conference resolved that the ACCC should work to amend the federal income tax laws so that corporations could deduct payments to charities as a business expense.

The day after the conference closed, the organization began this effort, coordinating it through the national office in New York. By April 1928, Burns recognized that the large corporations were leaning toward setting a fixed percentage for their donations, ignoring the particular needs of a community. To deal with this problem, the ACCC elected as its president, J. Herbert Case, the chairman of the board of the Federal Reserve Bank of New York, and established a special committee of influential business. The ACCC also promoted a study, *Corporation Contributions to Organized Community Welfare Services* (1930), which the agency distributed to leading businessmen. Ambitious plans for a conference in 1930—which was to have included a speech by that friend of big business as well as one of private social welfare services, United States President Herbert Hoover—were dropped because of the depression facing American business, an obviously inopportune time to try to drum up corporate support for welfare. A student of these events, Morrell Heald, concluded that perhaps more than any other factor, the ACCC and the chest movement shaped the social responsibility of business in the twentieth century.

Activities during the depression years of the 1930s brought the ACCC into the national social work community. In 1931, the agency conducted its important welfare relief mobilization campaign, begun in cooperation with the President's Organization on Unemployment Relief. Financed largely by the Rockefeller Foundation (RF), this campaign was an effort by private agencies to deal with the enormous problems of the Great Depression. The ACCC president, J. Herbert Case, headed this initial campaign. The ACCC began the drive with a survey of 376 localities, 244 of which had community chests, and before and during the campaign in the fall, the agency provided publicity information to communities and sent its experienced staff to localities to advise and generally to help leaders there. President Herbert Hoover opened the campaign on October 18, 1931, with a nationwide radio broadcast from Fortress Monroe, Virginia. Because the bulk of the funds raised by the drive in 1931 went for relief, Executive Director Burns and his assistant, Ralph Blanchard, urged the campaign in 1932 to provide more funds for traditional welfare recreational programs, which had been slighted in 1931. Under their leadership, the theme for the ACCC's convention in 1932 was "Man Does Not Live by Bread Alone," and to indicate this reorientation, the campaign for 1932 became "mobilization for human needs." The mobilization campaigns, which became an integral part of the ACCC's program, were annual events, always inaugurated by the president of the United States until the period of World War II and the beginning of the National War Fund (NWF) in 1943.

In 1936, the agency held a mobilization conference to stimulate interest in this drive. The campaign featured a national women's committee, chaired by prominent lay people. In 1936, the National Social Work Council* appointed a committee, led by Bertha McCall of the National Association for Travelers Aid and Transient Service,* to contribute to the drive. To help the field of social welfare generally, the ACCC initiated its Great Lakes Institute at College Camp, Wisconsin, to bring together representatives to discuss the problems of community organization in social work. In 1936, the national agency, called the Community Chests and Councils, Inc. (CCC), since 1933, appointed its committee on program materials to help local affiliates improve their publicity materials. Also, beginning in 1936, the CCC published its annual News Almanac for Social Work, a handy guide to key dates in social work. To advise and to serve regional groups that developed spontaneously, as well as to serve affiliates better, the CCC board of directors in early 1936 authorized the establishment of a field service. By 1937, changes in the mobilization campaigns, chiefly resulting in less pressure on the staff, allowed several staff members, including Executive Vice-President Burns, to conduct field visits. In the mid-1930s, the CCC developed a series of films for publicizing chest and council activities, and in 1938, it sponsored a play about their services. The CCC introduced a special training program in the field of chest and community council work at Boston College in 1938.

A highlight of the 1930s was the CCC's efforts to obtain an income tax deduction for corporations contributing to private social welfare. As early as March 1928, Pierce Williams of the staff met with representatives of the USCC to discuss the matter. In June 1930, Kellogg helped to draft legislation to change the income tax law. ACCC leaders hoped initially to clarify the issue through an administrative or judicial ruling rather than through legislation. Agency leaders spoke privately with influential administration and congressional leaders, and in 1932, the ACCC joined with the New York Telephone Company to fight a ruling of the Interstate Commerce Commission that its $75,000 contribution to the Unemployment Relief Fund was not tax deductible. By 1935, however, the organization, now called the CCC, supported the successful movement in 1935 to provide that up to 5 percent of a corporation's taxable income could be deducted as an expense. Continuing to court business support, in the late 1930s, the CCC established industrywide committees, such as for railroads.

In the 1940s, the CCC helped social service agencies and communities to deal with the problems of welfare related to World War II. Cooperating with the new United States Committee for the Care of European Children*—an agency established in 1940 to help bring threatened British children to safety in American foster homes—the CCC provided the first chance for community chests and councils to participate in program planning and in setting local standards. In the early 1940s, Burns and Blanchard not only urged community chests to become war chests but also promoted war chests in communities lacking community chests. In April 1940, the CCC held the first annual institute for chest executives at Ohio State University, under Charles C. Stillman, and on February 15, 1940, the agency held the first social service exchange day to popularize this activity. Late in 1941, the executive committee directed the staff to study selected local defense councils' health and welfare programs, to distribute the results to such communities, and to show the need to develop coordinated programs at the local level. Also in 1941, the CCC agreed to cooperate with the American National Red Cross* (ANRC) campaign to raise $50 million.

An important event occurred on July 2, 1942, when Executive Vice-President Burns resigned. The executive committee, however, quickly appointed Burns as special consultant for foreign relief and war-related projects, on the relation of federal taxes to community chests, and on labor organizations and chests and councils. Burns had been the key figure in the growth of community chests, and his leadership accounted largely for the growth to about 650 affiliates at the time of his retirement. Blanchard, Burns's assistant since 1928, became the new executive officer on January 1, 1943.

In the period after the war, the CCC strengthened its leadership in the field of fund raising and community planning. Another major event occurred in 1946 with the first use of the red feather as a symbol for the fund-raising campaign of that year. In December 1946, the board of directors adapted it as the official symbol and adopted a slogan, "Everybody Gives, Everybody Benefits," as the theme. Also in 1946, the CCC established the National Budget Committee (NBC), which resumed the review of national social service agencies' budgets, a project begun in 1942 by the NWF. The NBC grew into an important activity in the field of social welfare, providing the process for national agencies' requests for funds to be channelled to local communities. In early 1947, the CCC established its labor-employee participation department, headed by William F. Maxwell, the former director of the labor liaison of the agency. In 1947, an important joint statement with the National Social Welfare Assembly* (NSWA) recognized the CCC as the fund-raising leader in the field of social welfare. Also in 1947, the CCC cooperated with pioneering experiments in statewide planning and financing in Massachusetts, Michigan, and Oregon, and in December, with the National Federation of Settlements,* sponsored a pilot conference in Cleveland on neighborhood councils.

The CCC faced a stiff challenge in fund raising from the national voluntary health agencies, which were strengthening the telethons they had initiated. In June 1953, the agency moved to its new national headquarters in the Carnegie International Center in New York City, the home of other leading social service agencies, such as the NSWA. In late 1952, the CCC began a campaign to raise $100,000 from a hundred wealthy individuals. For the benefit of its local units, the CCC continued to hold public relations clinics before the organization's national conference. The board approved a name change to the United Community Funds and Councils of America, Inc. (UCFCA), in December 1956; the membership ratified it officially in 1957. The field service in the western states began to operate in early 1956. In 1958, responding to further pressures from the health agencies, the board of directors adopted a new "eight point program for united giving." Serving its constituents, in early 1959, the UCFCA held a conference in Pittsburgh for local affiliates that had organized or planned to organize state and local health funds. During this period, to develop a better flow of information between the larger cities than before, the UCFCA established its campaign research exchange. In 1958, the personnel department, which served all its affiliates, began a five-year program to obtain staffs for smaller communities.

In the early 1960s, as Professor Scott Cutlip argued, the UCFCA provided a "persuasive voice for philanthropy and [stood] as a bastion of defense" against the growing, aggressive, independent fund raisers, notably the national voluntary health agencies. The UCFCA also developed programs to deal with new trends in social service. In the early 1960s, the agency helped groups of communities to establish united health foundations to coordinate voluntary health activities on the national scene. In 1960, to help its affiliates deal with new issues in social welfare, the organization held "community organization" institutes for local chests. These institutes were conducted in eighteen localities. A grant from the Stern Family Foundation enabled the UCFCA to produce a film, *A Town Has Two Faces,* which was used by 125 communities. In 1960, the UCFCA established its institute of community service to assist local communities in strengthening their health and welfare programs, and with a grant of $500,000 from the Lilly Foundation (LF), it held a national workshop on the use of research in community planning.

In the 1970s, the agency, renamed the UWA in 1970, continued its basic services to affiliates and seemed to develop as a spokesman for voluntarism. Along with the name change in 1970 came a reduction of the board of directors from sixty-two to thirty-two members, and among other changes, the chief salaried officer, William Aramony, formerly the executive vice-president, became the national executive. A census project to use data from the national census of 1970 to determine needs and such began in 1970, when the UWA also began to plan a national academy for voluntarism, which was soon created. In the early 1970s, the UWA began its personnel development program to help serve affiliates. The UWA won a major victory in early 1973 with a successful lawsuit challenging the government's right to delegate fund raising in the federal establishment to locals. During this period, the UWA operated the committee on national agencies services to compile data to assist affiliates in deciding allocations to national organizations. In 1971, the UWA moved its headquarters from New York City to the Washington, D.C., area, in Alexandria, Virginia. One result of a self-study begun in 1971 was the appearance in 1973 of *Standards of Excellence for Local United Ways Organizations,* which articulated its goals. In 1975, with a grant of $450,000 from the LF, the UWA conducted a pilot project to experiment with the use of telethons to recruit volunteer hours, not money, in Richmond, Virginia, and Seattle, Washington. The agency was also developing a program with a government agency, ACTION, to test the capacity of local units to provide technical and management assistance to organizations assisting the poor, both UWA and non-UWA agencies.

The primary sources for studying the UWA's history are diverse. The most helpful source for this study proved to be the agency's variously named *News Bulletin,* which became the *Bulletin* in 1956. A few difficult-to-locate published *Annual Reports* also provided information, especially for the years since the late 1950s. A host of contemporary agency publications at the New York Public Library, such as *Yesterday and Today with Community Chests, a Record of Their History and Growth* (1937), also provided materials. William J. Norton, *The Cooperative Movement in Social Work* (1927), has only minimal information about the national agency. The agency's files, including minutes of meetings, are located at the agency's headquarters in Alexandria, Virginia.

Morrell Heald used these unpublished materials for his interesting discussion of the national organization in *The Social Responsibilities of Business: Company and Community, 1900–1960* (1970). This was the most helpful secondary source, even though it treats only a portion of the UWA's long history. Scott M. Cutlip, *Fund Raising in the United States, Its Role in America's Philanthropy* (1965), also deals with the UWA. Agency personnel have told me that the UWA plans to publish a full-length organizational history in mid-1977. Nevertheless, there seems to be room for scholarly historical studies of this veteran and leading national agency.

URBAN LEAGUE: see NATIONAL URBAN LEAGUE.

V

VOLUNTEERS OF AMERICA, THE (VOA). In 1887, General William Booth, the founder and leader of The Salvation Army* (SA) in England, sent his son, Ballington, and his daughter-in-law, Maud, to head his international agency in America. Under the administration of Maud and Ballington Booth, the SA's social work activities in the United States increased significantly. The organization, for instance, began to work with prisoners, developed its first day nursery in 1890, started the first food and shelter depot in 1891, and initiated the salvage corps, which featured a woodyard similar to that of The Charity Organization Society of the City of New York.* Maud and Ballington Booth also inaugurated the SA's inexpensive lodges for homeless men, a slum maternity, an orphan asylum, and the salvage brigade, which later became the SA's men's social service centers. In early 1896, however, General Booth ordered them to leave the United States after their successful nine-year administration. The couple decided not to follow these instructions and resigned. At the urging of such prominent Americans as philanthropist William E. Dodge, socially prominent and wealthy General and Mrs. Edwin A. McAlpin, and United States Senator Chauncey Depew of New York, Maud and Ballington Booth founded The Volunteers of America (VOA), a new national, religious social welfare organization in New York City on March 8, 1896.

The VOA, like the SA, was a paramilitary organization with uniforms, titles of rank, and military terminology. Unlike the SA at that time, however, the commander-in-chief was to be elected and policies established democratically by an annual grand field council composed of the higher-ranking officers. General Ballington Booth was chosen as the first commander-in-chief and was reelected until his death in 1940, when he was succeeded by his wife, General Maud Ballington Booth. At her death in 1948, their son, General Charles Brandon Booth was elected and served until his retirement in 1958. In that year, the national leadership passed from the Booth family to General John F. McMahon, who was completing a fourth five-year term in the mid-1970s.

Supported by a number of prominent American social, political, and philanthropic figures, including such diverse personalities as Theodore Roosevelt and William Jennings Bryan and social gospel movement leaders Josiah Strong and Lyman Abbott, the VOA spread quickly, and by the end of 1896, it was incorporated and had active posts in American cities from coast to coast. The social welfare program grew out of the religious evangelical work of the organization in urban slum areas. The earliest programs included summer outings for city children, shelters for homeless transients, and food and clothing distribution centers. The first VOA maternity home for unwed mothers was established in 1899, the same year that the VOA salvage and rehabilitation program for transient men (the sheltered workshop concept) began. Since each VOA post had a high degree of local autonomy, the programs varied widely as to type, number, and quality. Local needs and the ability of the local community to support the program determined the type of service in each place. A distinctive feature of the VOA throughout the country since the turn of the century has been the use of solicitors in Santa Claus suits to collect funds for Christmas dinners for the needy.

An early work of the organization, which continues to the present, was the emergency disaster service. The VOA helped during floods, fires, tornadoes, and other disasters. An outstanding example was its response to an explosion in Texas City, Texas, in April 1947. Seven trained officers were flown to the scene of the explosion from a grand field council meeting in Fort Worth. For three weeks they worked to collect and identify the dead and to provide food, shelter, and clothing for the living. One of the group alone tagged 370 bodies. While the "Texas City Seven" were engaged in relief work on the scene, the resources of the national organization were mobilized to collect clothing to ship to the stricken area.

The most important national program was the work in state and federal prisons begun by Maud Ballington Booth in 1896. Her work, which earned her the title, "Little Mother of the Prisons," included the organization of the Volunteer Prison League (VPL), an autonomous branch of the VOA under her direct supervision. The VPL provided aid for the families of prisoners, assisted prisoners after their release, and worked to improve conditions in the prisons themselves. Maud Booth not only spoke regularly in every major federal prison but, as a highly popular and effective Chautauqua lecturer at the turn of the century, she also publicized the cause of prison reform, advocating the parole system and effective educational and vocational programs in prisons. Through her lectures, books, and articles, she condemned the silent system, the lockstep, the striped prison uniforms, and the enforced idleness common in most prisons of the day. She was an active member of the American Prison Association,* served on several of its committees, was a member of its national board of directors, and in 1943 was elected a special honorary vice-president for life.

During its first half-century, the VOA as an organization was overshadowed by the personalities of its founders. The ten-year administration of General Charles Brandon Booth that began in 1948 instituted a period of transition from strong personal leadership to better institutional organization. Since 1948, the VOA has evolved from a movement of dedicated but largely self-trained workers to a modern social welfare agency utilizing professionally trained personnel and operating under accepted professional standards.

The administrative head of the VOA is the commander-in-chief, General John F. McMahon, with headquarters in New York City. General McMahon, whose parents were VOA officers, grew up in the organization, moving frequently with changes of assignment. He began high school in Fort Worth, Texas, and finished in St. Paul, Minnesota. He took courses to support a career in social work at the University of Louisville, Marquette University, and the University of Wisconsin at Milwaukee. He was in charge of the VOA post in Milwaukee, noted for its day care program, when he was called to New York as national field secretary in 1948, the position that led to his election as the fourth commander-in-chief of the VOA.

In addition to a national headquarters staff, four regional directors with the rank of colonel supervise the eastern, western, midwest, and southern regions, with offices in Binghamton, New York, Los Angeles, Minneapolis, and Atlanta, respectively. There are national secretaries for social welfare, religious activities, rehabilitation services, correctional services, and youth and the aging, reflecting the major program categories of the VOA. In 1971, the VOA had program centers in more than eighty cities in twenty-nine states. A VOA brochure in 1976 claimed 750 service centers in the country, but many of these are parts of multiple service programs in the same city or town. Each local post has an advisory board of prominent citizens, and there are advisory boards for several states and on the national level. Each year since 1952, a well-known personality from the field of social work, politics, entertainment, or philanthropy has been given the Ballington and Maud Booth Award at the annual meeting of the organization's grand field council.

In 1950, reflecting the shift to a modern agency, a VOA officer with a master of social work degree was elected national social welfare secretary, and in 1966, Belle Leach was brought to national headquarters. In 1950, the VOA participated officially in the White House Conference on Children and Youth and had a booth at the National Conference of Social Work, joining that organization in 1955 as an associate member. Since that time, VOA delegations have participated in each of the White House Conferences on Children and Youth, the White House Conference on Education, the White House Conference on Aging, the National Conference on Juvenile Delinquency, the National Conference on Aging, and the National Conference on Crime Control. VOA officers have been active in a variety of national social welfare organizations, such as the National Association of Social Workers,* The American Correctional Association,* and others.

Taking advantage of the federal Housing Act of 1959 and subsequent legislation, the VOA first built a multiprogram housing complex for senior citizens in Seattle in 1965 and went on to build twenty additional projects providing housing and a wide variety of services for more than fourteen thousand elderly and low-income tenants. Valued at more than $90 million, these projects have made the VOA the sponsor of one of the largest nonprofit housing programs in the country. Each of the projects has a range of social services, including counseling, day care facilities, health clinics, and adult educational and recreational programs, all operated by professionally trained personnel. The Kennedy Homes in Gainesville, Florida, opened in 1960, was the first VOA low-income family housing complex. North Hollywood, Florida, Apartments broke new ground by specializing in the needs of one-parent families. Other low- and middle-income housing projects are located in Houston, New Orleans, Oklahoma City, and Wichita. Two of the largest VOA residences for the elderly are in Denver and Minneapolis.

At the eightieth anniversary grand field council in New York City in 1976, the VOA summarized its current programs, listing twenty-one nonprofit housing complexes for low-income families and the elderly; nine nursing homes; twenty-five group homes for children with family or behavioral problems; twelve group homes for retarded children and adults; fifty-six halfway houses for rehabilitating alcoholics; and ten prerelease centers preparing paroled prisoners for their reentry into society. The focus of the 1976 meeting was on the future as well as the present. The VOA plans to continue to expand its services, in cooperation with the federal government, in the fields of low- and middle-income housing, housing and nursing homes for the elderly, day care centers, programs for the handicapped and retarded, and rehabilitation programs for juvenile problem youngsters, as well as continuing its traditional programs of emergency disaster services, aid to prisoners and those released from correctional institutions, and the rehabilitation of transient alcoholics.

The principal source for VOA's history is in its official publication, begun in 1896 as *The Volunteers' Gazette* and, since 1967, published monthly from New York as *The Volunteer*. The archives at the national headquarters, 340 West Eighty-fifth Street, New York, New York, contain the essential primary source materials. Especially useful for recent developments are the *Annual Reports* of the grand field councils containing the texts of the papers given. *History of the Volunteers of America,* published in 1954 by the VOA, by Herbert A. Wisbey, Jr., has been brought up to 1971 in a yet unpublished manuscript, "VOA Spells 'Service.'" References for the story of the beginnings of the VOA can be found in Herbert A. Wisbey, Jr., *Soldiers Without Swords: A History of the Salvation Army in the United States* (1955). *Look Up and Hope!* by Susan F. Welty (1961) is both a biography of Maud Ballington Booth and a history of the VOA during her lifetime.

Herbert A. Wisbey, Jr.

__ *W*

WAR RELIEF SERVICES OF THE NATIONAL CATHOLIC WELFARE CONFERENCE: see CATHOLIC RELIEF SERVICES—UNITED STATES CATHOLIC CONFERENCE.

WOMAN'S CENTRAL ASSOCIATION OF RELIEF (WCAR). Soon after the hostilities broke out between the Union and the Confederacy in early 1861, President Abraham Lincoln called for volunteer societies to aid the soldiers. Influenced by Lincoln's appeal and inspired by the example of Florence Nightingale during the war in Crimea in 1854, about fifty prominent women from New York City met at the New York Infirmary for Women to discuss how they could coordinate all the local women's societies that were collecting bandages and other supplies. At this meeting, a committee was appointed to pursue the organizational efforts. The committee drew up an "address," which was circulated widely. It called for a mass meeting at the Cooper Institute on April 30. The meeting, which was probably the largest gathering of women to that point in American history, formally organized the Woman's Central Association of Relief (WCAR) to aid the men fighting for the Union in the conflict. The WCAR chose as its president Reverend Henry Bellows of the All Souls' Church, and as vice-president, Dr. Valentine Mott of the Bellevue Hospital, who had been active in other philanthropic ventures in New York City.

The WCAR began its relief work quickly. Volunteer women in New York City sorted, marked, and packed goods headed for the troops. At the organizing meeting in late April 1861, the WCAR had appointed a committee to confer with federal officials about integrating the relief work with the war effort. The delegates traveled to Washington, D.C., but the government rejected their aid initially. Some members of the delegation, however, remained in the capital and, having witnessed the great confusion there, became even more convinced of the need for a national relief organization. From these observations and thoughts, the United States Sanitary Commission* (USSC) was born, and Frederick Law Olmsted, the famous architect of Central Park in New York, soon became its chief executive officer. With few exceptions, the WCAR volunteers distributed their goods according to Olmsted's directions, but they did use their own discretion in supplying hospitals and regiments in the area of New York City. The WCAR also established an eight-member registration committee on nurses in its first year. This committee handled the recruitment of nurses and arranged for training courses at both the New York and Bellevue Hospitals. Also, during the winter of 1861–1862, the WCAR conducted classes on nursing and sanitation for doctors at some hospitals in New York City.

Even before the federal government began to pay nurses' salaries, the WCAR provided the Union with over ninety nurses. After the government assumed responsibility for paying the nurses, the WCAR still paid their traveling expenses. The chairwoman of the committee handling this task was Elizabeth Blackwell, a pioneering woman physician from New York. The early structure of the WCAR included a board of managers, composed of the president, the secretary, and the treasurer. It also had a ten-member executive committee, which included Bellows and Dr. William H. Draper, a prominent New York physician.

The USSC developed as the major relief agency during the Civil War, but the WCAR continued to assist relief effort. During its second year, 1862–1863, the WCAR established a number of new associate managers, women to communicate with societies similar to the WCAR in local areas throughout the Union. The WCAR had a committee for special relief, which included Dr. Elisha Harris, an important reformer in nineteenth-century New York City. Because the government cared well for returning and discharged soldiers, this committee chiefly referred the men to appropriate organizations for help. In 1863, the WCAR noted the need to provide assistance to disabled soldiers, and in January 1864, the stability and contributions of the WCAR were recognized at the meeting of the Council of Women in Washington, D.C. The WCAR, which disbanded in late 1865, prompted women to develop important social services later. Dorothea Dix, Josephine Shaw Lowell, the noted reformer and the founder of the influential Charity Organization Society of the City of New York* (COS) in 1882, and Louisa Schuyler, the founder and leader of the State Charities Aid Association* (SCAA) of New York, each worked for and gained experience in social service with the WCAR.

The primary sources for studying the WCAR's history included the published *Annual Reports* and *Semi-Annual Reports* and pamphlets. *The New York Times* also reported the highlights of the agency's activities.

A few secondary studies, such as Marjorie Barstow Greenbie, *Lincoln's Daughters of Mercy* (1944), and especially Albert Deutsch, "Some Wartime Influences on Health and Welfare Institutions," *Journal of the History of Medicine* 1 (1946): 318–329, mention the WCAR. The standard social welfare histories, such as Robert Bremner, *American Philanthropy* (1960), and Walter Trattner, *From Poor Law to Welfare State* (1974), do not mention the WCAR. There does not appear to be a scholarly history of this agency.

WOMEN'S EDUCATIONAL AND INDUSTRIAL UNION (WEIU). In Boston in 1872, a group of women began to hold Sunday afternoon discussions on topics of interest to women at the home of Dr. Harriet Glisbey, a pioneer woman physician. During the formative years of these Sunday meetings, the idea of an organization whose purpose would be "to promote the best practical methods for securing the educational, industrial, and social advancement of women," germinated. To implement these ideas, the women founded the Women's Educational and Industrial Union (WEIU) in Boston in May 1877. The leader in its founding was Dr. Glisbey. The group of forty charter members who formally organized the WEIU and others saw that the lack of economic opportunity caused many social limitations that hampered the lives of women. One of the first activities of the WEIU was to appoint committees of volunteers to see what could be done to provide openings for women in need of employment and/or other kinds of help. The committees formed were of three types: industrial, educational, and social service.

The first of the major committees organized in the early history of the WEIU was the committee on hygiene and physical culture, which was very active in sponsoring lectures on health matters. Volunteer women physicians conducted free clinics for needy women. The work by this committee was carried on until 1903 when it became apparent that other agencies, schools, and hospitals were more fully addressing this purpose. The work of this committee was thus lessened. It was then renamed the committee on sanitary and industrial conditions and concentrated on issues such as abatement of smoke nuisance; ventilation in shops, streetcars, and schools; cleanliness of the streets; and decent health conditions in factories employing women and children. Studies were made of dangerous trades, sweatshops, and the enforcement of labor laws.

The committee on moral and spiritual development conducted Sunday afternoon meetings, continuing Dr. Glisbey's house meetings to discuss religious and moral questions. In 1895, this committee was renamed the committee on ethics and through members' interests began to work with and for the blind. This resulted in the appointment in 1904 of a Massachusetts State Commission for the Adult Blind. A subcommittee took active measures to find work for handicapped women and maintained an interest in industrial hazards, mental hygiene, and prevention of other handicaps from accidents and disease.

The committee on social affairs was in general charge of all matters pertaining to practical philanthropy, hospitality, the agency of direction (which compiled information of interest to women), the library, and the reading room. The committee for the protection of women collected money that had been wrongfully withheld from the wages of domestics, seamstresses, and other women. At first they used volunteers who became known as "the lady lawyers" and called in friendly lawyers when necessary. A woman lawyer was later employed, and cases needing extensive legal attention were referred to the Boston Legal Aid Society (BLAS) after it was organized in 1900, somewhat after the WEIU model. The WEIU continued its work because the BLAS had no women on its staff until 1921, when the WEIU attorney was asked to join the BLAS's staff. For many years, the WEIU studied the victims of installment buying and of small borrowers, and, under pressure from the WEIU, legislative protection against exploitation was passed. Capping the work of this committee was the establishment of a WEIU credit union in 1910 to enable the small borrower to get money without paying extortionate rates.

Responding to the third area, industry, the WEIU organized activities that resulted in the WEIU's being called the "mother of women's exchanges." The sale of goods produced by women in their homes was one of the earliest activities of the WEIU. All goods were accepted in the early years, but this was changed and emphasis was laid on quality, not only to build up a satisfied patronage of buyers but also to make labor honorable so that women could have pride in earning money. The food department worked with individuals and through classes to teach women to do well what they attempted, and the department held meetings with consignors to talk over common problems. Trade school shop classes were begun in 1904 in different kinds of needlework and were modified only in 1913 when the Boston Trade School for Girls, which the WEIU had aided in its early years, was able to give complete instruction in the needle trade. This was done in cooperation with the WEIU handwork shops to give practical experience to the girls in all phases of the industry. At that time the classes shifted focus to the teachers and conducted trade normal classes in cooperation with Simmons College.

The WEIU established the school of housekeeping in 1897 to train women for domestic service. This was the WEIU's effort to solve the servant problem. This school also concerned itself with the employers of domestics and provided classes for them. Ultimately this aspect grew as the primary purpose defaulted. As the course in home management grew, it invited the interest of Simmons College for Women and, in 1902, the WEIU transferred the school of housekeeping to Simmons College as the nucleus of its household arts department.

The WEIU's school of salesmanship was started in 1906 to teach women the art of selling. It developed gradually under the direction of Lucinda Prince as a training school for educational and personnel directors and other women executives for stores. Prince was well fitted for her pioneering work in department store education. Following graduation from Framingham Normal School, she taught in both public and private schools. She later continued her studies at Wellesley College and in Germany. Throughout her life she traveled extensively, was well acquainted with educators and philanthropists, and was interested in all social movements; she had been a resident in the first college settlement house in Boston. The salesmanship school was organized in cooperation with the leading retail stores in Boston, using the stores as working laboratories. In 1918, the school was taken over by Simmons College, moved to its own location, and took the name Prince School of Education for Store Service under the auspices of Simmons College.

The lunchrooms constructed by the WEIU in its building on Boyleston Street and in its subsidiary, the New England Kitchen on Charles Street, which the WEIU had taken over in 1907, provided an opportunity to use some of the food materials sent in by consignors and produced in the WEIU laboratory. In 1907, the WEIU took over the responsibility of providing school lunches for many of the public schools in the city of Boston. Over fourteen thousand pupils were fed each day in the twenty-four school buildings.

The appointment bureau, which grew out of the business agency in 1910, was also known as the department of vocational advice and appointment. The appointment bureau was the first of its kind in the country. Its purpose was to supply vocational advice and information and to place trained women. This agency assisted all women, including those who had had college training. The activities of the bureau also included a training course in vocational guidance and practical training for college graduates in placement work.

The WEIU has regarded itself as a social laboratory that for years has maintained a department of research, which offered fellowships to students who wish to engage in social research. Many improvements in the community owe their beginning to the findings of the students. Further consideration of the educational opportunities of young women were articulated in an extended program of work-study for students wherein the WEIU provided the laboratory experiences in all parts of its operation. As many as three hundred to four hundred students a year have worked in the various WEIU departments. The WEIU also provided a placement site for a number of agencies to allow a few of their people opportunities to learn the art of teaching through experience in a great many diversified areas. In keeping with the educational purpose very early established in the WEIU constitution, a bookshop for boys and girls was set up at the WEIU. The significant activities of the bookshop included exhibits, book conferences, publication of the magazine *The Horn Book,* compilation of bibliographies for schools, a bookshop car that toured New England selling books, classes for teachers, a loan library for educators, and encouragement of book buying by children.

The WEIU terminated some of these activities when it was determined that they had outlived their usefulness and need, but many have been continued with the necessary modernizing. The WEIU has not been less occupied or innovative in the more recent decades, but the organization has become more settled as its purpose and direction have been clearer through the experiments of the early years. Programs that were undertaken were less a spontaneous event in character, and they evolved slowly and deliberately. Indicative of the program's evolution was the introduction of the first family day care program in 1970. The day care staff recruits women who have the potential to become competent day care mothers and whose homes can qualify for state licensing. After comprehensive training, the mothers receive children in their homes through the family day care placement service.

Companions Unlimited, the WEIU's largest social service program, answers the needs of individuals who are isolated from society. Volunteers are recruited, trained to understand the handicapped, aged, chronically ill, and the blind, and assigned to persons who need their help. In addition to this activity and as an outgrowth of it, the WEIU operates Mini Mart, a food cooperative for persons over sixty and the handicapped of all ages. In addition to food, the project provides a weekly suggested menu and shopping list based on proper nutrition and economy. In another related program, homemakers are trained to take over in homes where chronic illness or an emergency exists. This WEIU activity concentrates on placing homemakers in short or long-term situations where householders cannot help themselves. The homemaker steps in and prepares meals, shops, runs errands, and provides general support. The WEIU is engaged in both the training and placement of homemakers.

The WEIU housing project is aimed at the elderly and handicapped population. It investigates and develops a wide range of living arrangements: furnished rooms, apartments, boarding houses, foster homes, or independent living quarters for the blind. Since 1968, the WEIU has researched and listed the only state guide to nursing homes and extended care facilities. Its findings are published in *Levels of Care Facilities in Massachusetts,* put out in cooperation with the Massachusetts Department of Public Health.

The most visible of the WEIU activities, the shops, which opened in 1877 to help women support themselves by work produced in their own homes, moved to a new location in 1976. The shops, which are found in the new quarters at the

"Sign of the Swan," include a gift shop, a collectors' shop, a food shop, a needlework shop, a children's shop, and a cards and stationary shop.

The WEIU's traditional trademark was chosen because Boston's famous swanboats were launched in the Public Garden the same year the WEIU was founded and because the WEIU, through decades of expansion, has always been located in the Public Garden neighborhood. Throughout the WEIU's history, a great deal of time, thought, and resources have been devoted to carrying out the WEIU's purposes stated by Dr. Glisbey. The continued effort has been made by WEIU volunteers, who have represented all social classes. At various times, as indicated in *Annual Reports,* the presidents have felt the need to emphasize that the WEIU is not an organization of advantaged women helping the socially or economically disadvantaged. The WEIU is composed of all women helping anyone in need of assistance in any area that can be answered by the WEIU membership. From its origin to 1976, the WEIU membership has and does exhibit real concern for members of society who are in need through the development of projects for direct assistance and the calling of existing public agencies to appropriate response to those in need of service.

The primary sources for studying the WEIU consist largely of its own publications and materials in their library, the Simmons College Library, and the Schlesinger Library at Radcliffe College in Cambridge, Massachusetts. Most helpful are the *Annual Reports,* an unpublished manuscript of the history of the WEIU by Agnes Donham, and existing publications issued in cooperation with state and federal agencies not widely available in libraries. There is no scholarly study of the history of the WEIU.

Robert Jennings

_Y

YOUNG MEN'S CHRISTIAN ASSOCIATIONS OF THE UNITED STATES OF AMERICA, NATIONAL COUNCIL OF THE (YMCA-NC).

During the early nineteenth century, a spreading evangelical Christian movement, which sought to imbue the middle classes—on both sides of the Atlantic Ocean—with its messages of moral and spiritual uplift, promoted a number of institutions and agencies. One of these was the Young Men's Christian Association (YMCA), founded in London, England, in 1844, with the purpose of improving the "spiritual condition of young men in the drapery and other trades by the introduction of religious services among them." The transmigratory influence of this reawakening was reflected in the fact that the founder of the YMCA, a dry-goods apprentice named George Williams, was a follower of the American preacher and abolitionist, Charles G. Finney.

From London the idea of the YMCA spread rapidly throughout Europe, and in 1851, Montreal, Canada, became the first North American city to establish a local association. Boston in 1851 and New York in 1852 were the first cities in the United States to boast YMCAs, and by 1860 there were already 205 local American associations claiming twenty-five thousand members. Most early YMCAs began their lives in rented quarters, often above a store; but in 1859, with the expenditure of $7,000, the Baltimore association constructed its own building, a practice quickly adopted by other YMCAs.

The United States proved fertile ground for the YMCA. During the 1840s and 1850s, countless similar organizations aimed at the moral regeneration of the young had proliferated in American cities and towns. With these homegrown precedents and the example of the London association to guide them, American YMCAs soon developed a pattern of service and organization that remained largely unchanged for decades.

Although they maintained close relationships with the Protestant ministry, YMCAs were completely under lay control, and they delighted in stressing their interdenominational character. Strongly urban oriented (by 1923, 74 percent of YMCA membership was in city associations), YMCAs geared their program toward the sons of the middle classes, especially those newly arrived in the city to seek their fortunes. Bible study classes, lectures, prayer meetings, and the opening of libraries stocked with religious tracts were all designed to keep impressionable young men from succumbing to the less savory temptations of city life. The maintenance of employment bureaus and boardinghouse referral services were two additional means of steering young men in the proper direction.

Local YMCAs, to varying extents, also engaged in a variety of community services, usually in the form of emergency relief. Visitations of the sick, the distribution of coal to the poor, the clothing of destitute children, and the provision of holiday dinners to residents of almhouses were but a few of the charitable works undertaken by local YMCAs. During a yellow fever epidemic in New Orleans in 1858, for example, the YMCA carried on extensive relief work, and throughout the economic depression of the 1870s, local associations used their facilities to help the general public. In 1875 alone, the Chicago YMCA found work for four thousand unemployed men, and, at about the same time, the Bowery branch of the New York association opened an emergency dormitory facility for the destitute. But the YMCA continually stressed that such services were only temporary and certainly subsidiary to its primary function of improving the spiritual life of the young. "To *save souls*," cautioned one YMCA official in 1888, "is the great work—the only *needed* work of the Associations." As soon as other organizations—charitable or governmental—proved able to provide for those in distress, the YMCA usually withdrew from the field.

The lay evangelical nature of the American YMCA network was reflected in its membership and organization. Few issues caused such long-standing dissension within YMCA councils as the question of who could belong. Because of their origins, most YMCAs normally limited full membership to young men who belonged to one of the orthodox evangelical, and thus Trinitarian, religions. The term "evangelical" was never really defined, and associate, nonvoting membership was available to others, but most associations adhered to this admittedly vague standard for full participation. Ratified on a national level at the convention in Portland, Oregon, in 1866, this so-called Portland test of evangelical orthodoxy remained the basis of YMCA membership until 1931, despite the constant efforts of religious liberals and secularists to modify or repeal it.

Beyond this, however, local associations maintained a high degree of autonomy, drawing up their own constitutions and selecting their own officers. While some smaller Ys determined policies by a direct vote of their members, most elected boards of directors, which in turn appointed executive committees. Most early YMCA work was performed by volunteers, but the practice soon developed of hiring salaried staff members. Of these, undoubtedly the most important were the local secretaries, perhaps the first of whom was twenty-one-year old John Wanamaker, the future department store magnate, hired by the Philadelphia association in 1857. The YMCA local secretariat soon emerged as a major force in the determination of national YMCA policy.

The national YMCA organization grew out of a conference of local associations in the United States and Canada, held in Buffalo, New York, in 1854, at which a loosely organized Central Committee was created. Ten years later the national convention, held annually, reorganized its machinery, establishing a five-member executive committee located in New York City. In 1879 this body, subsequently enlarged, was transformed into the important International Committee (YMCA-IC) which, under the guidance of an international secretary, remained the voice of national YMCA policies until it was replaced by the National Council in the mid-1920s.

In its activities and organization, the American YMCA movement experienced considerable growth in the late nineteenth and early twentieth centuries. State and local associations proliferated, organizing their own conventions; dormitory and restaurant facilities became permanent features of YMCA buildings; and a construction boom so expanded the physical plants of the associations that by 1929, total YMCA property in America was valued at $250 million. Indeed, the size and design requirements of YMCA buildings had become so specialized by the early twentieth century that, in 1913, the IC established a building bureau to provide local associations with professional advice on both architectural and financing plans.

Ever eager to expand its Christian mission, the YMCA-IC established successful overseas associations in many foreign countries, including Japan, India, and Brazil. At home, additional international secretaries were appointed to supervise the YMCA's growing role among Indians, industrial, especially railroad, workers, college students, and Negroes. The organization's efforts in behalf of blacks—notably in the South—were greatly enhanced by the philanthropy of Chicago merchant Julius Rosenwald, who donated matching funds for the construction of separate facilities for them. Increasingly, too, YMCA leaders became aware of the need to provide professional training for men seeking careers within the YMCA or other Christian social service organizations. As a result, several association-affiliated colleges were set up in the late nineteenth century, including Springfield College in Massachusetts in 1885 and George Williams College of Chicago in 1890.

Undoubtedly the most significant growth in YMCA activities occurred in the area of physical education and recreation. Spurred on by men such as Brooklyn clergyman Henry Ward Beecher, association leaders had early accepted the precept that a healthy moral spirit is best engendered in a sound body. By 1880, most YMCAs had gymnasiums for their members' use, and some, like New York City and San Francisco, even had bowling alleys. The swimming pool, which soon became the most popular attraction at local Ys, was first introduced by the Brooklyn association in 1885.

Under the guidance of imaginative local secretaries like Robert Ross McBurney of New York, the physical work program of the YMCA became an integral part of the organization's fourfold mission to enrich the "spiritual, mental, social, and physical" aspects of man's makeup. Extending their reach to boys, as well as to young men, associations conducted classes in body building and acrobatics, often taught by former prize-fighters and circus performers; and in 1885, the first of many YMCA summer camps for boys was opened at Orange Lake, near Newburgh, New York.

Dr. Luther Halsey Gulick, a physician and pioneer in the field of organized recreation—who later worked with the Russell Sage Foundation* and who founded the Campfire Girls of America* in 1911—brought a scientific and philosophical coherence to the YMCA's physical program. As the first physical work secretary of the YMCA-IC from 1886 to 1903, Gulick wrote and spoke widely on his theory of the "unified man," a theory that rejected the traditional mind-body dualism of earlier thinkers and argued that, like Christ, man's nature was an essential unity of "body, mind, and spirit." Exercise and recreation were, therefore, not merely useful but vital to the development of the "perfect" Christian man. To illustrate his notion of the tripartite nature of man's unity, Gulick devised an inverted equilateral triangle, which quickly became—and remained—the universally recognized symbol of the YMCA.

Under Gulick and his staff of professionally trained athletic directors, the YMCA-IC emerged as a major innovator of recreational programs. Seeking a simple group sport that could be played in any gymnasium, Gulick was widely credited with inspiring James Naismith, an alumnus of Springfield College, to invent the game of basketball in 1891. In the early years of the twentieth century, the YMCA-IC was a leader in the emerging playground movement in American cities. And, during the Progressive era, it and its affiliates around the country helped to promote first the Boy Scout movement and then, since its inception in 1910, the Boy Scouts of America.*

In addition to its programs for civilians, the YMCA-IC performed many social services for the American armed forces. In every armed conflict beginning with the Civil War, the YMCA set up centers at military posts at home and abroad to provide recreation and moral guidance to American soldiers. It also helped to collect and distribute supplies, ran supplementary kitchens in the field, and aided in hospital work. The association's most ambitious, independent initiative occurred during World War I, when it enlisted some twenty-six thousand workers and spent $172 million in the United States and Europe. Taking over the ''PX'' functions of the army, the YMCA-IC operated fifteen hundred canteens in France alone and was the first American agency to provide food services to American prisoners-of-war in Germany.

After the war, the YMCA's canteen operation was widely criticized by returning soldiers for charging excessive prices for items like cigarettes and candy that other private agencies distributed free. But a lengthy investigation, requested by the YMCA-IC itself, found the charges baseless and concluded that they arose from the mistaken impression that the YMCA-IC was a welfare organization similar to The Salvation Army.* During World War II, however, the YMCA-NC's military programs were coordinated with those of other private agencies under the banner of the United Service Organizations for National Defense, Inc.*

Despite its innovative development of programs to meet the changing needs of modern America, the YMCA, well into the twentieth century, clung tenaciously to the conservative religious and social tenets of the post–Civil War revival movement led by the Reverend Dwight L. Moody. Appealing to the middle classes and governed largely by businessmen, the YMCA rejected appeals to align itself with the social gospel movement of the late nineteenth century; and, with the exception of a few leaders, it resisted the acceptance of religious modernism until at least the 1920s. Following the religious orthodoxy of Moody, who exerted a strong influence on both the Chicago association and the YMCA-IC, the YMCA continued to define its purpose as the improvement of society through the moral regeneration of individuals rather than through a sustained attack on social and economic problems.

The failure of many YMCA activists, like Chicago settlement house worker Graham Taylor, to enlist the association in the social welfare movement was thus not surprising. In its limited forays into public issues, the Y's conservatism prevailed. Various local associations led temperance programs, supported Sunday closing laws, and crusaded against prostitution and gambling. The influential New York Society for the Suppression of Vice, headed by Anthony Comstock, began in 1868 as a YMCA committee aimed at censoring obscene literature. Insulated as they were from the problems of the working classes and fearing the spread of social disorder, YMCA spokesmen of the late nineteenth century often stood against labor protests and took special pride in opposing the Pullman strike of 1894. As one prominent clergyman put it, "The eruption of the social volcano, if it breaks out at all, will not break out in the basement of the YMCA in our town."

Gradually, however, under younger and more liberal leadership, the YMCA caught up with the mainstream of urban Protestantism in the 1920s and 1930s. A closer cooperation with the modernist Federal Council of the Churches of Christ in America began to develop; the YMCA-IC, long under attack as autocratic, was replaced in 1924 by the YMCA-NC, which gave local associations a greater voice in national policy; and the Portland test was finally abolished. In fact, by 1952, when the YMCA-NC declared that a member should be anyone who "agrees to cooperate with others" to achieve the association's goals, the agency virtually eliminated religious restrictions on membership. Participating in some programs and movements close to the national social work community, the YMCA-NC seemed to have programs for transients and the homeless during the Great Depression of the 1930s.

In the post–World War II era, the American YMCA movement continued to thrive. By the mid-1960s, there were more than eighteen hundred local associations with nearly three million members, the greatest growth in membership being among boys under the age of seventeen. Income was derived from membership dues, service fees, contributions, and the Y's share of community chest funds. Although studies suggest that the greatest proportion of YMCA members still came from Protestant, middle-class homes, association services were available to a much broader constituency than ever before. Continuing its record of innovative program development, the agency in the 1960s and 1970s has expanded its educational facilities to help dropouts to complete high school and college training; it has instituted vocational instruction; and it has extended its services to women and girls. Recognizing the special problems of American cities, it has also inaugurated programs like the National Center for Youth Outreach Workers to aid juvenile delinquents, the national drugs action team, and a host of local seminars designed to promote better understanding between young people and the police.

Now well into its second century, the YMCA, while changing with the times, remains loyal to its historic purpose: the moral, spiritual, intellectual, and physical improvement of the nation's youth.

The chief repository of YMCA materials is the YMCA Historical Library located at the headquarters of the National Council in New York City. The New York Public Library also has two file drawers of its general catalog devoted to YMCA sources, both primary and secondary. Much information can be gleaned from the association's numerous publications through the years, including the *Quarterly Reporter,* the *Association Forum,* and the *Yearbook and Official Roster.* Useful historical data can be found in a number of books written by men long associated with the YMCA, including Richard C. Morse, *History of the North American Y.M.C.A.* (1913) and *My Life with Young Men* (1918); Laurence L. Doggett, *Life of Robert R. McBurney* (1902) and *History of the Y.M.C.A.* (1922); and Edgar M. Robinson, *The Early Years: The Beginning of Work with Boys in the Y.M.C.A.* (1950). There are also many published histories of local associations. Easily the best general history of the YMCA movement by a historian is C. Howard Hopkins, *History of the Y.M.C.A. in North America* (1951), which was drawn largely from original sources in the YMCA Historical Library and contains extensive references. Among more recent secondary studies are Mayer N. Zald, *Organizational Change: The Political Economy of the Y.M.C.A.* (1970), and Clifford M. Drury, *San Francisco Y.M.C.A.: 100 Years by the Golden Gate, 1853–1953* (1963).

Philip De Vencentes

YOUNG WOMEN'S CHRISTIAN ASSOCIATION OF THE U.S.A., NATIONAL BOARD OF THE (YWCA-USA). During the mid-nineteenth century, as many young women flocked to industrial cities to work, a series of separate agencies to meet their needs developed in different parts of the country. Like other social institutions and movements in the United States during this period, the first such clubs for young women began in England a few years before they developed in the United States. In 1855, Emma Robarts of Barnet, England, the daughter of a wealthy businessman, organized a Prayer Union concerned with the welfare of young women in a turbulent time of industrialization and social change. In the same year, the Honorable Mrs. Arthur Kinnaird founded the "General Female Home and Training Institution" to provide shelter and services to nurses and other young women who had come to London from the provinces to seek work. These two organizations, which united in 1877, are generally recognized as the first Young Women's Christian Associations (YWCAs) in the world.

Both the British and American YWCAs were patterned in concept after the Young Men's Christian Association* (YMCA), which was established in England in 1844 and in the United States in 1851. The men's and women's movements, while sharing common concerns and pursuing similar ends, have always been organizationally independent and maintained separate identities.

On November 24, 1858, a group of thirty-five women met in New York City at the chapel of New York University to establish a "Ladies Christian Association" under the leadership of Mrs. Marshall O. Roberts. Mrs. Roberts, the wife of a prominent New York businessman, was elected the first director. The group of founders adopted a constitution, which included among the duties of members to "seek out especially young women of the operative class, aid them in procuring employment and in obtaining suitable boarding places, furnish them with proper reading matter, establish Bible classes and meetings for religious exercises."

At about the same time, Lucretia Boyd, a city missionary in Boston, was working with a group of church women to develop interest in the plight of employed young women in that city. She identified housing, recreation, employment, protection, and moral influence as areas of need. Boyd appeared before the Boston City Missionary Society in 1859 to propose the development of interdenominational work for young women. The effort was discouraged by the male clergy of Boston; it was March 3, 1866, before the Boston Young Women's Christian Association was formally organized with the object of fostering "the temporal, moral, and religious welfare of young women who are dependent on their own exertions for support."

Within a few years after the establishment of the New York and Boston YWCAs, women founded YWCAs in a number of different cities in the East and Midwest. The first national meeting was a conference held in Hartford, Connecticut, on October 8, 1871. Delegates from eight associations attended, and thirteen others sent reports out of a total of thirty potential member associations. The conference, held biennially in different locations, adopted a constitution in Montreal in 1877 and named itself the International Conference of Women's Christian Associations. This meeting included city associations from the United States and Canada. In 1891, the need for greater structure led to the development of a board, an executive committee, and a budget. The members also changed the name to the International Board of Women's and Young Women's Christian Associations.

The member associations were in the cities, and their activities covered virtually the gamut of known social services for young women: residences, employment services, libraries, sewing, typing, and nursing schools, cafeterias, travelers' aid, Bible classes, and recreation programs. YWCA volunteers visited prisons and hospitals, set up day nurseries, orphanages, and homes for unwed mothers and the aged, and engaged in other activities as needs were recognized and resources permitted.

In 1873, the first student YWCA was established at Illinois State Normal University, Normal, Illinois. As with community associations, student YWCAs developed independently and almost simultaneously on many campuses. The model for student work came from the student YMCAs, which dated from the 1850s. The purpose of student YWCAs was to foster Christian commitment and spiritual and social growth among women at colleges and universities. At first, they engaged in Bible study and prayer meetings and encouraged the development and support of missionary work abroad. The YMCAs and YWCAs on campus also provided orientation and counseling for new students and sponsored cultural activities and social service projects. The YWCA staff acted as the first deans of women on many campuses. During the twentieth century, the emphasis of student YWCAs broadened to include greater concern for social action and provision of experiential learning opportunities such as student-in-industry projects, citizenship seminars, United Nations seminars, and leadership training institutes.

A report of the work among students to develop YWCAs and YMCAs on campuses was received at the international conference in 1881. The conference went on record as supportive of such efforts and appointed a committee to promote the foundation of student YWCAs. In many respects, however, the first student YWCAs related more closely to student YMCAs than to the city YWCAs. In the early years, they often met with the men at YMCA state conferences, and the student YWCAs soon began to develop their own state organizations with paid staff, called state secretaries.

In 1885, there were seven state associations of student YWCAs. They united that year in drafting a recommendation for the creation of a permanent international organization composed of city and student YWCAs together, with fixed headquarters and an executive committee or board to act between meetings. This proposal was carried by representatives of the student movement to the international conference in 1885 but, for a variety of reasons and misunderstandings, it was not presented there. Instead, representatives of student associations called a constitutional convention in 1886 at Lake Geneva, Wisconsin, and established the National Association of the Young Women's Christian Associations of the United States of America, with headquarters in Chicago. The supervisory body, called the National Committee, changed its name twice in the next thirteen years to the International Committee in 1889 and then to the American Committee in 1889, when the Canadians formed their own national organization to affiliate with the World's YWCA. The National Committee (American Committee) was comprised of the state chairmen plus at least seven others; it met annually and carried out such activities as correspondence among members and publication of a journal called *The Evangel* and other resource materials. By 1889, there was a general secretary who attended state conferences and conventions and provided other staff functions.

For the remainder of the nineteenth century and into the twentieth, there continued to be two national bodies of YWCAs: The International Board and the American Committee, the former including predominantly city associations, and the latter, mostly student YWCAs. There were some philosophical differences, so aside from periodic communication, each pursued its own course until 1905, when the two bodies clashed over jurisdictional questions.

In Washington, D.C., there was a long-established Women's Christian Association, a city association affiliated with the International Board, when a group of young women sought help from the American Committee to establish a Young Women's Christian Association there. Grace Hoadley Dodge, a philanthropist from New York who had worked with women and girls for many years, offered to mediate the dispute. She held meetings with representatives of both groups; the focus of the discussion was the possibility of union. She was successful. Following agreement by the two bodies, a convention was held December 5–6, 1906, at South Church, Reformed, in New York City. This meeting created the YWCA-USA as the National Board of the Young Women's Christian Associations of the United States of America (NB-YWCA). The convention fixed the headquarters in New York and elected a national board, which in turn elected Dodge as the first president. A three-day conference of staff department directors, organizing secretaries, and superintendents met after the convention with an attendance of 149 YWCA workers. The NB-YWCA was incorporated according to the laws of the state of New York on June 7, 1907. Six hundred and sixteen member associations affiliated with the new national organization—469 of them student associations and 147 city associations—with 186,330 members. The establishment of the NB-YWCA took place thirty-five years after the first national structure and nearly fifty years after the founding of the first YWCAs in the United States.

The structure established between 1906 and 1909 has remained essentially the same to the present time. The YWCA-USA in 1976 is an organization of associations, governed by a constitution and bylaws. The National Board of the YWCA of the U.S.A. (YWCA-USA) is the legal entity incorporated to carry out the work of the national organization. The national convention, presently held triennially, is the membership meeting and legislative body. Delegates from member associations adopt policies and programs and elect the national board, which initially numbered thirty but numbered ninety in 1976, to act as the executive body between conventions. National board members and officers are all volunteers. There is also a national staff at the headquarters in New York and in four regional offices in Pasadena, Chicago, Atlanta, and New York City. Apart from meeting the conditions for affiliation, member YWCAs, both community and student associations, are autonomous units, with programs and activities determined by their members. The YWCA-USA affiliates member associations; since the 1940s, the convention has also adopted ongoing standards for YWCA administration and program development. There is a process of regular agency evaluation and accreditation called association review in which each member YWCA makes an in-depth self-study and receives an accrediting visit from a team of national board and staff once each six years. Financing takes place through membership fees, donations, united way support, and program fees. Men and boys may become associates and participate in coeducational activities, but the need for the YWCA to remain a women's movement has been reaffirmed consistently throughout its history.

As YWCAs were proliferating in the United States during the last three decades of the nineteenth century, similar programs were arising in other parts of the world. Frequently industrial development and urbanization led to new social problems, and influential women recognized the need for special services for women and girls in changing times. Missionaries who had been part of the YWCAs on college campuses and staff sent by student YMCAs and YWCAs to work abroad also helped carry the idea to diverse locations. In 1894, representatives of the YWCAs in England, the United States, Norway, and Sweden agreed to establish the World's YWCA (W-YWCA). They adopted a constitution and named a general secretary (executive director), Annie Reynolds from the United

States. Reynolds had previously served as director of a city association and organizing secretary at the state level and was a member of the staff of the international committee. The first world conference was held in 1898 in London. Over the years, many women from the United States have served as staff or advisers in other countries. The approach used in overseas work reported at the convention in 1906 of the NB-YWCA was that the national committee of the country involved gave direction to the worker from the United States. This policy of fostering autonomous national YWCAs continues to the present day.

The increasing use of paid staff and the need for skilled volunteers in both student and community YWCAs led to the establishment of training programs. There were at least two in existence in the nineteenth century, the Summer Bible and Training School, initiated in 1891 near Chicago, and the School of Domestic Science and Christian Workers in Boston, established in 1888 and offering courses for association workers from 1897. Because of the limitations of these programs and other factors, the American Committee decided to set up a training institute in 1904 to prepare YWCA secretaries, primarily for student work. Following the union of the American Committee and the International Board, the national training school opened in New York in 1908 and offered a one-year course of study until 1930. After that, regularly scheduled institutes, conferences, and leadership training workshops became the means of providing orientation and continuing education for YWCA staff and volunteers. The standards for volunteer training through the years have been high, and an extensive range of leadership training programs has been offered during each triennium.

As the YWCA moved into the twentieth century, it developed several new areas of endeavor. Women had established YWCAs in Negro colleges in the 1890s, and the first YWCA work began in Indian boarding schools in 1892. This work expanded rapidly, with the NB-YWCA employing special staff for its development. In 1908, the student department of the NB-YWCA added Negro staff, and in 1913 a secretary for Negro work in the cities was employed. During this period, there was rapid development of branch associations in Negro neighborhoods, staffed and led by Negro women. Such branches were administratively part of the community association rather than being separate organizations. The philosophy underlying the work was interracial rather than biracial, and the YWCA took positive steps toward integration and inclusiveness ahead of the rest of society as a whole.

Another specialized area of work was with foreign-born women. In 1910, the YWCA established the first International Institute in New York as a center where immigrant women could learn English and be provided social services by a staff fluent in various languages. These institutes were developed in many large cities until 1933, when the YWCA helped establish an independent organization to continue this work, the American Federation of International Institutes.* Similarly the YWCA, which had initiated the first travelers' aid work in Boston and had assisted women arriving in many major cities since the 1880s, promoted the formation of the National Association of Travelers Aid Societies* in 1917. Another independent organization that the YWCA helped found was the National Federation of Business and Professional Women (see *Fraternal Organizations*) in 1919.

Two other specific groups with which the YWCA developed programs and services were adolescent girls and women and girls working in industry. In 1918, the work with teenagers was formally organized into the Girl Reserve (GR) movement, in which girls between the ages of twelve and eighteen joined activity groups led by trained volunteers and staff. In 1920, there were 500 staff across the country working with younger girls and a membership of 80,000 GRs; by 1934, the number had increased to 325,000. In 1946, the program name was changed to Y-Teens. Teenage programs have often been carried out through clubs in schools, as well as camping and various activities in the community YWCA building. Based on this and other work, the YWCA gave leadership to the development of group work as a method of social work practice. Services to industrial women and girls are as old as the YWCA; the organization of this group nationally as a constituency with special assemblies at convention time began in 1922 and extended through the next three decades. The YWCA granted similar constituency group status to students, teens, and young adults, enabling them to hold assemblies to discuss their own interests and problems. These continue to meet in the mid-1970s.

The two wars created special problems, which YWCAs met by developing new services. In May 1917, the NB-YWCA established the war work council. The council conducted a wide range of projects, such as the creation of about 140 hostess houses for women visitors near military bases, the development of recreation centers, special programs for war brides and their babies, assistance with housing for women war workers, increased services to the foreign born, and industrial service centers. Council overseas activities included work with refugees and social services in eight countries in Europe and the Near East. Perhaps the most significant program the YWCA developed to respond to a war-related problem was the Commission on Social Morality, which became the official lecture bureau of the Division of Social Hygiene of the War Department. The activity of the commission was to develop a nationwide sex education program employing women physicians in an effort to combat the alarming increase in prostitution and venereal disease. Even after the war, the YWCA continued the lectures "to cultivate an attitude of honest, open scientific interest in the subject of sex."

During World War II, the YWCA engaged in many similar programs to serve women and girls in the time of crises. The NB-YWCA was one of six national organizations that cooperated to form a major social service agency for servicemen, the United Service Organizations for National Defense, Inc.* (USO), in

1940. Another example of cooperative endeavor was the American War-Community Services, which helped meet the needs of workers in war industries. Beginning in 1942, the YWCA offered services to Japanese-American women in ten relocation centers to which they had been sent. A world emergency and war victims' fund, established by the NB-YWCA in 1940, provided support for relief and refugee work in Europe and the Orient.

From its earliest days, the NB-YWCA has included the dual emphasis of direct services to women and girls and social action to improve their environment and living conditions. The formal public affairs program of the YWCA began in 1911, when the national convention adopted a resolution urging legislators to regulate the hours and wages of women workers. From that time forward, the convention took stands on social issues that enabled the national board and staff to testify at legislative hearings, join in coalitions with reform groups and government agencies, such as the Women's Bureau, and in other ways support progressive movements. One example of such work was the assistance given by the YWCA to Florence Kelley and the National Child Labor Committee* in the effort to prohibit child labor. Other resolutions the YWCA adopted in its conventions of the 1920s included ones outlawing war, urging entry into the League of Nations, and advocating better regulation of labor conditions and higher minimum wages.

In the 1930s, the NB-YWCA was in the vanguard of the New Deal with its support for the right of workers to organize for collective bargaining, for compulsory unemployment insurance and national health insurance, for public housing, and for greater economic opportunities for blacks and other ethnic minority groups. Subsequent social action targets in the postwar period through the 1950s emphasized open housing, support for the United Nations changes in restrictive immigration policies, extension and expansion of Social Security and minimum wage coverage, benefits for agricultural workers, and disarmament. The YWCA went on record in the 1960s and 1970s for the expansion of civil rights, conservation of natural resources, the enactment of equal rights for women, gun control, protection of civil liberties, and the restructuring of national priorities to provide more adequately for the social welfare of the people.

A continuing emphasis throughout the twentieth century has been work for conditions to foster dignity, respect, and participation of all groups in society, and, specifically, work for racial justice. At the convention in 1946, delegates adopted the interracial charter, which stated that the YWCA must actively protest and vigorously work for the removal of injustice on the basis of race, in the community, the nation, and the world.

Thus, the NB-YWCA began by studying itself and revising its own practices. Although the national staff had included women of all races for many years, the NB-YWCA tried consciously to increase their numbers at the local and national levels, especially professional staff members. To promote racial justice in all facets of association life, the NB-YWCA held workshops, seminars, and other programs on civil rights, intergroup relations, and community action to increase racial inclusiveness through the late 1940s and 1950s.

As the 1960s opened, however, there were still a number of community YWCAs in the South where a segregated pattern of services persisted. In 1963, the YWCA-USA set up a special two-year project with two staff members to provide assistance to those associations to ensure they integrated all programs and centers. During this period, the student YWCA sponsored a number of summer and spring vacation projects on voter education and registration and other aspects of civil rights.

Starting a new decade with an awareness of a continuing need for action, a national conference of the black women of the YWCA was held prior to the convention in 1970. The convention then pledged the YWCA to work on one imperative, "to trust our collective power toward the elimination of racism, wherever it exists and by any means necessary." The YWCA-USA held consultations during the next triennium, bringing together native American women, Chicanos, Asian Americans, and Puerto Ricans to explore further the role of the YWCA in promoting social justice. This priority has been reaffirmed in the two subsequent conventions; a program of training institutes and workshops has been held all over the country to educate YWCA members and leaders and to prepare them for direct action in eliminating racism.

The YWCA today, as at its inception over a century ago, is made up of many associations trying to meet the needs of women and girls in their communities and on campuses. Typical services include a wide range of classes in cultural, recreational, and educational subjects, women's consciousness raising groups, camping programs, clubs and activities for teenage girls, auto mechanics for women, health, physical education, and recreation programs, public affairs study and action groups, abortion and rape counseling, residences and cafeterias, "mother's day out," groups (Y-wives), women's support groups, and leadership training. A number of YWCAs have day care centers or "latch-key" programs of afterschool activities for children whose mothers work. Some community associations have converted all or part of their residences to halfway houses for women in correctional diversion programs or released from mental hospitals or other institutions. There has been a trend toward developing programs in cooperation with the government. One example is Job Corps YW residence programs and Job Corps centers, which the YWCA initiated under a federal contract. Residence accommodations, counseling, and educational services were provided in this program for eight years. Other significant demonstration projects initiated by member YWCAs with federal and state funds include residential programs for delinquent girls, services to women in prison and after their release, and nutritional and service programs for the elderly. Through purchase-of-service arrangements with state and county agencies, YWCAs often provide day care, youth recreation, and other needed services.

In 1975, there were 406 community and eighty-six student YWCAs in the

United States, located in all states but Alaska, with nearly 2.5 million members and program participants. Programs vary according to the needs of the community served. The present statement of purpose, revised in 1967, reads:

The Young Women's Christian Association
   of the United States of America,
a movement rooted in the Christian faith
   as known in Jesus and nourished by
      the resources of that faith,
seeks to respond to the barrier-breaking
      love of God in this day.
   The Association draws together into
responsible membership women and girls
   of diverse experiences and faiths,
that their lives may be open to new
understanding and deeper relationships
   and that together they may join
   in the struggle for peace and justice,
freedom and dignity for all people.

About a dozen histories have been written on the YWCA or some aspect of its program. The first work that covered the beginning through the present national movement was Elizabeth Wilson's *Fifty Years of Association Work Among Young Women, 1866–1916* (1916). Three subsequent basic histories, all by Mary S. Sims and all published by the NB-YWCA, are *The National History of a Social Institution—The Young Women's Christian Association* (1936), *The YWCA: An Unfolding Purpose* (1950), and *The Purpose Widens, 1947–1967* (1969). Two pamphlets on specific aspects of the YWCA work are *The Past Is Prelude: Fifty Years of Social Action in the YWCA* (1963), by Elsie Harper, and *From Deep Roots: The Story of the YWCA's Religious Dimensions* (1974), by Frances Mains and Grace Elliott. Significant primary materials include the *Reports* of the International Committee of YWCAs, 1886–1891; *Journals* of the International Conference of the Women's Christian Associations, 1871–1905; *Annual Reports* of the American Committee, 1891–1906; and the *Proceedings* of the National Conventions of the YWCA of the U.S.A., 1906–1976 (27 vols.). Information on these and other primary materials can be obtained from the National Board, YWCA of the U.S.A., 600 Lexington Avenue, New York.

Ann W. Nichols

RELIGIOUSLY AFFILIATED SOCIAL SERVICE AGENCIES

This appendix contains a list of social service agencies associated with or affiliated with the three main religious bodies—Catholic, Jewish, and Protestant—by either legal or traditional ties or by popular recognition. For instance, the New York Association for Improving the Condition of the Poor did not have formal religious ties, but in New York City it generally handled cases involving Protestants and was popularly recognized as a Protestant agency. Agencies identified as Protestant, except those clearly affiliated with denominations, are generally less concerned with Protestant clients and Protestant sectarian issues in social welfare than are the Catholic and Jewish agencies, many of which focus almost exclusively on sectarian issues and on their coreligionists.

CATHOLIC

CYO Federation, National
Catholic Charities of the Archdiocese of New York, The
Catholic Relief Services-United States Catholic Conference
National Catholic Community Service
National Conference of Catholic Charities
Society of St. Vincent De Paul, Superior Council of the U.S., Inc.
United States Catholic Conference, Department of Social Development and World Peace of the

JEWISH

American Jewish Joint Distribution Committee, Inc.
American Organization for Rehabilitation through Training Federation
Bureau of Jewish Social Research
Council of Jewish Federations and Welfare Funds, Inc.
Family Location Service, Inc.
Hebrew Sheltering and Immigrant Aid Society

Industrial Removal Office
Jewish Agricultural Society, Inc., The
Jewish Board of Guardians
Jewish Family Service
National Conference of Jewish Communal Service
National Coordinating Committee for Aid to Refugees and Emigrants Coming from Germany
National Jewish Welfare Board, The
National Refugee Service, Inc., The
United HIAS Service
United Service for New Americans, Inc.

PROTESTANT

American Christian Committee for Refugees, Inc.
American Friends Service Committee
Baptist Churches in the U.S.A., American Division of Social Ministries of the American
Brethren Service Commission
Charity Organization Society of the City of New York, The
Church World Service
Congregational Christian Churches, Council for Social Action of the
Disciples of Christ, Church in Society of the
Episcopal Church, Department of Christian Social Relations of the Protestant
Episcopal Service for Youth
Evangelical and Reformed Church, Commission on Christian Social Action of the
Lutheran Council in the United States of America, Division of Mission and Ministry
Lutheran World Relief
Mennonite Central Committee
Methodist Federation for Social Action, The
National Council of the Churches of Christ in the U.S.A., Division of Church and Society of the
New York Association for Improving the Condition of the Poor
Presbyterian Church in the United States of America, Church and Society of The United
Salvation Army, The
Unitarian Association, Department of Social Relations of the American
Unitarian Universalist Service Committee
United Church of Christ, Office for Church in Society of the
United States Christian Commission for the Army and Navy
Volunteers of America, The
Young Men's Christian Associations of the United States of America, National Council of the
Young Women's Christian Association of the U.S.A., National Board of the

CHRONOLOGY

In the listing that follows, the founding dates of the social service agencies included in this volume are arranged chronologically by year. A perusal of this appendix not only reveals periods of accelerated social services and social reform activity but also indicates the periods during which types of agencies began to organize. For instance, the Progressive years are heavily represented by issue-oriented and problem-solving agencies. The periods of wars, of course, represent years of organizing military aid organizations.

1825

American Seamen's Friend Society

1843

New York Association for Improving the Condition of the Poor

1853

Children's Aid Society, The

1854

Young Men's Christian Associations of the United States of America, National Council of the

1858

American Printing House for the Blind, Inc.

1861

United States Christian Commission for the Army and Navy
United States Sanitary Commission
Woman's Central Association of Relief

1870

American Correctional Association, The

1872

American Public Health Association
State Communities Aid Association

1874

Jewish Family Service
National Conference on Social Welfare
New York Society for the Prevention of Cruelty to Children, The

1876

American Association on Mental Deficiency

1877

American Humane Association, The
Fresh Air Fund, The
National Shut-In Society, The
Women's Educational and Industrial Union

1880

National Association of the Deaf
Salvation Army, The

1881

American National Red Cross

1882

Charity Organization Society of the City of New York, The

1883

National Children's Home and Welfare Association

1885

Needlework Guild of America, Inc., The

1889

Hull-House Association

1893

Henry Street Settlement Urban Life Center

1895

American Association of Workers for the Blind
Florence Crittenton Association of America, Inc.

1896

Volunteers of America, The

1897

National League of Girls Clubs

1898

National Association for the Study of Epilepsy and the Care and Treatment of Epileptics
National Association of Day Nurseries

1899

National Conference of Jewish Communal Service
National Consumers' League

1900

Army Relief Society
Jewish Agricultural Society, Inc., The

1901

Industrial Removal Office

1902

Juvenile Protective Association
Speedwell Services for Children, Inc., The

1904

American Lung Association
National Child Labor Committee
Navy Relief Society

1905

Goodwill Industries of America, Inc.

1906

American Association for Labor Legislation
Boys' Clubs of America, Inc.
National Recreation and Park Association
Young Women's Christian Association of the U.S.A., National Board of the

1907

American School Hygiene Association
Methodist Federation for Social Action, The
National Council on Crime and Delinquency
Russell Sage Foundation

1908

Foundation for Child Development
Girls and Boys Service League
Immigrants' Service League, The
National Council of the Churches of Christ in the U.S.A., Division of Church and Society of the
North American Civic League
Unitarian Association, Department of Social Relations of the American

1909

American Child Health Association
Episcopal Service for Youth
Hebrew Sheltering and Immigrant Aid Society
National Committee for Mental Hygiene, Inc., The
National Federation of Remedial Loan Associations

1910

Boy Scouts of America
National Conference of Catholic Charities
National Housing Association

1911

Camp Fire Girls, Inc.
Family Location Service, Inc.
Family Service Association of America
National Committee on Prisons and Prison Labor
National Federation of Settlements and Neighborhood Centers
National Legal Aid and Defender Association
National Urban League

1912

American Association for Hygiene and Baths
Baptist Churches in the U.S.A., American, Division of Social Ministries of the
Disciples of Christ, Church in Society of the
Girl Scouts of the United States of America
National Organization for Public Health Nursing
Survey Associates, Inc.

1913

American Cancer Society, Inc.
American Social Health Association
Council of the Southern Mountains

1914

American Jewish Joint Distribution Committee, Inc.

1915

American Foundation for Overseas Blind, Inc.
National Society for the Prevention of Blindness, Inc.
Society of St. Vincent de Paul, Superior Council of the U.S., Inc.

1917

American Association of Social Workers
American Friends Service Committee
Big Brother and Big Sister Federation, Inc.
National Jewish Welfare Board, The
Travelers Aid Association of America

1918

American Association of Medical Social Workers, Inc., The
Child Health Organization of America
Commonwealth Fund, The
Maternity Center Association
National Council on Illegitimacy
United Way of America

1919

American Relief Administration European Children's Fund
Bureau of Jewish Social Research
Episcopal Church, Department of Christian Social Relations of the Protestant
National Association for Hearing and Speech Action
Near East Relief

1920

Catholic Charities of the Archdiocese of New York, The
Child Welfare League of America, Inc.
Committee on Transportation of Allied National Agencies
Mennonite Central Committee
National Health Council, Inc.
National Society of Penal Information
United States Catholic Conference, Department of Social Development and World Peace of the

1921

American Foundation for the Blind
Foreign Language Information Service, The
Jewish Board of Guardians
National Easter Seal Society for Crippled Children and Adults, The
Planned Parenthood Federation of America, Inc.

1922

American Heart Association
American Legion, National Children and Youth Division of the
American Lung Association
American Organization for Rehabilitation through Training Federation
American Rehabilitation Committee

1923

National Assembly of National Voluntary Health and Social Welfare Organizations, Inc., The

1924

American Orthopsychiatry Association, The
International Social Service-American Branch, The

1926

National Rehabilitation Association, Inc.

1927

American Association for Social Security, Inc.

1929

Seeing Eye, Inc., The

1930

American Public Welfare Association
National Council on Naturalization and Citizenship

1932

Council of Jewish Federations and Welfare Funds, Inc.
Council on Interstate Migration, Inc.
National Housing Conference, Inc.
Osborne Association, Inc., The
Save the Children Federation

1933

American Federation of International Institutes
International Relief Association

1934

American Christian Committee for Refugees, Inc.
Congregational Christian Churches, Council for Social Action of the
National Coordinating Committee for Aid to Refugees and Emigrants Coming from Germany

1935

Alcoholics Anonymous
Evangelical and Reformed Church, Commission on Christian Social Action of the

1936

Presbyterian Church in the United States of America, Church and Society of the United

1937

Association for Voluntary Sterilization
Foster Parents Plan International, Inc.
Lutheran Council in the United States of America, Division of Mission and Ministry
National Foundation-March of Dimes, The

1938

National Industries for the Blind, Inc.

1939

Brethren Service Committee
Common Council for American Unity, The
Community Service Society
National Council for Homemaker-Home Health Aide Services, Inc.
National Refugee Service, Inc., The

1940

International Rescue Committee, Inc.
National Catholic Community Service
Unitarian Universalist Service Committee
United States Committee for the Care of European Children, Inc.

1941

AFL-CIO Department of Community Services
United Service Organizations, Inc.

1942

National Council on Rehabilitation
United Seamen's Service

1943

American Council of Voluntary Agencies for Foreign Service, Inc.
Catholic Relief Services-United States Catholic Conference

1944

Baruch Committee on Physical Medicine and Rehabilitation
National Council on Alcoholism, Inc.

1945

Cooperative for American Relief Everywhere
Girls Clubs of America, Inc.
Lutheran World Relief

1946

Big Brothers of America, Inc.
Church World Service
National Mental Health Foundation, Inc.
National Multiple Sclerosis Society
United Cerebral Palsy Associations, Inc.
United Service for New Americans, Inc.

1947

United States Committee for UNICEF

1950

Muscular Dystrophy Association, Inc.
National Association for Mental Health, Inc., The
National Association for Retarded Citizens
National Council on the Aging, Inc., The
United Community Defense Services

1951

Association of Volunteer Bureaus
CYO Federation, National

1952

Council on Social Work Education, The

1954

American Immigration Conference
United HIAS Service

1955

National Association of Social Workers, Inc.

1957

United Church of Christ, Office for Church in Society of the

1958

Day Care and Child Development Council of America, Inc., The

1959

American Council for Nationalities Service
National Committee for Children and Youth
United States Committee for Refugees

1960

American Immigration and Citizenship Conference

1961

American Freedom from Hunger Foundation

1967

Association of Black Social Workers
Fortune Society, The
National Welfare Rights Organization

AGENCY FUNCTIONS

This section suggests the types of traditional social service functions that the agencies in this volume conducted. In some cases, the category represents virtually the only function of an agency, while in other cases, such as with the Community Service Society and the category of aging, the specialization indicates only one—but an important one—area of agency commitment and activity.

The categories included generally represent subject headings gleaned from the *Social Work Year Books* and its successor, the *Encyclopedia of Social Work*. Some categories are not necessarily utilized in these volumes but seemed logical to me. Not all agencies in this volume are included in this section; many of them simply did not qualify according to these functions and specializations. It should not be assumed that agencies omitted from this appendix, such as the Association for Voluntary Sterilization, The National Assembly of National Voluntary Health and Social Welfare Organizations, Inc., and the Bureau of Jewish Social Research, contributed insignificantly to the development of American voluntary social services.

Aging

Community Service Society
National Council on the Aging, Inc., The
Salvation Army, The
Volunteers of America, The

Alcoholism: Prevention and Rehabilitation

Alcoholics Anonymous
National Council on Alcoholism, Inc.
Salvation Army, The
Volunteers of America, The

Aliens and the Foreign Born

American Christian Committee for Refugees, Inc.
American Council for Nationalities Service

American Federation of International Institutes
American Immigration and Citizenship Conference
American Immigration Conference
Common Council for American Unity
Foreign Language Information Service, The
Hebrew Sheltering and Immigrant Aid Society
Immigrants' Service League, The
Industrial Removal Office
International Relief Association
International Rescue Committee, Inc.
International Social Service-American Branch, The
Jewish Agricultural Society, Inc., The
National Coordinating Committee for Aid to Refugees and Emigrants Coming from Germany
National Council on Naturalization and Citizenship
National Refugee Service, Inc., The
United HIAS Service
United Service for New Americans, Inc.
United States Catholic Conference, Department of Social Development and World Peace of the
United States Committee for Refugees

Blindness

American Association of Workers for the Blind
American Foundation for Overseas Blind, Inc.
American Foundation for the Blind
National Industries for the Blind, Inc.
National Society for the Prevention of Blindness, Inc.
Seeing Eye, Inc., The

Child Welfare

American Child Health Association
American Humane Association, The
American Legion, National Children and Youth Division of the
American School Hygiene Association
Child Welfare League of America, Inc.
Children's Aid Society, The
Day Care and Child Development Council of America, Inc., The
Foster Parents Plan International, Inc.
Foundation for Child Development
Fresh Air Fund, The
Jewish Board of Guardians
Juvenile Protective Association
National Child Labor Committee
National Children's Home and Welfare Association
National Council for Homemaker-Home Health Aide Services, Inc.
New York Society for the Prevention of Cruelty to Children, The
Save the Children Federation
Society of St. Vincent de Paul, Superior Council of the U.S., Inc.
Speedwell Services for Children, Inc., The
State Communities Aid Association
United States Committee for the Care of European Children, Inc.
United States Committee for UNICEF

Community Organization

American Friends Service Committee
Association of Black Social Workers
Catholic Charities of the Archdiocese of New York, The
Community Service Society
Council of the Southern Mountains
Henry Street Settlement Urban Life Center
Hull-House Association
National Welfare Rights Organization
State Communities Aid Association

Correctional Services

American Correctional Association, The
Episcopal Church, Department of Christian Social Relations of the Protestant
Fortune Society, The
Jewish Board of Guardians
National Committee on Prisons and Prison Labor
National Society of Penal Information
Osborne Association, Inc., The
Salvation Army, The
Volunteers of America, The

Crippled, The

American Rehabilitation Committee
Baruch Committee on Physical Medicine and Rehabilitation
Foundation for Child Development
Goodwill Industries of America, Inc.
Muscular Dystrophy Association, Inc.
National Council on Rehabilitation, Inc.
National Easter Seal Society for Crippled Children and Adults, The
National Foundation-March of Dimes, The
National Multiple Sclerosis Society
National Rehabilitation Association
National Shut-In Society, The
United Cerebral Palsy Associations, Inc.

Day Care

Child Welfare League of America, Inc.
Day Care and Child Development Council of America, Inc., The
Volunteers of America, The

Deaf and the Hard-of-Hearing

National Association for Hearing and Speech Action
National Association of the Deaf

Disaster Relief

American Council of Voluntary Agencies for Foreign Service, Inc.
American Friends Service Committee
American National Red Cross
Brethren Service Commission

Catholic Relief Services-United States Catholic Conference
Church World Service
Cooperative for American Relief Everywhere
Lutheran World Relief
Mennonite Central Committee
Salvation Army, The
Society of St. Vincent de Paul, Superior Council of the U.S., The
Volunteers of America, The
Young Men's Christian Associations of the United States of America, National Council of the
Young Women's Christian Association of the U.S.A., National Board of the

Education for Social Work

Council on Social Work Education, The

Family Social Work

American National Red Cross
Catholic Charities of the Archdiocese of New York
Charity Organization Society of the City of New York, The
Community Service Society
Family Location Service, Inc.
Family Service Association of America
Jewish Family Service
New York Association for Improving the Condition of the Poor
Salvation Army, The
Society of St. Vincent de Paul, Superior Council of the U.S., Inc.
State Communities Aid Association
United Service Organizations, Inc.

Foundations in Social Welfare

Commonwealth Fund, The
Foundation for Child Development
Russell Sage Foundation

Health Agencies

American Cancer Society, Inc.
American Child Health Association
American Heart Association
American Lung Association, The
American Public Health Association
American Social Health Association
Child Health Organization of America
Maternity Center Association
Muscular Dystrophy Association, Inc.
National Association for Mental Health, Inc., The
National Association for the Study of Epilepsy and the Care and Treatment of Epileptics
National Committee for Mental Hygiene, Inc., The
National Council on Alcoholism, Inc.
National Easter Seal Society for Crippled Children and Adults, The
National Foundation-March of Dimes, The
National Multiple Sclerosis Society

National Organization for Public Health Nursing
United Cerebral Palsy Associations, Inc.

Housing

National Housing Association
National Housing Conference, Inc.
Salvation Army, The
Volunteers of America, The

Juvenile Delinquency and Juvenile Delinquency Prevention

American Humane Association, The
American Legion, National Children and Youth Division of the
American Orthopsychiatric Association, The
Big Brother and Big Sister Federation, Inc.
Big Brothers of America, The
Boys' Clubs of America, Inc.
Children's Aid Society, The
Girls and Boys Service League
Jewish Board of Guardians
Juvenile Protective Association
National Committee for Children and Youth, Inc.
National Council on Crime and Delinquency
New York Society for the Prevention of Cruelty to Children, The

Legal Aid

National Legal Aid and Defender Association

Mental Health and Mental Illness

American Orthopsychiatric Association, The
National Association for Mental Health, Inc., The
National Association for Retarded Citizens
National Association for the Study of Epilepsy and the Care and Treatment of Epileptics
National Committee for Mental Hygiene, Inc., The
National Mental Health Foundation, Inc.

Migrants, Transients, and Nonresidents

Charity Organization Society of the City of New York, The
Committee on Transportation of Allied National Agencies
Council on Interstate Migration, Inc.
Family Service Association of America
Volunteers of America, The
Young Men's Christian Associations of the United States of America, National Council of the

Military Social Service

American National Red Cross
American Social Health Association
Army Relief Association
National Catholic Community Service
National Jewish Welfare Board, The

Navy Relief Society
Salvation Army, The
Travelers Aid Association of America
United Service Organizations, Inc.
United States Christian Commission for the Army and Navy
United States Sanitary Commission
Woman's Central Association of Relief
Young Men's Christian Associations of the United States of America, National Council of the

Overseas Aid

American Council of Voluntary Agencies for Foreign Service, Inc.
American Foundation for Overseas Blind, Inc.
American Freedom from Hunger Foundation
American Friends Service Committee
American Jewish Joint Distribution Committee, Inc.
American National Red Cross
American Organization for Rehabilitation through Training Federation
American Relief Administration European Children's Fund
Brethren Service Commission
Catholic Relief Services-United States Catholic Conference
Church World Service
Cooperative for American Relief Everywhere
Foster Parents Plan International, Inc.
Hebrew Sheltering and Immigrant Aid Society
International Relief Association
International Rescue Committee, Inc.
International Social Service-American Branch, The
Lutheran World Relief
Mennonite Central Committee
Near East Relief
Save the Children Federation
Unitarian Universalist Service Committee
United HIAS Service
United States Committee for UNICEF
Young Men's Christian Associations of the United States of America, National Council of the

Poverty

Association of Black Social Workers
Charity Organization Society of the City of New York, The
Council of the Southern Mountains
Foster Parents Plan International, Inc.
Jewish Family Service
National Urban League
National Welfare Rights Organization
New York Association for Improving the Condition of the Poor
Society of St. Vincent de Paul, Superior Council of the U.S., Inc.
State Communities Aid Association

Professional Organizations

American Association of Medical Social Workers, Inc., The
American Association of Social Workers

American Association of Workers for the Blind
Association of Black Social Workers
National Association of Social Workers, Inc.

Recreation

National Recreation and Park Association

Settlements and Community Centers

Henry Street Settlement Urban Life Center
Hull-House Association
National Federation of Settlements and Neighborhood Centers

Unmarried Parents

Child Welfare League of America, Inc.
Episcopal Service for Youth
Florence Crittenton Association of America, Inc.
Jewish Board of Guardians
National Council on Illegitimacy
Salvation Army, The
State Communities Aid Association
Volunteers of America, The

Vocational Rehabilitation

American Rehabilitation Committee
Goodwill Industries of America, Inc.
National Easter Seal Society for Crippled Children and Adults, The
National Industries for the Blind, Inc.
National Rehabilitation Association, Inc.

Youth-Serving

Big Brother and Big Sister Federation, Inc.
Big Brothers of America, Inc.
Boy Scouts of America
Boys' Clubs of America, Inc.
CYO Federation, National
Camp Fire Girls, Inc.
Episcopal Service for Youth
Florence Crittenton Association of America, Inc.
Girl Scouts of the United States of America
Girls and Boys Service League
Girls Clubs of America, Inc.
Jewish Board of Guardians
National Committee for Children and Youth, Inc.
Salvation Army, The
Young Men's Christian Associations of the United States of America, National Council of the
Young Women's Christian Association of the U.S.A., National Board of the

SOCIAL SERVICE AGENCY GENEALOGIES

This appendix indicates the name changes and appropriate dates, mergers, and dissolutions of each agency included in this volume. When primary sources, such as manuscript collections, letterheads, published annual reports, and newsletters and journals, did not provide this information clearly, I relied on the information on national voluntary agencies in most issues of the *Social Work Year Book* and its successor, the *Encyclopedia of Social Work,* reports in *The New York Times,* the newspaper of record, and on entries in the volumes of the *Directory of Social and Health Agencies of New York.* Since its inception in 1883 as the *Charities Directory,* issued by The Charity Organization Society of the City of New York, this publication generally described national agencies headquartered in the New York area and even some of those outside the New York City region. Except for *The New York Times,* I am not convinced that these sources were always accurate, but in the absence of other data, I have had to rely on them.

These limitations have left some questionable dates, names, and dissolutions. Items in question are indicated by a question mark. Mergers and disbandments are described clearly.

Indented entries preceded by a ")'' indicate that those agencies merged to create the organization listed immediately below.

AFL-CIO Department of Community Services

AFL-CIO Department of Community Services, 1941–

Alcoholics Anonymous

Alcoholics Anonymous, 1935–

American Association for Hygiene and Baths

American Association for Promoting Hygiene and Baths, 1912–1930?
American Association for Hygiene and Baths, 1930?–1934?

American Association for Labor Legislation

American Association for Labor Legislation, 1906–1945

American Association of Medical Social Workers, Inc., The

American Association of Hospital Social Workers, 1918–1934
American Association of Medical Social Workers, Inc., The, 1934–1955
(Merged to form National Association of Social Workers, Inc.)

American Association on Mental Deficiency

Association of Medical Officers of American Institutions for Idiotic and Feeble-Minded Persons, 1876–1906
American Association for the Feeble-Minded, 1906–1933
American Association on Mental Deficiency, 1933–

American Association for Social Security, Inc.

American Association for Old Age Security, 1927–1933
American Association for Social Security, Inc., 1933–1944
(Disbanded)

American Association of Social Workers

National Social Workers' Exchange, 1917–1921
American Association of Social Workers, 1921–1955
(Merged to become National Association of Social Workers, Inc.)

American Association of Workers for the Blind

American Blind Peoples Higher Education and General Improvement Fund, 1895–1905
American Association of Workers for the Blind, 1905–

American Cancer Society, Inc.

American Society for the Control of Cancer, 1913–1944
American Cancer Society, Inc., 1944–

American Child Health Association

American Association for the Study and Prevention of Infant Mortality, 1909–1919
American Child Hygiene Association, 1919–1922
)Child Health Organization of America, 1918–1922
American Child Health Association, 1923–1935
(Disbanded)

American Christian Committee for Refugees, Inc.
American Committee for Christian German Refugees, 1934–1940?
American Committee for Christian Refugees, Inc., 1940?–1944
American Christian Committee for Refugees, Inc., 1944–1947

American Correctional Association, The

American Prison Association, 1870–1954
American Correctional Association, The, 1954–

American Council for Nationalities Service

>)Common Council for American Unity, The, 1939–1959
>)American Federation of International Institutes, 1933–1958
> American Council for Nationalities Service, 1959–

American Council of Voluntary Agencies for Foreign Service, Inc.

> American Council of Voluntary Agencies for Foreign Service, Inc., 1943–

American Federation of International Institutes

> National Institute of Immigrant Welfare, 1933–1943
> American Federation of International Institutes, 1943–1958
> (Merged to form American Council for Nationalities Service)

American Foundation for the Blind

> American Foundation for the Blind, 1921–

American Foundation for Overseas Blind, Inc.

> British, French, Belgian Permanent Blind Relief War Fund, 1915–1917
> American, British, French, Belgian Permanent Blind Relief War Fund, 1917–1919
> Permanent Blind Relief War Fund for Soldiers and Sailors of the Allies, Inc., 1919–1925
> American Braille Press for War and Civilian Blind, Inc., 1925–1946
> American Foundation for Overseas Blind, Inc., 1946–

American Freedom from Hunger Foundation

> American Freedom from Hunger Foundation, 1961–

American Friends Service Committee

> American Friends Service Committee, 1917–

American Heart Association

> Association for the Prevention and Relief of Heart Disease, 1914–1924
> American Heart Association, 1924–

American Humane Association, The

> International Humane Society, 1877–1878
> American Humane Association, The, 1878–

American Immigration and Citizenship Conference

>)National Council on Naturalization and Citizenship, 1930–1960
>)American Immigration Conference, 1954–1960
> American Immigration and Citizenship Conference, 1960–

American Immigration Conference

> American Immigration Conference, 1954–1960
> (Merged to become American Immigration and Citizenship Conference)

American Jewish Joint Distribution Committee, Inc.

> Joint Distribution Committee of American Funds for the Relief of Jewish War Sufferers, 1914–
> 1918

Joint Distribution Committee of Funds for Jewish War Sufferers, 1918–1931
American Jewish Joint Distribution Committee, Inc., 1931–

American Legion, National Children and Youth Division of the

National Children's Welfare Committee of the American Legion, 1922–1923?
National Child Welfare Committee of the American Legion, 1923?–1924
Children's Welfare Department of the American Legion, 1924–1925?
National Child Welfare Division of the American Legion, 1926?–1957?
National Child Welfare Commission of the American Legion, 1958?–1962?
National Child Welfare Division of the American Legion, 1963?–1970
National Children and Youth Division of the American Legion, 1970–

American Lung Association

United States Society for the Study of Tuberculosis, 1904–1904
National Association for the Study and Prevention of Tuberculosis, 1904–1918
National Tuberculosis Association, 1918–1968
National Tuberculosis and Respiratory Disease Association, 1968–1973
American Lung Association, 1973–

American National Red Cross

American Association of the Red Cross, 1881–1893
American National Red Cross, 1893–

American Organization for Rehabilitation through Training Federation

American Organization for Rehabilitation through Training Society, 1922–1936
American Organization for Rehabilitation through Training Federation, 1936–

American Orthopsychiatric Association, The

Association of American Orthopsychiatrists, 1924–1926
American Orthopsychiatric Association, 1926–

American Printing House for the Blind, Inc.

American Printing House for the Blind, Inc., 1858–

American Public Health Association

American Public Health Association, 1872–

American Public Welfare Association

American Association of Public Welfare Officials, 1930–1932
American Public Welfare Association, 1932–

American Rehabilitation Committee

American Rehabilitation Committee, 1922–1975
   (Disbanded)

American Relief Administration European Children's Fund

American Relief Administration, 1919–1919
American Relief Administration European Children's Fund, 1919–1926?
   (Disbanded)

American School Hygiene Association

American School Hygiene Association, 1907–1925?
  (Disbanded)

American Seamen's Friend Society

American Seamen's Friend Society, 1825–

American Social Health Association

American Social Hygiene Association, 1913–1960
American Social Health Association, 1960–

Army Relief Society

Army Relief Society, 1900–1976
  (Disbanded)

Association of Black Social Workers

Association of Black Social Workers, 1967–

Association for Voluntary Sterilization

Sterilization League of New Jersey, 1937–1943
Sterilization League for Human Betterment, 1943–1943
Birthright, Inc., 1943–1950
Human Betterment Association of America, 1950–1962
Human Betterment Association for Voluntary Sterilization, Inc., 1962–1965
Association for Voluntary Sterilization, Inc., 1965–

Association of Volunteer Bureaus, Inc.

National Association of Volunteer Bureaus, 1951–1953?
Association of Volunteer Bureaus, 1953?–1961?
Association of Volunteer Bureaus of America, 1961?–1973?
Association of Volunteer Bureaus, Inc., 1973?–

Baptist Churches in the U.S.A., American, Division of Social Ministries of the

Social Service Commission of the Northern Baptist Convention, 1908–1912
Department of Social Service and Brotherhood of the Northern Baptist Convention, 1912–1917
Committee on Social Service of the Northern Baptist Convention, 1918–1940
Council for Christian Social Progress of the Northern Baptist Convention, 1941–1961
Division of Christian Social Concern of the American Baptist Churches in the U.S.A., 1961–1973
Division of Social Ministries of the American Baptist Churches in the U.S.A., 1973–

Baruch Committee on Physical Medicine and Rehabilitation

Baruch Committee on Physical Medicine, 1944–1949
Baruch Committee on Physical Medicine and Rehabilitation 1948–1951
  (Disbanded)

Big Brother and Big Sister Federation, Inc.

International Advisory Council of the Big Brother and Big Sister Societies, 1917–1921
Big Brother and Big Sister Federation, Inc., 1921–1937?
  (Disbanded)

Big Brothers of America, Inc.

Big Brothers of America, Inc., 1946–

Boy Scouts of America

Boy Scouts of America, 1910–

Boys' Clubs of America, Inc.

Federated Boys' Clubs, 1906–1915
Boys' Clubs Federation, 1915–1929
Boy's Club Federation of America, 1929–1931
Boys' Clubs of America, Inc., 1931–

Brethren Service Commission

Brethren Service Committee, 1939–1947
Brethren Service Commission, 1947–1968
 (Merged into program of World Ministries Commission)

Bureau of Jewish Social Research

Bureau of Jewish Social Research, 1919–1935
 (Absorbed by National Council of Jewish Federations and Welfare Funds, Inc.)

CYO Federation, National

National Federation of Diocesan Catholic Youth Councils, 1951–1967
National CYO Federation, 1967–

Camp Fire Girls, Inc.

Camp Fire Girls of America, 1911–1912
Camp Fire Girls, 1912–1914
Camp Fire Girls, Inc., 1914–

Catholic Charities of the Archdiocese of New York

Catholic Charities of the Archdiocese of New York, 1920–

Catholic Relief Services-United States Catholic Conference

War Relief Services of the National Catholic Welfare Conference, 1943–1955
Catholic Relief Services-National Catholic Welfare Conference, 1955–1966
Catholic Relief Services-United States Catholic Conference, 1966–

Charity Organization Society of the City of New York, The

Charity Organization Society of the City of New York, The, 1882–1939
 (Merged to form Community Service Society)

Child Health Organization of America

Child Health Organization, 1918–1920
Child Health Organization of America, 1920–1922
 (Merged to form American Child Health Association)

Child Welfare League of America, Inc.

Child Welfare League of America, 1920–1928
Child Welfare League of America, Inc., 1928–

Children's Aid Society, The

    Children's Aid Society, The, 1853–

Church World Service

    Church World Service, 1946–

Committee on Transportation of Allied National Agencies

    Committee on Transportation of Dependents, 1902–1910
    Committee on Transportation, 1910–1921
    Committee on Transportation of Allied National Agencies, 1921–1934?
      (Disbanded)

Common Council for American Unity

)Foreign Language Information Service, 1921–1939
    Common Council for American Unity, 1939–1959
      (Merged to become American Council for Nationalities Service)

Commonwealth Fund, The

    Commonwealth Fund, The, 1918–

Community Service Society

)New York Association for Improving the Condition of the Poor, 1843–1939
)Charity Organization Society of the City of New York, The, 1882–1939
    Community Service Society, 1939–

Congregational Christian Churches, Council for Social Action of the

    Labor Committee of the Congregational Christian Churches, 1901–1904
    Industrial Committee of the Congregational Christian Churches, 1904–1913
    Commission on Social Service of the Congregational Christian Churches, 1913–1927
    Commission on Social Relations of the Congregational Christian Churches, 1927–1934
    Council for Social Action of the Congregational Christian Churches, 1934–1961
      (Merged with the Council on Christian Social Action of the Evangelical and Reformed Church)

Cooperative for American Relief Everywhere

    Cooperative for American Remittances to Europe, 1945–1952
    Cooperative for American Remittances to Everywhere, 1952–1958
    Cooperative for American Relief Everywhere, 1958–

Council on Interstate Migration, Inc.

    Committee on Care of Transient and Homeless, 1932–1938
    Council on Interstate Migration, Inc., 1938–1939
      (Disbanded)

Council of Jewish Federations and Welfare Funds, Inc.

    National Council of Jewish Federations and Welfare Funds, 1932–1935
    Council of Jewish Federations and Welfare Funds, Inc., 1935–

Council on Social Work Education

    Council on Social Work Education, 1952–

Council of the Southern Mountains

Conference of Southern Mountain Workers, 1913–1944
Council of Southern Mountain Workers, 1944–1954
Council of the Southern Mountains, 1954–

Day Care and Child Development Council of America, Inc., The

Intercity Committee on the Day Care of Children, 1958–1960
National Committee for the Day Care of Children, Inc., 1960–1967
Day Care and Child Development Council of America, Inc., The, 1967–

Disciples of Christ, Church in Society of the

Committee on Social Service of the Disciples of Christ, 1912–1913
Commission on Social Service and the Rural Church of the Disciples of Christ, 1913–1920
Board of Temperance and Social Welfare of the Disciples of Christ, 1920–1935
Department of Temperance and Social Welfare of the Disciples of Christ, 1935–1960
Department of Christian Social Action and Community Service of the Disciples of Christ, 1960–1969
Church in Society of the Disciples of Christ, 1969–

Episcopal Church, Department of Christian Social Relations of the Protestant

Commission on the Relationship of Capital and Labor of the Protestant Episcopal Church, 1901–1910
Joint Commission on Social Service of the Protestant Episcopal Church, 1910–1919
Department of Christian Social Service of the Protestant Episcopal Church, 1919–1939
Department of Christian Social Relations of the Protestant Episcopal Church, 1939–1968?
  (Disbanded)

Episcopal Service for Youth

Church Mission of Help, 1909–1919
National Council of the Church Mission of Help, 1919–1946
Episcopal Service for Youth, 1946–1964
  (Disbanded)

Evangelical and Reformed Church, Commission on Christian Social Action of the

)Commission on Social Service of the Reformed Church in the U.S., 1917–1935
)Commission on Christianity and Social Problems of the Evangelical Church, 1921–1935
Joint Commission on Christian Social Action of the Evangelical and Reformed Church, 1935–1938
Commission on Christian Social Action of the Evangelical and Reformed Church, 1938–1957
  (Merged with Council on Christian Social Action of the Congregational Christian Churches to form Council for Christian Social Action of the United Church of Christ)

Family Location Service, Inc.

National Desertion Bureau, 1911–1955
Family Location Service, Inc., 1955–1967
  (Absorbed by Jewish Family Service)

Family Service Association of America

National Association of Societies for Organizing Charities, 1911–1912
American Association of Societies for Organizing Charities, 1912–1917
American Association for Organizing Charities, 1917–1919

American Association for Organizing Family Social Work, 1919–1930
Family Welfare Association of America, 1930–1946
Family Service Association of America, 1946–

Florence Crittenton Association of America, Inc.

National Florence Crittenton Mission, 1895–
Crittenton Homes Association, 1950–1960
Florence Crittenton Association of America, 1960–1976
(Absorbed by Child Welfare League of America, Inc., as its Florence Crittenton Division)

Foreign Language Information Service

Foreign Language Information Service, 1921–1939
(Merged to become Common Council for American Unity)

Fortune Society, The

Fortune Society, The, 1967–

Foster Parents Plan International, Inc.

Foster Parents Plan for Children in Spain, 1937–1939
Foster Parents Plan for War Children, 1939–1956
Foster Parents Plan, 1956–1974
Foster Parents Plan International, Inc., 1974–

Foundation for Child Development

Association for the Aid of Crippled Children, 1908–1972
Foundation for Child Development, 1972–

Fresh Air Fund, The

Fresh Air Work, 1877–1882
Tribune Fresh Air Fund, 1882–1899
Tribune Fresh Air Fund Society, 1899–1920
Tribune Fresh Air Fund, 1920–1948
Herald Tribune Fresh Air Fund, 1948–1966
Fresh Air Fund, The, 1966–

Girl Scouts of the United States of America

Girl Guides, 1912–1913
Girl Scouts, 1913–1915
Girl Scouts, Inc., 1915–1947
Girl Scouts of the United States of America, 1947–

Girls and Boys Service League

New York Probation Association, 1908–1912
New York Probation and Protective Association, 1912–1923
Girls Service League of America, 1923–1963
Girls and Boys Service League, 1963–

Girls Clubs of America, Inc.

Girls Clubs of America, Inc., 1945–

Goodwill Industries of America, Inc.

Morgan Memorial Cooperative Industries and Stores, Inc., 1905–1910
National Cooperative Industrial Relief Association, 1910–1933
National Association of Goodwill Industries, 1933–1946
Goodwill Industries of America, 1946–

Hebrew Sheltering and Immigrant Aid Society

Hebrew Sheltering and Immigrant Aid Society, 1909–1954
  (Merged to form United HIAS Service)

Henry Street Settlement Urban Life Center

Nurses' Settlement, 1893–1903
Henry Street Settlement, 1903–1970
Henry Street Settlement Urban Life Center, 1970–

Hull-House Association

Hull-House, 1889–1962
Hull-House Association, 1962–

Immigrants' Service League, The

Immigrants' Protective League, 1908–1954
Immigrants' Service League, The, 1954–

Industrial Removal Office

Industrial Removal Office, 1901–1922
  (Disbanded)

International Relief Association

International Relief Committee, 1933–1936?
International Relief Association, 1936?–1942
  (Merged with International Rescue Committee to form International Rescue and Relief Committee)

International Rescue Committee, Inc.

)International Relief Association, 1933–1942
)Emergency Rescue Committee, 1940–1942
International Rescue and Relief Committee, 1942–1950
International Rescue Committee, Inc., 1950–

International Social Service-American Branch, The

International Migration Service-American Bureau, 1924–1926
International Migration Service-American Branch, 1926–1946
International Social Service-American Branch, 1946–1972
  (Merged with Travelers Aid Association of America to form Travelers Aid-International Social Service of America)

Jewish Agricultural Society, Inc., The

Jewish Agricultural and Industrial Aid Society, The, 1900–1922
Jewish Agricultural Society, Inc., The, 1922–1972
  (Absorbed by the Baron de Hirsch Fund)

Jewish Board of Guardians

Jewish Board of Guardians, 1921–

Jewish Family Service

United Hebrew Charities of the City of New York, 1874–1926
Jewish Social Service Association, 1926–1946
Jewish Family Service, 1946–
(Absorbed Jewish Family Welfare Society of Brooklyn)

Juvenile Protective Association

Juvenile Court Committee, 1902–1906
Juvenile Protective Association, 1906–

Lutheran Council in the United States of America, Division of Mission and Ministry

Department of National Lutheran Welfare of the National Lutheran Council, 1938–1939
Department of Welfare of the National Lutheran Council, 1939–1945
Division of Welfare of the National Lutheran Council, 1945–1966
Division of Welfare Services of the Lutheran Council in the United States of America, 1966–1973
Division of Mission and Ministry of the Lutheran Council in the United States of America, 1973–

Lutheran World Relief

Lutheran World Relief, 1945–

Maternity Center Association

Maternity Center Association of New York, 1918–1939?
Maternity Center Association, 1939?–

Mennonite Central Committee

Mennonite Central Committee, 1920–

Methodist Federation for Social Action, The

Methodist Federation for Social Service, The, 1907–1948
Methodist Federation for Social Action, The, 1948–

Muscular Dystrophy Association, Inc.

Muscular Dystrophy Association, 1950–1952
Muscular Dystrophy Associations of America, 1952–1974
Muscular Dystrophy Association, Inc., 1974–

National Assembly of National Voluntary Health and Social Welfare Organizations, Inc., The

National Social Work Council, 1923–1945
National Social Welfare Assembly, 1945–1967
National Association for Social Policy and Development, 1967–1973
National Assembly of National Voluntary Health and Social Welfare Organizations, Inc., The, 1973–

National Association of Day Nurseries

Federation of Day Nurseries, 1898–1915?
National Federation of Day Nurseries, 1915?–1938
National Association of Day Nurseries, 1938–1942
(Absorbed by Child Welfare League of America)

National Association of the Deaf

National Association of Deaf-Mutes, 1880-1889
National Association of the Deaf, 1889-

National Association for Hearing and Speech Action

American Association for the Hard of Hearing, 1919-1922
American Federation of Organizations for the Hard of Hearing, 1922-1935
American Society for the Hard of Hearing, 1935-1946
American Hearing Society, 1946-1966
National Association of Hearing and Speech Agencies, 1966-1974
National Association for Hearing and Speech Action, 1974-

National Association for Mental Health, Inc., The

)National Committee for Mental Hygiene, Inc., The, 1909-1950
)National Foundation for Mental Health, Inc., 1946-1950
)Psychiatric Foundation, The, 1946-1950
National Association for Mental Health, Inc., The, 1950-

National Association for Retarded Citizens

National Association of Parents and Friends of Mentally Retarded Children, 1950-1953
National Association for Retarded Children, 1953-1974
National Association for Retarded Citizens, 1974-

National Association of Social Workers, Inc.

)American Association of Social Workers, 1917-1955
)American Association of Medical Social Workers, 1918-1955
)National Association of School Social Workers, 1919-1955
)American Association of Psychiatric Social Workers, 1920-1955
)American Association of Group Workers, 1936-1955
)Association for the Study of Community Organization, 1946-1955
)Social Work Research Group, 1949-1955
National Association of Social Workers, Inc., 1955-

National Association for the Study of Epilepsy and the Care and Treatment of Epileptics

National Society for the Study of Epilepsy and the Care of Epileptics, 1898-1900?
National Association for the Study of Epilepsy and the Care and Treatment of Epileptics, 1900?-1915?
(Disbanded)

National Catholic Community Service

National Catholic Community Service, 1940-

National Child Labor Committee

National Child Labor Committee, 1904-1957
National Committee on Employment of Youth, 1957-1958
National Child Labor Committee, 1958-

National Children's Home and Welfare Association

American Educational Aid Society, The, 1883-1890?
National Children's Home Society, 1890?-1916

National Children's Home and Welfare Association, 1916–1938?
(Disbanded)

National Committee for Children and Youth, Inc.

National Committee for the Golden Anniversary White House Conference on Children and Youth, 1959–1960
National Committee for Children and Youth, Inc., 1960–1973
(Merged with Council of National Organizations for Children and Youth to become National Council of Organizations for Children and Youth)

National Committee for Mental Hygiene, Inc., The

National Committee for Mental Hygiene, The, 1909–1950
(Merged to form National Association for Mental Health, Inc.)

National Committee on Prisons and Prison Labor

National Committee on Prison Labor, 1910–1915?
National Committee on Prisons and Prison Labor, 1915?–1950?
(Disbanded)

National Conference of Catholic Charities

National Conference of Catholic Charities, 1910–

National Conference of Jewish Communal Service

National Conference of Jewish Charities in the United States, 1889–1919
National Conference of Jewish Social Service, 1919–1937
National Conference of Jewish Social Welfare, 1937–1951
National Conference of Jewish Communal Service, 1951–

National Conference on Social Welfare

Conference of Boards of Public Charities, 1874–1875
Conference of Charities, 1875–1879
Conference of Charities and Correction, 1880–1881
Conference of Charities and Corrections, 1882–1883
National Conference of Charities and Correction, 1884–1916
National Conference of Social Work, 1917–1956
National Conference on Social Welfare, 1956–

National Consumers' League

National Consumers' League, 1879–

National Coordinating Committee for Aid to Refugees and Emigrants Coming from Germany

National Coordinating Committee for Aid to Refugees and Emigrants Coming from Germany, 1934–1939
(Merged to form The National Refugee Service, Inc.)

National Council on the Aging, Inc., The

National Committee on the Aging, 1950–1960
National Council on the Aging, 1960–

National Council on Alcoholism, Inc.

National Committee for Education on Alcoholism, 1944–1950
National Committee on Alcoholism, 1950–1955
National Council on Alcoholism, Inc., 1955–

National Council of the Churches of Christ in the U.S.A., Division of Church and Society

Commission on the Church and Social Service of the Federal Council of the Churches of Christ in America, 1908–1932
Department of the Church and Social Service of the Federal Council of the Churches of Christ in America, 1933–1945
Department of Christian Social Relations of the Federal Council of the Churches of Christ in America, 1945–1950
Department of Social Welfare of the National Council of the Churches of Christ in the U.S.A., 1950–1973
Division of Church and Society of the National Council of the Churches of Christ in the U.S.A., 1973–

National Council on Crime and Delinquency

National Association of Probation Officers, 1907–1911?
National Probation Association, 1911?–1947
National Probation and Parole Association, 1947–1960
National Council on Crime and Delinquency, 1960–

National Council for Homemaker-Home Health Aide Services, Inc.

National Committee on Supervised Homemaker-Houseworker Service, 1939–1941
Committee on Supervised Homemaker Service, 1941–1946
National Committee on Homemaker Service, 1946–1962
National Council on Homemaker Services, 1962–1971
National Council for Homemaker-Home Health Aide Service, Inc., 1971–

National Council on Illegitimacy

Inter-City Conference on Illegitimacy, 1918–1936?
  (Absorbed by Child Welfare League of America, Inc.)
Committee on Unmarried Parenthood, 1938–1946
Committee on Unmarried Parents, 1946–1948?
Committee on Services to Unmarried Parents, 1948?–1953?
National Association on Services to Unmarried Parents, 1953?–1965
National Council on Illegitimacy, 1965–1971
  (Disbanded)

National Council on Naturalization and Citizenship

National Council on Naturalization and Citizenship, 1930–1960
  (Merged to form American Immigration and Citizenship Conference)

National Council on Rehabilitation

Council on Rehabilitation, 1942–1943
National Council on Rehabilitation, 1943–1949
  (Disbanded)

National Easter Seal Society for Crippled Children and Adults, The

National Society for Crippled Children, 1921–1922
International Society for Crippled Children, 1922–1939
National Society for Crippled Children of the United States of America, 1939–1944
National Society for Crippled Children and Adults, 1944–1967
National Easter Seal Society for Crippled Children and Adults, 1967–

National Federation of Remedial Loan Associations

National Federation of Remedial Loan Associations, 1909–1946?
  (Disbanded)

National Federation of Settlements and Neighborhood Centers

National Federation of Settlements, 1911–1949
National Federation of Settlements and Neighborhood Centers, 1949–

National Foundation-March of Dimes, The

National Foundation for Infantile Paralysis, 1937–1958
National Foundation-March of Dimes, The, 1958–

National Health Council, Inc.

National Health Council, Inc., 1920–

National Housing Association

National Housing Association, 1910–1936
  (Disbanded)

National Housing Conference, Inc.

Public Housing Conference, 1932–1933
National Public Housing Conference, 1933–1949
National Housing Conference, Inc., 1949–

National Industries for the Blind, Inc.

National Industries for the Blind, Inc., 1938–

National Jewish Welfare Board, The

Jewish Board for Welfare Work in the United States Army and Navy, 1917–1918
Jewish Welfare Board, United States Army and Navy, 1918–1919
Jewish Welfare Board, 1919–1943?
National Jewish Welfare Board, The, 1943?–

National League of Girls Clubs

National League of Associations of Working Women's Clubs, 1897–1899
National League of Women Workers, 1899–1920
National League of Girls Clubs, 1920–1928
  (Disbanded)

National Legal Aid and Defender Association

National Alliance of Legal Aid Societies, 1911–1923
National Association of Legal Aid Organizations, 1923–1949

National Legal Aid Association, 1949–1958
National Legal Aid and Defender Association, 1958–

National Mental Health Foundation, Inc.

National Mental Health Foundation, 1946–1946
National Mental Health Foundation, Inc., 1946–1950
  (Merged to form The National Association for Mental Health, Inc.)

National Multiple Sclerosis Society

Association for Advancement of Research in Multiple Sclerosis, 1946–1947
National Multiple Sclerosis Society, 1947–

National Organization for Public Health Nursing

National Organization for Public Health Nursing, 1912–1952
  (Merged to form new National League for Nursing)

National Recreation and Park Association

Playground Association of America, 1906–1911
Playground and Recreation Association of America, 1911–1930
)National Recreation Association, 1930–1965
)American Association of Zoological Parks and Aquariums, 1924–1965
)American Institute of Park Executives, 1898–1965
)American Recreation Society, 1938–1965
)National Conference of State Parks, 1921–1965
National Recreation and Park Association, 1965–

National Refugee Service, Inc., The

)National Coordinating Committee for Aid to Refugees and Emigrants Coming from Germany,
    1934–1939
National Refugee Service, Inc., The, 1939–1946
  (Merged to form United Service for New Americans, Inc.)

National Rehabilitation Association, Inc.

National Rehabilitation Association, 1926–1935
National Rehabilitation Association, Inc., 1935–

National Shut-In Society, The

Shut-in Society, 1877–1945
Shut-in Society, Inc., The, 1945–1965
National Shut-In Society, The, 1965–

National Society of Penal Information

National Society of Penal Information, 1920–1932
  (Merged to form The Osborne Association, Inc.)

National Society for the Prevention of Blindness, Inc.

National Committee for the Prevention of Blindness, 1915–1917
National Committee for the Prevention of Blindness, Inc., 1917–1928
National Society for the Prevention of Blindness, Inc., 1928–

National Urban League

National League on Urban Conditions Among Negroes, 1911–1918
National Urban League, 1918–

National Welfare Rights Organization

National Welfare Rights Organization, 1967–1975
(Disbanded)

Navy Relief Society

Navy Relief Society, 1904–

Near East Relief

Near East Relief, 1919–1930
(Merged to become Near East Foundation)

Needlework Guild of America, Inc., The

Needlework Guild of Philadelphia, 1885–1891
Needlework Guild of America, 1891–

New York Association for Improving the Condition of the Poor

New-York Association for the Improvement of the Condition of the Poor, 1843–1847
New York Association for Improving the Condition of the Poor, 1847–1939
(Merged with Charity Organization Society of the City of New York to form Community Service Society)

New York Society for the Prevention of Cruelty to Children, The

New York Society for the Prevention of Cruelty to Children, The, 1874–

North American Civic League

North American Civic League for Immigrants, 1908–1934
North American Civic League, 1934–1946?
(Disbanded)

Osborne Association, Inc., The

Osborne Association, Inc., The, 1932–

Planned Parenthood Federation of America, Inc.

American Birth Control League, The, 1921–1939
)Birth Control Clinical Research Bureau, 1923–1940
)National Committee on Federal Legislation for Birth Control, The, 1931–1936
Birth Control Federation of America, The, 1939–1942
Planned Parenthood Federation of America, Inc., 1942–

Presbyterian Church in the United States of America, Church and Society of the United

Department of Social Education and Action of the Presbyterian Church in the United States of America, 1936–1947
Division of Social Education and Action of the Presbyterian Church in the United States of America, 1948–1952

Department of Social Education and Action of the Presbyterian Church in the United States of America, 1953–1958

Department of Social Education and Action of the United Presbyterian Church in the United States of America, 1958–1960

Office of Church and Society of the United Presbyterian Church in the United States of America, 1961–1965

Church and Society of the United Presbyterian Church in the United States of America, 1965–1972
(Absorbed into the Unit II of the Program Agency of the United Presbyterian Church in the United States of America)

Russell Sage Foundation

Russell Sagè Foundation, 1907–

Salvation Army, The

Salvation Army, The, 1880–

Save the Children Federation

Save the Children Fund, 1931–1939
Save the Children Federation, 1939–

Seeing-Eye, Inc., The

Seeing-Eye, Inc., The, 1929–

Society of St. Vincent de Paul, Superior Council of the U.S., Inc.
Society of St. Vincent de Paul, Superior Council of the U.S., Inc., 1915–

Speedwell Services for Children, Inc., The

Speedwell Country Homes Society for Convalescent and Abandoned Children, 1902–1912
Speedwell Society for Convalescent and Abandoned Children, The, 1912–1914
Speedwell Country Homes Society for Convalescent and Abandoned Children, 1915–1923
Speedwell Society, The, 1923–1960?
Speedwell Services for Children, Inc., The, 1960?–1976
(Disbanded)

State Communities Aid Association

State Charities Aid Association, 1872–1967
State Communities Aid Association, 1967–

Survey Associates, Inc.

Survey Associates, Inc., 1912–1952
(Disbanded)

Travelers Aid Association of America

National Travelers Aid Association, 1917–1920
National Association of Travelers Aid Societies, 1920–1934
National Association for Travelers Aid and Transient Service, 1934–1938
National Travelers Aid Association, 1938–1966
Travelers Aid Association of America, 1966–1972
(Merged with International Social Service-American Branch to form Travelers Aid-International Social Service of America)

Unitarian Association, Department of Social Relations of the American

Department of Social and Public Service of the American Unitarian Association, 1908–1917
Department of Community Service of the American Unitarian Association, 1917–1925?
 (Inactive)
Department of Social Relations of the American Unitarian Association, 1927–1941?
 (Absorbed by Department of Adult Education and Social Relations of the American Unitarian
 Association)

Unitarian Universalist Service Committee

)Unitarian Service Committee, 1940–1963
)Universalist Service Committee, 1945–1963
Unitarian Universalist Service Committee, 1963–

United Cerebral Palsy Associations, Inc.

United Cerebral Palsy Associations, Inc., 1949–

United Church of Christ, Office for Church in Society of the

)Commission on Christian Social Action of the Evangelical and Reformed Church, 1935–1957
)Council on Christian Social Action of the Congregational Christian Churches, 1901–1957
Council for Christian Social Action of the United Church of Christ, 1957–1974
Center for Social Action of the United Church of Christ, 1974–1975
Office for Church in Society of the United Church of Christ, 1975–

United Community Defense Services

United Community Defense Services, 1950–1957
 (Disbanded)

United HIAS Service

)United Service for New Americans, Inc., 1946–1954
)Hebrew Sheltering and Immigrant Aid Society, 1909–1954
United HIAS Service, 1954–

United Seamen's Service

United Seamen's Service, 1942–

United Service for New Americans, Inc.

)National Refugee Service, Inc., The, 1939–1946
)Service to Foreign Born of the National Council of Jewish Women, 1902?–1946
United Service for New Americans, Inc., 1946–1954
 (Merged to form United HIAS Service)

United Service Organizations, Inc.

United Service Organizations for National Defense, Inc., 1941–1950
 (Inactive)
United Service Organizations, Inc., 1951–

United States Catholic Conference, Department of Social Development and World Peace of the

Department of Social Action of the National Catholic Welfare Council, 1920–1920
Social Action Department of the National Catholic Welfare Council, 1920–1923

Social Action Department of the National Catholic Welfare Conference, 1923–1966
Department of Social Development of the United States Catholic Conference, 1966–1972
Department of Social Development and World Peace of the United States Catholic Conference, 1972–

United States Christian Commission for the Army and Navy

United States Christian Commission for the Army and Navy, 1861–1866
(Disbanded)

United States Committee for the Care of European Children, Inc.

United States Committee for the Care of European Children, Inc., 1940–1953
(Disbanded)

United States Committee for Refugees

United States Committee for Refugees, 1959–1975
(Absorbed by the American Freedom from Hunger Foundation)

United States Committee for UNICEF

United States Committee for the International Children's Emergency Fund, 1947–1949
United States Committee for the Children's Fund, 1949–1953
United States Committee for UNICEF, 1953–

United States Sanitary Commission

Commission of Inquiry and Advice in respect of the Sanitary Interests of the United States Forces, 1861–1861
United States Sanitary Commission, 1861–1878
(Disbanded)

United Way of America

American Association for Community Organization, 1918–1927
Association of Community Chests and Councils, 1927–1933
Community Chests and Councils, Inc., 1933–1948
Community Chests and Councils of America, Inc., 1948–1957
United Community Funds and Councils of America, Inc., 1957–1970
United Way of America, 1970–

Volunteers of America, The

Volunteers of America, The, 1896–

Woman's Central Association of Relief

Woman's Central Association of Relief, 1861–1865
(Disbanded)

Women's Educational and Industrial Union

Women's Educational and Industrial Union, 1877–

Young Men's Christian Associations of the United States of America, National Council of the

Central Committee of the Young Men's Christian Associations, 1854–1879
International Committee of the Young Men's Christian Associations, 1879–1924

National Council of the Young Men's Christian Associations of the United States of America, 1924–

Young Women's Christian Association of the U.S.A., National Board of the

National Association of Young Women's Christian Associations of the United States, 1886–1889
International Association of Young Women's Christian Associations, 1889–1899
American Committee of the Young Women's Christian Associations, 1899–1906
National Board of the Young Women's Christian Associations in the United States of America, 1906–1949
National Board of the Young Women's Christian Association of the U.S.A., 1949–

INDEX

ABOUT THE EDITORS

PETER ROMANOFSKY, editor-in-chief, is assistant professor of history at Jersey City State College, New Jersey. Specializing in the history of social and child welfare, he has published in such journals as the *Missouri Historical Review, New York Historical Society Quarterly,* and *Jewish Social Studies.* Presently he is preparing a book-length study of urban community organization.

CLARKE A. CHAMBERS, advisory editor, is professor of history at the University of Minnesota and director of the Social Welfare History Archives Center.